Analyzing the material remains left by Maryland's colonists in the eighteenth century in conjunction with historical records and works of art, archaeologists have reconstructed the daily life of an aristocratic British family, whose head was governor of Maryland. In this large household people from different cultures interacted, and English and West African lifestyles merged. Using this fascinating case-study, Anne Yentsch illustrates the way in which historical archaeology draws on different disciplines to interpret the past.

A Chesapeake family and their slaves

NEW STUDIES IN ARCHAEOLOGY

Series editors

Colin Renfrew, *University of Cambridge*
Jeremy Sabloff, *University of Pittsburgh*

Archaeology has made enormous advances recently, both in the volume of discoveries and in its character as an intellectual discipline; new techniques have helped to further the range and rigor of inquiry, and encouraged inter-disciplinary communication.

The aim of this series is to make available to a wider audience the results of these developments. The coverage is worldwide and extends from the earliest hunting and gathering societies of historical archaeology.

Some recent titles in the series

Steven Mithen : *Thoughtful foragers: a study of prehistoric decision making*
Roger Cribb: *Nomads in archaeology*
James Whitley: *Style and society in Dark Age Greece: the changing face of a pre-literate society 1100–700 BC*
Philip Arnold: *Domestic ceramic production and spatial organization*
Julian Thomas: *Rethinking the Neolithic*
E. N. Chernykh: *Ancient metallurgy in the USSR: the early Metal Age*
Lynne Sebastian: *The Chaco Anasazi: sociopolitical evolution in the prehistoric Southwest*
Anna Maria Bietti Sestieri: *The Iron Age community of Osteria dell'Osa: a study of socio-political development in central Tyrrhenian Italy*
Christine A. Hastorf: *Agriculture and the onset of political inequality before the Inka*
Richard E. Blanton, Stephen A. Kowalewski, Gary Feinman and Jill Appel: *Ancient Mesoamerica*
Laura Finstein: *Ancient Mesoamerica: a comparison of change in three regions*
Richard Bradley and Mark Edmonds: *Interpreting the axe trade: production and exchange in Neolithic Britain*
Dean E. Arnold: *Ecology and ceramic production in an Andean community*

ANNE ELIZABETH YENTSCH Armstrong State College, Savannah

A Chesapeake family and their slaves

A study in historical archaeology

Illustrations by Julie Hunter

Published by the Press Syndicate of the University of Cambridge
The Pitt Building, Trumpington Street, Cambridge CB2 1RP
40 West 20th Street, New York, NY 10011–4211, USA
10 Stamford Road, Oakleigh, Melbourne 3166, Australia

First published 1994
Reprinted 1997

A catalogue record for this book is available from the British Library

Library of Congress cataloguing in publication data

Yentsch, Anne E.
A Chesapeake family and their slaves: a study in historical archaeology /
Anne Elizabeth Yentsch.
    p.   cm. – (New studies in archaeology)
Includes bibliographical references.
ISBN 0 521 43293 6
1. Annapolis (Md.) – Antiquities. 2. Calvert family.
3. Archaeology and history – Maryland – Annapolis. 4. Material culture –
Maryland – Annapolis. 5. Maryland – Social life and customs – to 1775.
I. Title. II. Series.
F189.A647Y46   1994
975.2'56–dc20   93–24740 CIP

ISBN 0 521 43293 6 hardback
ISBN 0 521 46730 6 paperback

Transferred to digital printing 2003

For St. Clair Wright, whose faith, strength, and sense of the past never faltered. Her vision was an inspiration and her encouragement steadfast.

For the staunch support of my son, Timothy C. Yentsch, and for two consummate teachers, Robert Jay and Ferdinand Jones.

CONTENTS

ILLUSTRATIONS

TABLES

Charts

FOREWORD

In the mid-twentieth century, anthropology was a profoundly different field from what it has become today. A simple division of labor existed among scholars whose interests were the cultural domain of human life. There were the so-called socio-cultural anthropologists – an awkward designation soon shortened simply to "anthropologists" – who ventured into remote areas of the world to study isolated, small-scale societies very different from their own, and there were the archaeologists whose task it was to unearth the remains of vanished communities and piece together the story of the vast sweep of human prehistory, a sweep more than three million years long. What the two groups held in common was a professed interest in the phenomenon called culture, the shared concepts and plans used by human societies to make their way through the world, to make sense of it, and to make it work in an efficient manner for the good of the whole. Anthropologists like Franz Boas, living among the Kwakiutl of British Columbia, Bronislaw Malinowski, telling us about the people of the Trobriand Islands, or Margaret Mead, under-standing how Samoan children were made into "proper" adult members of their society, strove to present complete pictures, or so-called ethnographies, of the cultures they studied.

Archaeologists, on the other hand, having no informants from whom to elicit information, relied on the fragmented remains of time past. For the most part, they constructed culture histories – essentially narrative accounts of the development of human culture – rendered in broad strokes and ponderously descriptive. For these reasons, it was the anthropologists who had the "right stuff," if only they could make sense of it; the archaeologist's status was often perceived as somehow second-rate, or at least derivative. "I'm just an archaeologist" was a statement heard all too often at gatherings of scholars of both persuasions in conferences, faculty meetings, and in the home. One definition of archaeologists current at the time was "persons with more grey matter under their nails than between their ears." But archaeologists, always a stalwart bunch, persevered and began to pay close attention to concepts of culture then prevalent. By the 1960s, they were fashioning a robust body of explanatory theory in which a concept of culture was central.

As the century moved into its later decades during the sixties and seventies, the world of anthropology underwent major change. Anthropologists were running out of people to study. More and more, anthropologists were forced to turn to their own society as a proper subject for analysis; the field took on a decidedly sociological tinge. Courses with titles such as Peoples and Culture of . . . (fill in the distant geographical area of choice) became fewer; courses in urban anthropology, on ethnicity, on gender studies, or on the homeless in American society took their place. While the concerns reflected in courses such as these are both important and timely, part of the underlying reason for their appearance in the seventies and eighties is the virtual impossibility of doing research such as that conducted by earlier generations of anthropologists. As the world's global villages began to merge into one vast global city, many small, formerly isolated groups of people were rapidly absorbed into the world system. Those who remained apart became increasingly intolerant of people coming among them asking personal questions. As Floyd Westerman, a Sioux Indian composer and singer of protest music in the seventies, put it, "Here come the Anthros, better hide your past away; here come the Anthros on another Holiday." Certainly, by the mid-seventies, the course of anthropological research had been altered irreversibly.

Yet all the while something else was happening too. Pioneered in large part by folklorists with interests in material culture (the physical tangible world fashioned by human activity), scholars began to see objects more and more as possessing significance far beyond the technological realm. They began to recognize that objects came freighted with both social and symbolic significance. This was also the time when historical archaeology assumed an increasingly important position within the broader field of archaeology. But historical archaeologists had access to something beyond the reach of prehistorians: a rich body of written material about the very people whose broken dishes and house foundations they were excavating. The components for a critical mass were at hand. These included a combination of more sophisticated archaeological theory; a proper appreciation of the importance of material culture in understanding any culture's workings; and a rich documentary data base to contextualize the findings about the material world.

So it is that as the century draws to a close, it is the archaeologists who are able to present us with richly detailed ethnographies. Instead of images of contemporary but exotic societies, they give us descriptions of the people of the past. Appreciating the inherent biases of the written record, and making proper allowances for them, archaeologists are now fashioning sophisticated accounts of cultures as exotic as those once possessed by remote and isolated peoples of the late nineteenth and early twentieth centuries.

A Chesapeake family and their slaves is such a study. It is a state-of-the-art presentation of the culture of eighteenth-century Maryland. Incorporating historiography, oral history, archaeology, and material perspectives, it can properly be described as a study in historical ethnography or anthropological history. Through a detailed examination of one family in eighteenth-century Annapolis, the Calverts, Anne Yentsch leads us into a world very different from our own, and makes us feel at home there, intimately acquainted with everything from fine china on the table to the foods consumed, to the house, garden, and work spaces in which the story of the family plays out. It is, furthermore, the story of a household, and through skillful use of a wide variety of objects and sources, she makes visible those who otherwise may not have been: people such as the African and African-American slaves, equally members of the household and critically necessary to its functioning in the manner in which the Calvert leaders saw fit.

Books such as this naturally invite comparisons, and two other works come immediately to mind. Henry Glassie's masterful *Passing the Time in Ballymenone* is a skillful synthesis of the same kinds of material that Dr. Yentsch has so effectively employed in her study. A collaborative work by an anthropologist, Marshall Sahlins, and an archaeologist, Patrick Kirch, *The Anthropology of History in the Kingdom of Hawaii* is yet another superb study in historical anthropology. That such a body of literature, grounded in distant encounters, artifacts, and time past, is now emerging is surely a sign of renewed vitality in the more traditional, culture-oriented, world-based anthropology, and offers great hope for the field as a whole.

James Deetz
Berkeley, California
September 1992

PREFACE

In the 1960s when James Deetz and Ivor Noël Hume wrote their pioneering studies – *Invitation to Archaeology* and *Here Lies Virginia* – most American archaeologists gave their attention to Native American or prehistoric sites: places where Indian tribes lived before European expansion. Deetz and Noël Hume were instrumental in increasing the number of studies of European colonization and Deetz, in particular, initiated research on the peoples of different ethnic origin – English, Spanish, African, Chinese, French, Dutch, and so on – who created historic sites. The environmental impact legislation of the 1970s was a third catalyst for historical archaeology as highway development and urban renewal projects cut through large numbers of sites, threatening their destruction. In the 1980s, "public archaeology" came to the foreground; Annapolis was in the forefront. Mayors, such as William Donald Schaefer of Baltimore, realized that the fascination archaeology holds for the public provided an immediate tourist attraction highly useful in promoting public awareness of state history. Still, the perceptions that the public holds of archaeological techniques and artifact interpretation are imperfect. This is particularly true in historical archaeology and because of it sites are impacted or destroyed before they can be preserved or fully studied.

This book is written in part as a response to a situation I saw develop where it became crystal clear that my discipline could be misunderstood, cast as ahistorical, and seen as an unnecessary frivolity. Trained archaeologists take things for granted, such as the relationship between a layer of soil, its artifact contents, and the strata lying above or below, which are critical in determining the age of a building, a fence line, a burial. They also take for granted the importance of material things ranging from garbage and graffiti to monuments, lost ships, and buried paths. These values and relationships may seem mysterious to the man- or woman-on-the-street, but they need not.

Greater awareness of what historical archaeology is and what it can do would increase the capacity of people interested in the history of their own local neighborhoods, towns, and cities to know what to preserve and how to do it. Archaeology is not an esoteric calling; it holds vital importance for local historians, architects, city planners, historic house owners, developers, museum officials, roadway engineers, environmentalists, and landscape designers. Because it can tell us things we did not know and reveal facets of life presented in texts from a single point of view (i.e., that of the dominant culture or gender), or never discussed at all, archaeology is an enfranchising link with the past. It speaks to the issue of cultural pluralism, to the potent effects of culture contact, and it helps us see where myth and history intertwine.

Archaeology is also a topological discourse tied to time and place. Archaeologists work outward from their data. Here I began with the information from a single site – the Calvert site – buried beneath the surface of a three-hundred year old capital city, Annapolis, Maryland. The first research among documents was directed to giving the Calvert site a set of owners and to delineate the household composition of the families who lived there. Then I looked for information about specific features and gradually began to build an interpretive context for the Calvert artifacts drawn from (a) the artifacts and features themselves; (b) comparative information on other sites; (c) local history; and (d) a worldwide framework that let us place the immigrant Annapolitans of 1720–40 within their different cultural contexts.

Annapolitans came from different places in those days. Some, like the Calvert men, came from an English background and were members of minor noble English families; others were indentured Irish servants, Welsh gardeners, or Scottish physicians. Men, women, and children were also brought to the Chesapeake from West Africa, from Madagascar, from the continent of India, and from the islands of East Asia. It was an era of intensive and often problematic culture contact; social interaction frequently progressed across cultural boundaries. People expressed their cultural identities in a variety of ways; many found expression in material goods that left tangible remains as mute proof of the different lifestyles which characterized the region.

In analyzing data from the Calvert site, I deliberately blurred genres to explore what historical archaeology would be like if it was fused with the constructs of anthropological history, and I set aside the constraints of processual archaeology to see if a detailed understanding of social process could be gained through an interpretive approach that paid close attention to local context. Local context was further defined to include more than the few important individuals well known in the town's history; here it contains a variety of individuals, some named and some unidentifiable, whose lives in one way or another touched those of the Calvert family. While this is a book that grew from an archaeological excavation, at its heart it is not so much about archaeology as about the ways one can use the historical record and a knowledge of anthropology to supplement traditional artifact interpretation. A fuller view of the artifacts, however, was not seen as an end in itself; the ultimate goal was to see the people through the things they left behind.

This synthesis is the culmination of ten years' research in Annapolis. The study uses an anthropological approach to past life sometimes seen in folklore, increasingly seen in history, and characteristic of ethnohistory, but less often applied in post-processual archaeological research. It is based on the premise that the nitty-gritty of archaeological sites – their features and artifact assemblages – is derived in large measure from repetitive, ordinary behavior whose origins stem as much from the symbolic domain of daily existence as they do from the pragmatic workaday world: emptying rubbish, butchering a calf, building a fence, stealing a sheep.

Material culture provides a strong focal point, but not the only one. Attention is paid to small and ordinary objects like household pots and oyster shells, and to larger entities such as town plans and major landmarks; attention is given to both the pragmatic and symbolic roles of material things. Consideration also is given to what people take for granted (and which they describe using "vernacular concepts" based on conventional expectations or customary procedures). I began to develop this view of artifacts in an earlier dissertation, and first applied it to Annapolis in two 1984 papers on the Georgian order, the Annapolis townscape, and the importance of orangeries. Primarily, it has evolved from reading and re-reading a series of contemporary anthropological studies as well as classic social anthropology. This study also owes a debt to the demands of feminist archaeologists, to their insistence that women are not muted people, shadows and shades that only reflect men's beliefs or male social action.

The Calvert site was located at 58 State Circle in the center of the Historic District of Maryland's capital. It lay beneath an urban city lot on which stood one large, partially collapsed building. The excavation was carried out in short, intensive spurts of activity primarily by a 3–5 man field crew as (1) funds became available, (2) the construction schedule permitted archaeologists on site, and (3) unstable portions of the building were provided with additional shoring to make their rooms safe work areas.

The excavation of the site was sponsored by Historic Annapolis, Inc. It was funded by an emergency grant (RO-20600-83) from the National Endowment for the Humanities, by the Maryland Commission for the Capital City, by the Annapolis Institute, by the Colonial Dames of America, Chapter 1, by the Society for the Preservation of Maryland Antiquities, the City of Annapolis, and the Historic Inns of Annapolis, Inc. Public interpretation at the site was funded, in part, by grants from the Maryland Humanities Council and the National Endowment for the Humanities. Analysis of the material from the site has been funded by the Historic Annapolis Foundation, the National Endowment for the Humanities (RO-21482-87), the College of William and Mary, and the Colonial Dames of America, Chapter 1 (especially the conservation of the small finds such as the buttons studies by Steven Hinks [1988]) and by matching funds from local businesses and private donors. Hence it seems appropriate to describe the work at the Calvert Site as a community effort to preserve and recover endangered evidence on the city's earlier history.

Historic Annapolis Inc., a private, non-profit preservation agency, hoped that the remains buried below ground (as much as 6–8 feet deep below the present level of the Circle in some units) would provide information that scholars and preservationists could use to further their understanding of the material development of the town over time, including the evolution of its economic growth and the impact of its bureaucratic institutions on the social organization of the community. The institution then was involved in a comparative study of wealth and consumer consumption patterns utilizing probate inventory data led by Drs. Lois Green Carr and Lorena Walsh. Preservationists hoped that the material evidence obtained from archaeological research would also supplement that provided by the documentary study.

These links between artifacts, texts, historical events, and everyday Annapolitans were not immediately visible for a number of reasons. First, we were doing preservation-based archaeology; communities tend to pull together and to exhibit the most passion for preservation and archaeological mitigation when local heroes celebrated in town and county history lived on a site. They are far less vocal when it is ordinary folk, people from poor backgrounds, or those who were disenfranchised who lived on a plot of land slated for development. Of course, the Calvert family is not presented in this monograph as an ordinary family but it was not firmly linked to the site when we began. The family was unusual in many ways. This provides a provocative counterpoint to the archaeological narrative because the family was also one whose life in Annapolis was all but forgotten in oral tradition and in local histories.

McMahon (1831: 313), in his explanation of why the Calvert family dropped from sight, also demonstrated the power of culture (with its attendant beliefs, ideas, and foci) to guide thought:

> The period of which we are treating [ca. 1714–60], is so far removed from us
> in time and character, that not only the actors and their motives, but even
> the transactions and the results which belong to it, have in a great degree
> ceased to interest. When events are forgotten, the individuals connected with
> them cannot hope to be remembered.

What this study demonstrates is that although the Calvert family may have been set aside in the local history of Annapolis, it is as deeply entangled with the persona of the city today as it was in the past. For, just as Maryland-based events and ideas left an imprint on the Calvert family households residing on both sides of the Atlantic, the Calverts in turn left an indelible stamp on Maryland.

ACKNOWLEDGMENTS

This is a book that was written in the corner of a kitchen and with much encouragement and support from my son Timothy Yentsch, St. Clair Wright, John Arbuckle, Mary C. Beaudry, Lois Green Carr, James Deetz, Carmen Weber, Melva and Bill Bailey. John Hague, Director of the American Studies Program at Stetson University, secured borrowing privileges at the Du Pont Ball Library. Special assistance was given by the Maryland State Archives, especially its director, Edward C. Papenfuse, but also Phebe Jacobsen, Susan Cummings, Robert Oszakiewski, Greg Stiverson, and Mimi Culver, as well as the other archivists who located old records and daily carried them back and forth from storage shelves to reading room, then back again. In the early phases of the project, while I was beginning to learn Chesapeake history, Lois Green Carr, Phebe Jacobsen, Lorena S. Walsh, Nancy Baker, John Hemphill, and Pierce Middleton provided advice and support, as did the staff at Historic Annapolis, Inc.

None of the work could have been done without an able fieldcrew which included Beth Acuff, Beth Ford, Esther Reed, Carmen Weber, and occasionally my brother, Frederick David Langenheim, or my son, Timothy Yentsch. Students from the University of Maryland at College Park and from the College of William and Mary also worked at the site as did local volunteers. Anne Mullins, Jim Sorenson, Robert Sonderman, Larry McKee, and Gary Norman served as field directors at different times. I am especially grateful to Joe Dent and Henry Wright for their thoughtful advice on field strategies. Richard J. Dent and Mark P. Leone, who served as co-directors of Archaeology in Annapolis with me, were also helpful as were Constance Crosby, Curtis Moyer, and Parker Potter.

I would also like to thank the librarians at the Library Company of Philadelphia, the Maryland Historical Society, the Philadelphia Horticultural Society, the reference and inter-loan librarians (and their assistants) at the Du Pont Ball Library (Stetson University) and the Lane Library (Armstrong State College), and the History Department, Armstrong State College. In addition, other archivists and curators were particularly helpful in locating old manuscripts, illustrations, and a variety of material. It would be difficult to list these one by one, yet on both sides of the Atlantic – from the Royal Society of London to the University of Florida at Gainesville or the special collections at the University of Miami, from the Boston and Baltimore Museums of Art to the Metropolitan to the smaller University Art Museum in Lafayette, Louisiana – individuals helped with information on the

Calvert family, on African-American culture, and on the whole range of topics represented among the Calvert artifacts.

Lois Green Carr, Patrick Coggins, Rhys Isaac, Arthur Pierce Middleton, Naomi F. Miller, and Henry T. Wright carefully read earlier drafts of the manuscript and provided consistent and cogent suggestions. Comments by an anonymous reader at the Maryland State Archives prompted more revision and the inclusion of the detail on Annapolis in Chapter One. Patrick Coggins of Stetson University gave me the courage to revise the African-American chapters and add more information on black women; Theresa Singleton, Mark Bograd, Christopher DeCourse, Roderick and Susan McIntosh provided additional information on African and African-American archaeology. Thad Tate supplied a blueprint for a final reorganization of the book and if the book is now less technical and more readable, this is due in large measure to his efforts. Ronald Hoffman and Jean Russo sent copies of inventories; Jean together with Marian Creveling also arranged for artifact illustrations; Stephen Patrick searched out illustrations as did the curators at the many museums who supplied final copies. Curtis Moyer supervised the artifact conservation (generously funded by the Colonial Dames of America, Chapter 1, whose assistance will some-day enable an exhibit of Calvert artifacts that would otherwise have disintegrated once out of the ground). Curt also pointed out the more unusual small finds; Jean Lee and Jim Deetz let me read portions of their unpublished manuscripts. Sue Crilley devoted a long fourth of July weekend to reading the manuscript with an eye to its visual material and the final figure list. Both she and Jim Deetz urged more pictures, not fewer, and stressed their importance.

The last stages of work on the manuscript, its tables and illustrations, was made possible by grants from the Anne Arundel County Heritage Trust; the Colonial Dames of America, Chapter 1; Paul Pearson and the Historic Inns of Annapolis, Inc.; the Maryland State Archives; a generous contribution to the project by Chesapeake archaeologists and historians, and faculty development funds from Armstrong State College. Russell Wright and Marion E. Warren donated fine examples of their work to help provide the visual information that archaeologists depend on. Celia Pearson, Merrick Posnansky, Henry Miller, and Wayne Clarke also contributed photographs. Without their help, the book would remain unfinished or contain but one or two photographs; without the kind assistance and guidance of the editorial staff at Cambridge University Press, it would not appear at all. Books, I came to realize, are cooperative projects in much the same way that excavating a site is. Sometimes they come into being because of technical skills; at other times, it is the quiet steady support of a son, a sister, a mother, a brother that pushes them further. The laughter and pride of my nephew, Brian Eastman, assisted too.

Finally, Julie Hunter-Abbazia was exceptionally generous with her time, advice, and artistic skill. I am delighted that she was able to put her talent to work on the manuscript, and that my son brought the two of us together. Artifact analysis and the interpretation of material culture is a visual experience; form is the third dimension of archaeology, but it loses much of its impact when it is described in words alone. Julie's drawings of small artifacts, her suggestions as to which ones would show their tone and texture best as photographs, and her renderings of African women in their homeland are a welcome contribution to the volume.

Illustration sources

The author gratefully acknowledges the following for their kind permission to reproduce photographs and other illustrations and for the help of their respective staffs in procuring these materials.

Julie Hunter-Abbazia	1.12; 2.2; 2.7; 5.3; 6.3; 6.4; 6.5; 8.2; 8.3;
Daytona Beach, Florida	8.4; 8.5; 9.5; 9.6; 9.7; 9.9; 10.1; 10.2;
	10.3; 10.6; 11.2; 11.3; 13.3; 13.10; 15.6;
	16.2; 16.3; 16.5; 16.7
Archaeological Society of Maryland	2.5; 2.6
The Baltimore Museum of Art, Baltimore, Maryland	3.1; 4.1; 9.4; 13.1; 13.2; 13.4; 14.3
The Boston Museum of Fine Arts, Boston, Massachusetts	5.2
The British Library, London, England	1.10; 9.3
The British Museum, London, England	15.2
Cambridge University Press	9.1
Newell Cannon, Harwood, Maryland	14.5
The Chesapeake Bay Foundation, Annapolis, Maryland	16.8
The Colonial Williamsburg Foundation, Williamsburg, Virginia	4.4; 7.1; 7.4; 7.6; 14.1; 14.4
Dumbarton Oaks, Washington, DC	4.2
Enoch Pratt Free Library, Baltimore, Maryland	1.5
Leland Ferguson, University of South Carolina, Columbia, South Carolina	10.5b
The Georgia Department of Archives and History, Atlanta, Georgia	10.4
Henry Francis duPont Winterthur Museum, Winterthur, Delaware	7.2; 7.3
Jefferson-Patterson Park, Leonardstown, Maryland	8.1
The Library of Congress, Washington, DC	3.3; 14.6
Mariner's Museum, Newport News, Virginia	1.9; 6.8
The Maryland Historical Society, Baltimore, Maryland	9.2; 12.3

The Maryland State Archives, Annapolis, Maryland	1.1; 1.2; 1.2; 1.6; 1.8; 1.11; 1.13; 4.6; 6.6; 6.7; 12.2; 13.5
Hannah McKee, Nashville, Tennessee	2.5; 5.6
The Metropolitan Museum of Art, New York, New York	3.2
Henry Miller, St. Mary's City Commission, St. Mary's, Maryland	1.4
Naomi F. Miller University Museum, University of Pennsylvania, Philadelphia, PA	11.1
The National Archives of Canada, Ottawa, Canada	12.1
Celia Pearson, Annapolis, Maryland	6.1
Paul Pearson, Annapolis, Maryland	2.4
The Society for Historical Archaeology, Tucson, Arizona	11.1
The University Art Museum, University of Southwestern Louisiana Lafayette, Louisiana	15.5
The Virginia Historical Society, Richmond, Virginia	15.1
Marion E. Warren Annapolis, Maryland	1.7; 2.1; 2.3; 2.8; 3.5; 6.2; 7.5; 7.7; 8.6; 8.7; 8.8; 9.8; 10.5a; 13.8; 13.9; 13.12; 13.13; 13.14; 14.2; 16.1; 16.4; 16.6
Russell Wright, Bridgton, Maine	3.4; 5.5; 13.7; 13.11

GLOSSARY

Above-ground archaeology. The study of material remains from prior cultures which remain standing in the present landscape.

Acculturation. Social and cultural change arising through intensive and continuing social interaction with people of a different culture.

Achieved status. Rank in a society which is acquired by individuals who successfully apply special talents and abilities to their daily lives.

Archaeobotanists. Another word for paleoethnobotanists who are people who study plant remains found at archaeological sites or plant remains used by people in the past.

Archaeological context. Where artifacts or features are located – the soil matrices, associations with other objects, and placements within stratigraphic layers (i.e., provenience); the position in time and space of archaeological finds.

Archaeological data. The remains of material objects left by past cultures. These include data found above and below ground which are normally grouped into four main classes: artifacts, features, building remains, and food remains. It also includes evidence on the use of space and land alterations.

Archaeological record. The material remains of people's lives and past cultures which survive in the ground.

Artifact typology. The classification of artifacts based on similarity of form.

Ascribed status. Rank in a society which is conferred by birth, i.e., hereditary positions.

Assemblage. All the artifacts found at a single site. These are normally divided into different classes associated with specific activities (pottery, glassware, weaponry, faunal and botanical remains, etc.) which are then analyzed as sub-assemblages to provide information about the different activities which took place at a site.

Builder's trench. The material remains left by construction trenches dug into the soil as men excavated cellar foundations or built brick walls.

Cognitive archaeology. Research which focuses upon the way archaeological data reveals how people in the past perceived and ordered their universe.

Comparanda. Artifacts from the same classes of material remains which are found at comparable sites within a region (i.e., from the sites with the same function or from sites with the same date range).

Conspicuous consumption. A practice whereby people acquire and use surplus material goods as a way to display their position in the social structure or the political hierarchy of a culture.

Cultural context. A holistic framework which includes the individuals, beliefs, social action, and cultural elements of a community which surround, shape, and give cultural meaning to material culture.

Cultural relativism. The idea that social action and its meaning is best understood when interpreted in terms of the culture of an individual (i.e., from the native's point of view using his or her frame of reference), and that cultural traits are explicable when viewed in terms of the cultural system of which they are a part. Cultural relativism is the opposite of ethnocentrism in which judgments about others are based on the values of one's own culture.

Division of labor. The division of work tasks by age, gender distinctions, social rank, or skill within a society.

Enculturation. The process by which children in a given culture learn traditional beliefs, customs, values, and patterns of behavior as they grow up.

Ethnicity. A way of dividing people into different social groups based on culturally perceived differences in their national origins, their spoken languages, or on variations in religious beliefs.

Ethnocentrism. The belief that one's own culture (or sub-culture) is superior.

Ethnography. A description of the behavior, customs, beliefs, values, and material culture of peoples from specific ethnic groups or distinct cultures.

Ethnohistory. The study of history using evidence primarily from documentary sources or oral traditions to understand peoples without written histories. Ethno-historical research normally focuses upon non-Western cultures that existed during the period of European expansion (i.e., from the 1400s onward), cross-cultural contact, and ensuing culture change.

Feature. Artifacts that cannot be removed from the ground without destroying their integrity. They are things which can be recorded for later study but cannot be carried to the laboratory as a ceramic sherd or a broken piece of tobacco pipe can. Common features on historic sites include postholes, cellar walls, wells, trash pits, garden walks, fence-lines, field patterns, and military fortifications.

Household. People who share a common residence. Extended or complex house-holds may include two or more generations of adults, and have lateral extension (i.e., cousins, aunts, uncles), or non-kin (servants, slaves) among their members.

Kill-off patterns. The differences observable in faunal remains which tell of the way livestock was raised and utilized for food (e.g., age at slaughter, sex, size, food sources utilized, etc.).

Kinship. The social relationships between people that are based on the way individuals are related to one another in real or imagined (i.e., fictive kinship) ways. These include blood ties and social relationships created by marriage. Associated with these ties are rights and obligations. Kinship relationships form one of the essential social institutions found in all human societies. A bilateral kinship system is one in which descent as well as rights and obligations extend through the generations on both sides of a family; a matrilineal system is one in which relation-ships traced through the mother's side are dominant.

Material culture. All products shaped and influenced by human thought and action.

Deetz specifies it as that aspect of the physical environment which is modified through culturally determined behavior while Rhys Isaac notes that it is all intentional human shapings of the environment. Many archaeologists prefer to limit the concept to those objects whose shapes endure over time, dismissing ephemeral examples which do not survive in the archaeological record.

Minimum numbers of individuals (MNI). A technique used by zooarchaeologists to estimate the number of whole animals represented by the bone elements within a collection of faunal remains.

Minimum vessel counts. An analytical procedure in which pottery sherds are separated by ware type, by decoration, and by form (using primarily rim sherds and/or base sherds) to derive the approximate number of vessels represented within a ceramic assemblage.

Modes of production. The different ways that people work to obtain and create products which can be used in the home or exchanged in the marketplace for other goods, services, or money.

Network. A web of social ties with different levels or fields of action. Anthropologists often study kinship networks, whereas zooarchaeologists look at procurement networks (how food is obtained) and distribution networks (how it is dispersed). Other types of network analysis are possible, but these are the three most useful to historical archaeologists.

Oral tradition. Information on traditional patterns of behavior, genealogical ties, manufacturing techniques, or knowledge of an event in the past which is passed down from one generation to another through verbal testimony. Eye-witness accounts and rumors are two other distinctive types of verbal testimony, but are not considered by Vansina (1961) to constitute oral tradition.

Pan-African. Cultural patterns which are observed throughout much of Africa.

Performative structures. Social action in which people creatively reconstrue the patterns of daily life (see Sahlins 1985).

Post hole. At many historic sites, men excavated holes in the ground in which they then placed posts to support a building or a fence, filling in around the post once it was placed in the ground. Often yard trash was dumped into the hole together with the soil and both were tamped down together. When the post rotted or burned, it left a distinctive stain in the soil of the same diameter it possessed (the post mold). When a post was pulled from the ground and new refuse used to fill its place, small refuse deposits were created. The forms of the post holes in the ground are clues to the shape of a building or direction of a fence while the material contained within the post holes enables archaeologists to date them.

Prescriptive structures. Social action which is highly organized according to traditional patterns of behavior, and in which there is little room for spontaneous or creative alteration (see Sahlins 1985).

Racism. The unfounded belief that there are inherent mental differences or emotional traits among individuals which derive from racial origins. Using race to explain cultural and social facts which are the result of social circumstances and historical process (see Murphy 1979: 17–23).

Recursivity. The ability of material culture to feed back upon and affect other elements of people's lives throughout a variety of social institutions. It is this aspect of things which gives them a dynamic role in human culture.

Scarification. A type of bodily adornment consisting of symbolic designs that are incised into the human skin using techniques that ensure the incisions will produce raised scars.

Sealed deposit. A feature which normally results from rapid, short-term deposition and which is then sealed by a layer above it. Wells filled and then capped with a layer of soil or rubble, or cobble-driveways covered with 5–6 inches of new soil are examples of sealed deposits which have been found at historic sites.

Seasoning. A period of acclimatization, usually accompanied by chills and fever, which immigrants experienced in the Chesapeake until their bodies adapted to the new environment.

Site. Archaeological sites are often defined by their function (i.e., domestic, industrial, burial, etc.). They are places where artifacts, features, or elements of the natural world (animal remains, botanical remains, the landscape) have been altered by human activity.

Social class. The division of society into hierarchical groups of individuals or categories of people in which those in the upper classes – elites – control portions of the lives of those in classes below them by virtue of privileged access to and control over the society's resources.

Social rank. Hierarchical positions occupied by individuals within a society.

Status and role. The differential positions of individuals within a culture (status); the range of activities which are associated with each individual status position (role). Note that any individual holds multiple status positions and plays a variety of different roles within a culture throughout his or her life cycle.

Strata. Individual layers of cultural deposition which are visibly distinct from those above and below by virtue of either soil characteristics (sand, clay, loam, etc.) or artifact contents (building debris, artifacts of different age, charcoal-mottling, etc.).

Stratigraphy. The superimposed layers of cultural deposition that exist at archaeological sites, or, in geology, the natural layers of the earth.

Symbol. An object, a spatial relationship, verbal behavior, or social action which arbitrarily stands for (or represents) another entity; the relationship is normally that of concrete to abstract, particular to general (e.g., a rose may symbolically represent love; a flag may represent a nation). The symbol itself generally appears capable of "generating and receiving effects otherwise reserved for the object to which it refers." Such effects are often highly emotionally charged (see Firth 1973: 15–16).

Synchronic/diachronic. A synchronic analysis considers a community at a single period in time whereas diachronic analysis looks at a community over time and sees it as composed of a sequence of historical events. Because the passage of time is built into archaeological sites, most archaeological analysis emphasizes diachronic aspects of culture.

Syncretism. The process by which new ideas and objects (introduced by culture contact) become fused with older, traditional ways of behavior.

Taphonomic processes. Animal and plant remains are altered after their deposition in the soil through chemical changes in their composition, through decomposition, scavenging by animals, and other events such as alternate cycles of wet and dry, cold or warm weather. The study of the way these affect the archaeological record is called the study of taphonomic processes.

Terminus post quem. The date after which a well was filled or a post hole dug; these dates are normally obtained from artifacts with well known and/or obvious date ranges (i.e., white salt-glazed stoneware which was not produced until ca. 1715, or a penny dated 1773).

Tradition. A behavioral pattern, a cluster of behavioral patterns, or a set of artifact attributes which existed over a long period of time, often within relatively small spatial areas.

Zooarchaeologists. Scientists who study the animal remains found at archaeological sites.

It is the archaeologist's sadness to have to study people through material remains, chipped flint, burnt clay, but it would be the ethnographer's madness to try to comprehend the complexity of culture through one kind of expression.

Henry Glassie, *Passing the Time in Ballymenone*

I

STARTING POINTS: REGION, TOWN, AND SITE

Now, if I would be rich, I could be a prince. I could goe into Maryland, which is one of the finest countrys of the world. I can have all the favour of my Lord Baltimore I could wish. His brother is his Lieutenant there; and a very good-natured gentleman . . . Plenty of all things [there are in Maryland]; ground there is 2,000 miles westward. I could be able, I believe, to carry a colony of rogues, another of ingenious artificers; and I doubt not one might make a shift to have five or six ingenious companions which is enough.

John Aubrey, 1676, *Brief Lives*

Transforming space into place

He who out of curiousity desires to see the Landskip of the Creation
drawn to Life . . . [may] view Mary-Land drest in her green and
fragrant Mantle of the Spring.

G. Alsop, 1666, *A Character of the Province of Mary-land*

"The past is not dead"

The past is a bridge to the future; it permeates the present. Despite the convictions
of some historical archaeologists, it has yet to die, although we neither witness it
directly nor live in it. The past remains alive in familiar ways: when older women tell
family legends to younger ones, teach them to make pots, or old men teach their
grandsons to fish and sail. It matters little whether they are Indian, African, Asian,
or Euro-Americans. The past is also with us in ways that are unrecognized or
unfamiliar.[1]

Many people in Maryland do not know there are material remains lying outside
their doorsteps that tell, sometimes with exquisite detail, of the everyday experiences
of colonists who lived here while it was still a province, a land of rich black "mould,"
or soil, dense woods, interspersed with tobacco plantations and farms in small
clearings, governed by the Calvert family through Royal charter. The question is just
who and what these material remains tell us about – black people, white people,
men, women, lifestyle, world view. Does one's social status, ethnic identity, or
gender affect what the future can learn of the past? Are those who were most visible
in earlier societies those who left the most indelible imprint on the archaeological
record or can we, with skill, learn how to read artifacts so that additional individuals
appear with clarity and grace? If so, would it make a difference? Do artifacts have
import beyond a narrow frame?

Many people, especially those whose goals necessitate the reuse or reallocation of
land, cynically believe archaeology is an obstacle to economic growth and expansion. Their view is similar to Samuel Johnson's 1751 statement, "Life is surely given
to us for higher purposes than to gather what our ancestors have wisely thrown away,
and to learn what is of no value, but because it has been forgotten." Sometimes
disparaged as piles of dirty trash, archaeological artifacts remain a fragile, vital
bridge between past, present, and future. Essentially they are things lost, set aside,
thrown away, misplaced, buried, and then forgotten.[2]

Because they are direct derivatives or surviving examples of material culture – all products shaped and influenced by human thought and action – the value of artifacts transcends their origin as things discarded and displaced. Artifact analysis is capable of disclosing beliefs so fundamental that they were taken for granted by the people who left behind an archaeological record – ideas that were unspoken assumptions essential in a culture's world view, ideas which existed at the interface of conscious and unconscious activity. These beliefs were the bedrock of human social action, encapsulating and framing daily life. This aspect of past culture is often less visible in written records such as wills, merchants' invoices, legislative records drafted for specific, well-articulated goals than in broken pieces of glass, clay, and bone, in the spatial constraints of old buildings, or in patterns made by fence lines crossing the land which shaped social space (fig. 1.1).[3]

The value of Maryland's historical archaeological record is increased because in its years as a province, men and women also left a wide variety of other cultural texts: documents in court, town, and state records, folk narratives maintained by individual families or communities, and illustrative portraits of family, favorite animals, landscape paintings, and maps. All of these can be used to create a cultural context for the artifacts and features that archaeologists excavate. The texts are collateral sets of independent evidence that enable us to draw stronger inferences about past behavior from information derived from artifacts, soil layers, and features than from data at sites that come naked, without parallel documentation. Texts strengthen and enrich archaeology; they bring individuals into focus. They let us situate an old culture, like that of the Chesapeake, in time and space (fig. 1.2).

The tobacco coast: a settled land

Historian Edmund Morgan began *American Slavery, American Freedom* asserting the importance of tobacco, by stepping back to bring in native peoples. Rhys Isaac began a more anthropological interpretation, *The Transformation of Virginia*, by surveying the landscape. He moved quickly to show culture's imprint in configurations of social space and among the marks of tobacco production. Tobacco trade governed the placement of plantations, the outlines of fields, and the shapes of houses no matter who built them. Chesapeake tobacco was food, cloth, and drink. The use of tobacco as coin helped create a society where interaction was close, personal, not mediated by electronic device. There are various points of entry to the study of its past.[4]

As a start – and it is the beginning here – one might take Maurice Bloch's point that "environment is not neutral, but is itself culturally construed" and try to gain some grasp of the colonial Chesapeake as a distinct space. It was, after all, the environmental setting in which most of the social action that fills these pages took place. If we were dealing with the era ten thousand years ago when the Susquehanna still ran in its riverbed, a different approach would be required. But we are not.[5]

From clues in old documents, evocative descriptions of a Chesapeake garden of Eden, disparaging remarks in the heat of the day, and reminiscences of crossing the Bay, the environmental context – the Maryland ecosystem – takes on a cultural hue. It also can be approached experientially by seeking out less settled areas in the

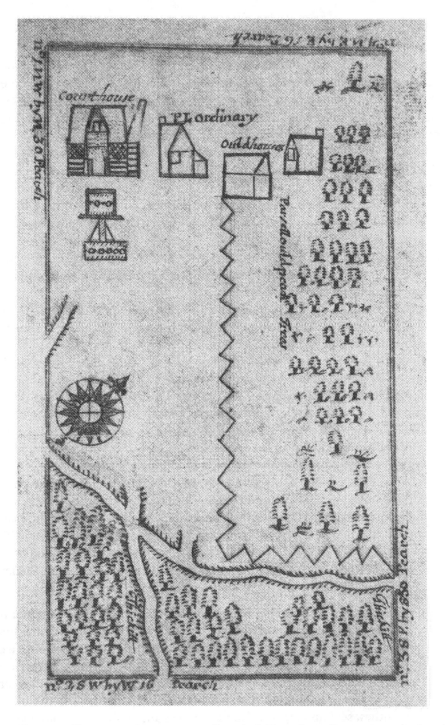

Figure 1.1. Zigzag worm fence protects a "parcel of old peach trees" on a surveyor's 1697 plat of the Charles County courthouse and ordinary. The plat inserts the cultural landscape into the wilderness: a wooden clapboard courthouse with diamond-paned windows and crib chimney with pillory and stocks outside its door. Close to a tavern lie old homes; thickets of uncleared forest abut a road. (Maryland State Archives, Charles County Court Records V No. I, MDHR 8132.)

region, by listening to wind and weather, by recreating in the mind's eye a day when travelers climbed into log canoes, paddled by people of color, or using the eyes of an artist: "all about land cradled water. Beyond the coves and harbors, loblolly and maple brushed a feathery sky. Here and there, among the myrtle and the cord grass, the honeysuckle and the pine, were weathered brick facades." The spirit of place can be heightened by thinking of the pigs of the sea, as men called dolphins, that leapt and dove, pacing ships, playing in waves, overturning canoes, and forcing Edward Kimber to swim for his life near Yorktown in the 1730s. This is not recreating past thought, but actively imagining a world that might have been, using this to structure questions and evaluate answers. As Greg Dening reminds anthropologists: "It is no breach of scientific method to claim to see the time before in the time after."[6]

Naturalists introduce the Chesapeake by writing of its subtle beauty, its shallow tide-washed shores and gentle, reserved tides, its history "bound in sand and clay and water." Ecologist Eugene Cronin views it as a "biological treasure" while earlier men saw it as bountiful, teeming with life, a garden of earthly delights. Seventeenth-century promoters also were exuberant about its soil, a loam capped by two feet of "blacke mould wherein you shall scarce find a stone, . . . like a sifted Garden-mould." Expressing a cosmology that metaphorically connected the human body and the natural world, Rev. Hugh Jones likened "the many Rivers, Creeks, and Rivulets of Water . . . to veins in humane Bodies" while others wrote of the many ships the Bay could harbor in its capacious bosom. The physical context of land and water is evocatively captured in *Tobacco Coast* by Arthur Pierce Middleton: "a vast inland sea thrusting its deep estuaries and long tidal reaches far into the wooded coastal plane . . . The presence of the Bay profoundly affected the history of Virginia and Maryland by providing an unsurpassed network of natural waterways . . . [opening] 10,000 square miles of hinterland to immediate settlement."[7]

In 1634, Father White believed the Bay was "the most delightful water I have ever seen" and contrasted the Potomac – the sweetest and greatest river he had seen – with London's Thames, "but a little finger to it." Carefully watching the weather like an anxious planter, he observed: "from the South comes Heat, Gusts, and Thunder; from the North, or North-west, cold-weather, and in winter, Frost and Snow; from the East and south-east, Raine." John Hammond contrasted it with England's climate:[8]

> The Country is as I said of a temperate nature, the dayes in summer not so long as in England, in winter longer; it is somewhat hotter in June, July and August than here, but that heat sweetly allayed by a continual breaze of winde, which never failes to cool and refresh the labourer and traveler; the cold seldom approaches sencibly untill about Christmas, . . . and when winter comes, (which is . . . no worse then is in England), it continues two monthes, seldom longer, often not so long and in that time although here seldom hard-weather keep men from labour, yet there no work is done all winter except dressing their own victuals and making of fires.[9]

Dr. Alexander Hamilton wrote an intimate letter, extracted below, to his brother containing an informative account, contrasting the region's climate with Scotland's, revealing the underlying strain the British emigrants felt, their expectations and fears:

> We have here in this country very hot weather in the summer time, of which you can have no idea. I write to you now in my shirt and drawers with all the doors and windows open upon me to receive the Breeze and yet I sweat excessively. The grass and herbage here would all dry to snuff, were it not for the frequent heavy rains we have in the summertime, which come up for the most part in the evening with violent thunder and lightning . . . our winters are for the most part exceedingly cold – your breath will freeze upon the sheets in a night, cold iron will take the skin off if you handle it, the

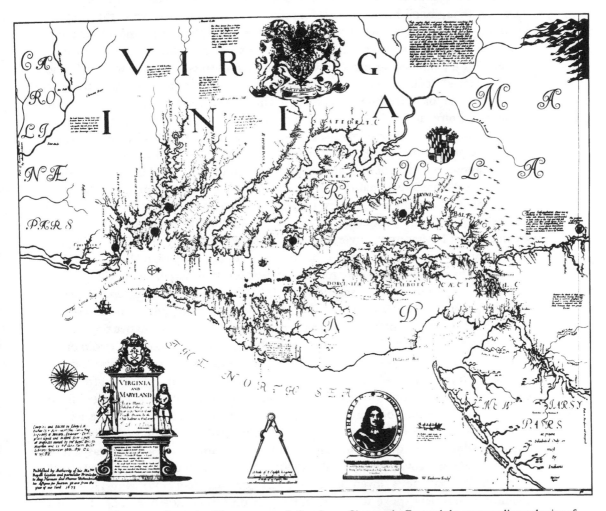

Figure 1.2. Augustine Herman map of 1673 shows Chesapeake Bay and the surrounding colonies of Maryland, Virginia, and New Jersey which was "inhabited only or most by Indians." The settlements at Norfolk, Yorktown, Williamsburg, St. Mary's City, and Annapolis are marked with circles. (Maryland State Archives, Huntington Map Collection, MSA SC 1399-679.)

noscdrops will freeze to one's nose who rides out or walks in the air. It sometimes rains and freezes here at the same time, so that the trees in the woods are sometime broken [by] the icicles upon them . . . a bowl of water or punch will freeze standing near a pretty large fire of wood and sometimes as one endeavors to warm himself, he shall roast upon one side and be almost frozen on the other.

. . . I wish well to all men and mind carefully my gallipots and vials, which are my basic stock, and I daily pray to God, that I may never be disabled by distemper, or arrive to a helpless old age in this part of the world.
Letter to B.G.H. from Annapolis, June 13, 1739.[10]

When the British arrived, the Chesapeake was already a settled land (fig. 1.3). Thus in 1634, Englishmen travelled upriver to negotiate first with the original inhabitants, stopping at two Algonkian Indian towns: Patomeck and Piscataway. Bonfires lit along the river's edge spread news of their coming; 500 bowmen gathered at a palisaded stronghold with their "Werowance" (hereditary chief) and "Cockarouses" (counselors). The Maryland Piscataways perceived the settlers as strong because of noisy English guns that announced Leonard Calvert's passage along the Potomac. This they likened to thunder, and because English ships appeared as reincarnations of mythic wonders – bewitching floating islands – curious men came aboard the vessels to see "where that tree should grow, out of which so great a canow should be hewen, supposing it all of one peece, as their canows use to be." Father White wrote that the "king of Yoacomaco" and his people, who lived across the embayment from the proposed location for St. Mary's, increasingly threatened by hostile Susquehannocks, hoped an English presence would bring greater safety. Higher up the river, Piscataways spoke of bloody raids by the Virginia settlers, by the northern Erie, and other members of the Iroquoian alliance. And so the native peoples traded Leonard Calvert a recently deserted open village, one where the Yoacomaco had recently lived, whose occupation extended seven thousand years or more back to a time when the land was still an upland forest.[11]

The English settlement of Maryland resulted in retrenchment, a native population decimated by European diseases, and ultimately a long journey north to rejoin other Native Americans in upstate New York. Throughout this process, Maryland Indians were able to preserve many elements of traditional culture. In 1715, the fifth Lord Baltimore filed a petition with the Crown asking that the province be excepted from a regional military plan because his council believed Maryland Indians were peaceable and their numbers were too small for effective warfare. At the same time, they formed a fringe community; negotiations with Native Americans were one aspect of Captain Calvert's governorship in the 1720s. Men continued to wear Indian dress (e.g. Mark Challoner's inventory), to trade for furs (e.g., William Holland's inventory); travelers spoke with Indian couples on woodland roads (e.g. Edward Kimber at Snow Hill); a few Indians worked in menial jobs within towns (such as selling lamp black and cleaning chimneys); Indian bowls were used on some English farms; a few planters sold tomahawks in their stores. Some Indians taught the

English how to tame turkeys. A few native place names remained; others such as *portobaco* were anglicized (i.e., Port Tobacco). Here and there, to those such as Henry Parker who could speak their language and lived among them, they taught medical skills prized by the colonists.[12]

The English province

The Indians gave Maryland settlers a gift of inestimable worth – the opportunity – and a product – tobacco – which the English adopted and used to build their own dominion. The Chesapeake's network of creeks and rivers provided ready access to the interior, and facilitated a supplemental fur trade. The cleared fields of the Yoacomaco village gave the English a head start with farming tasks; a few alterations to a native long house provided Father White with a chapel to celebrate mass (fig. 1.4).[13]

Figure 1.3. Detail from the Herman map showing the Indian villages at Pamunkey and Piscataway in Prince George's County. The encroaching English plantations have begun to line the Potomac along its Maryland shore as far up river as St. Thomas. (Maryland State Archives, Huntington Map Collection, MSA SC 1399-679.)

To the English, the Chesapeake was a place filled with opportunities for profit and for pleasure. From an economist's and a demographer's perspective, the society "was open enough to allow a man who started at the bottom without special advantages to acquire a substantial estate and a responsible position." Historian Jack Green provides a succinct summation:[14]

> Chesapeake society was highly materialistic, infinitely more secular, competitive, exploitive, and very heavily devoted to commercial agricultural production for an export market. Its high demand for labor and high mortality rates combined to produce a population that was disproportionately male, young, single, immigrant, and mobile. The process of family formation was slow. Social institutions were weak, authority was tenuous, and individualism was strong.

In the countryside where families cleared the woods to build small tobacco farms, living standards were not high; life was difficult. Men had to build homes for their women and children, barns for their cattle, shelter for the hogs and the hens, dig wells for water, cut firewood, and put up worm-panelled fences to protect fields and orchards. Then they had to care for the animals and tend crops, although women helped by feeding pigs, milking cows, and mothering chickens. Women also worked in the fields. Since tobacco was labor-intensive, there was little time for anything else; Chesapeake housewives rarely had time to spin and weave, to sew and cook. The simplest foods, coarse and meager, sufficed; the plainest clothes made do. Men complained because there were not enough women to go around; the sex-ratio was skewed. Rural families bought necessities at storehouses on wealthy plantations where enterprising merchant-planters extended credit.[15]

Here and there archaeologists have excavated the sites these households first left behind. The evidence is sparse. At Martin's Hundred there were coffin nails, pins from body shrouds, and evidence of war. Stains in the soil signalled the presence of post holes left from fences and buildings. Other soil stains in the floor of a St. Mary's chapel mark where bodies, including the earlier Calverts, were laid to rest. Zooarchaeologists who age animal bones say Chesapeake bones reveal how families used livestock for food *after* its productive farm days were done. The dominant pottery forms were utilitarian vessels of earthen and stone. The meager possessions of ordinary folk are overshadowed by the artifacts rich families left; there were great gaps in styles of life. Still, even the wealthy adopted lifestyles in which comforts were limited.[16]

Furthermore, the economy stagnated ca. 1680, not recovering until ca. 1720, although by then more craftsmen lived in the region, especially coopers and carpenters whose products were essential for marketing tobacco. Some farmers made shoes on the side and took up other trades to supplement incomes; a few women knit stockings, charging 2 shillings a pair. Ordinary planters lived simply, their incomes ranging from £10–£15. Great planters had incomes of £200–£250, but through diversification, by serving as merchants, money-lenders, lawyers, land speculators, by holding public office, and adding activities that cross-cut ordinary economic and

Figure 1.4. Plan of an open village with Native American long houses and tobacco fields. (Original drawing by John White in 1585 first published in *Thomas Hariot's Virginia, 1560–1621*; photograph by Henry Miller courtesy of the St. Mary's City Commission.)

legal boundaries, a planter could make an additional £200–£350 per year. To do so, however, required indentured labor or slave-holdings; neither servants nor slaves were always treated well.[17]

Calvert leadership

From 1634 to 1689, the Calvert family governed the province from a personal base inside it. Members of the family who made Maryland their home included Leonard Calvert who led the first settlement and was the younger brother of Cecilius, the second Lord Baltimore. He served as governor for the first fourteen years (1633–47). Philip Calvert, the youngest brother of Cecilius and Leonard, also served briefly as Governor (1660–1), but held a variety of administrative positions throughout his life that gave stability and leadership to the Province. Finally, the 24-year old son and heir of the second Lord Baltimore, Charles Calvert, was also sent to Maryland to govern (1661–75), assuming the proprietorship with his father's death in 1675 (chart 1.1). The Calvert family consistently drew on the strength of kinship alliances to tighten their political networks, but like other aristocratic families they also used material contrasts to designate and legitimate their status and authority.[18]

With the 1689 revolution (when the third Lord Baltimore was abroad in England), political power went to the Crown. But the 25 years that elapsed before the Calverts regained control in 1715 were insufficient to eradicate the Calvert charisma built during prior years. Memory in oral cultures is retentive. Imagery of sight and sound is strong. Although the Calvert family had no mnemonic devices (buildings, church graveyards, ancient trees surrounded by legend) in the Annapolis landscape like those that stood in Lower Maryland, they were silent members, through marriage, of select Maryland families. Calvert family legends were part of the province's folk history, imprinted upon Maryland's territory in many ways. Thus the family charisma, although diminished, still endured in 1715. The fifth Lord Baltimore built on it by once again sending Calvert men to rule the province.[19]

Yet, with the re-establishment of proprietary rule in 1715, the anti-proprietary movement also gained cohesion and strength. In fact, the dance of power, the tug and pull of Court and Country party in the 1720s, as expressed in legislative records, makes the years of the Calverts' personal governorship (1720–32) especially valuable for ethnographic study. These years were ones in which deft power plays are particularly visible, making accessible the way humor, wit, and subvention were used in unanticipated ways (from a modern point of view) to assert the legitimacy of different factions to exist and to possess political power.[20]

The young fifth Lord Baltimore (initially through his guardian, Lord Guilford) first moved to re-assert the proprietor's authority in the province by sending his "cousin" Captain Charles Calvert, and then his own brother, Benedict Leonard Calvert, to Maryland to govern. When Benedict Leonard encountered opposition, if not treachery, within family circles, Lord Baltimore sent a second brother, Edward Henry, to provide support. In 1732, he came himself. All of the Calvert men and their wives had personal servants; Benedict Leonard also brought an English housekeeper and a cook with him. Then too, he had a secretary and, like his great-grandfather, a young black attendant (fig. 1.5). His cousin, the Captain, further invested in slave-holdings and at his death thirty-one slaves were attached to the urban household while twenty-four more lived on rural farms. No other wealthy *town* household kept as many domestic servants; most Maryland men in the early 1700s used servants and slaves to build a productive labor base and not to designate wealth. Thus, the social and cultural complexity that characterized all Calvert households over time was seen in the Calverts' Annapolis household also, but further intensified by the presence of black slaves from exotic homelands.[21]

Of the Calverts that passed through the doors of the house on State Circle, none possessed more power than the fifth Lord Baltimore himself. Yet he was in Annapolis too briefly (about six months) to associate changes in the home or

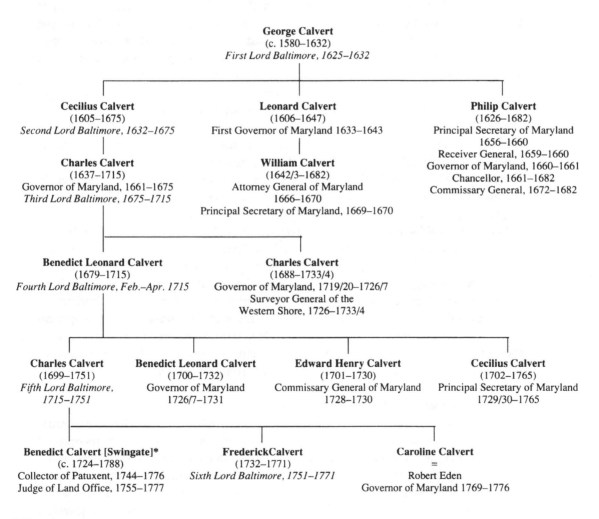

* Natural sons

Chart 1.1. Kinship chart of Calvert men who held political positions in Maryland

household lifestyle with his presence. Edward Henry Calvert, the youngest brother to come to Annapolis, died too young – at age 29 – and too soon – fifteen months after his arrival – to become an active force in Maryland society or in its political structure (chart 1.1). Edward Henry Calvert would be a minor actor in the social drama that created the archaeological record of the Calvert Site were it not that, as a young married aristocrat, he was head of a household whose material expectations were formed by intimate knowledge of and enculturation in the norms of the English country gentry. The things he and his young wife, his cousin Margaret Lee, brought or bought were the objects English gentry believed to be necessities.

The couple's household possessions are seen, in part, among the artifacts recovered from the site. Certainly there are remnants of objects Captain Charles and Rebecca Calvert owned; there are also fragmentary pieces of Benedict Leonard's possessions. The impression received from the probate inventories and what is known of the background of the two Calvert wives, Rebecca Gerard Calvert and Margaret Lee Calvert, is that Margaret had a more intimate knowledge and sophisticated view of courtly hospitality. She was also the great-granddaughter of a Stuart king in a town where Scotsmen constituted a significant, forceful, upwardly mobile sector of the population. In a town as small as Annapolis, her royal ancestry was common knowledge. Of more archaeological importance is the entertaining implied by the couple's possession of eighty-four pewter plates and sixty drinking glasses. These suggest the ostentation and labor base required to support hospitality in the Calvert home. Yet in the end, responsibility for the archaeological record of the site is divided. Benedict Leonard Calvert's influence can be seen in various ways; his cousin's impact can also be traced. The slaves too left their imprint.[22]

With the establishment of a proprietary Governor's household in Annapolis, the Calverts could once again influence life in the colony as the third Lord Baltimore did when he lived in Maryland (1661–84). It was necessary to do so if the fifth Lord Baltimore's prerogatives were to be maintained and enhanced. The influence both the earlier and later Calvert households wielded was based in part on charisma, a form of symbolic power. It was facilitated by the number and variety of reciprocal relationships that kept many Maryland people in contact, however tangentially, with the Calvert family. It drew on a cultural precedent, the property of visual contrast in the material realm of life. It extended outward from Annapolis.

Annapolis, a capital "cittie"

Annapolis lies on the western shore of Anne Arundel County (fig. 1.2). Anne Arundel County was formed by an act of the General Assembly in 1650; its original settlers were religious dissidents from the Norfolk-Nansemond area at the foot of the Bay. Ridgely listed the different names for the settlement: Arundelton, Severn, Proctor's, Anne Arundel town, and, finally, Annapolis. Reps concluded "the rather bewildering set of names may indicate the informality of its legal status and physical form."[23]

The town itself is located on a small peninsula between the Severn and South rivers. Thomas Todd (hence Todd's Creek) first obtained title to the peninsula through a patent in the 1670s. The locale is filled with gently contoured hills, knolls, and bluffs ranging from 25 to 40 ft above sea level (fig. 1.6). Many extend to the water's edge where their wave-cut headlands drop sharply to the shore. The high land is pierced by deep, steep-sided ravines or gullies hiding fresh meadows at their bases often yielding small springs and clear, freshwater pools. Lower and closer to

Figure 1.5. Cecilius Calvert, second Lord Baltimore, with his grandson and a black attendant. (Painting by Gerard Goest; illustration courtesy of the Enoch Pratt Free Library, Baltimore, Maryland.)

the shore, a tracery of brackish estuaries merges with tidal creeks and flows to the Bay.

In 1682, legislators chose Arundelton as a good place to develop under Maryland's first Town Act. Supposedly no more than half a dozen families (fewer than thirty to fifty people) resided in the hamlet. To facilitate its growth, Richard Beard surveyed the town in 1684/85, griding the land into rectangles 9 perches by 16 perches (148.5 ft × 264 ft) and squares 12 perches by 12 perches (198 ft × 198 ft), a plan similar to grids for Chestertown and Wye and his earlier layout for Londontown. His new plan integrated the natural terrain: hills, creeks, coves, marshes, shore, and outlets to the Bay; the latter he assessed using a mariner's criteria of tide, wind, and sail. The plan made space for families already here; it outlined narrow streets that ran southeast–northwest, aligned parallel to Acton Creek (then Todd's Creek), bypassing a series of steep ravines and gullies. These streets were cut at right angles by other streets running southwest to northeast. By and large it was a paper plan.[24]

In 1696, for military, political, religious, and environmental reasons, legislators selected Annapolis as the new provincial capital. Although the move, made during the Royal administration (1692–1714) took the capital away from counties largely settled by Catholics, ease of reach (centrality) was the reason cited when the General Assembly overruled St. Mary's protest. The change broke the tie between the Calvert family and the seat of power; the Calverts owned no land and had minimal influence among Anne Arundel's protestant households. In Annapolis there were no commanding locations, no ancient trees or tall chapels that evoked the Calvert past, whereas in southern Maryland Mattapany, the mansion house of the third Lord Baltimore still looked out from the headlands towards the shipping lanes – a ruin left standing as a deliberate reminder of Calvert power. Additional testimony that the Calverts knew the impact of visual imagery can be seen in baroque elements they introduced at St. Mary's City. Hence the attention paid to Annapolis vistas and ascending topography once Queen Anne restored the family's power is significant (see Chapter 6).[25]

An earlier governor, Francis Nicholson (1694–8), evaluated potential locations for the new capital using criteria similar to those used by Leonard Calvert in 1634. Jerome Hawley recorded why Calvert accepted the Indians' offer of St. Mary's lands: "a very commodious situation for a Towne, in regard the land is good, the ayre wholesome and pleasant, the River affords a safe harbour for ships of any burthern, and a very bould shoare [i.e., steeply rising, abutting deep water]; fresh water, and wood there is in plenty, and the place so naturally fortified, as with little difficultie it will be defended from any enemie." Annapolis had the potential to be a place healthful, fruitful, easily fortified, accessible for trade, even as St. Mary's did. Like families in Charleston, South Carolina, Annapolitans could write of their town as "a verie convenient place . . . , free of swamps and marshes, a high bloffe land excellently well watered [with] wholesome air." Yet Oldmixon's 1708 caution must be remembered: what Maryland men called towns "would not pass for anything but little villages in other countries."[26]

Inhabited space

Yet even frontier settlements that were splendid only in men's minds might be grandly planned. Thus Governor Nicholson created a formal baroque design while his years in office gave new names to places. Busby's Cove became the Governor's Pond, Weathering Cove became Nicholson's Cove; lands above the harbor also took his name – Nicholson's Pasture – as did the hills northwest of Annapolis known as Nicholson's Vineyard. Although the same solitary blue heron stood one-legged in the mud at the cove, pecking at fish and watching, the displacement of original settlers' names with symbolically charged designations related to the politics of space changed the community's orientation from local to provincial. It didn't matter that the heron didn't recognize the governor walking past; the waterways remained as major roadways. Continuity and change co-existed. People continued to enter town by sea, sometimes via the bay-side road that "leaps the fishing creek," sometimes departing from Pig's Point, Lyon's Creek, or Indian Landing. Water routes crisscrossed the Bay and creeks near Annapolis. There were at least four anchorages off the shoreline.[27]

Rivers and creeks virtually encircled the town except for a narrow band of land on which men grubbed out a rough dirt road, ditched on either side, and running west beneath the wooden gatehouse to the tobacco lands (fig. 1.7). The general belief among historians has been that the locus of settlement in the earliest years was along

Figure 1.6. In the 1858 Sachse lithograph, the Annapolis terrain is less wooded than it was in the early 1700s; there are more and better built homes, among them the 1760s Georgian mansions of the Golden Era. To the right, the U.S. Naval Academy stands on reclaimed land; the former location of the Governor's Pond shows as a wooded thicket. (Maryland State Archives, Marion E. Warren Collection, MSA SC 1890–1919.)

Acton Creek in the southeast sector of the town and that the nucleus of the settlement was a family of shipbuilders. Shipwright Street, one of the earliest in the city, is a remnant of this occupation (fig. 1.8). At the Calvert site, however, a few 7/64" pipe stems (most prevalent from 1650–80), and the remains of a post-constructed, earthfast building inside an old fence line are tantalizing clues that may indicate the existence of another neighborhood in the early town, one directly opposite the old town of Providence across the Severn River.[28]

With the construction of the first State House in 1696 and the church in 1700, Nicholson's grand plan was implemented. The prominence it gave to church and state buildings gave these visual mastery of town space. All other structures existed in tandem with or in reaction to the arenas of social activity represented by these two major buildings. The subordinate position of the church was seen in the original positioning of its door to the east, facing the State House, whereas the State House faced away from the Church to oversee the Bay. Its visual domination of the town continued into the twentieth century.

While most of the other buildings in the town, including "a parcel of wooden houses," were frame constructed, a 1701 deed mentioned the "small brick house" of John Perry's lying on two lots above Conduit Street which Perry prized for the view from his garden across the shore to the water. Another described a 44-foot-long stone house situated in a waterfront garden that may be older than Perry's home. And Benjamin Tasker had inherited his father-in-law, William Bladen's house and garden that overlooked the creek (now Spa creek) which he willingly negotiated easements for in order to protect. Thus the town had an architectural range seen in

Figure 1.7. A broad hoe and a scythe are but two of the agricultural implements used to clear the land which were recovered from the site. (Photograph by Marion E. Warren.)

court records that explicit descriptions (e.g., Hugh Jones' 1698 letter or Ebenezer Cook's 1708 poem) in other texts do not convey.[29]

In 1736, Englishman Edward Kimber compared the larger houses at Yorktown to London homes: "equal in Magnificence to many of our superb ones." He also saw smaller wooden structures "differing very little from booths" at a country fair. Most houses were wooden; rebuilding began with renewed prosperity ca. 1720. Annapolitan homes ran the gamut and sat side by side with commercial outbuildings – bakers' ovens; meat houses; brew houses; butchers' shops; a ropewalk; tanning yards; a forge; a potter's kiln; a print shop; market house; a carpenter's complex on the sandbar; for protection, a powder magazine and small fort:[30]

> [by 1740] a Small Semi-Circle of 15 Guns, Six pounders, raised about 4 Feet above the Level of the Water Fixt Fast by the Brick & Trunions in 2 Circular

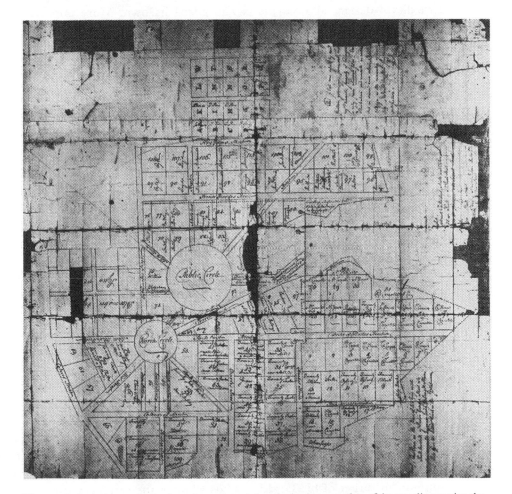

Figure 1.8. Some street names have been altered, but the basic town plan of Annapolis remains the same as it is in this eighteenth-century map based on the Stoddert Survey of 1718 and drawn by John Callahan. (Maryland State Archives Map Collection, MSA SC 1427-501.)

pieces of Timber so that of Course they cannot Traverse, & no Breast work, so that a person is Exposed down to the Calf of his Legs, that a Small Privateer might drive Every Person out of it or Destroy them in a Few Minutes.[31]

But these are bare facts that do not get beneath the surface of the city. We could begin again with the land and its people, placing things upon it. For example, an eighteenth-century sketch (fig. 1.9) of Yorktown shows a typical Chesapeake town with middling and larger homes on the bluff, and smaller wooden houses, shanties, and warehouses just above the tide line. In harmony with this model, men positioned the original home at the Calvert site on high ground. The lot they chose was secure, guarded from hostile attack by the city walls and gate, and protected by its elevation from the Chesapeake's flood and storm tides. A stout palisado, or "paling" fence was unnecessary because the massive two-story city gates, based on a medieval design, allowed the city to guard its own. More importantly, as the Province emerged from the tobacco depression, life in the city was bustling, its population growing; daily life in Maryland had improved greatly in the decade that the Calvert men moved to Annapolis.[32]

Waterfront activities

Annapolis was a market town, a capital town, that contracted and expanded. Sometimes it was a busy place; at other times it slept, especially when tobacco kept people busy from dawn to dusk. Situated on the dividing line between South and North, today it still keeps southern time, awakens slowly in the morning. Men carved it from woods and marsh so that the town sat on seven hills shorn of much of the foliage that made the Chesapeake coast a forest-land, a place where families could not "see their next neighbor's house for trees." Like most frontier towns, trees sat ever ready to encroach from its landward side. Like most coastal communities, its better buildings sat high above the water while small, ramshackle buildings and odd wooden docks perched on the lower reaches, vulnerable to storm tides. In this land, many viewed nature as an enemy.[33]

People were wary of ground near the water where fog clung, attacking the low lands first, leaving them last as it burned off or receded to sea. Disease, they thought, accompanied the mist. William Byrd II revealed such a world view in praise of land "far above swamps and savannahs . . . [without] any great bodys of water to fill the atmosphere with fogs and foul exhalations." The "foul exhalations" were not all due to natural causes; families often tossed their refuse in the harbor, and mariners swept all sorts of things overboard in the hustle and bustle of commercial trade. Not that the unruly behavior sometimes seen along the waterfront was always tolerated. Two Annapolitans were brought to court for firing their muskets across the wharf, another for dropping stones in it, while Margaret Steele, the goldsmith's wife, was called "a common disturber of his Lordship's boats" after she carelessly dropped a lighted "brand" in a neighbor's scow. Fined five shillings, Mistress Steele may simply have been dumping hot coals from her hearth into the nearest water receptacle.[34]

The difference between the lower lands and the higher could also be seen in the shape, composition, size, and use of buildings lying close to the water. Annapolitans placed few public buildings near the water's edge: the jail and, at times, the market house. Here, in public view, the pillory stood where men were placed, clothed or bare-breeched, to face the ridicule of their peers. Here too, women were whipped for giving birth to bastard children and men for stealing turkeys and lambs or for lying. The waterfront was often a busy place where black dockhands worked side by side with white. Yet it was also where soul-drivers sold African-born slaves at auction, especially in spring and summertime so slave-masters could benefit from their labor before the onset of the sickly, malaria months – the Chesapeake's days of death – exacted its toll.

Figure 1.9. Yorktown, Virginia, in 1754–6, had a hierarchical ranking of buildings which depended, in part, on size, building material, and location. Only the most elaborate homes had landscaped gardens. Insets show the terraced pleasure garden in front of one Georgian mansion (the Nelson house now opened by the National Park Service) and the small, irregular buildings that huddled along the shore. (Drawing by John Gauntlett reproduced through the courtesy of the Mariner's Museum, Newport News, Virginia.)

The only African sold who was freed and later wrote about it was Ayuba Suleiman (fig. 1.10) who arrived on a ship from Gambia in 1731; Thomas Bluett, who wrote down Suleiman's oral account, passed over his sale in Annapolis. It was not the first time that Suleiman was sold; only in hindsight was it the most important.[35] Some grasp of what was involved, however, survives in an account by an English convict, William Green: chained to another convict, the two men were

> driven in lots like oxen or sheep [and inspected by purchasers who] search us there as the dealers in horses do those animals in this country, by looking at our teeth, viewing our limbs, to see if they are sound and fit for their labour, and if they approve of us after asking our trades and names, and what crimes we have been guilty of to bring us to that shame, the bargain is made.[36]

Men who bought convict laborers or indentured servants were often quite specific

Figure 1.10. Portrait of Ayuba Ben Suleiman (known by the English as Job Ben Solomon) drawn in 1733 when he was in England to see King George II while on his way home from Maryland. (Illustration originally from the *Gentleman's Magazine* of 1755, courtesy of the British Library.)

about their wants in terms of age and honesty. At heart, however, the town did not expect the latter. To sell slaves, traders brought prospective buyers out to their ships, took slaves ashore, exhibited them in dark, smoky taverns, and sailed up creeks and bays marketing their wares. It was a dirty business, and the cellars of some homes were built to serve as slave stalls.

Men also unloaded other live, less heart-wrenching cargoes. Sloops such as John Brewer's regularly made dock overflowing with live oysters and crabs. One could buy basketsful for a few pence or a whole sloopful for less than £1. In winter, Nanticoke deer hunters brought venison in their canoes to sell; Hugh Jones, an observer sent by the Royal Society in the 1690s, wrote of their hunting: "They take delight in nothing else." Small coastal vessels filled with pigs, goats, sheep, cows, and chickens also docked at Annapolis. These were ventures commissioned by local butchers who supplied the town with meat. Once ashore, most animals were slaughtered, but some became sea travelers, held in wooden crates tied down on decks, who provided food for sailors. In great storms, they washed overboard, but through this mechanism of trans-Atlantic live shipments, more exotic creatures reached Maryland: muscovy ducks from South America (possibly entering via the Caribbean or West Africa), guinea hens from West Africa, pheasants from Asia via Europe, parrots from tropical forests, perhaps a monkey or two. Rats came too. Always the "dump ducks" or sea gulls wheeled overhead or sat in guard rows on ridge poles. Feral cats, skunks, and racoons may have been occasional visitors; cart horses regularly stood around, flicking flies with their tails, neighing, contributing to the wharfage refuse.[37]

The sights and the sounds of this nether region of the town gave it a flavor of its own, one distinct from New Town where craftsmen's homes clustered, different from the old shipyards to the east with their aroma of sawdust, tar, or rosin, unlike the currier's yards riddled with tan vats near the city gates, the butchers' shops near the market, the ropewalk. This region contained small warehouses filled in season with fragrant tobacco leaves, taverns for seamen and travellers, and tiny kitchen gardens in the nooks and crannies of house yards. The tide ran further inland; then as now waves sometimes drove against the hill (fig. 1.11). And each time it rained the sandbank at the base of the hill got larger with the soil the stream through Pinkney Street brought down. It is no wonder that men promised to build houses raised "at least two feet above the ground."[38]

Two shops

Each time I read John Davisson's 1721 inventory,* the image of his home resides near the Annapolis docks. Davisson, a Scotsman, barber, trader, and medicine man ("Dr. Sure and Certain") kept a house that epitomized the "organic" quality of seventeenth-century living. He slept upstairs on a feather bed in a room filled with bushels of red and white wheat, malt, 1,000 pounds of sea-biscuits, four casks

---

* Probate inventories are lists of the personal belongings of an individual at death (i.e., assets), and the debts owing to and from an estate.

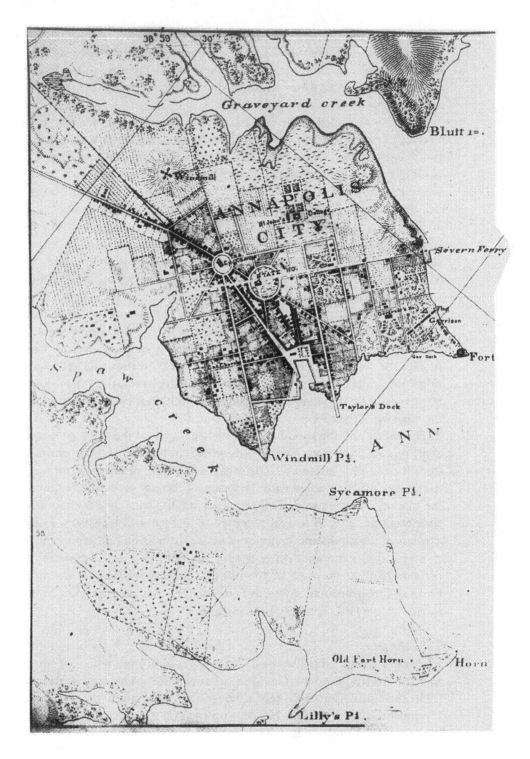

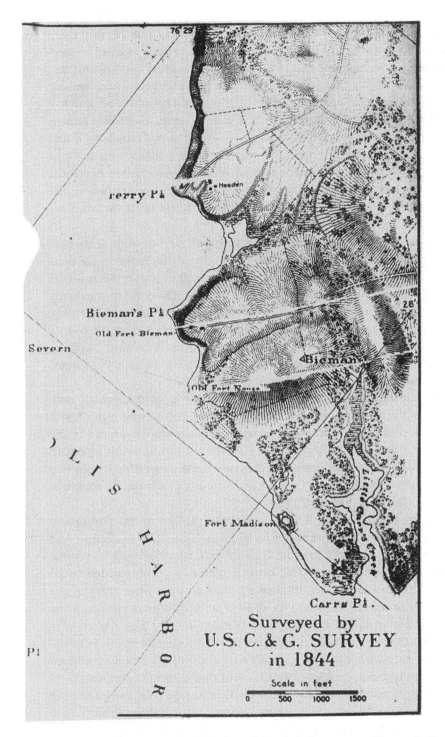

Figure 1.11. 1844 U.S. Coast & Geodetic Survey map of Annapolis shows a narrow harbor which originally extended inland to the back edges of the market square (shown here on filled land). (Maryland State Archives Map Collection MSA SC 1427-10.)

holding 400 pounds of chocolate nuts, and another 96 pounds of processed chocolate. Much of his clothing was filthy or "foul." Downstairs he stocked a store-room with an amazing assortment of goods: bushels of nails, child-sized drums and fiddles, sixty-four hats, silk caps, more chocolate, combs and head-rolls, looking glasses and fans, razors, tobacco boxes, pendants, seals, a little bit of thread, and five lawn-searchers. It was a treasure-trove for boys and girls: whistles, children's horses, birds, and other small toys, eighty-eight "babies of several sorts," chalk men and beasts (see fig. 1.12), and school supplies. It was also well stocked with wooden wares; in his adjacent "small store" families purchased cheap pottery (see Appendix A-1). The barber shop was simply a lower-level room in the dwelling where the family cooked, customers drank as needed, and seventy dozen buckets sat safe from the rain.[39]

Almost as many items, however, were stored in the yard. Barrels of tar were kept in the "north shade" while the "southeast shade" held foodstuffs central in the diets of servants, slaves, and other poor folk: flour, hops, rum, salt, sugar, molasses, tubs and barrels of hog-lard and pickles, soap, preserved meat, dried codfish, mackerel, hominy beans, as well as more coarse earthenware and thousands of tiny glass vials. Pottery, food, buckets, damaged fish, knitting needles, and small pictures were sold in the yard together with "bunches" of beads and necklaces of bastard pearls or colored gold. Davisson's prices were cheap; many of the things he sold were items people could do without but wouldn't wish to.

If his store was near the waterfront (as the ship's stores he sold suggest), then children sent on errands from craftsmen's homes in New Town (where the Naval Academy now stands) could easily pass his way walking to the store operated by the servants of lawyer Charles Carroll of Annapolis. Carroll was a Roman Catholic with a small chapel attached to his home, who held favor in the proprietor's eyes. His wife's grandmother was also a Calvert. Yet the Carrolls too kept a store. Its contents, however, were unlike those of Davisson's.[40]

An Irish immigrant himself, Carroll knew the temperament of the population well. He kept prodigious quantities of rum – 62 hogsheads or 10,692 gallons – and a modest supply of wine. With the exception of food (a small offering of plums, currants, sugar, and one or two spices), the other essentials a family needed could be readily obtained from Charles Carroll's store. It held an impressive array of dry goods: some good, some damaged; most were coarser fabrics for work clothes; a few were luxury cloths. The range of colors was restricted, but the necessaries were present (i.e., more than 22,000 buttons; ninety-six hooks-and-eyes; needles, thread). For the few times when a wife couldn't sew a suit of clothes, Carroll also had a few pieces of ready-made apparel as well as stout shoes, hose, sheepskin gloves and fancier pairs. The family orientation to his retail trade, however, can be seen in the emphasis on cooking utensils, on plain dishes and breakfast basins (see Appendix A-1), maple-hafted knives and forks, pewter plates, sieves and strainers, iron lanterns, brass candlesticks, bedding, and tools for cleaning: scrubbing brushes, mops, hair brooms. Certainly his storekeeper sold some frivolous items: a few silver rings with glass stones, ear-pendants set in gold and silver, silk-covered clogs; silk nightgown sashes, silk girdles – one of tinsel and gold – and a lace hat. Practicality appears, however, with the eye glasses: forty monocles, three pairs of silver-rimmed, seven of tortoise shell, and eight of leather. It is clear, then as now, eyesight failed with age.

Practicality also lay behind the coarse-milled caps for Negroes, 250 straw hats to wear in the fields, and farming tools of all kinds including at least four types of hoe. There were several hundred drum, perch, and rock-fish hooks with assorted fishing lines; gun flints and bullet molds; saddles and assorted horse tackling. But the store did not cater solely to domestic needs or to those of rural planters. Clerks might purchase stationery and inkhorns; students might buy grammar and vocabulary books. It was also well stocked with tools and building supplies for craftsmen. A mariner could buy a ship's compass. A would-be pirate could purchase a buccaneer's gun.

But the black woman who wanted to string a beaded necklace or the washer-woman who wanted a "baby" for her niece had to trade elsewhere. The socially conscious families who wished to buy a tea cup, coffee pot, or Chinese porcelain punch bowl found that Amos Garrett, a former ship's supercargo and now the wealthiest man around, catered to their tastes. Nearby Thomas Bordley ran a very discreet store; no one now knows what John Brice sold. Yet, any consideration of their shops discloses different planes of social interaction.

Town folk

At least four different "social fields" are immediately visible: the planter-gentry; ordinary planters; artisans and craftsmen; servants, slaves, and unskilled workers. Information in court records suggests others: boatmen, clerks, convicts, laborers, widows, migrants, and occasionally a prostitute or "woman of ill fame." Tavern-

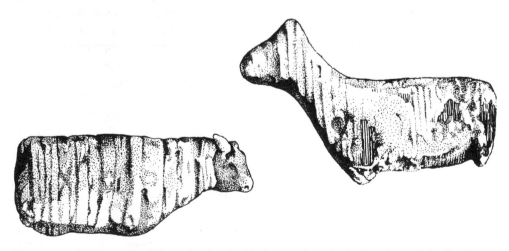

Figure 1.12. Children at the Calvert site played with tiny wooden animals (less than 2 inches long), painted white. According to his inventory, John Davisson sold similar "beasts" in his Annapolis store in 1720. Toys such as these are not often recovered archaeologically because wood decomposes readily in soil. (Illustration by Julie Hunter-Abbazia.)

owners and innkeepers were intermediate and provided the social space that cross-cut the ranking system. But there were also age distinctions in the community. Some people were very old, upwards of sixty, who showed up in Court to plead for tax relief. These included the poor: unskilled men, widows left with small means of support, and aged African-born slaves. William Peele, for example, brought Old Bob, Old Sarah, and Old Saltwater John to court – personal appearances were required – in November 1734 to have them declared "levie-free"; Henry Hill brought Bess and Hannah who each had been in Maryland "above 40 years" (since the 1690s). Elderly and indigent or enslaved, these were people who did not leave probated estates and were not readily visible in business transactions. Little is known of their lives.[41]

Another group was much younger. Indentured servants, apprentices, and household slaves formed a set of young, single people who intermingled freely around 1720–30. Approximately one third of the children born out of wedlock in Annapolis were mulattos, the offspring of liaisons between black men and white women.* Friendships between black and white men can be inferred also from occasional glimpses of servants and slaves drinking together in taverns, outwitting their masters. Not that it always worked. Henry Tudor Williams and John Sutton were caught entertaining the mayor's servants and fined "for swearing they left after one bowl of punch whereas they stayed longer." The system of written passes – permission slips, really, such as schoolchildren sometimes carry – that slaves needed to go about on their own grew out of a system originally designed to regulate servants.[42]

Of all these, people most feared transported convicts. They were seen as people who would lie at the drop of a hat to protect themselves; their word was unacceptable in a court of law. No judge asked a convict maidservant who fathered her child. No one could believe the answer. What was worse, convict servants ran off as opportunity arose. In 1720 at least nine plotted to seize the town's arms and ammunition, steal a boat, and sail away. The Mayor's court considered the situation seriously and carefully. The town, after taking depositions in investigative sessions, collected sizeable sureties from the masters and mistresses of those it believed were involved; two ringleaders were taken before the governor, Captain Calvert, for further questioning.[43]

Overall, however, the range of behavior that brought individuals to the local courts was not characterized by violence directed at the community. Crime was sporadic. Two spinsters broke into one man's home; another stole a canvas petticoat

---

* The term "mulatto" in the eighteenth century was initially used to designate a combination of attributes, i.e., a mixed racial heritage (white and black; red and black) or non-European heritage (Native American) which also carried with it rights to freedom. These were not absolute; mulatto children born to white mothers had to serve an indenture (until age 31) before they could obtain freedom; they might be classified as mulatto at any time after birth. The offspring of black women and white men, however, were classified as *mulatto slaves* if the mixed ancestry was discernible, and they had no rights. Some were manumitted by their fathers (cf. Callcott's discussion (1991: 378–84) of examples in the nineteenth century); most were not. Thus the definition of this term in its early eighteenth-century usage was more restrictive, evolving to include children born to black mothers as time passed.

and white apron. Thomas Holmes, a "common drunkard," beat his wife and was jailed; like many men, he persuaded her not to testify. Someone beat the town drums at an unseasonable time of night purely for the hell of it. A man under undue influence of liquor behaved "indecently," said things derogatory to "the Dignity of the Court and to the ill example of others."[44]

One tanner stole a hide from another. Country folk sometimes sold stolen goods in the town (pigs, lambs, turkeys). Occasionally, counterfeit money circulated; unpaid debts were often brought to court. The emphasis on financial gain, on getting one's due, was clear, but the level of knowledge about what went on in the community and who did what to whom made it difficult to escape detection. Laborer Darby Callahan, for example, was found guilty of unlawfully bartering, dealing, and receiving a pine plank from Tarrence Magriger which belonged to a local bricklayer. If identifying a stolen turkey seems hard, surely identifying a pine plank defies the odds. Obviously very careful attention was paid to the appearance, condition, and disappearance of things.[45]

Maryland men had long memories too when it mattered. Benjamin Tasker came to court in 1745 to remind the town that it had not entered on its records an agreement he had made with them 20 years earlier "as Captain Gordon very well

Figure 1.13. Small Maryland house and a coastal sailing vessel shown in a sketch of the town fort on Severn River (drawn ca. 1800 by Benjamin Ogle). (Maryland State Archives, Special Collections, Maltby collection G779-7.)

remembers." Tasker, whose house and garden sat on part of Market Street, had agreed to leave a right of way with room for carts to travel eastward (towards the creek) so that by providing an alternate space "convenient as said street," he would not have to move his house or terraced garden. Accommodations such as these were made more than once in the town's life. More than one family built or extended its land onto someone else's. The reasons why boundaries were mutable can be inferred from the following deed for land at the Severn ferry landing: "[beginning at] a locust post standing on the brink of a small bank on the south-west side of the said [ferry] point near a black walnut tree and just by the rising of the clift or banck from the said of the shore and lower ground."[46]

Benedict Leonard Calvert described boundaries like these as "perishable." One might also describe many homes as almost ephemeral shelters: a room and a half; two and a half feet above the ground; free access to hogs, dogs, and poultry; no plastered ceiling; a leaky roof only covered with shingles ("when it rained I moved my bed"); one window without glass or shutter, sealed from the storm by a square board and a worn out rail. Others were still smaller (fig. 1.13) and leases were written for garden plots 10 ft × 12 ft![47]

Although this Chesapeake world was one of encroaching standardization, Annapolis ca. 1730 was still free, open, a toe-hold of European civilization fraught with possibility. It contained people from two oral cultures and comprised a society where people spoke of the past saying, when I was a little Boy . . . , when I was a child . . . , when we lived beyond the sea . . . , when the Piscatawy left and came no more . . . It was a land where old crones like Ann Seaborn, a full hundred years old, perhaps born on the passage west, knew how things once were, that they would be different; many told time by the season of the year: "twas at the pulling of corn time when corn was in tassle." Others drew on nature to foretell death: "I knew his time was come; the whip-poor-will cried all night." They spoke of social structure in a myriad ways: "This mole was once a man; see, master, it has got hands and feet like you and me. It was once a man, but so proud, so lofty, so puffed up that God to punish his insolence, condemned him to crawl under the earth."[48]

In their socio-cultural discourse, Annapolitans used the artifacts now found throughout the town wherever archaeology is carefully, systematically, and skillfully done. Artifacts are Annapolis' hidden legacy, one that tells of a faraway time and place as archaeologists unravel its strands. Yet, whereas artifacts were originally objects in motion, appearing here and there, and not necessarily tied to place when they were in active use, once they entered the archaeological record they became frozen in time and space, locked to a site. To recover them and begin to understand how they once operated as part of a large, fluid, and dynamic cultural system, archaeologists normally start with the precise investigation of a given site or, in this case, the Calvert site.

2

Beginning the research

You may trace [a Man] . . . in the Place where he has lived.

Joseph Addison, *The Spectator*, No. 583

Zeroing in on the site

Archaeological interpretations begin earth-bound and object oriented. To obtain data, archaeologists, like gardeners, stoop down and put their hands in the dirt. Then, they cut the soil away with tools – shovels, trowels, hoes, sometimes grade-alls, and other heavy machinery, occasionally with dental picks – in careful, methodical stages. Good sites are always fixed in time and place by reliable stratigraphic sequences, and, on historic sites, tracked through historical documents too.

My site, 18AP28, was among a growing number of endangered sites in Maryland, and located deep inside a small modern city (fig. 2.1). Because it was threatened by urban development, its excavation was driven by the need to save cultural resources for the future; it was not a site chosen for its research potential nor to illustrate how artifact interpretation could answer the specific questions addressed here. Many of the issues raised in this book, particularly that of making a range of people visible in archaeological data, arose as I studied the site, read old records, and looked at artwork hanging in local museums. Located at 58 State Circle in the center of Annapolis' Historic District, it lay beneath a lot (# 83) on which a large and damaged building stood.

In 1982, impending hotel construction endangered the lot. Construction workers in the 1970s had gutted its old house, stripping away architectural elements such as chamfered beams and wall paneling. Excavation for a large basement foundation undermined the building, causing the roof and north side walls to collapse. Work-men made partial repairs, but no one could restore the missing architecture and a segment of the original yard was lost. What remained was a remnant of a small eighteenth-century house that had grown large with time while its historical integrity degenerated. No one knew what survived below ground.

In March 1982, Russell Wright, A.P., and St. Clair Wright visited the site with me to make a brief architectural and archaeological survey. We collected surface materials beneath a brick addition in an exposed crawlspace. Their ages indicated a ca. 1700–70 occupation. Russell Wright pointed out the architectural details on the window frames of a later, standing wall that indicated its ca. 1770–5 construction

date. Based on this information, Historic Annapolis Inc., raised preliminary funds
to begin excavation of the area sealed when the addition was built.

Archaeologists working in the crawlspace found a dense and qualitatively rich
deposit of artifacts: gold-gilded porcelain, hand-painted fine white saltglaze, ornate
delft, jewelry, personalized bottle seals, book bindings, ivory game pieces, gold-
plated, embellished hooks-and-eyes (fig. 2.2). The extant architecture suggested a
simpler building than the quality of its artifacts implied. Meanwhile, documentary

Fig. 2.1. Aerial photograph of Annapolis with site at its center. (Photograph by Marion E. Warren.)

research by Nancy Baker revealed the site was once the home of Captain Charles Calvert, Governor of Maryland from 1719–27. The site appeared paradoxical, tugged at our minds, and demanded attention. Ivor Noël Hume, retired Director of Archaeology at the Colonial Williamsburg Foundation, suggested thinking of it as a Chinese puzzle and playing "if then" with the pieces. Emergency funding was sought from the National Endowment for the Humanities (1) to complete the excavation of the crawlspace, (2) to test for the presence of an earlier post-built structure, and (3) to procure information on land use.

The threat of ensuing construction and the construction itself, including demolition of major portions of the standing structure and underpinning of others, significantly affected the process of excavation. Luckily, the developer, Paul Pearson, knew the archaeological record was a potentially rich resource for local history, that it could supplement information in the documentary record, and that it should not be squandered. Pearson, highly sympathetic to the research needs of scholars working with Historic Annapolis Inc., also had a schedule to maintain and financial

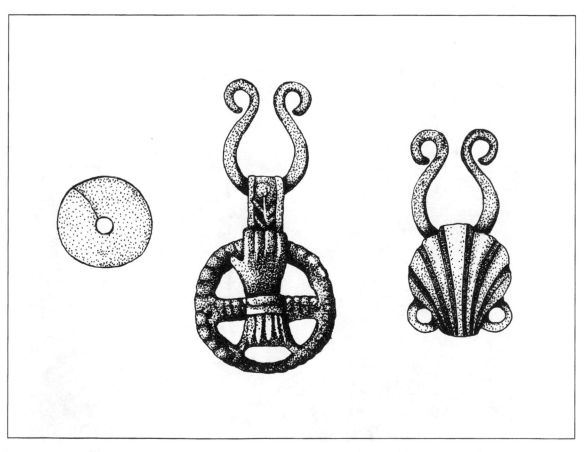

Figure 2.2. Tiny, silver-plated hooks-and-eyes and sequins gave a stylish flair to women's clothing. The scallop shell fastener is .3 inches; the hand-shaped one is .5 inches. African-Americans attributed to the latter protective power over witches. (Illustration by Julie Hunter-Abbazia.)

resources to shepherd. Thus the excavation team was faced with a situation in May 1983 where, with funding in place, builders would begin work in seven days. Contracts in hand, the construction firm forcefully ordered all archaeologists off the lot.

The site lay at the edge of the Circle roadway below the domed eighteenth-century statehouse; it received heavy visitation. During the spring, thousands of school children visit the capital; tourists flock to the historic district; graduation at the U.S. Naval Academy draws families to town. Thus many "outsiders" walked past the site, stopping to look and to question. Town residents also visited regularly, some daily. The field crew answered countless questions about the nature of archaeological research; the flow of work was measurably slower than at more secluded sites.

Because of the high visibility of archaeology, once we knew the construction firm wanted the work stopped, we moved to excavate rapidly the fill layers over the ca. 1730 features. These strata had been thoroughly sampled and tested. They covered remains of a brick-paved kitchen courtyard and brick well that fascinated visitors (fig. 2.3). I hoped that by raising public awareness in a town that was

Figure 2.3. Well at the Calvert site and the archaeologists down in it consistently drew the attention of Annapolitans on State Circle. (Photograph by Marion E. Warren.)

extremely attentive to its past, community pressure to conserve the historical resources of the site might secure more time for its study. The visual impact of the courtyard meant it was an archaeological feature whose existence could not be denied. This, for example, differentiated it from more amorphous soil stains marking the remains of a post building.

Some information was lost in the rapid excavation of some units in the front yard, but with Pearson's intervention, we gained extra time from the builders who also promised us a second season of fieldwork. By the time this arrived, some portions of the site that it would have been informative to study were destroyed (fig. 2.4). Yet we were able to complete work in an eighteenth-century well and to excavate another sector of the front yard, recovering evidence of a ca. 1690 occupation. The second season's work has been vital in the interpretation of the site.

This is a situation often seen in preservation-based archaeology. In many cases the support of the developer is less forthcoming and less courageously given. In Annapolis, the community and the developer were firmly behind the preservation agency working to record the site. This taught a valuable lesson: namely that if a developer expresses his consideration for the historical record of his local

Figure 2.4. The original Calvert house, much changed, during renovation. It stands behind and to the right of the excavation pit for an underground garage which now lies beneath the Calvert House hotel. (Photograph by Stewart Brothers Photographers, Inc., courtesy of Paul Pearson.)

community in a straightforward, forthright manner, the architects, engineers, and construction firms involved in urban development quickly find ways to help and raise far fewer barriers against archaeology than they do otherwise. At the Calvert site, they gave modest donations of labor and equipment, and expansive goodwill. One engineering firm also designed and donated a safety system for work in the well.

Still, the archaeological study of the Calvert site represents an accommodation between the requirements of finely-tuned research archaeology in an urban setting and the organizational constraints created by work in a construction environment. It was also the study of an incredibly rich site.

What is a rich site? A site can be described as rich when it contains many artifacts and features or when its artifact assemblages speak of wealth within the community. Using either criteria, the Calvert site fits within the framework. But in retrospect, the real reason why the word "rich" best characterizes the site is that it stretches the imagination. From the onset, it has provided a series of paradoxes. The first was simply that any of it survived the activities of subsequent generations living above it. The second was the contradiction between architectural style and material goods. A third was the presence of the most avant-garde horticultural practice for its era recorded in Maryland to date (namely an orangery where exotic plants were grown). A fourth was the fact that the site apparently functioned as a family compound for a household whose social structure was extended by any definition of the term. Its members included siblings, cousins, nieces, in-laws, servants – English, Irish, and Italian – as well as one of the more unusual large groups (thirty-one) of slaves in the province, comprised primarily of young children with a ratio of almost two adult women for each man. A fifth is the degree to which the archaeological evidence suggests the continuation of African lifestyles.

These attributes were paradoxes because they turned upside-down conventional expectations based either on normative assessments drawn from quantitative social studies or on assemblages seen at other sites. In each case, the contradictions initially perceived were resolved as further evidence was gathered by following the Boasian strategy of going out and finding what is there. This included historical research to find out who owned or lived on Lot 83. Eight periods can be distinguished, each associated with different families or, between 1854–1978, with significant changes in the style of the housing.

Before the Calverts

The first years (ca. 1680–1718)

The first occupation coincided with the early growth in the northeast quadrant of Annapolis. The earliest information on who owned Lot 83 is in a 1702 deed between two innkeepers which mentions a corner post on land that belonged to (or was owned previously by) Samuel Chew, presumably at the northeast corner of the lot (fig. 2.5). Three or four men with the name lived in the county from 1690–1710; no documents link Lot 83 to a specific Samuel Chew. Whoever built the first house, however, probably built a frame dwelling of post-in-the-ground construction.[1]

The first known landowner, William Taylard, does not appear in the records until later. However, analysis of the pipe-bore diameters associated with the early features (i.e. those that date to or before ca. 1735) and with the feature in the crawlspace area (which contained mixed materials from earlier features as part of its fill) suggests occupation of the site began prior to 1700. Included among the early features are a series of refuse-filled post holes where the Calverts removed timbers, refilled and leveled the soil. Their disturbance has made it impossible to determine whether the original house was constructed in the 1680s or 1690s. However, the structure did not align with the Circle. This suggests it was built before 1695 when Governor Nicholson carved the Circle into State House hill.[2]

How the land passed from Samuel Chew to William Taylard remains a mystery. Taylard also purchased Lot 92 which fronted on Prince George Street and abutted Lot 83 on the west. He was a striving, opportunistic man who bought land whenever he could, investing in varied money-making ventures. Taylard held a series of minor government posts and lived in the first capital before settling in Annapolis. In 1698 Philip Clarke described him as "being poor and Indigent and for an Imploy would doe aney thing." These seem harsh words for a man who, while not wealthy, earned an adequate living for himself, his wife, and stepson. Taylard successfully made his way through the convoluted web of Maryland politics. His estate was valued at

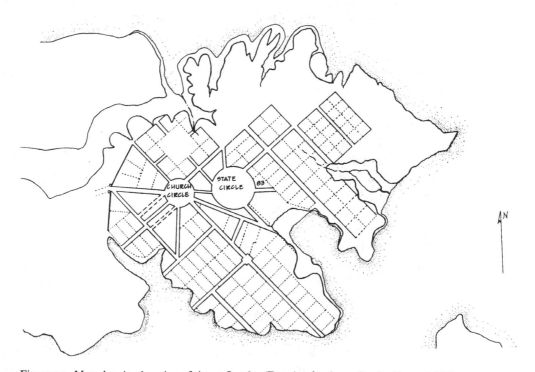

Figure 2.5. Map showing location of site on Lot 83. (Drawing for the author by Hanna McKee courtesy of the Archaeological Society of Maryland.)

£58.1.8 in 1711, which placed him below the median for the city, yet he kept four servants. Not surprisingly, given Taylard's occupation as a clerk-attorney in the provincial bureaucracy and his involvement with local politics, he lived so close to the Public Circle that to all intents and purposes he could tumble out of bed and into the State House chambers. Nor was there anything odd in Philip Clarke's attack on Taylard's character. Taylard, after all, successfully regained favor with Governor Nicholson by informing him of John Coode's plans for a fourth rebellion (1696–8) whereas Clarke, a member of the Lower House from St. Mary's County, served six months in jail for insulting Nicholson and leading (1698) the rebellious Lower House against him.[3]

The intrusion of politically-based social action into everyday activities was constant with respect to the activities of all the households who lived at the Calvert site. Often Maryland politics were tumultuous; a myriad ways of expressing opposition appear in the historical records which also hold a wealth of colorful details about the people who lived on the Circle's perimeter. Yet, in differentiating between small men such as Taylard and more powerful men like the Calvert governors, the imprint of the latter on the archaeological record of both town and site was immeasurably greater than that of the former.

There was a dwelling listed in the deed of sale from Taylard's widow, Audrey, to Philemon Hemsley, but its price was low and William Taylard's household possessions were so jumbled and old that it seems unlikely he had the money to build something more substantial than the average small frame dwelling. The clapboards shown in his inventory were undoubtedly intended for use in repairing its wooden walls; the single ewe and pigs probably grazed and grubbed in its yard. Yet the inventory also indicates a number of small indulgences – a bird cage; pictures; a silver tankard; books – that more fiscally conservative, agrarian families with equivalent wealth did not own.[4]

A merchant-planter buys the site (1718)

Philemon Hemsley and his second wife, a wealthy widow, next purchased Lot 83. In all likelihood, they built its first brick home – a building 20 ft wide and possibly 44 ft long – and used one of its outbuildings to house a mercantile venture. Hemsley died shortly after buying the property, leaving an estate valued at £3,034.1.9 (including forty-four slaves and seven servants). His inventory indicates that renovation of the house and yard was then in progress.[5]

Philemon Hemsley's 1720 inventory also lists the house contents. It is not a room-by-room inventory so it is difficult to gain an impression of the size or shape of the home from reading the list. It is notable that there were perhaps as many as three chamber rooms (assuming each *complete* set of bed clothes, curtains, and bed was contained in a separate chamber). It is also noteworthy that the family owned a large quantity of delft and Chinese porcelain including six small Chinese porcelain flowerpots. Comparing the delft and porcelain listed in the inventory (ninety-four vessels comprised of 10% earthenware, 45% porcelain, 45% delft) with the quantities found at archaeological sites for the same period or sold in local stores (see

Chapter 7), suggests that conspicuous consumption in the Hemsley household was high, possibly higher than in most planter-gentry homes (fig. 2.6).[6]

Mary Townsley immigrated to Maryland with her cousin, Governor John Seymour (1704–9) and married a wealthy widower, John Contee, in the same year. She married another one, Philemon Hemsley, a few years later. After remaining a widow for five years, Mary entered yet a third marriage in 1723 with Captain William Rogers. By the time of Rogers' £220 mortgage to Charles Calvert, Mary Rogers had died; her young husband was remarried. The following year Rogers sold the house and land to cancel the mortgage.[7]

The value of the property rose between 1718 and 1727 from £30 to over £400. This reflects the combined effect of inflation on the tobacco economy, the growing population (an increase from 405 Annapolitans in 1715 to 776 in 1730), the city's economic growth and prosperity, and property improvements. With its purchase by Captain Calvert, the house and lot became more important. Its archaeological significance also increased dramatically beginning with the Calvert occupation because of the wide variety of social, economic, and political events or activities that their family and household members participated in or were connected to throughout Maryland.

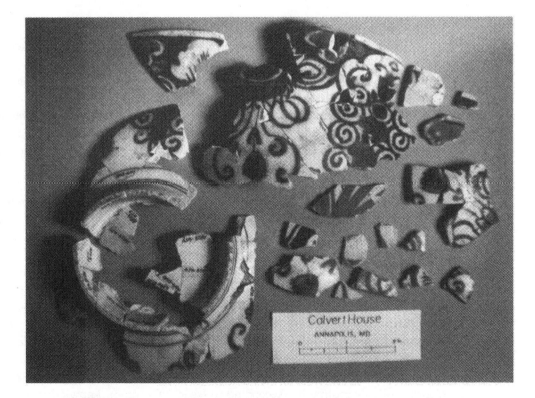

Figure 2.6. Sherds from a delft punch bowl. Punch bowls of porcelain or delft ware were the most common vessel form found in features associated with the Calvert governors. (Photograph by the author.)

Table 2.1. *Selected household goods in Annapolis and Anne Arundel County inventories for estates valued below £50 (after Carr and Walsh 1993: 120–1)*

	Rural		Urban	
	1700–9 %	1710–22 %	1700–9 %	1710–22 %
Item				
Linens: bed and table	15	9	50	50
Ordinary pottery	34	28	50	27
Table knives	9	7	0	0
Table forks	5	7	0	0
Spices	2	1	0	7
Fine tablewares	2	0	0	13
Wigs	3	6	33	20
Clocks and watches	2	0	0	7
Books, religious	23	20	67	57
Books, secular	5	0	33	0
Paintings	2	0	17	20
Silver plate	2	4	17	20
Tea and tea services	2	0	0	0

Who lived at the site from 1727–34?

In June 1727, Benedict Leonard Calvert, Lord Baltimore's younger brother, arrived in Annapolis to govern the Province. In June 1727, Captain William Rogers and his new wife, Lucinda, mortgaged their home to Captain Calvert. Although he had the right to live in the house, no one today knows whether or not Rogers moved immediately to Northeast Street (Maryland Avenue). Capt. Calvert was already living in the house when he paid Rogers an additional £220 and obtained the deed to the property in December 1728. He had begun to purchase adjacent lots earlier, some containing simple dwellings, in February 1728.[8]

No official governor's residence stood in Annapolis; Governor Nicholson (1694–8) lived on Prince George Street in a house near the later Calvert home. I do not know where other early eighteenth-century governors (Blakiston, Seymour, Hart) lived. Captain Calvert maintained private lodgings elsewhere in town when he was governor. Lord Baltimore decided to replace Captain Calvert in the spring of 1725. The timing of this change is a tantalizing clue that the property was not purchased for Charles and Rebecca Calvert's sole use. It seems significant that the sale fell immediately on the heels of an eighteen-month period (1725–7) in which Governor Charles Calvert lived in Prince George's County, awaiting Benedict Leonard's arrival and maintaining political calm by the simple expedient of not calling the legislative houses into session.[9]

A second clue is that it required skilled organization to make a Chesapeake plantation truly profitable. According to Isaac, "Common knowledge . . . dictated that the yield would be closely proportioned to the intensity of labor applied to the [tobacco] fields." Tobacco plantations required active, on-site management to

Table 2.2. *Household goods in Annapolis and Anne Arundel County inventories for estates valued at £50–£94 (after Carr and Walsh 1993: 120–1)*

	Rural		Urban	
	1700–9	1710–22	1700–9	1710–22
Item	%	%	%	%
Linens: bed and table	30	41	100	82
Ordinary pottery	44	48	50	100
Table knives	4	15	100	36
Table forks	0	11	0	36
Spices	4	7	0	27
Fine tablewares	0	4	18	25
Wigs	7	0	0	27
Clocks and watches	4	0	0	9
Books, religious	48	59	0	91
Books, secular	7	0	0	9
Paintings	4	0	0	36
Silver plate	4	15	100	27
Tea and tea services	0	0	27	50

prosper. A planter, his sons or white overseers (often Scots) usually provided this. At one Calvert tobacco plantation the overseer was African. This unusual situation would have been more so if Charles and Rebecca Calvert had not spent substantial portions of the growing season nearby. Any reading of diaries by tobacco planters shows close supervision was required. Landon Carter wrote that he "looked into every hole and corner" of his plantation; another wrote of daily morning rides to tell slaves what to do. Jonathan Boucher was explicit on the matter. Combine this practice with the fact that ultimately the size and splendor of an Englishman's country estate – not his town house – and its productivity were the visible markers of gentlemanly rank, and it becomes difficult to envision a situation in which Captain Charles Calvert was an absentee landowner for extensive periods of time. Further, estate accounts show active participation in tobacco trade.[10]

Early eighteenth-century planters who realistically anticipated increasing their wealth spent their cash on items that would increase the productive gain at their rural farms, and did not spend extensive sums on ostentatious and unnecessary household goods. There is nothing in the inventory of household goods kept at the Prince George's County home to suggest Captain Calvert followed a different pattern (compare, for example, the value of its "amenities" with those of the Annapolis residence as shown in table 2.3). Balanced against this is the fact that the degree of conspicuous consumption displayed in the site's artifacts from the early period (ca. 1730) is unusually high and extends across all categories of material goods. It is my impression the Hemsley-Rogers house and lot was bought as a familial effort or joint venture and not intended to be solely home to Captain Calvert's own small family (himself, his wife, his daughter).[11]

These bits of information converge to serve as related clues that the house and lot were associated with members of a complex household. In England, it was not unusual for extended families – i.e., households with three or more generations or lateral members such as aunts, uncles, nieces, nephews, cousins – to occupy a town house during the London season. Occupied seasonally, sometimes rented rather than owned, London town houses supplied transitory dwelling space; this is one reason why English family identity remained linked to the landed gentry estate. Relatives also visited country estates, sometimes staying for months at a time. In his childhood, the household in which Benedict Leonard lived from age six onward included his grandfather, his grandfather's third wife, a great-aunt, his father, and his own brothers and sisters, possibly his cousin, the Captain, as a young man, or other cousins, and a host of attendants. The household composition of Woodcote Park was extended with at least three generations of Calverts making it their home, a situation characteristic of the earlier Cecilius Calvert house at Kiplin.[12]

In terms of ties to places, whereas Captain Calvert's future lay in Maryland, his cousin Benedict Leonard saw the Maryland years as exile. Family allegiance and loyalty drove him overseas, not personal advancement (see Chapter 4). Benedict Leonard's reluctance to come, in fact, argues against a desire to invest in Maryland. On the other hand, the fact that Benedict Leonard hoped to be here temporarily, only long enough to resolve his brother's political problems, could argue for a willingness to live on a cousin's town estate.

The household possessions inventoried in 1730 at the death of Edward Henry Calvert, younger brother of Benedict Leonard, are repeated, in many instances, in the 1734 inventory of Captain Calvert. Further, when one considers the ca. 1728–30 construction of the orangery, it is evident that Benedict Leonard Calvert's interests, knowledge, and education made him far more apt to have built this exotic structure than his cousin Charles (see Chapter 6). There is also the question of where the other Calverts lived if not at the house on the Public Circle, and the fact that it was used as an occasional meeting place for the Governor's Council from 1727 onward, even after Captain Charles Calvert's death in 1734. Then too, Captain Calvert bought in his name, but for the family, the land on the north side of the Public Circle where Lord Baltimore planned to raise a governor's mansion (see Chapter 5).[13]

English historian G. E. Mingay wrote that England's "great" families subordinated the individual's interests to those of the family. It is clear from the behavior of the Calverts in the early eighteenth century that while they divided some assets (e.g., land) among themselves on an individual basis and became financially entangled by loaning each other money (defining as kin anyone married to a sister, mother, brother, etc.), family generosity and Lord Baltimore's patronage had its limits. The expectation was that family resources would not move beyond Baltimore's control. When death created such a possibility, family members coalesced to reinstitute their claim. His lordship's kindness tacitly carried with it the expectation of attendant care for or consolidation of Calvert interests (expressed as the interests of his lordship, or Baltimore's need) rather than individual profit or advancement.[14]

For these reasons it is most likely that the Calvert site contains the residue left by the social action of three Calvert men, Governor Charles Calvert, Governor Benedict Leonard Calvert, and Mr. Edward Henry Calvert, and their related households. Hence information from the archaeological excavation is not presented as indicative of the behavior of one man and his small, upwardly mobile family nor is it seen as reflecting the ideas of a single individual. Rather the archaeological record at the Calvert site is conceived as expressive of the ideas and action of an extended family with a prominent political role in the province whose members sought to enhance and maintain their "prerogatives" and those of their immediate kinsman, the proprietor Lord Baltimore.

Calvert lifestyle

But how did the Calverts live? In the next two chapters historical texts are considered at length in terms of what they reveal about the Calvert men and women. Before moving on, it is also useful to consider quickly what comparative probate inventory research reveals. Wills and inventories are one of the most informative sets of documents about the early eighteenth-century Chesapeake. For the Calvert household there is a series of wills and probate inventories filed at the deaths of Edward Henry Calvert (1730), Benedict Leonard Calvert (1733), and Captain Charles Calvert (1734). The Calvert inventories list the items necessary to maintain an aristocratic household. The fullest, most complete set of household goods, equipment, servants, slaves, livestock, and so on was maintained by Captain Charles Calvert, who not only owned Lot 83, but also seems to have acquired possession of his deceased kin's household goods as first (1) Edward Henry died, (2) his widow Margaret Lee Calvert and then (3) the Honorable Benedict Leonard returned to England.[15]

In a will made shortly before sailing, Benedict Leonard left most of his English estate to his younger brother, Cecilius, and wrote that its worth was in the range of £10,000. Much of what he brought with him originally, goods insured for £1,800 on the voyage out, were taken home. His appraised belongings (£51) were the things he left behind. Among the discards were two tea tables, two large porcelain punch bowls, an incomplete set of China teaware, a set of red watered (silk?) curtains and covers for his bed. Benedict Leonard also left his bedstead. All were luxuries Maryland families strove to own. The remnants of the ex-governor's household goods were worth as much as or more than most Maryland families had invested in their own worldly goods. Fifteen years later, in the 1770s, Benedict Leonard's leavings would not have been extraordinary possessions, although their total value still would have represented a significant portion of the average family's household wealth.[16]

The inventories of Benedict Leonard's brother, Edward Henry, and his cousin, Captain Charles, reiterate and amplify the emphasis on luxury goods visible in Benedict Leonard's inventory. This can be seen by comparing their goods against the standards for contemporary families developed by Lois Carr and Lorena Walsh. Carr and Walsh studied patterns of household consumption using probate

Table 2.3. *Household amenities owned by Annapolitans ca. 1730*

Amenities	Captain Calvert	Captain Calvert	E. H. Calvert	Mark Challoner	Thomas Britte	Jane Burrel	Cornelius Brooksby	John Davisson	Samuel Harvey	Philemon Hemsley	Charles Carroll
1. Linens: bed and table	£4	£40	£23	£1	—	£4	£2	£3	£10	£28	£70
2. Ordinary pottery	£2	*	£5	—	—	£2	£1	£1	£2	£1	£4
3. Knives	—	£7	£1	£1	—	£1	£1	—	£1	£1	£9
4. Forks	—	£7	£1	£1	—	£1	£1	—	£1	—	£8
5. Spices	£1	*	£5	—	—	—	—	—	£1	—	£3
6. Fine tablewares	£1	£7	£13	—	—	—	—	—	£3	£8	£16
7. Wigs	—	—	—	£2	—	—	—	£2	—	—	£5
8. Watches and clocks	£5	£4	£5	—	—	£2	£3	—	£5	£2	£3
9. Books (all kinds)	£1	£7	£3	£1	—	£31	—	—	—	£1	£1
10. Paintings	£1	£6	—	—	—	—	—	—	—	£4	£56
11. Silver and gold	£14	£192	—	—	£1	£2	—	£3	£8	£37	£372
Value of amenities		£270	£55	£6	£1	£43	£8	£9	£31	£82	£544
Inventory total	£594 (P.G. plantation)	£1650** (Annapolis)	£389	£25	£57	£115	£222	£397	£487	£681	£4897
Occupation		Governor	Council	Trader?	Mariner?	Widow	Food Merchant	Barber & Merchant	Merchant Planter	Merchant Planter	Merchant Lawyer

* Presumed present in Annapolis because shown for the Prince George's County home.

** Inventory total shown does not include debts due to the estate

inventories from Maryland counties on both the Eastern and Western shores.[17] They summarize the trends they saw:

> While the material culture of the seventeenth century was most remarkable for its sameness, changes can be seen at the very top beginning about the mid-1680s . . . by 1700 [the wealthiest] could be distinguished far more readily . . . Over the first quarter of the eighteenth century, change accelerated in the households of the rich and powerful . . . By the 1760s many of [their] notions of comfort and ways of using objects to advertise status appeared not only in wealthy but in middling households, and even the poor were participating to some degree . . . Conspicuous consumption of the kind described by Thorstein Veblen was beginning to appear, although not to the degree practiced by the English aristocracy.[18]

Carr and Walsh measured consumption using two indices in which the presence or absence of key items on an inventory were noted and given single-digit scores. Their first index measured amenities (i.e., non-essentials) and of these, they considered only items 9–11 listed on Tables 2.1 to 2.3 to be true luxuries, found in few homes. Although Carr and Walsh use only presence/absence in their scoring procedures, Table 2.3 also shows the approximate quantity and value to demonstrate that members of the Calvert family possessed more than token numbers of each luxury, and that they integrated these luxuries into daily life.

Carr and Walsh found that by 1700, the emerging elite (defined as those whose wealth was above £491) frequently had purchased one or two luxuries, but that acquisition of specific items varied on an individual basis. Individual variation across the population is also mirrored by small differences in the two Calvert inventories. On the one hand, Edward Henry had only one timepiece; Captain Charles had three watches, two silver and one gold. On the other hand, Edward Henry had five wigs. Each man owned silver swords, a time-honored emblem of courtly status that no gentleman would willingly relinquish. One might note that Charles Carroll of Annapolis, despite his wealth and the stock of weapons in his score, did not own a sword.[19]

The data in Table 2.3 also include Annapolitans at different wealth levels: an adventurer, a butcher, a mariner or coastal trader, a craftsman, a widow, and a merchant-lawyer. How inventories for people in these economic ranks usually scored can be seen in Table 2.4. Captain Calvert's luxury goods, appraised at £277, were worth more than the average estate value for 95% of Chesapeake decedents whose inventories were filed before 1750; indicative of the vast gap between the average family and rich families, only 11% of decedents in Anne Arundel County owned goods worth £1,000 or more during the 1720s–30s; the Carroll and Calvert inventories fell at the peak of the wealth pyramid (see table 3.3). Considering their social status and political power, it is not surprising that the consumption score for the Calvert men was significantly higher than mean consumption scored for other inventories filed in both Annapolis and Anne Arundel county.

Carr and Walsh also used a "modern index" to measure the use of commonplace

Table 2.4. *Average scores on amenities index for decedents whose estates were inventoried in Annapolis and in Anne Arundel County. (From Walsh 1984c).*

Wealth group	Rural parishes	Annapolis and Londontown
£0–49		
1723–32	1.14	2.40
1733–44	1.48	2.58
£50–225		
1723–32	2.86	6.80
1733–44	3.16	6.21
Above £226		
1723–32	6.17	7.46
1733–44	7.02	7.67

household furnishings which modern Americans take for granted. These included tables, chairs, beds, mattresses, sheets and blankets, lamps, table forks, pottery food vessels, iron pots for boiling, and other utensils to fry, roast, bake, or spit-grill foods. They note that more than half the households in the region owned less than half of the items on this list up until the Revolution (1775). While their absence correlates with purchasing power, wealth levels alone do not explain why many Chesapeake families led such a spartan lifestyle. Simply put, the culture was different; many objects were not perceived as essentials.[20]

In summary, using the Carr–Walsh "modern index" as a measure of transition from post-medieval to modern lifestyle, the two Calvert inventories score 10 out of 10 possible points of 100%. The Calverts had at least as many beds and tables as found in other wealthy Annapolis homes and, on the average, twice the number of chairs. Their furniture included pieces made of walnut and mahogany – the most fashionable woods for English furniture – and the forms were elegant ones: dressing tables, bureaus, chests of drawers. Some were japanned. Some were special purpose, especially the tea tables and the card table. These were accompanied by other items that bespoke education, culture, and leisure – gaming pieces (fig. 2.7) and gaming table; musical instruments; books, religions and secular; a compass, Brazilian ruler, and multiplication wheel. An appreciation of the visual arts was shown by the number of paintings within the house whereas Calvert sponsorship of printed volumes of poetry and plays by local authors indicated their appreciation of other humanistic, creative endeavors. Together with the quantities of teawares, such items enabled the family to entertain visitors and their home to stand as a center of provincial hospitality.

Yet the point is not that the Calvert men saw themselves as living on the cutting edge of change or thought of their lifestyle as epitomizing new fashions and new ways of doing things. The change in lifestyle one sees in analyzing the inventories might suggest this, but it would be erroneous. The Calvert men built on tradition. They drew on older beliefs like Sir Henry Wooten's idea that a gentleman should locate his home apart from those of greater neighbors for otherwise "it will mean living on Earth as Mercury in the Heavens . . . ever in obscurity under brighter beams than his own." The symbolic image of brighter lights did not rest solely in gardens or homes, but extended to daily dress, and the illusion of light and brightness provided by clothing or a sparkling house and yard. Brightness was an old metaphor for social standing adapted by the Calverts.[21]

Further building on cultural precedent, the Calverts also made their town house a center of hospitality in part because gracious entertaining facilitated their roles as power-brokers. Whereas other men in Maryland built their fortunes on tobacco or, to achieve greater wealth, on tobacco and mercantile activities (as Oldmixon pointed out in 1708), the Calverts utilized family ties and their Annapolis estate to wield power and influence in the Province. It was, in essence, their Maryland executive court, an institution of state, a counterfoil to the upper and lower chambers of the nearby State House. Within its walls they behaved as aristocrats applying known and familiar strategies to legitimate and convey power and prestige.

Lawrence and Jeanne Stone have separated the English aristocracy into parish and country gentry using as a measure distinctions in economic resources, occupational

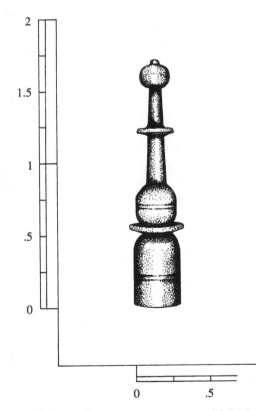

Figure 2.7. Ivory chess pawn recovered from the orangery deposits. (Illustration by Julie Hunter-Abbazia.)

profiles, and range of "cultured" interests and activities (i.e., lifestyle). The country gentry were better educated, more sophisticated, wealthier and wielded greater power. They often held membership in parliament, most undertook a Grand Tour of Europe, staying abroad for several years. As a consequence, these men possessed minds whose horizons or aspirations ranged beyond their parish borders to London, or further abroad to international realms. They had landed wealth, participated in local government, possessed country estates. Their depth of knowledge about the expanding Western world was more detailed than their compatriots' grasp of colonization and its profits. An economic and status elite, the country gentry comprised "a pool of talent from whose ranks emerged the ruling class that ran both the [English] counties and the country."[22]

In retrospect, knowing what is written in the chapters to come, it is easy to point out how the Calverts fit within this social group. Yet when the archaeological study began I had a very different impression of the family than I do now. Because their lives are not emphasized in English history, where they almost drop out of sight, historians have written off the Calverts as insignificant, a minor noble household. In reality, their generations represent the society in microcosm and once one learns how it operates, more detail on their lives appears. The Calverts who lived in Maryland gain historical dimension by their connections to a range of different and interesting individuals: Lady Blanche Arundel, gentlewoman (and great-great-grandmother) who managed the defense of Wardour Castle, with its very small garrison, so well that it took Cromwell's forces more than a week to capture it; Robert Talbot (a cousin) whom King Charles II sent into France to cure Mademoiselle d'Orleans because of his medical knowledge; Thomas Hearne, an "outspoken" archivist at the Bodleian Library in Oxford whose diary reveals he didn't suffer fools gladly; Fitzroy Henry Lee, governor of the Leeward Islands, and Samuel Pepys, who knew of the Mynnes (in-laws of the Calverts) and wrote of their house and forest. If one considers the information that documentary sources contain and looks carefully at what these reveal of education, attitudes, family position, political activities, and demonstrable interests within an anthropological perspective, it is apparent that the Calvert family was connected to the "leading institutions" of their times through multiple channels. Tracing these connections is one way to reconstitute context.[23]

When we began work at the site we were presented with a sparse list of historical events in the lives of the site's occupants. There was a lack of local context as well in that we knew little of what had occurred in the community in the early eighteenth century. African culture and African-American lifeways were not fully integrated into Annapolis' historiography – its elements were simply glossed. The seventeenth-century or later years were more important in the development of Maryland as a state. The early eighteenth century was a backwater; the town had reached its apex or Golden Era in the 1760s. Historians concentrated upon these phases in their local and regional studies from the 1820s onward creating a superb series of studies which tell in detail of Maryland past and of its most important buildings while overlooking the below-ground remains.[24]

Figure 2.8. Archaeologists recovered a small silver teaspoon made by an English silversmith (4½ inches in length) bearing the initial "R" from beneath the doorsteps of the original house. Discarded 1727–35, this spoon is unusual because it bears a single initial. (Photograph by Marion E. Warren.)

Below-ground remains are part and parcel of context and context, as considered here, is essential to archaeological interpretation, one way to zero in on a site. One can take the artifacts and move with them. Or, one can work an interpretation backward as well as forward, take what is known or knowable about a family in its different ranges of activities, and use these as clues that suggest how individuals would use material objects. This is what is done in the next section. It is done with a broad brush, but the final objective is to see if it is possible to discern how the role of family members in the community and its household composition might reasonably be played out in the material world. Can one see ways in which they differed from other Chesapeake gentry; were they colonials or English at heart? The following questions were a guide:

> What did it mean to be a member of the English ruling class?
> Were the Calverts living in Annapolis members of this social group?
> What might there be about an aristocratic English lifestyle that would leave distinctive marks in the archaeological record?
> Would English expressions of an aristocratic lifestyle be different from Chesapeake ones?

Jack Greene wrote recently of the way rich Chesapeake planters desired to be seen as British and not as colonials. The three Calvert men living in Annapolis at the start of this era *were* English gentry, and stood at the apex of the political structure of the province. Still, it seemed insufficient simply to say that their household was aristocratic and affluent even though the inventory analysis clearly demonstrated this. It showed that in some ways the quality of life within the family (which has a direct impact on the archaeological record of any site) differed from the qualitative experiences of other Maryland families. But it did not indicate adequate ways in which the Calverts might, through their participation in the developing culture of the tidewater gentry and their intimate knowledge of contemporary English culture – displayed and illustrated in their behavior – have set trends that others emulated as Maryland families sought to replicate English custom (fig. 2.8). Answers were sought through more detailed knowledge of their Calvert backgrounds, training, and social networks. In doing so, the archaeological record of the site was momentarily set aside to look at the individual histories of two proud and autocratic governors, Captain Charles Calvert and Benedict Leonard Calvert, and at other close kin.

II

RULING THE PROVINCE

Relationships . . . supply the threads of which social fabric is woven. The quality and patterning of such threads in a society, or in a milieu, will largely determine the texture of its members' lives.

Rhys Isaac, 1982, *Transformation of Virginia*

3

On behalf of his Lordship

I am afraid some Evil Spirits walk among us and it would be a matter of Great pleasure to such, to have your house [Maryland] and mine [Baltimore's] att Variance, but for my own part, I defy the Devill and his Works to do it.

Captain Charles Calvert, 1725, Speech to the Maryland Assembly

A brief Calvert history

In 1709 at age 21 (if his birthdate was 1688 as written on the back of his portrait by his daughter), young Charles Calvert Lazenby dropped his surname and entered the British military as an ensign in the prestigious Grenadier Guards. He purchased the position with funds obtained by selling Maryland lands given him by an older relative, Charles Calvert, the third Lord Baltimore. Baltimore had strongly supported the British military previously, and had served as a General in European campaigns under Marlborough in 1696 and 1707. Charles Calvert Lazenby may have been illegitimate, but even so his family took steps to ensure his well being. Baltimore knew the advantages and disadvantages of military service, knew that many British officers later assumed positions of power in the colonies, and knew that with training the young man could usefully assist the Calvert family. Further, command was a family tradition.[1]

The beginnings of this tradition can be traced to the early 1600s when George Calvert began to move in Stuart circles after serving James I in Ireland. James I rewarded service with honor, knighted George Calvert in 1617, and awarded him an Irish baronetcy in February 1624/25. The status, prestige, and political powers of the Calvert family were on the rise. Still, the family was not among the greater English nobility and did not possess the wealth of the aristocratic families that maintained major estates like Boxwood or Chatsworth. The aristocracy at that time evaluated its members according to a variety of cultural criteria including length of pedigree and location. The Calvert baronetcy was recent and Irish, not English; the family seat of Kiplin was in Yorkshire, distant from the Court.[2]

Kiplin's Jacobean design in 1622, however, contained Italian elements of the Renaissance architecture that would become immensely popular in years to come. Its continental influence led architect Christopher Hussey to assert that the first Calvert house was "the product of a fertile mind working in a traditional style, but independent of conventions." In many ways, this balance between tradition and innovation became a leitmotif of the Calvert family; a blending of cultural precedent and praxis can be seen in many of their endeavors.[3]

George Calvert, as principal Secretary of State (1619–25) to James I, was favored by the King. The wealth to build his new home was one sign, as was the design of Kiplin and the richness of his clothing. Of more enduring value was the strength of the prerogative powers granted in the Maryland charter to his son Cecilius by Charles II shortly after George's death. Drawn by the Calverts' future prospects and the family's Catholic faith, Thomas Arundel (Lord Arundel at Wardour) asked the second Lord Baltimore, the young Cecilius, to wed daughter Anne. The couple were married in 1627/28 and may have lived briefly at Arundel's own home, Wardour Castle in Wiltshire, before settling at Hook Manor on the Wardour estate. There Anne gave birth to three daughters, an infant George (1634–6), and finally Charles, the third Lord Baltimore (chart 3.1). Charles had two sons, Cecilius (who died at 13) and Benedict Leonard (Sr.) born in Maryland (chart 3.1).[4]

By that time the Calvert family was politically allied through a network of marriage and financial alliances with some of the most talented families in England. George Calvert forged the initial connections when he became a junior secretary to Sir Robert Cecil (1563–1612), who rose to be the Earl of Salisbury and was principal Secretary of State of James I. Among the circle of families linked to the Calverts were the Arundels, the Somersets, the powerful Irish Talbots (Lords Tyrconnel), the diplomatically astute and fiscally prudent Hydes (Earls of Rochester and Clarendon), and the literary, mathematical, and political Digges. The third Lord Baltimore built upon this network during his Maryland residence (1661–84), using the mechanisms of judicious land grants, marriages, and political appointments to create his own small cadre of prominent Catholic families in Maryland, including Sewalls, Talbots, Digges, Darnalls, Lees, Lowes. Maryland's Catholic gentry reciprocated by providing strong and effective political support and service, and gradually the lines extended to include other wealthy families including the Eastern Shore dynasty of Quaker Lloyds.[5]

The third Lord Baltimore spent many years in the Province; his children were born in Maryland. Yet Charles Calvert, the third Lord Baltimore, returned to England after his father's death in 1675 to oversee the broader Calvert network. Successful, influential interaction with the nobility, in that era, could not be initiated from a colonial outpost. In England, Calvert's close association with Catholic lords (cf., his uncle, Henry Arundel) resulted in accusations of treason soon thereafter and King Charles urged a return to Maryland. Soon after Calvert reached his Chesapeake home, he sent his eldest son, Cecilius, to school in England. Lord Baltimore too returned in 1684 to argue the Maryland–Pennsylvania boundary dispute and was abroad when revolution in Maryland gave Protestants power in 1689. Thereupon, Charles Calvert was effectively barred from the Province. His wife, surviving son, and unmarried daughters soon joined him in England. Yet he never gave up the idea of regaining control of Maryland.[6]

The third Lord Baltimore was adroit at establishing strong political alliances and kin-based support networks, providing for the future by laying subtle foundations well beforehand, generously rewarding his supporters, surviving rebellions, uprisings, and most political crises. He put his political acumen to good use in the training he provided for his grandsons. He drew upon it in the plans he made for Charles Calvert Lazenby.[7]

In 1715, the third Lord Baltimore died at age 76; his son and heir, Benedict Leonard Calvert, Sr., died within a few short months. Charles Calvert, the fifth Lord Baltimore, was but 15 years old at the time. His older cousin, who shared his name, was serving in the Grenadier Guards. Francis North, Lord Guilford, was appointed guardian of the Calvert children.[8]

Captain Calvert becomes Governor

In February 1719/20, Captain Charles Calvert (fig. 3.1) was appointed Governor by his twenty-year-old cousin on the advice of Lord Guilford and the privy council. To regain control of the Maryland hegemony after a thirty-five-year break, the Calvert family needed loyal, diplomatic men working on its behalf. Captain Calvert was old enough, had administrative experience, and by virtue of his birth was enough of a Calvert to become their Maryland leader. Genealogists have not identified Captain Calvert's parents; some have assumed he was an illegitimate son of the third Lord Baltimore. A careful reading of the Lowe correspondence reveals his mother was the Countess Henrietta who died ca. 1728. She is also called "Mother Calvert." It is possible that a further search of English records would clarify his relationship to the grandchildren of the third Lord Baltimore and to the Lazenby family. Like the Calverts, the Lowes, and the Bordleys, the Lazenbys were a Yorkshire family, but until English records can be mined for the maiden names of Margaret Lazenby (wife of Henry) and that of the Countess Henrietta, their kinship ties remain elusive.[9]

When Charles Calvert Lazenby dropped his surname, he was neither behaving unusually nor reaching for fame. Lawrence and Jeanne Stone point out that Englishmen sometimes altered their surnames to indicate either fictive or actual blood ties between their wives, mothers, or other benefactors. Thus Charles Calvert Lazenby was simply following tradition. His possession of a middle name was not, however, customary for most children born in the 1600s, but it was traditional among the Calverts.[10]

Although it was not possible to establish Captain Charles Calvert's parentage, it is clear that he received substantial financial backing from the Calvert family and benefited from their political patronage. In their book *An Open Elite?* Lawrence and Jeanne Stone discuss the position of younger sons of the nobility, noting that access

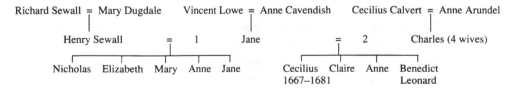

Chart 3.1. Kinship chart for Charles Calvert, the third Lord Baltimore (showing children and step-children)

to business apprenticeships in the great overseas trading companies "was only open to the sons of rich and generous fathers" because apprenticeship fees cost £1,000, a sum that by 1700 only the wealthiest merchants, farmers, squires, or nobility possessed. The Stones also note that an option for many younger sons was to obtain a commission in the armed services, but to rise in the ranks required "substantial capital to buy the office."[11]

According to Erickson, a man advanced in the military by purchasing a commission, paying "sale prices" to the previous holder of the lowest office to which he was eligible. With promotion to higher rank, an ensign or lieutenant paid "an additional and larger sum to the officer whose place he took, and partly offset the expense by selling the old rank to someone else." Cavalry commissions were more costly than those in the infantry. Positions in the prestigious Guards were most expensive. In 1718, after serving in the war against France and Spain, Charles Calvert purchased the office of lieutenant and soon thereafter that of a captain. Assuming that his young "cousin" or Lord Guilford helped Captain Calvert buy the commissions, the promotions only strengthened his allegiance to Lord Baltimore. When he was sent to Maryland holding an appointment as Governor of the Province, his young cousin assumed he would steadfastly represent the family's interests above all else. The reasons for sending Captain Calvert, however, were phrased in terms of his faithful, loyal service to the king, his ability to make the interests of Province and Proprietary one, and his intention to live permanently in Maryland.[12]

Captain Calvert as Governor

Initially, Captain Calvert's appointment blocked the "malicious designs" of Col. Thomas Brooke II, a converted Protestant then serving as President of the Council, whose activities were seen by Calvert allies and loyal Council members as detrimental to the Proprietor. The appointed Council had a dual function: as the Governor's council it advised the Governor; as Upper House, it was the highest legislative body. The Council quietly expressed their gratitude to Guilford and former governor Captain John Hart for the appointment.[13]

Captain Calvert arrived in Annapolis during late summer. His mission, wrote Aubrey Land, was "soothing tempers and making peace." He was also directed to create a better balance – one more to the Proprietor's advantage – between Baltimore's prerogatives and the colonists' "privileges" set forth in the Maryland charter. Lord Baltimore directed Captain Calvert to work out a settlement between the colonial and proprietary positions, and to negotiate with the Indians. He was more successful in the latter than in the former, meeting with representatives of different Algonkian tribes to secure treaties. The Captain personally negotiated with Towena, sachem of the Senecas; with George, king of the Tuskeroras; and with members of the Onandogas, Nanticoakes, Shuano [Shawnee]. He helped resolve tensions created by the encroachment of English farmers upon the Pocomoke and Assateague lands of Maryland's Eastern Shore as well as upon lands belonging to the River Indians.[14]

Glimpses of Captain Calvert in action reveal a pragmatic man who could resolve issues by cutting through the tortuous, convoluted ruses characteristic of early eighteenth-century politics. His opening speech as Governor was short, "let time and my actions" show that I have Maryland's interests at heart. When petitioned by Mr. Slye to solve a dilemma created when Richard Lewellyn (stepson of William Taylard) hired the only two attorneys in the Province competent to comprehend fully the legal issues in a lawsuit, Calvert agreed to discharge one so

Figure 3.1. Portrait of Captain Charles Calvert (by John Wollaston; illustration courtesy of the Baltimore Museum of Art.)

that Slye could hire him: "If such a method is usual, I can't but think it very reasonable."[15]

Calvert resolved another troublesome matter that arose when Philemon Lloyd asked his clerk to arrange the removal of a land patent from the records. Lloyd's man found an indiscreet clerk in the land office named Geist willing to "extract" the deed for six pistoles (gold Spanish coins). Word spread. Lloyd soon complained to friends of the "scandalous story told publically at the Governor's table," and of Captain Calvert's "forward" behavior in repeating it. Yet Calvert turned over to Lloyd (a member of the Council; a Deputy Secretary of the Province) Geist's "Memorial" or written account with only a mild rebuke and a comment that the two clerks "had been playing into one another's hands, and at length fell to quarreling about the stakes."[16]

But the Governor grew as "hot" as Lloyd when news circulated about his own plans. He asked both legislative houses to discourage "parties, factions, and newsmakers." Angry at unsound advice and assuming it to be purposefully divisive, Captain Calvert summarily dismissed Thomas Bordley from the Council in 1721 for "counsel of pernicious consequence." Inexplicably, Calvert thought this would not affect Bordley's eligibility to serve as a member of the Upper House. He refused to re-appoint Bordley when it did. Whereupon Bordley ran for office in the Lower House and was elected by Annapolitans in the very next election.[17]

The Captain spent much time resolving what he termed "little heats," prematurely concluding in 1721 that these were at an end within the legislature; it was not so. During the sessions between 1722–5, the alignment of Maryland political interests began which eventually coalesced into the "Country Party." The removal of Bordley from the Council was pivotal in its development since it forged an alliance between Thomas Bordley and Daniel Dulaney inimical to proprietary interests. The controversy over adoption of English statutes, which Maryland men favored and Lord Baltimore fought, increased during Captain Calvert's governorship; McMahon credits the dispute with awakening an intense and lasting concern over colonists' rights and privileges. Everstine writes that it was the great debate of the decade, pitting the full Assembly *against the Governor* and Lord Baltimore.[18]

The way in which the rights of the people contrasted with the proprietary prerogatives is laid out in clear detail by Charles Barker in a masterful study, *The Background of the Revolution in Maryland*. The proprietary benefited financially when sales of Maryland tobacco prospered, but high sales also depended on the quality of the tobacco sold. An unpopular bill prohibiting transport of "trashy" tobacco provided qualitative control of the crop; the proprietary saw its enactment as essential. To ensure its passage, Captain Calvert called a special session of the legislature at the critical start of the tobacco-planting season. This strategy was a raw expression of his lordship's power. By taking tobacco planters away from their fields, Captain Calvert made plain Lord Baltimore's ability to weight issues on his own behalf. The tobacco planters responded with other expressions of resistance more difficult to suppress.

The moves of different factions within the legislature are a striking illustration of how different groups negotiated their self interests within early eighteenth-century Maryland. Their postures, positions, voices, excuses, tactics, and strategies reveal the way political power was symbolically charged. In the interchanges between the Lower and Upper Houses, Maryland men applied metaphors of authority, stressed knowledge of protocol or etiquette, and withheld funds to purchase paper supplies. The argument rolled from the sublime to the ridiculous; it was an active and heated debate.

The stakes could be phrased in economic terms. Maryland planters foresaw a loss of income through passage of the "trashy" tobacco bill, and moved to redress this loss by subtracting revenues and financial prerogatives from the proprietor. For example, Captain Calvert encountered insurmountable difficulties trying to mediate a dispute between the Upper and Lower Houses over payments (£150 in tobacco per day) to the Upper House owed its members when they served as the Council of State. The pointed messages exchanged between the two legislative bodies showed the hardening of lines between the two factions – Court and Country. In proroguing the General Assembly, Captain Calvert gave his opinion, Baltimore "will be surprized at your Endeavouring to load his Revenue with the Charge of maintaining the Council after his Lordship has so generously Sacrificed his private Interest for the Public Good."[19]

The controversy was renewed again in 1725 and Calvert was no more able to dissuade the Lower House from its position than were negotiators in the Upper House. The smaller politicians were adamant over the vested relationship between the Upper House (or Governor's Council) and the Proprietary: "You are appointed and intrusted by the prerogative, we by the people. Give us leave to make the distinction and to mind the discharge of our own trust." One suspects that by the end of the session, Captain Calvert shared his Council's view that members of the Lower House were "Obstinate people." The Lower House, in turn, offered to show the Upper House how it had departed from its "boasted Superiority in good manners." Civility and protocol were commonly supposed to distinguish those in higher stations; they were signs of gentlemanly behavior. Common planters were presumed to exhibit a different and rougher set of manners, but they well knew how to turn the world upside down and use the symbolic expressions of one station in life to designate another.[20]

Earlier in the session, Calvert spoke bluntly to the legislators: "I am afraid some Evil Spirits walk among us and it would be a matter of Great pleasure to such, to have your house and mine att Variance, but for my own part, I defy the Devill and his Works to do it." He saw his task: to "confound theire devices"; and thwart their plans. Captain Calvert subsequently maintained control of the political process by not calling the legislature into working session, a tactic his successor, Benedict Leonard, would also use.

Captain Calvert loses ground

Yet, the Captain's administrative skills and diplomacy were not sufficient to dispel the unrest. His English "house" was dissatisfied and uneasy with the thought of

Table 3.1. *Appointed offices held by Captain Charles Calvert and considered among the most "lucrative" positions in Maryland's provincial government*

Year	Position	Estimated annual income
1720–7	Governor	£1,000
1720–6	Surveyor General of the Eastern Shore	£130
1726–34	Surveyor General of the Western Shore	£200
1725–7	Chancellor	£200
1727–9	Commissary General (Judge of Probate)	£300–£700
1730–4	Commissary General (Judge of Probate)	£300–£700
1727–34	Upper House and Governor's Council during legislative sessions	£150/day (in pounds of tobacco)
1727–30	Second position on Council (Vice-President?)	None?
1730–4	President of Council	None?
1729–34	Judge of the Admiralty Court	£250?

Note: By way of contrast, the ordinary planters on the Eastern Shore lived simply, their average incomes in the range of £10–£15 (Clemens 1980: 87–9; Hoffman 1988: 213). Great planters had incomes of £200–£250 (Main 1982: 84), but some through the addition of a set of diversified activities that cross-cut economic and legal boundaries – mercantile, money-lending, legal activities or office-holding – made an additional £200–£350 per year. Placement in higher government echelons could bring as much as £500 more.
Source: Donnell MacClure Owings, *His Lordship's Patronage: Offices of Profit in Colonial Maryland.* Studies in Maryland History No. 1, Maryland Historical Society, Baltimore, 1953.

losing any of its power or funding base (which capitulation to the Lower House might have precipitated) or its political supremacy (which the "obstinacy" of the legislators put at stake). Lord Baltimore preferred and Captain Calvert worked to promote a metaphorical image of the youthful proprietor as a "bountiful, indulgent father" working on behalf of dutiful, deserving sons (Maryland men, many older than either of them). Captain Calvert evoked the imagery unequivocally – "the most tender, endearing Father could do no more for his own private family" – knowing that in Maryland families, custom dictated that sons uphold paternal authority. Meanwhile, the Lower House gave the proprietor a less exalted position by pointing out that he was "paid by the people," and therefore should use his own revenues to pay his "assistants," the men he appointed to the Upper House.[21]

As a result of these political events, prompted in part by the growing population, increased prosperity, individual striving, or discontent among the general population, in 1727 Charles, the fifth Lord Baltimore, replaced Captain Calvert with his own younger brother and proprietary heir, Benedict Leonard Calvert. Yet Captain Calvert's years of bureaucratic service were financially beneficial, an asset no Calvert ever forgot. Whatever his birth, Captain Calvert's education "as a gentleman thoroughly schooled in the graces" and his family connections enabled him to obtain positions within the proprietary bureaucracy that produced substantial income –

Table 3.2. *Values of the top one per cent of estates appraised in Maryland, 1720–39*

Year	Decedent	Residence	Value
1728	Amos Garrett	Annapolis	£24,450
1726	Thomas Bordley	Annapolis	£9,416
1737	Samuel Chew III	Anne Arundel	£7,667
1736	Samuel Chew II	Anne Arundel	£7,384
1733	Samuel Peele	Anne Arundel	£6,530
1737	Thomas Cockey	Anne Arundel	£5,276
1722	Charles Carroll	Annapolis	£4,897
1734	*Charles Calvert*	*Annapolis*	£4,401
1729	James Carroll	Anne Arundel	£3,900
1735	Amos Woodward (Garrett heir)	Annapolis	£3,606
1722	Richard Colgate	Baltimore	£3,165
1721	Samuel Galloway	Anne Arundel	£3,099
1733	Samuel Harrison	Anne Arundel	£3,048

Note that at this time (1726–42), 35% of the inventoried population left estates worth under £50; 56% under £100; 76% under £225. 11% left estates of £226–£400; 6% between £401–£659; only 7% had more than £650 (Burnard 1988: 22).
Source: Burnard 1988: 410–12.

offices that Owings termed "positions of profit." These are shown in Table 3.1 which also records estimates provided by Owings of the annual incomes obtained from the lucrative posts. Captain Calvert emigrated to Maryland without extensive wealth, as did Thomas Bordley and Amos Garrett (also listed in Table 3.2), but died one of the richest men in the province. "His lordship's kindness" paved the way for the Captain whereas Amos Garrett made it on his own, while Thomas Bordley and Charles Carroll used their legal knowledge in legislative matters and applied practical knowledge in others.[22]

The importance of family can be seen in the fact that Captain Calvert was replaced, but not displaced, when Benedict Leonard arrived. However, his appointed positions were not kept without controversy. A nasty altercation with Benedict Leonard Calvert ensued when the Captain relinquished the governorship but not his expectation of receiving fifty per cent of the three pence per hogshead (or tobacco duty) as specified in a legislative act of 1727 that he helped pass while Benedict Leonard was still learning the gubernatorial ropes. The latter was outraged and demanded a change. Cecilius Calvert, the youngest brother, wrote Benedict Leonard that his English relatives found Captain Calvert's behavior astonishing, and "thinks him mad." Charles Lowe expressed his opinion that "designing Men" had exerted an "evil Influence" for the express goal of setting the two Calvert family members at odds with one another so that their combined talents – Benedict Leonard's steadiness and ability, and the Captain's popularity – could not be used against the partisan interests of the Country Party. Lord Baltimore wrote that he never intended that Benedict Leonard, as Governor, should obtain less than the same, ample gratuity for his services that his predecessors received and attributed the dispute to "deadly Malignants, & such as live but in the Shipwreck of Friend-ship."[23]

The family promptly made plans to send Edward Henry Calvert to Maryland to serve his brother as President, Commissary General, and ranking member of the Upper Council. At the same time, Baltimore, through Lowe, also suggested another patronage office for Captain Calvert that could produce £250 per year. Benedict Leonard, however, needed a loyal helpmate and eagerly awaited his brother's arrival. He knew he could trust Edward Henry.[24]

A promising branch of the family

As the third son, Edward Henry's expectations were limited by his birth rank (chart 4.1; chapter 4). Raised in a lordly household, he also developed a keen awareness of what constituted the appropriate deference due people of rank. It is perhaps in this light that a 1727 letter written to his older brother should be read. Edward Henry conveyed an expectation that he took for granted: Maryland's people "will always Endeavor upon all occasions to shew the regard and respect that is due to you as Governor," firmly believing that Benedict Leonard would continually have at heart the best interests of Maryland's colonists. This, of course, conflated the interests of two separate interest groups – the people of Maryland, and the proprietor with his network of family retainers. The letter also reveals the regard, respect, and affection in which the younger brother held the older.[25]

> I hope soon to have an other oppertunity of writing to you, which will always be very acceptable to me, to acquaint you the state of affairs in particular relating to our family as well as I can & to Endeavor to convince you how much I have at heart the desire of keeping up that Brotherly affection and friendship their ought to be between us & tho' fortune hath now separated us so far distant from one the other, hope you will accept this as not comeing from the Pen alone but spoke from the Bottom of the Heart.

Ned, as Edward Henry was fondly called, and Margaret Lee Calvert, his young wife and cousin, set sail in late November 1728, reaching Annapolis in January. They came to provide Benedict Leonard with loyal family whom he could depend on; they came to support a beloved older brother. A glimpse of how Edward Henry viewed his prospects abroad is contained in a letter from his younger sister Charlotte: Ned "says he shall like the Company there as well as anny he did here, and that he is certain, on that Account, he shall never return." Unlike Benedict Leonard, he did not view the trip to Maryland as punishment, but rather as adventure. He was also close to his cousin, the Captain. Benedict Leonard celebrated Edward Henry's arrival with a ball in the Council Chamber using the birthday of Queen Caroline as the occasion.[26]

Unfortunately, although he had visited Maryland as a youth, Edward Henry still fell ill with the "seasoning" that few immigrants escaped. The experience was commonplace and for those who survived could have long-term effects. As Dr. Alexander Hamilton wrote to a friend: "As to the warmer suns of America increasing my genius – this I am sure of, that the warmer suns have much impaired my health." Edward Henry never fully recovered. Benedict Leonard expressed his concern over Ned's deteriorating health nine months later in a letter to Lord Baltimore: "Ned Continues very thin, and his Cough and Spitting very troublesome. I much fear the Approaching Winter will hardly relieve it." Still, sister Charlotte feared Ned's intemperance more than illness for she had been told "they drink verry hard in those parts." Charlotte's correspondence also reveals Margaret's view of Annapolis:[27]

> Its a great comfort to me to hear both [Ned] & his wife is So well pleas'd & Satisfied with the place & people. I hope Peg by this time has quite gott over the continual aprehensions she lay under of the Negroes, & yt by use your town will prove equally easy & agreeable as the Mall or anny other parts of London. She Speaks much in favor of the Ladies, but not once mentions the gentlemen. So I conclude they are creatures.

On April 24, 1730, Edward Henry made his will. His brother, Captain Calvert, and the family doctor witnessed it. Within two weeks he passed away. Somewhere in Annapolis his remains lie buried, possibly on Church Circle underneath St. Anne's church. When the legislators began their May session, they offered Benedict Leonard condolences. Edward Henry, they said, had been "a promising branch of the family," someone who could well have become an "Ornament" to the country. His young widow, drawing £80 in mid-August from her brother-in-law, left her household possessions and returned to England with her maid. Benedict Leonard turned back to his cousin, the Captain, and appointed him Commissary General once again. Life, all realized, was a fleeting thing.[28]

Margaret Lee Calvert spent less than two years in the province, years filled with sorrow and with fear. Why did she leave Maryland? The toll taken by the "seasoning," the effects of fever and ague on both Edward Henry and Benedict Leonard were surely one reason. It could not have been pleasant nursing them nor could the two men have been the best of company while in ill health. A missionary for the Society for the Propagation of the Gospel, Commissary Johnson, was blunt in 1708 about the way he felt: "It is no pleasing task to flesh & blood, to be Ministering to Sick or dying Persons, & to be exposed to all the filth & Nauseous Smells & Ghostly Sighs." Then too, there was little time for Maryland to become home and in some cases, even a dozen years did not suffice. One Anglican minister spent sixteen years in the Province and still wrote of it as a "strange land" in his own epitaph.[29]

Captain Calvert in society

Unlike his young cousin, Captain Charles Calvert lived long enough (fourteen years) after his immigration to leave his imprint on Maryland and Annapolis in various ways. He worked hard to establish decent clergymen in different parish churches and authorized the construction of a Chapel of Ease for St. Anne's Parish. He served as a vestryman for St. Anne's and worked towards the improvement of education in Prince George's County. These, however, were duties in which his role also denoted his status as Governor.

Cosmopolitan, well travelled by virtue of military duty on the Continent, Captain Calvert thoroughly enjoyed horse racing – an interest he shared with relatives, other gentry, and the average man. The first of a long series of quarter-mile horse races in Annapolis, honored with a hefty prize for the winner, began the year Captain Calvert arrived. The race was September's celebration after the tobacco harvest. Hawksters sold goods at the race grounds where town merchants too set up booths to sell food and beverages (contributing toward the prize for their use of space). Jones (1724) wrote that next to cock-fighting in which men "greatly delight," horse racing was the people's passion. Horseriding also symbolized human triumph: "As he curvetted and bounded, galloped and turned, or skilfully shuffled sideways, the rider of the great horse proclaimed both his social superiority and his conquest of the animal creation." The belief that people of lower social rank were impressed by gentlemen on horseback is expressed in Sir Thomas Elyot's statement that "the spectacle of a gentleman daunting a fierce and cruel beast created a majesty and dread to inferior persons, beholding him about the common course of other men."[30]

Horse racing and its symbolism has been insightfully placed in a cultural context for tidewater Virginia by Timothy Breen, but Rhys Isaac's reminder of "how essential it was to be proudly mounted when one entered the stages of significant action in the social landscape" is also pertinent (fig. 3.2). At his death, the most valuable animal Calvert owned was a gray racing horse valued at £18! At this time, the average value of a riding horse in Anne Arundel County was £5–£7 while that of a working horse was between £1 and £2. The appraised values on his cousins' horseflesh did not approach the worth of Captain Calvert's animal. Even the first recorded Arabian imported to the Colonies – Samuel Galloway's Selem – was not appraised much higher. Isaac's evocative description of rich Virginians as "proud men on horseback" held true throughout the region.[31]

Maryland gentry saw hunting, fishing, gaming, and horse racing as manly exercise, and thus appropriate leisure activities. Other social pursuits included drinking and dining with friends, music, dancing, a variety of sedate games as well as the socially cross-cutting cockfights. Here, the historical records provide snippets of information in which Captain Calvert appears. Reading them, Aubrey Land concluded, "The arrival of the new Governor was a grand occasion and opened the houses of Councillors and officers of state with displays of family silver and glass brought to sparkling perfection." Here, Captain Charles Calvert met the women of Maryland. Possibly at one of these occasions, Calvert met the young landed heiress, sixteen-year-old Rebecca Gerard, whom he wed.[32]

Marriage and family

The social structure of the society and the symbolic imagery central in English world view gave married men greater prestige than bachelors. In a study of Charles County, Jean Lee includes a statement by a rich young man: "The whole neighborhood of Marlbro [Prince George's Country] . . . has made free enough to tell me that

I only wanted a good wife to render me quite respectable." A respectable husband also complemented a woman's character; together, especially among the planter-gentry, the stature of a married couple symbolically stood for the members of their household or others associated with it. The alliances formed by gentry marriages were one mechanism through which economic activities, political affairs, and even religious belief systems were activated.[33]

One has only to read carefully the Calvert correspondence to realize that financial assets were always of consideration when evaluating the marital merits of young, eligible women. Captain Calvert knew that a good marriage was to his advantage. On November 21, 1722, the rector of Queen Anne's Parish married Captain Calvert to Maryland-born Rebecca Gerard for love, perhaps for money, or for other considerations. Miss Gerard, an only child, inherited her father John Gerard's estate when he died in 1715. She lived with her mother, Elizabeth Gerard, on a plantation near Queen Anne's Town in Prince George's County. Although her mother was still alive, control of John Gerard's estate went to Captain Charles Calvert upon the marriage.[34]

Aubrey Land wrote that Calvert's marriage in 1722 "enlivened the whole winter season with entertainments for the new first lady." The next autumn, his mother (the Countess Henrietta) accompanied by young Mrs John Ross (Alicia) made preparations to sail for Maryland where the family hoped "they will find the Governor and his Lady well." On November 2, 1723, Rebecca gave birth to their

Figure 3.2. Proud hunters on horseback ca. 1725 are shown in a folk painting. Scottish artist John Watson (1685–1768), who lived in New Jersey, may have painted these colonists at play. (Metropolitan Museum of Art, gift of Mr. and Mrs. Samuel Schwartz, 1979.299.)

first-born child, a son Charles who lived less than three months. During his brief life, however, his grandmother arrived from England to greet the infant. Daughter Anne was born in 1726; she died between age 9 and 11. The third child was daughter Elizabeth, born February 24, 1731. She was named for Rebecca's mother Elizabeth (present at the baptism), and was the only one of the couple's three children to live beyond childhood (see kinship chart 3.2 and fig. 13.1).[35]

Wealth and possessions

In 1726, the couple still resided in Prince George's County, probably in Rebecca's family home, for there is no record of a sale of the Gerard property during the Calverts' lifetimes. Her father's room-by-room inventory indicates this was a story-and-a-half or two-story dwelling. Knowledge of traditional Maryland architecture suggests it was of post-hole or frame construction. Charles Calvert's room-by-room inventory of his Prince George's County tobacco plantation taken in June 1734 lists a dwelling with a hall chamber, hall, lower room, and two outlying quarters (see figs. 3.3 and 3.4). Its contents closely match those shown on the Gerard inventory. Meanwhile Captain Calvert actively began to amass additional land in Prince George's County and Anne Arundel County. The £12 rent charged for his agricultural holdings after his death, considered in light of farms that rented for £6 (table 3.3), suggest that they were well apportioned. Captain Calvert also bought fifteen lots in the city of Annapolis, but these may have been purchased to advance Lord Baltimore's ambition to build a governor's mansion on an undeveloped hill.[36]

The Captain's business activities are more difficult to trace. Interestingly, in light of a £300 debt to Thomas Bordley, Calvert appears as one of the plaintiffs in the suit that Edmund Jennings brought against the Proprietor on behalf of the Bordley family and other Annapolis landowners to secure land titles. The accounts presented by Calvert's executors show his widow purchased £282-worth of goods from a London merchant the year following his death. Calvert also had advanced over £300 to merchant Samuel Hyde although the Hydes had encountered a drop in trade with Maryland planters. The Hydes were not directly related to Captain Calvert, yet his support of their mercantile ventures in the Province was another facet of his relationship with Baltimore's extended network and financial associates. The debts alone due the estate (in the range of £2,000) were sufficient to place

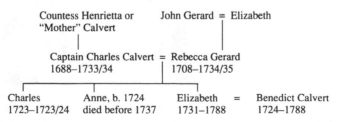

Chart 3.2. Captain Calvert's family chart

Figure 3.3. Patuxent Manor, built ca. 1730, was a small brick hall and parlor house typical of those built by wealthy planters. (Photograph by Frances Benjamin Johnson, courtesy of the Library of Congress.

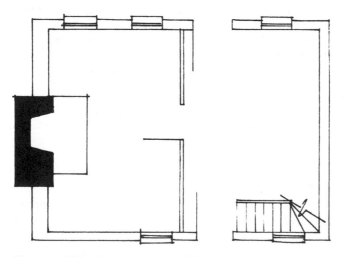

Figure 3.4. Floor plan of a house at 43 Pinkney Street in Annapolis is typical of wooden hall and parlor houses found throughout Maryland in the early eighteenth century. (Drawing by Russell Wright, AIA.)

Table 3.3. *Thomas Rutland, the real estate he holds for orphans, viewed by Thomas Worthington and Charles Guff, June 1735*[37]

1. The property of Moses and Charles Maccubbin.

One dwelling house, 40 × 15, with a brick chimney, two rooms below with plank floors below and above, a partition below of clapboards, and a part above of the same. One of the rooms filled in with brick on edge; the chimney fast, a closet on one side the chimney, a pair of stairs the other side. A stone celler under one part of the house 15 feet square from outside to outside. A shed at the end of the house, 7½ feet wide, part thereof being a milk house [and] the other part a pair of stairs to the cellar. That part over the cellar being posts in the ground of cedar and locust. The house double-covered except about one-third of one length of one side.

A dwelling house, 40 × 16, with brick chimneys at each end, plank floor above and below, a plank partition below, both chimneys fast, two closets in one room and one and a pair of stairs in the other. The rims lathed and filled in, the floor good except one room below. An 8' shed at one end, the shed and the one other single-covered and post in the ground, cedar and locust.

A 10' stable, double-covered; an old meat house, 10 × 8; a hoghouse, 25 × 8, but it is built by the guardian; one brick oven with a 10' square house over it. One 15' kitchen with a chimney and shed on the side, the width with the house being 13 feet. An old hen house with partitions, 20 × 12. An old house, 20 × 12, all open below and very much decayed. One tobacco house, 30 × 20, overjeal with 5 ft wide sheds on one side and double-covered. 290 feet of paling round the yard joining to the garden which consists of about 400 feet as also a small yard of 70 ft more of old paling. 79 apple trees in an orchard yard surrounded within a pretty good worm fence; a nursery of apple trees, about 200, the greater part ready to place out. 20 old peach trees, 6 cherry with a worm fence; a cornfield with a worm fence; a pasture with a worm fence and part thereof a hedge or brush fence. One 50 × 20 tobacco house. Rent at £7-00-00 per year.

2. The property of Benjamin Howard.

One dwelling house, 40 × 60 with old plank floor, pair of old stairs, outside wooden chimney, double covered but old. One 10 ft square hen house, double covered but old; one 10 ft square house very old and good for very little; one old dwelling house with a shed, 20 feet long, 19 ft wide; one 50 × 22 foot tobacco house, old but pretty good; one 50 × 22 tobacco house, pretty good. One dwelling house, 28 × 12 feet, very bad, seems of little or no use; one house 12 × 8 feet without any doors, settled to one side; one tobacco house, 40 × 20, part blown down. One house, 20 × 15 feet, with a shed on each side, all very bad, all open below. A cornfield . . . enclosed with a worm fence; some other worm fences. An orchard with apple trees, a cherry walk of about 16 old cherry trees; a parcel of scattering peach trees, about 15; a small parcel of old apple trees.

[some information on fields and fences has been deleted]. Rent set at £6 current money.

Calvert's financial assets well above the average holdings (under £100) of most Maryland decedents.[38]

Charles Calvert Lazenby owned a dozen black slaves in 1709 whom he sold to another uncle or cousin (Henry Darnell). Their numbers were unusually high; most slave-owners had far fewer this early in the century. At the Captain's death, his slave-holdings were again among the largest in the province. This is highly significant in assessing the archaeological assemblages recovered from his Annapolis town lot; its probable effects are the subject of chapters 9–12. Investments and slave purchases were both means the Captain chose to build wealth. His cousin, Benedict Leonard, wrote in 1724 that Italian families rejoiced when one of their men was elected as Pope for it meant increased riches, especially for his oldest nephew. In the same paragraph, Benedict Leonard noted that often death came too soon for a new Pope, frequently before his relatives had the time to consolidate their new social position or amass a stable fortune. The same might be said of Captain Calvert.[39]

Captain Charles Calvert died on February 2, 1734 aged 46 after suffering briefly from premature senility. The three inventories filed listed material goods worth more than £2,300; combined with debts due, his estate was worth £4,000. Table 3.2 indicates that Calvert's estate placed him at the very top of the wealthy (families with estates worth more than £1,000); only seven men in the province left larger estates in the twenty years that bracket his death. The expenses (£60) incurred for his stately funeral were more than the net worth of a full third of Maryland's families.[40]

Calvert's widow, Rebecca, was 28 years old. Her marriage had lasted 12 years. She survived her husband by only one year and, at her death in March 1735, left a will requesting that a young French woman, Elizabeth Razolini, take care of her daughters: Anne, age 9, and Elizabeth, age 4. These children were orphans not only in the legal sense of the word (i.e., those without living fathers), but in all senses of the word. To the best of anyone's knowledge, by 1737 Elizabeth had no close living relatives left in Maryland except her second cousin in Annapolis, who lived with George Stuart and went by the name of Benedict Swingate, not yet acknowledged as Lord Baltimore's natural son. Like other children who experienced similar tragedies, her affairs were placed in the hands of community men; unlike other young orphans, "Mistress Betsy" did not have to work. A further difference was that the men concerned with her welfare – Benjamin Tasker, George Plater, Onorio Razolini, and Daniel Dulaney – were politically powerful men who owed allegiance to the Calvert family (fig. 3.5). The clear expectation was that they would carefully steward the Calvert estate.[41]

In Maryland, a small family size or a family with a single child was unusual. This element of their respective family situations gave Rebecca Gerard and her daughter, Elizabeth Calvert, financial assets they would not have possessed ordinarily. It made each heiresses, which in turn undoubtedly made them doubly attractive to the Calvert men they married. Since Captain Charles Calvert's slaves and lands, gifts from the third Lord Baltimore, were sold to pay for his commission in the British army, he was more bereft of assets than most Calvert men. Without doubt, the Gerard family capital was beneficial in the Captain's acquisition of wealth. Rebecca's land and slaves effectively became his to use with their marriage – assets that could be turned to good advantage in improving an estate. In terms of real estate, Captain Calvert acquired land (a) above average and yet (b) not fully the equivalent of other wealthy men in early Maryland. In contrast, his slave-holdings were well above the average (see table 3.4).

Yet, by the mid-eighteenth century most native-born white men reached their late 40s or 50s before death struck while almost three-quarters of the women lived to age

40. Neither Captain Charles nor Rebecca Calvert lived as long as neighbors born within the same decade in either Prince George's County or Annapolis. Each, however, outlived the Calvert brothers – Benedict Leonard and Edward Henry – but ironically not long enough to ensure the continuation of their own branch of the family. This feat awaited the arrival of Captain Calvert's younger second "cousin," Benedict Swingate, born in the mid-1720s within a few years of the birth of Charles and Rebecca's oldest son and daughter.[42]

In summary, despite his access to or control of political patronage from 1720–34, the means whereby Captain Charles Calvert obtained his most solid financial worth – marriage to an heiress – was a pattern oft practiced in Maryland families. In addition to his reputation for integrity, one reason for the esteem and popularity that Captain Charles Calvert held in the Province may have been simply that he was much like the native-born Chesapeake gentry: endowed with a passion for horses, married to a Maryland woman, a Maryland land and slave owner who grew tobacco

Figure 3.5. Seals on wine bottles brought to the Calvert home. The "O.R." seal was probably associated with the younger son of a Venetian nobleman, Onorio Razolini, who arrived in Maryland about the time Lord Baltimore visited the province. Razolini represented the Calvert family's Maryland interests until he returned to Asolo, Italy in 1748, and lived at the site in the 1730s and 1740s. (Photograph by Marion E. Warren.)

Table 3.4. *Slave-holdings among the*
inventoried population 1726–42
(Burnard 1988: 58)

Size of slave-holdings	Per cent
None	1.2
1–5 slaves	8.1
6–10	13.8
11–20	34.5
21–30	18.4
31–50	14.9
Over 50	9.2

and worked towards a future for himself, his children, and grandchildren within the Province. These characteristics, which were the ostensible reasons Lord Baltimore first sent him to Maryland, distinguished Captain Calvert from the two younger brothers of the Proprietor who also resided at the Calvert site between 1728 and 1732.

4

Governor Benedict Leonard Calvert

I am very glad you have not consented to Castrating any of the [Maryland proprietary] officers fees for I will never be so dismembered . . . I hope you are so well acquainted with your & the whole family's interest as not to suffer, throu influence or present advantage, any thing to pass Contrary to the honour & interest of the whole.

Lord Baltimore to Governor Benedict Leonard Calvert, 1729

My weakenesses I doubt are many, but yet sure I am, they cannot outnumber my affections to your service. For I am most sincerely and entirely devoted to you.

Benedict Leonard Calvert to Lord Baltimore, 1729

Authoritative influences

Benedict Leonard Calvert was the second son of the fourth Lord Baltimore. As the fifth Lord Baltimore's closest brother and next in line to succeed, he was most apt to have ordered or directed the activities discernible at the Calvert site. There is no gainsaying that Benedict Leonard Calvert believed he was an aristocrat highly capable of ruling Maryland. He had been trained to do so since his birth at Ditchley in the low, old timber-framed home of his maternal grandparents, the Lees.[1]

By 1700, the Calvert family's English headquarters was the third Lord Baltimore's home at Woodcote Park which he inherited from his aunt (Elizabeth Mynne Evelyn). Celia Fiennes described the estate in 1702: "encompass'd with a wall at the entrance, a brest wall with pallisadoes, large courts one within the other, . . . old but low, tho' large run over much ground; in front six windows, and in the top just in the middle 12 chimneys in a row . . . look into a court which is built round." Its advantageous Epsom location in the county of Surrey gave the family easy access to London and court life; Hampton Court was but a short ride away; many of the gentry assembled regularly in the town to enjoy the races or its beneficial springs.[2]

From his new home, the third Lord Baltimore arranged a marriage between his eighteen-year-old son and the lovely Charlotte Lee, granddaughter of Charles II. This added another dimension to the Calvert network of kith and kin. Benedict Leonard's cousin, Fitzroy Henry Lee, came to serve as Governor of Newfoundland

(1735–8) and later as commander in chief of the Leeward Islands while his uncle, Francis Lee (1661–1719), a physician, was known as a man of "great learning" who drew up plans for charity schools in England. The marriage served to preserve the family lineage, but was abusive.[3]

The third Lord Baltimore supported his son's children and gave them a home at Woodcote after their young mother, having given birth to seven children in the first six years of their marriage, left Benedict Leonard (Sr.) in 1705 (see chart 4.1). With the dissolution of the marriage, her father, the Earl of Litchfield, filed suit to have the couple's home – Woodstock Park – sold and the profit returned to the Lee family. The children remained with their father during the ten-year separation or boarded at private schools, yet they also sustained ties with their mother, her family, and later with her second husband and their half-brothers and -sisters. Childhood memories were surely one reason the fifth Lord Baltimore named his first yacht the *Charlotte*.[4]

The third Lord Baltimore not only made a home for his grandchildren after his son's marriage dissolved, he financed their education, withdrawing funding only when their father removed them from Catholic schools and placed them in Protestant institutions. According to his son, Lord Baltimore had reassured Benedict Leonard (Sr.) that his allowance would not be cut if he converted to the Anglican church. However, the old gentleman "resented this So much that he withdrew four hundred & fifty Pounds per annum" which created deep financial problems as Benedict Leonard (Sr.) then had to live on his marriage settlement of £600 per annum, support his wife, and pay for the children's schooling. Citing "hard usage from his Father & his slender Fortune," Benedict Leonard (Sr.) petitioned Queen Anne for relief. She granted him £300 per year from the "Royall Bounty" to maintain the children and also requested Maryland's governor to provide an additional £500 from the profits of the Province.[5]

Lois Green Carr wrote me that Jesuit records indicate the fifth Lord Baltimore left the Catholic school of St. Omers with great reluctance, but that his Jesuit teachers, well aware that the fate of Maryland Catholics might rest on his father's shoulders (and within a few years they rested on the boy's own shoulders), urged obedience rather than rebellion, and treated him with great kindness. Perhaps the 75-year old Lord Baltimore would have relented and continued to fund the Calvert boys' educations if he had not died so soon. The proprietary revenues and property which the third Lord Baltimore retained after the Maryland revolution left him significant assets; he continued to plead for the return of full rights. However, it is certain that the allowance provided by Queen Anne fused his son's loyalties to the Crown and made it in Benedict Leonard's own interests to support its administration of the Province. However, without the conversion from "Romish Errors," it is unlikely that Benedict Leonard (Sr.) would have regained proprietary control of the Province which had been his birthright. He had no time to take advantage of his new powers before his death two months after his father's.[6]

In the long run, it proved vital that the third Lord Baltimore ensured his grandsons were given education and training to prepare them to rule the Province. Through their schooling, he broadened the brothers' networks by enrolling them first in a Belgium school, St. Omer's. Afterwards the Calvert boys were entered in the most prestigious English schools which gave them an opportunity to form friendships and acquaintances among the more powerful aristocratic families. Three attended Oxford. At least two, Charles and Benedict Leonard (Jr.), made lengthy European tours while one of the younger brothers, Edward Henry, was sent to Maryland as a teenager.[7]

English younger sons often received an education markedly inferior to that of the eldest son; the third Lord Baltimore broke with this custom. Benedict Leonard's education was equivalent to those given the wealthiest English noblemen, and qualitatively better than many eldest sons of aristocratic families received. His broad-based knowledge gave him the intellectual foundation to pursue the arts (music, poetry, drama, painting), architecture, history, horticulture, and science. Further, the Calvert brothers honed their minds to considerations of political and legal matters. Their education and training provided a cosmopolitan outlook that differentiated Benedict Leonard from almost all other men in Maryland ca. 1730 (fig. 4.1). His intellectual reach can be seen in lengthy letters to his older brother from Naples, Italy in which he summarizes what he has learned of Italian military defenses, taxation, wealth, towns, churches, antiquities, libraries, gardens, vistas, paintings, and wine, together with succinct descriptions of the effects of papal government and the rise of Renaissance thought. Consistently comparing what he saw with England, he concluded "they adorn for the ages and we only for years."[8]

Benedict Leonard's inquisitive outlook is paralleled in his youngest brother Cecilius Calvert's plea of August 29, 1724 to observe carefully when Mt. Vesuvius erupted: "I hope that when that Combustable Mount has vented itself you will be so kind as to favour us with an Account . . . because People Differ much Concerning those Mountains." Benedict Leonard was later recommended for membership in the Royal Society. While the fifth Lord Baltimore also became a Fellow of the Royal Society, Benedict Leonard's interests were more scholarly and had a broader, humanistic reach. As seen through the writings of his friends, Hearne and Lewis, he was also practiced in literate discourse and displayed interest in the wide variety of topics that gave a gentleman mental stature. Whereas some saw his older brother as "not so bright within as without," Benedict Leonard indisputably possessed a keen

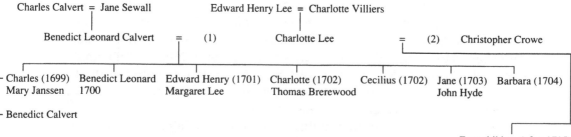

Chart 4.1. Kinship chart for the fifth generation of Calverts

Figure 4.1. Portrait of Benedict Leonard Calvert at Woodcote Park ca. 1726 by Francis Brerewood. Some of the statues shown standing in wall niches may have been collected during his Grand Tour of Italy in 1724–5. (Illustration courtesy of the Baltimore Museum of Art.)

intellect. Oxford archivist Thomas Hearne, after meeting the three younger Calvert brothers and hearing tales of the elder, concluded that "all the Learning of this Family is lodg'd in my Friend [Benedict Leonard]."[9]

Yet, whatever their mental capabilities, English country gentlemen were, like Maryland families, at the mercy of births, deaths, and childbirth traumas. While a family might wish for a son to carry on the lineage – and a prudent family wished for more than one to insure it – the actual number of sons and daughters born in a family was seen as God's will. Only one of the third Lord Baltimore's sons survived to adulthood. It is noteworthy that despite an unhappy marriage, the legal separation of Charlotte Lee Calvert and her young husband did not occur until she had given birth to seven children, including four sons. The fifth Lord Baltimore, named Charles Calvert to honor his grandfather, was less concerned about insuring his succession, an attitude derived perhaps because he had three younger brothers. He did not marry until after Edward Henry's death, when Benedict Leonard was in poor health, and Calvert himself was thirty (a dozen years older than his father and mother when they wed).

To preserve the family's interests, the fifth Lord Baltimore also continued tradition by surrounding himself with a loyal staff, many with close family connections. The proprietor kept as secretary his cousin, Charles Lowe, who was succeeded in 1729 by the youngest brother, Cecilius Calvert, at Lowe's death. Cecilius stayed in the post until his mid-fifties, serving his nephew too. Their sister Charlotte's brother-in-law, Francis Brerewood, became Baltimore's "man" and oversaw much of the construction and renovation at the various Calvert homes, working for Baltimore's son, Frederick, after the fifth Lord died. Other kinsmen were given positions with political and executive power: Captain Calvert as Governor; Thomas Bladen as Governor (brother-in-law through his marriage to Barbara Janssen); William Janssen (another brother-in-law) as principal Secretary of Maryland; cousins Nicholas and Bennett Lowe as the Maryland Agents. Within this framework, it was inevitable that Charles Calvert's brothers would be asked to play major roles in the administration of provincial government and in the maintenance of the province's economic resources as defined by the way in which each domain promoted the family's private interests and the proprietor's prerogatives. Benedict Leonard's analytical skills were thus directed at enhancing the family's fortunes.[10]

A gentleman's education

Educated as a young boy on the Continent, Benedict Leonard learned French and became acquainted with French culture. Still a Roman Catholic, he entered the socially exclusive school of Weston in his early teens where he was converted, possibly before his father, to the Anglican faith. At age seventeen he followed his brother to Christ College at Oxford where the eminent antiquary, Thomas Hearne, befriended him. Hearne's diary tells of their activities. They sallied throughout England, visiting locations that possessed ancient relics and old curiosities ("Valuable Things"), went to visit Ditchley, and walked the countryside. Essentially, the young scholar and the older one were both interested in material things that were clues to the early history of England and, more broadly, of Europe. Educated in Latin and Greek, Benedict Leonard transcribed manuscripts for his mentor. Hearne's influence can be seen in Benedict Leonard's description of classical Rome and in his enthusiasm for the city: "For some time after a man comes to Rome, he knows not which way to turn himself amidst such an infinite variety of curiosities."[11]

Hearne taught Calvert well. As he travelled throughout Italy on his prolonged Grand Tour (1723–5), Benedict Leonard visited archives and repositories, noting the difficulties created by inadequate cataloging of records and general "disorder," gaining insight he later put to good use in Maryland. He also began to acquire the collection of rare books that his brother, Cecilius, inherited at Benedict Leonard's death. He became acquainted with a wide variety of people. He stretched the boundaries of his mind.

From an archaeologist's perspective what is most fascinating was the attention Calvert paid artifacts, large and small: England's Roman ruins and ancient monasteries, Italy's villas, France's gardens, Greek and Roman coins, manuscripts, statues, and jewelry. Benedict Leonard wrote of ancient walls, roads, aqueducts, and of living conditions in medieval cities:[12]

> [Ferrara] has very visible marks of Papal tyranny upon it – a vast city deserted and as it were uninhabited, whole streets in possession of rats and mice, and even they, I believe, in a starving condition . . . This [its water] is a natural fortification to Venice and which they endeavor to preserve at a vast expense by cleaning these channels often which would otherwise be choked up by the rubbish and dirt which come from the city . . . crabs and oysters [are] neither savory nor wholesome because of the filth in the canals.

Applying an archaeologist's (or art-historian's) eye for detail, Benedict Leonard wrote Hearne that the shape and form of the fleur de lis and crosses decorating a monument in Gloucester, England, indicated it was installed long after the Conquest rather than before as historians believed. Taking a preservationist's stance, he wrote that Romans protected their works of art by placing them inside churches whereas "we at St Paul's and the Church on the Strand have placed it without where our London smoke will soon wear out those beauties and philagree niceties. St. Peter's on the outside is as plain as architects will permit it!" And with a collector's instinct he disdained the trumpet, spur, sword, and battle axe excavated (pot-hunted doubtlessly) from Windsor Forest by a clergyman, but attempted to buy the Roman coins in this collection on sale in a London bookshop. The era was one in which miscellanies or curiosities were collected individually and exhibited as entities by themselves. Their possession conferred prestige on their owner, but they were not collected to form a series of objects which would represent another way of life in a collective sense as modern museum exhibits of material culture attempt to do. Instead, artifacts and ruins served as symbolic reminders of the temporal frame of life and man's fragility. They were components of a metaphysical discourse. "Endowed with moral virtue" as Plumb notes, each spoke of the fleeting nature of material things, man's own susceptibility, his heritage, and place in the universe.[13]

Men learned the art of visual discourse embedded in exotic curiosities or in classical architecture, and its symbolic content, during their Grand Tours of Europe. Some visits were narrow in geographic scope; others reached to Rome or beyond. But most tours began with France and thus at age eighteen on a summer tour of France with his nineteen-year old brother, Lord Baltimore, Benedict Leonard visited the palace of Versailles with its famous gardens (and orangery). After this visit Lord Baltimore began to plan a series of landscape changes to his English home that are relevant to the building episodes at the site in Annapolis (see Chapter 5); he started them during Benedict Leonard's second and last visit to the Continent, one in which he spent almost two years in Italy. A passage from Johnson informs us of the country's standing among the aristocracy, giving Benedict Leonard's journey a context: "A man who has not been in Italy is always conscious of an inferiority." However, Joseph Addison's remarks are also apropos: "There is certainly no place in the world where a man may travel with greater pleasure and adventure than in Italy." A man could visit and write accounts of "pictures, statues, and buildings," or he could "search libraries, cabinets of rarities, and collections of medals," said Addison in dividing the attractions, although some preferred to "take up inscriptions, ruins, and antiquities." All were of passionate interest to Benedict Leonard. He neglected none.[14]

Benedict Leonard's second European tour began with a summer in Paris and autumn in Montpellier, a medieval university town in southern France. Then, he searched for antiquities in Burgundy near Lyons and inspected its Hermitage. Crossing the Alps, Benedict Leonard made himself at home in Leghorn, one of Italy's great market cities. He spent the spring of 1724 in Rome (and attended the Coronation of the Pope) where the attention of papal authorities was drawn to his earlier renunciation of Catholicism. During that year he also went to Tuscany, Venice, Padua, Bologna, Florence, Ferrara, Nimes, and Lucca, visited gardens and villas (fig. 4.2) and possibly toured the nascent archaeological excavations at Herculaneum.[15]

The trip was made in search of health and knowledge, but it was not all pleasure. His brother asked him to assist initially by negotiating a tobacco contract with the French Farmers General of Tobacco. Benedict Leonard did this exceptionally well to the family's pleasure; his success brought benefits to the Province when the French market for tobacco renewed growth of Maryland's faltering economy. Benedict Leonard also took time to write Captain Charles Calvert concerning the English statutes and the disadvantages that would ensue if Maryland's legislature was allowed to make them part of Maryland law. Within the year, Benedict Leonard was informed by Lord Baltimore that he should return in 1725 and prepare to sail for Maryland to oversee the family's legislative domain.[16]

Overall, Italy was good for Benedict Leonard's health and his spirit. In the spring of 1725 Benedict Leonard partied in Florence while friends in Leghorn wrote of more gay parties and begged his return. Letters home described Italian horse races, operas, masquerades, and games of chance. He was entranced by a Venetian courtesan who had wit, good sense, and beauty. Cecilius envied his brother meeting a woman with this rare combination of womanly assets. But if Benedict Leonard had to go to Maryland, he felt an English wife would better suit. Lowe, pragmatic as ever, believed finding a Good Wife willing to be "transported to the Plantations (as the Women call it) out of the world and dear London" would be exceedingly difficult. He suggested following the path of Captain Charles: "When your Excellency comes to be cloathed with Authority in your American Dominions, you may fling your Handkerchief at whom you list, and happy will the fair one think herself to have your Mantle thrown over her." Benedict Leonard departed for England after spending the spring in Florence with his thoughts on domestic pursuits, and after a few summer weeks in Paris, crossed the channel to home.[17]

Postponing his departure, perhaps feeling he need not go, Benedict Leonard stood for and was elected as MP for Harwich, a post his father held briefly ten years before. At the same time he began preparations to move abroad and assume oversight of the family's Province, its profits, and its prerogatives. Captain Calvert's increasing difficulty with the Lower Assembly and the stormy interchanges between Upper and Lower House made it a necessity. By the spring of 1727 Benedict Leonard was aboard a vessel bound for Annapolis. It was likely he left with trepidation because his health was never strong; friends warned of the dangers and hazards of crossing the ocean and living in a "more sultry and scorching climate."[18]

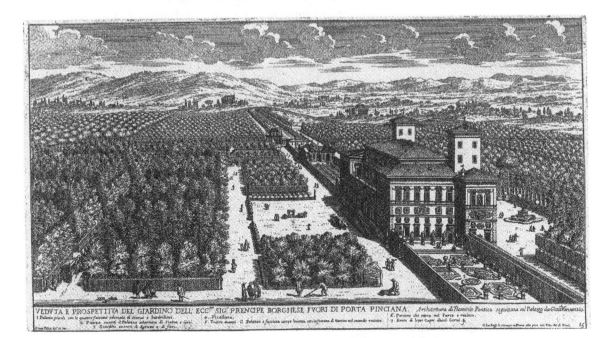

Figure 4.2. Statues and orange trees in containers decorate an ornamental garden seen by Benedict Leonard Calvert at the Villa Borghese gardens in Rome in this seventeenth-century illustration from Giovanni Battista Falda's *Li giardini di Roma*. (Illustration courtesy of Dumbarton Oaks.)

Benedict Leonard Calvert once told Thomas Hearne he expected to live a short life. In 1719 a physician suggested he take the waters at Bath and the following year he drank those near his home at Epsom. Hearne kept track in his diary of his friend's lengthy illness throughout 1720 and 1721. One reason that Lord Baltimore funded the lengthy Grand Tour was his brothers' and sisters' belief that a different climate might improve Benedict Leonard's health. Despite an overall improvement, however, he was ill in Rome and again at Leghorn. He could not have looked forward to arriving in Maryland and the "seasoning" all newcomers faced with its accompanying fever, chills, and threat of death. Did he remember, as he sailed, the folk belief which physicians also professed, "that which is a man's native soyle, and Countries ayre is best . . . [and] preserveth him"? If so, there was no way to prepare except with stoic humor and prayer. In terms of earthly pleasures and material comforts things were different.[19]

The material start of a new life

In 1635, Cecilius Calvert reprinted Captain John Smith's list of necessities to begin farming in the Chesapeake; the cost was minimal – less than £20 per person. If only a list survived of what Benedict Leonard shipped to make life in the "Plantations" more comfortable. A letter from his brother's secretary indicates Lowe acted too late to increase insurance upon the goods from £1,600 to £1,800. The sum of £1,800 was large enough to buy whole storeloads of goods! The commotion as Annapolis dockhands unloaded the bales and barrels containing the new governor's possessions and the impact it created must have reverberated through the town. The procession of boxes, barrels, and trunks up the hillside streets towards the State House could not have gone without notice.[20]

There is no mention in any correspondence I have found of additional orders to London merchants except for books and wine. These were sent out to Benedict Leonard on a regular basis by friends, relatives, or at his own request. While the books were sent for spiritual pleasure, the pipes of port were sent for social occasions and less lofty purposes: "Pray when you wait on the Widow [Rebecca] Bowles," Lowe wrote, "convince her what a Melancholly thing it is to lie alone; Mr. Crow will take care to provide some Good Wine to push you on." The family's interest in the young and wealthy Widow Bowles was prompted both by their wish to see Benedict Leonard wed and because an alliance with the Bowles family would reiterate and strengthen earlier ties. It is also dramatic evidence that Annapolis gossip networks reached far afield.[21]

Yet there were no gossipy tidbits in the family correspondence about daily life in the Calverts' Annapolis household. Archaeology has produced the best and virtually the only information (fig. 4.3). On the other hand, there is documentary evidence about the way Benedict Leonard began to set his legislative house in order, beginning with the Council Chamber (sometimes called the Armory) built a decade earlier. This is important because it demonstrates the way in which he approached those buildings where he would spend time and how he set about bringing them up to snuff.

Legislators first ordered construction of the Council Chamber building near the State House to gain safe storage space for arms and ammunition, to provide a meeting room for the Upper House (or Governor's Council), and to give the Governor a special place to receive "the County and Strangers" on public occasions. Financing was derived from a tobacco duty "appropriated for arms and

Figure 4.3. Small and large sections of old bottles testified to wine consumption in the governor's era. Bottle glass was found across the site; bottles might be almost whole in abandoned post-holes, but were broken in half or in smaller fragments to catch moisture when recovered from old planting beds. (Photograph by the author.)

ammunition." In other words, the small building was intended for state occasions, ceremonial, practical, and secure. Its association with the Council gave it symbolic significance, positioning it clearly within a sphere wherein the Calverts were active. Because its windows were not on a par with those of the State House, Captain Calvert, as Governor, with his Council, oversaw installation of three eight over eight sash windows with cedar frames of approximately three feet wide and four feet high. These made it "in full proportion and Uniform to those of the State House."[22]

Visual images of authority were one means men chose to legitimate their roles as leaders. Benedict Leonard must not have felt the windows by themselves gave the Council Chamber a level of elegance requisite for his needs nor that it was a suitable seat from which to govern (fig. 4.4). He ordered changes to the Council Chamber upon taking office, beginning with essentials: the floor was supported and propped; the doors and windows were painted. A painter applied new pigments to the walls; steps were built; window shutters were installed. All this was done within three months of Benedict Leonard's arrival. Once the chamber was in good structural shape and had an orderly appearance, the new governor requested additional embellishments. A "handsome" table was purchased for Council meetings together with a handsome carpet for protection and/or to muffle sound. A large elbow chair, and twelve strong Russian leather chairs with high backs were bought; the added comfort of the elbow chair signified the Governor's higher rank. Twelve single brass sconces were fastened to the walls, and a lacquered candleholder containing twelve tapers was also placed in the room. Additionally, forty-eight flagstones were laid in front of the foundation to the Council room to make the entrance more impressive to the messengers from the Lower House, and so men in the Upper House could stand outside without muddying their feet; finally, the city guns were fixed.[23]

Benedict Leonard also turned his attention to St. Anne's, the parish church (where both he and Captain Charles served as vestrymen). During the first years of Benedict Leonard's time in Maryland, new pews were added at the front for the Governor, the council speaker, and members of the legislature. The "state" bore the cost. A second-floor gallery was added the year he arrived; it gave additional room for slaves and others of lower rank to attend religious services, seated, of course, in positions whose spatial bounds foretold their social roles. Before God as well as man, placement in society was visually represented. Further, the pageantry of the civil body – the legislature – was conjoined to that designed for God, aligning the mysteries of the state with more divine institutions.[24]

It would seem that the new governor was not accustomed to rooms that were neither in tip-top shape nor elegantly furnished. This should be borne in mind when considering the changes made to the house on the Circle shortly after his arrival (see Chapter 5). Also significant is his successor, Governor Ogle's, comment in a plea for additional monies from Lord Baltimore, "I am sure you cannot be served well unless your Governor also lives something like one." Status and rank, in this era, depended in large measure on visual representation, an exterior radiance that bespoke inner strength.[25]

Literary discourse in an "unpolished" part of the world

Annapolis was a small town when Benedict Leonard Calvert arrived. While some men were exceptionally well educated, Annapolis could not be called an intellectually sophisticated community. Many of the leisure activities enjoyed by the Calvert family in London or at Epsom were missing: theater, opera, court balls. Benedict Leonard wrote Hearne that he spoke with the Indians at every opportunity; their language and religious beliefs provoked his curiosity, and he believed Hearne would take pleasure in hearing more of them. Nine months after his arrival, he was more sanguine about the prospects of diverting, lively conversation on other topics. "You cannot expect from me in this unpolished part of the Universe any entertainment worthy your consideration," he wrote; there are no antiquities, learning is rare, classic authors and the muses absent. "Our Conversation runs on planting Tobacco and such other improvements of trade." Believing that provisions for a "regular Clergy and Learning" were better provided for in Maryland than elsewhere in the colonies, Benedict Leonard told Hearne of his ambition "to see a real foundation for literature, well and prosperously established."[26]

Benedict Leonard had already befriended the poet Richard Lewis, an old Etonian who taught Maryland youths in the private school that Francis Nicholson and Captain Calvert had promoted. Lewis, in Benedict Leonard's view, was a man of real "ingenuity," and "well versed in poetry." Lewis later wrote of his honor's

Figure 4.4. Council chamber built in the 1720s contained stylish architectural elements that complemented the second state house but made the chamber the more elegant house of government. (Drawing by Julie Hunter-Abbazia based on an illustration generally attributed to Charles Wilson Peale in the *Columbian Magazine*, February 1789.)

grace, skill, humor, gallantry, and good breeding. He also recalled dinner conversations at the Governor's mansion where "round the social bowl," Calvert delighted his friends by discussing "what e'r was beautiful in Italy . . . gardens, grottos, and labyrinths." Walter Norris attributes a "period of surprising literary activity in Maryland" to Calvert's scholarly and artistic interests. During his period in office, the *Maryland Gazette* was established, and the *Sotweed Factor*, an account of Maryland's history (set to poetry) by Ebenezer Cook, reprinted and distributed as well as Lewis' translation of a Latin work (*Musicapala, or Tale of a Mousetrap*; the first Latin text printed in the province according to its publisher). Support for the latter was provided by subscriptions from those close to the Calvert circle: Benedict Leonard himself (ten), Captain Charles Calvert (four), Nicholas Lowe (two), John Ross (two), and Daniel Dulaney (three). Copies were sent to Hearne at Oxford.[27]

If Benedict Leonard Calvert was successful in introducing a modest, elevating, cosmopolitan flourish into the Annapolis milieu, he was not well-liked by the politicians elected to the Lower House. Less accommodating, more reserved than Captain Charles Calvert, he constantly longed for England, asking his brother to let him return. Benedict Leonard felt he had little in common with Maryland men, describing the majority as "proud, petulant, and ignorant planters." In contrast to him, they were; using Lawrence Stone's contrast between the parish gentry and the country gentry, urbane, well-educated, intellectually meticulous Benedict Leonard Calvert fell within the latter set, whereas most of Maryland's families possessed a world view congruent with the English country squires and yeomen farmers.[28]

Setting the house in order

One of the ways in which Benedict Leonard Calvert's actions expressed his membership in the English country gentry, their changing attitudes toward human life and its relationship to the natural world, can be seen in his passion for order. The probate inventory that he prepared when Edward Henry died, for example, is a masterful example of the distinctions and increasingly separate categorization of things beginning to develop within the pre-modern world view. The inventory is not the usual jumble of items, written down in either the order they appeared in a home or the order they came to mind (and sometimes appraisers used both), but a separate, precise listing of objects by function and material composition. It reveals a modern organizational framework.

The passion for precision was instilled in Benedict Leonard's soul in part through his scholarly studies done with and for Thomas Hearne. Hearne instructed him to pay attention to the form of the letters and other characters on inscriptions for these will "be of service in determining their Age, after the same manner as we judge of the Age of MSS. by Specimens of the Hands." Consult *de regionibus urbis Rome* by Victor, Hearne added, to find out what Rome was before you visit the city. Return to Lucca and study the Oactantius, "compare it accurately, especially since there are some Things in it of great value, not printed" in Montfaucon's published version. Hearne's letter was written the same month as one by Charles Lowe telling Benedict

Leonard he would soon be made Governor of Maryland. Once in Maryland, the new governor began to put its records in order, drawing on the standards Hearne instilled and on his own experiences abroad.[29]

Benedict Leonard charged his cousin, the Captain, and Col. Richard Tilghman to inspect the record books and make lists of what each contained. He was particularly concerned with the rent rolls and the land records; he gave them priority because without a good grasp of the information they contained, it was impossible to protect the economic assets of the Calvert family. He presented the process to the legislature in its best light, speaking of the "Public Good" as he did so: "nothing can be more desirable than a certainty in matters of property" and therefore advised "a separate Repository for Our Old Records." This was essential to "preserve the rights of this and future generations" from accidents, i.e., the loss of records.[30]

While it would certainly benefit ordinary landowners, the tightened curation of land records and rent rolls was advantageous to the proprietor. Benedict Leonard was blunt in writing to his brother: "Your Mannor of Pangayah is they say already Swallow'd up, for people pretend, that no one knows where to find it." He advised Lord Baltimore to resurvey all his manors or lose them, since "many daily incroach upon them." He observed that the fault to some degree lay with the custom of specifying property lines by utilizing living trees as boundary markers – trees that "daily grow old and drop off."[31]

The superb condition of the colonial records of Maryland today stands as testament to Benedict Leonard's care, circumspection, and admonishments regarding these documents. He was thanked by the Upper House, who noted the concern was testament of "your Excellency's good Inclinations" and evidence of his regard for the "Publick Weal." The Upper House further expressed its gratitude for the way in which the actions of Benedict Leonard advanced "the United Interests of His Majesty, the Lord Proprietary, and the Good People" of the Province and promised to make "Loyalty, Moderation, and Justice" the basis for their deliberations, adopting a standard of "right Reason and a Calm Reflection." The speech was read by Edward Henry Calvert, and noted the legislators' resolution to keep to the path Benedict Leonard thought wisest. His brother's words, on behalf of the Upper House, were ones the Governor wanted to hear. However, there were also those in Maryland who felt differently.[32]

Differences of opinion and man's fallible nature

The decade of the 1720s was one of constitutional and economic turmoil. Problems with the tobacco trade menaced the prosperity of Maryland planters. Captain Calvert, in his term as Governor, attempted one solution by forcing through legislation prohibiting export of trashy tobacco. Many were unhappy with this law. In Captain Calvert's term the Dulaney–Bordley faction also began to pressure for legislative reform, and the Captain had even signed a bill that set aside Lord Baltimore's prerogative to veto legislation not in the proprietor's interests. The crisis was one that was to pit the new Governor against the growing Country Party; it had already deepened the schism that existed between Upper and Lower House. There was little Benedict Leonard Calvert could do, at times, but rail against those who mistrusted him simply because he was their governor.

The political reasons for the challenge and the way in which it was fought out on the floors of the two Houses have been thoroughly analyzed by Charles Barker and Aubrey Land. One problem was that deference was an even less well developed social more in the New World than in the Old, and that the Maryland legislators recognized as valid their move to increase the people's rights – prerogatives akin to those the Proprietor possessed. However, the autocratic Calverts perceived these as privileges they should bestow as long as the rights did not interfere with maintenance of the family's governance and economic interests. Benedict Leonard Calvert described the context to his brother this way: "This Superiority, as I may term it, of the people not the Government, seems Unnatural, and is I am sure repugnant to the very End for which Government was Instituted, Viz. an Authoritative Influence for the good order of Society."[33]

Everywhere, attitudes and beliefs were changing. Daniel Defoe, in 1724, saw the decline in traditional demeanor as disintegration of the fabric of society: "The Common People of this Country have suffer'd a Kind of general Revolution, or Change, in their Disposition, Temper, and Manners . . . a general Change, such as I believe no Nation has undergone but themselves." People no longer consistently adopted a subordinate posture towards those of higher rank. In Maryland, people found a variety of ways through the political process, often encapsulated in the exchanges between Lower House and Upper House and Governor, to express their own points of view. There were counter-currents visible in the traditional political structure of the Province that required negotiation.[34]

Benedict Leonard appealed to the people by establishing a link with the past, pointing out that he was honorably and by blood descended from "the nursing Fathers of this Colony," and asked men to grant him the same confidence their ancestors had given his forefathers. The Lower House replied that they were sure his intent to pursue the public's welfare was as strong as any of his "noble Ancestors." They promised to try not to offer legislation the only due of which was a veto, but also asked him, if they did so, not to attribute it to "sinister Designs" or a disbelief in his sincerity. The fallible nature of mankind, they said, "is not always capable of infallibly discerning truth" and hence men sometimes pursued the "same good end by different methods."[35]

Defoe did not see the new spirit of social consciousness as a change for the better nor, from what Benedict Leonard writes, did he. This is understandable. He had barely been in Maryland a year when he had to deal with rumors in October of an armed uprising involving men from Prince George's County and Queen Anne County, i.e., from both the Eastern and Western shores. The focus was tobacco. Next there was the question of a revolt by the Piscataway acting in concert with black slaves. This was resolved when one of the primary instigators among the blacks, an African named Negro Harry, was whipped (twenty-five lashes) for "his equivocation and evident falsities." Benedict Leonard's charge to the jurymen hearing the case in Prince George's County was calm and reasoned, asking them to listen carefully to the evidence, and expressing his concern. It contrasted with the furious taking-to-task he gave from the State House to the unidentified tobacco farmers who nailed notices on Prince George's County gateposts urging support for their uprising against him. Then, in November, Benedict Leonard had to assuage the concerns of the clergy that a new tobacco law would lessen their tobacco tax-based incomes. "A Grievous Offence against God," they protested; a pernicious act, Jacob Henderson wrote, adding, we "will pray."[36]

Finally, Benedict Leonard had to find government positions wherein his Councillors could obtain payments to balance the funds withheld by the Lower House which righteously claimed that a per diem for the Upper House, when it acted as the Governor's Council, should come out of the Proprietor's pockets, not theirs. There were insufficient patronage positions, he wrote his older brother, which made it difficult to find men to serve on the Council, because few "Care for an Empty Honour attended with trouble without some recompense." At the same time, he thought one would work in vain "to gain the Country" to pay them, for, as Land observed, the people's representatives in the Lower House "were busily concocting schemes for improving the staple [tobacco], every one of them in some way a threat to proprietary revenues."[37]

The proprietary revenues provided Maryland's governors with an annual income well above that of most Maryland households, perhaps only outstripped by the incomes of a few of the wealthiest merchant-planters. It was emblematic of his Lordship's kindness. Benedict Leonard Calvert received, for example, payments totalling almost £3,500 in a three-year period that came from a tax levy on tobacco. Clearly the value, monetary and symbolic, of the income that could be derived from "His Lordship's Kindness" was weighed and assessed carefully by all concerned.

Captain Charles Calvert, whose view differed from Benedict Leonard's, prudently set his contrary opinion aside when the issue grew inflamed. It was an issue that aroused the Governor to great heat and drove him to upbraid the legislature in an impassioned speech. It revolved around the relation between money and social worth. Benedict Leonard told the Lower House in 1729 that it had ridiculed any pretensions he had to its esteem by firing an "affront" directly at him. The three half-pence per hogshead of tobacco tax which the legislature for many years had given the Governor was a monetary incentive with active and deep symbolic value. By taking his share of the tobacco tax (a "present") away, the legislature showed a lack of concern in expressions of kindness or respect towards its Governor. Such expressions, the Governor insisted, custom (i.e., cultural precedent) demanded of anyone who pretended to the "name and free nature" of an Englishman (and hence to the English statutes Maryland planters insisted were their right).[38]

The legislators' act signalled the "Dawn of an Ensuing Day, wherein Slights & Disregards to His Lordship and His Family, were to appear in the full Gloom of dark Envy & unreasonable Malevolence, the unhappy Produce of some few discontented minds." Benedict Leonard's self-esteem had been sacrificed; his share of the tobacco levy degraded. It showed a "Superlative Degree of Disregard." It showed clearly the "Marks of a public Resentment." Restore my reputation, he pleaded, let me appear in an honorable robe (i.e., grant me a worthy fee) or tell the whole world that I am your "Oppressor," and an "Enemy of the Good People of Maryland."[39]

Charles Lowe wrote Benedict Leonard Calvert about the role Captain Calvert played in this. The Governor in the meantime had dismissed the Captain from his Council. Perhaps the ways in which Lowe's own interests were mediated by those of the family enabled him to see Captain Calvert's options with special insight:

> What turn Mr. Charles Calvert may take on these Occurrances, is hard to determine. If he leaves Maryland, he puts it out of his power to do hurt, or good, but should he remain there, he probably may have Influence to do the One, or the Other, as he shall be inclined or biassed: for my part, were I in his Situation, I should soon see my Error, & by future Conduct endeavor to reconcile myself to his Lordship and you, by making use of the Talents and Interest I had in the Country to the End you should think proper to direct them, *in hopes of some future favor* [emphasis added].[40]

Captain Charles Calvert did so, mediating his own self-interest with those of the larger interests of the proprietor. His decision perhaps followed Baltimore's own inclinations seen in advice to Benedict Leonard: "Leave that to time which by good Nature you cannot effect."[41]

Letting time take its course was not in Benedict Leonard's nature to do as is clearly expressed in a letter about a lawsuit involving the border dispute he wrote to Governor Gordon of Pennsylvania in September 1731. "I have but lately finished a tedious Session of Assembly," he began. After summarizing the case's status in the Maryland Court proceedings, he wrote that he had sent Mr. Edmund Jennings "to inquire more particularly into the matter" since he was "desirous of contributing towards peace and good neighborhood." With respect to another incident in Kent, he claimed that Pennsylvania judges were the "real infringers of that peace" which he and Governor Gordon wished to promote. The owner of the land, Benedict Leonard reasonably explained, merely sought to resurvey some long-held property bounds, marked by "trees – such perishable things."[42]

It seemed unreasonable, however, for the Pennsylvania magistrates to take into custody the Maryland commissioners and sheriff involved in the matter particularly because the issue was disputable, "as those of bounds between Us are." And so, Benedict Leonard warned, "if your People please to continue to use such short methods with ours, a just Retaliation may serve to convince them of the unreasonableness as well as hardships of such proceedings." He then stepped back to assure Gordon that the most effective way to quiet such disturbances was "a settlement upon the spot of such boundaries." Yet if that could not come to pass, he would be:

> sorry to find your people so eager in their menace toward ours. I believe they had better let pacific measures take place Wherein I shall be always ready to concur with you; they may be assured that we shall as cautiously avoid doing

anything on our part that may argue Fear, as they shall do; Nothing doubting but that we shall be as ready and capable of maintaining our own rights and possessions as they can be.[43]

Finally, Benedict Leonard sent his regards to the governor's wife and family, and apologized for any omissions or imperfections in the letter, noting that he was "at present in so very weak and disordered condition through sickness, and the daily expectation of my Brother's [Baltimore's] arrival." The last few lines he penned himself as a gesture of his esteem for Gordon.

Fifty years earlier, his grandfather, the third Lord Baltimore, faced the issue of the border conflict also, but in his words a more forceful approach can be seen. Writing to Penn about the "inlet or back door in the head of my bay," he pointed out that without it much of what the King had graciously given Penn would be naught but a "dead lump of earth." Driven further, he finally stormed that Penn had attempted "to make me believe I am as black as hell," which, he cautioned, were it true, "I must then conclude 'twere not safe for you to breathe in the same air with me."[44]

The effects of Chesapeake heat

Despite his own colorful rhetoric, Benedict Leonard Calvert was a milder, cautious man who harked back to the earlier years of the Province, and to tradition, as a way of asserting authority. In September 1731 his days as Governor were almost over. He was disappointed that his replacement, Samuel Ogle, and not his brother, Lord Baltimore, crossed the ocean that fall. Although Benedict Leonard was prompted by an inner resolve to succeed in his post, and as he told Hearne, to do "what service he could for the Family," that is to say, to do well by his older brother despite the crises in government that existed, Benedict Leonard was never able to meet completely the older brother's expectations. Some were especially difficult.

Among these could be listed Lord Baltimore's wishes that Benedict Leonard not "be alarmed at every vexatious Noise, and Report," move steadily, ignore the headstrong Maryland planters and lawyers who had no intention of being swayed by his arguments in any event, and let time take its course. Re-establishing Calvert hegemony and instilling it with authoritative, legislative order was a demanding task. The younger man couldn't easily escape on leisurely voyages to the Mediterranean or the Baltic as his older brother did. As one consequence, Benedict Leonard's health grew worse. It had never been robust.[45]

After Samuel Ogle arrived in Maryland, he wrote to Lord Baltimore that Benedict Leonard was "much worse than I imagined, and which I believe has not been mended very much by the help of Physik, of which he takes more of than anyone I ever knew in my life." Sister Charlotte Brerewood's letters provide information on one tonic that the ailing Governor tried, and found useless. An infusion of bark, it was said to have cured Lord Baltimore when he bled repeatedly and went into convulsions after a tennis ball hit him on the nose. Archaeology, of course, provides minimal evidence of the use or composition of folk medicines. However, in raw quantity alone, the number of drug or ointment pots recovered from the State Circle site stand out when compared with those from other Chesapeake sites.[46]

Despite the fact that he had been ill for sustained periods of time in England, Benedict Leonard attributed his illness to the hot, hostile Chesapeake summers: "The Cold Season is a relief to me . . . with the Sharpness of the weather I began to have a little appetite, which for the Summer Six Months I was an Utter Stranger to." Noting a similar relationship, Alexander Hamilton wrote of the gaunt faces of Maryland men and women; their countenances "like so many staring ghosts" gazed out at him from their windows and doorways as he rode into northern Maryland one late September morn. Folk took for granted the onset of disease with changes in weather. The warm, moist air that blows in off the Bay over Annapolis in July and August was viewed with suspicion; spring dew, mist, and fog were considered unwholesome.[47]

By the time Benedict Leonard arrived, much of the forest in the region had been cleared near the coast for planting. This, in the eyes of the inhabitants, made the air more wholesome and eliminated one cause for disease. Yet overall folk believed, as Governor Hart observed, "The climate is unhealthy, especially to strangers, occasion'd by the excessive heat in summer, and extreme cold in winter; the vernal and autumnal quarters are attended with fevers, pleurisies, etc." Within the prevailing English world view, each climate had its own particular balance of the four elements – air, fire, earth, and water – represented in the body by blood, yellow bile, phlegm, and black bile. The folk remedies that restored these were legion; the Calverts believed in the efficacy of bark tonics and bloodstone necklaces. Few effectively promoted healing.[48]

Yet the world exists for people as they perceive it; perception is informed by cultural precedent, enculturation, and contemporary observation. The activities associated with the Calvert site were informed by the beliefs and attitudes its occupants held. There was also a certain amount of creative alteration, although how much is difficult to assess. Did the family set aside their customary English clothing – the heavy Bombays, broadcloths, camblets, plushes, rosselles, and satins – in favor of the lighter-weight textiles that made the heavy summer days more bearable? Did they alter their diet to accommodate the excessive heat? Were the changes they made to the physical landscape done in concordance with English custom or did they show creative adaptations?

Within this chapter there is much evidence which would suggest cultural precedence was extremely important to the Calvert family. At the same time, their education and travel gave them a broader outlook than many men and women professed. An archaeologist would probably be safe in assuming that like other aristocratic families, they believed in hospitality, in visual representations of rank, spent money in conspicuous ways, sometimes with frivolous extravagance, and were attuned to changing fashions. Historical documents provide a bulwark for this position. Lord Baltimore, for example, when he wished to impress the young and beautiful Widow Pendarvis, hired a barge and filled it with musicians so that they could float down the Thames in his own boat while accompanied by music.

Were similar pleasures sought by his brethren in Annapolis? We may never know.[49]

The historical record, however, points out ways in which their tastes and standards of living were changing as the times changed. There is, for example, the contrast one would expect between the inventories of the eighteenth-century Calvert men and that of their great-great-grandfather (George Calvert) who died in 1632. His inventory, however, was similar in many respects to that of his granddaughter (Mary Calvert Darnell) who died in the 1690s and to those of numerous Maryland decedents who died from 1700–25. Yet the thought worlds of these men and women were different from their forebears, particularly when it came to things close to the heart such as the profits from their labor.[50]

Benedict Leonard Calvert and his Council attempted to do a variety of things to improve the Province. His intellectual values led him to set as goals during his administration the establishment of two free schools, at Annapolis and on the Eastern Shore: "two schools well provided of Masters were better than 12 indifferently suited with one each." As he wrote Hearne, he also tried to improve the literary ambience of the community. He worked to promote the well-being of the poor, assessing possible changes in the Prerogative Court system, and gave money to church and chapel.[51]

In practical fashion, his Upper House laid out an incentive system that would rid the countryside of predators – wolves, bears – and smaller varmints such as crows and squirrels. The plan was to pay a bounty of two lbs. of tobacco for squirrel scalps; 200 lbs. for wolves; and 100 lbs. for bears in Somerset County. Yet here one can see the tension created by societal interaction. The Lower House made changes, the Upper House demurred, and the Lower House insisted: "It must certainly be more Advantageous to have [squirrels] killed after [our] manner than to expend one million and 300,000 lbs of tobacco per year in maintaining a war against those little animals" (fig. 4.5). Their tobacco profits were not to be spent on frivolous measures, nor, in many men's minds, on his Lordship's councillors who helped institute a tobacco law partial to the large planters.[52]

With a new consciousness rising slowly in the region, the country's people were learning to ask for various "rights." Because they were fluent in non-verbal discourse, one of these was improvement in the symbolic representation of their collective identity. Build us a small cupola on the State House, they urged Captain Calvert before Benedict Leonard came; it won't cause the roof to leak and the present practice of "hoisting a [flagg] upon a pole stuck in the open field [is] rather a ridiculous than a decent ornament to the Public" (fig. 4.6). In a culture such as this, with emerging and creative opposition, the Calvert family had varied options open to establish and affirm their legitimate authority. Captain Calvert gave the people their cupola and standard, and obtained in return their blessing and favor; beneficent towards widows and orphans (as Commissary General), he aroused awe or fear by a highly visible hanging of a black woman who had bludgeoned to death a white man. In fact, in a culture such as this, where social institutions – church, state, family – often blended one into the other, and the separation of different spheres of action followed organizing principles unknown in today's world, it would have been unusual not to have utilized visual symbols of power and rank in every aspect of life that could comfortably accommodate them. Benedict Leonard and his kinsmen were as fluent in this form of cultural discourse as were the people they governed.[53]

Bequests for the future

Before he set out to sea on an April tide, Benedict Leonard made a will providing funds to hire a schoolmaster for the Free School (established by Nicholson), or a glebe for St. Anne's church if the school closed as well as giving a legacy of £40 per annum to Theodosia Lawrence for each year she had nursed him. He provided for a chapel on the Eastern Shore. He remembered his sisters with small legacies, gave Captain Calvert's child, his god-daughter Elizabeth, a negro boy (Osmyn), and left a small amount for the poor of Annapolis. He dispensed money to his servants, including the cook. The bulk of the estate (which Benedict Leonard believed was in

Figure 4.5. Squirrels on delft plates were welcomed in Chesapeake homes while simultaneously men paid tobacco bounties on the heads of live squirrels. (Illustration courtesy of the Colonial Williamsburg Foundation.)

the order of £10,000) he gave to his youngest brother, Cecilius, and then to the children of John and Jane Calvert Hyde.[54]

Benedict Leonard Calvert died of consumption on the passage home; his body was coffined and cast into the waters from the family's swift ship, *Charles*. Hearne mourned his death as did other friends and kin. Aubrey Land, in 1966, concluded that Lord Baltimore had lost one of his ablest allies when his younger brother died, and noted that the elder brother, in subsequent years, followed most of the advice provided him in a lengthy letter from Maryland that was one of Benedict Leonard Calvert's most significant legacies. The letter candidly outlined the political situation that existed in the Province, albeit from the autocratic position of the English landed aristocracy. The letter was concise, thoughtful, analytical, and practical. Although an intended history of Maryland was never written, Benedict Leonard's correspondence with his brother, Land concluded, "brought more decisive consequences than any formal history he might have written."[55]

In providing him with a broad education equivalent to his elder brother's, his father and grandfather had knowingly laid a foundation to insure the family's continuity. He was thus enculturated in a set of attitudes which formed his posture as a Maryland governor, and given a superior intellectual background that did not

Figure 4.6. Second Annapolis State House was adorned with a cupola while Captain Calvert was governor. This illustration from Radoff's *Buildings of the State of Maryland at Annapolis* was based on an architectural study of documents. (Courtesy of the Maryland State Archives.)

impede his administrative abilities, although the management skills the young Governor possessed were perhaps less than those of his predecessors. Their ages and military backgrounds (cf. Governor Francis Nicholson, Captain Charles Calvert) gave them greater contact with individuals of more varied social backgrounds. These men were similar in that respect to the inhabitants of Maryland who lived in communities where cultural pluralism was the norm even if sustained interaction was minimal between the different groups.

Benedict Leonard Calvert also helped introduce a graceful, urban quality to the daily life of the Calvert household in Annapolis, a way of life which incorporated music, dance, the other arts, horticulture, social dining, *and* one in which visible, symbolic reminders of the authoritative position of the Calvert family were expressed in a variety of different material domains. His influence on Maryland town life among the local merchant-planters, it is suggested here, continued to be felt for many years as families in the Chesapeake sought to express their identities as people of wealth and status through the acquisition of material goods emulating, in part, a way of life that he and his kinsmen practiced while resident in Annapolis.

III

BIG FEATURES AND TOPOLOGICAL DIMENSIONS

If we are digging an eighteenth-century home site, we cannot give up once we have dug all the exciting artifacts out of the cellars. There are still outbuildings to be located, fence post holes around the yard to be plotted, and walkways to be traced, all demanding much time and hard work and often giving very little entertainment in return. Nevertheless, these features are an integral part of the whole, and without them the physical appearance of the site cannot be reconstructed.

Ivor Noël Hume, 1969, *Historical Archaeology*

5

"A house well built and with much strength"

> Think of a house. It is a matter of form, of the sculptural
> arrangement of masses and voids. It is decorated. Its walls display
> the colors of stone or wood or earth, whitewash or paint . . . Its parts
> fuse in use. Seen, the house is used as an emblem for its occupants.
> Entered, it is used as a stage for social drama, as shelter from the
> storm.
>
> Henry Glassie, 1989, *The Spirit of Folk Art:*
> *The Girard Collection at the Museum of International Folk Art*

The shape of the land

Like the town lots where Virginians placed Yorktown's stylish mansions – "equal in Magnificence to many of our superb [London] ones" – the Calvert lot stood on high, airy ground, on a knoll at an elevation between 25–28 feet above sea level on the southeast slope of the highest hill in town. The site lay beneath two of the most politically important buildings in the Province – the second and third State Houses. Its placement gave its dwelling visual representation among buildings of rank in Annapolis. Men back then would have looked at it and known there was no way it danced fifth flowerpot. Through contiguity, the house and its land assumed greater symbolic importance than if it had been located elsewhere. Even if the Calvert house had been located on another Annapolis hill such as the one where Charles Carroll of Annapolis' waterfront home sat, its placement apart from the "heart" of the Province, or the Circle, would have diminished its place in the hierarchy. The ascending location – the spirit of place symbolically defined – was an essential element in its persona.[1]

To exploit this element, builders overcame topographic obstacles. It is likely that a gully, converted into the boundary ditch mentioned in a 1747 deed, ran east-northeast from the higher reaches of the hill along the slope near the site in the general direction of Maryland Avenue. The original ground surface was also irregular with a greater degree of slope than exists today. A similar situation existed on the crest of the hill where the Council Chamber was built. It required Governor Hart's on-site guidance to ensure an advantageous placement of the council building. Various drainage devices were installed at each location. However, the topographic attributes of the site were probably not as strategic in the cultural framework of daily life as the symbolic association which its topology enhanced.[2]

The first home

In 1694, Governor Francis Nicholson redesigned the town to give it a capital air, a touch of the Italian Baroque flair he saw on the European continent during military travel. Nicholson collapsed old lot boundaries and established new ones, combining bits and pieces of older ones to make his plan visually effective. He closed old roadways; sometimes occasional pieces survived intact in the new plan, but in most instances no trace remained. In the process, the lot on which the site is found lost its original form and took on the unusual truncated triangular shape it possessed for the next 150–200 years (see fig. 2.5).[3]

By ca. 1690 there was a wooden house on the lot, perhaps located near to a spring on its northwest side. The original western boundary of the land was indicated by a post and rail fence running northwest–southeast parallel to the old southeast dividing line 9 perches distant. The material remains of the fence line include four post holes. These post holes appear at the base of a rich soil layer of "black mould, fat and thick laid" now called Collington sandy loam at elevations of 26.96, 26.93, 26.86, and 26.07 where they cut into the red-orange subsoil. More critical in their interpretation is the fact that they extend to equivalent depths, depths which deviate from the bases of other post holes in their vicinity, and run downhill. The distance between each post hole is roughly 8 feet (or a half-perch). The presence of each was signalled first by small, irregularly shaped dark humic midden layers that appeared above each feature at the base of the garden soil used to grade the site. But because the fence posts were not allowed to rot in place, the refuse (i.e., artifacts) dumped when the posts were both erected and removed were mixed within the holes. It includes baking dishes and tea bowls.[4]

Sadly, with the exception of the fence lines and a few other isolated features, we know little about the actual use of the lot from 1680–1720 in terms of distinguishing culturally-defined activity areas or of separating one spatial locus from another. There is limited evidence of occupation, a small amount of material from ca. 1680–94, mixed within the Calvert period garden soil in the yard next to the orangery and in the yard adjacent to the Circle.

When the Hemsleys moved to Annapolis in 1718, they were a prosperous merchant-planter family who could easily afford renovations to the house. Their new home probably did not fully face the Circle. One door opened towards Northeast Street (now Maryland Avenue). The cellar foundation was cut into the hillside; its door opened at ground surface at the rear of the house – a pattern repeated in many Annapolis homes including Charles Carroll's of Annapolis waterfront home. No builder's trenches survive from the Hemsley renovation.

The floor plan of the Hemsley house showed its architectural adaptation to the Chesapeake climate. It was a single room deep; the windows provided ventilation and a smooth flow of air. The fireplace furnished warmth and the brick cellar was a cool storage area. The house may not have been complete when Philemon Hemsley died in 1719 less than a year after its purchase. His probate inventory hints this for it includes hinges, 15,000 brads, a parcel of seasoned blanks, 3,000 oak shingles, 500 clapboards, 1,000 bricks, more than 70,000 assorted penny nails, and 40 locust garden posts. Further, Madam Hemsley paid Timothy Sullivan, an Annapolis bricklayer, an overdue £4-01-06 bill for masonry in 1721, another suggestion that construction was in progress.[5]

Preservation architect Russell Wright, who remembers an informal visit to the site twenty years ago, believes that the south half of the building had chamfered beams and older architectural details not present in the northern half, but he was unable to take measurements for scaled drawings. Throughout its history, families subjected the house to a myriad of changes; it was assembled and reassembled, almost but not quite built in shreds and patches: a cellar here, a new wall there. Sometime after 1860, the Claude family even lopped off the roof and upper story to add three more floors, but they were not the first occupants to change its appearance drastically (fig. 5.1). The Calverts too took off at least one roof. It is difficult to know which segment was the earliest or core, which one was built by the Hemsleys (or the Chew or Taylard families), and which one was added by the Calverts. The best estimate is that the southern half was once a small wooden house; neither the Taylard nor the Hemsley inventories are rich enough in household furniture to be read as evidence for a large, spacious house.

The archaeological evidence is indisputable on one point: the builder's trench for the east wall of the south half (the half that has the earliest cellar foundation) post-dates the builder's trench for the hypocaust foundation in the orangery. Materials found in the builder's trench for the east house wall include fine, white *slipped*, salt-glazed stoneware. English potters began to produce this ware ca. 1715. Is it more likely that the Hemsleys or the Calverts built the orangery?

The answer is clearly the Calverts. Two types of collateral evidence converge on this point. First, Benedict Calvert's interest in gardens is documented as is the enthusiasm for horticulture his brother, sister, and brother-in-law displayed. Second, the abandoned post holes from an old wooden building removed to make room for the orangery contained artifact-rich refuse used to fill and seal their cavities. The refuse yielded the following diagnostic pottery:

> *Coarse earthenware*: milk pans made by William Rogers, the Yorktown potter, beginning in the 1720s after Hemsley's death.
> *Coarse stoneware*: porous yellow-bodied stoneware storage jars with a date range of 1725–40.
> *Fine white saltglazed stoneware* [no slip] with a date of 1720–80.

Since potters did not begin making these wares until the 1720s, they provide a TPQ – *terminus post quem* – or date after which carpenters and masons raised the orangery. If these men had erected the orangery beforehand, the broken bits of pottery could not have found their way into the refuse layers left during the construction process. The presence of potsherds made by the poor potter of Yorktown is a clue that the Calvert household was responsible for the major building episode ca. 1720–35. When Captain Charles Calvert purchased it, the Hemsley house may have been a wooden house with brick ends (as seen in two other Annapolis homes ca. 1720 and at Tuckahoe in Virginia), a brick dwelling, or a simpler structure. Whatever, its form was soon to change and its appearance to assume a more graceful air. The Calverts, their relatives, and friends were blessed with a desire for style and fashion, and a hunger to rebuild old homes.

To unlock the house and use it as a document in writing local history, we needed to do no more than follow Henry Glassie's lead, observe carefully what happened to it, provide it with a context, and "ask a few reasonable questions." One place to begin was in England.[6]

Rebuilding family homes in England

The first Lord Baltimore build the Calverts' first great home, Kiplin, at the very end of an epidemic of country-home building (1580–1620). Kiplin is an excellent example of homes that grew as King James' courtiers, among them Sir George Calvert, rivaled one another, each seeking a more stunning architectural feat to outdo the other. Some architectural historians attribute Kiplin's design to Inigo Jones, thus placing it four-square within a classical aesthetic tradition that drew on Palladio. In the 1700s the first Calvert relative to rebuild extensively was their uncle, Henry Lee, the second Earl of Litchfield, who razed their grandmother's old home at Ditchley. The earl then spent £33,000 in the 1720s to erect a magnificent dwelling, still one of England's stately homes. Its five-mile avenue, allees, and park were famous in the Calverts' time. Landscape historian David C. Stuart writes of homes like Ditchley as sitting "like spiders at the confluence of immense avenues whose only function was ceremony." Benedict Leonard Calvert visited Ditchley often and was fully aware of its ceremonial aura. He must have known of the way in which its buildings and grounds created awe in people such as Thomas Hearne.[7]

All around them in England, aristocratic Georgian families rebuilt the homes of their grandfathers. Reed observes: "This building left no part of the country untouched, and in due course penetrated almost all ranks in society. What the great ones did lesser men imitated." Cecilius Calvert's letters to Benedict Leonard reveal that their older brother at Woodcote Park, had "pulled down everything," "finished nothing, and what he does is done out of his own head." In deciding to rebuild his home using his own scheme, Lord Baltimore placed his country home among a group of similar estates where most work was done in accordance with plans devised by their owners rather than by skilled designers. The implications of this practice, in Annapolis, is that the traces of change in the house and yard also stem from the personal skill, talent, and architectural knowledge of the Calvert family.[8]

Cecilius passed judgment on Woodcote's architectural changes in his letters. "What gives me the most trouble is that he has cut down vast numbers of trees, which one would have thought would have been the last thing that would have [been] done . . . there is no such thing as Contradicting of him." Yet by removing trees, Lord Baltimore also opened up a vista over the valley to a ridge. On July 6, 1724, Woodcote was still in disorder; two large grass areas and the gravel walks in the garden had been removed. A foot of earth had been stripped from the yard to provide the house with a ground surface level with it (fig. 5.2). Celia Fiennes wrote that a back drive led to the Woodcote stables and its "pretty horse pond." Lord

Figure 5.1. Two stories and an attic added to the eighteenth-century Calvert home gave it a Victorian appearance. The earliest section of the house, built ca. 1718, is the first-story, right-hand corner; stucco was added to protect the brick and make it appear more modern. (Photo by the author.)

Baltimore rebuilt the stables and erected four classical pillars near the horse "trough" to frame the vista "up the valley towards the Downs." Cecilius concluded that "only the Lord knows when everything will be finished."[9]

Finally, several years later, Lord Baltimore completed the exterior rebuilding consisting of new outbuildings, a new fountain, an orangery, a two hundred foot wall and a cross wall over the grove. Interior renovations included new wainscoting (of cedar and Maryland walnut) in the Westminster "Hall" and a much higher ceiling plus newly whitewashed ceilings and painted walls throughout the home. After Lord Baltimore bought a new set of bed furnishings for the "Maryland parlor" and Benedict Leonard's room, he was temporarily satisfied. With this architectural face-lift, he gave his home greater splendor, added a French flair, and brought it up to par with the other fashionable homes in Epsom. Possibly at the same time, he had

Figure 5.2. Woodcote Park, Epsom, Surrey, was the Calverts' country estate and home. It is shown here after alterations made by the fifth Lord Baltimore changed its seventeenth-century appearance. (Anonymous engraving courtesy of the Boston Museum of Fine Arts.)

the altar in his grandfather's chapel removed to nearby Ashtead Church, although its Verrio ceilings and carvings by Gibbons remained. Throughout Baltimore's life other exquisite touches were added. The home also had a library ceiling by Rubens, a sector of the drawing-room ceiling by Verrio, and another by Zuccarelli while the grand staircase had both walls and ceilings by Verrio. Painted panels designed in 1717, by Philip, Duke of Orleans, were installed in the gallery. Silver and brass locks containing the Calvert coat of arms, and said to be crafted with skill and delicacy by French refugees, were another elegant addition (fig. 5.3).[10]

Celia Fiennes gave thumbnail descriptions of five Epsom homes; these suggest high-style homes, each surrounded by elaborate gardens, topiary trees, painted and gilded fences, strong gates. Lord Baltimore knew at least one mansion intimately – Durdans, which was first his guardian's, Lord Guilford's, home and later that of a good friend, Frederick, Prince of Wales. Like his grandfather's era, that of Lord Baltimore was a time when architectural feats were a measure of a gentleman's progress. Did the flurry of building make as much impression on Benedict Leonard as it did on his youngest brother? It is the topic of many letters from Cecilius; it crystalized the focus of Francis Brerewood, Benedict Leonard's travel companion, who later helped Charles Calvert stylishly maintain and adorn Woodcote Part. In

Figure 5.3. Brass key-plate with Janus motif recovered from site. This stylish decoration used on door and locks brought classical allusions into family homes as Janus was the traditional Roman guardian of portals. (Illustration by Julie Hunter-Abbazia.)

1723, Benedict Leonard, who had first visited Versailles with his older brother, took Brerewood to see its gardens (fig. 5.4). That fall, Brerewood put this knowledge to use in designing an elaborate garden with canals and a pavilion for brother Thomas and Charlotte (Calvert) Brerewood. An article in the *Gentleman's Magazine and Historical Chronicle* notes the family

> laid out a large sum of money in improving the house, garden, and canals . . . being young men of spirit and fashion, they did much to improve this old mansion to the taste of the time. Across the principal canal they threw an arch, on which they built an elegant pavilion, which was fitted-up with much expense of furniture, carving, and gilding as a library.

Brerewood also supervised more rebuilding at Woodcote – work that lasted throughout his life and Lord Baltimore's.[11]

Wealthy Chesapeake families also began to rebuild grandly in the 1700s. In Virginia one can point to the Rappahannock mansion, Corotoman, built by Robert "King" Carter or to Governor Spotswood's home, Germanna, above a Piedmont river facing the Blue Ridge mountains. Each is archaeologically documented. In Maryland too, men built large, gracious homes. On the Eastern Shore, Col. James Holliday erected Readbourne, a home which shares stylistic attributes both with Bladen's Folly in Annapolis and, in a fainter but still discernible way, with Woodcote Park. Not surprisingly, family legend linked its design with the 1732 trip to the Province of Lord Baltimore, although others inferred "a master builder."[12]

This is the architectural milieu in which the Annapolis Calverts moved ca. 1730. How should their own building activity be interpreted? It can be viewed in two ways: as architecture to be used – a context and framework for daily life – and as an end in itself, a creation to be seen and appreciated aesthetically. It can also be analyzed in terms of orientation: improving buildings or landscaping grounds.

Rebuilding the Annapolis house

By the late 1720s, the house and its related outbuildings spread over two town lots was a home for a complexly structured household that included, at different times, perhaps as many as sixty different individuals. Its members included Governor Benedict Leonard Calvert, his younger brother, his cousin, their spouses, his cousin's children, attendants, servants, and slaves. Briefly in 1732/33, the proprietor of Maryland, Charles Calvert, the fifth Lord Baltimore, and his wife probably were resident guests. Obviously the small original house had insufficient social space for this active household nor did it possess requisite style or visible, stalwart strength.

Englishmen achieved social status, in part, by ostentation; conspicuous display was *de rigueur* among the gentry. Understandably, the Calverts resident in Annapolis decided renovations to the property were in order. Perhaps Benedict Calvert brought to this activity the same dispatch with which he restyled the Council Chambers, giving them the ambience so useful to authoritative governance. Across the street and down the hill from the Council Chamber doors, and maybe simultaneously, craftsmen, builders, gardeners, servants, and slaves soon altered the Calvert house and yard to fit its new role in Annapolis society.

The archaeological evidence can be summarized in terms of what it tells about the rebuilding. Changes to the house, whose floor plan is shown in fig. 5.6, included:

- Brick walls and an addition extending its length to 44 ft.
- New fireplaces and chimneys.[13]
- An expanded cellar running the full length of the house.
- A northeast addition to the original core of the house.
- Construction of an orangery with its brick hypocaust.
- A center door and passageway opening onto the gardens and facing toward Prince George Street.

Architectural logic also suggests the following were part and parcel of the renovation: a new, hipped roof; new sash windows (if not installed by the Hemsleys); new floors; new doors. Alterations to the yard (fig. 5.5) included:

- Construction of a large brick well with a brick well-head.
- Installation of brick steps and a small portico at the Circle doorway.

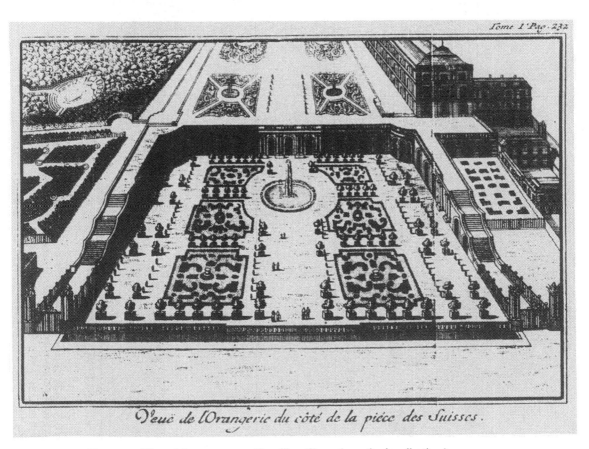

Figure 5.4. View of the orangery at Versailles. (From the author's collection.)

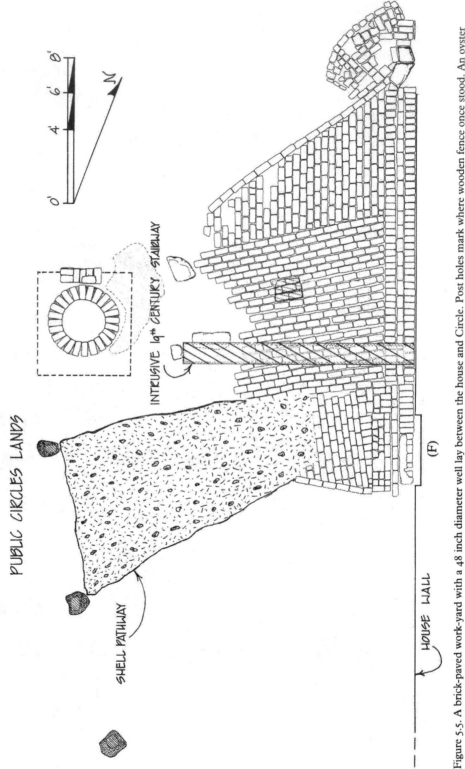

Figure 5.5. A brick-paved work-yard with a 48 inch diameter well lay between the house and Circle. Post holes mark where wooden fence once stood. An oyster shell path led to the brick-floored portico at the door while a brick-lined drainage bed by the house fed water towards the hill slope to the north. Planting beds (not shown here) were located on the south side of the door and there is some suggestion that a small wooden outbuilding may have stood in the south yard between house and fence. (Drawing by Hannah McKee courtesy of the Archaeological Society of Maryland.)

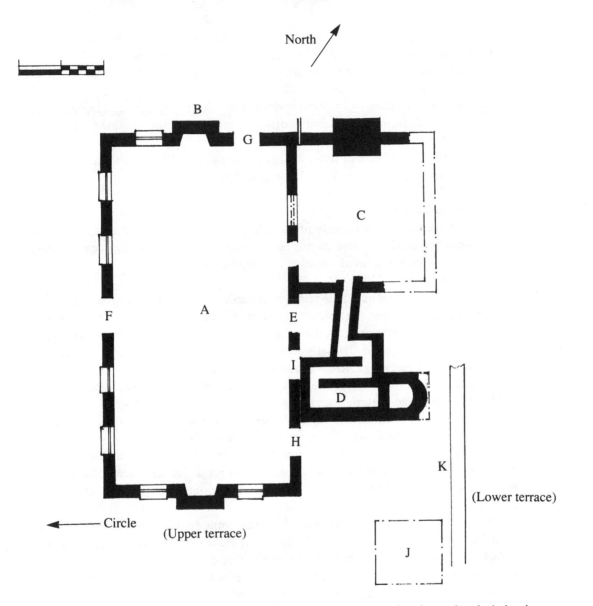

North

B

G

C

F

A

E

I

D

K

(Lower terrace)

H

Circle

(Upper terrace)

J

Figure 5.6. Conjectural floor plan of the Calvert home ca. 1730 based on archaeological and architectural remains. North half of house (A) was added to an earlier core; chimneys were renovated and/or added (B); a brick addition was built (C) and a wood-and-brick orangery built over the hypocaust foundation (D). A central doorway at location E served as the main entrance although its precise dimensions could not be determined since walls were partially destroyed along the eastern sector of the building. At least four exterior doorways were located (F, G, H) as well as an interior entrance to the orangery (I). A rubble-filled cellar, presumably the remains of a garden outbuilding (J) was located near the north garden wall (K) which appeared as a robbed-brick wall trench. (Illustration by Russell Wright, AIA.)

- Brick paving to provide the kitchen or domestic work area with drainage.
- Erection of a new post and rail fence between the Circle and yard.
- Installation of an oyster-shell path directing foot traffic from the Public Circle to the home's west portico.
- Raising and leveling the ground surface through the addition of a layer of rich garden soil, possibly procured outside the town if not obtained when the terracing was installed.
- Construction of brick garden walls, in particular one dividing the east sector of the house and its facade from the rear, or Circle-side yard.
- Terracing.
- New garden parterres.
- Other garden improvements for which no archaeological remains now exist probably include: (a) tree plantings; (b) major garden walkways; (c) statuary; and (d) a fountain, pond, or small drainage canal.

The alterations necessitated the removal of earlier outbuildings, fences, and so on. This work, especially the post removals, formed refuse deposits used to pack and level the ground surface prior to the addition of the new garden soil. As workmen disturbed and demolished the early features, their activities produced a blend of seventeenth- and early eighteenth-century materials inside the features and in the refuse that covered them. The preparation of bedding areas for plants required the addition of drainage material, and in some cases oyster shell was added whose function may have been to alter the soil's pH. The brick paving also needed a base which oyster shell and household refuse provided. In the end, a sequence of archaeological features was created which contained an array of artifacts whose attributes can be made to tell of a range of activities inside the "great" house and within the town. Linkages to the county and throughout the Bay can also be delineated.

When the family completed its rebuilding, the home sat on a level terrace or stage on a newly landscaped lot. It stood amidst an elaborate, formal terraced garden embellished by exotic fruit trees and other visual delights. Orange trees in large wooden tubs were a seasonal decoration; they provided a sweet perfume to the air. But what of the house as architecture to be used?

Certainly it provided shelter from the winter storms and with five or more fireplaces it should have been warm. One new problem, however, was that its cross-ventilation was cut by the brick additions to the original core building which made it two rooms deep. Put bluntly, the house was hot in the Chesapeake summer. It was hard for the prevailing southwest breeze to penetrate. The house had been forced into an accommodation with English norms; its Chesapeake heritage had been negated. This was doubly difficult for the home's inhabitants because as English men and women, they were used to wearing heavy clothing. Complaining of the heat, Benedict Leonard sought a cooler residence elsewhere.

As a "stage for social play," however, the house worked well. It was an arena for social activity; people entered and left through formal and informal portals to the work areas, to the garden walks. Even late at night, lacking plumbing, some of its occupants rose and left its doors. Yet, there they become lost to view, for little remained that could be analyzed to reveal traffic patterns in the yard and garden. And inside, no central hearth or core of activity can be discerned within the residual floor plan. Thus there is much that remains confusing. Yet, there is a suggestion that in their use of interior space the Calvert family was conservative and blurred or merged the spatial boundaries in a manner characteristic of seventeenth-century households; the clear-cut separation of sleeping, eating, cooking, and working that framed activity in the later Georgian period is not readily apparent in the house's ca. 1730 guise. The recovery of any personal, inner dimension must be left to other aspects of archaeological analysis; the architecture tells more of the public family than of the private one.[14]

The Calverts followed the same plan used by their grandfather who built a "handsome" house at Mattapany "more for convenience than magnificence," placing it where it would be a landmark visible at sea. Their house remained simple as befitted a London townhouse or a suburban villa among the English, who rarely spent sums on their city homes equivalent to those expended on country estates. The latter, with their gardens, statuary, horses, libraries, exotica, paintings, and other *objets d'art* provided the measure of a man in his home community. London residences were centers of social activity from which personal and family networks radiated out into the broader society at a national level; the horizons of activity originating from a country estate were of smaller scope.[15]

The same principles applied in Maryland in terms of action spheres, although by ca. 1760 if not earlier a few planter-gentry broke with tradition to spend large sums on town homes whose architectural scale was more magnificent than that of their country estates. This may have been precisely because these formed the spatial loci from which Maryland family networks reached out and penetrated the wider horizon. In the case of the Calvert home, it was also a center of state patronage. The sense of awe that needs to be attached to patronage if it is to provide its full aura of munificence to donor and recipient was provided, in part, by the physical formal surrounding of the house and its material contents rather than by the home's inherent form and style. And, just as the relationship and reciprocal debt that was thereby established between the patronage donor and his recipient was asymmetrical, so too was the tension between the Calvert's town lot and the town landscape in which it was embedded. This can be seen by considering other visual contrasts.

Visual contrasts and social fields

On their side of the Circle, the Calverts used a brick drainage system and a wooden portico rather than the shell drainage apron and brick portico found at the State House and at the smaller Treasury Building. Instead of a palisade fence, they installed one of open posts and rails. After removing the earlier post and rail fence, replacing it with one that encroached five additional feet onto the Circle (appropriating physically what they could not control visually), the Calverts terraced their land. They created a series of wide terraces descending from the level of the Circle (28.5 ft) to a level of 24.5 feet at East Street and to a lower level along the interior boundary line. The exact depth and number of terraces is unknown. Benedict Leonard Calvert used his knowledge of Italian garden design and geometric logic as inspiration: the double squares, from which the house was formed, are based on classic proportions. The dimensions of the main block of the house (as it existed ca. 1730) in turn were generated out into the landscape to form design units for the garden. For example, these proportions locate the first terrace boundary. There was thus an interplay between the natural elements and the artificially carved landscape at the Calvert site that contrasted with the more formal stylistic details and the naturally sloping hill of the Public Circle. The social actors that used each stage also set up visual contrasts.

The exterior boundary of the Public Circle was not demarcated by a sidewalk or roadway. Instead it was indicated simply, perhaps by locust posts. The sturdiest fencing – a palisade fence – was placed away from its outer edge, close to the State House building, for its protection. Horses were tethered on the Circle's grassy incline and pissduits were cut into its soil. A food market operated every Wednesday and Saturday beneath its flagpole from dawn till mid-morning. Butchers fought, militia marched, and garbage accumulated on its grounds, washing downhill to the harbor with heavy rain.[16]

In contrast to the formal garden beds that edged the Calvert yard along East Street, the approach to the yard from the Public Circle differed. The approach moved from a region with minimal visual boundaries (the outer limits of the Circle) into a clearly demarcated spatial zone. People strode along an earthen footpath or cart path, walked through a wooden gate onto an oyster shell path, and then either stepped down into the brick-paved kitchen yard with its elaborate, wide well (built at the edge of the fence into the hillside) where African or African-American slave women worked, or into a garden area on the south side of the yard that led around to the east where the orangery stood. The elaborate treatment of the kitchen yard was one means whereby domestic activity at the site was set apart from domestic activity at other Chesapeake homes. Its cleanliness too was distinctive, but this was perhaps a consequence of West African cultural tradition and nothing the Calverts intended.

Bilateral symmetry had no place here yet. The alignment of the house with its fence, gate, path, or kitchen yard was asymmetrical. The materials were drawn directly from nature – wood and oyster shell – except for the social space immediately adjacent to the house where brick paving created a well-drained working platform for the black slaves. Clearly, the asymmetry characteristic of medieval houses, as pointed out by Deetz in his classic, *In Small Things Forgotten*, was found at the Calvert site ca. 1730. The asymmetry created a context in which the domains of politics and tobacco commerce, domesticity and governance, elected officials (Maryland men) and appointed officials (Calvert kin and allies) intersected and merged into one another without a sharp division of any one sphere of activities from the other except for one between the formal walled garden, behind its walls, guarded by the house, and the informal landscape of the town, wharfs, and business establishments which overflowed with informally arranged goods, a polyglot of languages, and odors that people saw as potentially maleficent.[17]

Another contrast with the town existed by virtue of the small quantity of refuse that accumulated, to a slight extent, in and close to the house. The yard surface on its eastern side was also kept relatively clean. One other Maryland site had a yard next to its house that people kept relatively clean. This was St. John's during the 1660s when it was briefly the residence of the third Lord Baltimore. Given the emphasis on housecleaning utensils in the Calvert inventories, an archaeologist might place responsibility for keeping the kitchen courtyard clean with the English housekeeper were it not for a provocative essay on "West African Reflections on African-American Archaeology" by Merrick Posnansky. Posnansky described a pan-African use of space whereby people cooked, ate, and made things in courtyards and other exterior areas, reserving interior space for sleeping and storage. Posnansky writes of African women sitting on steps and using compound areas to work, to weave, to pot, and to spin. He could have added to chatter, gossip, and maybe sing as working women are wont to do.[18]

There is much about the Calvert lot and its western court that reminds one of a compound. This is one reason why it is a social space that has few counterparts in the Chesapeake region. Posnansky wrote of African women and children who "constantly sweep compounds and the areas in front of their houses with grass whisk brooms" thus obliterating the telling marks of their activities. Earlier scholars also wrote of how compound space was used in African villages as an area for eating, cooking, and task-related social action. Did African women and their Chesapeake-born children do the same in this foreign land, transporting an African convention that gave them comfort even as the Calverts brought English goods and conventions? The archaeological evidence is suggestive, but no more. Yet as one draws these people in and positions them on the site, it loses its skeletal appearance to become a rich melange of individuals, ordinary and exotic, who further distanced the site from others in the community.[19]

Some pieces of this can be seen in records which reveal details of African sociability, night-time gatherings of men and women in kitchen quarters to eat and talk, of slaves abroad at night, of far-flung inter-plantation networks which connected the town with the countryside. Records also describe the gatherings that took place on Sundays, "the only days of pleasure" where slaves ate, danced, and wrestled all day long. The extension of these rural events to smaller social groups formed by the slave households of the urban town-dwellers is a natural analog; the increased geographic proximity in fact suggests the contact was more frequent and more intense.[20]

With the deaths of its most important occupants between 1730–4, the house entered an unstable era. Its guardianship resided in the hands of the younger son of a Venetian gentleman, Onorio Razolini, and two other executors. In 1738, Razolini petitioned the court for £35 to pay for unspecified repairs to the house. The house and family all but disappear into the Chesapeake mist for the next decade until Elizabeth Calvert turned eighteen in 1748 and wed her handsome cousin. As the young couple lived in the house, they made changes that left archaeological traces. These included removal of the orangery, an artifact of the earlier era that epitomized the cosmopolitan worldview of the earlier Calverts, their elegant lifestyle, and the luxurious possessions with which they sought to surround their lives. The structure left its trace in the ground: the firebox or hypocaust which gave it warmth on the clear, cold days of a Maryland winter.[21]

6

Ordering nature: the Calvert orangery, garden, and vista

> Do not those live contrary to nature who require a rose in winter, and who by excitement of hot water and appropriate modifications of heat, force from winter the later blooms of spring?
>
> Seneca

How extra-ordinary events leave ordinary remains

The Calvert home became the house that Jack built; its additions multiplied, compacted, and grew into a multi-storied Victorian mansion that contained no more than a few hints here and there of what had gone before. People forgot its past and reworked its gardens. Soon, they too vanished except for one or two aged trees. Even those fell into the bulldozer's maw together with weeds of gigantic proportions. Birds, squirrels, skunks together with the wild, white, red and gold kittens of the town sought new homes. An unrecognized, mini-wildlife refuge in the heart of the city, the land on lot 83 had lost its power years before.

Riches buried in a chest have no power if the men who buried the gold are dead and its resting place is forgotten. Power is a force that dries up if it has no channels for expression. Benedict Leonard Calvert knew its nuances. When he railed at the Maryland legislature about tobacco "presents" and spoke of his need to wear honorable robes, he was directly referring to power, its balance, and expression within the province. The orangery attached to the Calvert home was a more covert expression. Wealthy men – curious about nature, plant-lovers, avid horticulturalists – built orangeries in the Chesapeake to assert prestige and compete with their peers. Orangeries, with their exotic contents, socially accrued the luminescent qualities that made a man a "brighter light." Orangeries spoke to the issue of power within society.

Gardeners built orangeries to grow tropical plants or to keep others alive and blooming out of season, something ordinary farmers could not do. Owning an orangery gave a family symbolic control over the plant kingdom. Why might a man or woman want to do something that would make it clear to neighbors that he or she possessed mastery of the natural world? The answer to this question requires two levels of analysis: anthropological and archaeological. First, symbolic control of nature was and continues to be a way in which humans define and demonstrate cultural mastery. Nasayih-i Iskandar (a counsel for Alexander of Macedonia) put it this way: "The world is a garden for the state to master." Human cultures express this control in a myriad of ways; one of the best analyses of the human need to order things can be seen in Henry Glassie's work on folk housing. His conclusion? Namely that design in architecture (house or land) is, like a folktale, an "attempt to contain fancy" and, like scholarly exegeses, an "attempt to control reality."[1]

When working with archaeological sites, however, the anthropological basis has to be inferred from the material residue, using objects as action statements. By joining inferences drawn from the archaeological record to collateral evidence, the strength of a particular item in the symbolism of the society and its recursive role in the material dimension of everyday life become easier to see. Following this technique, discussion here moves from a consideration of artifact evidence and its provenience to placement of the data within their historical and ethnographic setting. Gradually the meaning that gardens and vistas possessed emerges. Since one object which had an unambiguous meaning for Annapolitans ca. 1730 was the Calvert orangery, it provides a good place to begin looking at the things, large and small, that we found as artifacts in the Annapolis soil.

Feature 5: the hypocaust foundation

Almost as soon as excavation began inside the crawlspace of the 1770s brick addition (fig. 6.1), we uncovered one corner of the south exterior brick wall of a hypocaust demolished prior to the Revolution (fig. 6.2). The foundation lay only 2–3 inches

Figure 6.1. Removal of floor inside a 1770s house addition revealed a rich deposit of artifacts and garden soils used to cover the foundation of the earlier orangery. (Photograph by Celia Pearson, April 1982.)

beneath a dry, powdery topsoil, but it was not until eight months later that its outline was fully defined and its function identified. For a long time we were tantalized by the dramatic deep-red color of its earth floor, first revealed when construction workers began to shore the crawlspace. This suggested that the interior of the

Figure 6.2. Hypocaust exposed inside the 1770s brick addition. (Photograph by Marion E. Warren.)

foundation was subjected to high temperatures which altered the color of the local subsoil, turning it a different shade from the subsoil visible in an exterior soil profile. Bricks still attached to its wall indicated components had been arched.

Vaulted features in Annapolis have been assumed in the past to be the remains of wine vaults. There are examples throughout the city of arched, subterranean features ranging from the immense vaults built by the Redemptorist fathers at St. Mary's to the small one reburied by Professor Sturdy, but none whose depth was as shallow as that of Feature 5. Its design initially made no sense. There were few landscape features we could relate to it. In retrospect, its presence was fully explicable, perhaps predictable. We simply did not know enough of the early eighteenth century to begin to place it within a cultural context when excavation began. As we have learned more of the logic whereby people constructed and used their garden space, the principles they utilized have become active elements in designing modern research strategies for recovering earlier landscapes.[2]

The brick foundation was 10 feet square and 1.5 feet deep. Its south wall, 1.5 feet thick, was unusually thick in terms of colonial construction and strong enough to support a large superstructure. The other walls varied from 8 inches to 14 inches thick. The interior was designed to create a snaking, shallow barrel vault, 2.5 ft wide and 1.5 ft high; an apse-shaped firebox was attached to its southeast corner, and a narrow brick runway sloped upward and extended north until it passed through a secondary wall supporting the new, formal front door opening on the garden (see figures 5.5 and 6.2). When an Old World archaeologist, Henry T. Wright, identified the foundation as the base of a hypocaust similar to ones excavated at Roman sites in Britain and on the Continent, there was great delight among the preservationists who had sponsored the excavation. Their premier work in Annapolis had been done on another horticultural landscape feature: the 1760 William Paca Garden (excavated by Glenn Little in the 1960s). The Calvert feature indicated that earlier gardens in the town had set the tone of later ones.

Initially the feature was an anomaly. Its chronology was not clear, and its function was unknown. As in many eighteenth-century constructions, its brick was laid almost flush against the edge of the builder's trench. The remaining space was not more than 3 inches wide and contained no readily datable artifacts. Its builder's trench was cut by an equally narrow one for the exterior brick east wall, one that we presume, because of the cellar configuration, was built to encase an earlier wood structure. This trench contained a few early eighteenth-century pipe stems and some finely potted, buff-bodied, combed-and-dotted wares. The best chronological data, however, was provided by two trash-filled pits which were created when earlier building posts or fence posts were removed to clear space for the orangery. The posts were torn out of the ground and household refuse was used to fill them; this included a few ceramics that provided tight 1720–30 dates.

Tracing the import of the Calvert orangery has provided a key to understanding much of what went on at the site. The first step was researching orangeries using the library of the Cambridge Botanical Gardens. Reading documents written in the 1600s and 1700s, rather than secondary sources, was a key step in perceiving how various horticultural activities fit into the stream of social action that characterized an elite lifestyle. This is because the "thought-world" or belief system that eighteenth-century horticulturalists used was implicitly and explicitly expressed in these documents far more clearly than it has been conveyed in any subsequent history.

Giving the feature its historical dimension

The average American archaeologist is not familiar with the technical workings of a Roman hypocaust; orangeries were transformed into conservatories and then into greenhouses long enough ago that the esteem in which they were held is no longer part of an American's local knowledge. Their technical function was easy to discover. Orangeries were protected, sheltered places where people could place tender plants to survive the cold. The practice was described by Columella in the first century BC. Wilhelmina Jashemski and her co-workers uncovered a structure at Pompeii used for this purpose. The Renaissance revival was described by Senesis in an Italian garden book; he may have drawn from Latin sources, although there is also evidence that knowledge of hypocaust heating systems survived in monasteries. The renewed use in the 1500s was related to the development of botanical gardens. As Renaissance thought spread, the practice of revealing the depths of one's botanical knowledge and skill by raising rare or difficult plants became an important mechanism for social competition. In 1691, John Gibson drove around the London countryside and found a dozen or so individuals who had built orangeries. Chesapeake planters also competed using social arenas that spanned the spectrum of gentlemanly pursuits. What better mark of ability could one have than the skill to keep plants alive when the nippy frost and the cold north wind brought death to those of your neighbors? It is no wonder men took the concept from the Old World and made it part of the new.[3]

The ways of keeping plants warm and thus alive varied from the simple to the complex. Some are still in use today in rural areas where smudge pots are lit in orange groves on frosty nights. Romans began to grow cold-sensitive plants in containers that could be moved inside when the weather changed. Men heated simpler orangeries, or plant rooms, with small charcoal fires maintained in metal pots or wheelbarrows. Better orangeries were provided with "stoves," as hypocausts were then termed, to heat their interior space even as Roman baths were. Chemical methods were also used: caking the back walls with thick layers of dung, held in place with wooden lathes. While writing that dung was "not so sightly & sweet, a retreat for rats and mice," La Quintinie, a well-known French horticulturalist, still insisted it was better to live with the rats and mice than to let deadly frost kill an orange tree.[4]

Rat tunnels ran through the crawlspace where the hypocaust was located. It was obvious the area had been a haven for the creatures for centuries. There is also evidence in the firebox that the Calverts altered it in an attempt to improve its heating capability by placing two rows of dry-laid, unmortared brick in the threshold between the fire-box and the chamber ducts after construction. Henry T. Wright (personal communication, 1988) notes that similar alterations have been made in Japanese pottery kilns to raise temperatures within their chambers, and a row of unmortared brick can also be seen in a firebox for a garden outbuilding at Drayton Hall in South Carolina.

The way in which the Calvert hypocaust differs from its Roman prototypes is the use of enclosed, vaulted brick ducts. Romans built theirs in a columnar or radial form. It is unclear when and where the innovation observed in Annapolis was developed, although botanical historians agree that ducts were utilized by the seventeenth century. In this regard, Benedict Leonard's visits to Versailles with its formal gardens and elaborate orangery together with his tours of Italian gardens and villas become pertinent to understanding the orangery outbuilding and its technological refinements.[5]

His brother, Lord Baltimore, may have built one himself before or after Benedict Leonard did for there was an orangery (of unspecified age) at Woodcote Park. Lady Baltimore sent pineapples grown in it to Court in the 1730s, much to the delight of the queen's ladies-in-waiting. The family stuffed old correspondence and papers within the foundation of another, selling them in the late nineteenth century at the urging of a Maryland historian who retrieved these documents from "the litter and rubbish of an old conservatory." And, as shown in Chapter 5, Lord Baltimore extensively altered his gardens by leveling land, framing vistas, installing a fountain, laying new walks (see figure 5.2).[6]

According to Agricola's 1719 advice, "stoves" worked best when placed in the ground and stoked from outside the building. This is the pattern that the Annapolis Calverts followed. The hypocaust is also similar to one illustrated in Philip Miller's 1731 *Gardener's Dictionary* which had a small shed for the firing unit on its east wall. In 1693, La Quintinie advised a southern exposure to admit as much light as possible, facilitated by large windows up to 6 feet wide from floor to ceiling. He also suggested a narrow chamber only 10 feet deep to facilitate light penetration into its back reaches and a stout brick wall on the north. The Calvert orangery was built to accord with La Quintinie's advice on exposure, protection from the north wind, and room depth. Loudon, however, described seventeenth-century orangeries as "chambers distinguished by more glass windows in front than usual in dwelling rooms" which, if followed in Maryland, would imply simple structures more rudimentary than later Georgian examples such as the Wye House orangery in Talbot County.[7]

Very little is known about the appearance and style of the Calvert orangery above its hypocaust base. Almost all architectural evidence was destroyed when the new brick wing was added in the 1770s, by construction of an early twentieth-century cellar, or by the 1970s foundation pit. Architectural study of the extant building by Stephen Harris and myself revealed there were two doors in the wall of the main house next to the orangery. One, south of the hypocaust foundation, was set lower than the joist pockets for the orangery's wooden floor, indicating it opened at a lower level; this door undoubtedly provided access to the terraced side yard extending towards East Street. The side yard contained planting beds lined for drainage at their bases with broken bottles whose form corresponds to those used ca. 1730. It is also likely that in summer it provided a decorative stage for the large containers of wood or earthenware in which the orange trees grew (fig. 6.3). And, off the southeast corner of the orangery, it also held a small building whose function and precise dimensions are unknown, but whose placement suggests a garden structure. Shelter, privacy, and support for espaliered fruit trees was provided by a nearby brick wall.

The second door opened into the main house, perhaps through a small hall. This

Figure 6.3. Garden imagery ca. 1730. Orange trees were grown in pots so they could be taken inside in winter and displayed outside in summer. Exotic birds, especially peacocks, were also decorative additions in pleasure gardens; bones from a peafowl (its sex undetermined) were identified among the faunal remains. (Illustration by Julie Hunter-Abbazia.)

was in keeping with Richard Bradley's advice of 1724 to install an interior door opening directly into the orangery so that cold air could not enter without first being softened by the warmth of a fire. Note too that the placement of the firebox enabled the garden staff to maintain the winter fires without disturbing anyone in the main house. Descriptions of other orangeries in their first English florescence suggest that the Calvert building was a small structure of wood and brick construction, perhaps 12 feet tall with 3-foot-high and 5-foot-wide arched windows facing south. In winter, it would have been crammed with small trees, tender plants, and potted herbs. Two small post holes and a rotted sill beam are evidence of the wooden components, and probably the remains of the entrance steps. The south brick wall was located 2 feet north of these in the location recommended by Miller for placement of the first flue. To the north, the orangery abutted the main entranceway to the house which may have incorporated a projecting portico and formal entrance stairs. No one will ever know since only half of a post hole was left intact by subsequent construction.[8]

The orangery perhaps fitted well the advice Van Oosten gave in 1703:

> Doors must be so wide that orange trees may be easily carried in and out. Windows must be large and high, reaching quite to the ceiling from the breast work which is commonly 3 feet high. The breadth of the windows must be 5 or 6 feet that when you open them in winter, when the sun shines brightly . . . the sun may shine on them all at once . . . Walls must be good and without least hollowness . . . those are best that have on the north side some other building.[9]

Obviously such orangeries in the early eighteenth century did not possess the visual impact and elegance of later ones with their immense facades of glass. An example from Wye House illustrates how much more elaborate horticultural buildings grew with time (fig. 6.4), but the first ones built were simpler. The Calvert orangery could even have been one of the tomb-like buildings Nichol felt were characteristic of the first hot-houses.[10]

In Benedict Leonard's time, people were sensitive to the quality of the air they breathed and accorded it various properties beneficial to their health and well-being, or to that of the plants and animals they kept, but the importance of light per se was not universally accepted. While botanists like Van Oosten or Richard Bradley understood that plants needed light, such knowledge varied among gentlemen who gardened as a status-marking tactic. Despite the fact that they had more windows than ordinary rooms, many conservatories remained too dark for plants to prosper inside. John Gibson observed that access to light was frequently ignored in the placement of seventeenth-century orangeries; at Lambeth, the archbishop of Canterbury placed his where it fell beneath the church's shadow until 11:00 a.m. all winter long. The orangery on the Calverts' town lot was, in contrast, placed to take full advantage of the Chesapeake sun during the winter season, but it undoubtedly admitted less light than the Lloyds' building at Wye House for we found no significant deposits of window glass associated with its removal.[11]

We may never know what the Calvert family raised in its orangery. The botanical remains reported by Dr. Naomi F. Miller yielded no orange or lemon seeds. Many fruit and nut seeds from a range of plants commonly cultivated in the early eighteenth century Chesapeake entered the archaeological record when the orangery was dismantled. These included edible nuts (almonds, Brazil nuts, hazelnuts, hickories, pecans, and walnuts), fruits (apricots, cherries, olives, peaches, and plums), and other foodstuffs (corn, grapes, cantaloupes/muskmelons, peanuts, pumpkins/squashes, and watermelons), but they were recovered from the fill rather than from the yard surfaces, although some mixing of the two did take place. However, the Calverts' concern to further protect the plants they grew from cold can be seen in the numerous pieces from broken bell jars (fig. 6.5) which were recovered.[12]

The significance of the orangery rests not on what it provided the family in terms of fruit or edible foodstuffs, but on its role in maintaining and enhancing their prestige. In each society there are cultural mechanisms which men and women use to participate in a series of discourses concerning status and power. One discourse in which the Calvert household was an active participant revolved around horticulture. Although they were not primarily planters and raised few crops themselves, the Calvert men demonstrated their mastery over nature with their orangery. The extraordinary value of orange trees was such that their command of its realm gave the Calverts symbolic control of the plant kingdom. This can be seen by considering the historical evidence about oranges, orange trees, their value in the society, and using this to recreate their role in the social world of the Chesapeake.

Oranges and orange trees ca. 1730

Like tulips, orange trees were introduced to the European continent via the Near East in the early modern era. Their popularity was at its peak in the early eighteenth century. At least 169 different kinds were grown, many with special virtues. It was Dutch horticulturalist Van Oosten's opinion that "in all the compass of gardening,

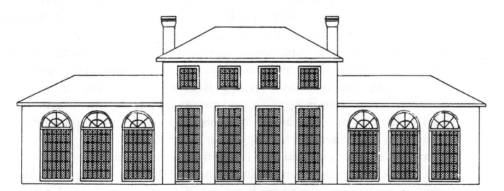

Figure 6.4. The Wye orangery well illustrates how Maryland gardeners merged architectural elegance with utilitarian horticultural requirements. (Illustration by Julie Hunter-Abbazia based on an architectural drawing by Henry Chandler Forman [1967: 72–3].)

there is not a plant or tree that affords such extensive and lasting pleasure" as an orange tree. Oliver de Serres believed there were no words to convey fully the beauty of these "precious" trees that produced a lush, brilliant green foliage against which the ripe fruit showed, dazzling the eye and creating an image of exotic fertility. The fragrance of the blossoms and of the fruit was also highly praised for providing a delicate perfume to rooms where unwashed bodies – belonging to people of all social strata – contributed their own aromas. Since strong odors were potentially malevolent, the fragrance of the orange was mask and counterbalance.[13]

The resources required to grow oranges year-round were extensive. The glass was expensive; the fruit trees themselves were more so. Skilled servants were required to maintain the facility – men trained for horticultural tasks. It was unthinkable to let an unskilled boy water such trees, and a woman's touch was deadly. The degree of skill required to grow an orange tree is one reason why orange groves were not planted as money-making ventures, although at the best orangery in England (Beddington Gardens), Sir Francis Carew's staff produced 10,000 oranges and lemons in 1690. Queens such as Henrietta Maria (1609–69) had gardeners to raise the royal orange trees, but primarily cultivation was a focus of activity for educated, intelligent gentlemen, deeply interested in medicine and botany, whose enthusiasm for learning "spilled over into the fields of mathematics, meteorology, antiquarianism, experimental philosophy, and invention." Benedict Leonard's inquisitive mind placed him within this group; the Calverts' membership in the Royal Society was also emblematic of their esteem for intellectual activity. These traits defined the Calvert men as gentlemen as much as the knowledge they sought broadened their world view. As Rhys Isaac wrote, it was an era characterized by revolutions of the imagination.[14]

Historical practice thus was construed in such a way that the skills to maintain the trees were mysterious, out of reach of an ordinary man or woman. Having grown oranges myself, I know full well this was an illusion. Defined as rare and special plants, man's control over them symbolized potency and this power, in turn, extended beyond the immediate scope of the orange tree itself to become associated with other domains of culture. Among people for whom agricultural pursuits are closely enmeshed in the fabric of daily life, gardens and skilled gardeners assume a significance akin to that of a hunter's prowess in simpler societies. Fifteenth-century Italian noblemen and noblewomen boasted of their green thumbs. La Quintinie, gardener to Louis XIV, was acclaimed because he could procure early and out-of-season fruits and vegetables: fresh asparagus in December, lettuce in January, strawberries and peas in April, figs and melons in June. In other words, La Quintinie had learned to order nature in its seasons by forcing plants contrary to nature; therein lay his power and his fascination to the English aristocracy whose country estates and gardens defined their position in the social hierarchy.[15]

The fascination that learned Englishmen exhibited with respect to the procurement of exotic plant specimens is evident in a range of texts, and it prompted the charisma that attached to men such as the Tradescants, Peter Collinson, John Evelyn, or, in the New World, John Bartram. It speaks strongly to the rising role of botany in the cultural discourse surrounding horticulture, a discourse in which the gentry maintained preeminence for many years. Further, it was a discourse in which words were less vivid marks of successful participation than a healthy, rare, hard-to-grow botanical specimen happily situated and prospering in one's garden or hothouse.

Did the Calverts' plants grow tall and strong in the Annapolis sun? Did they wither and die young as the Calvert men did? This is something which we may never know and it lends a touch of mystery to the daily activities at the site that this book

Figure 6.5. Eighteenth-century garden with raised beds and bell jars that gave plants warmth and shelter from the cold. Insets show bell jars protecting a strawberry plant and spring lettuce and the profile of a glass fragment from the base of a jar. Although the glass is shown as translucent here, in actuality it was semi-opaque. (Illustration by Julie Hunter-Abbazia.)

attempts to describe. It also lent a touch of mystery to the aura that surrounded the Calvert household in the early eighteenth century; it was one of the elements, unique in Annapolis ca. 1730, that gave the Calverts a mystique which functioned usefully in their management of power within the province, in part because it made the way they wielded power seem natural and intelligible to the population at large.

Pragmatically, the hypocaust that now lies beneath a glass floor in an Annapolis hotel worked once as a heating system for an orangery when nights were cold and punch turned to ice in Alexander Hamilton's delft bowl. It was an apparatus derived from antiquity, a bit of ancient technology that provided a symbolic association by connecting the Calverts who ruled the province of Maryland with the Romans who had ruled the Old World. Control of it gave the Calvert household control over nature, something no one else in Maryland had accomplished by 1730. The orangery presided over their garden realm even as other men used brick privies and dove-cotes to anchor their own garden landscapes.

The pleasure garden

Although we know very little about the Calvert pleasure garden in Annapolis, it is possible to provide an impressionistic image and to be quite sure that within its walls there were a series of gravel side paths, cross walks, and an extra-wide center avenue defining the spine of the garden as well as formal parterres and a park-like setting. Assuming the Calverts living in Annapolis did no differently than their brothers and sisters living in England, the garden also contained statues, urns, and watery elements – possibly a canal, fish pond, or gurgling fountain to lend joy and lightness. A summerhouse, grotto, arbor, or open air room would have provided shade and relief from the Chesapeake heat. Probably a mocking bird called, sweetly or wildly, from a tree while small black and gold birds – the Baltimore oriole – wore the Calvert colors as plumage in flight. Exotic tones were added whenever the peacock spread its wings. Wild animals too would have been appropriate residential ornaments in this setting.[16]

The garden would have had an Italian air for if Benedict Leonard loved to entertain guests with discussions of grottos and falling terraces, then he surely drew on these for inspiration. In fact, his notations on Italian gardens suggest other dimensions of the garden landscape. First, and the one fact that *was* verified through the archaeology, was that he did not plan a level garden. Florence gardens, Benedict Leonard wrote after visiting one in 1724, did not pique his fancy because they had no variety, "being all a flat level." He did, however, admire a hedge of elms, "neatly cut like our garden hedge in England." "The gardens of Borghese please me the best," he continued, because they are "much in the English or French taste" (fig. 4.2). His comments on a rural garden north of Florence are also suggestive.[17]

> The outlets round Florence are very agreeable, particularly the Caseine [?], a mile north of Florence, which is a large wilderness cut out in Vistas, very full of Hares, Pheasants, and all sorts of wild game which none dare touch under

pain of the galleys. However, it is common for people to walk in and divert themselves. Indeed, it must be a very pleasant place in spring.

Yet it was not necessary for the Calverts to go as far afield as Italy to find ideas about what gardens should be like. Their family home in Epsom with its own garden sat amidst a circle of ornamental gardens famous from the mid-seventeenth century into the eighteenth. John Evelyn wrote of the gardens at Durdens (belonging to their guardian, Lord Guilford, in the Calverts' day) as among the best in England in 1658. Celia Fiennes described six town gardens in detail in 1702. She wrote of walls; fences of wood and iron; brick walls with piers; courtyards; cascades; tree-lined avenues; ponds, canals, spouting fountains; ice houses; summerhouses; mounts; cherry arches; flower borders; mazes; greater and lesser flowerpots, some blue, some red; box for long private walks; curious cut trees and hedges in forms like sugar loaves, mushrooms, and pyramids; flowers; greens; parks; coddling hedges and hot beds; dwarf fruits and berries; gates and decorated ironwork; shady garden seats for one or two or, court-like, for many, and paintings of the seasons to decorate the walls (fig. 6.6).[18]

What Fiennes did not discuss was the care required to keep a garden in tip-top shape. Peter Martin wrote that without constant work, pleasure gardens such as those in Maryland grew untidy and out of sorts. Volunteer plants quickly became rampant in the long growing season, as any Chesapeake gardener well knows, and so attention was always required. Yet summer rains were not routine; wilting plants often demanded water in the hot, dog-days of August when the heat shimmered and fire-flies hid. Black slaves and indentured servants provided the labor in Annapolis gardens. And so to this image of the Calverts' pleasure fields one must add black women and children gracefully carrying buckets or pots of water on their heads, walking to and fro, well to planting bed, planting bed to well or spring, their bare feet carving another well-trodden path from water source to plant through foliage and grass. And add again: men hoeing, pruning, carving, weeding, carrying buckets and baskets of manure to fertilize the plants. Think of black men taking orange trees in and out in their hefty pots, shifting plants to get the sun, sheltering them from the frost, capping some with bell-glass, swinging a scythe when the grass on the garden green reached knee-height.

If the imprint of a town plan is a constellation of ideas in material form on a large scale, surely that of a garden is one on a minor tone. And this garden was not small. The sector on the south side of the house was at least 8 perches (132 ft) in width and its grounds fell over an expanse 12 perches (198 ft) deep; the full garden may have been twice that size (i.e., as large as the extant William Paca Garden). It backed up to the stables and other working spaces, encroached on the town road and grew across the old north–south dividing line. It likely combined food-producing plants with ornamental materials. It likely held English and African vegetables as well as New World specimens like the unicorn plant (fig. 16.3) we recovered from the well. Here and there in its nether reaches, far away from the formal forecourt, slaves had their own small plots where they grew herbs, edibles, and flowers. They cared for these early in the morning, late at night, and sometimes under the moon. For some, the plants grew and their gardens were filled with brilliance as if by magic. As a stage for social display, the Calvert garden offered many views to those who strolled along its private ways.[19]

A garden changes day by day and shows the seasons of the year encompassed within its frame. Nature marks the time as do the cultural rhythms of workday and promenade. Yet a garden judiciously planned, as assuredly Benedict Leonard's was, also presented a changing sequence of vistas.

Vistas: public and private

Why did the Calverts purchase Lot 83? Initially, there seemed little to recommend it except closeness to the State House. Its proximity to the Circle, its elevation, and

Figure 6.6. The decorative ironwork guarding ornamental plants at Robert Bowie's Georgian mansion in Prince George's County was one of the more fashionable ways to enclose garden space. This stylish trend began early in the century and it is tempting to postulate that some elements of it appeared on gates and fences erected by the Calverts. Drawing by Benjamin Ogle. (Maryland State Archives, Special Collections, Maltby Collection G779-2.)

wholesome air were cultural criteria undoubtedly important, for on coming to Annapolis in 1732, the fifth Lord Baltimore, selected a similar location as the best place to build his own governor's palace.[20]

While Lot 83 stood slightly in front and east of the State House knoll, the one Baltimore wanted stood to the northeast, a quarter mile distant, on a lot of land large enough for a park-like setting and to distance the mansion from the town, symbolically locating the governor above other Annapolitans. Noting the view it would have possessed, Lord Gordon observed that its situation was elegant for it stood "on an agreeable rising ground in a beautiful lawn commanding the view of the town, the River Severn, the Bay, and all the creeks running into it. Nothing," he emphasized, "could be better chosen."[21]

The Calvert house, located on a high terrace on the hillside above a formal, ornamental garden, also furnished its owners with a panoramic view of the town and Chesapeake Bay, and provided townfolk in turn with evocative status-telling imagery. Looking out, the view spread in a wide arc, extended south to the head of the cove (now the town dock) and encompassed the lower slope of the hill where milk cows grazed on the town common, and poor families in tiny wooden houses held squatters' rights (fig. 6.7). The view also extended easterly to the ferry landing on the Severn River, the tidal shoreline of Governor's Pond, and the distant high

Figure 6.7. An 1858 Sachse lithograph of the panoramic view from State House hill suggests the vista from the Calvert garden. To the left Maryland Avenue runs straight to the Severn ferry; to the right Main Street appears as a diagonal roadway lined with houses and ending at the town dock. Two large houses, the modest Claude house, and a small saltbox fill the two lots to the forefront which once contained Calvert's "stack" or "row" of buildings. Thomas Bordley's 1720s mansion can be seen to the left while Governor Eden's pre-Revolutionary home is visible in the distance. (Maryland State Archives, Special Collection SC 1890-1919.)

rolling hills of Providence (now Navy grounds). Joseph Alibone described the view in his journal ca. 1770: "commands an extensive and pleasant prospect of the lands around as also of the Bay, which opens to view down the River and between the woods on each side, . . . as though a natural avenue."[22]

The house overlooked the most public sectors of the city. People entering the city from Chesapeake Bay (i.e., from the south and east) had an unimpeded view of the hillside where house and garden stood. How these elements combined to give the Calverts additional control over nature can be seen by considering their land in terms of its vistas. A lovely vista gave the gentry two ways to express social status: as public view and private prospect. This depended on whether one was outside looking in or inside looking out. Consider the public dimension – the image of house and garden Annapolitans saw from outside looking in. In the processional land-scape, as one moved through the community, it was almost omnipresent. It was next to impossible to stride across the State House grounds without being aware of the Calvert compound; at the same time a viewer looked down upon the house, confronting its working court. The more prestigious portions remained hidden. The house and garden were almost equally visible to people on the lower streets near the docks. Such highly accessible visual images enhanced the power symbolism implicit in the house and its garden, but the telling contrast came with the juxtaposition of public and private views. Eighteenth-century elites contrived not only to control a public vista, but to own a private one.

The private view was the panoramic vision of the town, anchorage, sailing "road," bay, islands, and Eastern Shore which the Calverts could either make available or restrict because it radiated out over town and countryside from a central point within their garden. Its dynamism was enhanced by an ever-moving flotilla of small ships crossing the bay, moving up the bay or heading down to the ocean, ships which, in William Eddis' words, in "various sizes and figures are continually floating before the eye . . . [adding] to the beauty of the scene, [exciting] ideas of the most pleasing nature" (fig. 6.8). By keeping a workaday entrance court adjacent to the Circle, the family isolated their private view from casual visitors, clerks, and trades-men. One had to enter and pass through the house or climb a garden wall to reach it. As Humphrey Repton wrote a century later, the power of such a private vista rested on the fact that its basis was "appropriation . . . that charm which only belongs to ownership, the *exclusive right* of enjoyment, with the power of refusing that others should share our pleasure." Unlike many of the later gardens, such as the William Paca Garden, which were hidden from public view by tall, brick walls with only small, narrow fenestrates at their bases and barricaded by buffer zones of private land (see, for example, fig. 13.5), the garden at the Calvert Site and the people strolling in it were designed to be seen.[23]

Finding the past

Although the research reported here was not designed as an application of middle-range theory, it made use of one of its techniques. Answers to archaeological anomalies were sought in documents. Like Woolley's description of Ur, the archaeological results were "worked out independently and then brought into relation with the records." The process, however, became spiral and interactive; movement to and from the two data sources was constant. Each was used to inform the other until, using Charles Taylor's strategy, what was once puzzling became coherent and comprehensible. With each move artifacts and texts yielded more data or new ways of seeing the old. Would the information in chapters 3–4 have enabled us to predict what might be recovered before entering the field? Is what an anthropological historian learns through immersion in documents useful in interpreting artifacts and archaeological features? Yes, and had the documentary data been available earlier, a different excavation strategy would have been used to recover, as one example, Benedict Leonard's ornamental garden, and, as a second, the full spread of the earliest post hole buildings on the lot. With permission from adjacent lot owners, we might also have begun a search for the working buildings – stables, slave quarters, dovecotes, wash house, provisioning grounds, etc. – that surely existed.[24]

What we knew when we started work at the site was that it was possibly (because it had not then been established) the home of a governor of Maryland. There was nothing in the extant architectural fabric of its building to suggest former glory. And it was unclear how, if it had been occupied by a governor of the Province, he had used his material possessions as an active force in the negotiation of power or how they set apart his household from others in the town. With further historical

Figure 6.8. This view of ships circling the island at Halifax, Nova Scotia illustrates how sailing vessels in Chesapeake Bay created small, visually exciting flotillas. (Illustration by John Gauntlett, 1754–6, courtesy of the Mariner's Museum, Newport, VA.)

research, done after excavation was finished, different ways in which the Calvert household was distinct began to emerge. In the next two chapters on dining and cooking, this distinctive quality is explored further by looking at smaller artifacts. In the process, it becomes possible to see a range of activity in which routine events provided the material contrast, and the mystery, or aura, that power requires to be effectively wielded in a hierarchical society.

As one begins to learn about events in the Calvert years, the symbolic forms through which their social world was displayed and articulated begins to emerge. The terms of the symbolic forms and the way they were defined, by black and white, in daily life are neither familiar nor comfortable. Yet it is clear that for a relative of Lord Baltimore, resident in Annapolis and governing the province with his lordship's best interests at heart, building an orangery and filling it with rare plants, common flowers, and useful herbs was sensible and appropriate. The vistas, the ornamental gardens, and the orangery served the needs of politically powerful individuals by displaying their mastery over nature, by denoting that the center of power in the town was indeed the center, by visually reminding men and women of the way Chesapeake society was structured.

IV

MOSAICS BUILT FROM LITTLE ARTIFACTS

In the seemingly little and insignificant things that accumulate to create a lifetime, the essence of our existence is captured.

James Deetz, 1977, *In Small Things Forgotten*

7

Touches of Chinese elegance: pottery and porcelain

Indices in non-verbal communication . . . do not have meaning as isolates, but only as members of sets.

Edmund Leach, 1975, *Culture and Communication*

Social trappings

A family could amass a fortune in Maryland and not adopt the pleasure gardens, costly cloth, or array of luxurious goods that surrounded the Calvert family. Amos Garrett, who rose from a modest job in shipping to become the richest man of the time (whose inventory survives), is an excellent example of someone who lived plainly. People at various levels of the wealth ladder could buy one item or another and make them part of their lives in varied ways. As status designators, things assumed their most evocative powers when their non-verbal messages were repetitive, replicated in different channels. Among the more fluid symbolic artifacts historical archaeologists recover are tiny pieces of eighteenth-century teawares. The Widow Smith kept a small delft set – only six pieces – and a Chinese teapot in her chamber at the inn (now Shiplap House) apart from customers drinking ale below. The teacups and saucers gave her pleasure, but were not important elements in the tavern's visual backdrop since they were seen only by the few friends she entertained upstairs. It was different in the Calvert home; teawares formed a goodly proportion of the ceramic artifacts (20% in the early deposits; less than 10% in the later).[1]

As at many sites where the rich lived, pottery and porcelain sherds revealed touches of Chinese elegance in sociable dining and drinking at the governor's mansion (fig. 7.1). Then as now, ceramics were markers of distinctive lifestyles. Yet, the broken pots were also directly related to food. Hence, to the extent that food was common and everyday – made, served, and eaten in a folk mode – the Calverts' household pots were the remains of common and everyday objects. But because food was also central in social display, to the extent that families used food in conspicuous consumption, they surrounded themselves with uncommon ceramics. Elegant dining required a different setting: a social space surrounded by ceremony; fine glass and fine china; generous and hospitable behavior, i.e., secular rituals. The tea ceremony was one, as were traditional "toasts." Edward Henry's letters contain written proof that the Calverts toasted each other while drinking wine or ale; the quantities of Chinese porcelain teawares, porcelain and delft punch bowls, large and small, interspersed with mugs for beer, ale, and cider provide archaeological evidence that the family instilled social ceremony into their beverage consumption (figs. 7.2 and 7.3).

Without doubt, hospitable drinking was part of the social scene at the governor's mansion. We have only to consider the ceramic assemblage and place it within a framework provided by *comparanda* from other sites and documentary sources to see its residue emerge. Two information sources are primary. First, probate inventories reveal (a) what ceramic vessels merchants kept in their stores, and (b) the range of pottery and porcelain possessed by households at different wealth levels throughout the region. Second, artifact assemblages from other Chesapeake sites are strategic. Together the information provides the *comparanda* or comparative material that reveals the Calverts' pottery and porcelain had an elegant fashionable flair (see list in Table 7.1).[2]

Ceramic offerings in Annapolis stores

At first, many merchant-planters operated "little markets," sometimes in nearby outbuildings, sometimes in attached sheds or wings (cf., the Bordley residence), and sometimes further away (as at the Addison plantation in Prince George's County). Breen writes these small shops were a "badge of class, a means of distinguishing the great planters from those of lesser status." "Great" men saw them as a profitable sideline integral in an overall package of financially productive plantation activities,

Figure 7.1. In the 1730s, Chinese porcelain tea vessels such as these were expensive and used primarily by the wealthy. Shown here are examples similar to ones recovered in Annapolis. (Illustration from Audrey Noël Hume (1978) courtesy of the Colonial Williamsburg Foundation.)

but they also may have been seen as a means of expressing individual largesse or service to the community, providing necessities to smaller planters, servants, and laborers whose lower incomes prevented direct orders or stockpiles of goods. "Little markets" also created debt relationships binding small planters to the gentry.[3]

Similarly, no Annapolis shop owner below could be accurately described as a "shop-keeper." Each accepted goods from British merchants which he sold on consignment as one element in a broader set of money-making ventures. But the material goods inside most homes were dependent upon the choices such men made and what they chose to sell to their neighbors. The shop inventories contrasted with the goods in their own homes (table 7.2). In fact, the close reins these quasi-merchants kept over what was sold sometimes prompted smaller planters to sign aboard voyages to New York – "the land of social joys" – in return for "the free passage of goods they bought." The discrepancy between what small merchants offered and what the Calverts owned is one reason scholar Stephen Patrick believes that wealthy families only occasionally patronized such stores, preferring to order directly from London agents even after an influx of mercantile Scots co-opted the network of country stores and broadened the selection. A few merchant-planters, men not originally part of the Maryland elite, followed suit.[4]

The fact that the overall quality of the pottery offered for sale did not match the fine ceramics the merchant-planters kept in their own households is a further sign of the symbolic importance held by impressive, decorative wares. It also gave one set of families the ability to monitor if not to control the acquisition of status-

Figure 7.2. A foot-wide tin-glazed, hand-painted blue and white punch bowl dated 1722 similar to those produced at Bristol, England potteries. Its interior is inscribed "Drink Fair, Dont Swear." (Illustration courtesy of the Henry Francis duPont Winterthur Museum, vessel no. 60.1014.)

Table 7.1. *List of minimum vessels from the c. 1730 features at the Calvert Site in Annapolis, Maryland (data from Yentsch, Bescherer, and Patrick n.d.)*

Vessel form and functional artifact class	Coarse earthen and stoneware	English slipware	German stoneware	Delft	Chinese porcelain	White saltglaze	Total
Preparation and storage							
(A) Foodstuffs							
Bowls	1	—	—	—	—	—	1
Butter pots	5	—	—	—	—	—	5
Cooking pots	2	—	—	—	—	—	2
Iberian storage jars	1	—	—	—	—	—	1
Jars	3	—	2	—	—	—	5
Milk pans	4	—	—	—	—	—	4
Subtotal	**16**	—	**2**	—	—	—	**18**
(B) Beverages							
Bottles	5	—	—	—	—	—	5
Food distribution							
Chargers	—	—	—	3	—	—	3
Condiment jars	—	—	—	—	—	1	1
Dishes	—	7	—	6	1	3	17
Platters	—	—	—	—	1	—	1
Salts	—	—	—	1	—	—	1
Saucers	—	—	—	1	—	—	1
Subtotal	—	**7**	—	**11**	**2**	**4**	**24**

Food consumption							
Plates	—	—	6	4	—	1	11
Porringers	—	—	1	—	—	—	1
Subtotal	—	—	**7**	**4**	—	**1**	**12**
Traditional beverages							
Cans (tankard)	2	—	—	3	—	1	6
Drinking pots	—	4	—	—	—	—	4
Jugs	4	3	—	—	—	—	7
Mugs	5	1	5	—	—	8	19
Subtotal	**11**	**8**	**5**	**3**	—	**9**	**36**
New beverages – punch	1	—	—	7	12	—	20
New beverages – teawares	—	—	—	4	24	4	32
New beverages – coffee/ chocolate	—	—	—	—	—	1	1
Subtotal	**1**	—	—	**11**	**36**	**5**	**53**
Other							
Basins	—	—	—	3	—	—	3
Candlesticks	—	—	—	1	—	—	1
Flowerpots	—	—	—	1	—	—	1
Inkpots	—	—	—	1	—	—	1
Ointment pots	—	—	—	12	—	—	12
Subtotal	**0**	**0**	**0**	**18**	**0**	**0**	**18**
Total	**33**	**15**	**7**	**50**	**42**	**19**	**198**

Table 7.2. *Ceramics sold in Henry Lowe's store in Kent County on the Eastern Shore and those within his home (Lowe served on the Governor's Council)*

Pottery and porcelain	Store	Home	Value in pence per vessel
Butter pots, small	5	—	4
Butter pots, large	—	4 (at the Home Quarter)	
Earthen pans	5	—	10
Mustard pots	3	—	4
Assorted dishes	—	11	11
Plates, coarse earthen	12	—	2.5
Plates, white earthen	18	—	2.5
Plates, earthen	—	20	2.5
Porringers, earthen	4	4	3
Bottles, stone	—	2	18
Jugs, small stoneware	4	—	6
Jugs, brown	3	—	8
Jugs, large painted	5	—	8
Jugs, great stone	—	1	12
Mugs, half-pint (stone?)	—	5	5
Mugs, pint, stone	2	2	12
Mugs, quart, stone	—	4	12
Mugs, pint, earthen	11	—	4.5
Mugs, quart, earthen	10	—	9
Bowls, large earthen (delft punch?)	2	4	12
Bowls, small earthen (delft punch?)	6	2	6
Cups, small Welsh	6	—	2
Cups, small chocolate	—	24	3
Teacups, China	—	6	*
Tea saucers, China	—	6	*
Teacups (ware not specified)	—	45	2
Tea saucers (ware not specified)	—	24	2
Cups and saucers, coarse China	—	12	*
Milk pot, stone	—	1	*
Sugar pot, China	—	2	*
Sugar dish, earthen	1	—	12
Teapot, stoneware	—	1	*
Teapots, small stoneware	—	3	*
Saucers (stone?)	—	3	1
China jars, small	—	(quantity not given)	*
Basins, earthen	4	4	4
Chamber pots, earthen	—	6	6.5

* Values were lumped together for these items by the appraisers who saw them as two "sets" of teawares.

Source: Probate inventory, 1723 (Maryland Hall of Records, Kent County, Box 5.F.63).

designating items within a broader spectrum of less-advantaged households. Ordering directly from London required trade connections and cash or credit outlays that few possessed. Then too, poorer households had to balance their actual purchasing power and knowledge of pottery's fragility against the desire for fancy goods.

By ca. 1740 Scottish merchants had opened a number of stores in Maryland – "places where," according to Rhys Isaac, "men gathered, drank, swore, and even boxed or wrestled among themselves." With the spread of the Scottish shops, operated with unambiguous, directly structured, profit-making goals, the general population acquired greater access to the full range of pottery and porcelain vessels in the areas the stores served. By mid-century the gentry were entrapped in a cycle of renegotiation over the status of pottery and porcelain vessels. Different ones were continually elevated to prestigious positions, only to drop down. John Rousby, a member of the Governor's Council appointed as Captain Calvert became Governor,

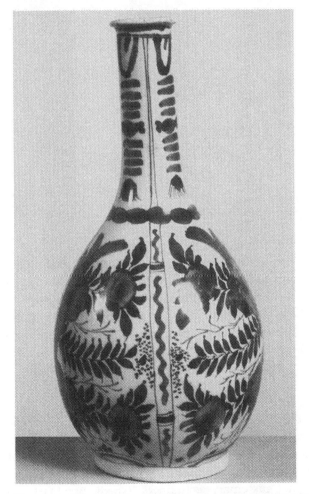

Figure 7.3. Tin-glazed, hand-painted water bottle with chinoiserie decoration probably made in Bristol, England. (Illustration courtesy of the Henry Francis duPont Winterthur Museum, vessel no. 59.0004.011.)

Table 7.3. *John Rousby's Chinese porcelain*
(Calvert County Inventories, 1747, L35: f. 83)

Dining and serving ware	
Dishes, large	3
Plate, butter	1
Plates	60
Drinking vessels	
Mugs, quart	2
"About Quarts"	5
Punch bowls, gilded and large	2
Punch bowls, gilded and middling	1
Punch bowls, gilded and small	4
Punch bowls, enamelled	1
Punch bowls	5
Chocolate cups	8
Coffee cups	12
Coffee dishes	6
Teacups, gilded	32
Teacups and saucers, no gilt	8
Tea saucers, gilded	31
Teapots	3
Milk pot	1
Sugar cups and stands	2
Sugar pot	1
Tea cannister	1
Slop basins	2
And a large number of serving dishes . . .	

continually upgraded his Chinese porcelain so that what he owned could not be mistaken for the possessions of a poorer man (table 7.3). But the passion for fashionable ceramics among *all* social classes had not impacted the older marketing system within the town ca. 1730. What Annapolitans could buy can be seen in inventories for four shops (Appendix A-1), owned by Charles Carroll, John Davisson, Amos Garrett, and Thomas Bordley. Although more small stores undoubtedly existed, these are the ones whose merchandise is listed in extant probate inventories. Each one had a slightly different character.[5]

The Carroll store

This establishment was described in Chapter 1 as a general store. Perhaps the most important point to remember about it here is that it catered to fiscally conservative farmers, artisans, craftsmen, and others of the "middling" sort with tight purse-strings. Its pottery offerings emphasized cooking utensils, food storage, traditional drinking vessels, and the customary containers (small breakfast basins and earthenware porringers) for the gruels and potages associated with folk cooking (see following chapter) (fig. 7.4).[6]

The Davisson store

At barber John Davisson's death, appraisers made a careful list of his household goods and store merchandise while consuming wine punch, bottles of beer, and salted mackerel worth 30 shillings (subtracted from the inventory). Note, however, that no items on the list were made of the finest wares. Davisson offered but two choices of drinking vessels: quart mugs of stoneware or small earthenware drinking pots known as pannikens. Most of his delft was described as "coarse blue and white earthen." The average cost per item was low (a penny or two). It is unlikely that the Calvert servants and slaves purchased many items from Davisson for household use because there were at least three stores closer to the home, one kept by Thomas Bordley's servants on the Circle, the other by Amos Garrett in his home on Prince George Street next door to the store operated by the Brice family.[7]

The Garrett store

Appraisers valued the stock in Amos Garrett's store at £1,300, or more than three times that of Davisson's. Garrett stocked less pottery; in terms of raw vessel counts, his ceramic inventory was one third of Davisson's. It consisted primarily of earthenware milk pans, but like Carroll, Garrett also sold a wide variety of ordinary drinking vessels. He also stocked more punch bowls than the other stores and had one of the few establishments where anyone, no matter his or her social rank, could purchase China coffee or custard cups (rice bowls?).[8]

Figure 7.4. Sturdy stoneware storage containers were sold in some Annapolis stores; these examples were recovered from a site in Williamsburg. (Illustration from Audrey Noël Hume [1978] courtesy of the Colonial Williamsburg Foundation.)

The Bordley store

Thomas Bordley's stock was much smaller than the other three stores, of higher quality and more expensive. Bordley himself was well educated and elite. The small store that he maintained on his town lot was neither a major source of income nor a major focus in his life. But if a measure of a man was where he bought goods, Bordley's store was one the Maryland gentry could patronize with no shame. For those who wished to cook in high style, he offered more saucepans (300) or specialized cooking utensils (153) than other stores. The lack of ordinary drinking vessels (ten) suggests he did not cater to plebeian tastes. His shop, also, had all the items necessary to celebrate the convivial tea ceremony: delft and Chinese porcelain cups, saucers, teapots, milk pots, sugar dishes, and tea stands.[9]

There was an informal ranking of stores in the community and concomitant variation in the pottery and porcelain each sold. In other words, out of four shops in town, only one was an establishment where Annapolitans could buy truly elegant table wares. This may or may not have been dependent on the vagaries of the British consignment system. Three or more Annapolis shops were clustered on Prince George Street midway between the artisans in New Town and the legislators on the hill; one was near the waterfront, and another was adjacent to the private Catholic chapel. More existed. Robert Alexander perhaps ran one in New Town while Edward Lloyd had one on Main Street. No Annapolitan had to walk far to have access to a shop. The one closest to the Calvert home was a block away and sold high-quality ceramics, although if a house servant cut through the garden, Garrett's store and butcher's shop was equidistant.[10]

Overall, the approximate number of vessels marketed in Annapolis, based on this sample, consisted of coarse earthen and stoneware (59%), delft (19%), wood (15%), and Chinese porcelain (7%). Because wood disintegrates in the soil and thus vanishes from the archaeological record, let us subtract wooden vessels from the storekeepers' inventories. The percentages of ceramic vessels are then as follows:

Coarse earthen and coarse saltglazed stoneware	69%
Delft	23%
Chinese porcelain	7%
Fine white saltglazed stoneware	0%

These are much like the percentages seen in small shops that merchants in London-town such as Samuel Peele maintained or those shown for the probate inventories of the merchant-planters with country storehouses (e.g., Henry Lowe in table 7.2.).

Relating the store inventories to the Calvert ceramics

Table 7.1. shows the minimum vessels list for the features associated with the first Calvert household. Delft, which constituted 60% of the sherd count, is under-represented. Chinese porcelain remains at 25% in both sherd counts and vessel counts. The variation between sherd counts and vessel counts for prestige ceramics matters little here because the percentage representation by ware type using either sherd counts or vessel counts differs so sharply from the wares stocked in Annapolis stores that decreasing the porcelain and increasing the delft would not alter the symbolic dividing line. Where coarse earthen and stoneware constituted approximately three quarters of the vessels available for purchase in Annapolis shops, they were less than one third of the Calvert assemblage.[11]

There are no other minimum vessel counts from Annapolis sites for this period to use in an archaeological comparison. In terms of sherd counts, a small, sealed refuse deposit at 199 Main Street contained ceramic sherds in the same approximate proportions as those from the merchants' inventories. At the Sands House near the dock, the frequency of ceramic sherds was very low and most were coarse earthen or stoneware. Preliminary testing of the Bordley-Randall site, occupied by Thomas and Stephen Bordley, produced artifacts from a ca. 1730–40 level that had ware representation equivalent to that seen in the merchants' inventories but with the addition of fine white saltglaze.

The limited archaeological data from other Annapolis sites suggests that the minimum vessel list from the Calvert site constitutes a different assemblage than would be formed by the ceramics used in other homes. This suggestion is strengthened by data from contemporary sites in southern Maryland, on the Potomac, or the Virginia tidewater, which are analyzed elsewhere. The ceramic vessels from these sites were remarkably similar. The number of Chinese porcelain sherds from different-sized plates and serving vessels, as well as the teaware vessel forms recovered at the Calvert site, is highly significant, for these vessels symbolized the family's social and political rank in the province. It also illustrated that clear distinctions in the two procurement patterns – direct order through British factors or purchases at local stores – can be seen in the archaeological record.[12]

These distinctions are also paralleled in the glassware with examples of cruets, salts, jelly glasses, and decanters recovered at the site as well as elaborate wine glasses. All of these were rarely seen in the shop inventories analyzed here. One could point out also that whereas few inventories list truly extensive quantities of bottles – there are some exceptions – broken bottles were used as drainage bases in the Calverts' garden planting beds.

Pottery and porcelain in wealthy homes

Information from probate inventories was used earlier (cf., chapter 2) to see where the Calvert family stood in terms of the Carr–Walsh indices of modern lifestyles and to measure their luxuries on a scale of 1–12. A limited comparison was made with other Annapolis families using the same source. If other Maryland families bought pottery and porcelain from local sellers, then the archaeological record at their sites should be a parallel representation of the ceramic assemblages recorded in the inventories. Similarly, it should be noticeable if the Calvert family used pottery and porcelain as a means of distinguishing themselves from others. Then, their ceramic assemblages should differ in inventories and in feature fills. This is especially so if the other excavated sites were occupied by families lower on the social or political scale.

At the same time, the opinion of scholars like Barbara Carson, Lois Carr, Lorena

Walsh, and George Miller has been that governing towns, such as Annapolis or Williamsburg, or burgeoning cities such as Philadelphia, Norfolk, or Boston, provided their inhabitants an opportunity to purchase small and fashionable amenities before their country cousins could do so. While research on this phase of the project was not completed, several trends did appear. Those with the least wealth owned vessels used to drink traditional simple beverages (such as beer, ale, cider). The price of tea was too high for them to afford it, and Maryland had not yet been hit by the craze for fashionable drinks and containers rocking English towns:

> Such is the expensive humor of the times that not a family, no, hardly of the meanest tradesman, but treat their families with wine, or punch, or fine ale, and have their parlors set off with the tea-table and the chocolate pot; treats and liquors all exotick, foreign and new among tradesmen, and terrible articles in their modern expense.

People of middling wealth and status obtained small numbers (three or fewer) of vessels associated with wine-based punch or tea; these numbers gradually increased. As wealth levels grew, the quantity of tea vessels and punch bowls rose.[13]

With respect to teawares and ware types, it is significant that no fine white salt-glazed stoneware was found in the inventories of ordinary folk as early as 1730. One large and one small white stoneware teapot do appear on Thomas Addison's 1727 inventory, and another that could be a dipped and sprigged Crouch ware vessel or produced in white was in the possession of the wealthy Eastern Shore Lloyd family by 1723. Four more were owned by a Calvert relative, Henry Lowe. Although thick-walled, white stoneware mugs with slipped-dipped rims were made in traditional forms and utilized as tavern wares in the early eighteenth century, the implication is that initially, use of the finer examples of this ware type (especially the teawares) was confined to the planter gentry. These wares are found on elite archaeological sites in the Chesapeake beginning with Robert "King" Carter's Corotoman that burned in 1729 and were found in small, but significant quantities in all the ca. 1727–33 architectural features at our Annapolis site. In the 1720s fine white stoneware was one of the most expensive types of pottery sold, but soon dropped in price to become commonly available. By 1737 for example, white stone teapots were found on Brian Taylor's shelves in a rural shop north of Baltimore whereas in 1727 Madam Addison sheltered hers inside her bedroom chamber (fig. 7.5).[14]

The rough distribution of pottery forms and wares by wealth groups was paralleled in the sets of vessels associated with food consumption. With reference to dinner plates, these rarely appeared in the inventories of lower-wealth groups before 1730 despite their presence in the Davisson store. This suggests that the archaeology done to date on Maryland sites, where plates are present, has not touched thoroughly upon the more ephemeral dwellings of the urban and rural poor.[15]

Even an individual as aspiring and primed for upward social movement as the roguish and brilliant Annapolis attorney Thomas McNamara, who put coffee cups and tea bowls in almost every room in his home – the silver room, the parlor, bed chamber, green room, store room, and even the small room above the cellar – ate from earthen or pewter plates and not Chinese porcelain. The Hemsley family, who also lived at the Calvert site and who had both wealth and high status (see Chapter 2) owned a dozen porcelain plates. Two other men with a dozen plates apiece are also present in a sample of Maryland elite drawn on the basis of appointments to the Governor's Council between 1715–33. These are James Bowles, husband of the Widow Bowles mentioned in Chapter 4, and Thomas Addison, who journeyed to England with his wife and saw how the English really lived.[16]

Against this backdrop must be included the knowledge that the Calverts had substantial quantities of pewter plates, an unknown number made of silver, and at least two dozen of expensive Chinese porcelain. Only four of the latter made their way into the ca. 1730 archaeological features, but more of these older plates show up in later deposits, suggesting they were carefully curated and cared for by the governor's household while they were new. The enthusiasm for porcelain is conveyed by a mutual friend of the Calvert family in a letter from London dated 1728: "China is risen mightily within this month. My Aunt Stanley liked them so well for the oddness of them that she bought a set of cups, saucers, bason, sugar-dish and plate cost fourteen shillings" (168 pence).[17]

The Calvert pottery and porcelain were visible marks of a distinctive lifestyle. It

Figure 7.5. Hand-painted white saltglaze teapot (from Feature 121, the Calvert well) conveys the robust shape and style of earlier teapots. (Photograph by Marion E. Warren.)

is useful to think of them as props in a performance, although one that Maryland people took for granted (fig. 7.6). Conspicuous splendor was a useful way for the gentry to set themselves apart. Fancy ceramics, ca. 1730, were masculine tools for status acquisition. Men carefully compared, selected, ordered and used fine pottery and porcelain, although the individuals who cared for them, or washed, dusted, and stored them, were the women of the household, often black slave women. Men sometimes gave full sets of opulent china to their daughters as wedding gifts. Thus they ensured that their young daughters would be treated with the proper deference due members of their family who had left the family home and become allied with other households. In this way honor accorded to the father and family who gave the gift as well as to the bride and her new family. Further, in a bilateral kinship system, properly speaking, the monies spent did not go outside family lines, for daughters were considered members of their birth families for life as were their children and grandchildren.

Figure 7.6. A gold-gilded Chinese porcelain plate decorated in overglaze red and underglaze blue. This vessel from the second quarter of the eighteenth century is representative of porcelain recovered from Chesapeake sites, including the Calvert site in Annapolis, and listed in probate inventories (e.g., the list shown in Table 7.3 of John Rousby's china.) (Illustration from Noël Hume (1969) courtesy of the Colonial Williamsburg Foundation.)

Honor, deference, and dignity were behavioral principles ingrained into the fabric of society. Lawrence Stone writes that the English country gentry had a moral obligation to live in a style that harmonized with their ascribed dignity. This they did through the expenditure of large sums of money on buildings, furnishings, clothing, entertainment, and transportation (horses, carriages, etc.). Conspicuously splendid ceramics were commensurate with their dignity and enabled their lives to be bright starbursts overshining a darker social field (fig. 7.7).[18]

The candlelight from the sconces in the Calvert home glistened and reflected from burnished pewter plates, shining silver vessels, rarely seen colors such as famille rose and verte on Chinese bowls, and crystal decanters. It shed soft rays on the table where Benedict Leonard Calvert sat with his friends, the literati of Annapolis, and told them of his days in Italy, the Venetian courtesans, the difficulties of translating old Latin manuscripts, and the politics of the Vatican. With certainty he spoke of grottos, labyrinths, and perfumed blooms in ornate gardens. His cousin, the Captain, told of military adventures with Marlborough; his sister-in-law spoke of London fashions, other bits of feminine wisdom, and perhaps whispered her fears of the black house servants and the "outlandish" people in the streets.[19]

In defining their identities as magnificent, the Calvert family also defined the identities of others who existed in relation to them and in tension against them. Symbols of a greater collectivity (the ruling British aristocracy), their lifestyle acquired meaning in part because it stood in opposition and contrast to those of other individuals who occupied positions of differing rank in Chesapeake society.

Figure 7.7. A small Chinese porcelain coffee or chocolate cup was found remarkably intact in a 1770s soil layer. (Photograph by Marion E. Warren.)

The repetitiveness of the visual message and its replication in the social dynamics of the different kinds of entertainment hosted by the family within their home gave the message of wealth and power a dynamic clarity well understood within a community whose members were enculturated to its nuances.

Pottery and porcelain can be studied as indicative of consumption patterns and monetary expenditures and this is an important and useful way to trace the visual messages such items conveyed. Fashion trends as revealed through quantified studies of household consumption had an impact on Chesapeake society. Elements of material culture are recursive and hence the purchases, the small things that families acquired, had an effect of their own, acting back on the pre-existent system and the historical precedents on which it was based, altering these as the new items were incorporated into the prior cultural framework. At the same time, it is hard to argue, even given their symbolic importance, that the position of pottery and porcelain in the cultural system was as central and as strategic in defining the social relationships on which the community operated as that of the food domain.

8

Fine foods and daily bread

> To the savage and to the civilized man alike there is nothing more
> important perhaps than what he eats and how he eats . . . The
> natives of the Trobriand Islands . . . do not eat man and shudder at
> the idea of eating dog or snake. They abhor their neighbours as
> cannibals and dog-eaters or snake-eaters. These neighbours in turn
> despise the Trobrianders for their lack of culinary discrimination in
> neglecting such excellent viands as man, snake and dog.
>
> Bronislaw Malinowski, 1932, *Hunger and Work in a Savage Tribe*

Social distinctions in daily food

"What we like, what we eat, how we eat it, and how we feel about it are phenomeno-
logically interrelated matters; together they speak eloquently to the question of how
we perceive ourselves in relation to others." This was Mintz's conclusion after
studying the ways that people incorporated sugar into their daily diet: how they
surrounded it with economic schemes, myths, domestic rituals, barter and
exchange, legend and lore. Raymond Firth, on the other hand, used food to show
how activities were organized in a small community where getting the daily bread
was the daily work of the entire village. In Maryland, a fat corn-stuffed goose resting
in a delft dish on a dining table was the culmination of many decisions and activities;
the understanding that people had of these or the way they ranked them were
elements in the social value of a goose. Those who valued goose less might cook it
in any old pot, those who valued it more, such as the members of the Charles Carroll
of Annapolis household, might even spend 3 shillings and 6 pence on a special tin
roasting pan.[1]

Cooks normally prepared food in informal or less accessible areas of the home,
often in exterior kitchens or yard compounds. The cook's role, within the home, was
subservient to others enacted within a household's public space. As cook, she
entered the social arenas less often and, if a servant, her salary denoted this. Thus
Benedict Leonard Calvert paid his cook (a woman) less than he paid Theda
Lawrence, his housekeeper, and left her a legacy of only £10 whereas Theda
received £200. His successor, Samuel Ogle, purchased Negro Joe, who cooked the
night away and when he was sold, years later, ran away. More often the cook in a
Maryland home was a black woman. And should a planter's wife cook a meal and
then act as hostess in the dining room, her social roles in each were distinctive and

held different status. Understanding the tasks that people do in the social places where food is prepared and the varying roles they hold also enables an archaeologist to understand better the symbolic import of food as it is served and consumed in dining rituals, how elaboration enhanced its symbolic worth, and the paths by which substitutions were made.[2]

Elaboration in the food domain

Seventeenth-century Chesapeake women cooked meals and taught their daughters and granddaughters to do so in one of two cooking traditions: an English folk tradition centuries old, and a courtly or elite tradition that showed recent Continental influence. By the eighteenth century, these were joined by a West African tradition incorporated into the culture by slaves. Yet, Chesapeake cookery in the English folk tradition remained medieval in form throughout the seventeenth century, and into the eighteenth. While change became more apparent in the nineteenth century, elements of this tradition survive today as do elements of the African heritage.

Utilization of the elite tradition was restricted, however, to a small number of families throughout the pre-Revolutionary period. Conflicting needs within the home left English women little time for the labor required in elaborate cookery while small, simple houses gave them little space for it. Waverly Root highlights this: "It was usually not practical, in a kitchen that was in essence only the enlarged base of the chimney, to prepare dishes requiring, during their preparation, manipulations more complicated than simple basting [fig. 8.1]. Boiling, and roasting meat and poultry on a spit, ordinarily exhausted the available possibilities." English historian Stephen Mennell provides additional testimony: "The method of slow boiling dominated the cooking of all but the richest."[3]

Criteria for the extraordinary food prepared in the courtly tradition are described by William Edward Mead:[4]

> Into the mortar went the most heterogeneous ingredients: meats, vegetables, fruits, spices, sugar, nuts, particularly almonds . . . Nearly every dish, whatever its name, was soft and mushy, with its principal ingredients disguised by the addition of wines or spices or vegetables. The skill of the cook was attested by the fact that his strange compounds were actually eaten . . . practically everything had to be mashed or cut into small pieces and mixed with something else, preferably of so strong a flavor as to disguise the taste of most of the other ingredients. Nearly every dish was a riddle.

Evidence that some households in the region preferred the elite tradition beginning ca. 1620 can be seen at a few archaeological sites from tidewater Virginia, by the Calvert deposits in St. Mary's City, and in a few probate inventories. Lists of kitchen utensils and foodstuffs in probate inventories of the wealthy merchant-planters contain increasing evidence of its accoutrements in the early years of the eighteenth century.[5]

However, the folk tradition was the dominant mode throughout the seventeenth century and prevailed in the early eighteenth century. It is the context that provides the gustatory contrast for food served in the Calvert home; the informal practices associated with it were familiar to Chesapeake families. When they became guests in the Calvert home, Chesapeake men and women were inescapably attuned to the values embedded within the folk tradition, although the Calvert men as English aristocrats were not attuned to these. One element within the folk tradition that must have provoked thought, since it created a clash of values between provincial standards and those of the English aristocracy, was dependence on domestic animal meat and the high cultural value given this food source. This, no doubt, grew out of unsettled earlier times when livestock production was a tenuous endeavor on the Maryland frontier, when men hunted and gathered many wild food resources for

Figure 8.1. Archaeologists at the Jefferson-Patterson Park in Maryland have recreated the appearance of a simple seventeenth-century kitchen recorded from the King's Reach Site; it is perhaps more neat and tidy than many kitchens actually were. (Drawing courtesy of Jefferson-Patterson Park, Leonardstown, Maryland.)

their families, and when venison was a common table meat. As beef, pork, kid, and mutton became available routinely, Maryland families, rich and poor alike, ate them in increasing quantities. The variety introduced by wild game such as their forebears ate through necessity was not a strong component in status food consumption among Maryland families of the early eighteenth century (fig. 8.2). If the older English value system, in which game ranked higher than meat from domestic animals, had remained in force, the Chesapeake environment provided ample opportunity for families to adopt it as a strategy expressing upward mobility; evidence of its continuation should be apparent through faunal analysis. That wealthy families adopted a newer pattern with a different set of meat values is seen instead.[6]

On the other hand, in England hunting continued to be a prerogative of the rich; seventeenth-century aristocrats strengthened the poaching laws as the century progressed. Hence game retained its prestige. The Calverts brought with them a perception of game as a desirable, if not always a delicious, food. They also brought the knowledge that variety was the spice of sociable dining, a way to honor guests and denote the pleasure taken in serving them. What also set apart ceremonial dining from an ordinary meal was the delicacy and the quality of the food, as well as the manner in which it was served.[7]

Variety could be provided in two ways: first in the different kinds of meat, vegetables, and beverages servants served, and second in the way wives or household servants cooked it. Taken together, these two aspects of food preparation enabled food to possess delicacy, culinary quality, or a combination thereof. The qualitative importance of meals to the Calvert household can be inferred from Benedict Leonard's complaint about Italian meals to his brother Cecilius which prompted this response: "As to the Italians sobriety at their own Tables, and that they love to eat at another man's Table, . . . you must remember some people here at home dont overload their Guest's stomach with Cheer, and yet love to see another Man's Table well spread."[8]

Variety in daily meals

Variety was not a wide-spread characteristic of Chesapeake cuisine in the early eighteenth century. Devereux Jarratt wrote that his mother served no tea or coffee, only bread, milk, and meat appeared at ordinary meals in his childhood. Breakfast was the cold remains of the prior night's dinner; dessert consisted of pies and puddings; supper was much like dinner which was based on a selection of different meats and small offerings of other foods. Food preparation was deeply tied to the rhythm of agricultural labor. Carr and Walsh point out that in homes without servants, many tobacco planters' wives also worked in the fields whenever they could, tilling, hoeing, picking worms off leaves, removing suckers, and otherwise helping produce the bountiful tobacco crops on which family income depended. This left English women little time, after grinding grain for bread, washing, or mending, to introduce variety into meal preparation. It also gave them little time to work in a kitchen garden or to tend fruit trees although these proliferated to a degree that in 1697 Thomas Lawrence wrote an English friend that Maryland hogs ate better peaches than "Duchesses eat in Hyde Park." Lists of vegetables grown repeated names of familiar English plants – potherbs (basil, sage, rosemary, and thyme), beets, rape, kale, colewort, spinach, leeks, shallots, onions, cabbage, carrots, French beans, parsnips, turnips, radish, cucumber, lettuce, spinach, and garlic. Yet some forgot how to grow plants like "carrots, spinach, red beets, and onions." The importance of fruit and the dishes or drinks women prepared from it can be inferred from two sources: accounts sent to England and property descriptions. Apples, peaches, and cherries were the most important, but other fruits were grown too; these exhibited the range of variation typical of English species. Detail on vegetables appears in random comments such as journal entries which show that a range of different varieties of peas and beans were grown – Rouncival, Hot-spur, Dwarf, and Miraculous, or, among beans, the Indian Bonavis, Calivance, and Nanticoacks. The plea for tax abatement by old John Juitt tells of one woman's talent at providing food and money for her family from a market garden and of its demise: "that his wife, when the petitioner lived near Annapolis, used to raise things of several sorts which she disposed of in town and thereby raised a little money, . . . " but now, Juitt testified, "being removed up in the woods, a great distance from Annapolis, has not the like opportunity."[9]

Seasonal variation in food production limited options, although foods available in one season might be preserved for later seasons by salting, smoking, drying, pickling,

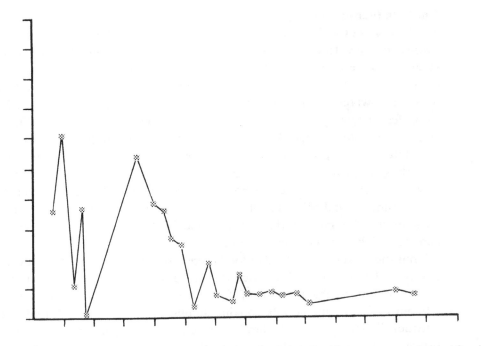

Figure 8.2. The use of wild game in daily diet decreased as the land became more settled and farming improved. (Graph drawn by Julie Hunter-Abbazia after Miller 1984.)

or the inclusion of liquor (fig. 8.3). Five entries in John Davisson's 1721 inventory illustrate the perils of food preservation.

Item	*Value*
seven barrels of Irish beef	£10.10.00
a tub of stinking beef of no value	[left blank]
five barrels of mackerell	£8.05.00
about ½ barrell not so good	0.15.00
136 [lbs] of damaged fish	0.08.00

The seasonal variation in domestic meats available for sale in Annapolis food markets shows the intercession of preservation attributes, animal birth and growth cycles, the mesh between farm tasks associated with crop production and those of animal husbandry, and holiday food requirements. Lamb appeared first in the spring, with calf meat present by the Easter holiday; shoats, except for some very small suckling pigs, were generally butchered starting in late summer. Chickens, ducklings, and green goose were sold in the summer; pullets (young hens) appeared in September. Farmers rounded up their older cattle and sheep to sell in August and September after the peak of tobacco cultivation, taking advantage of the weeks tobacco leaves hung to dry. These meats appeared, in different proportions, on Maryland dining tables depending in part on the social status of a family, on the location of its home (urban or rural), on cultural precedent, and on personal preference.[10]

Cooking techniques

Most families owned only an iron pot or frying pan for cooking purposes, and were overwhelmingly dependent on braised meat, stews, and boiled dishes. Cookbooks reveal the style by their emphasis on cooking techniques. For example, Susanna Carter, the only American cook to publish in the eighteenth century, divided her meat and fowl recipes among broiling (4); frying (12); roasting (34, of which 21 were for different types of birds); and pot-meals: boiling (22), stewing (23), fricassees (13), and ragouts (9) together with potted dishes and soups. A similar scheme is found in women's private notes on food cookery. Edward Kimber, in a late winter or early spring journey down the Eastern Shore, drank "thin-fretting cider," water served in a calabash, "excellent beer," and ate "mush (Made of Indian Corn, or Rice, pounded) and Milk of Molasses." He also dined on "hominie" (Indian corn-meal, pounded or ground with its husks, and fried) and ate "Great hominie," which had meat, fish, or fowl as an addition.[11]

Thus the most basic method of food preparation shared attributes with an African tradition. The use of meal and rice with inclusions of meat or fowl is very close to the one-pot meals characteristic of West Africa. The spices would have marked the difference, for traditional folk cooking among the English was "simple, spiceless, nutritious" (see, for example, how few inventories list spices in tables 2.1 and 2.2). African cookery, on the other hand, made use of varied spices to introduce a heat and sharper flavors. Octavio Paz describes the secret of the spicier food: it unites "the fresh and the piquant, the salty and the sweet, the acid and the hot, the harsh and the delicate." Yet the utensils used in its preparation were remarkably similar to those that produced the blander English meal described above, and ones most people owned.[12]

Henry Miller's analysis of cooking equipment indicates that between 1692–1705, 99% of the households in lower Maryland (St. Mary's County) had the iron pots necessary to prepare food by braising or boiling. Only 63% could fry foods and only

Figure 8.3. Fruits were often preserved in liquor. William Kelso recovered examples from a well at Kingsmill where whole bottles dropped from baskets and fell, without breaking, to the bottom below. Two similar sealed bottles from the Calvert Well have yet to be opened. (Illustration by Julie Hunter-Abbazia.)

50% could roast meats if one takes it as a given that cooks used only metal implements. Inventories recorded in Lancaster County, Virginia, across the Potomac river from St. Mary's County, reveal fewer deep pots (72%), fewer spits, but equal numbers of frying pans (62%). Since spits (an indication meat was roasted) and frying pans were not mutually exclusive kitchen tools, families who chose to diversify their food preparation techniques might own either one or both. And as an example of how historical precedent could be practically reconstrued, Lois Carr suggests some women may have used wooden poles stretched across the hearth as temporary, substitute spits; travelers' accounts also describe roasting birds on sticks. Iron spits were perhaps one of the first small luxuries Chesapeake housewives asked their husbands to buy (fig. 8.4).[13]

Still, it is obvious that women in a full third of the households in lower Maryland only owned the utensils to prepare food in one way while only about half owned those that enabled them to use more than two ways. The evidence from early Annapolis was remarkably similar but began to change faster than in the counties. The Annapolis inventory for Philemon Hemsley was valued at £631, placing him among its wealthier families in 1718. While Hemsley's household furnishings included some amenities and one or two luxuries, the kitchen equipment was spartan in contrast to the Calverts' (table 8.1). Mary Hemsley, like many contemporary Annapolitan women, owned the tools to roast meat, to fry or saute, and to boil or braise, yet she possessed but six pots and pans, and two were earthen. Throughout the Chesapeake, cooking techniques were simple ones, taught to daughters by their mothers, stepmothers, or indentured female servants, and plain fare was the order of the day celebrated in song by aristocrats such as Thomas Jennings, a member of the exceedingly exclusive men's group, the Annapolis Hominy Club of the 1760s, who wrote "verses in praise of hominy": "No foreign dish shall fire my heart, Ragoust or Fricasse, For they can ne'er such sweets impart as good, boiled Hominy."[14]

Fancy foods and high-style dining

Plain fare was not the order of the day in the ca. 1730 Calvert household; even their outlying slave quarters were provided with modest sets of kitchen tools. The Calverts' town kitchen was as fully equipped as any in the region. Its extensive and sophisticated utensils were equal to the ca. 1760 kitchen of the Governor's Palace in Williamsburg – a kitchen that curators at the Colonial Williamsburg Foundation believe to be the most elaborate kitchen for its time in the Chesapeake. Given the explosion of material items that Chesapeake households purchased between 1730 and 1760 and the incredible difference in the quantity of goods used within their homes, the fact that the ca. 1730 Calvert kitchen is comparable in any way to the 1760 kitchen in Williamsburg is remarkable.

The specialized utensils in Table 8.1 are listed under the cooking techniques for which they were employed, thus showing the range of different techniques the kitchen staff used in the Calvert home. These techniques vary from simple to complex. Of note is the variety, quantity, and quality of the utensils; the list shows brass or copper in contrast to iron or bellmettle, two coffee, tea, and chocolate pots each (fig. 8.5). The value of Edward Henry's kitchen utensils was approximately £42 while that of Charles Calvert was slightly lower. Their values were insignificant amounts in terms of the personal estates of each man; each had more wealth concentrated in silver, pewter, glass, porcelain, and delft, but in terms of the money

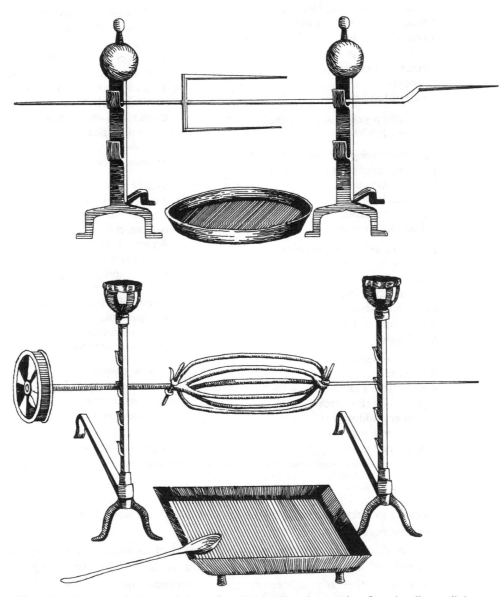

Figure 8.4. Spits came in sizes and shapes from the simple to the complex. Occasionally, small dogs were placed in drums where their movements caused the spit to rotate without human motion. In many kitchens, young black children helped rotate the spit. In families without slave labor, it was a housewife's task or one assigned to her daughters. (Illustration by Julie Hunter-Abbazia.)

Table 8.1. *Cooking utensils used in Captain Calvert's and Edward Henry's households (as shown on their probate inventories) permitted a greater degree of elaboration in food cookery than in ordinary homes with small sets of utensils*

Fireplace tools:
2 brass hearths, each with dogs [and irons], bellows, 2 pr of brass tongs and shovels

Utensils for boiling and braising:
A brass ladle, a brass skimmer
A copper dish kettle (weight 15 lbs, 6 oz.)
4 copper porridge pots
3 iron pots (weight 150 lbs)
2 coppers
A pair of [pot] racks

Utensils for poaching and steaming:
A copper fish kettle

Utensils for frying and sauteing:
4 copper sauce pans (with covers)
3 copper flat pans
A copper frying pan
A bellmettle skillet
2 [iron] frying pans

Utensils for grilling and roasting:
4 French larding pans
1 jagging iron
A copper dripping pan
3 spits and wheels
A winding-up jack
3 gridirons

Utensils for baking:
A brass slice
A brass flour box
A paper box (for parchment?)
A copper pudding pan
Earthenware patty pans
6 dozen patty pans

4 dozen biscuit pans
An apple roaster

Other:
Earthen pans of assorted sizes
A copper coffee pot, and a coffee mill and another coffee pot
A black copper tea kettle and another copper tea kettle
Two copper chocolate pots
A [chocolate] mill
Brass scales and weights
An iron chafing dish
A copper cistern
An iron hibbert

Small kitchen tools:
2 chopping knives
2 flesh forks
An iron cleaver
An iron ladle and a dozen wooden ladles
A copper basting ladle
6 sieves and 2 rolling pins
A bellmettle mortar and pestle
A brass mortar and marble mortar
A sugar hammer
A pewter funnel
A pewter colander

Storage vessels:
3 cannisters
10 dozen bottles
1 two-gallon bottle

For distilling liquors:
A copper still and worm

invested in kitchen utensils by the average Maryland household, the sums expended were outrageous.

This affluent Chesapeake household might, if its members so chose, prepare in a variety of ways a range of foods from Italian ices and ornately sugared fruits to roast pig. In the early eighteenth century, elaborate food preparation for ceremonial dining required an array of specialized utensils; the Calvert family owned these. Fine cooking took time and labor. The large number of household slaves was more than sufficient. Further, Benedict Leonard's long sojourn in France and Italy (1723–5), his curiosity, and his fluency in foreign languages gave him opportunity to learn first-hand of the qualitative elaboration that distinguished courtly Continental cuisine, an elaboration slowly being incorporated into English high cuisine. At the very least, one Calvert had knowledge of French techniques (and these were not yet translated into English cookbooks). The family's financial resources were fully adequate to cover the price of scarce or costly ingredients such as cinnamon (two shillings an ounce), cloves (one shilling apiece), almonds from Jordan (almost two shillings apiece), hart's horn from Germany (table 8.2), fresh ginger from the West Indies (one shilling per pound), rice (one shilling per pound), or coffee (8 shillings per pound) in an era when an entire "buttock of beef" could be bought for only four shillings, a loaf of bread was six pence, and small chickens could be two pennies each.[15]

"Courtly fashion moved towards the proliferation of small, delicate, and costly dishes," wrote food historian Stephen Mennell. "Knowledgeability and a sense of delicacy in matters of food became something of the mark of the courtier." This, in itself, might have been sufficient reason for the Calverts to prepare these dishes in Annapolis. The questions, of course, are whether they did and whether the ingredients were available for them to do so. Mead observed that the ingredients

Figure 8.5. A wheel-turned spit was appraised in the Calvert inventory as well as an extensive set of fireplace cooking utensils (Illustration by Julie Hunter-Abbazia.)

required for elite cookery included fruits, spices, sugar, and nuts, particularly almonds. Earle enumerated ships that carried voluminous cargoes of currants and raisins from North Africa or the eastern Mediterranean to English ports and, at different times of the year, of lemons and oranges. Archaeological remains do not illuminate the fruit, spices, herbs, vegetables, and sugar used in the Calvert house. Quantities of peach pits were found, but none came from early features. Yet the orangery itself denotes the horticultural interest and expertise that might have enabled the family's gardeners to raise exotic fruits. Of the nuts and spices there is no record for the 1730s except what is listed in the probate inventory: raisins, almonds, nutmeg, cloves, ginger, mace, sage, hartshorn, three kinds of pepper. The Calvert inventories also list three kinds of sugar. Such were the ingredients required by haute cuisine. While the shopkeepers of Annapolis also stocked these items (see Table 8.3), and they were listed in inventories of merchant-planter gentry families in the countryside, most inventories do not show the quantities listed in the Calvert records, and since the nuts and spices rarely appear in the inventories of ordinary planters, either these foodstuffs were not used or were present in quantities so small that they had no resale value.[16]

It seems significant that the quantity of spices in the house decreased from 1730 to 1734, i.e., after the departure of Lady Margaret Lee Calvert, Benedict Leonard, and his cook. Carr and Walsh conclude that few Maryland women had access to or used fancy spices in the late seventeenth and early eighteenth centuries. Often, on the few inventories where they do appear, they are sequestered from other food products, stored in a closet or box in a woman's private bed chamber. Unlike her in-laws, Rebecca Calvert was brought up in rural Maryland. Exotic spices did not appear in her father's inventory. Maryland food cookery was a folk art; recipes were passed from one generation to another as part of a woman's heritage. It is unlikely (even if she did try) that sixteen-year-old Rebecca Gerard Calvert had much knowledge of courtly cookery before her marriage or had fully mastered English haute cuisine when she died at age 28.

Yet, the available evidence strongly suggests that the Annapolis Calvert family used food to embellish their state dinners in a manner akin to the way it was used in the country estates of England. Certainly later governors did so for in 1744 William Black ate a splendid dinner at Governor Bladen's with a "Great Variety of Dishes, all serv'd up in the most Elegant Way, after which came a Dessert no less Curious; Among the Rarities of which it was Compos'd, was some fine Ice Cream." His journal entry lists three key elements in this form of social display – variety, elegance, and rarity – and, as will be shown later, the Calvert faunal remains exhibit qualities useful in producing variety, elegance, and uncommon dishes (figs. 8.6 and 8.7).[17]

Food creolization

At the beginning of this chapter it was suggested that the critical symbolic attributes signifying prestige could transfer from a visual realm to one of taste and texture when food was consumed. This chapter has sketched the ways that ordinary people in the Chesapeake cooked because this was the backdrop, the conventional point of

Table 8.2. *Hartshorn jelly from* Penn Family Recipes *(Benson 1966) shows the use of exotic and expensive ingredients, including some listed on the Calvert inventory*

"Take 4 oz. of the shavings of harts horne
one oz. of the shavings of Ivery,
Infuse it all night upon embers in a possett of Running watter,
with ½ a pound of Raisons of the sonne stoned,
with a Little mace in an earthen pipkin,
in the morning boyle it up with a Little saffron,
if you Like it a Littel Licorish and sum opening Rooses,
if you please serching [sprinkling] it with a Litel sugar."

view, which guests to the Calvert mansion brought with them when they were invited for dinner, supper, or an evening's entertainment. Setting a table with a wider variety of foods or more and better-quality wines than were normally served in Chesapeake homes was one way that the Calverts could distinguish their house from others; it was a way that was as recognizable to the guests (or recipients) as it was to the hosts (or donors). But the distinguishing elements in these meals existed at deeper levels too.

Power and prestige are enhanced by mystery, puzzlement, and complexity. Consuming a superb meal, one is aware of its qualitative difference through the medium of taste. The texture and flavor of young meat, well cooked, is qualitatively different from that obtained from older animals. To produce similar results in their own kitchens, the Chesapeake gentry had first to acquire the utensils necessary to prepare the meal, its raw ingredients, find the leisure or labor to practice the skill, and then begin to master a complex set of food preparation techniques that reached out from the kitchen to include methods of butchering animals. Such knowledge was not necessarily shared with anyone who asked, although neither was it necessarily hidden.

In summary, while the greatest English households imported French chefs, the blunt fact is that it was senior women of a household who normally handled the organization of the kitchen. Their managerial skills and cooking secrets were ones that mothers taught to daughters or to other close female kin. The Calvert women did not have extensive kin networks in the province. In fact, their networks were minimal and hence their obligations to teach such skills were few. The knowledge may actually have been possessed as much by skilled servants as by the two young Calvert wives, in which case, through a different vein of power brokerage, flattery, and cajolery, the techniques may have passed piecemeal into the community.

By the nineteenth century, there are descriptions of black women "who deservedly took great pride in their cooking." They planned, procured, and prepared food for the families they served and for their own fathers, husbands, brothers, and children. The meals, of course, were not identical for a variety of reasons; time was one of the most critical factors. Yet, black slave women took time and taught their daughters to cook; one can trace the imprint of their knowledge through genealogies for three

Table 8.3. *Foodstuffs sold in Annapolis stores, ca. 1730, and shown on Edward Henry Calvert's inventory*

	Davisson	Garrett	Carroll	Bordley	Calvert
Spices					
Allspice (pound)	—	X	—	—	—
Alum	—	X	—	—	—
Cinnamon (ounce)	—	X	X	X	—
Cloves (ounce)	—	X	—	X	X
Ginger (pound)	—	X	—	X	X
Mace (ounce)	—	X	X	X	X
Nutmeg (ounce)	—	X	X	X	X
Pepper, black (pound)	—	X	X	X	X
Pepper, Jamaica (pound)	—	—	—	X	—
Pepper, white	—	—	—	—	X
Hartshorn	—	—	—	—	X
Sage	—	—	—	—	X
Snake root (pound)	—	X	—	—	—
Fruits & nuts (*indicates botanical materials recovered at the site)					
Apricots	—	—	—	—	X*
Cherries	—	—	—	—	X*
Currants	—	—	X	X	X
Currants, candied	—	X	—	—	—
Peaches	—	—	—	—	X*
Plums	—	—	X	—	X*
Raisins	—	X	—	X	X
Raisins, candied	—	X	—	—	—
Jordan almonds	—	—	—	—	X
Brazil nuts	—	—	—	—	X*
Peanuts or ground nuts	—	—	—	—	X*
Coconuts	—	—	—	—	X*
Foodstuffs					
Cabbage knots	—	X	—	—	—
Florence Oil (quart)	—	X	X	—	—
Flour	X	—	—	—	—
Hog's lard	X	—	—	—	—
Hominy beans	X	—	—	—	—
Hops	X	—	—	—	—
Linseed Oil	—	—	X	—	—
Malt	X	—	—	—	—
Pickles	X	—	—	—	—
Rice (pound)	—	X	—	—	—
Red rice (pound)	—	X	—	—	—
Salt	X	—	X	—	—
Sorghum	—	—	?	—	—
Tamarind (sold elsewhere in town)					
Oatmeal (bushel)	—	X	—	—	—
Wheat, red (bushel)	X	—	—	—	—
Wheat, white (bushel)	X	—	—	—	—

Table 8.3. (*cont.*)

	Davisson	Garrett	Carroll	Bordley	Calvert
Sugar products					
Clay'd sugar	—	X	—	—	X
Loaf sugar	—	X	X	X	X
Molasses	X	X	—	X	X
Muscova sugar	—	X	X	X	—
Beverage ingredients					
Chocolate or cocoa nuts	X	X	X	—	—
Coffee, raw	—	X	—	X	—
Bohea tea	—	—	X	—	X
Green tea	—	X	X	X?	X
Preserved meats and fish					
Beef, Irish (barrel)	X	—	—	—	—
Beef, stinking	X	—	—	—	—
Codfish, dried	X	—	—	—	—
Damaged fish	X	—	—	—	—
Mackerel	X	—	—	—	—
Smelt	—	—	—	X	—
Whiting	—	X	—	—	—

and sometimes four generations. None in Maryland, however, goes back as far as we would need to connect them with our site.[18]

But by moving outward one can bring these women into view. Elizabeth Fox-Genovese's *Within the Plantation Household* does this for the nineteenth century. Implicit in her narrative is the idea that black women were active agents; she highlights this by describing a black cook in Mississippi who decided she would rather work in the cotton fields than stay in the kitchen after her mistress' death. The family found they could not "beat good cooking out of her." Records reveal the woman "systematically disobeyed orders and stole or destroyed the great part of the provisions given to her for the table." It is reminiscent of Robert Carter's slave at Nominy Hall who systematically sent her children to milk the cows at midnight so that they would grow strong. One can turn this around slightly by noting that many discussions of women in North American slave societies do not tell of women's assertive behavior but focus instead on unpleasant tasks, the things that women were forced to do such as grubbing marsh land during the dead days of winter, clearing icy fields for tobacco or rice, on sexual exploitation, and on asymmetrical power relationships in which all people – white men, black men, white women, white children, Indians, and Asians – except their own offspring held higher social rank.[19]

Chapter one posed the question of who and what material remains tell us about. The answer depends to a large extent on the position taken by an analyst and who or what she considers worthy of study (fig. 8.8). Of course, important persons are often visible. Myth and history ensures that this will be so because their roles dramatically and publicly intercede in the events that affect ordinary men and women. So, time is compressed and space bridged to create what Edmund Leach calls mythic-history: "a charter for beliefs or actions in the present" tied to known heroes and heroines, things, buildings, and landscapes evocative of the past.[20]

Archaeology is so rooted to place that archaeologists normally work from their site outwards without the historian's freedom to go here and there collecting ideas and information that can then be woven together in a comprehensive manner. Rhys Isaac speaks of this as the *"topological"* dimension of our discourse. Archaeologists do not see people in action as anthropologists or folklorists do and so they have less

Figure 8.6. Small individual glassware vessels were used to serve fancy desserts – molded jellies, blancmanges, flummeries, steeple creams, custards, and ices (sorbets or ice creams) – decorated with blossoms, comfits, and small bits of jelly that brightened the table. Edward Henry had twenty-four such vessels; Captain Calvert had more than 144. (Photograph by Marion E. Warren.)

awareness of the communities and societal interaction that surrounded each and every one of their sites. There are ways to bridge the gap.

One is to recognize that in crowds or aggregates, social roles simplify when people are seen merely as consumers or producers. In this view eighteenth-century Annapolitans and Anne Arundel families become analogs of Henry Glassie's rural folk, "a little lost, standing alone . . . country people, dressed neatly, poorly, on the streets of big cities." We might imagine some as tobacco planters bringing their wives and children into Annapolis for a rare holiday. But this is a view in which it is easy to forget that in rural counties and in small towns men and women are "neighbors first, part of a cooperative enterprise" or within their families, kinfolk

Figure 8.7. Stems from fragile drinking glasses survive more frequently in archaeological deposits than the glass bowls that held beverages. In this example, the stem is adorned with a twisted collar and a ball knop. (Photograph by Marion E. Warren.)

first and foremost and, for the most part, working for the benefit of household or family rather than for themselves as individuals in the way that modern society values. Glassie eloquently shows how shifting the view can create new insights in his study of Ballymenone; he demonstrates that people who may seem silent when placed in a crowd are actually highly articulate. "Society," he writes, "is composed of communities simultaneously occupying space and time at the same human level. Some are composed of upper-class fox-hunters [cf., the Calverts], some of middle-class scholars [cf. the physicians and lawyers who kept a variety of shops in Annapolis], some are poor farmers [or black slaves]. All seem reasonable from within, strange from without, silent at a distance." And it is distance that models of society as essentially consumption or production units create.[21]

Glassie urges instead that we study ordinary people by working from the inside out, beginning with the dimensions of daily life in which they are articulate and pushing the boundaries forward. Another way is to take the concept of space on lot 83, which has heretofore been described as a Calvert place, and see what view of it emerges when we look at it in terms of the others who simultaneously dwelled within its boundaries, sleeping in nooks and crannies, in halls, closets, stables and on kitchen hearths, and who were black, with African birthplaces or African ancestors. They did not have the same freedom as the Calvert men and women, but cultural

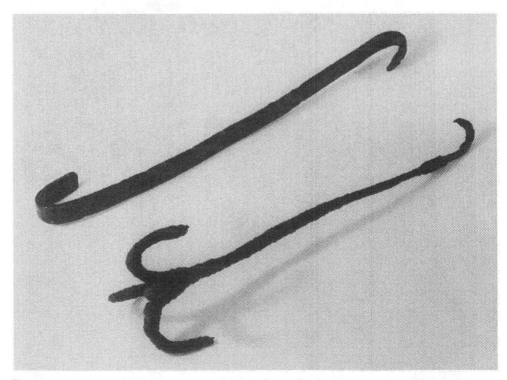

Figure 8.8. Simple tools such as the iron pot-hook and grappling hook shown here enabled cooks to hang pots on the hearth or food in a well. They were common utensils used by women of European or African heritage. (Photograph by Marion E. Warren.)

identity does not require freedom to find expression and cultural mechanisms can easily manipulate objects of foreign manufacture (cf., European-made) into tools that serve different ends – as markers of ethnicity *and* as items of production and consumption. People can confer multiple meanings upon artifacts, but normally they do so within systems of social relationships; these, for black men and women of the Chesapeake, were in a state of flux.

V

BUILDING BLACK IDENTITIES

There were among them a great number of slaves, called Negroes, . . . of whose souls there was no manner of care taken.

Missionary for the Society for the Propagation of the Gospel, 1703

The inescapable fact in the study of Afro-America is the humanity of the oppressed, and the inhumanity of the systems that oppressed them. But not all slavery systems oppressed all slaves equally, and not all slaves dealt with their oppression in the same ways . . . people in Afro-American societies . . . quite literally built their life-ways to meet their daily needs.

Sidney W. Mintz and Richard Price, 1976
An Anthropological Approach to the Afro-American Past

9

The face of urban slavery

Of the categories that we have been examining in this last section, gu, hku, ga, hka, and nam, only gu and nam are kinship categories in the ordinary sense. But, in Kachin usage, the whole set of words is intricately tangled up. The kinship relationship gu-nam cannot be separated from the rest of the tangle. If we are to understand what the kinship terms may mean we must examine the non-kinship words as well.

Edmund Leach, 1967, The language of Kachin kinship

The first view

Intricate tangles – that is what sites create; the more varied the people that inhabit a land, the more intricate are the marks they leave on the ground. Yet it was in inventories that I first saw African-born slaves as a strong presence in the Calvert household. Here they stood out in contrast to the average Maryland slave-holdings, although their impact on the ca. 1730 archaeological record was not initially visible; its artifact assemblage seemed dominated by English activity. It was only as I patiently sifted through both documentary and archaeological evidence that information about the black occupants became visible; it began to emerge as the ethnographic context was recreated. First, items that previously had seemed simply British (fig. 8.8) became ones that could have dual functions, and then their roles in symbolically maintaining African ties became clearer. Artifacts that were signs of African influences became easier to see the more I knew about old West Africa.

Although Captain Calvert did not possess the hundreds of slaves that Virginia planters like Robert "King" Carter kept in 1732 – at more than 700, the Carter slave population was equivalent to the population of Annapolis ca. 1730 – Calvert's life also was not dominated by tobacco production. Yet, whatever the yardstick, Captain Calvert owned more slaves in 1734 than most Maryland families. Like other chattel property in the Chesapeake, the names, age labels, and appraised values of the Calvert slaves were shown on the Captain's probate inventories (see table 9.1), and it is likely that like others, they too were primarily from countries adjacent to the Bight of Biafra, from Angola, the Gold Coast or Senegambia (fig. 9.1). The statistics can be compared with generalized patterns of slave populations drawn from other inventory studies (see tables A.2, and 9.3).[1]

Table 9.1. *Slaves listed on Captain Calvert's inventories in 1734**

Annapolis
Old men and women
  George, a very old man (£2);** Old Toney (£18)
Men and women
  Jacob (£35); Shrewsberry (£20); Samy (£20); Will (£20)
  Sew (£30); Nan (£30); Patey (£30); Nell (£26); Matty (£26); Sarah (£25)
Boys and girls
  Benja (£12); Jack (£10); Ned (£10); Samm (£10); Solomon (£10)
  Toney (£7); Stephen (£5); Charles (£4)
  Beck (£15); Ruth (£10); Kease (£10); Rachel (£9); Sew (£7)
  Jane (£6); Rachel (£6); Sarah (£5); Patt (£4)
Infants and toddlers
  a one month old child (£3)

At the Prince George's County Plantation House
Old men
  Mingo, a very old man (£1)
Men and women
  Charles (£25); Nom (£27)
  Hann (£28); Lucy (£22)
Boys and girls
  Harey (£22); Nell (£20); Hannah (£16); Jenny (£18); Betty (£12); Doll (£8)
Infants and toddlers
  A negro child about two years old (£5)

At Cubit's Quarter
  Cubit (£30); Abigale (£28); Girdle (£18)

At the Garrison Quarter
  Men and women
  Peter (£25);
  Tydoe (£28); Liby (£23)
Boys and girls
  Peter, a boy (£26); Frank (£22); Hercules (£15); Easter (£15); Betty (£8)
Infants and toddlers
  A child named Cusey about six months (£2)

 * No ages are shown for many of the young people. Some idea of age can be gained, however, from an inventory filed for William Locke in Anne Arundel County in 1733 which lists both age and value.
** A man named Tony, aged 30, is shown on the inventory of Capt. Calvert's father-in-law, John Gerard, in 1716.

Slave hierarchies: men, women, and children

How to take this bare-bones data, enhance its ethnographic range, and see different dimensions of black life? One might begin by observing that if Onorio Razolini, the Italian nobleman who became Captain Calvert's daughters' guardian, was among the highest-ranking men who served the Maryland household, then child slaves

Table 9.2. *Ages of the Calvert slaves*

	Infants	Girls	Boys	Women	Men	Old men	Total
Rural estate							
(Prince George's County)							
Main dwelling	1	5	1	2	2	1	12
Cubit's Quarter				2	1		3
Garrison Quarter	1	2	3		2	1	9
Subtotal	2	7	4	4	5	2	24
Annapolis*	1	9	9	7	2	3	31
Total							55

* The inventory contents suggest the presence of a second house or quarter, but not its location.

belonging to it were among the lowest. Yet they worked; as children they were made to be productive workers. What did they do?

Child slaves who lived at the rural plantation and were aged seven to ten helped in the fields and may, like other youngsters (Indian, free African, or English), have helped scare blackbirds and other pests from the ripening corn. "Old Dick," an Anne Arundel slave born about 1730 in Virginia, said that as soon as his young sons became old enough and strong enough to hoe, his children were sold. As I learned more about them, I realized the wide variety of children's work: they thinned corn, weeded potato patches, fed the hens, carried water, set tables, waited at table, gathered feathers, ran errands, and were companions, sometimes friends, for young white boys and girls. Occasionally their faces appear in portraits of young Chesapeake gentry. Yet in the ranking system, children stood beneath the men and women who were field hands, drivers, sloopers (boat or watermen), artisans, house servants, or overseers. Some of the thirty-two black children who were Calvert slaves may have been born in West Africa and transported, but the youngest, Cusey (aged six months; named for the day of his birth, Sunday) and the infant without a name (a month old), were surely born in Maryland (see table 9.1).[2]

Most adult slaves in the Chesapeake throughout the 1720s, however, were immigrants. Russell Menard estimates that an average of 300 a year arrived from 1695–1708; then the trade increased. Wax estimates 25% of the population on Maryland's Western Shore was black ca. 1710; by 1750 it was close to 40% (see table A-3). Most were men; few lived on plantations with equal sex ratios (16% of the men; 23% of the women). But all plantations were not alike and in their gradations the opportunity to maintain a strong Afro-centric cultural identity waxed and waned. It was particularly strong ca. 1730 because of a constant infusion of African-born peoples whenever a slave-ship unloaded. Since historians know more about the rural framework of African-American life in the countryside than in the towns, it provides an apt starting point to trace the interaction between black and white in urban Annapolis.[3]

In rural Maryland ca. 1730, nine out of ten black men and almost all black women

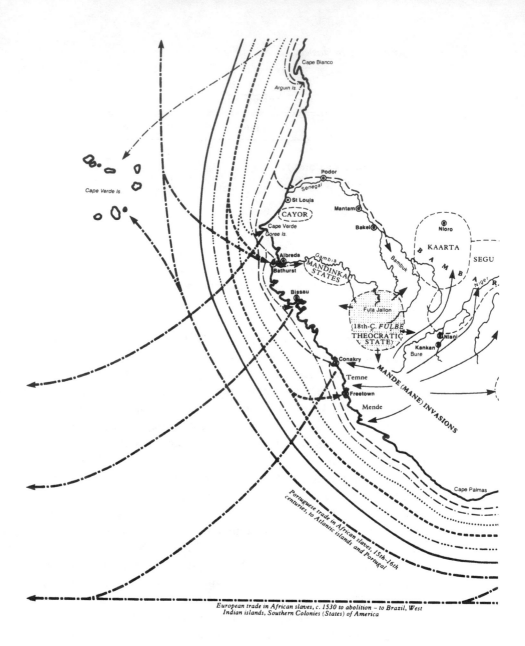

Figure 9.1. Map of West Africa and European trade routes in the seventeenth century.

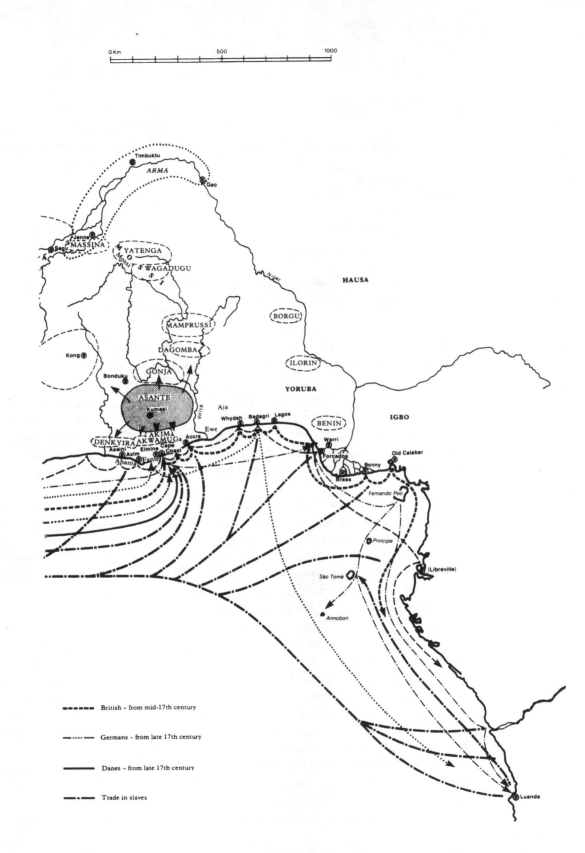

ARMA

Timbuktu

Gao

MASSINA

Jenne

Segu

YATENGA

M O S S I

WAGADUGU

Niger

HAUSA

Kong

MAMPRUSSI

BORGU

DAGOMBA

ILORIN

Bonduku

GONJA

YORUBA

IGBO

ASANTE

Kumasi

Volta

BENIN

Aja

Whydah Badagri Lagos

AKIMA

Ewe

Warri

DENKYIRA AKWAMU Ga

Accra

Assini

Elmina

Forcados

Axim

Cape

Old Calabar

Ahanta

Fante

Coast

Bonny

Brass

Fernando Poo

Principe

[Libreville]

São Tomé

Annobon

Luanda

0 Km   500   1000

- - - - - British – from mid-17th century

- · - · - Germans – from late 17th century

——————— Danes – from late 17th century

— · — · — Trade in slaves

Table 9.3. *Demographic characteristics of slave-holdings in eighteenth-century Maryland*

	Prince George's inventory	Annapolis inventory	"Urban"* (Walsh) 1723–32	1733–44	Prince George's and Charles Cty (Menard)
Per cent reported as					
Children	0.54	0.61	0.30	0.36	0.39
Male/female sex ratio	0.66	0.29	1.56	0.92	1.56
Ratio of children to adults	1.30	2.00	0.62	0.83	0.66

* The urban data is drawn from Table 1 in Walsh (1984c) and includes all inventories filed in Annapolis between 1723 and 1744. This includes Captain Calvert's own inventory. Since the urban inventory sample only contains a modest number of inventories, column 4 shows the effect of the Calvert inventory.

worked in the fields; most were born in Africa, but a few were one generation removed, possibly two. They worked side by side with mulattos who served thirty-one-year indentures (if their mothers were white) or were slaves themselves (if their mothers were black). They worked in ragged garments that saw hard use; some had almost no clothes. Old Dick's description of working for an Anne Arundel planter – "I was put to work on the hoe, I was up an hour before sun, and worked naked till after dark" – is paralleled by an advertisement for a runaway, Pete, who "was almost naked when he went away, having nothing but an old cotton waistcoat and half a spotted rug."[4]

As a group, they drew distinctions among themselves: "I was born on a plantation on the Rappahannock River. I have no mixed blood in my veins; I am no half and half breed, no chestnut sorrel . . . my father and my mother both came over from Guinea." They spoke in African dialects, sang Guinea love-songs, and mapped their world within an African frame of reference. That is to say, they measured distance by days of travel, used nature as a clock, and remembered years by distinct and outstanding events: a flood, a war, a drought.[5]

Allan Kulikoff estimates that 1% were boatmen, 4% were carpenters or coopers, making barrels for the tobacco trade, and 1% were house servants. Black feminists point out that slave women worked longest of all; after a day in the fields that began before sun-up – hoeing, raking, shoveling, mucking out stalls, slaughtering animals, cutting wood and clearing bush, weeding, planting, and harvesting – they still cooked and cared for their families, laundered, made clothes, wove fish nets, hushed a child, rubbed away its aches and pains or soothed its soul. Some women estimate that in the early eighteenth century, these mothers lost two out of every three children born, while African historians point out that the average West African woman who continued to live in Africa had seven children; mortality rates were high; small children might be sold and taken away; some were removed as toddlers (i.e., under 3) from their homes. It was an agonizing, pain-filled existence. To survive, people drew on inner strengths and every resource at their command.[6]

Subtle differences

There is no indication that the Calvert slaves in Prince George's County were other than field hands, except for Cubit, an overseer. However, Captain Calvert's choice of an African as overseer (this occurred on at least one of the quarters) set the Calvert slaves apart and made them part of a tiny minority. There were other differences. The level of their material possessions was slightly higher than listed in inventories for many slave quarters. The earthenware at the Garrison, for example, together with a hand mill, was worth £1.06.06; many poor white families owned less. And whereas many slaves, because of the disproportionate number of men taken, lived in all-male groups bonded by necessity, not kinship, the Calvert slaves lived in family-like enclaves, had a higher percentage of young children in their household units, and kept African names as often as not.

In the 1690s, a Dutch slave-trader, William Bosman, wrote of West African naming practices among the cultures he knew; three names were given then to a child:

> One for the day of the week
> One for the grandfather or grandmother
> One for some special talent or achievement

And if a child was the eighth, ninth, or tenth offspring, this too was noted. Names were exceptionally important; names told of origins; names were a reconnecting link, one way that ancestral spirits were kept alive. Travellers observed that the practice of using African naming patterns continued in the Caribbean. However, Kulikoff reported only 3% of 456 Virginia slaves (or fewer than a dozen) kept African names. He concluded that slave children in the Chesapeake were almost always given English diminutives, and that slave masters forbade the use of African equivalents. By way of contrast, almost 40% of the rural Calvert slaves kept African names, and if one adds English homonyms for common African names, the percentage comes close to 80%. Thus there were social factors that lessened the degree of isolation and cultural severance at some slave quarters, and where this occurs, one might expect to find other forms of African-related material culture.[7]

Further evidence that the Calvert slaves possessed a degree of autonomy and stature within the black community is the fact that one of Charles Carroll of Annapolis' runaways sought sanctuary with them and was "harbored" for a long winter's month in 1729. He was not immediately returned. Perhaps Captain Calvert's Annapolis house slaves gave the runaway directions to reach their rural brethren. Perhaps he went because there was no longer an option to join the Native American settlement at Monocacy after Captain Calvert's negotiations with the tribe and after "Negro Harry" bandied about news of a planned revolt the summer before. The fact that "Negro Stephen, a cooper" ran to Cubit's Quarter reveals a sphere of black interaction reaching from the western shores of the Bay into the farmlands near today's town of Bladensburg outside Washington, D.C. Join that to the fact that late one night well after midnight Governor Nicholson met a group of six or seven black travelers returning from the Potomac falls and add the recollection of another Anne Arundel slave, Old Dick, who married a house servant at an Elk Ridge tavern: "It is a good 25 miles from Annapolis to The Landing Place; but a Negur never tire when he go to see his sweetheart, and after work on Saturday night I would start for Elk Ridge, and get to my wife before supper was put away." Advertisements in the Maryland Gazette indicate similar dispersed networks: "Celia . . . is entertained by Negroes and has been conveyed by them through most of the counties of the Western shore."[8]

The networks were one way slaves built and maintained black identities within the Chesapeake; the fact that they were operative from the 1690s onward and that the rural slaves in Cubit's Quarter had positions within them is important for understanding what the urban slaves might have done at the Annapolis site.

"Tumultuous meetings"

The point above is simply that the more one can demonstrate interaction among members of an ethnic or cultural group, the more one can begin to see dimensions of daily life not readily visible in artifacts that suggest how objects could be used to reinforce cultural identities with different value systems than those characteristic of the dominant group. The fact that Englishmen placed European forms over essentially African words (i.e., Joe over *Cudjo* or Venus over *Benah*) is but one example of how cultures mesh yet maintain independent value systems. The "tumultuous meetings" slaves held at night (then called "Negro day-time") and on Sundays are another example.[9]

A series of eighteenth-century accounts reveal that slaves drew together to dance, wrestle, drink, eat, sing, chant, and conduct heady conversation in all the African dialects they understood. At these gatherings, men played banjos, fiddles, flutes and horns, beat drums, and kept time with bone rattles. This is why the English used the word "tumultuous" (i.e., "full of commotion; marked by confusion and uproar; disorderly and noisy; violent and clamorous") to refer to the socializing. African-Americans today might speak of it in terms of *gumbo ya ya*. These social events are recorded at Philadelphia (before 1693), New Orleans, Charleston, Norfolk, every town in the West Indies, and assuredly took place in Annapolis. Men washed, shaved, and dressed up first (fig. 9.2); women donned rings, bracelets, necklaces, earrings, and favorite clothes. Sometimes the celebrations took place in public areas of a city or town – areas where blacks felt free to go – or at a quarter. Folklorist Roger Abrahams is clear about their role: "tumultuous meetings" were events where "shared expectations, attitudes, and feelings emerged, drawing upon common features of past experience in Africa and in the New World."[10]

In Virginia, Governor Spotswood found such expressions of African values and the sight of Africans at play unnerving. Not able to understand everything that was being said (and the messages were multiple), he wrote that "tumultuous meetings" were social arenas for planning revenge and urged Maryland governors to join with Virginians and enact legislation outlawing them. Captain Calvert acquiesced in part, signing a bill in 1723 that placed responsibility for the gatherings on the shoulders of slave-masters even as he helped Annapolitans collect bonds from other masters that were surety for good behavior by convict servants (see chapter 1). No legislation, however, could hide the African presence in the community nor in the tobacco counties where blacks almost outnumbered whites (table A-3).[11]

Visual images: Africans as different peoples

Folklorist Charles Joyner from South Carolina recorded an old Yoruba proverb, "However far the stream flows, it never forgets its source." The source, for most African-born slaves in Maryland, was the African hinterland stretching for 3,400 miles from the river Senegal to Benin and Old Calabar behind a coast dotted with English or European forts, penetrated by rivers, and lined with market towns where caravans brought people to sell. Some were criminals, some were prisoners of wars, others were simply stolen, tied with leather, tied to poles with "wicker bandages" around their necks, and loaded with other goods – hides, gum, ivory, beeswax, gold – or provisions to be traded at market for salt, cloth, iron pans, and glass beads. They wept as they gazed back to the East, and wailed when their fiber bonds were exchanged for cold, iron fetters. They were drawn from sedentary tribes and sub-Saharan nomads; they were young, old, male, female. Even well-born, educated,

Figure 9.2. Men dressing to enjoy a Saturday night in Norfolk, Virginia (drawing by Benjamin Henry Latrobe, courtesy of the Maryland Historical Society).

literate men were sometimes captured, shaved to hide their rank, and sold. Witness the psalms of David that one wrote out carefully on a sheet of rag paper in Arabic script.[12]

African people did not look alike or share the same language. Some were Muslim; others worshipped different gods. In Virginia, they came ashore often wearing nothing but "corals of different color around their neck and arms" (fig. 9.3). A few women may still have retained coral beads or small bells woven into their braided hair.[13]

Slave buyers preferred Africans to Madagascans because the latter ate meat and were "too choice in their diet." However, concluded one slave trader, "If they are young likely Negroes it's not a farthing matter where they come from." Yet slave buyers also consistently expressed preferences based on shade of color and other elements of physical appearance which they correlated with personality traits. Maryland buyers wanted people from the Windward and Gold Coasts. The cultures in this region were pluralistic; some were highly advanced. Suleiman, a Fulani sold on the Annapolis docks (fig. 1.10), came from a group described as tawny, tall, well-limbed, robust, and courageous, with loose wavy hair. Fulani women were "handsome" and wore their hair long, forming it into plump ringlets by applying oil. The Wolofs from Senegal and Gambia were short with tightly curled, or "wooly" hair sometimes worn in intricate braids (see fig. 9.4). They were noted for the blackness of their skin, the beauty of their features, and among women their talent at spinning. Africans could be short (54 inches; 4.5 ft), broad-shouldered and stout, middling (62 inches, 5.2 ft), or "tall and majestic" (above 6 ft). Mandingos, sought for breeding, had black skin with a hint of yellow, regular features, and great strength. The Whidah were "gentlemen-like," a people "abounding with good manners and ceremony to each other." The Ibos, not usually robust, were well-formed and of moderate height, a mild and engaging copper-colored people who would share "the last morsel of meat amongst each other thread by thread." Their enemies, the ferocious Quaws, were a blacker folk who filed their teeth so they looked like a "saw." This fact alone would have made a Quaw visually distinctive among any group of Annapolis slaves ca. 1730.[14]

More African-born people, however, were distinctive because of ritual scarification – bodily patterns that identified tribal affiliations (figs. 9.5 and 9.6). Englishmen described these as including parallel facial scars on the temples, diagonal or curving stripes, and "printing works" (i.e., scarification) upon women's backs and stomachs. Many women also wore distinctive jewelry that identified the wearer to others in the society or "with respect to particular deities and spirits," conferring power on and hence protection to the wearer. This range of varied physical appearance is important to recognize when imagining the town's people. It meant that when Africans from disparate tribes came together at a town "quarter" on lots adjoining the Circle or in the market place, the sight other Annapolitans saw was culturally diverse. It was also an exotic image and in "owning" it (by virtue of the number of slaves they held), the Calvert men marked ways they too stood apart. Here, a modern ethnographer's words point the way:[15]

Figure 9.3. Wearing coral necklaces and little else, slave women and children leave a ship in the Caribbean after the journey westward. (Illustration from John Stedman's *Narrative of a Five Years Expedition to Surinam 1772–1777*; illustration courtesy of the British Library.)

She sat on the edge of her seat, her hands folded in her lap, her feet tucked neatly behind the chair. She lowered her head, her rather big eyes raised, expressionless towards the door. She seemed remote inside her extreme blackness, as though she had withdrawn herself from the events that were taking place around her. Her hair, carefully plaited beneath the white tiko, the three tiny scars on each cheek, seemed marks of her differentness, her

Figure 9.4. Detail from a portrait of a Maryland infant, Gustavus Hesselius, Jr., which shows the young black woman who was his nurse (painting by John Hesselius courtesy of the Baltimore Museum of Art). The full portrait is shown to the side.

unapproachability. I suddenly saw her, not as an individual person, but as a "Mandinka woman" – a fragile, exotic presence.[16]

Archaeologists need to visualize the different West African peoples, to try to see them as others saw them, and then place them in the Annapolis landscape (see table 9.4; slave descriptions). It is a necessary analytical step in understanding the flow of people within a community, the corridors connecting one social space with another, and the activity areas, or social spaces, such routes encompassed and accessed. As Dell Upton points out, members of different cultures could inhabit the same space but utilize it differently. Thus in sifting for evidence of eighteenth-century activity in Annapolis, two interlocked views must be kept in mind: the model that structured the way the English passed through the community and the paths utilized by Indians and Africans. Different messages were encoded within the physical structure of the town for each subgroup. It is useful to remember that as slaves walked the highway westward to the farmlands, red dust swirling up around their feet, they passed the West Street gallows where a black woman, guilty of murder, was hung in Captain

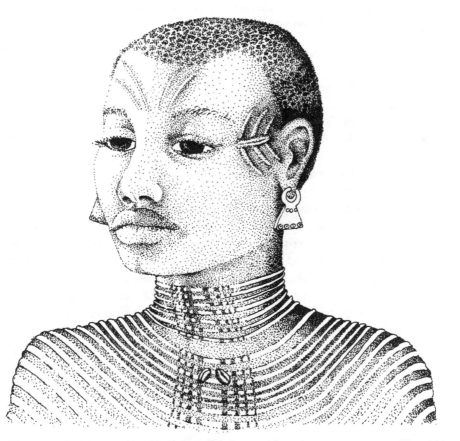

Figure 9.5. Facial marks identified tribal affiliations and gave clues to status among West African women in the past even as they do today. (Drawing by Julie Hunter-Abbazia derived from visual evidence in photographs of modern Fulani women shown in Angela Fisher's *Africa Adorned.*)

Table 9.4. *Examples of advertisements for runaways in the* Maryland Gazette, *1745–1750*

A tall, slim wench, full-eyed . . .
A mulatto man with short black hair, a little curled; he plays very well on the fiddle . . .
A negro marked between his eyebrows . . .
A tall slim fellow, a mulatto fellow, a deep dimple in his chin, a lively pleasant look, and is a mighty singer.
A Negro man, Harry, so fair as to be taken for a white man. He was wearing an old blue coat, a blue flowered stuff-damask waistcoat and leather breeches with white metal buttons, brown linen trousers, two checked shirts, one brown, and one fine white shirt. He stole from his mistress a blue coarse cloth coat and vest trimmed with blue mohair buttons, lined with red tammy stuff, the body of the vest lined with fine white dimity, a pair of fine white cloth breeches and rode away with a small, well turned gray horse.
Toby – a tawny complexion. He took with him a canoe, a new fiddle, a banjo, on both of which he at times plays, a Howel with an iron-maker with which he makes bowls, and an old hat which he usually wears cocked . . .
A negro man 26 [who] called himself Peter Harlitt. He ran away 12 months ago and changed his name to Hercules Kelly and John Dave. He speaks slow, is somewhat hopperars'd, and his beard is red; he was almost naked when he went away, having nothing but an old cotton waistcoat and half a spotted rug.
A mulatto, 25, named Dan, much the color of an Indian . . .

Calvert's time upon his "dead warrant" with the express intent "that after She is Dead she be hanged up in Chains on the said Gallows there to remain Until She be Rotten" as a reminder of Maryland justice which could be directed towards them. And people did remember; among the Maryland slave narratives collected in the 1930s is one that gives a very precise account of a law that specified punishment for slaves who carried out violent crimes that Governor Benedict Leonard Calvert had enacted two hundred years before.[17]

Africa was a country whose oral traditions were as strong as if not stronger than those in England, a land of rich cultural complexity, but it was also little understood. In their apprehension of its difference, upper-class English drew upon the precedents of shame and public spectacle to instill fear in the Africans brought to their shores. Chesapeake people described Africans as "outlandish" because of the foreign tongues in which they spoke, their delight in the hot summer heat, their measure of time by the moon, their unfamiliar appearance, and "country-marks." The fact that their "seasoning" in the region had a different pattern than that of the English was yet another contrast. The first steps in assimilation took place when Africans began to wear western clothing and hair styles (which owners could enforce) and learned to speak English (a capability partially controlled by the slave). Here, locale and the quality of black–white interaction entered the equation.[18]

The face of urban slavery
Most Chesapeake historians believe that the isolation of a rural quarter inhabited primarily by African-born slaves retarded cultural assimilation because it provided

few opportunities to learn English or the "sensible" demeanor the English preferred. At the same time, historians cite the bewildering variety of African dialects and the different configurations of African culture as factors working against the strengthening of African ties or cultural expressions at these quarters. Opportunities for assimilation were greater in the towns and cities where Africans had more chance to interact with a wider range of English people. Yet, Herbert Klein believed that because the urban African or African-American population in Chesapeake towns was never large (i.e., remaining below 38%) it was possible to single people out, isolate and control their non-working habits, and minimize the development of social cohesion among them. On the other hand, black town dwellers had higher proportions of house servants (waiting men) among their members and greater contact with black watermen. Since house servants and watermen stole away more often than others (running to places like the mixed African–Indian community on the western edge of Prince George's County in 1728–9), some awareness of the range of options surely existed among urban black Annapolitans.

African-American women today write how their mothers mentally recorded "all the facts about the people and community" in their home towns, teaching their daughters to know them as they did. Private behavior, public behavior, inter-related relationships, institutional histories, and kinship trees built a mentally held record of local lore or "speeches, ideas, and actions" recalled by a mother for her daughter

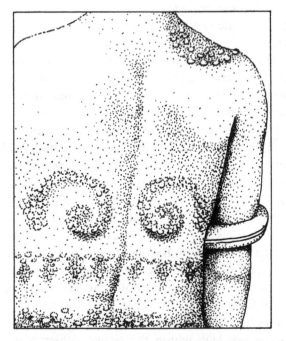

Figure 9.6. Decorative patterns created by scarification of a woman's back or abdomen were another means of social identification that women proudly displayed. In Jobson's words, "it appears they take extraordinary pride [in the printing upon their back], because they will turn themselves [so] wee should take notice of it, and be very well pleased, wee should touch or handle it, as a matter to bee esteemed or set by" (1623: 55). (Illustration by Julie Hunter-Abbazia.)

when she had need to know. This style of learning was undoubtedly passed down for generations. It takes little hindsight to believe that some version of this didactic form of oral history existed in Annapolis ca. 1730.[19]

Demographers estimate one-third of the population was black, but Lorena Walsh notes Annapolitans depended on indentured servants and skilled apprentices long after planters adopted slavery as their major labor base. She and others argue that in Chesapeake towns, large groups of Africans were a rarity. Ira Berlin adopts the same point of view: under cramped, urban conditions, "few masters had more than one or two slaves." He also writes of the strain put on the family because of higher mortality rates for children in cities and because masters "discouraged their slaves from establishing families." Berlin notes too where urban slaves lived: lofts, closets, makeshift alley shacks, back rooms to which we could add stables, kitchens, pantries, cellars, halls, and practically any unlocked tiny space that their masters thought would hold a floor mat, including their own bedrooms.[20]

Overall, there is no consensus about the quality of early urban African-American lifestyles and its perceived impact in a town with only 700 residents. Yet into this setting, one must fix the black people living at the Calvert lot, and consider what black Annapolitans did and did not do, in order to interpret even-handedly the artifacts recovered.

The workaday world

Numbers of women and older slaves increased in towns like Annapolis, because elite town homes greatly needed domestic servants, a need created by more intensive social interaction and higher levels of entertaining than characterized country plantations. A Governor's lifestyle further opened his house; many servants were required. Most household tasks were gender-specific and this overrode racial distinctions within Chesapeake homes. After all, it was women, not men, who scoured the floors, stirred kettles of dirty clothes, made the beds. So it is perhaps not unexpected that the Calverts had seven female slaves. What is surprising is that there were two children for every adult shown on Captain Calvert's inventory. The usual ratio was less than one, sometimes considerably so with Walsh reporting ratios of 0.62 and 0.83 for combined Londontown–Annapolis inventories and Kulikoff reporting 0.66 for Prince George's County (table 9.3).[21]

How to place all these people? We might begin with the black man who had the most status in the household. Jacob's value can be measured in two ways. First, when Rebecca Calvert died, she asked Onorio Razolini to see that Jacob had a good home if he had to be sold. Next, his value in pounds sterling was considerably higher (£35) than the average for a slave (£21) throughout the province and higher also than the black overseer at Cubit's Quarter. What Jacob did is not known; he probably oversaw implementation of household policy in one or more realms of domestic activity, thus placing him high within the servants' hierarchy. In their homeland, African slaves could also "occupy high positions within households" while still held in slavery.[22]

Spheres of activity in the Calvert home varied from those associated with the care of livestock on the outer reaches of the lot or possibly on lots separate from the house, to those which were private upstairs or "chamber" regions. Thus in one activity area there were ostlers and stable hands who groomed the horses, mended harnesses, cleaned out stalls, hitched the chaise to harness, and cared for sick or injured animals. The care of other nearby animals, such as the dairy cattle, the sheep, and the pigs, may have been women's or children's work. The Calvert gardens also required labor year-round; the orangery suggests horticulture was especially important, maybe more demanding than at other town houses (see Chapter 6). Some tasks required more skill than others, but most slaves had little opportunity to specialize. They would be asked to overlap tasks such as butchery and gardening, and were expected to be good hands both with a hoe and in the house. Old Dick considered himself a gardener, flax-beater, and a good judge of horseflesh.[23]

In other social spaces women held, fed, suckled, changed, bathed, told stories to, or rocked the master's children to sleep. Black women washed, ironed, mended, sewed, dusted, made candles and soaps, stocked the cellar and storerooms, swept and scrubbed floors and took out garbage (fig. 9.7). Some were healers; the Calvert family records reveal how their sons and daughters were born with the help of African-American midwives. The English ideal for slave behavior throughout much of the social space in colonial homes was for slaves to work quietly if not invisibly.[24]

Figure 9.7. A house servant scrubs the hearth. (Illustration by Julie Hunter-Abbazia based on a sketch of "Cook Tydoe" perhaps drawn by Benjamin Ogle ca. 1800; it is a bit of eighteenth-century graffiti that decorated a court document.)

Elsewhere, dishes had to be washed and copper kettles cleaned; often women worked together: "shucking corn, snapping beans, shelling peas, kneading dough, mending and heming, folding cloths," talking and assisting one another as they did so. Kitchen boys and girls worked under the baker, the cook, the butler; more children ran errands. Some were involved in presentation duties which put them on public display so that their demeanor was especially important as was their ability to anticipate the needs of their master and mistress (e.g., Benedict Leonard's boy, Osmyn). Slave women also spun, knitted, pickled fruit, went to market, gossiped, and became pregnant.[25]

Walsh believes Annapolis' more mixed population (old, young, male, female, African-born, creole) facilitated family formation. These two factors – more people and a greater degree of social interaction – were among reasons why there were more black children in the household. Yet, the birth rates for immigrant women are assumed to have been low, with first pregnancies coming when a woman reached her mid-twenties. In all cases, infant and child mortality were extremely high. Yet children outnumbered the adults on Captain Calvert's inventory; no one yet knows why.[26]

Thinking of the children raises other issues. It would be easy to use Menard's statement – "the ability to reproduce is a fundamental indicator of well-being" – to argue the well-being of the Calvert slaves. One basis for it is that undernourishment and overwork or strenuous labor result in low fertility rates, as men knew in 1708 when Oldmixon wrote, "if female salves were treated more gently," and their burden of labor lessened, childbirth among Caribbean slaves would increase. Today, Kulikoff uses the existence of children as an indicator of family formation, defining marriage as a "sexual union" or a "stable sexual union." Jean Lee points out that more than an intimate sexual relationship is involved. She is correct and any consideration draws one back to the meaning of family life within African cultures, its African-American equivalent, and the adverse conditions that families lived in under slavery.[27]

Whatever the reason or the social and cultural context surrounding it, the larger number of slaves and the fact that a significant proportion of them were young children further set apart daily life on the Calverts' town lot from everyday experience elsewhere in Annapolis. And, in a small town where everyone knew to some extent or another what was happening, the contrast this created cannot be over-emphasized. By surrounding themselves with an extensive domestic establishment, the Calvert family made a statement about their own importance to the community while the varied activities of their household servants and the ways in which these intersected with the rest of the community gave the message extra potency.[28]

Material expressions of black identity

Many African traditions would not normally leave marks in the archaeological record and others could as easily be left out of the historical record or set aside as whimsy. Take as one example working patterns that incorporated one-way dialogues, a patter of ongoing speech, with inanimate objects, that was as much a part of their social context as the area of a site where their remains were disposed. Atkins, for example, wrote that Ibos, "when employed at any kind of labour, continually talk to their tools, and that in an earnest manner, as if they were addressing a human being." Olaudo Equiano recorded that his people would prepare to eat first by washing, then "libation is made, by pouring out a small portion of the drink on the floor, and tossing a small quantity of food in a certain place, for the spirits of departed relations." These were part of a ritual discourse with the spirit world and a way to incorporate older generations, no longer living, into everyday life and strengthen kinship bonds. Thus some of the more significant elements of the discourse that joined African artifacts and people cannot ever be recovered. And what is present is less than one would like.[29] Here, it is considered in terms of a few representative examples.

Dwellings

The mean number of slaves per quarter in Anne Arundel County ranged from 5.4 to 9.8 between 1723 and 1743; inside the city the range was 5.6–6.2. Walsh shows no quarters holding more than fifteen residents. This raises provocative questions vis-à-vis housing for the Calvert slaves which the archaeology did not answer. Obviously there was not room in the main house for the sixty-plus people (family, servants, slaves) to work, eat, and sleep. We found nothing that could be classified as a slave quarter in the excavation, but work was concentrated around the main house and not on its periphery – much of which no longer fell within the present property bounds. An adjacent lot purchased in 1728 held at least one small dwelling.[30]

In the early 1800s, an old woman recorded her memories of Annapolis and included "a large range of buildings . . . called 'Calvert's row'." By inference, a fire reported in a 1762 *Maryland Gazette* at Governor Calvert's old, high wooden house also suggests more buildings since the present structure is and was brick from 1730 onward. Lithographs of eighteenth-century African port towns show a harmonious combination of traditional, rectangular European houses and circular African dwellings merged together, side by side. This would leave a highly distinctive imprint in the ground and nothing resembling it has been reported in the Chesapeake. Instead, the houses where slaves lived as known through excavation resemble small English houses, a fact understandable given that the data base is largely drawn from areas immediately surrounding large plantation homes, where control by the master would be most strongly felt, and where visual symmetry with the main house was part of landscape design.[31]

Smaller finds

If slave quarters have no inherent African tag, what about other artifacts? Douglas Armstrong's work in Jamaica further addresses this question. He located hearth stones corresponding to historical descriptions of ones West Africans used to cook food (see chapter 10 and fig. 16.7). Armstrong also found evidence of crudely constructed cooking sheds built from wattle and daub walls with thatched roofs, and signs of related, intensely used yards or activity areas. He found Afro-Jamaican earthenwares and evidence of re-used materials including delftware sherds formed into round gaming pieces. He wrote of the analytical problems facing archaeologists who recover only a "small proportion of surviving artifacts that can be directly attributed to a specific, or even a generalized, African ethnic identity." Slave sites appear much like Anglo-American sites, he concluded, because the predominant artifacts are English-made.[32]

There are at least two other types of African artifacts found on New World sites – clay tobacco pipes and glass beads – also recovered on West African sites. Clay tobacco pipes of various sorts are ubiquitous here; the remnants – broken pipe stems and fragments from the tobacco bowl – include ones of Indian manufacture, ones that came from England (the largest percentage), and others made of a red clay decorated in a series of lines and dots reminiscent of the technique Jobson described for ritual scarification. Matthew Emerson has laboriously studied these terra cotta pipes, and concluded that some exhibit a series of African design motifs.[33]

The evidence that Africans smoked pipes is unequivocal. Francis Moore identified the clay Gambians used as red in 1730, but an older description gives more insight on the role of tobacco pipes in African society:

> Only one principall thing they cannot misse, and that is their Tobacco pipes, whereof there is few or none of them, be they men or women doth walke or go without. They do make onely the bowle of earth, with a neck of the same, about two inches long, very neatly, and artificially colouring or glazing the earth, very hansomly, all the bowles being very great, and for the most part will hold halfe an ounce of Tabacco; they put into the necke a long kane, many times a yard of length, and in that manner draw their smoake, whereof they are great takers, and cannot of all other things live without it.

Thus Richard Jobson, writing in 1632, and Matthew Emerson, writing in 1988, provided an answer to a puzzle: the presence at the site of small numbers of broken pipe stems from red earthenware pipes, some glazed, others not. I had assumed they were anomalous derivatives of the millions that English merchants shipped abroad. The evidence of importation was clear, in the archaeological record and in the documentary record. Some merchant planters and innkeepers kept as many as twelve dozen gross on hand. Yet there were so few overall near the Calvert home that I had gradually concluded the Calvert men rarely smoked tobacco or, if they did, used the great silver pipes of their great-grandfather's time – pipes one would not discard as the smoke clogged the bore hole, but would carefully clean instead. Red earthenware pipes also show up here and there on Caribbean sites that are demonstrably linked with the culture of slavery. But the more provocative artifacts were small glass beads.[34]

Beads

Anderson concluded that the "presence of glass beads [at Drax Hall] suggests the continuance of African practices of body adornment" among Jamaican slaves. This is an oversimplification of a rich, complex area of cultural expression which survived, though not without change, in the New World. It is also one that gives insight on women's lives and helps us see black women as individuals despite the way in which much of their documented history masks both individual personality and the solidarity necessary for survival. It is also an unfamiliar topic for historical archaeologists on the North American continent where bead studies are usually linked to research on Native Americans.[35]

The jewelry recovered from the Calvert site includes a fine gold stickpin that was probably never worn by a slave, together with a wide variety of glass beads as well as some of semi-precious stones and coral (fig. 9.8). These are not beads included in burial goods where one would find the remains of whole necklaces or entire waist strands and so their numbers are not as large as those recovered in graveyards. The Calvert beads were individual pieces sporadically lost which fell between the floorboards inside a single room of the main house. Their modest presence (approximately one hundred were recovered) – while higher than that recovered at most slave quarters – denotes an even larger quantity in "real life." Further, their presence inside the main house indicates that the jewelry was not something black women had to hide or could wear only when slaves gathered. It seems to suggest instead that various forms of African-based body adornment were part of the everyday black experience in eighteenth-century Maryland. How to sort out the significance of this relatively unknown dimension of ethnic interaction?[36]

It is clear that in West Africa jewelry was a significant mark of cultural and social identity and that traditional patterns of body adornment had great time depth. Archaeologists find glass beads in contexts that date before the trans-Atlantic slave

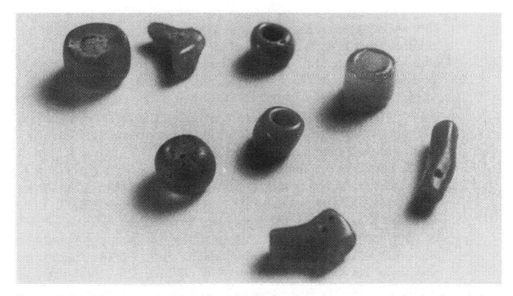

Figure 9.8. Small fragments of coral and ivory, beads of semi-precious stone, and glass beads made in the Far East and in Europe were once strung as jewelry to be worn by African women; slave women in the Americas continued the tradition. (Photograph by Marion E. Warren.)

trade began. At the Diakhité sand pit, east of modern Dakar, workmen have found thousands of beads in or near clay pots which lie beside fragile skeletal remains. Many of these date to the eighteenth and nineteenth centuries, and are contemporaneous with slave sites in the New World. In fact, some of the beads from Diakhité are remarkably like those recovered in Annapolis.[37]

This is not surprising. In 1623, Richard Jobson wrote about a transaction he made with a Fulbie (i.e., Fulani) woman who traded him her dairy products for beads, knives, and other trifles. Descriptions of women's jewelry can be seen in most travellers' accounts. Matthews, for example, wrote in 1788 that African women "are also very fond of ornaments, such as beads formed into necklaces, bracelets, &c., silver rings, lockets and chains, manillas (which are hoops of silver made flat or round to wear on the wrists), strings of coral and use a variety of paints." In 1705, Bosman specified strings of a white coral, "Conta de Terra" and gave the native name for a blue stone, "Agrie" or "Accori." Today, the Yoruba know the latter as "aggrey," an ancient blue bead made of powdered glass that retains its symbolic value in part because of its age.[38]

It is easy to trace the use of body adornment to the Caribbean where Mrs. Carmichael described the dress of women as including handkerchiefs, turbans, gold earrings, rings, coral necklaces, gold chains, lockets, and other ornaments. She specified that each woman has "one really good necklace, but they also often wear along with it, half a dozen or so necklaces of combined glass beads, light blue, yellow, white, and purple. Every negro has a garnet necklace . . . little girls are dressed much as their mothers are." There are, in addition to the beads – primarily red, blue, or white – recovered by Armstrong, other archaeological examples from the Caribbean which supplement the written evidence.[39]

The more provocative examples were associated with the Barbados graves of men. First there was a simple necklace worn by a slave with one carnelian stone strung among varied glass beads. A second, elderly man was also buried wearing an elaborate necklace with a single carnelian stone that showed its African derivation in the mix of materials – cowrie shells, fish vertebrae, canine teeth, and beads. His copper and brass bracelets and his finger rings were also emblematic of West Africa. Because the jewelry was found in the graves of men, archaeologists associated it with obeah men or shamans, individuals who had "great influence and prestige in plantation slave communities."[40]

The jewelry is not limited to West Indies sites but appears at other places associated with Africans and African-Americans. William Adams found ten blue, yellow, red, and black beads at a Georgia slave cabin. Marvin Smith analyzed a small collection of twenty-five (which includes four red glass beads – cornaline d'Aleppo – imitative of chalcedony (i.e., carnelian) from Yauhan and Curriboo plantations along the Cooper River in South Carolina. Now, one of the largest samples of glass beads found in Maryland has been recovered in Annapolis at a site where many of the slaves were women or young girls. What do they mean?[41]

Like many women, West African women delighted in and still enjoy dressing finely. English travellers specified the pride in clothing: "the women's dress is richer than the men's. Ladies plat their hair very artfully, and place their fetiches, coral and ivory, with a judicious air and go much finer than the men." Black women continued to dress well whenever they could in the New World too. In the 1790s, John Davis observed, "the girls never failed to put on their garments of gladness, their bracelets, chains, rings, and ear-rings, and deck themselves bravely" before setting forth on Sundays to visit their neighbors. But the issue is not one simply of dressing for joy, but of using a variety of means to tell the world about cultural identity while simultaneously gaining other benefits.[42]

Handler and Lange believe that glass beads were not regularly obtained and so became highly valued items in the slave populations of the Caribbean. They attach particular significance to carnelian beads, imported from India, and important in Africa for generations. Others stress the importance of blue beads. But what most historical archaeologists do not talk about is the magic of beads. Prehistorians such as George Hammel have written of their metaphorical roles in Native American cultures: crystal (i.e., glass) "as light, bright, and white things . . . are reflective substances, literally and figuratively, and substances in which native ideological and aesthetic interests are one." Thus their trade became "a trade in metaphors"; one culture's "truck" – its baubles, bangles, and beads – were another's treasure. The concept can be transferred to considerations of African trade at that time as well. While many of the beads and bangles African women wore were British trade goods (thus "truck"), their expressive roles in the cultures remained African; thus European beads became symbolic extensions of African human bodies and of African gods.[43]

Like other forms of body decoration so richly illustrated in *Africa Adorned*, jewelry conveyed information, was emblematic of cultural identity in a heterocultural society, and provided protection to its wearer. Nicholas David and his co-workers observe that variations in the style of African bracelets distinguish parents of boy twins from parents of girl twins from parents of single-birthed children. Jewelry (as with body scarification) helped separate one sex from another, older from younger, marked rites of passage, and told of special talents in life and death. Body adornment told of a person's social identity; it said to others, "you are my relative and I am yours," or spoke of social taboos.[44]

It accomplished this feat through its imagery, variations in width, length, decorative detail, color, and material components. Jewelry was made from valuable metals such as gold and silver or from natural objects symbolic of wealth (cowrie shells), from natural objects valued in their own right, and from others symbolically associated with gods and spirits. The color blue could be identified with a god by one tribe because it possessed the color of the sky where he lived or, among another, green glass with the color of vegetation after rainfall. Ivory might be given magical properties while lions' teeth could symbolize strength. The possibilities for substitution were endless and whereas bells and shell were once the common items women wove into hair designs, as time progressed, they used coins and glass buttons with equivalent creativity (fig. 9.9).[45]

Beads were not routinely worn by European women until the mid-nineteenth century. Yet they were prevalent at the Calvert site and included, in addition to a single, large carnelian bead, jade, coral, turquoise, lapis (?), and white quartz. Glass beads of varied colors – red, blue, orange, green, yellow, white – were found in large sizes suitable for jewelry and in smaller versions, as seed beads to sew upon cloth. West Africans today still use tiny seed beads to create intricate designs, sometimes on ritual masks, sometimes on common cloth. If the Calverts' slaves were allowed to use traditional African items of adornment, such as beaded necklaces, bracelets, and anklets, it raises the question as to whether they were also allowed other things (African cloth perhaps or hair styles) that spoke to their African heritage. That some creole children continued to carry African names is evidence that their families sought to maintain connective links with their homeland. And if African men were given responsibilities beyond the norm (i.e., as overseers) by the Calverts, were women too allowed to participate in some of their traditional activities such as marketing goods, raising poultry, growing foods important in an African cuisine, and cooking them using African methods of food preparation?[46]

One of the arguments in this book is that a certain sense of mystery surrounds many expressions of power and that it is deepened when it also conveys an image of mastery over exotic elements, natural and cultural, existing in the everyday world. The visual imagery of numbers of African slaves in a town setting, living, reproducing, possibly even prospering (to the extent that someone considered a chattel ever can), effectively set the Calvert household apart from others. Was this deliberate? Was it a by-product of other cultural patterns based on a different, perhaps pragmatic, rationale? No one will ever know.

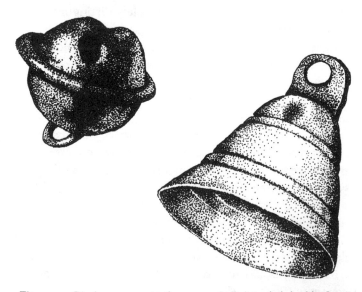

Figure 9.9. Black women sometimes wove bells into their braids. Small bells were also found at the Calvert site in association with glass beads. (Illustration drawn by Julie Hunter-Abbazia.)

What is seen instead is the fragility and disruptive elements that so easily and capriciously affected servants and slaves. When the Calverts died, the standards of behavior shifted because no one survived who had the power, wealth, and rank to maintain life in the family home as it was lived between 1727 and 1734. To give estate administrators funds to sustain her orphaned daughters, Rebecca Calvert authorized the sale of all slaves except "old George." Because of his age, his inventory value (£2) was less than an infant's. Because he was old, he was undoubtedly held in esteem by the other black household members, for Africans revered age, feeling it brought wisdom. Death took from the African and African-American people who lived on the Calvert land the few privileges they possessed when the household was at its peak. And in the next few years six of their own died too: Mingo, Lucy, Doll, Jemy, Shep, and Beck. Perhaps some of the others were sold to households who treated slaves well, but the generalized patterns that appear in historical studies suggest this was unlikely. One would like to know even as one would like to know more about their lives and to have the detail that persists in the records with respect to Euroamericans.[47]

Leach wrote that to understand the different nuances of kinship among the Kachin he had to understand that kin terms and non-kin terms for both were "intricately tangled up." This chapter has tried to show that to understand the Calvert family, one must understand its household from the highest to the lowest individual, from old to young, English to African, and to get a sense of how it worked internally, and how it intersected with the broader society. This, in turn, provides a background which gives the material remains added meaning. The approach is followed further with a discussion of West African food in Chapter 10 because it too provides a way to understand and amplify what the faunal remains reveal of life on the Calvert site.[48]

West African women, foods, and cultural values

> Still, if I could balance water on my head I can juggle worlds on my shoulder.
>
> Olive Senior, *Ancestral Poem*

The passage of ideas

Of the African or "country-born" slaves at the Calverts' town house, seven were women whose tasks included cooking. While the cooks surely oriented the Calvert family food to English or Continental tastes, the meals the black women prepared for themselves and their families as readily could have used techniques and ingredients important in West African cookery. An archaeologist who ignores this possibility can easily misread the archaeological record and diminish what she learns about the different cultural dimensions of Annapolis life. Raising it, however, opens Pandora's box because distinguishing African elements from English elements within refuse deposits that merge the materials used by the two ethnic groups is complex and tricky. Here, the consideration of West African food traditions brings front and center the question of carryovers: the beliefs, ideas, and material objects African peoples brought with them.[1]

There is a rapidly growing body of literature on archaeological assemblages from slave quarters in the far south and in the Caribbean, yet very little exists about those from the early Chesapeake. Archaeologists have not had an opportunity to excavate sites where blacks lived in the years when African-born people formed the dominant part of the slave population. There is a modest start on sites where African-Americans lived at mid-century that William Kelso began with excavation at Kingsmill. Kelso's later work at Monticello also stresses a range of late eighteenth- and early nineteenth-century features associated with African-Americans; Diane Crader's faunal analysis of these indicates variations that derive from dietary differences among master, house slaves, and field hands, with an expectable presence of tenderer, meatier animal parts near the mansion, and bones ground up (i.e., shattered or highly fragmented) as for stews near an outlying storehouse. But more critically, the extent to which decisions were made with respect to food by the slaves themselves is not visible yet in the Monticello data.[2]

Accepting that black women actively tried to maintain elements of their own heritage, it becomes necessary to consider to what extent the one area of daily life where slaves *were* allowed an opportunity to be autonomous (i.e., to do what they decided to do) reveals evidence of continuing West African traditions.

But on a regional basis, comparative archaeological data sets are not very helpful. I can point to one or two assemblages from southern Maryland and say that I think they exhibit evidence of an African presence but, in reality, I think so because of what I know of my own site. This is not a satisfactory way to proceed. When sources run dry, in the words of James Axtell, ethnohistorians who study Native American groups turn two ways. Because an essential element of culture is the preservation of cultural values even in the midst of change, they look at descendant cultures of earlier groups. They also consider what is happening with related cultures in the same general area, looking at groups whom they could reasonably expect to share cultural traits. Chapters 11 and 12 adopt the first strategy and apply knowledge of black foodways to the archaeological record at the Calvert site.[3]

This chapter looks at related cultures, but jumps traditional archaeological times and space lines to do so. The idea is simply that wherever West African women were taken as slaves, they brought similar sets of internalized ideas with them. This is based on the premise that if two women from a village were enslaved, say a generation apart, and one went to Charleston while the other went to Annapolis, their ideas about what constituted proper food still would be similar because as children they were enculturated to the way women prepared food in their home village. We can learn about these core values by studying the cultural precedents recorded in West Africa where the Ibo preferred yams while in villages along the Gold or Windward Coasts, rice and corn were held in high esteem. But we can also learn what these women viewed as the essence of African cooking in their villages by looking at its expression in the West Indies, in the Carolinas, and even in Brazil. The idea is to gain knowledge of what women might have done and the food configurations they might reasonably have used as a model for creating a creolized cuisine in early Annapolis.[4]

West African food traditions in old texts
Old documents often vividly tell of some things people thought and did. Many – court records, ledgers, probate inventories, legislative proceedings, wills, tax lists – are what Daniel McCall calls "witnesses in spite of themselves." Glassie calls them "inadvertent bits of information" because they were never meant to be used to reconstruct culture history. The reasons why people wrote them can be assessed, however, and their evidence usefully combined with that in the archaeological record. Another set of sources, ones that historians call "narrative sources," were written by people "who consciously intended to inform [or misinform] their readers." Travelers' accounts fall within this set. However, anthropologists who work with living informants have considered the problem of intentionality and worked out ways of resolving its bias within written texts.[5]

The historical record for the seventeenth and eighteenth centuries, in particular "narrative sources," has a lot to say about the food domain of West African culture from shared traits that form a basic core to individual variations within different

Table 10.1. *An excerpt from John Leo's description (ca. 1526)*

This countrie [Benin] aboundeth with long pepper called by the Portugals Pimienta dal rabo, which is as much to say, as pepper with a tayle. This tailed or long pepper so far excelleth the pepper of the East Indies that an ounce thereof is of more force than half a pound of that other . . . there hath bin great quantitie secretly conveyed from thence by the Portugals: as likewise the English and French nations, and of late yeeres the Hollanders . . .

Lower to the south the province of Meleghete, a place very famous and well knowne, in regard of a little red graine which there groweth, being in shape somewhat like to the Millet of Italy, but of a most vehement and firy taste: and these little graines are by the apothecaries called Grana Paradisi.

. . . Ghinea is so named, according to the chiefe citie thereof called Genni, being situate upon the river of Sanega. The people of this countrie towards the sea-coast live upon fish; and they of the inland sustain themselves with Lizards and such like creatures; & in some places more temperate their food consisteth of herbes and milk.

groups. Visual images also survive in art. While archaeological evidence indicates freshwater fish, rice, and beef were eaten in West African cities (cf. Jenne-jenno) from AD 100 to 1200, the first Arabic descriptions for sub-Saharan Africa (two centuries before the Portuguese entered the slave trade) mention goats, fish, and millet. Among the first English accounts is one dated 1623 from Richard Jobson's probe of the Gambia River. The careful environmental observations that explorers inevitably made in writing of the New World from ca. 1500 onward are paralleled in the accounts of travelers to Gambia, Senegal, Calabar, Benin, and Timbuktu. There is redundancy because authors often plagiarized older accounts, but some repetition comes from continuity in time and space of food and drink. Men almost always described the beverages they drank, sometimes with exquisite detail on brewing, contrasting the results with familiar European drinks. Thus we know from Francis Moore that in Gambia, "the liquor is palm wine, ciboa wine, honey-wine (not unlike mead), brandy, and rum," while the Caribbean variants were more experimental: "mobbie, brew'd with potatoes, water, and sugar; kowwow of molasses, water, and ginger; perino of cassavy root; plantain drink; kill-devil; and pine drink."[6]

According to Moore, who worked for the Royal African Company, West African women worked with a modest set of food implements: "the moveables of the greatest among them amounting to only a few earthen pots, some wooden utensils, and gourds or calabashes; from these last . . . they are abundantly stocked with good clean vessels for most household uses, being of different sizes, from half a pint to several gallons." The use of these was soon adopted in New World towns and cities (figs. 10.1 and 10.2).[7]

The base of the West African diet was vegetarian – rice, spices, vegetables – with fish, fowl, or the flesh of bullocks, goats, and sheep as additive elements. Meat was given religious symbolism by its use in food offerings to gods and dead ancestors. Writers from the late 1600s like Bosman indicate goat was preferred to sheep; it still holds a niche in contemporary feasts: "And so three goats were slaughtered and a

Table 10.2. *Excerpts from Richard Jobson and Gustavus Hesselius (1714)*

Now because I speak of gourdes, which are growing things, it is fit I tell you, they doe grow, and resemble just that wee call our Pumpion, and in that manner are placed, and carried upon their walles and houses, being of all manner of different sorts; from no bigger than an egge, to those that will hold a bushell . . . [Jobson writing of Senegal in 1623]

    There is also a strange fruit called a Callibis [calabash] which grows like pumpkin in tall vines, one cannot eat them, but they are good to make different vessels of, such as scoops, bowls, etc. [Hesselius describing Philadelphia in 1714 to relatives in Sweden]

number of fowls. It was like a wedding feast. There was foo-foo and yam pottage, egusi soup and bitter-leaf soup and pots and pots of palm-wine."[8]

By the late eighteenth century, political leaders ordered food for special occasions – cordial meals where West Africans negotiated with Europeans – prepared with European preferences in mind: "The king has always a succession of cooks trained up in the European sorts . . . he is able to treat his visitors with victuals dressed after their own country manner . . . in plates, and dishes of pewter and earthenware." But this was courtly cuisine with dining rituals akin to the hospitality and fine foods dispensed by the Calverts in their roles as Maryland leaders.[9]

Among ordinary folk in some places (cf., the pastoral Fulani), women made butter; primarily palm oil was its fat substitute, adding a strong, distinctive tone to the semi-dry, nutritionally rich potage made from small millet seeds (Guinea "corn") or rice. The potage was scooped from a calabash or from earthen pots that women made, fired in the stumps of burning trees, possibly simultaneously with wood and field fires set to catch "Ginny hens." People "boiling up their grain, roll it up into balls," Jobson wrote, "and so eat it warm, and even to us is it a very good and able sustenance." Crow observed folk using their hands "even to sup up their soup with an agility and ladle-like convenience." This knack was afterwards observed in the Antilles among Creole ladies: "They picked up their food with such lazy but skilful grace," said a Frenchman, "that not a drop fell onto their pale dresses."[10]

Portuguese ships (who carried free blacks as crew) introduced new elements into West African cuisine – maize, cassava, peanuts, tomatoes, sweet potatoes, hot chili peppers, the French bean, and Muscovy ducks – and new utensils – European iron cooking pots. Thus people recorded among their oral traditions that when "white men arrived in ships with wings which shone in the sun like knives; they brought maize and cassava and groundnuts and tobacco." Simultaneously Portuguese ships carried African foods to the New World – okra, coriander, dasheen, sesame, black-eyed peas, pigeon peas, white yams, kola nuts, varieties of rice and millet, tamarind and watermelon, Guinea fowl, African sheep, calabash gourds and fluted pumpkins, and the West African oil palm. How did the foods arrive? Stories of seeds carried abroad hidden in black ears are legends, part of an African-American mythology; the reality is more complex.[11]

Birds, beautiful and pleasing – peacocks and Guinea hens – were "brought into

England [by 1623], and given as presents to those of note, and worthy persons who preserve and keep them." Other animals were taken in crates to be eaten at sea and with good fortune reached shore alive. However, the situation with many plants was different. Men transported these as seeds, tubers, or live specimens potted in

Figure 10.1. Bitter gourds known as calabash plants grew on vines along fences or building walls and sprawled across the ground. They were used for storage and as eating or drinking utensils. Jobson (1623: 132) wrote that they were "carried upon their walles and houses, being of all manner of different sorts; from no bigger than an egge, to those that will hold a bushel." (Illustration by Julie Hunter-Abbazia.)

wooden crates. Sometimes greens were grown aboard ship to add a touch of class to the captain's meals; when this was the case, guards stood by to protect them from rats and hungry men. At other times, plants were brought as rarities – curious things, gifts that delighted the recipient and set his collection apart, increasing his own social esteem. And at still others, edible plants were cargo destined to provide the root stock for agricultural experimentation (for example, rice and sesame, sorghum and millet).[12]

Tracing the exchange pathway reveals that some foods were carried from South America to Africa and then men took them back across the sea to Caribbean or North American ports. Bosman, who knew West Africa in the late seventeenth century, believed that Muscovy ducks came from South America (and this agrees with what ornithologists say today) while Hans Sloane recorded their presence in the West Indies in 1687–9, noting that they had come on ships from Africa. But actual origins are not as important as how people incorporated new materials into old cultural patterns. Ducks slipped right into African food traditions to sit side by side

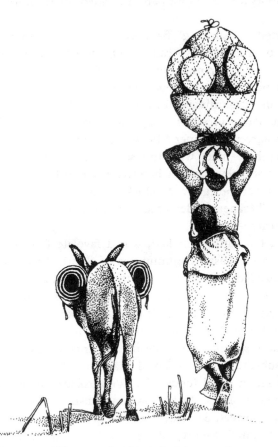

Figure 10.2. Often carved and inscribed, because they were organic, the gourds rarely survived in the archaeological record. However, their use as storage vessels continues today among West African peoples where ethnographers have photographed them and depicted the designs with which they are carved. (Illustration by Julie Hunter-Abbazia based on information in Angela Fisher's *Africa Adorned*.)

with Guinea hens; very little accommodation was required for their assimilation. So, too, one might say, African ways of handling cattle slipped right into New World husbandry practices.[13]

Core ingredients in West African cuisine

The cuisine blended different tastes and textures. Sweetness was provided by honey. Families strung reed and sedge-grass baskets along the "outbows" of trees near their homes to hang like giant fruits. Honey was harvested from the bees that hived there. African families, especially the women, also bought and sold foodstuffs. In cities like Jenne-jenno, copper and salt from the Sahara were traded for rice, fruit, millet, honey, nuts, spices, dried fish, fish oil, cotton, and cotton cloth. Men who lived inland traded slaves for salt at coastal locations while women in country villages purchased dried fish from traders whose routes led inland from the sea. Fish, in fact, held central importance in the cuisine and were used as design motifs on Asante weights, were incorporated into divine manifestations of the god Olokun, at Benin, were carved on doors for decoration, and provided the form for small boxes (fig. 10.3).[14]

Dried fish (usually listed as "stinking" fish) was regularly mentioned by Europeans; some equated its odor and the African taste for it with their own gourmets' preference for "high" game. Bosman noted that boiled fresh mullet or dried fish was combined with yams or potatoes and a few boiled herbs in various areas of the country. In others, "for an extraordinary dish, they take fish, a handful of corn, as much dough, and some Palm-oil which they boil together; and this they call Mallaget." It is not a "disagreeable dinner," he wrote, adding later, "a lover of fish, as I reckon myself, may here meet with full satisfaction." The poor, Bosman concluded, "subsist in a miserable manner when there is no fish." Shellfish too were important foodstuffs wherever they grew. Mollusks eventually were over-harvested and, like oysters in the Chesapeake, decreased in size because people ate them before they reached maturity.[15]

Fish, whether dried in the sun or smoked, was a favorite food in Gambia. It maintained its importance in coastal communities of South America and in the Caribbean where it had excellent preservation in the heat and, unlike meats which lasted only a short time even with preservation, was still edible months later. In 1707, Sir Hans Sloane wrote that blacks "covert [salt mackerel] extremely in pepper pots and oglios [stews]." Mrs. Carmichael believed they were a "favorite food." Jessica Harris, a food historian, adds shrimp as another integral dried ingredient, suggesting that salt pork became a substitute in New World adaptation.[16]

In addition to a core set of dried foodstuffs, West African markets also were usually well stocked with goats, hogs, ducks, fowls, and fish. At Annamaboo, there were also "plenty Crabs, Lobsters, &c. [so] that you need not ever want for fresh provisions." In fact, wrote Francis Moore, "there is scarce anything they do not eat: large snakes, guanas, monkeys, pelicans, bald-eagles, alligators, and sea-horses [hippopotamus] are excellent food." Turtle weighing a hundred pounds, another man wrote, "has been purchased for a single flask of brandy." Bosman's account also mentions dog-flesh, but he clearly specified that people "like cats and find them useful; they do not eat them." The cuisine, in other words, drew upon a large number of food resources and many came from wild sources in contrast to an English dependence on domestic animals. It also had its food taboos. Markets in Zaire today still sell a wide variety of foodstuffs including wild resources: crocodile, snapping turtle, river crayfish, caterpillars, and palm grubs.[17]

The list of identified animals from the free black community at Fort Mose in Florida and from coastal Georgia slave sites, reported by William Adams and Elizabeth Reitz – deer, shrews, rabbits, squirrels, bobcats, black bears, opossums, raccoons, turtles, terrapins, alligators, lizards, snakes, toads, frogs, salamanders together with birds such as pelicans, egrets, cormorants, and many species of fish – implies a similar wide-ranging use of animals for food. Elizabeth Reitz was one of the first workers in the southeast to point this out; she observes too that it is also an element, more narrowly drawn, within the Calvert faunal remains, particularly the ca. 1770 deposits.[18]

European travelers consistently wrote that Guinea fowl, turkeys, and a variety of birds were the basic source of the meat in West African cuisine. The most common were cocks and hens raised in small areas beside domestic buildings, and there were all sorts of ingenious methods of catching them. This traditional emphasis was carried over. Its continuation is evident in planters' views of African-American Virginians as "chicken merchants." One could also cite the accompanying economic devaluation of the poultry trade which prompted a late eighteenth-century Virginian to ask, "Pray why is a fowl more disgraceful in the sale of it at market, than a pig, lamb, a mutton, a veal, a cow or an ox?" The answer, of course, is that it was first women, white, who sold domestic fowls in the Chesapeake, and that later the source

Figure 10.3. Ashante men cast gold weights in various fish forms that mimicked the fish they caught and ate. (Drawing by Julie Hunter-Abbazia based on styles of Ashante weights seen in Western museums.)

became African-Americans. The original evaluation, based on gender distinctions, was readily transferred to one based on race.[19]

West Africans too, like the English, maintained small kitchen gardens close to their homes. Perhaps because these were also cultivated by women, they are only briefly discussed by male travelers. However, the custom continued in the New World. Some planters viewed these gardens as a means of keeping slaves from Sunday mischief. Mrs. Carmichael reviewed what women grew on Jamaica plots: sweet cassado, tomato, lima beans, calialou, tanias, capsicum, gub-a-gub (black-eyed peas), weedy-weedy, pigeon peas, grenadillos, watermelon vine, creole beans for soup, christophone, and cucumber; English peas, carrots, turnips, pumpkins, and cabbages for market. Another clue that it was in part a women's activity is an early nineteenth-century law on Montserrat that gave slave women "who had borne five or more live children" relief from most field work to cultivate their garden plots. Frederick Douglass' Maryland grandmother was known as wise in her knowledge of planting, sent for by many to place her hands upon their plants, settling them softly in the hills or drills because she was "born to good luck." As one modern scholar has written, it was not luck she exhibited but skills taught her by older women: how to protect sweet potatoes from the winter frost by storing them in the floor near the cabin hearth, placing the seedlings the right depth in the soil, recognizing accurately the signs of spring, setting aside bruised plants. Then there is a contemporary report on gardens in Gambia: "Every women in the village had a garden," noted Mark Hudson, giving the spatial detail archaeologists admire: "Those who did not have a place in the Kurung Kafo garden cultivated tiny plots, squeezed into the corners of their compounds, behind the washing areas and the rubbish heaps, or between the walls of the houses and the walls of the streets – always tightly fenced with millet stalks or baroum-barow." The garden crops might have been less varied in the past, holding a role minor to that of the field crops, yet in their form and content they still denoted cooperation among women. Feminist black historians stress this is why women, not men, created the field chants – the hum, the call and response – that continue in modern music with African-American roots.[20]

The field crops, which women (and also men) tended with primitive short-handled hoes, distant cousins of the ones they would use in Maryland, included rice, sorghum, and millet. Making the furrows for sowing seed was, in Jobson's belief, "painful labor," but since people worked in groups, he also saw it as evidence that "many hands make light worke." The process of grinding the grains and turning them to meal was also tedious and time-consuming. Like the Chesapeake white women who had little time left for fancy cookery after helping their husbands in the fields, West African women prepared food simply. Like the English food, it carried symbolic import. A man drew identity and meaning, still visible in African folk beliefs, from the foods he grew: "yams stood for manliness, and he who could feed his family on yams from one harvest to another was a very great man indeed." Food was also useful in expressing territorial distinctions. Thus one eighteenth-century tribe ate shark "because it was an idol at New Calabar" (an icon of the people), and in eating it, they were consuming their enemy. People at New Calabar retaliated by "eating iguana" (the "idol" of their foe), a meat source that to the English taste was "good and delicate, like a chicken." This "associative rule" in the cultural grammar that dictated food choice in tribal cuisine was familiar to the English who disparaged the Dutch for being "butter-boxes" and the French for eating snails and frogs.[21]

How West African women cooked

In the late eighteenth century, Joseph Corry wrote of eating "a country mess of rice, boiled with fowls" among the Mandingos and also observed that West African food in general consisted of "rice or millet seasoned with palm-oil, butter, or the juices of the cocoa-nut tree mixed with herbs of various kinds. They frequently regale them-selves with other dishes, kous-kous [made with millet], and country mess, to which they sometimes add fowls, fish, and flesh, heightened in the flavor by a variety of savory applications." The latter came to include ground-nut sauces and others based on hot peppers as their uses became known. Corry's description is similar to ones written almost two hundred years earlier. In between, in 1738, Francis Moore noted that the women used Guinea corn, or millet "beaten in a wooden mortar, and sifted through a fine basket till it is about as fine as coarse flower." He watched Gambian women place it "into an earthen pot filled with holes like a cullender which is luted to the top of an earthen pot in which is boiling water and sometimes broth in it, the stain of which colors and hardens the flower." Finally, he observed, "when it is done, they mix these together and eat it with their hands."[22]

"The Negro women," Francis Moore wrote another time, "dressed my victuals in earthenware, sweet and clean." The use of earthenware pots rather than iron prevented some African vegetables, like okra, from turning black. This might be one reason West African women turned to making their own pottery in the New World or sometimes substituted Indian vessels. In their homeland, African women continued to simmer soup in earthen pots; Corry wrote in 1806 of eating an especially tasty okra version made by a Mandingo woman. Leland Ferguson quotes a Southerner's view (ca. 1840): "It was a confident faith among the old ladies, that okra soup was always inferior if cooked in any but an [earthenware] Indian pot." Harris' discussion of modern "canari" vessels used in slow-cooking West African stews and her recipe for a "kedjenou" with its traditional Guinea hen or chicken base to be served over rice provides one more link between flat-bottomed, bowl-shaped colonoware vessels found at southern sites or in the Chesapeake and West African food traditions, joining the more purely ceramic connections established by Ferguson and others. To this add Edna Lewis' belief that Guinea fowl stays more moist if cooked in an earthen pan. Yet none of the ceramics at the Calvert site was of African or Indian origin, a fact that may be related to its urban locale, ready proximity to stores where cooking pots could be reasonably bought, and the more open pockets of its owners.[23]

Iron kettles and brass skillets, standard tools in English homes, were also essential elements in the cargoes European traders brought to sell in West Africa. Their use, in fact, spread throughout the world. Today, Harris writes, "heavy black cast-iron pots, caldrons, and skillets are a leitmotif of Black cooking" whether one is in

Nigeria, Brazil, Barbados, or the American South, while in the 1880s, Mary Kingsley watched African women use them as well as "native-made, rough earthen pots. These pots have a very cave-man look about them; they are unglazed, unlidded bowls. They stand the fire wonderfully well," but she concluded, you have got to put up with the "soot-like color they impart to . . . white rice."[24]

Whether it is rice or millet, pepper pots or garden plots, older food accounts are echoed in recent ones from two hemispheres, constituting a long-standing set of cultural values surrounded by behavior embedded in tradition. The Herskovits described food among Suriname blacks in Dutch Guinea in 1928 and 1929: "stews in which a bit of salt-fish or meat is added to rice and okra." Mark Hudson, in a 1989 ethnography, wrote of African women and children roasting field corn, noting its harvest in September signalled the end of one hunger season, while in Virginia, Edna Lewis remembered the field corn of her childhood, a sign of summer, baked in the oven with its inside leaves, as "a little bit crispy." Hudson also gave directions for *dempetengo*, another meal that marked the passage of the seasons, and repeated the cycle of earlier years.[25]

> First [the women] gathered wood for the fire, then Jarra Njai pounded a
> small portion of the new rice and shook away the husks. It was then heated
> in a cracked old cooking pot, until it began to jump out. Then it was
> pounded again. All three women took part, pounding in rotation into the one
> mortar, building up speed till the thudding of their pestles sounded out
> across the salt flats like the beating of a great drum.

The resultant substance was seen as a great treat. Old black women on Carolina rice fields made it too in three-legged iron pots with wooden covers. Men ate it when they could: "brown-rice cakes, in the centre of which are snow-white grains, each thoroughly done and each separate." The grey flakes still warm from the pot would be agreeably crunchy and dry, enlivened by charred bits and green flakes of the grains not fully ripe. "It was extremely laborious to prepare . . . the pounding was a small ritual in its own right – something by which the time of year could be identified." A "culinary treat," said men to each other in Carolina, find it if you can. Whether it is described from South Carolina or the heart of Africa, such foodways speak to the deep knowledge women held and to feminine cooperation (fig. 10.4).[26]

Another description, of an African compound "busy as an anthill," tied modern yam food preparation to folk traditions: "Temporary cooking tripods were erected on every available space by bringing together three blocks of sun-dried earth and making a fire in their midst. Cooking pots went up and down the tripods, and [yam] was pounded in a hundred wooden mortars." Men who were not cooks themselves were not precise in the nomenclature they used for cooking utensils and thus there is a merging of pots, kettles, and skillets in these examples. It was a Victorian gentlewoman who specified the difference: "Any woman knows a kettle must have a spout." These African utensils, wrote Miss Kingsley, "are spoutless and round with a handle across the top." Foods wrapped in leaves are placed inside to steam

Figure 10.4. Nineteenth-century women living on the sea islands of Georgia pound rice using tools and techniques that derive from West Africa. (Photograph courtesy of the Georgia Archives.)

and the "whole affair is poised on the three cooking stones over a wood fire, and left there until the contents are done."[27]

While colonists in Africa used male chefs (as they also did in the West Indies), Kingsley found native cooking was women's work. She specified different ingredients for seasoning: bark that tasted like an onion; Odeaka cheese made from the kernel of the wild mango. She told how women began by wrapping fish in leaves, then either buried it in the ground, lighting a fire above it or buried the packet among hot coals. She added snails, snakes, and crayfish (and humans in certain districts) to the men's list of meat resources. She wrote of pots, kettles, and skillets and gave a recipe for pot-less meals:[28]

> Reduce the fire to embers, and make plantain leaves into a sort of bag, or cup; small pieces of the meat should then be packed in layers with red pepper and odeaka in between. The tops of the leaves are then tied together . . . the bundle, without any sauce pan of any kind, stands on the glowing embers, the cook taking care there is no flame. The meat is done, and a superb gravy formed, before the containing plantain leaves are burnt through.

Three generations later, Sylvia Leith-Ross studied Ibo women and noted too their interest in food. "There are several ways of varying the pounded foods," she wrote, "and all sorts of flavorings . . . Real interest is taken and imagination exercised." Like all good cooks, she continued, they "describe with enthusiasm the preparation of a good dish."[29]

New World echoes

Hearths and small charcoal pits where slaves cooked are found in the New World. Cooking pots, varying in size and shape but holding essentially the same foodstuffs and perched on fires of similar form, are signs of a shared cultural tradition, modified in the New World, which archaeologists recover. Thus for Caribbean artifacts associated with African-American foods, archaeologists record grinding stones, used to mill grain or to crush the peppers and spices used in piquant sauces, from excavation units close to kitchens; a similar pestle was recovered from the kitchen/slave-quarter sector of the William Paca site on Maryland's Eastern Shore. They also tell of *three flat stones* used to form simple hearths at slave compounds in Jamaica (cf. fig. 16.6), but the few flat stones found *in situ* in the kitchen courtyard area of the Calvert site do not appear to have been used in this fashion.[30]

Here we see a historical record that reveals Arabic sources of medieval age, that identifies new foodstuffs introduced by the Portuguese, then assimilated, and provides information both on seventeenth- and eighteenth-century West African cuisine. Modern culinary artists such as Edna Lewis or Jessica Harris, and anthropologists like Sylvia Leith-Ross or Mark Hudson, provide testimony of the strength of historical precedent in African-based foodways. The retention of core ingredients and techniques, incorporated and imaginatively transformed while maintaining African style, can be seen elsewhere in eighteenth-century documents for Barbados,

Jamaica, Brazil, New Orleans, and the Carolinas. Survivals are readily visible in descriptions of twentieth-century food use by anthropologists in South America, and by African-American scholars such as Robert L. Hall in the United States. Unfortunately, much of what these data reveals about African food traditions and their vegetarian base will never be readily visible in the archaeological record because of the way that plant remains decompose in the soil.

Because the full spread of activity areas at the Calvert site could not be sampled and excavation clustered close to two sides of the main house, there is even less information on hand than at broadly worked sites like Monticello, Kingsmill, King's Bay, Curriboo, or Cannon's Point. What we recovered is more equivocal than it would have been if recovered from a trash pit just outside a quarter's wall or a "hidey hole" – a rectangular pit dug to store yams or personal possessions – inside a slave dwelling. Further, because no fully-formed comparative Chesapeake data base exists to help place it in context, the Annapolis data remain ambiguous. Yet there were artifacts recovered which could as easily have been used in preparing African-style foods as English dishes. These included a number of large iron pots, cauldrons, and smaller, glazed earthenware cooking pots (figs. 10.5a and 10.5b). Spices used in

Figure 10.5. Vessels made by Africans (Senegambia), African-Americans (South Carolina), and Europeans (Annapolis) show similarities in form that would have enabled black women to utilize African methods of slow cooking in the New World. Rice, for example, would have cooked almost as well in these pots as they sat in the ashes as it does in modern rice-cookers. 10.5a: An English "jar" found at the Annapolis site charred from use in fire and close in form to 10.5b. 10.5b: Colonoware "jar" also used as a cooking pot was recovered from the slave quarters at Curriboo plantation in Berkeley County, South Carolina (Wheaton, Friedlander, and Garrow 1983). (Photographs by Marion E. Warren and Leland Ferguson.)

African cookery include Jamaica pepper (allspice), melegueta pepper (cardamon or "grains of paradise"), ginger, and African nutmeg; three of these are listed on Edward Henry Calvert's inventory. Other ingredients – rice, sorghum, tamarind – could be bought in local markets or obtained through illicit barter. Finally, some attributes of the faunal collection also hint at African influence.

Drawing on the work of Melville Herskovits, Sidney Mintz and Richard Price were among the first of the new scholars of Afro-America to reiterate Herskovits' insight of the way memories and ideals could remain intact, gaining strength and coalescing within the individual as more extraneous earthly things disappeared. What remained was a core essence expressed in a walk, a gesture, a cadence, a blues song, or, for food, an appreciation of a salty taste, a heated flavor, a leafy green sauce. Knowledge of how to blend ingredients to produce familiar tastes balanced by innovations, substitutions of New World greens for Old World plants, and acquisition of original foodstuffs mediated the processes of recreating a folk art ripped apart by the slave trade. It helped women renew the connection between past and present required among a people whose lifestyle maintained as a touchstone the presence of ancestral spirits and contact with them; it gave pleasure to their men. It is one face of the African-American experience in the Chesapeake and it is one, as we will see, that archaeological information suggests found expression on the governor's lot below the State House.[31]

It is not far-fetched to see at the Calvert site echoes of folk beliefs about food that African women brought with them. After all, when one looks at the larger artifacts the Calvert men left behind one can see how they too carried ideas across the sea about the way the world should be. If the Calverts could recreate a house and garden set in a culturally created natural surrounding that followed aristocratic English precedents, what reason in the world do we have for thinking that others would not do likewise?[32]

In fact, when one reads texts carefully, many incidents that tell of cultural carryovers and West African survivals appear. These range from ways to build homes, weld iron, herd cattle and treat illness, to ways of cooking foods in the home. But to understand the patterns these take in the archaeological record also requires looking at the relationships between slaves and masters and, in particular, how foods were rationed. As one will soon see, what black people were fed by slave-masters was often insufficient to provide nourishment to working folk and contained little to ease their hunger for home.

Slave diets

Eurocentric history has often asserted that African slaves were stripped of most vestiges of their tribal identities on the passage westward to make them more tractable, whereas the belief that some individuals were able (or in some cases allowed or even encouraged) to maintain the cultural connection that food, cloth, jewelry, or music expressed imparts a more complex dimension to the slave presence in Chesapeake society from any vantage point. African-born slaves and their creole offspring were not a people without a past. Certainly, as Mintz and Price stress, the

Table 10.3. *Excerpt from Virginia court records, 1728–9*

They built a town of boughs and grass houses in the manner of the homes of their native land, and set up a tribal government under a chief, who had been a prince among his own people . . . near Lexington.

Source: T. E. Campbell, *Colonial Carolina: A History of Caroline County*

dominant power base wielded by European slave owners had a strong effect on the ways in which African customs and social relationships were maintained; it influenced innovations that disparate Africans, as they drew together in slave communities, used to build new identities. The desire to retain their African heritages must also be paired with the "increasing body of evidence that slave owners interfered as little as possible in the nonwork lives of their labor force." Mechal Sobel is very clear on this: "A quasi-African body of values functioned in almost every African household in America." And that brings an archaeologist face to face with some of the most common artifacts on colonial sites: bones and other food remains. Many of the basic eighteenth-century African ingredients – beans, peas, okra, squashes, pumpkins, melons, ground-nuts (peanuts), rice, and millet (Guinea corn) – were not ones normally listed on probate inventories, but inventories listed items that were not highly perishable and that had known prices within a defined, male, English market system. Using a conservative approach, we have attributed the uncharred squash, pumpkin, peanut, and watermelon seeds from the site to squirrel encroachment, but note that squirrels maintain relatively small territories which implies that these items were grown or used within relatively close proximity to the Calvert mansion (i.e., probably within the grounds of their land on lots 82 and 83). Further, some were also found deep in an abandoned kitchen well (a deposit capped ca. 1785) unaccompanied by squirrel remains. There is also evidence of African crops grown further south – sesame, two varieties of Guinea corn, Guinea grass, Guinea gourds, African potatoes (tubers) as well as the ground-nuts and hot peppers assimilated within their cuisine by Africans in the 1600s.[33]

Sparse records on these foodstuffs appear during the late 1690s and in the first decade of the 1700s in the Carolinas and then as the century passes, in a wider range of colonial communities. The few that initially appear also indicate some of the difficulties in growing tropical plants in the more moderate Chesapeake climate. Families, for example, had to learn to store yams in root cellars near the hearths to preserve them through the winter. Virginian farmers in the seventeenth century wrote of the difficulty in keeping these tubers from rotting until they learned to do so.

Earlier sections of this chapter stressed various aspects of West African cuisine. Within African towns and villages, eating was a cultural mechanism that day by day meshed family life into the larger society. For almost all African peoples, getting their daily meal was their daily work. Yet, the overriding fact in the New World was that the cuisine had to be incorporated within the culture of slavery. Its priority, from the slave-owners' perspective, fell below the productive labor needed to generate cash crops; the guides used in allocating food did not center on rights and obligations of African kinfolk or village neighbors. Yet, as in West Africa, meals were built from a vegetarian base and many were portable (breads, roots, etc.); the preparation techniques (cf., burying tubers in hot ashes) were almost identical; meats were additive and not the essence of made dishes.

Oldmixon wrote in 1708 that the food allotted slaves comprised a "coarse diet" while Lawson, in the Carolinas, said they were fed "nothing but Indian corn and salt." The choicest fare was plantains or bread made of Indian corn in the Islands with the addition of rice dishes and variations of "hommony for the Negroes" on the North American continent. Other plants incorporated into the black cuisines of the Chesapeake included "red and white" potatoes, "very nice and different from ours" according to Hugh Jones, with "roots and pulse [peas and beans]." "Year in and year out they receive nothing but Indian or Welsh or Turkish corn," wrote Johann Martin Bolzius in 1740.[34]

Allotments were given on a weekly or monthly basis; the division was based on a ranking system that incorporated factors such as age, work tasks, and favor in the owner's eyes. Slave-masters gave more ample rations to head drivers, foremen, coopers, carpenters, and masons than to less willing or less able workers. Using information in Thomas Jefferson's *Farm Book*, Diane Crader reports that "the largest quantities of fish and meat were given to some house servants, to single hired men, to some very old field workers, and certain other favored slaves . . . while less was usually given to regular field hands and children; exceptions included spinning girls and nail boys who received more." Jefferson's beef ration was 0.5 to 1.5 pounds per adult; fish were rationed in quantities ranging from 4 to 8 lbs. On rural plantations, breakfast was the heftier meal; dinner was irregular and slight: roasted yam, sweet potato, corn, a salted fish.[35]

The basic meat rations were salted fish, mackerel, pork, and occasionally beef. Some slaves were fortunate to have masters who would let them roast a shoat. Others were given less meaty portions – innards, gizzards, snouts, and trotters. Some were given almost no meat at all: "If they have benevolent masters, or prove themselves loyal, they may receive a little meat a few times a year." Yet, continued Bolzius, "they love to eat meat, and sometimes roast mice or steal meat. Some have permission to catch fish on Sundays."[36]

To obtain more food, many drew on a variety of nondomestic resources. They gathered plants and shellfish, hunted game (mammals, birds, and reptiles) or fished. Women applied their knowledge of food preservation to pork. As one slave mistress wrote, the women "understood well the composition of sausages" and took to dressing pig's head as a souse which could be eaten cold and would "keep a week at least" even in the heat.[37]

Finally, slave sites in the southeastern United States are characterized by high percentages of fish remains, and by bones that have been cleaved apart. McKee also found that bones from a root cellar in a Virginia slave quarter had been mashed as if cut to fit in a single pot or, perhaps, to facilitate access to bone marrow. He concluded this was evidence of meat re-use, and that roasts, after having served the master's table, were then removed from the kitchen so their remains could be incorporated into the slave family's meal. This would fit with English norms, for one way a wealthy medieval household who could eat bountifully benefited the larger community was as a food redistribution point for those of lesser means. And it would fit, too, within a system of pilferage by slaves wherein what belonged to the master was seen as a resource that might assuage the slave's need as well.[38]

Additionally, food rations were supplemented by plants slave women grew in small gardens, by the goats, swine, and poultry that slaves raised themselves until, almost across the board and almost simultaneously, legislation by slave-holders in one decade forbade this practice. It was imperfectly enforced, and funds obtained by selling animals and plant crops gave some slaves money to purchase other items. Resourceful individuals also found food by collecting wild plants, by petty theft (milking cows in the night, stealing from the kitchen, slaughtering and cooking animals "lost" in the woods or those who died by "accident"), by hunting (well documented for the far south), and by fishing. The black cuisine was not defined by choice, but adapted to a variety of different circumstances. Gradually African-American cookery assumed a distinctive, vigorous guise while simultaneously elements within it were assimilated into the "sweet" cuisine of the slave owner. It is hard to imagine its configuration ca. 1730, for this was an era when greater latitude

Figure 10.6. Guinea hens, birds of "extreme caution," roost at night in trees near dwellings on old tobacco plantations in Maryland today even as they used to do in West Africa (Jobson 1623: 38). (Illustration by Julie Hunter-Abbazia.)

existed vis-à-vis expressions of Africanisms, when most adult slave women had actually learned to cook as young women in Africa. There had not been time enough, however, for African food practices to penetrate and become integral to the elite domain of courtly cuisine or to flow over into its folk parallels in the Chesapeake. These effects would take a generation or two to emerge.[39]

As West African foods and cooking techniques were merged with English styles of cooking, the origins were misplaced. Many clues remain, however, that point to their homeland. Mrs. Carmichael, for example, gave an Afro-Jamaican recipe for souse (originally an English dish) in which the addition of lime juice and country peppers enhanced the flavor and its keeping qualities. Mrs. B. C. Howard gave numerous variations of okra soup in her *Fifty Years in a Maryland Kitchen* (published in 1893). Moving further back in time, calabashes were common by 1714 in Philadelphia while in New Jersey soon thereafter watermelons appeared; some travellers observed they were so plentiful that it was their belief no farmer or poor person planted a garden without watermelon.[40]

Guinea hens also represent the transfer of an indigenous African fowl to the New World and its thorough incorporation into the foodways and wildlife of whole regions such that people today know Guinea hens as a rural bird, nesting in trees, serving as a watch-dog and screeching – "they are birds of extreme caution and suspicion" – whenever a stranger comes near. They can be seen running through fields on Long Island, and living near farms in southern Maryland; William Kelso observed them at Carter's Grove in the 1960s, but their homeland is Africa where they were carved in wood or clay by ordinary folk and cast in silver by the rich

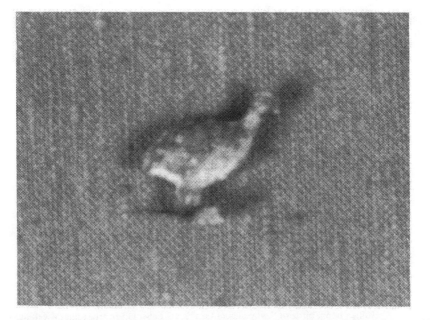

Figure 10.7. In the fill above the orangery, archaeologists recovered a painted tiny metal bird, less than one inch tall, whose form is reminiscent of a Guinea hen. (Photograph by the author.)

(figs. 10.6 and 10.7). The trick, of course, is to see whether one can discern some of these West African elements in the faunal record of Annapolis, but to do that one has to know whether or not there is anything distinctive about the animal remains from a site.[41]

VI

ARTIFACTS IN MOTION

Does not our life consist of the four elements [fire, water, earth, and air]? Faith, so they say but, I think, it rather consists of eating and drinking.

William Shakespeare, *Twelfth Night*, Act II, Scene 3

Faunal remains: putting meat on the bones

For an illustration of an anthropological analysis of symbolism I have taken the theme of food. In contrast to the more common anthropological studies of symbolism . . . I have deliberately chosen as material and pragmatic a field as one can get. Granted that meaning is ultimately "in the head", in this case as Tikopia would probably agree, head and stomach are closely allied . . . The Tikopia use food as a symbolic instrument to express ideas of social co-operation and social status, by many subtle variations in amount, composition and style.

Raymond Firth 1975, *Symbols, Public and Private*

Archaeological evidence of food

Anthropologists are familiar with the cultural insight they gain from studying a people's food. Sidney Mintz tells of its role: "People who eat strikingly different foods or similar foods in different ways are thought to be strikingly different." Food is also a simple, carnal pleasure that divides the day and punctuates the seasons of the year. As importantly, it leaves wide-ranging footprints in the archaeological record. The tracks are formed by organic plant remains (seeds, nuts), sea shells, and pieces of cut, sawn, cleaved, mangled, splintered, gnawn, and otherwise mutilated bone, some with teeth marks and some knife-scarred. Most of the destruction, to be sure, took place at the hands of man, and hence its archaeological import, but not all. An analyst must consider the effects of taphonomic processes that further degrade the bone. She must also decide which animal bone is the remains of food that was left by commensal animals, and which is the remains of commensal animals, taking into consideration what predators or scavengers (hungry dogs, rats, pigs) did to the original refuse deposit (fig. 11.1). These questions are not simple, and to obtain answers an interpretive archaeologist must set aside issues of eighteenth-century hospitality, cooperation, and status, and cross a border zone into another realm of inquiry, highly specialized, objective, quantitative, and generalizing. Past peoples and their actions are momentarily left behind.[1]

Fortunately, we were able to ship the organic remains from critical sectors of the Calvert site to specialists at the University of Georgia (Dr. Elizabeth J. Reitz) and at the University of Pennsylvania's Museum Applied Science Center for Archaeology (Dr. Naomi F. Miller). With their scientific reports in hand, it was possible to begin constructing an ethnographic interpretation, reinserting people and their social action, pushing the data beyond the level of the site itself until it converged with collateral evidence from historical records. What we learned, however, was dependent upon what was available; the faunal data were richer than the plant remains, and bone elements outnumbered seeds and nuts by more than 100 to one. The latter show an undue amount of activity from squirrels; there are strong indications that these little creatures were busy gathering, eating, and storing nuts from nearby Annapolis trees within the Calvert yard and house, making it difficult to sort out which seeds and nuts were present because of human activity and which ones were there because of squirrel activity. Although this may be a clear sign that the Maryland legislature lost the campaign it began under Benedict Leonard against squirrels (see Chapter 4), it has had a result they surely did not intend: an interpretive emphasis on meat remains rather than plant remains within this book.[2]

In contrast to the ceramics discussed earlier, most of the skeletal remains described here were never meant to be seen. They operated within a sensory domain where tactile sensations of taste and texture conveyed non-verbal messages about social distinctions. Whereas tablewares were seen by guests, most household procedures related to food preparation and its meat contents took place privately in service areas, i.e., off-stage, or even off-site. What servants brought into the dining area was a finished product, a flavorful dish. It was created from ingredients whose distinguishing marks or contrasting elements, in terms of the way these survive in the archaeological record, were less apparent in its prepared state than in prior phases of the food preparation cycle.

Archaeologically analyzing food remains

Identification of bones from the Calvert site involved the use of standard analytical procedures set out in Dr. Reitz's technical reports. Essentially, after initial sorting into broad categories, laboratory workers identified the faunal remains through comparison with a study collection of animal skeletons – wild and domestic mammals, birds, reptiles, fish, and so on. While doing this, Dr. Reitz and her assistant, Barbara Ruff, attempted to assign each bone element to a precise taxon and thus to identify it to the genus and species level. This is not always possible, so bones that have fewer distinguishing criteria, sometimes because they were pulverized in the preparation of meals or because they were small, fragile, and broke easily in the soil, were put into more general categories. Sheep and goat are particularly difficult to distinguish, unfortunately, since New World uses of these two species reflected to some extent cultural attitudes. Many West Africans often ate goat – it is still popular in West Africa and in the Caribbean – whereas medieval Englishmen preferred sheep. Thus from the outset archaeologists face difficulties delineating the marks of ethnic food preferences in their artifact assemblages.[3]

Bone analysis is customarily presented in tabular form (Table 11.1) by species and genus, using a taxonomic order distinct from the habitat ordering used in Chapter 12 (Table 12.1). This gives the data a very firm and finite appearance that is deceptive. The bone reflects what was eaten during a brief period of time at the

Calvert site, but it does not tell the whole story. Some of its pieces have disappeared. Once each bone specimen was part of a whole, living animal. Most of these entered Annapolis on the hoof to be slaughtered, then butchered and sold. The separation of animal parts began immediately, with skins sent to tanners who submerged them in deep "curing" pits, charging different fees for currying based on the size of a hide. The carcass meanwhile progressed through the channels that transformed it into food and then into garbage. Larry McKee charted this progression for food remains recovered at rural Flowerdew Hundred, and his chart is reproduced here with modifications for an urban locale (Chart 11.1). The chart, however, does not adequately express the fact that the first four stages (the raw material to discard phases) take place within a very brief time while stage five, which includes a bone's residency in the archaeological record, may last centuries.[4]

In looking at the faunal assemblage that Dr. Reitz sorted, weighed, identified, and aged, the issues are whether the faunal remains constitute evidence that the meat people ate in the Calvert home was varied, prepared in ways that differed from the ordinary (i.e., possessed elegance), provided quality food, and exhibited other attributes that can be related to high-style cuisine or might partake of rarity. In other words, can one see evidence of a high-status English presence and whether the family set a generous (and therefore hospitable) table? Or, is there anything unusual about the deposits that might be related to other styles of food preparation and procurement? A good beginning is a review of what is known about meat consumption in the Chesapeake. Another entry is provided by considering what the Calvert household might have purchased and what they had to raise or catch themselves since a common presumption is that ordinary families, and even most of the planter-gentry, supplied most of their own food needs. We will start with familiar

Figure 11.1. Black walnuts gnawed by Calvert squirrels. (Photograph by Naomi F. Miller reproduced with permission of the Society for Historical Archaeology.)

Table 11.1. *Species list for ca. 1730 features. Left to right: abandoned post holes (F34 and F40) and small, circular planting hole (F101)*

	Abandoned post holes			Planting bed		
	NISP	MNI		NISP	MNI	
	CNT	CNT	%	CNT	CNT	%
Unidentified mammal	1,324			418		
Unidentified large mammal	384			153		
Unidentified small mammal	6			1		
Oryctolagus cuniculus (domestic rabbit)	1	1	1.7			
Sciurus spp. (squirrel)	1	1	1.7			
Muridae (rats and mice)	12	3	5.3			
Rattus spp. (rat)	9					
Artiodactyl (ungulates)	106			64		
cf. *Sus scrofa* (pig-like)	1					
Sus scrofa (pig)	127	9	15.8	10	2	8.3
Bos taurus (cow)	81	7	12.3	18	3	12.5
Caprine (sheep/goat)	70	9	15.8	44	3	12.5
Capra hircus (goat)	3			1		
Ovis aries (sheep)	5			5		
Unidentified bird	265			136		
Anatidae (ducks)	6			6		
Anas spp. (dabbling ducks)	3	2	3.5	1		
Anas platyrhynchos (mallard)				15	2	8.3
Anser spp. (domestic geese)	2	1	1.7			
Aythya spp. (diving ducks)	4	2	3.5			
Branta canadensis (Canada goose)	11	2	3.5	3	1	4.2
Cairina moschata (Muscovy duck)	3	1	1.7			
Phasianidae (quail, partridge, and pheasant)	17					
Colinus virginianus (bob-white)	2	1	1.7			
Gallus gallus (domestic chicken)	40	5	8.8	30	6	25.0
Maleagris gallopavo (turkey)	24	3	5.3	1	1	4.2
Pavo real (peacock)	3	1	1.7			
Muscicapidae (flycatchers)	3	2	3.5			
cf. *Corvus* spp. (jays, magpies, and crows)				1	1	4.2
Unidentified fish	164			247		
Acipenser spp. (sturgeon)	6	1	1.7	1	1	4.2
Morone spp. (striped bass/white perch)	16	3	3.5	5	1	4.2
Serranidae (butterfishes?)	3	1	1.7			
Paralichythus spp. (summer flounder)	1	1	1.7			
Sparidae (porgies)	20			1		
Archosargus probatocephalus (sheepshead)	4	1	1.7	17	4	12.5
Total	2,992	57	99.6	1,178	24	100.1

NISP indicates number of identified faunal elements ("specimens"); MNI indicates the minimum number of individuals represented among the identified faunal elements; CNT refers to the actual bone count.

These data were drawn from Tables 27, 32, and 37 in Reitz 1989a.

English barnyard animals since these constituted the major source of meat eaten in Annapolis.

Meat from domestic animals

Henry Miller's dissertation on the changing food patterns in the Chesapeake, combining ecology, archaeozoology, and history, remains the best study of regional diet to date. It is supplemented by the work of faunal analysts at the Colonial Williamsburg Foundation, by McKee's research on slave diets, by David Langdon's and Justin Lev-Tov's studies of later Annapolis sites, and by Lois Carr's analysis of nutritional information in probate inventories. Because the number of sites north of the Potomac where detailed faunal analysis has been done is small in comparison to the number of households whose livestock holdings can be read in probate inventories, the image that emerges from archaeology is spotty. Nonetheless, it demonstrates that most Chesapeake farm families wrung the last shilling out of their livestock by using cattle as draft beasts, cows as sources of milk or as breeding stock, and sheep for wool production until the animals were no longer productive. They were then slaughtered and butchered for food.[5]

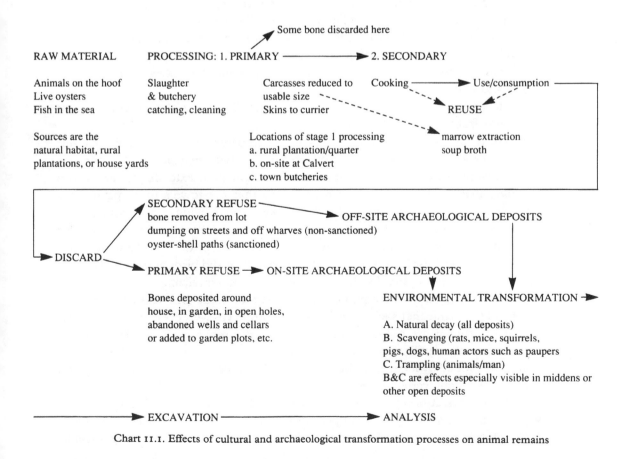

Chart 11.1. Effects of cultural and archaeological transformation processes on animal remains

Carr estimates that a cow's productive life was over by age twelve, a steer's between five and six and a sow's after three years. Providing nourishment at the end of their lives, farm animals were scrawny in comparison with modern animals, and not raised for the quality of their meat. However, scattered throughout the area, especially on the Eastern Shore where land was less suited to tobacco, families did raise animals for the Annapolis market. Lois Carr and Lorena Walsh first searched for information on the town's market by analyzing the inventories of rural families living in Anne Arundel County within 10–15 miles of Annapolis, basing their study on land-based transport criteria. They found scant evidence, leading Walsh to conclude that market transactions linking "Annapolitans with country residents defy any simple classification." She noted the absence of a cluster of suppliers near the town, and decided few planters "chose to concentrate on producing meat, produce, fodder, and firewood" for the urban market. Instead, Walsh envisioned large landowners who "supplied many of their own needs and some of those of their town neighbors from their own far-flung plantations." This is probably accurate, but only in part, for the town aldermen drew up a very careful set of market regulations and fined those who broke their rules.[6]

Oldmixon wrote in 1708 of a town with a twice-weekly market supplying its food needs. Annapolis was small, but artisans, craftsmen, mariners, the governor's staff, and other government clerks lived in the capital. There was an in-pouring of Upper and Lower House members, their families, servants, and slaves during the legislative sessions, and the maritime community expanded whenever ships made port. The town differed from the self-sufficient farm communities of New England, New York, and Pennsylvania. Annapolitans could not raise all they wished to eat. They were dependent on many outside sources except for the legislators who brought foodstuffs from their rural homes.

I looked for the track of butchers in the documents to find out if the Calvert pattern of food acquisition and use differed from other townspeople. Gradually it became clear that the procurement network for Annapolis extended up and down the Bay, that it drew on water transport, and that the town's more prosperous butchers, men like Cornelius Brooksby, went on buying trips through the countryside to obtain animals. They certainly did not raise them. Yet the town also maintained a communal herd of goats until its goatkeeper died in 1722. Evidence that poor women raised market crops also appeared, as did birds and animals stolen for sale in the town. Finally, here and there, were tantalizing clues that black Chesapeake men and women participated in the food trade (see next chapter).[7]

One of the points that social anthropologists stress vis-à-vis pre-industrial culture is that institutions are not divisively segmented nor separate. Reflecting this, the evidence on Annapolis food use, presented here as *comparanda* for the Calvert bones, was found by looking at the storehouse inventories of men who bought and sold a bewildering variety of goods while making their primary living as planters, land speculators, attorneys, even as town barbers (for example Col. Thomas Ennalls who bought and sold pigs and salt pork in addition to growing tobacco – see Table A-5). Information on food also appeared in lists of unpaid debts owed by artisans, craftsmen, and unskilled laborers that smaller merchants, ordinary families, or widows brought to court. Here one sees the foodstuffs that women sold – sugared tarts, loaves of bread, a dozen fowls, two dozen oranges, a week's diet for a servant – and the supplies they purchased as part of the genderized nurture of male boarders or for the old and the sick whom they nursed. Annapolis and Anne Arundel men were also very precise in listing the expenses of finding runaway servants, presumably because the court would add additional days, weeks, or months of "runaway time" to a servant's indenture in compensation. The costs included provisions eaten on wide-reaching searches.

Amidst all these data, two documents were outstandingly helpful. These were the debts run up with two meat-merchants: Cornelius Brooksby and Amos Woodward. The first contained the purchases of a bricklayer, Timothy Sullivan, for himself and possibly for his workers during a three-month period (August to October 1721), while the second revealed the meats the family of a young English gentleman, Nicholas Hammond, bought between 1731 and 1734 (fig. 11.2). The account of food use obtained from the Calvert faunal assemblage is not precisely like the picture that emerges from the lists of Sullivan's and Hammond's unpaid debts, but neither is it like that which is seen in analyzing the faunal assemblages from Reynolds Tavern (ca. 1740–60) or St. Mary's City.[8]

To start with, the numbers of faunal elements in the two town deposits (at Reynolds Tavern and Calvert) are higher than many of those in the countryside where larger expanses of land may have prompted a more dispersed refuse disposal pattern. The Reynolds deposits came from features with a larger cubic capacity than the Calvert ones, and actually contained more bone, but cooking methods in the tavern produced greater bone fragmentation which resulted in a smaller number of identified bone (16% vs. 25%). Between September and November while workmen built the orangery, the governor's servants and slaves tossed household food refuse into three small holes left by two uprooted posts (from a dismantled post-in-the-ground building) and an uprooted bush or small tree. These formed three very small trashpits deposited rapidly and sealed beneath a layer of garden soil or the orangery floor. The cubic capacity of each "receptacle" was less than the average 20 gallon aluminium garbage container used by today's single family, probably half to three-quarters of its size. The garbage was dumped quickly; there were no stratigraphic distinctions to show that food refuse had accumulated gradually as it does in middens (unsealed, open-ended yard depositions) over six months, a year, a decade, a generation, or longer. What we see is the daily diet of the household and its guests over a short time, a month to six weeks at most.[9]

Large deposits at less wealthy sites such as Reynolds Tavern contained less bone (measured in terms of volume of bone per size of feature), providing one of the first insights from this material. It is simply that the Calvert household consumed more meat on a daily basis than many other households in the town and province. Carr estimates ½ lb per day for an adult man; less for women, children, and slaves. The three trashpits contain the remains of meat in excess of this: portions of eleven pigs; ten cows; twelve sheep or goats. Not surprisingly, the number of people associated with the Calvert household created a large demand for food, and the Calvert family had the money to feed them well. Its cooks were also able to introduce variety into daily meals. The contrasts can be seen by considering first the young domestic animals, and then the older, by looking at the fish, the fowl, and the oysters, the tame and the wild, moving from the most expensive foods to the cheapest, inserting delicacies where appropriate.

In the process, the fact that most nourishment from meat was obtained by eating beef is a fact that will be set aside because it derives from an etic analysis. It is true that the dominant element in any English Chesapeake faunal assemblage of the eighteenth century is usually the remains of old cattle. However, when people looked at food and thought about what they would like to eat, beef did not always come to mind. And, as Crader points out, pork sausage or bacon as well as organs – non-bony meat – never appear in the archaeological record. Additionally, some of the household's African members came from cultures where beef was not focal. Other meat sources were more highly valued among Anglo-Americans and were priced accordingly (cf., veal) (Table 11.2). The pricing scheme that existed used the following criteria: small ducks and chickens were cheaper than large birds like geese and turkeys; birds were cheaper than mammals; young animals were more expensive than older ones; little distinction was made between hindquarters and forequarters; seasonal considerations affected the cost as did method of preservation; tougher meats (i.e., neck and breast sections) were priced the same as tenderloins; species distinctions were paramount; country or place of origin was also relevant. Nonetheless, the cuts of meat that slavemasters distributed on a routine basis to slaves were not those that they themselves ate; this hierarchy gradually came to govern meat preferences throughout the society.[10]

Throughout the colonies, food use drew upon culturally perceived differences of the worth of meat. Similar price schemes were seen elsewhere together with similar schedules for seasonal animal use (Table 11.3). The information given on a 1740 questionnaire on animals and meats in Georgia and the Carolinas was like that seen in Maryland documents and European paintings: "The planters mostly slaughter oxen and pigs in the autumn and at the beginning of winter when they are fat, and the meat keeps well" responded Johann Bolzius. They salt or smoke it for winter's use, hanging the meat in chimneys or smokehouses. Then, he continued, "they keep chickens, geese, ducks, Calcutta chickens, sheep, lambs, calves as fresh food for an emergency, and whoever has time and skill goes deer hunting, or shoots wild Indian or Calcutta chickens, wild ducks, etc."[11]

Food delicacies: young animals and tasty heads

Calves

Ordinarily, calf meat was holiday fare or a special treat. This can be inferred from the Hammond account in which a loin of veal was served at Christmas one year and breast of veal appeared two years in a row in April after a 4–6 week period (Lent) when no meat at all was purchased. As shown in Table 11.2, veal was the most

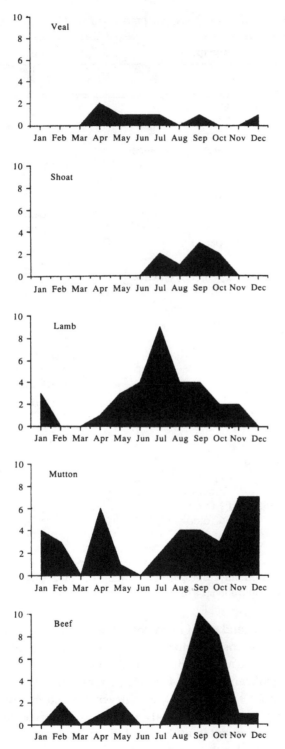

Figure 11.2. Graph showing seasonal variations in meat purchases by the Hammond family. (Drawn by Julie Hunter-Abbazia.)

Table 11.2. *Food prices in Maryland (Annapolis, ca. 1720–40) and Virginia (1705)*

	Annapolis	Virginia
Fresh meat		
Young meat		
kid (side)	£3	
veal (lb)	6 pence	
lamb (lb)	4 pence	
shoat	2 shillings, 6 pence	
deer		8–12 shillings apiece
Older meat		
mutton (lb)	4 pence	
beef (lb)*	2 pence	1–2 pence
pork		1–2 pence
dung-hill fowls (ea.)	2 pence	
Heads		
calf	2 shillings, 6 pence	
pig	2 shillings	
lamb	9 pence	
sheep	9 pence	
Poultry		
chickens (per dozen)		3–4 shillings
turkey cocks		2 shillings
turkey hens		15–18 pence
geese		1 shilling
duck		8–9 pence
capons		8–9 pence
poulets, large and fat		6 pence
Dairy products and preserved meat		
butter (lb)	10 pence	
pork (barrel)	£2.00.00	
beef (barrel) (Eastern Shore)	£1.15.00	
Irish beef (barrel)	£6.10.00	
gammon (ea.)	7 pence	

* Seasonally this could rise to 3 pence in the spring and early summer; there is also some yearly variation (i.e., 2 pence normally, but 2½ pence one year in September in the Hammond account, and 3 pence in Sullivan's bill).

expensive meat sold in Annapolis, and a calf head cost almost a shilling more than a pig's head or over three times the cost of a sheep's head. Depending on the weight of a calf, its whole side would have been priced equivalent to the £3 charged for kid, if not higher. It is probably significant that the Hammond family purchased veal in small quantities, pieces useful for a single meal, and never ordered as much as a hindquarter. The archaeological evidence from Calvert does not illustrate the use of young calves, but neither does it discount it, as the age designation most appropriate in the analysis grouped all cows under 18 months of age into one set. These constituted the major portion of beef eaten in the household.[12]

Table 11.3. *Food prices in Charleston and Savannah ca. 1740 and Philadelphia in 1797*

	Charleston or Savannah	Philadelphia
Fresh meat		
Young meat		
calves' head		3 shillings, 9 pence
veal (lb)	2 pence	9 pence
lamb (lb)		9 pence
shoat	2 shillings, 6 pence	
chickens and duck	8 pence	
Older meat		
mutton (lb)	5 pence	6 pence
beef (lb)	2 pence	9 pence
tongue		3 shillings
fowl (pair)		3 shillings
geese and Calcutta chicken (ea.)	2 shillings	
venison (per lb)	1 penny	
wild Calcutta hen	10 pence	
Preserved meat		
gammon (smoked)	4 pence	
bacon	5 pence	
Fish	"quite cheap"	

Lamb

Lamb was ordered frequently in the Hammond household and constituted 42% of their purchases. The Hammonds bought the hindquarters, forequarters, or lamb's head. Bricklayer Timothy Sullivan also included it in his diet, but less often (8%). It appeared on the table at Reynolds Tavern and at the craftsman's home on West Street (Gott's Court), but was of minimal importance at sites in southern, rural Maryland. It also appears to be rare at most slave sites. Conversely, lamb was of equal importance in urban Charleston, South Carolina, which may be a hint that it was obtained from small herds raised specifically in each region for urban markets. Lamb, together with kid, was also served in the Calvert household despite the fact (archaeologically evident) that the season was autumn, a time of year when traditionally fewer lambs were sold.[13]

Shoats

Planters raised swine almost solely as a food resource, although many Lower Eastern Shore families sold them and not all were destined for a planter's own table. Piglets were born in the spring. English and southern colonial recipes indicate that some were used as a food source while still young weanlings, yet the seasonal cycle contained in the Hammond account indicates they purchased shoats only from July through October. Barbecued shoat slow-roasted over a fire was considered a delicious meat, but one that was more labor intensive than other forms of cooking.

Gradually, barbecued pork became associated with the fall "corn-shuckin" feasts on southern farms. It is notable that the bricklayer bought no shoats, although his invoice spanned the season when they appeared in the Hammond account.[14]

In summary, young animals were eaten at specific times of the year; they were readily available in Annapolis markets based on the three-year Hammond account. Their meat was not purchased as often by craftsmen as by the gentry. Young pig remains were recovered from the Calvert site, Reynolds Tavern, and mid eighteenth-century deposits near the City Gates (Gott's Court). Given that Amos Garrett's store, which Amos Woodward inherited, was but one block from the Calvert Site, the Calvert family had a ready source. Young animals were also raised on Captain Calvert's outlying farms and plantations. However, the difficulties of differentiating between animals of less than a year of age – the folk distinction – and those still young enough not to have fused bones – the objective, etic measurement – shifts the frame of faunal reference to one that more readily reveals the presence of young, prime animals than of kid, lamb, calves, or shoats. There is only an illusionary congruence between the folk hierarchy and the age-grades (under 18 months; over 18 months; immature, juvenile, etc.) that most Chesapeake faunal analysis has produced. However, the latter classifications can indicate use of animals slaughtered in their prime for meat.

Heads as food treats

Modern families in the Chesapeake rarely eat calf's head, pig's head, sheep's or lamb's head, although souse remained important among African-American farm families into this century. These animal parts were delicacies, served whole in medieval England, and fell into disfavor in the nineteenth century, although as late as the 1770s American cooks recommended them to housewives as winter food. By 1833, however, English women in Jamaica found special inducements were needed to feed souse to their families. When blacks kill a hog, "they are very loathe to sell the heads and feet," cautioned Mrs. Carmichael, "and if you wish these, you must coax them for a favor." The pricing scheme shown in Table 11.2 reveals pig's head continued to hold a special role in the colonial Chesapeake while the purchase of one on December 11 may indicate the continued English Christmas custom of serving boar's head, or brawn, on a platter, celebrated by song. During the remainder of the year, the elite Hammonds chose lamb's or sheep's head in preference to pig, but were unwilling to shell out the funds for more than one calf's head. Timothy Sullivan bought two lambs' or sheep's heads also. Skull fragments were recovered from Reynolds Tavern, but in lesser quantities than at the Calvert site where there were more teeth from the pricey pig's head than from other animals.[15]

Prime meats

Meat obtained at the end of an animal's productive farm life is much tougher than from animals slaughtered in their prime. Butchers stand by the saying: "the younger the animal, the more tender the meat." This is one criterion that faunal analysts use in searching for evidence of animals raised for market and it causes them to pay special attention to kill-off patterns. They also look at species diversity. While Near Eastern studies suggest a more restricted range of animal species was used in ancient urban centers than in the countryside, the data from Charleston, South Carolina indicate that eighteenth-century urban dwellers had a greater range of domestic animals available and ate more types of fowl than their country cousins. Town families also ate wild animals less often than rural people. This pattern has also been observed in Annapolis; it may result from the more ethnically diverse town population, from the larger numbers of slaves living in a concentrated area, or from the greater range of occupations that gave the town social and economic heterogeneity. It is beyond the scope of the present study to consider whether the market developed in response to demand or whether greater opportunities for the sale of meat prompted an expansion of the trade.[16]

Cattle

At rural southern Maryland sites, Henry Miller found the dominant kill-off pattern resulted from slaughter of domestic cattle four years of age or older. Additional research by Bowen at Williamsburg, Virginia, produced similar findings. While the best beef for food consumption is and was obtained from young, tender animals (18–24 months), faunal analysts conclude it was rarely eaten in Chesapeake households, although Hugh Jones praised the beef and veal Virginia families consumed as "small, sweet, and fat enough," a tribute that could not have been written with old cows in mind. The contrast between the findings from other Chesapeake sites and the kill-off pattern for the ca. 1730 features at the Calvert site illustrates two very different patterns of beef utilization: (1) a regional Chesapeake pattern and (2) an aristocratic, possibly urban Annapolis pattern.[17]

Captain Charles Calvert maintained livestock on his Anne Arundel farm, and on each of his Prince George's County quarters (Table A-4). One implication of his inventory is that the family used their rural lands to raise beef cattle for consumption at Annapolis since beef cattle can be marched long distances. Between 22–30% of the cattle were used as draft animals (i.e., steers, yearlings); the majority were heifers and cows. No implements used in the production of cheese were listed in his inventory and cheese production, in fact, was not part of the regional cuisine. Captain Calvert's grandfather, the third Lord Baltimore, refused to send any Chesapeake cheese back to England, writing his own father in 1672 it was "soe Ranke and soe full of Eyes, that your Lordship would bee angry with me should I send such."[18]

The household served young, prime beef at their dining table; the faunal data indicate that 78% of the slaughtered cattle were from animals less than 36 months old. Assuming roughly equivalent male and female births among the livestock, the lack of male cattle in the inventories (cows, heifers, and calves total 68%) suggests that one source of beef at the site was the young bull calves born on the Captain's outlying farms. It would have been incompatible, given their political and social status, for the family to have engaged in a retail sale or trade of beef, although it would not have been unreasonable to dispense with some as gifts or favors. Of course, they might have let their slaves run the trade, but their herd sizes contain no hint of largesse such as that seen among men known to have been involved in commercial meat sales (e.g., the 96 cows or the 180 shoats and barrows in Col. Ennalls' inventory shown in table A-5).

The herd sizes on Captain Calvert's plantations were not as large as those seen at some others in Anne Arundel County; his herd was one quarter the size of Col. Thomas Ennalls' on the Eastern Shore. Col. Ennalls' cattle-holdings were as large as geographer Samuel Hilliard estimated a herd should be for commercial beef production. Ennalls bought and sold animals, pigs and cows, possibly processing some into salted meat and probably exporting that to the West Indies, whereas Captain Calvert increased his financial assets in other ways. Although his animal herds were much larger at the outlying quarters in Prince George's County, near Annapolis the Captain kept a modest nine cows. This raises the question of whether the household also bought beef from town butchers or depended on their own resources.[19]

Timothy Sullivan purchased just over 100 pounds of beef each month from Brooksby; the average number of pounds per piece was 12–15 except in October when he purchased two quarters (36 and 67 lbs apiece). The Hammonds ate less beef on a monthly basis, but consistently bought larger pieces of beef (averaging 23 lbs apiece), obtaining meat every 2–3 days (on average) for the first year, and approximately once a week thereafter. It is a safe bet that neither man was providing food for as large an establishment as the Calvert household. While the beef represented in the identified faunal elements (approximately 96 lbs) is close to that purchased by Sullivan, a whole cow weighed far more (about 400 lbs). Although the estimate is undoubtedly an under-representation, given the attrition that results during different stages of the progression from usable animal part to archaeologically recovered bone, the fact that skeletal parts are not equally represented has to be taken into consideration as well. One has to conclude that either the Calvert slaves butchered animals and used only specific body segments in the family kitchen, disposing of the rest elsewhere, or that the family also purchased specific portions from a town butcher on an as-needed basis.[20]

The kill-off pattern for domestic cattle from the Calvert site is also remarkable in that it indicates a strong preference for young beef. Not much old beef was ever served in the Calvert home, although it did turn up in the Reynolds Tavern dining room and in the homes of artisans throughout the community. When the Calvert cattle were no longer productive, slaves slaughtered and disposed of the beef elsewhere, undoubtedly sharing some of it among themselves and/or with servants and friends. There is no evidence the family dined on old beef in their town house, whereas its use was characteristic of family dining patterns elsewhere in the region. Within the Calvert home, decisions about which meats to eat were not based on economic prudence. This is a subtle but significant sign of affluence and suggests the degree to which the family had options other families did not.

Sheep

The Calvert family ate young lamb, but also ate mutton; they did so to a much lesser degree, however, choosing lamb two-thirds of the time. The patrons at Reynolds Tavern consumed more mutton. Nicholas Hammond, who was designated a "gentleman" on his overdue account, also bought three pieces of lamb for every two of mutton; meat from sheep comprised 67% of his purchases and must have been one of his family's favored meats. The Irish bricklayer included only a sprinkling of lamb among the meats he bought, choosing mutton over lamb four out of five times; more than half his purchases were beef. If Chesapeake farm families were as economically prudent with their sheep herds as with their cattle, the kill-off patterns for sheep should show a slaughter of older animals. There is no comparable published data, however, for the Chesapeake except for Reynolds Tavern in Annapolis and the small Gott's Court assemblage. Although meat preferences in the eighteenth century were shifting from a medieval pattern to a modern one which downgraded mutton, and cooks recommended its use less often as the century progressed, there is no way to assess the implications of the Calvert data without more comparative material. Yet, if the Hammond account is a model of meat preferences among the Maryland gentry, then the presence of both sheep and mutton among the Calvert faunal remains is its archaeological parallel.[21]

Pork

Table A-4 indicates that Captain Calvert raised pigs for food use in Anne Arundel and Prince George's Counties in moderately large quantities. Chesapeake families kept swine almost solely for food; they were raised by black and white alike. Some pigs were eaten young, but the traditional livestock practice with swine was to butcher and consume some animals, as "shoats," in the late summer and early fall, salt others for the winter, and to let the remainder fatten for consumption the following year. The swine remains in the Annapolis sample cannot be compared against a Chesapeake norm because the age data are not available. Crader shows age distributions for pigs by MNI (minimum number of individuals) for a Monticello deposit from a slave quarter that indicates most of the pork was derived from animals 18 months or older (i.e., not shoats). What the average Chesapeake planter used is still not clear.[22]

There is evidence however, that particular sections of the body were eaten by individuals at the site depending on the date and location of features. Missing entirely from all early deposits are the ribs (which may be in part an identification bias), but the forequarters and hindquarters are well represented as are cranial elements. The presence of large numbers of head elements might be read as an indication that brawn, a delicacy, was served. People do not normally identify foot elements from swine with delicate food, although calf's foot jelly was an important medicinal food and the historical record shows sickly people at the site. The "missing" ribs were a part of the body often cooked fresh and if the pigs were slaughtered outside town, say on the Captain's rural farms, then they may have been eaten there too.[23]

Here one comes face to face with the problem of whether the Calverts rationed less meaty portions of swine (fig. 11.3) to the household slaves – feet, heads, stomachs, intestines, backbones, ribs – and whether the larger number of bones from head and feet (78% of the identified pig elements) than from other parts of the body should be taken as an indication that refuse from both slave meals and master's meals were dumped into one trashpit. Actually, three trashpits were analyzed; two of these were inside a garden wall and adjacent to or underneath the orangery wing within 15 feet of the main house. The third, Feature 101, was on the opposite side of the garden wall, and 20–25 feet from the house. The first two trashpits differ primarily in terms of the raw numbers of bone recovered from them. Feature 101 had a bone count (1,178) intermediate between the first two; there are subtle differences in its contents which may have great significance or none at all. There were fewer bones from the meatiest animal parts recovered from this pit; there was also much more fowl.[24]

Variation in body elements represented in the faunal remains may be an indication that the Calvert family had begun to perceive meat cuts using the French standards then being incorporated into English cuisine. Traditional meat preferences among English aristocracy drew on a hierarchy based on animal age and species, but this changed to an evaluation relating body parts (pigs' feet, calves' feet, etc.) that cross-cut species lines. Governor Nicholson drew on custom in 1699 when he ordered mutton served on Sundays to people seeking medicinal cures at a southern Maryland "miracle spring." The evolving fashionable meat preferences, however, were based on a French scheme of good cuts of meat versus "gross meats" or low-grade cuts. The better, or meatier, more tender body parts (which are the same for cow, sheep, and goat as for the pig shown in fig. 11.3) comprised the greater proportion of the sheep/goat remains (64%) and of the cattle (54%).[25]

The French downgrading or rejection of various parts of animals began with pigs' ears in 1659, moved to pork chops, to fry (viscera, stones, or pluck from the head), lard, and then feet, snout, belly, back, chitterlings, and pork butchery by-products (offal) by ca. 1670. As different cuts became less valued, their prices dropped, but the trend was gradual and had little impact on American food markets until some-time after the Revolution. However, by the late nineteenth century in America differential evaluations of body parts had created a formulaic pricing schedule in most urban areas (there was regional variation though) whereby some meat cuts were more costly than others. Schulz and Gust in a 1983 California study introduced the use of the price schedules into the analysis of faunal remains because these provided a basis for observing the relationship between relative prices of different cuts of meat and its use by households with varying access to wealth; this enabled California zooarchaeologists (Sherri Gust, Peter Schulz, Dwight Simmons) to correlate the socioeconomic status of site occupants with body parts recovered at sites in Victorian Sacramento. In Annapolis ca. 1730, the pricing distinction was by age and species; a cut of meat cost the same no matter what portion of the body it came from. However, directions for meat fed to slaves that survive from the later eighteenth century (written for the most part by wealthy planters) quite clearly apportion head and pluck, fatback, necks, and other coarse cuts, chicken innards and gizzards to the slave diet, indicating attitudes towards meat were beginning to correspond with the French paradigm. To complicate matters further, cookbooks of the period (read by all strata of the literate society) continued to present recipes for pigs' ears, pig's pettitoes (little feet), calf and hog feet, and brain cakes. Clearly societal standards for food preparation were in a state of flux, one which eventually separated a northern cuisine from its southern counterpart.[26]

The introduction of new European cultural standards also left its imprint on the faunal remains of the Chesapeake, although the distance overseas and the dominance of the folk tradition slowed the introduction of changing food consumption patterns at most locations. In isolated areas, the older folk practices were followed for two centuries more. Yet, it may be these newer standards which are, in part, responsible for the emphasis on different body elements that can be observed in the faunal remains of swine at the Calvert site. It would not be surprising nor would it be unthinkable if some of the faunal remains were also a direct result of the presence of African-born slaves. Selectivity can be discerned in various ways within the faunal assemblage.

Additional variety in the Calvert diet is indicated by the presence of domestic rabbit remains and goat (see Table 11.1), but the more striking differences were

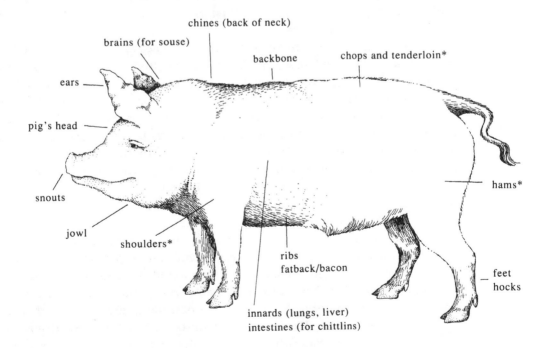

* designates the more tender, meaty portions

Figure 11.3. Meaty and non-meaty parts of a pig and some of the names these go by. (Illustration by Julie Hunter-Abbazia.)

introduced by fowl and fish. These raise the issue of how black and white men and women interacted in the Chesapeake, and whether the imprint of West African cookery survived and was felt in the early town of Annapolis.

Fowl remains

The significant quantity of bird bone from the site points also towards possible African influences. Reitz didn't find what would have sealed the case: bones from a Guinea hen (*Numida meleagris*), a wild bird much like the English pheasant (see fig. 10.6). Guinea hens were introduced into Jamaica where flocks became abundant by 1700; they were also introduced into Virginia where they appear, with Muscovy ducks, on a mid nineteenth-century list of plantation fowl, but the date of their first appearance in the Chesapeake is unrecorded.[27]

Elsewhere in Maryland, with the exception of the waterfowl and a few turkeys, far fewer wild birds are reported in the faunal assemblages. St. John's I had a mourning dove, a passenger pigeon, and a red-tailed hawk, a goose, and four kinds of ducks for a total of twelve MNI, but this, with nearby Pope's fort, is the most extensive representation seen until the eighteenth century. Deposits at St. John's I are also connected with the Calvert family; a surviving bit of minutiae in the provincial records indicates that an earlier Calvert and his Council feared they had been poisoned by a duck pie. Maryland cooks simply didn't use many species of birds in their cooking; not, however, because of fears they might be poisoned. But, since wild birds were part of courtly cuisine, we first interpreted their presence as markers of the Calverts' aristocratic lifestyle.[28]

Yet when studied more thoroughly it also becomes apparent that black hunters trapped and shot wild fowl; historical records from South Carolina indicate restrictions confining slave hunting to their master's property were passed in 1712. Wildfowl, together with a wide range of wild animals, are also routinely recovered from slave sites in the South where scholars take these as evidence of cultural stress and attempts to augment poor rations. Hunting was part of an African way of life. In the Chesapeake, hunting was initially controlled by Indians, but the argument, made by a number of African-American scholars, that Africans accustomed to tracking animals would soon become adept hunters in the New World, is a cogent one. That their quarry would include wild fowl also seems inevitable, given its centrality in West African cuisines (cf. Chapter 10), once one accepts the premise that African-born slaves did indeed hunt for or with their masters.[29]

The quantity of chicken bone too takes a significant leap above that seen at other Maryland sites, but whether the quantities recovered at the site have anything to do with knowledge of cookery, with a larger African population and especially the young black children normally given the task of feeding chickens, or with increased grain production on the Eastern Shore is unsortable at the present time. Jobson wrote in 1623 that he had met African peoples who were knowledgeable poultry farmers, even castrating male birds, as the English did, to raise fat capons for the cooking pot. Guinea "corn" continued to be used as poultry feed in this country among some blacks in the south. Mrs. Carmichael in Jamaica wrote that all her servants kept poultry; a list exists of those put "in the care of Old Betty": geese, turkeys, dungle hens, and ducks. Further, black women are credited with the development of methods of deep-fat frying by various food writers who assert, on good grounds, its importation from Africa in the seventeenth and eighteenth centuries.[30]

Reitz's analysis of medullary bone reveals that the Calvert household butchered female hens in laying condition, indicating a possible dietary preference for tender chicken – the type of chicken best suited for the frying pan. This can be tied to Carter's inclusion of pullets (plump young hens just beginning to lay eggs who reach that stage of their development in the fall of their first year) in her eighteenth-century dinner menus for September and December. But its more tantalizing link is with an urban market.[31]

Twelve chickens in six weeks is a consumption of two per week. The next highest number recovered was six from a large cellar hole at the Van Sweringen site deposited over a period of months. Overall, however, chicken remains were recovered in very modest amounts (six or fewer) at rural Chesapeake sites inhabited by white families, whereas chicken elements at a free black homestead (ca. 1740–60) were a significant element of the faunal remains. However, one has to pair both sets of data with knowledge of a 25-foot-long henhouse, complete with interior wooden partitions, on the McNamara farm in Anne Arundel County, with the painter's bill for "priming" the Annapolis hencoop of Rev. Humphrey, and with the fact that Reynolds Tavern customers ordered chicken for dinner too, although probably the poultry-based meals consumed at the tavern were eaten over a longer number of weeks or months. Chicken consumption may be more of an urban phenomenon in the Chesapeake ca. 1730, although if so, the Williamsburg pattern is different from what is seen at Annapolis and more like the rural countryside. Certainly by 1798 a commercial market existed, for one Annapolitan built a 100-foot-long chickenhouse just outside the city. But to thrust his marketing talents and agricultural experimentation back into the 1730s seems brash.[32]

At the same time we are left with the remains of a dozen chickens, assorted songbirds, tropical ducks (Muscovy), wild fowl, geese, and more turkeys than turn up elsewhere ca. 1730. How to make sense of them? Were these there because the Calverts were an aristocratic family? It is true that songbirds were "baked in a pie" in many a noble English house. It is also clear that West African women would have been quite familiar with the preparation of fowl, and might have sought it for their master's table (cooked curiously under the watchful eye of the English housekeeper or as Rebecca Calvert directed) or for their own dinners (using different herbs, spices, and sauces). The fact that more birds turned up in the trash pit outside the garden wall where there were also fewer of the meaty animal parts is tantalizing, but it remains a fact that sits by itself.

Finally, bones from a peafowl (the generic peacock) were also found at the site. This bird, however, may have played a more obvious role prior to its death as an ornamental bird residing in the pleasure garden as a companion to another, one of a pair of male/female birds. Peacocks were noted for their display value in medieval feasts and their ornamental value in pleasure gardens. The one in Governor Calvert's garden would have strutted the grounds and could have been heard throughout different sectors of Annapolis screeching at inopportune times, joining a cacophony of sounds as birds sang to each other in the early morning, perhaps matching the cock's crow in tone and strength. It was part of the pleasure of living in an aristocratic household to have the ability to incorporate exotic curiosities into daily existence; peacocks and peahens fit this bill. Caged songbirds, in fact, were found in many wealthy homes; falcons too, for hunting, were a symbol of class. Hunting in fact mediated between culture, nature, high, and low in a variety of ways. So, one has to ask, what happened on the fringes of the town where it intersected with creeks, bays, fields, and streams? How did the different elements of society penetrate this region and take advantage, symbolically and practically, of its resources? We know that congressmen, when they remembered Annapolis after the Revolution, wrote one another. "Don't you long for a good fat turkie, the fine fish and Delightful Oysters?" We know that the Calverts had these in abundance. We simply do not know for sure how they were obtained, yet that question, which pulls an archaeologist beyond the scientific identification of bones, is one that must be asked.[33]

12

Hunting, fishing, and market trading

> We meet with kingdoms whose monarchs are peasants, towns that
> are built of nothing but reeds, sailing vessels formed out of a single
> tree; where we meet with nations who . . . transact business without
> writing.

Loyer, Godefroy, 1714, *Relation of a voyage to the Kingdom of Assinee, West Africa*

Artifact entry onto a site

In a world of written words, it is hard to see the things that no one wrote about.
Archaeology provides clues. Following them in Annapolis brings both domestic and
wild things into closer view, raising provocative issues. As a start, one should
recognize that the decisive moment for an artifact is often seen as its arrival at a site;
analysts' research questions and resulting observations give the artifact's value.
Chinese porcelain cost more and came further; hence its prestige. There is less
attention given to the channels by which an artifact comes and how these denote
interaction patterns between a site's occupants and others in a community. Among
historical archaeologists, those who have paid the most attention to this have been
zooarchaeologists (cf., Bowen on herding and marketing).

As living animals, faunal remains were artifacts in motion riding a one-way ticket
to death and disposal as refuse. Whereas prestigious ceramics were purchased by the
head of household (see, for example, letters of tobacco planters with orders and
instructions for London factors), food items came in by a different door. Men
maintained the accounts that recorded the overseas purchases; occasionally they
recorded the meat, but more often food supplies were bought and paid for with a
housewife's allowance. She, in turn, sent servants or slaves away from a house and
its yard (i.e., off-site) to find what was needed. The relationships so established and
the accompanying social interaction took place in a social field quite different from
that belonging to fine ceramics. The latter involved factors, mariners, slave-masters,
and international trade; the former centered around women, black and white,
butchers, bakers, greengrocers, market ladies, hucksters, oystermen, small-scale
markets, and local trade.

Provisioning a black and white household

The mistress of a Maryland home made decisions on a daily, weekly, or longer basis
concerning the composition of meals and the number of people to be fed. In many

cases, a meager allotment was given to the slaves and that was that. But where family was concerned, servants and slaves put in long hard hours to prepare meals. Among the Calvert household, such work at times took men, women, and African-American children only as far as the cellar, a locked storeroom, the bi-weekly market, or occasionally to the small shops on Prince George Street. Some days they went down the hill to the waterfront shops where goods spilled out of small, crammed rooms into yards and almost onto the docks.

At other times provisioning the Calvert household involved getting items from its own or other outlying farms, sending messengers with requests that prompted transport of animals on the hoof (cattle) or in wagons (for swine never travelled well afoot) or in baskets (domestic fowl and rabbits). The liquor arrived in wooden hogsheads on horse-drawn wagons. Transport through the city did not go unnoticed even if it was so common an event that townfolk merely noted it in passing. We know they watched the carts and wagons roll by because of fines imposed on men such as Negro John, the elder and Negro John, the younger, for riding on cart shafts and on Mulatto Will for galloping his horse through the streets. Unfortunately we do not know precisely what came from where – in very few cases do good records exist – but as one thinks about the absence of records, about markets in Charleston and in the West Indies, as one considers the later Baltimore pattern, and inserts information on household composition, the food landscape and network system assume a blacker guise.[1]

Analytical questions that begin to suggest movement across this social landscape are where and how meat was procured. This is a different question than one that organizes the faunal analyst's traditional species list (table 11.1); it creates table 12.1. However, table 12.1, with its emphasis on food sources (i.e., the "where") begins to suggest the types of relationships involved in meat procurement, and prompts the related question of how these were initiated and maintained. Answers are not necessarily in the bone elements themselves, although some contain indications. More answers are found in texts that tell how other people in the Chesapeake obtained similar items and reveal the broader procurement networks.

Begin with goats whose absence in Captain Calvert's probate inventories might be seen as evidence he had none. Ever mischievous animals in orchards, Chesapeake planters found them troublesome and smelly. Goats were not in William Reynolds' inventory either; in both cases, their bones appeared among the faunal remains, although not in large numbers. So where did they come from? I first postulated families in rural homes – thinking poor and white – and saw the goat distribution network as bringing town families into contact with people from the hinterlands, for the town's goatkeeper died in 1722 and was not replaced. This was before I knew that the town reinstituted its laws regulating goats as its black population increased. This was before I realized the permutations of a market system in which blacks, whether slave or free, bartered and sold a whole range of small items to the white community.[2]

The town's lower-ranking butchers – the ones who sold meat in market stalls –

Table 12.1. *Selected animals eaten by Chesapeake families arranged according to the location where they were raised or normally lived in the wild*

Barnyard:	Horses, cows, pigs, goats Domestic rabbits Dunghill fowls Domestic ducks, Muscovy ducks, geese, pigeons, Guinea hens
House and barnyard pets:	Dogs and cats
House and barnyard vermin:	Squirrels (edible); rats and mice
Pleasure garden:	Peahens and peacocks; songbirds; sometimes turkeys, pheasants, and exotic animals
Slave quarters:	Guinea hens, pigs, goats
Fenced pastures and meadows:	Sheep, cows, goats, horses
Tilled fields, old fields, and meadows:	Pheasants, bob-whites, mourning doves, Canada geese, turkeys, quail
Deciduous forest and forest edge:	Deer and other forest animals Cattle and swine (allowed to forage) Passenger pigeons, bob-whites, mourning doves, quails, and turkeys

"Fresh" marshes or swamps	Ducks, geese, frogs, turtles; venomous snakes;
	  also racoons, beavers, minks, muskrats,
	  and otters

Creeks, marshes, and bay shoreline:	Dabbling ducks (shallow waters) including mallards and teal Diving ducks (deeper, open waters) Canada geese and whistling swans
Freshwaters:	Gar, pickerel, white catfish, brown bullhead catfish, yellow perch, large mouth bass, shad

Shallow estuarine waters:
  (with lower salinities)
	Butterfish, striped bass, bluefish, Atlantic croaker
	Sturgeon, shad, anchovies, and menhaden
	  (seasonal)
	Summer flounder, white perch, yellow perch
	Oyster toadfish
	Oysters
	Blue crabs (seasonal)

Moderately salty bay waters:	Oysters (abundant) Blue crabs (seasonal) Striped bass, shad, summer flounder, white perch Sturgeon (seasonal), oyster toadfish
Deeper bay waters: (with higher salinities)	Red and black drum, butterfish Scup, spotted sea trout, weakfish, jack Sheepshead (esp. oyster reefs), tautog, kingfish Sturgeon (seasonal), sea bass, shad, white perch Oysters (abundant), oyster toadfish Blue crabs (seasonal)

Table 12.2. Maryland Gazette, *October 1730 (CLXXII)*

A person who came into Town on Saturday . . . to sell some beef, was insulted, threatened, and hindered from using any of the stalls in the Publick Market House by some of the Town Butchers.

were contentious, and not above sly practices such as "blowing wind" into dead calves to make them seem alive. When country farmers brought animals or meat to sell, things got nasty. Disputes escalated from insults and threats to blows, gouging, assault, and battery. Sometimes these were reported in the newspapers and sometimes clerks made careful notations in the minutes of the county court (Table 12.2). The idea that the butchers had black suppliers came while reading the transcript of Negro Frank's court appearance.[3]

In 1734, Frank – possibly a free black – was charged with stealing five lambs while William Metcalf, an Annapolis butcher, was charged with receiving them. Frank was fined £300-worth of tobacco, lashed thirty times, and spent one half-hour in the pillory; Metcalf was found not guilty. If blacks did not normally sell livestock to town butchers, Metcalf would have had no grounds for asserting that he did not know (or expect) that the meat was stolen. No one would have believed him. There is no notation that links Frank to anyone, although the usual procedure was to specify a slave's owner whenever he or she appeared in court. For example: "Negro Jacob, the property of Mrs. Elizabeth Bordley, [presented to the Grand Jury] for keeping one hogg contrary to by-laws." It is also unclear why Frank would have been fined if he was a slave with no funds or if it was unusual for slaves to raise their own animals to sell. Conversely, it was traditional English practice to levy large fines on Indians – presumably the tactic worked with free blacks too – which could not possibly be paid, thereby forcing culturally marginal inhabitants into lengthy labor indentures. Here court and capitalist interests fused. However, the physical punishment was no worse nor less than what whites received for trading in stolen pigs and turkeys. The implication, however, is that it was because the animals were lambs (no owner was identified) that authorities believed they were stolen, not because of the transaction itself. In other words, sheep just seemed an unlikely animal for a black man to own.[4]

Goats, on the other hand, were sold in the well-stocked African markets and had a long and honorable history in food traditions of African communities, whereas they faded fast from most English communities in North America. And in most regions of the New World where blacks appeared, they soon had roles in food procurement (fig. 12.1). In the West Indies in 1708, Oldmixon wrote of slaves who "breed goats, hogs, or fowl, which they sell or eat." A Grand Jury Presentment in 1734 at Charleston set forth how black people were "Hucksters of Corn, Pease, Fowls, &c. whereby they watch Night and Day on the Several wharfs, and buy up many Articles necessary for the Support of the Inhabitants and make them pay an exorbitant price." Similar records of market activity by blacks are given for Georgia, for Wilmington, North Carolina, and for Virginia. Other documents dating to the

Figure 12.1. A black woman selling rolls and chicken legs at the train station in Richmond, Virginia, October 6, 1860 (drawing by Sir Henry Wentworth Acland (1815–1900), courtesy of the National Archives of Canada, Accession No. 1986-7-232.)

period of the Calvert site (the 1720s and 1730s) show that the Ball family who lived near Charleston bought eighteen fowls (£1.10.00), hogs (£8), and rice (more than £50 worth) from male and female family slaves. North of Baltimore (and at a later date), the Banneker family supplied food for workmen at Ellicott mills.[5]

Sometimes what people sold was their own and sometimes what slaves sold belonged to their masters. The practice of forestalling inserted an intermediary, and in many markets the intermediaries included African women. These individuals anticipated the market by buying outside the city gates and made their profit by enhancing the price they sold goods for within the town. It was also tricky to tell the difference between legal and illegal foodstuffs (hence some of the new laws). Mrs. Carmichael, in Jamaica, complained that all her servants kept poultry and sold her the eggs whereas "strange to tell" her own hens were never known to have laid an egg. She also told of cows milked in the night for milk to be sold on market mornings. Sloane wrote that Jamaican butchers slaughtered animals before daybreak; the market for flesh was closed by 7:00 a.m. An unintended result of the early hour was more difficult identification of stolen animals taken before their owners awakened.[6]

There is limited information on the sums people made selling goods in local food markets as well as some indication that men and women specialized in the sale of such items as poultry, fish, green vegetables, and prepared foods. Old Dick thanked the Lord that his mistress gave him "Alexandria market price" for his poultry while another slave noted that whereas his master often took his fish for free, "Sometimes when [another] white man take away my fish I go to my master, and he get my right."[7]

In other words, there is fairly good evidence that at the onset of American slavery, Africans became involved in local markets. While selling foodstuffs brought financial gain, these were not markets in a capitalistic mode. Many prices were fixed (sometimes by law) and the exchanges consolidated mutual assistance networks even as they moved goods from one household to another. African-born slaves were familiar with such small-scale transactions; they could look to the market economies in their homeland as a guide for what to do. West African markets had long histories (Jennejenno and Timbukto had been market cities for centuries); many Africans had intimate knowledge of barter and trade, and women were especially active in the food markets. Dr. James Africanus Beale Horton, for example, observed that "the [Akus] women make excellent traders; within a very short time they would double, treble, and even quadruple a very small amount." Furthermore, many were also proficient at wheeling and dealing in a language other than their own since different dialects prevailed throughout the region.[8]

The discussion of domestic meats in the last chapter suggests that some, including poultry, were purchased by the Calverts. One can go further and insist that if the town butchers who monopolized their trade through fair means and foul had been the "chicken merchants" of Annapolis, some record of poultry sales to Nicholas Hammond and Timothy Sullivan would have survived in each man's list of debts. I first found prices of domestic fowls in a lawsuit filed by Eleanor Tracy and she was the seller. Combine this with John Juitt's plea for relief because his poor wife lived too far from town to sell her produce, and the modest idea of female participation in a market for perishable foodstuffs emerges. Market specialization is hinted at in John Davisson's inventory which contains goods obviously oriented to a lower-status clientele, and to extend this line of reasoning further and suggest that other people had goods they sold that were not part of centralized storehouses controlled by the wealthy is not far-fetched.[9]

In the food trade, poor women obtained licenses to peddle wares on the streets of Boston throughout the seventeenth century. Hawking items for sale on town streets had English precedent. In Annapolis in 1717, three years after Charleston moved to restrict the market activities of its "Negroes," town fathers tried to limit door-to-door sales by confining purchases of "flesh or fish, living or dead, eggs, butter, or cheese, (oysters excepted)" to the market. The restriction did *not* work in Charleston; one does not know what took place in Annapolis nor precisely why townsmen thought they had to regulate food sales on the city streets. Yet as the black population in the town grew, more regulations appeared in the town's records, an indication that the marketing networks were not confined to the Wednesday and Saturday sale days when stalls opened from dawn until 10 or 11 a.m.[10]

Two ideas come to mind. First, space in a town is culturally divided and appropriate town activities are not sanctioned if they are carried out in inappropriate areas. In Annapolis, this meant that middlemen were not supposed to buy goods from producers before they passed through the town gates. In particular, they were not to buy goods whose ownership might be difficult to trace: dead meat, live produce. By the 1780s, the only foods that could be sold outside the market or on a door-to-door basis were oysters, beef, dried fish, salted fish in barrels or large casks; cattle, sheep, and hogs alive; flour in barrels; wheat, Indian corn, dried peas and beans, oats, rye, and brans. All of these were goods normally produced by small farmers or ones whose origins could readily be traced.

Thus laws against forestalling made the market house a sanctioned zone for trade, and commerce by the side of the road an illegal activity. Market-trading was primarily done by producer-traders (i.e., those who made/grew/raised the foods were the ones who sold it). Second, sanctioned behavior may be perceived as non-sanctioned depending on age-grades (as in drinking ages), on gender (as in women fighter pilots), or, in the era under study, on color of skin. Hence the prohibition against slaves purchasing and/or selling items in the 1780s. The onset of these laws can be traced to the 1717 market regulations which might have been written because appropriate people had encroached into inappropriate space, but could also have been imposed in an attempt to control the use of appropriate, if not highly regulated space, by a new group of individuals whose activities were not fully sanctioned.[11]

To get a better image of what *might* have taken place, one should join the limited bits of surviving testimony on Annapolis produce markets with descriptions of food markets in cities like Norfolk, Charleston, and in the Caribbean for the early eighteenth century, ones in which African women were active; the evidence too could be merged with descriptions of seventeenth- and eighteenth-century African markets in which women also participated. We could add Brazil where black women peddled trays of sweetmeats, cooked meats, and African foods and drinks (*acaraje, uatapa, carurú,* and *aloa*) on the streets, while free blacks were go-betweens in a "black" market for foodstuffs in which they "largely governed" sales of fish and meat by 1800. *Acaraje* are small fritters made from black-eyed peas, fried to a "golden crisp," slit, and filled with a pepper sauce containing dried shrimp; they are sold today in Nigeria as "*akara,*" and food historian Raymond Sokolov likens them to hush puppies, crediting Africans (he does not say "women") with the introduction of deep-fat frying into southern foodways and Caribbean towns.[12]

In Charleston, legislation was offered in 1738 to prevent "slaves from buying goods during market hours and to prohibit them from buying fish, fruit, or vegetables at any time." Wealthy people opposed the proposed law because it would have curtailed the range of market errands their black slaves could do. The law was proposed because of the brisk trade that Africans had begun to control and their outrageous abilities to monopolize distribution of country produce within the city (for that is how Charlestonians saw it). One should think of this from different points of view, realizing it was an activity that black men and women enjoyed, a small part of their lives in which some free choice was possible, and one that they probably did their utmost to protect. And one should keep in mind that in modern Africa, as women began to make substantial profits from their market activities, men usurped the commerce. This is not to say that anyone ever made much money selling foodstuffs in Annapolis market stalls nor that women, white or black, were a demonstrable presence within them. It does make one wonder how to find out if they were and whether John Smith's wife, an African-American woman known familiarly as Aunt Lucy, and her bake shop on Prince George Street (ca. 1790–1820) and the few black men in the Wells family who rented market stalls, were ties in an old but unbroken chain with West African roots.[13]

In nineteenth-century Baltimore, African-American women also sold foodstuffs. Baltimore in 1824 and 1831 had eighteen hucksters. Dell Upton notes that this was "a common occupation of black women . . . which most cities tried to forbid, and which meant buying day-old food in the market and selling it at reduced prices from door to door or from the curb." The number dropped in 1841, but rose to twenty in 1850 and to forty-one in 1860. James Wright wrote that "garden and dairy products, eggs and poultry" were the major items sold; fish and oysters (commonly sold by black men) were also part of the trade. Often accused of "foul practices," (or theft), some blacks sold farm and truck produce in the actual market itself. Others operated black grog-shops, catered, maintained cakeshops, and ran food booths set up on vacant lots, at picnic grounds, and at street corners where they sold patties, small delicacies, and occasionally more substantial food (fig. 12.2). Wright's brief summary of African-American foodsellers in Baltimore sounds much like summaries of other food markets in southern towns – ones which began in the early eighteenth century in places which, unlike Annapolis, prospered after the Revolution to become thriving nineteenth-century cities.[14]

Following the food route brings one into contact with a variety of different individuals living and working in Annapolis ca. 1730, and it will bring us still further if we explore its possibilities. It does this because food was central in the daily life of the pre-industrial town, and, for many people, the workaday world revolved around activities associated with food. A series of reciprocal relations can be traced by following the food data at a site outward into the community. Here the ties food established are not with known individuals, but with unknown men and women who had different social statuses and ranks. Understanding how they fit into the web of culture brings the past into closer view. Its image becomes richer when wild living things are incorporated.

Hunting wild

If it is plausible that the Calvert men demonstrated their mastery of "cultured" nature (exotic plants and horseflesh), leaving tracks in the archaeological record as they did so, then it is also appropriate to consider where they stood with respect to wilder forms of life. As background, English kings established hunting preserves with royal hunting lodges (maintained by the peers of the realm) which their majesties visited with great pomp and ceremony. The visual pageantry of an English

Figure 12.2. A fruit peddler selling strawberries on an Annapolis sidewalk in 1893. (Photograph by Frances Benjamin Johnson, courtesy of the Maryland State Archives; Special Collections, Robert G. Merrick Collection, MSA SC 1477-3589.)

hunt symbolized the power of its lords. James Cleland emphasized its importance in 1607, "he cannot be a gentleman which loveth not hawking and hunting." But tension also existed between aristocratic hunting and folk hunting (i.e., poaching), between the way the high and the low hunted wild creatures. Thus King James I, who gave George Calvert his baronetcy, also visited the hunting lodges used by his predecessor, Queen Elizabeth, including Ditchley Park. The Calverts' mother, Lady Charlotte Lee, grew up at Ditchley and her sons often visited their grandfather and uncles. On one visit Benedict Leonard's inquisitive mentor, Thomas Hearne, carefully described the house and its contents, including evidence of hunting's import among English aristocrats. Impaled in a parade of dead creatures around the walls of Ditchley's ancient hall hung a rogue's gallery of stags' horns, half a dozen with engraved brass plates detailing their last day alive: "King James made me to run for Life from Dead man's riding, I ran to Gorcil Gate, where Death for me was biding, 1608, August 26, Monday." Thus, clearly identified, were the stags killed August, 24, 26, and 28 in 1608 who "fled," "ran," and "flew" from the Stuart King.[15]

Maryland's charter, drawn up in James' time, gave the first Lord Baltimore the right to the royal game of the province – deer, turkeys, herons, and other wild fowl. His Council retained the right to grant leave to use "nets, hounds, or other means of taking them," exempting Indians by granting treaty rights to gather oysters, clams, to fish and hunt. Oral tradition in Maryland today still maintains that the third Lord Baltimore, Charles Calvert, set up a network of hunting lodges spread throughout the province. A number of small brick buildings survive from the early eighteenth century which are alike in form and design, associated with his name, with hunting, and containing, in one case, remains of an earlier house hidden within its brick shell. Perhaps the lore has associated Captain Charles Calvert with his namesake, or the Calvert brothers – Edward Henry and Benedict Leonard – with their grandfather, for Charles Calvert, the fifth Lord Baltimore, was here too briefly in 1732 to inspire legends.[16]

There is no way of knowing how the folklore arose; it may have grown up much earlier, when Leonard Calvert was governor and hired men to hunt, sometimes joining them himself, and then merged Leonard with later Calverts. Folklore often does that, bridging time and collapsing boundaries to bring events together. Still, it is clear from two different types of evidence that the Calvert men who lived in Annapolis from 1720–34 did hunt: the inventories listing their weapons, and the bones they left behind.

Edward Henry owned two pistols and four guns together with gunpowder, gun flints, a powder horn, and bullet molds. Captain Calvert left gunpowder, 75 lbs of bird shot, three guns, and seventeen fishing lines. The fishing lines, since they were made from an organic material, did not survive in the archaeological record, but weapons, different gun flints, and varied types of lead shot were found at the site. This array of equipment gains significance when combined with the species list in Table 12.1. It is well known that fish and game were used to add variety to British meals and were traditional elements in dishes served in aristocratic English homes and at feasts. Their relative abundance at the Annapolis site indicates that they created a variation on or embellishment of Calvert dinners in their Chesapeake home and perhaps served other purposes too. A general lack of hunting expertise, on the other hand, can be inferred from the faunal remains at many early eighteenth-century sites. By the late eighteenth century, however, an abundance of fish and game characterized the faunal remains left by wealthy slave owners throughout the rural south.[17]

This is not to say that the faunal remains from wildlife create such a dramatic difference that nutritional measurements or observations on biomass derived from the bone elements would imply a radically different diet within the Calvert household. But a difference is present. The fish and bird bone suggests that, in one way or another, the Calverts had greater dominion over the fish in the sea and the birds in the marsh than ordinary Chesapeake folk. Not surprisingly, the sites that exhibit the closest parallel are two in Maryland's first capital, St. Mary's, occupied in the mid-seventeenth century by a great-great-uncle, Governor Leonard Calvert, and his associates.

But who really hunted?

It is impossible to determine who were the most effective or enthusiastic hunters in the Calvert household. The one who came to mind first was Captain Calvert; I assumed that his English upbringing and years as a soldier created a greater passion for hunting than Maryland men seem to express (at least, by virtue of the faunal remains they left behind). Yet the situation is more complex.

Indians, adult men and young boys, did much of the hunting throughout the seventeenth century, selling game, large and small, to settlers. Among the English, some men learned Indian tactics for hunting and increased their prowess. Others, tied more tightly to farms and the labor these demanded, did not. The lack of intimate knowledge which many held can be seen in William Byrd's account of a 1733 trip to map the dividing line between Virginia and North Carolina. Indians accompanied the commissioners and surveyors to serve as guides and obtain food from the wild. Each day the Indian men "brought down" animals for the cooking pot, their worries increasing as the English paid no attention to the deep-seated beliefs expressed in native protocol for the preparation of wild meat:[18]

> Our Indian was very superstitious in this matter, and told us, with a face full of concern, that if we continued to boil venison and turkey together, we should for the future kill nothing, because the spirit that presided over the woods would drive all the game out of our sight . . .
>
> The Indian likewise shot a wild turkey, but confessed he would not bring it to us, lest we should continue to provoke the guardian of the forest, by cooking the beasts of the field and the birds of the air together in one vessel.

Byrd commented, as a "true woodsman," that bear meat tastes better in the fall when it has "high relish," and that it is "nearest to that of the pork, or rather of wild boar." He also discussed the taste of "rackoon, which is also of the dog kind, and as big as a small fox, . . . and when fat has a much higher relish than either mutton or kid." Byrd's mention of an opossum, which he called a "harmless little beast," suggests a little less familiarity: "The flesh was well tasted and tender, approaching nearest to pig, which it also resembles in bigness." Lawson was more outspoken: because of its appearance, eating a possum was like eating a rat.[19]

The use of Indians as meat suppliers on the surveying trip was not a singular event. In Maryland, the Nanticoke Indians used to leave the Eastern Shore in the winter to hunt deer which they sold to the English. As more forests on the Western Shore were cleared for tobacco, as the numbers of Indians dwindled, and the wild deer disappeared, the Nanticoake gave up this small bit of transhumance (or seasonal shift of abode).[20]

Yet as their population grew smaller and Maryland's Indians retreated to upstate New York, another group of native hunters were forced into the region. These were West African men, people also sensitively attuned to a wild environment of forest, marsh, and stream. They had to transfer their familiarity and knowledge, as well as having to learn its New World permutations, in order to eat: "I had no food but Homony, and for fifteen months did not put a morsel of any meat in my mouth, but the flesh of a possum or a racoon that I killed in the woods," said Old Dick, a slave born in the 1730s of African parents, of the years he lived in Anne Arundel County. He remembered his childhood: "When I was a lad, I used to track wolves on the snow . . . and there was such mighty herds of deer, the woods was feasted with them." By 1737, in the Carolinas at least, both possum and racoon, hunted at night (the animals were rarely seen in the day), became a food source; their meat, frequently eaten, was held in esteem by Indians and slaves, and in the case of possum, preferred to pork. Jack Lubber, a slave of Landon Carter's on Virginia's northern neck, also was a "vast progger in Catching fish, Beavers, Otters, Muskrats, and Minxes with his traps."[21]

Not all black men used traps or nets to catch their prey. Some masters gave slaves guns, a fact that dismayed anxious legislators in the South. Maryland legislators enacted a law in 1715 that slaves were "not to carry guns or offensive weapons off their master's land without leave from the master." Yet dextrous blacks, using guns or nets, were extremely proficient at hunting wild creatures. African-born slaves taught their sons to hunt and young African-American boys, as playmates and companions of planters' sons, taught them the skills too (fig. 12.3). The difference, however, is encoded in Hugh Jones' 1724 discussion of Virginian planters who hunted rabbits for sport (releasing them) or went after "vermin" (racoons). "Vermine Hunting", he wrote, was "very diverting . . . It is perform'd a Foot, with small Dogs in the Night, by the Light of the Moon or Stars."[22]

Night, an excellent time for hunting, was a most familiar time of day for African-born and African-American men to fish as well. They were highly adept on the water, skilled at maneuvering "punts," "a small and dangerous sort of Canoa, liable to be overturn'd by the least Motion of the Sitters in it," in the words of Edward Kimber who watched black or "sable" men dextrously paddle these bay craft in

1736. Almost concurrently, Michel Adanson wrote of flotillas of 500 or more 13–14 ft canoes which Gold Coast fishermen daily paddled sometimes as far as two leagues to sea in the Bight of Benin. In this country, their skills as watermen gave Africans access, in a land of creeks and wetlands, to a wide variety of wild resources:

Figure 12.3. A black youth holding a game bird is shown with his eight- or nine-year-old master, a cousin of the Calvert boys, who holds a bow and arrow in this ca. 1710 painting. (Portrait of Henry Darnall III by Justus Engelhardt Kühn, courtesy of the Maryland Historical Society.)

the Canadian geese that came in October; the pigeons that flew southward in the fall; wild turkey hens, fat and delicious after a summer's feasting. Although oysters were still gathered, much of this activity died in winter, and a good thing too for a people unaccustomed to the bone-chilling winds that blew across the water and for men who shivered in sparse clothes, awaiting the "violent heat" of summer more like their homeland. Each year the cycle began with herring in March, shad in April, and then fish in plenty during late spring, summer, and early fall: rockfish (bass), perch, large trout, drum, sturgeon, sheepshead, bluefish (tailor), channel catfish, porgy, and blue crab. Women joined in the effort, knitting seines, standing waist deep in the waters of Eastern Shore creeks, giving long hours to seine-hauling side by side with the men.[23]

Lévi-Strauss writes of the understanding that many non-Western peoples have of their land and environment as built from "passionate attention" and "precise knowledge." He might have added "an intimate understanding of the habits and ecology of other species," but he did not. All of these are things people learn and hence skills – "carryovers" – that can easily transfer from one land to another, although the actual habitat itself does not. The ethos, in other words, of hunting fish, flesh, and fowl came with West African men and did not disappear as they sailed westward. The marks of their skill are there, subtly discernible in old documents, but more vividly expressed in the faunal assemblages from the places they lived or those of the masters they served. Some of the pleasure too shines through in a planter's comments that, with a task done and a day off, men "usually" went down to the sea to "lay in a supply of fish and clams."[24]

I have no assured knowledge that meat from wild animals was plentiful and readily, routinely obtained in West Africa in the seventeenth and eighteenth centuries. It was not a common theme in the British travellers' accounts whose authors focused more on marketable commodities and the people. It is certainly present in the few sites excavated that date to the period and is also expressed in Benin art. DeCorse found in sites at Elmina that fish was well represented, shellfish was certainly eaten, and that wild fauna made up "a consistent though varying portion" of the faunal remains. Somehow there seems no doubt but what West African men were "ingenious" hunters; they also came to practice their skills in a land of plenty, not of milk and honey, but one where prodigious numbers of birds flew through the skies, and down the coastal flyway. The autumn migration some-times turned the skies black and, among some species of birds, the ground overnight, beneath the trees where they sat and roosted, became thick, six-inch pads of dung. It is clear there was seasonal abundance.[25]

The English roasted duck and baked it in pies; the Africans fried small birds and used them in spicy dishes. And at the Calvert site we have two groups of individuals who shared a passion for hunting, for fish, and for fowl. The actual interaction in procuring wild foods is not retrievable from the artifacts. But comparative analysis shows that more wildfowl was found at the site (36 to 42% in the early features and 57 to 65% in the later ones) than at most contemporaneous sites in the upper Chesapeake. People in the household ate pheasant, quail, turkey, and a range of ducks – some esteemed by the English and some considered by them naught but food for "Indians and Negroes." Brickell sets the tone for mallards: "Their Meat is not to be compared to our tame Ducks for goodness, and [they] are accounted one of the coursest sort of Water-fowl in all this Province [North Carolina]." At the same time, dabbling ducks who fed at the bay's surface in marshes, creeks, coves, and shallow river corners were ubiquitous in Maryland species lists from ca. 1620 onward. It is the range of species diversity and the raw counts, despite the narrow band they fill, that distinguish the Calvert site.[26]

Scarce game is not the reason for the small percentages observed elsewhere nor the reason why planters did not hunt as actively in the Chesapeake in the 1730s as they had 100 years before. Once hunger drove them, but good farming also demanded a farmer's time, while the small return or poundage of most game birds made them less cost effective than a tame, fat duck. A wealthy man with many servants and slaves did have leisure to hunt or could set his slaves to the task. With respect to the Calvert men, they grew up overseas where "the pursuit of wild birds and animals remained an obsessive preoccupation of the English aristocracy until modern times." It was, as Markham wrote in 1607, perceived as "a refined pleasure," one which incorporated nature into culture in a particular way.[27]

The sedentary/wild dichotomy was handled differently among the very wealthy who took wilder things, exotic or rare, and integrated them into their lifestyle to make them emblematic of privileged position; there was also an inversion whereby items associated with the very low appeared at the very top. This could be done because there was no possibility of symbolic confusion for groups at opposite ends of the continuum whereas for those at middling points along the spectrum, the inclusion of one item or another could tip the scales and shunt them down the ladder. The anomalies at the interface between the natural and the cultural world caused confusion, sometimes becoming a source of active inquiry. How did the wild and the tame mix? Where did people fit? Naturalists wrote of wild animals that Indians raised as tame – wolves, among others – but exhibited as much fascination with the mechanics of turkey domestication.[28]

Taming nature through turkeys

Indians, appropriate carriers, brought turkey eggs out of the wild sphere and to the "Christians" (read "English") who hatched them "under Hens, Ducks, tame Turkies, &c." Yet, brought up with chickens, at maturity (18 months) they would start running wild in the woods, coming home only to roost in a tree at night near houses, leaving at sunrise to feed and returning at sunset to perch. Dip a wild turkey egg in a bowl of milk or warm water – domesticated products these – when it is just at the point of hatching, advised John Lawson in 1709, and "it take off their wild Nature, and make them as tame and domestick as the others." Breeding wild turkeys with the tame produced a hardy creature that, for its excellent food, was worth the try. And here again we see the experimentation with the unfamiliar that the orangery emphasized, for turkeys were numerous – whether wild or tame – within the Calverts' faunal remains.[29]

These were not data immediately at hand when Elizabeth Reitz first wondered whether the turkeys from the site were wild or tame. Usually she categorized them as wild in southeast assemblages, but there were so many from Calvert, she questioned her designation. And so more attention was paid to texts about turkeys. It was when Charles Carroll of Annapolis wrote in a 1716 account book that his wife had bought a dozen that evidence for domestication or, more accurately, utilization for profit first appeared. Similarly, the court indictment of a local innkeeper who bought a live but stolen turkey also suggested domestication. If a thief could steal one then turkeys could be owned, but were they really domesticated? Turkeys would not have been listed on John Maccubbin's 1722 inventory – two worth 18 shillings (almost ten times the cost of a pound of beef) – if they were not. Yet before that was seen, a passage in an agricultural report explaining that the turkey's great hunger for horned worms, which arrived in July to eat tobacco, gave planters of the 1760s reason enough (a) to encourage them to roost nearby and (b) to grant them liberty to grub about among the plants, suggested a commensal bird, one no longer fully wild, but perhaps not fully tame.[30]

Symbolic dimensions of hunting

In summary, hunting, while an informal expression of status not tightly woven into activities that surrounded formal governance, was also highly visible. The hustle and bustle attending any hunting party with its bewigged gentlemen, its horses, and servants, as it came and went, was always observed by someone. Further, the foray through the countryside necessarily raised eyes, for men rode furiously. The standard pace was "a good sharp-handed gallop." Timothy Breen writes that the characteristic racing pace as a gentleman rode his quarter horse down highways and byways not only raised a cloud of dust which followed behind, but created a visual, emblematic signal to others in the neighborhood that the gentry were abroad. Thus, in a symbolic sense, hunting provided more than the simple pleasure of tracking across the countryside and bagging a bird.[31]

Geertz observes that one way in which kings mark territories as their own is by traveling from one sector of their realm to another. Assuming that both black and white men hunted, the sorties mounted by the Calvert household served a similar purpose, one in which the edible product so obtained was consumed as part of the social dining practiced within the home, but one in which the surrounding social action had more far-reaching effect in society than provision of food itself. The basic premise is that one of the dividing lines between men of power and wealth and those of lesser means was the breadth of the ecological domain (or natural world) which their households controlled and used. This is why for centuries foraged wild resources were a privilege of high-ranking English families.[32]

Yet the ways that the high and the low, the white and the black meshed together created a situation in which one of the highest emblems of status – triumph in the hunt, prowess with a gun – was also the leitmotif of the lowest social order. Foraged wild resources were their sustenance and without them, many would have starved.

Tracking across the land, becoming intimately acquainted with fog-shrouded coves and inlets, some black people established broad networks, found danger zones, and acquired the knowledge to subvert the social order. Side by side, different models of social space were built and to be in one was not to be in the other.

VII

TIME MARKERS AND THE SOCIAL HIERARCHY

Of all the human sciences and studies anthropology is most deeply
rooted in the social and subjective experience of the inquirer. . . .
Obviously, there is much that can be counted, measured, and
submitted to statistical analysis. But all human action is impregnated
with meaning, and meaning is hard to measure, though it can often
be grasped, even if only fleetingly and ambiguously.

Victor Turner, 1986, *The Anthropology of Experience*

13

Generations of change

One generation passeth away, and another generation cometh.

Ecclesiastes

Elizabeth and Benedict Calvert

Throughout the book, the emphasis has been synchronic, tying the site to Annapolis in the early eighteenth century. A synchronic slice of time lets an archaeologist see how different groups within a community interacted with and influenced one another. This is a key to understanding social process. However, when using artifacts as a base, the different social domains that together form a cultural pattern appear with varying intensity depending upon which one we look at. Some are highly visible in the archaeological record; others are more visible in documentary sources. For many, their illumination depends upon weaving contexts from artifacts *and* documents.

The dimension provided by passing time is also critical to understanding social process. It is one way of seeing the increments whereby small shifts in daily life (almost imperceptible in the short run) are a mechanism through which cultures change. Because historical archaeology allows us to make fine-grained time distinctions, the measure can be as short as the years between one generation and the next. Looking at the children and grandchildren of Captain Calvert and the fifth Lord Baltimore who also lived at the site on the Circle lets us see how a shift in the positional relation between the family and the political power base brought about a symbolic renegotiation of space and introduced other elements of culture change.

Most of the earlier chapters described how the ca. 1730 archaeological features and their artifacts demonstrate the Calvert family was at the center of society and because of this position possessed social, political, and economic power unsurpassed in Maryland for its era (1720–40). It did not stay unsurpassed long. As pointed out before, the Calverts who lived in Annapolis ca. 1730 died young; only one child survived. Five-year old Elizabeth Calvert, who inherited the family estate in 1735 with her older sister Ann, who then died too, was an orphan without close Chesapeake relatives. Her mother placed her in the care of Onorio and Elizabeth Razolini. A girl, she could not inherit the political power her father, Captain Charles, or her godfather, Benedict Leonard, wielded. As a female, she was not seen by society and its legal system as a person competent to manage a small financial empire no matter her age. The Calvert family did the best they could to protect the estate by appointing as executors men of wealth and status who were indebted to the family in different ways and loyal to Lord Baltimore. Yet Elizabeth Calvert's material and symbolic assets made her a potentially valuable "power" within the political, social, and economic networks of the province. She was not someone the English Calvert family could forget (fig. 13.1).

While "Mistress Betsy" grew up, few changes were made to the property; almost none were visible in its archaeological record. Some silt began to accumulate in the drainage duct beneath the Circle-facing doorway, but this, except for a repair or two to fence posts, was all that was found. Mistress Betsy grew up in an old-fashioned house with an overgrown garden – a house whose empty rooms were turned into dancing chambers where Elizabeth Razolini taught Chesapeake youths the proper steps, where Onorio discoursed passionately with Alexander Hamilton, and may have tutored her cousin Benedict Swinket. Surrounded by black women and children as a very small girl, never at a loss for companionship, it is unclear how many remained through her childhood.[1]

When Elizabeth was five or six, the fifth Lord Baltimore sent her illegitimate cousin, ten or twelve year old Benedict Swingate (or "Swinket") to Annapolis to live with Dr. George Stuart, an Edinburgh-educated physician. Benedict was Baltimore's eldest son, although this may not have been widely known in Annapolis (fig. 13.2). He lived around the corner from Elizabeth in an old-fashioned house on Francis Street. At least once, if not more often, he was beaten by a town bully and thief. His assailant was brought to the County Court and whipped; the court record places young Benedict in Annapolis in the mid 1730s. Family tradition says that King George had Admiral Edward Vernon of the British Navy escort him to the Province. Benedict Swinket witnessed a will in 1738 under his childhood surname, but in the early 1740s swore an oath in court under his new one: Benedict Calvert. Other witnesses testified that the two men were one and the same.[2]

As Benedict grew up, his father, the fifth Lord Baltimore, and uncle, Cecilius Calvert, turned over some of the family's Maryland holdings to him, and made provision to give him the first of the patronage jobs Benedict held until the Revolution. In 1745 he became the customs collector for the Patuxent District and its Naval Officer, a post which paid him a portion of the collected custom fees. In 1755, he joined Dr. Stuart as Judge of the Land Office. In 1748, possibly at the instigation of his father, Benedict married his 18-year old cousin and moved into the house on State Circle. In the 1750s, he toyed with the idea of joining the Tuesday Club and attended one or two of their meetings, but extended his city network instead by serving as an Annapolis Councilman. By this time his relationship to Lord Baltimore was well known (see table 13.1).

Elizabeth and Benedict Calvert made minor changes to their home, cleaning the well in the front yard, but none of the activities – the massive house cleanings and renovations – that often mark the transition between one generation and the next and create artifact-rich sealed deposits at a site, left any imprint on the site at State Circle. It is questionable whether much was done. Benedict's move into the house and assumption of responsibility may have been a more gradual merging of the past and present conditions than a sharp transition. A laissez-faire attitude towards the property might be inferred by town fines for disposing of garbage in the nearby street and for the dirty fireplace flue that caused a chimney fire "to the great detriment of the town . . . "[3]

A year after their marriage, Elizabeth gave birth to daughter Rebecca, the first of thirteen children; the house on State Circle filled with children's voices again

Figure 13.1. Elizabeth Calvert, daughter of Captain Calvert, at age 24 is captured in this portrait by John Wollaston which she sent to Elizabeth and Onorio Razolini in Asolo, Italy. (Illustration courtesy of the Baltimore Museum of Art.)

Table 13.1. *Excerpt from letter of Charles Calvert, fifth Lord Baltimore, to Benedict Calvert*

Pray do not think of Marrying till you hear from me, having some things to Propose to you, much for your Advantage, and believe me I will never force your Inclination, Only Propose what I think will make you most Happy . . .

Chart 13.1. *Family chart for Elizabeth and Benedict Calvert*

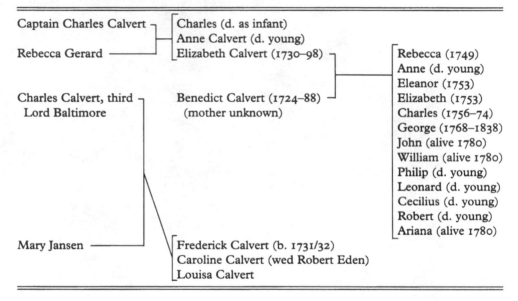

(chart 13.1, fig. 13.4). The remains of their toys were among the more whimsical artifacts recovered from later deposits (fig. 13.3). Captain Calvert's copy of *The Education of a Daughter* may still have stood on a shelf.[4]

Benedict's position in the Maryland bureaucracy was well-placed, but he did not immediately enter its inner circles. His father died in 1751 without additional provision for him in the will. Benedict received far more than most "natural" children, but unlike them, he was never told his mother's name. Legend says this was because she was the sister or daughter of the king. Lord Baltimore had already given Benedict much land with his gift of Mt. Airy. Through these gifts and marriage, Benedict Calvert acquired more than 4,000 acres of prime tobacco land. Benedict's relationship with his legitimate brother, Frederick the sixth Lord Baltimore, was distant. His uncle, Cecilius Calvert, had handled Maryland matters for many years for the dissolute Frederick. As Cecilius (in his sixties) withdrew from an active role in administering affairs for the fifth and sixth Lords Baltimore, Benedict turned his attention to developing the Mt. Airy estate. According to local legend, it had originally been a hunting lodge for Charles Calvert, the third Lord Baltimore, placed in the care of a cousin, Henry Darnell.

Benedict, Elizabeth, and their children moved to Prince George's County in the early 1760s, where they added a two-story wing large enough to become the mansion house itself, and created a wilderness garden next to the terraces. The couple also added new dependencies including a kitchen, meat house, smokehouse, carriage house, carpenter's shop, and twenty "negro quarters." A very small hothouse also

Figure 13.2. Benedict Calvert, natural son of the fifth Lord Baltimore, six years after his marriage to Elizabeth Calvert (Portrait by John Wollaston, courtesy of the Baltimore Museum of Art.)

may have been built about this time. It is unclear how the family afterward used their Annapolis town house, although advertisements indicated that they rented the stables to be run as a business in 1764. Benedict also let his business partners, Wallace, Davidson, and Johnson, sell occasional cargos of British goods from the property in 1772. Its proximity to the market house on the Circle made it a natural choice, and one can readily envision the brick-paved courtyard area as a display area for merchandise.[5]

In 1769, the sixth Lord Baltimore appointed Robert Eden, recently wed to Charlotte Calvert, as Maryland's governor. The Edens purchased the "Capital Mansion House" with its waterside vistas from each room, a small mount over-looking the city, and maintained, if not installed, its extensive ornamental garden (fig. 13.5). The Edens also drew their Maryland relatives into the Governor's circle of intimate friends. Benedict's love of horse racing was shared by his brother-in-law and the two men may also have shared racehorses, raising them on Benedict's Prince George's County estate, running them in Annapolis and throughout Maryland or Virginia, sharing the winnings, the stud fees, and selling various offspring. Jolly Chester won the race for Calvert in 1763; Regulus, son of the Arabian Godalphin, raced and won in 1766 for him, but in 1769 Regulus raced for Eden. The governor soon appointed Benedict to the Governor's Council.[6]

By the 1770s, Benedict Calvert possessed an extensive country estate and upwards of 150 slaves, including skilled craftsmen. Extrapolating from the acreage and the size of the slave-holdings places his wealth in the upper echelons of the province. There was a substantial income from fees collected at the Land Office and as customs duties at Patuxent where ships of the larger Maryland merchants and slave dealers made port. Benedict Calvert had sufficient wealth to adopt an upscale lifestyle. Abbé Robin, who traveled through Maryland in the Revolution, described plantations and slave-masters similar to Benedict Calvert:[7]

> [Maryland houses] are spacious habitations, widely separated, composed of a number of buildings and surrounded by plantations extending farther than

Figure 13.3. A wooden block with the letter "R" was left behind a fireplace when it was bricked up in the 1770s. (Illustration by Julie Hunter-Abbazia.)

the eye can reach, cultivated . . . by unhappy black men whom European avarice brings hither. . . . Their furniture is of the most costly wood, and rarest marbles, enriched by skilful and artistic work. Their elegant and light carriages are drawn by finely bred horses, and driven by richly apparelled slaves.

Figure 13.4. Young Rebecca Calvert, named for her grandmother (Rebecca Gerard Calvert) clutches a doll dressed in silk as fine as her own. Gilded buttons identical to those shown on her dress were recovered from the Feature 5 fill above the orangery. (Portrait by John Wollaston courtesy of the Baltimore Museum of Art.)

Benedict Calvert's membership among the planter gentry was secure. His alliance with the Stuart family and the Scottish businessmen in Maryland was strong. His children were being raised as befitted the family's rank. In 1772, his oldest son (Charles Calvert, see fig. 14.3) was sent to Eton to be educated; a younger son studied under Jonathan Boucher alongside George Washington's stepson, John Parke Custis, who courted and married one of Benedict's twin daughters.[8]

At the same time, Benedict Calvert's position was not equal to that of the earlier Calverts. His ties to the central social and political institutions in Maryland rested on a tenuous patronage relationship with his legitimate brother, on his wife's ancestry and wealth, on gifts from his father, and on an anomalous relationship with his English kin whose economic and political interests were not always aligned with his. Within the Maryland hegemony, his position was tangential, not pivotal. Calvert's closest and tightest ties were with the Scottish businessmen. His loyalty to this group of men was ensured, in part, by his purchase of Alexander Stuart's indenture in 1748 and its immediate resale to Scots who freed the Scotsman transported in 1747 after the Battle of Culloden.[9]

Change on the Circle

As his association with Governor Eden strengthened, Benedict Calvert began a series of changes to the State Circle home. It is not coincidental that these took place as the new State House was being built on the Circle. The 1770s was a time when many public material symbols were renegotiated, infused with new meaning. It followed on the heels of the "Golden Era," years of immense prosperity and town growth when major elite families built large and ornate mansions in Annapolis to clarify their rising positions and consolidate social status. A rage for buildings and pleasure gardens marked the social competition among the gentry whose lifestyles were characterized by opulence and splendor. Abbé Robin who saw urban and rural estates wrote that "We especially observe this opulence in Annapolis." The large mansions and their elaborate gardens cast into shadow the smaller Calvert house and its out-of-date orangery and ornamental garden. The new houses also outshone the second Maryland State House; hence its replacement.[10]

It is questionable in my mind whether Benedict Calvert would have rebuilt his Annapolis home if his brother-in-law had not become Governor of Maryland. My suspicion is that the house might have been sold, but Eden's appearance in Maryland provided an opportunity for Benedict and Elizabeth personally to renew and strengthen their Calvert contacts. At the same time, Benedict had to do so in a way that was not detrimental to his networks among the planter gentry and the Scottish community. Benedict Calvert was in a position very similar to that of Captain Charles Calvert. His future lay in Maryland. To the extent that the interests of the English Calvert family were congruent with those of the Maryland gentry, there was no conflict. When the interests diverged, Benedict had to move carefully. The changes he made to the house on the Circle took each power domain into account. In essence, the alterations constituted a symbolic renegotiation of Calvert social space. Through this process, it was defined as local, given a Maryland orientation.

Calvert brought the house into visual accord with the Georgian mansions built in Annapolis during the 1760s. The changes he made to the house and the yard in the early 1770s almost eradicated its medieval legacy. He reversed the major front facade to face west towards the Maryland State house, shifting the earlier orientation which faced east across the Bay towards England. The reversal, which was perhaps the major design decision in the renovation process, made the house symbolically responsive to the State House differently than before (fig. 13.6). It altered the positional relationship of the two structures, making one clearly subordinate to the other.

The ca. 1730 work yard (fig. 13.7) became a symmetrical formal facade facing the new State House. At least partially in response to the overflow soils accumulating on the Circle as large cellars for the new state house were dug, Benedict Calvert built

Figure 13.5. Governor Eden's mansion and its accompanying dependencies, some within and some without the garden, spoke to the social standing of its occupants while revealing spatial configurations characteristic of other Annapolis mansions. (Drawing by Benjamin Ogle, ca. 1800, from Rutland's Wharf across the shore; Maryland State Archives, Special Collections, Maltby collection G779-6).

an octagonal forecourt with strong brick walls that held back the raised grade of the hill. He formally demarcated the threshold between the Circle and the entrance to his home with a cobble-paved entryway between the forecourt gate and the Circle's dirt road. One could read the sturdy cobble-paving at the threshold of the site as a small, symbolic gesture invoking the former political importance of the house. The center point of the new brick forecourt gate precisely aligned with the center point of the main door, giving the entrance courtyard bilateral symmetry. A new oyster shell path was installed proceeding at a 90 degree angle directly from front door to gate, burying segments of the older, oblique path. Levels of doors and windows were raised; the building now looked as if it had been placed on site well after Nicholson planned the Circle in 1695. Inside there was additional renovation which made it a more sophisticated arena for entertaining and greeting friends, allies, and neighbors.

Workmen also dismantled all service buildings in the old work yard, partially filled the large, brick-lined well, covered the ca. 1730 paved surface and added new soil to the yard to give the forecourt a level surface. They then dug a new kitchen well in the southwest yard. Building crews demolished the orangery, laid a layer of fill over it, and then put a new addition onto the house, thus covering and inadvertently preserving the materials beneath its crawlspace. The archaeological deposits created during the process contained almost 100,000 artifacts, including old-fashioned household items tossed out as part of the stylish revamping and some that were politically disadvantageous (figs. 13.8, 13.9). Later the family added a square brick office to the "back" of the house. All this was accompanied by extensive

Figure 13.6. Merchant's bottle seal dated 1769 found at the site helped date the renovations made by the Calvert family after their brother-in-law, Robert Eden, arrived to govern the province in 1769. (Photograph by the author.)

landscaping, but the effect sought was not that of terraced gardens like those surrounding William Paca's house or Upton Scott's home. The ground surface was raised; gardeners hid the old terraces under a layer of garden loam.

When workmen finished, the house on the Circle no longer overlooked Chesapeake Bay. What was originally the ornamental garden had become a service yard with a well, privy, smokehouse, and stable – a locus for mundane activity separated from the eyes of people walking around the Circle. The grandeur of the extensive pleasure garden disappeared. Reduced in splendor, the house was domesticated and no longer served as a potent symbol of political power. This was appropriate since the Calvert family in Maryland no longer possessed it themselves. They had stepped back, off center stage, waiting to see how the change (and one could feel it in the wind) would alter their situation, maneuvering for position as they did so.

Benedict Calvert was a popular figure in the Province and reluctant to give up the power vested in him by his father – power that also legitimated his Calvert identity. He refused to surrender his office as a Judge of the Land Court until forced to do so on May 13, 1777. This must have had as much effect among Maryland's antiproprietary dissidents as Calvert's earlier actions in 1770. Although Benedict

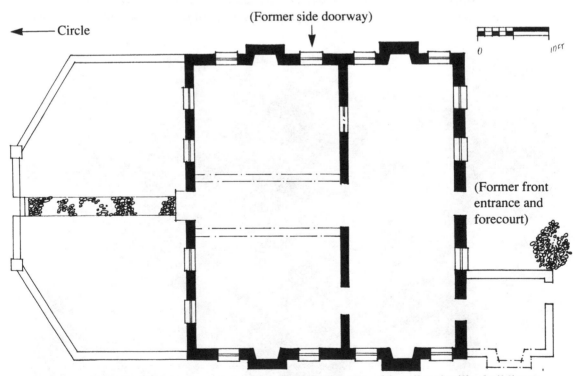

(Former side doorway)

Circle

(Former front entrance and forecourt)

(Location of former gardens becomes a service area with well and utility buildings)

Figure 13.7. Plan of house and front yard shows changes made by Benedict Calvert and his sons. (Drawn by Russell Wright, AIA.)

Calvert never signed the loyalty oath, the new government did not confiscate his rural estates. Unlike other avowed loyalists, his lands and holdings were never sold. There are many possible reasons why this was so and probably not all will ever be known. But living in country seclusion created its tensions.[11]

Six months after resigning the Judgeship, Benedict Calvert pleaded that he and his family be allowed to leave Maryland (table 13.2). No one knows how his plea was answered or if it was. In the long run, Benedict and Elizabeth Calvert survived the war with their fortune almost intact, although the triple taxes imposed on loyalists were onerous; Benedict may not have been as fearful as he presents himself. While his "step"-father, Dr. George Stuart, legally turned his estate over to his Maryland-born wife, Anne Digges Stuart, and returned to Scotland, his younger "step"-brothers in the Stuart family served in the Continental Army. Two of Calvert's sons-in-law (John Parke Custis and Charles Stuart) also were well placed in the Continental Army. While none of his own sons seem to have served either side in the war, Benedict occasionally supplied the army with horses, grain, and other provisions. And much to the chagrin and outrage of more patriotic men, George Washington, unable to make it across the Potomac to Mt. Vernon before the winter night set in, spent his first night after resigning his commission in Annapolis on December 23, 1783 with Benedict and Elizabeth at Mt. Airy.[12]

Benedict Calvert died in 1788. During his lifetime, his family formed few ties through marriage to the major Maryland families, but instead formed alliances with

Figure 13.8. Scratch blue tea saucers stylish in the 1740s and 1750s were discarded across the site in the 1770s. (Photograph by Marion E. Warren.)

neighboring Virginians across the Potomac. In 1774, with some reluctance (because of his youth, because of her lack of money) George Washington gave his permission for his stepson, John Custis, to wed Eleanor Calvert. Her younger brother, George, began to cross the nearby Potomac to hunt in the early morning with the older Washington after the War ended. Elizabeth Calvert saw her sons successfully enter Maryland politics, although one had married into a loyalist family.[13]

During the next decade the two Calvert brothers – Edward Henry and George – were repeatedly elected to serve in the Maryland House of Representatives. Both men sought political power from a system based in America rather than from one centered across the sea. The Annapolis house was not sold until the younger George married a Belgian heiress, Rosalie de Stier, and assumed control of her father's Prince George's County estate at Bladensburg. Earlier, while the 27-year old George was in residence at the house on the Circle, George Washington's grandson, John Parke Custis, was placed in his care, with Washington observing, "I can manage men; I can't manage boys." And as the years progressed, the family's association with political activity in the new nation's capital strengthened; Calvert men served on behalf of their country in a variety of ways. Since their activities were not oriented towards Annapolis, and since their Calvert ancestors were associated primarily with

Figure 13.9. As the Revolutionary spirit strengthened throughout Maryland, someone in the Calvert household threw down the well a delft punch bowl with the unpopular epigram "Success to the British Navy." (Photograph by Marion E. Warren.)

Table 13.2. *Benedict Calvert's wartime request to move his family*

Sir:

Mr. Richard Dent went this morning to my plantation with a gun and a number of people with him a got to pulling of my corn. I went and spoke to him and asked him what he did there. He pretended it was his. I told him that if he had a Right that was not the proper manner to get it. He informed that he was determined to proceed and lifted up his gun at me, upon which I came away. I received the inclosed note after I came away. I live under your Excellency's government and while I behave myself well, I put protection for my family and property [first], if you can't afford it to me. My family has been made so uneasy by these frequent outrages that I hope you will permit me to remove my family and property where I can get protection and you'll oblige.

proprietary rule, memories of the family's days in Annapolis passed from local view and were no longer conveyed in the town's own dynamic oral tradition.[14]

This is why when the archaeology began, almost no one in the town knew anything of the site's illustrious past.

Annapolis redresses

Physically, Annapolis in the 1780s was vastly different from the 1720s and not solely as a result of the economic prosperity of its Golden Era. The changing town also reflected a change in cultural patterns. Mental constructs derived from a medieval English heritage – the old order – played a lesser role in the way people thought about the world, in their attitudes, perceptions of daily life, and organization of activity. Association through contiguity, which created a co-mingling of people and activities within small, bounded spaces, was displaced by newer modes of association in which institutions – church and state – or individuals defined their social identity and expressed their power by the degree to which they could separate themselves from others. Privacy was equated with individualism and with liberty. One means of separation was to organize activities into discrete spatial areas and it is this change in the use of space that the archaeologist readily perceives in the landscape of Annapolis. Gradually, over the century, the co-mingling of activities lessens and one sees the start of the trend in which spaces became distinctively domestic or commercial, public or private, black or white.

There are many signs of this narrowing frame; Annapolis regulations provide one set. They show increased concern over unruly, wandering sheep, goats, swine, and geese inside the town, over "large and fierce dogs infesting streets and alleys," over slaves buying and dealing or being entertained without their master's knowledge. Town laws began to forbid fires in wooden chimneys (most characteristic of the homes of the poor or of slave dwellings), fires in iron pots, and/or tubs of wood filled with dirt (or like contrivances). This was one means they chose to restrict black. socializing. Another was to condemn houses "in ruinous condition" used for "meeting places or as shelters for servants, slaves; and other loose, idle, or disorderly people." Thinking about the situation, the aldermen prohibited the latter from entering town and, while they were at it, ruled against digging pits for garbage, against "bog-houses, house of office shambles or stalls" (i.e., privies) that were nuisances. They made it illegal to put "carrion, stinking fish flesh, dead creatures, broken glass bottles, loose oyster shells or other filth" in the passages next to houses, in the streets, or in the alleys unless these were removed within half a day. They wanted a clean town and their insistence gives us some reason for thinking it was a changed town they wanted too. There was to be no sale of winded or blown meat, no galloping of mares or geldings in the streets, no gambling (except billiards) and no prostitution.[15]

The reorganization was accomplished by activities – new construction, alter-ations, renovations, landscaping – that left an imprint on the archaeological record and evidence in the archives. It was helped along, in Annapolis, by damage to the town during the Revolution, when facilities were strained to capacity by the military and governmental activity. Officers and soldiers were quartered in Annapolis homes and, in part because of overcrowding, wore them out (fig. 13.10). The town was not attacked. Many rent payments (made by the State of Maryland and later reimbursed to the State by the Continental Army's Quartermaster General) specify both rents and damages paid to Annapolitans. Included among these were payments to Benedict Calvert.[16]

With the Revolution, political power passed from the English nobility into the control of Maryland men. The process began earlier as did accommodation to it. The cutting edge of the cultural transformation appeared in Maryland with the emergence of a native-born elite in the early 1700s. Yet, in terms of the material evidence there was little in particular to distinguish the Calvert yard before the 1720s. There was also nothing in particular that distinguished the artifact assemblages from ca. 1690s features except the paucity of artifacts and the relative absence of the delft and porcelain that characterized the ca. 1730 deposits. Yet the earliest features and their contents – a few sherds of earthenware, a few bits of glass or pipe stems, some bone – are clearly contrasted with the elaboration that set apart the yard areas at the site (as demonstrated by the kitchen and garden-related features) and the artifact assemblages of the ca. 1730 Calvert era when the occupants were members of a wealthy, politically powerful household.[17]

The elaborate yard ca. 1730 was also asymmetrical since the visual balance of its constituent parts was not fully achieved through bilateral symmetry. There were brick buildings and wooden buildings without an integrated architectural design. Ad hoc additions created the extra space required to house the extended family, comprised of at least two nuclear families, numerous servants and slaves, and its varied possessions. There is a strong contrast between the division of space during the first three periods (Taylard, Hemsley, ca. 1730 Calvert) of the site's occupation when compared with the use of space and its demarcations at the site in the early 1770s. The changes made to the yard were radical and, to the best of my knowledge, these were made in response to social and political change in Maryland that resulted in the physical alteration of the public buildings and public lands at Annapolis. The relocation of its well, for example, was brought about in response to these factors rather than to any mechanical defect. The changes in the spatial configuration of the site were not due to a series of incidental events; the reorientation of the front facade to the interior of the Province symbolized the deeper transformation within the social and political structure of Annapolis.[18]

It is hard to know to what extent Benedict Calvert was consciously aware of the symbolic structure that he was altering; his evaluation may well have been cast in terms of what seemed appropriate and what seemed out-of-date. The fashionable changes made to the house, and in particular its front forecourt, also presented Maryland natives with an opportunity for symbolic inversion. This provides a more vivid example of the way Annapolitans consciously knew of and used the visual symbols that dominated their cultural landscape. It occurred with the construction of the large, ornate, octagonal privy beside the State House in the 1780s (figs. 13.11 and 13.12). While the replication of style may have been a political act of

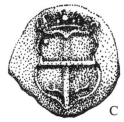

Figure 13.10. Military buttons testify to the use of the house as an officers' barracks in the Revolution. (A and B) In 1779, George Washington ordered that the use of "M" on a uniform button would stand for the state of Maryland; thus the "3M" and "4M" markings on buttons designate the third and fourth Maryland regiments. (C) The 1773 Virginia halfpenny has a shield and crown motif almost identical to the button shown here which was used on uniforms worn by Virginia troops in the 1770s. (D) The general service Continental Army pewter waistcoat button with the intertwined USA on its face was used by troops as early as 1777. (E) Pewter waistcoat button marked "NC" was issued to regiments from North Carolina. (Illustration by Julie Hunter-Abbazia.)

appropriation (symbolically inverting the prior order), or the emulation and use of a newly fashionable form, in terms of the positional relationships it set up on the State Circle landscape, an opposition between the octagonal forecourt at the Calvert house and the outhouse was clearly set in place. And shortly thereafter, the octagonal forecourt at the Calvert site was removed.[19]

In terms of the dynamic and recursive qualities of cultural discourse, the ensuing diagram of the events above would appear as in Table 13.3.

The archaeological study of the site and its relationships to the town demonstrates that town landscapes were not passive entities, but conveyed symbolic information. In the 1690s, Governor Francis Nicholson chose the crests of two Annapolis hills as placement points for a capital building and a church. He worked with entities that were natural – trees, hills, creeks, ravines – but the form these assumed in the Annapolis landscape was cultural. The process through which the townscape grew was additive but certain principles were maintained. In the 1730s, the fifth Lord Baltimore chose an Annapolis hill crest for the Governor's mansion, as did his son-in-law, Robert Eden, in 1769. Other wealthy families (the Pacas, Ridouts, Chases, Carrolls, Hammonds, Brices, and Ogles) placed their homes on high land, elevated above the tiny wooden houses of the poor that lay just above the Annapolis waterfront, and above the commercial warehouses, shacks, and quays that lay below an escarpment at an elevation almost level with the tide line. These events illustrate the prescriptive mode within landscape utilization; they were elements that Marshall Sahlins would say were "valued for their similarity to the system as constituted."[20]

There were gardens in eighteenth-century Annapolis, ornamental and practical. Working gardens could be as small as 10 ft × 12 ft, maybe smaller. Pleasure gardens

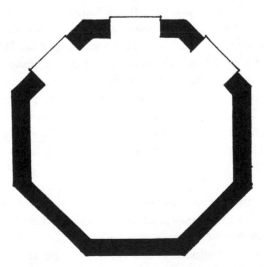

Figure 13.11. Footprint of the octagonal privy echoed the shape of the Calvert forecourt facing it across the Circle but its three individual doorways provided easier access than the single gate at the Calvert yard. (Floorplan drawn by Russell Wright, AIA, based on eighteenth-century illustrations of the State House buildings published in the *Columbian Magazine*.)

Table 13.3. *Chart of change: point and counterpoint*

1770s. Construction of stylish octagonal forecourt, symbolically associated with the elite, by Benedict Calvert.

1780s. Construction of stylish octagonal privy for use by Maryland legislators ordered by the new *state* legislators.

1800. Removal of octagonal forecourt, now no longer stylish or associated with the elite, by Benedict Calvert's sons.

required more space. Nicholson made provision for them when he designed Bloomsbury Square in imitation of the ca. 1680 London town squares with their fashionable town houses and enclosed gardens. A house set on a lot surrounded by a garden created a home atmosphere that was airy and healthy. However, the Calvert governors also used their garden to tell people of Calvert rank by embellishing it with an orangery, by growing other exotics, and undoubtedly by adorning it with statuary. The placement of houses, the use of social spaces, the creation of gardens, and the growth of specific plants were elements in a non-verbal discourse that told of relationships within the social order.

By the 1770s, the lifestyle of wealthy families in the Chesapeake was characterized by extravagance, luxury, and ostentation; witness Abbé Robin's journal. The sealed deposits that the Calvert family created as they altered their house and garden provide ample evidence of these qualities of the gentry's lifestyle. If one were to judge the quality and quantity of the ca. 1730 deposits by the contents of the later ones, one could only conclude that the wealth and power of the family had grown, not decreased (fig. 13.13). But the later deposits are not the appropriate *comparanda* by which to judge the earlier. Historical practice in the Chesapeake was altered, creatively reconsidered, to the point that a measure of one's position was the rapidity with which new fashions were adopted and material goods acquired. Hoping to improve their social position, to consolidate the advantages they did possess, and to remain as active well-connected participants in Maryland society, Benedict and Elizabeth Calvert bought as many fashionable ceramics as other planter-gentry (fig. 13.14). The quality of the items purchased remained as high as it was earlier; the quantity rose tenfold; minimum vessel counts demonstrate this with a total of 166 from the early (and smaller) features and almost 1,000 from the later.

Retrospect

Although familiar with much of the early history of Annapolis when archaeological research began in 1981, I overlooked the power of classificatory schemes to order perception. Preliminary ideas on the use of space at the Calvert Site were based on the organizing principles used in contemporary society. Yet whenever the present was used to interpret the past, there were contradictions such as a front yard that contained quantities of kitchen debris and a back yard that was almost pristinely clean. The present was not a good analogy to use in understanding an early eighteenth-century site and it clarified few of the archaeological clues that were found.

The continuum between past and present masked the reality of the cultural separation that existed through time. Ivor Noël Hume sat down with me one day in 1982 to discuss the site and what we were finding. He asked a number of questions, pointing out what a fascinating site it was since, in his view, it appeared to be one in which archaeology was going to tell us things that documents could not. In such a case, he said, you had to treat the site as if it existed in a foreign land, as if it were a Chinese puzzle.

The site possessed a coherence or order derived from different assumptions about the way the world was built; it worked according to unfamiliar rules. The site represented a household contemporaneous with the emergence of the Georgian Order, but one that was itself not fully representative of that order. The Calvert household was situated on the cutting edge of time at the end of an old era and the start of a new one. Its members transformed customary social practice even as they sought to reproduce it. There is a direct, immediate sense in which our modern world is linked to late eighteenth-century culture that makes it relatively easy to

A Front View of the State-House &c. *at* ANNAPOLIS *the Capital of* MARYLAND.

(From The Columbian Magazine of February, 1789)

Figure 13.12. Statehouse, council chamber, privy, and treasury in 1789. The sizes of the various buildings also signified the new political relationships between different sectors of the government. (This drawing, attributed to Charles Wilson Peale, first appeared in the *Columbian Magazine* and is provided courtesy of Marion E. Warren.)

understand how it operated or to understand, in Deetz's terms, the Georgian world view. It has a coherence and clarity for us not characteristic of other times and places. We not only comprehend the Georgian world view because we still share many of its basic assumptions, but also because elements of its deeper structure still underpin contemporary culture. Surviving features surround us and are readily visible in buildings standing today in the Historic District of Annapolis. Brice House, Hammond-Harwood, Chase-Lloyd, and other Georgian mansions are symbols of our mytho-history set in the land. The way it chose to treat its "others" in lore, legend, and models for social interaction live on.

Culture exists only as we ourselves construe it; it has no immutable form. The categories by which we organize our world, the classificatory systems we impose on

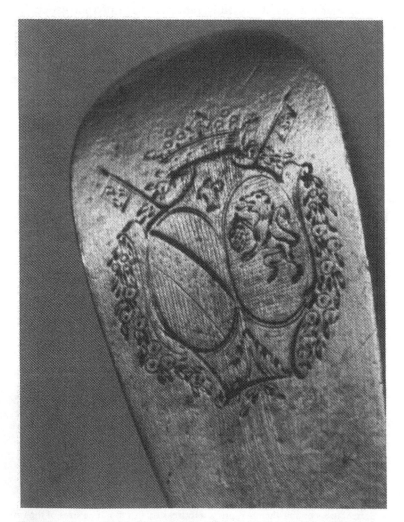

Figure 13.13. A graceful silver spoon bearing a coat of arms with a ducal coronet, probably made by a European silversmith, was recovered from deposits above the orangery. (Photograph by Marion E. Warren.)

it, and the reality that we perceive stem from culture. Hence it was, at one level, a very simple matter for Georgian men and women to create new designs and even new forms of nature. At another level, it was very difficult because these forms were the symbolic expressions and representations of the culture itself. One could not change their form without altering the structure of the society. The inter-relationships involved here are not fully understood, but are also visible in other studies of British encounters in the New World. What Marshall Sahlins saw in a study of Hawaii could be applied to the Chesapeake: "Responding to the shifting conditions of its existence . . . the cultural order reproduces itself in and as change." Continuing, he noted that this was especially true when a culture was one that licensed its subjects, notably the "heroic aristocracy," to construe the going values creatively and pragmatically, to depart from existing arrangements, to subject them to continual negotiation and renegotiation, and thus to reconstruct their own social

Figure 13.14. Creamware vessels with twisted handles, beaded rims, and exquisitely detailed, sprigged leaf or molded decorations – milk pitchers, sugar pots, coffee pots, and chamber pots – were among the fine ceramics used in Benedict and Elizabeth Calvert's home. (Photograph by Marion E. Warren.)

condition. In the Chesapeake, the provincial elite, including the wealthy merchants, formed a social stratum equivalent to the Hawaiian aristocracy, one that began actively to define itself as an emergent colonial elite by the third quarter of the seventeenth century, and hence one whose present and future were open, subject to continuing redefinition through verbal and non-verbal discourse – the language of buildings, grounds, fences, walls, and small "China" teapots.[21]

14

Charisma and the symbolics of power

> At the political center of any complexly ordered society . . . there is
> both a governing elite and a set of symbolic forms expressing the fact
> that it is in truth governing.
>
> Clifford Geertz, 1983, *Local Knowledge*

As variations on a theme, the message that the Calvert family possessed power was
sent and repeated through images and events in different cultural domains of daily
life. The message was of a legitimate claim to rank in the social hierarchy and to
the legitimate possession of political hegemony within the Province. It not only
depended on words and deeds, but also drew strength from a potent, visual
symbolism – pomp, ceremony, conspicuous consumption – that had worked for
hundreds of years in European countries where few men knew how to read written
words, but all people knew how to decipher the tangible, touchable, seeable
evidence of power. The Calvert household's position on the power continuum
gave it wide latitude while its geographic distance from England (combined with
Benedict Leonard Calvert's desire to return home) perhaps lent its customary
expressions a certain flamboyance. The linchpin for its analysis was provided by
Geertz:[1]

> No matter how democratically the members of the elite are chosen (usually
> not very) [assuredly not in eighteenth-century Maryland] or how deeply
> divided among themselves they may be (usually much more than outsiders
> imagine), they justify their existence and order their social actions in terms of
> a collection of stories, ceremonies, insignia, formalities, and appurtenances
> . . . that mark the center as center and give what goes on there its aura of
> being not merely important but in some odd fashion connected with the way
> the world is built.

Geertz describes these as consisting of images or rites or "crowns and coronations,
limousines and conferences." He stresses the connection between active centers of
the social order and the symbolic power that some men possess. In essence, the more
closely one is related or tied to the center, the more charisma or symbolic power one
embodies. Geertz points out that the center, in such cases, is not a geographic or
mathematical point on the physical universe. It is "the point or points in a society
where its leading ideas come together with its leading institutions to create an

arena in which the events that most vitally affect its members' lives take place . . . It [charisma] is a sign . . . of being near the heart of things." Among eighteenth-century Annapolitans, the signs signifying a place "near the heart of things" included trade beads, gratuities, and Indian alliances, Chinese teawares and social entertaining, Irish servants, black slaves, and slave children (an accompaniment of young boys and girls), exotic plants and animals, race-horses and town fairs, gun salutes and birthdays, hunting lodges, fish, fowl, and lordly peregrinations, and finally but not least, communiques and encounters between the upper and lower legislative "houses" that met in the buildings on the Public's Circle which lay immediately above the Calverts' town lot.[2]

Early eighteenth-century Maryland was not an industrialized, machine-based society; its communities were small (even on the large plantations, they normally consisted of fewer than 200 persons), of a personalized character. Like English medieval society, members of the dominant white culture "broadly shared the same set of values and interpretations." In this society, the Calverts stood proxy for Lord Baltimore who in turn stood proxy for the King and England. Residing in Annapolis, strategically and geographically centered in the Province, the Calvert family and their culturally variegated household also stood visually and symbolically at the center of power in the town.[3]

Active centers of the social order, however, normally have less to do with their placement in geographic space than with their connectedness to the primary institutions in a culture. The leading institutions of any culture are conceived as those that substantially affect its members' lives. Kinship and family networks often form a metaclassificatory system; in Maryland society they held central importance and were pervasive, framing activities that took place within various spheres of activity, such as the political, the economic, and the social. Besides family, other leading institutions were the provincial bureaucracy (one in which kinship affiliation played a strategic role), and the generalized exchange system of the Chesapeake oriented to tobacco. The growth of slavery also took an incremental leap in the eighteenth century, introducing a new verticality into social relations (fig. 14.1). As black people became more numerous, the society responded to their presence in a variety of ways, while African-born men, women, and children themselves struggled to re-establish cultural order in their lives and maintain their own distinctive cultural identities. Social ceremonies, public and private, were important structures too because of the way that they dovetailed with the cultural emphasis on hospitality. The social trappings of power included events in the public domain and the private, in science and the arts. Each of these domains formed a locus where "leading ideas" came together with the leading institutions to create an arena for social action in which the Calverts were active and prominent. Their political authority, in part, was defined by this cultural frame.

To put this argument as plainly as I can, let us assume that the Calvert family and household were both defined by their position vis-à-vis the center and in turn defined it. This dynamic, two-way relationship between family and center was expressed in more than one cultural domain. The relationship one sees – the family and household position on the power:non-power continuum (defined as nearness to or distance from the "center") is seen when analyzing the order of space (visible archaeologically; for example, the change in the use of space described in the preceding chapter) and is repeated in the order of things, in fact in a range of different object categories (also visible archaeologically). Because they drew on contrasting forms for meaning, the principles of spatial organization observed at the Calvert site become coherent when cast against comparative architectural studies

Figure 14.1. Men were set apart in many ways; the social divisions were shown on objects as ephemeral as paper tobacco wrappers. (Illustration courtesy of the Colonial Williamsburg Foundation.)

of other, early eighteenth-century building forms, vistas, house placements, and landscape activities. The relative positions these and other forms of archaeological evidence denote vis-à-vis the Maryland "center" are reiterated in other social domains less accessible through archaeology. However, they are reachable through family reconstitution charts (cf., kinship networks), through account books (cf., monetary redistribution and mercantile activities), through a range of activities and attitudes revealed in court records, letters, and diaries, through legislative disputes, and laws made to regulate and constrain the culture of slavery.

The interpretation here has focused on the analysis of artifacts and features recovered from one of the most prestigious households in the eighteenth-century Province of Maryland. Yet it is insufficient simply to say a household is rich or poor, powerful or powerless, because this assumes that an audience knows precisely what these labels meant in terms of the everyday behavior of the past. It also implies that there is a one-to-one correspondence between individuals at particular levels in the social structure and their social action. In the fluid social settings that characterized communities at the outskirts of the British colonial empire, customary social practice was frequently creatively reconsidered and reconstrued. Some identifiably powerful and charismatic men first arrived as immigrants, indentured servants, supercargos. Although their names were unknown, there were black men and women too who rose to positions of power and respect within the region; this fact is inescapable once one grasps certain dimensions of black culture. A person could grab power from either end, move up or move down; it existed at all social levels. The signs of power differed, however, depending on one's position in the culture. Whereas the signs of Calvert power rested in their garden and their Chinese porcelain, the symbols of black power included necklaces of carnelian beads or coral, sometimes intertwined among animal teeth and plant materials (or shell, bone, stone) (fig. 14.2).

Finally, it is of particular importance in studying colonial settlements to recognize that social action, whether or not in England and Europe it was usually comprised of "prescriptive structures," had necessarily to incorporate and accommodate a high degree of "performative structure" in New World communities. These terms, as used by Sahlins in *Islands of History*, refer to the degree to which prior cultural practice constrains ongoing events. They draw on the anthropological concepts of ascribed social status (obtained by virtue of birth – or past events) and achieved (obtained by virtue of one's own actions throughout life). Where tradition is highly valued and there are many social sanctions invoked when it is broken, people less often creatively reconstrue behavior, and prescriptive structures hold sway. In more open cultural systems or where the traditional social order has been shattered, people as social actors frequently seize opportunities to rework the traditional forms of behavior in day-to-day life (praxis), creating a situation where performative structures are dominant. Part of their cultural survival, in fact, can be a stealthy refusal to alter core values, a stubborn refusal to forget. Such refusal can be charismatic.[4]

Social scientists point out that charismatic attraction is an element that seems inextricably linked to power. The *Oxford English Dictionary* defines "charisma" as a grace or talent, a free gift from God. Charisma is an element of culture visible in living societies, less so in dead ones. Still, its presence and role can be discerned in the narrative of Maryland given here. Annapolis in the 1720s and 1730s was home to a number of dynamic households headed by vibrant men whose activities gave new life to the town and province. There were men with brilliant legal minds who became astute politicians, such as Thomas Bordley, Daniel Dulaney, and Charles Carroll of Annapolis, fortune-builders like Amos Garrett, unrepentant rogues such as Thomas McNamara, enterprising innkeepers, barbers who substituted as folk doctors, and a number of Scottish physicians turned entrepreneurs. Other important households in the town were established by men who came to Maryland to serve in official positions for Lord Baltimore (John Ross and Edmund Jennings), aligned with the family (George Stuart), related to the Calvert family (Darnalls, Digges, Lowes, Sewalls) or otherwise part of Baltimore's political network. Maryland had its share of vibrant, charismatic women such as the Widow Dent, but these are harder to see than one would wish. Overall, the charisma of the Calvert family outshone the rest. Some fought its magnetism, others forged their futures through it. It could be described in terms of raw power, or economic blessing, but

Figure 14.2. A red carnelian bead originally from India was recovered in the slaves' working area near the well. These beads are rare on North American sites, but one other has been recovered from St. Augustine, Florida (Deagan 1987). (Photograph by Marion E. Warren.)

that would be reductive, for the symbolic images of the family were thoroughly entangled in people's ideas of what Maryland was and should be (i.e., integral in their world view).

The Calvert men and women who came to Maryland were near the center or "heart" of the Province not only in the political domain, but in a number of different and allied domains. This is partially what made the Calvert power so extensive. It is, in part, the fascination the family evokes. It was inevitable that its residue should remain in the artifacts they left behind. The artifacts indicate that the Calvert family used ostentation (visibly conspicuous, magnificent objects out of the realm of the ordinary) as one means of enhancing their political and social power, and to make it appear numinous (fig. 14.3).

Yesterday's people

Another theme that runs through the book is that of a cultural discourse. Put simply, as the Calverts "spoke" to Maryland men using the media of speech and visual imagery, was their message as effective as they wished it to be? Or, were Maryland people already far enough along the road of change that the forms of discourse and their associated symbols of hierarchy and authority used by the governing Calverts were outmoded? These questions were raised by an earlier reader of a draft of this book, and in considering them it is my belief that the political discourse reached an impasse by ca. 1730 which existed until the Revolution. The Country Party was adroit at turning their governors' political discourse back on itself, contesting it. It is also fair to say that while Benedict Leonard Calvert represented a lifestyle that was forward looking in many respects, he also believed firmly in authoritative governance. Autocracy was continually undermined in Maryland. Yet, simultaneously, elements of the Calvert domestic life that gave them charisma in the town – the fine china, the fancy foods, the passion for horticulture, and the large number of servants – were emulated by almost every upwardly mobile family in the province to one degree or another (fig. 14.4). Each and every one wanted to be touched by the numinous aura that surrounded the gracious life of the Calvert family.[5]

The results are awe-inspiring at all ends of the social spectrum. On the one hand, exceedingly wealthy men like Samuel Galloway and Charles Carroll built magnificent homes surrounded by extensive, terraced gardens, raising the symbolic imagery of home and country seat to levels that approached what the English Calvert family possessed at their country estate in Epsom Park (fig. 14.5). These homes are one of Maryland's proudest legacies; some shine even today, encapsulating an image which should be protected, and often is not. On the other hand, the incorporation of smaller luxuries into daily life led to some odd juxtapositions.

> [1791]. We slept in a private home which only took in travelers. The exterior of that home presented a picture of poverty; it was falling into ruins . . . We were served tea in beautiful china cups, in a parlour the floor of which was full of holes, and where daylight came in through cracks in the walls. The sugar-bowl, the cream-pitcher, and everything was tastefully arranged on a

Figure 14.3. In this painting of young Charles Calvert, grandson and namesake of the fifth Lord Baltimore and Captain Calvert, at age 5, his sumptuous dress is matched if not outpaced by the finery worn by his young black companion. (Painting by John Hesselius, 1761, courtesy of the Baltimore Museum of Art.)

round and extremely clean, mahogany table . . . I was amazed to see pretty dresses of muslin trailing along over the worm-eaten, but well washed floor. The mixture of wealth and poverty, of studied elegance and negligence, made a very striking contrast.[6]

Socially conscious, this Maryland family chose a few small ways to express its rank and to indulge in luxuries that once were reserved for their betters. There was a certain amount of freedom in the province to do as one willed; there was also a vitality to the early Chesapeake that entices one to look further at its artifacts, large and small. If we excavated the site where the women above lived, their long swirling dresses would not be there, but the Chinese porcelain tea cups would speak to the fineness of the cloth. And how about the cracks in the floor? Well, at the Calvert site we found some 300 buttons, over 100 beads, and 800 common pins in the crawlspace above the hypocaust foundation; most had clearly fallen through the floor. Yet these remind one that "to recover the realities of a remote past and to appreciate its ethos, we have to . . . recover something of the sense of it that its possessors had, each in their own generation."[7]

Figure 14.4. Maryland families who could not afford peacocks in their gardens could have proud peacocks on delft plates. (Photograph courtesy of the Colonial Williamsburg Foundation.)

But there are elements of ethos – wit, wisdom, human grace – often not accessible through pure archaeology. We would never know that Mark Challoner wore an Indian suit of deerskin dress and that half of his moveable wealth in 1722 (cf. table 2.3) was a debt due him from Captain Calvert, then governor, who was in the process of negotiating with the Indians. We would never know that Gilbert Falconer shortly before his death in 1736 urged London to send men to Maryland to live with the Indians, learn their language, and record their ways: "I hope thou wilt give me leave to tell thee as Secretary of the Royal Society, that we in America wonder that they have several times sent Gentlemen over at their expence to take Account of our Insects, but never any to learn from the Indians the Use of our plants and herbs . . . The Indians have many valuable Secrets among them."[8]

We might find the skeletal remains of the slave whose rage, and its cause is unclear, drove her to take an axe, hide in an Anne Arundel home one dark night in 1722, and bludgeon Samuel Galloway, the son of a slave-dealer. Hannah killed Galloway seeking justice for wrongs a woman can well imagine. The results were haunting and tragic. The Province recompensed the Galloway family for their son's death and it was long years before white men and women in Anne Arundel County forgot Hannah's act.[9]

Who is "the other" in this case that an archaeologist sees? Caution would say that two "others" existed: one a black slave woman and one a white Quaker man. It has been easier reading the texts that survive to see the Quaker, and even to "think like" him, to follow the lines of his culture and begin to see why he did what he did. And thus I have followed Captain Charles and Benedict Leonard Calvert through their site and through their deeds. I know some of the ideas that informed their thinking and were integrated within their belief system. Many are not comfortable to think about. Their elucidation or expression is encoded in the material world of the Chesapeake. Yet when one looks at these objects more closely,

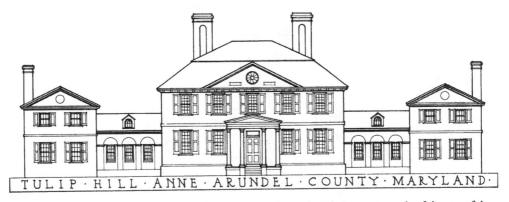

Figure 14.5. Tulip Hill, built by Samuel Galloway in 1756, stands today as an example of the graceful Georgian mansions that were set off by pleasure gardens and reigned over the Maryland countryside. Architectural drawing by George Lindsay originally appeared in the Domestic Architecture of Anne Arundel County, *Monograph Series: Recording the Architecture of the American Colonies in the Early Republic*, No. 5, vol. XVI. (Courtesy of Mrs. Newell Cannon, Harwood, MD.)

other people appear. People did not speak with one voice in the eighteenth-century Chesapeake.

Those of us who like certitude find it unsettling to face a plural history that appears in one light or another depending on the perspective that is chosen as a guide. Yet this is the record of Maryland's past. Any careful look at its material record reveals different dimensions; by shifting position on the structural scale, other people come into view, bringing their own systems with them. We can consider the implications of the Arabic text of the ancient Psalms of David written out ca. 1730 by a black man on Maryland's Eastern shore and wonder if like David he too "danced before the Lord with all his might." We can read portions of a letter from an indentured English servant in Prince George's County and worry at her plight: "scarce any thing but Indian Corn and Salt to eat and that even begrudged, many Negroes are better used. Almost naked, no shoes nor stockings to wear . . . what rest we can get is to rap ourselves up in a Blanket and ly upon the Ground. This is the deplorable condition your poor Betty endures."[10]

Within the dominant culture, the points of view of many people, black or white, were irrelevant, but within a humanistic archaeology, these other divergent perspectives become keys to understanding the social interaction that created Chesapeake culture. It is the joy of ethnohistory and historical archaeology to see each in the "ceramics, glass, and little things" that fell between the cracks and under the floorboards of an old Maryland home.

VIII

THE VITALITY OF CULTURAL CONTEXT

Context is the source of interpretation, the environment of significance. Outside context there is no understanding.

Henry Glassie, 1989, *The Spirit of Folk Art:
The Girard Collection at the Museum of International Folk Art*

15

Archaeology as anthropological history

> The basic similarities of history and anthropology, and therefore the usefulness of one study for the other, are concealed under opaque layers of jargon. History is ethnology, vertically ordered, and the historian's interpretive difficulties parallel those of the ethnographer.
>
> Henry Glassie, 1978, *Meaningful Things and Appropriate Myths*

The native's point of view

When I first wrote a proposal to the National Endowment for the Humanities to analyze artifacts and prepare a final report on the Calvert site, the projected monograph was tied tightly to archaeological data. Its goal was to describe and present the findings from the site so that they constituted and preserved the site record scientifically, as a set of observations, measurements, stratigraphic profiles, and so on, drawing the material out to make modest links between the archaeological record and historic events as in Otto's *Cannon's Point* or Kelso's *Kingsmill Plantation*. But as Larry McKee, Karen Bescherer, Stephen Patrick, Meryl Burgess and I worked through the Annapolis data, it became clear that method in historical archaeology had not focused on the articulation between archaeological data and anthropological "events"; social process and social relationships remained masked in archaeological patterns derived through standard procedures. Ordinary methods were inadequate to relate the material manifestations of Chesapeake life to the structure of the society that created them, define different dimensions of experience within the Calvert household, or find connections between household and community. In other words, historical archaeology as customarily practiced did not enable the artifacts and features from the site to tell us about yesterday's people.

I began anew with an archaeological reworking of Marshall Sahlins' suggestion that history could be exploded by the concept of anthropology and anthropological insight increased by adding a historical dimension. I reread Malinowski, paying attention to his belief that the goal of ethnography was to grasp the native's point of view, his relation to life, to realize *his* vision of *his* world. Today, this view is presented as classic anthropological strategy: the attempt to see another way of life in its own terms. The concept is reiterated by modern anthropologists who stress that culture "does not present itself neutrally or with one voice." According to Edmund Leach, modern anthropologists use one of two approaches. Either they base their interpretation on ideas derived from first-hand observations made in the field, or they base them on a priori models to which convenient ethnographic evidence is fitted. This can be seen as the process of working outwards from the data (an interpretive model) or of imposing a familiar conceptual scheme on the data (i.e., using an abstract set of ideas about what ought to happen and seeking evidence of it).[1]

In reality, both intersect, and anthropological fieldwork is a dialectical process, as James Boon emphasized when he observed that all interpretation is culturally embedded. Historians, realizing this, made subjectivity an issue in their discourse: "The dilemma of historians is that they want to see the past 'as it actually was,' but can see it only through the medium of their own and other people's ideas." Archaeologists have an added complication. Without people, archaeological artifacts are meaningless lumps of clay, bones, stone, and brick. An artifact data base is always fragmented, and archaeological encounters with past societies are distant ones. Since we work only with material residues, we have no opportunity to observe the stream of social action that surrounds objects (i.e., their social fields) or the people that give them shape. Artifact interpretation requires the imaginative reinsertion of people from the past into each distinctive context.[2]

Archaeologists build models of past life by combining and recombining patterns in their data; these are the effects of numerous "individual" choices made by men and women long ago. Of import here is the anthropological distinction between individual relationships and individual action, and person-to-person relationships and social action. To the extent that an archaeological pattern is a product of individual choice, it tells little of a culture; to the extent that it is derived from repetitive social action, it tells more. Nonetheless, it remains a built, empirical model. Some anthropologists believe a genuine cultural order is not recovered through this means, and without doubt there are many people from the past who would not recognize the cultures archaeologists have built for them from material remains.

This is one of the impasses that archaeological theorists try to overcome by stating that the past is dead and cannot be recovered through ethnographic means. They thus close the door on much of the informative dialogue that historians value so highly: the "unending dialogue between the present and past"; the reciprocity between now and then; the interaction of tradition and breakaway thought. When considering preliterate societies, the impasse, however, is of far different magnitude than it is when studying literate societies. Evidence of social action resides in the ground, but also in a wide variety of cultural texts. These tell of the deeds of people who were center stage (cf., the Calvert men), or those who were supporting actors (their women and children; the servants; the slaves), and even of those whose activity took place off-stage (butchers, merchants, princes).[3]

While ethnographic study superficially seems to depend on participant-observation among living peoples, the basic idea behind the injunction to discourse with the natives until you know their point of view is also held by historians who say, "Go on reading until you can hear the people talking." Historians see discourse with the past as an active, intellectual endeavor, describing it as a "communicative process built on the model of a dialogue." Personal knowledge obtained from documents is not isomorphic with knowledge obtained through fieldwork. It does, however, increase with increasing familiarity with the informant, i.e., the texts (or primary sources) for a particular area at a particular point in time. This process develops as a deepening understanding, and scholars caution others in words much like those that anthropologists use: "Having a historical sense is to conquer in a consistent manner the natural naivete which makes us judge the past by the so-called obvious scales of our current life, in the perspective of our institutions, and from our acquired values and truths."[4]

What is meant by an anthropological experience of culture? It is sometimes glossed in the phrase "other fields, other grasshoppers." During a sultry, steamy Florida summer in which eight-inch grasshoppers began to munch on leaves and plants, this took on a new meaning. Newspapers reported the recommendation of state horticulturalists: carry a big stick, use pruning shears, bite their heads off, do whatever works. Whatever works can be defined in many ways and in this volume it has been defined to include a series of assumptions about anthropological analysis, well expressed by Edmund Leach, including the beliefs that human volition, foresight, and planning are important elements in culture change. The individuals, black and white, who lived at the site, were viewed as active participants in the creation of the material record; it was assumed that they drew upon their individual cultural backgrounds, English, Italian, and West African, in shaping the world around them. At the same time, because they lived in a pluralistic society, what survived in the ground was expressive of a variety of folk beliefs about what to do and what not to do in cooking a meal, welcoming a guest, giving birth to a child. And, by virtue of the close proximity in which members of the different cultures lived at the site, it was also assumed that things changed in unforeseen and unplanned ways. The separate cultures were in transition, fusing to become part of a regional lifestyle which would eventually subsume them (fig. 15.1).

Culture and culture change in brief

Culture is a complex concept. There is no agreement on its definition. To some, culture is "the nonbiological mechanism of human adaptation." For many, it resides in the human imagination and is primarily a mental phenomenon; others insist it is a set of values, beliefs, ways of doing things that are shared, activities that take place in the streets and market spaces. Whatever it is, culture is tenacious and mutable.[5]

If there is little consensus among anthropologists and archaeologists as to what constitutes culture, there is also great agreement that it is extremely important and structures people's lives. Humanistic anthropologists stress the dialectical aspect of existence, that some elements of life are over-arching and bridge time or space while others are culture specific; they consider the physical nature of human experience together with environmental constraints and potentials as a unitary dimension, but also posit an essence that lies in individual and cultural differences. Clifford Geertz phrases it this way: "Becoming human is becoming individual, and we become individual under the guidance of cultural patterns, historically created systems of meaning in terms of which we give form, order, point, and direction to our lives." As individuals we have options to reconstrue practically cultural precedent as we live; this is done as much by thought as by action. Life consists of continuity and change.[6]

Outside anthropology, however, there is often a misreading of culture and how it works; it is seen as a possible *marker of* social phenomena, like group identity, but not as *models that shape* social phenomena, creating social and historical process. The dialectic is unrecognized. The relationships of culture and history, structure and praxis, are emphasized by Marshall Sahlins: "History is culturally ordered, differently so in different societies, according to meaningful schemes of things. The converse is also true: cultural schemes are historically ordered." The position that culture is a mark of, instead of a model for, leads some historians to reject the ethnographer's insight. But today, as history and anthropology grow closer, historians also point out distinguishing criteria for work in their genre that call to mind studies in classic and contemporary anthropology.[7] Take Peter Burke's list of what constitutes the new culture history:[8]

A. A focus on microscopic, detailed case studies qualitatively framed.
B. In-depth portraits of small communities, combining the scholar's and writer's crafts to describe with wit, wisdom, and color past life, breathing life into dry accounts by a careful scripting of the historical narrative. This includes an emphasis on writing that demystifies the past by making it accessible to an informed reader.
C. Use of a society's own norms and categories as the basis for objective analysis. Causal and global explanations are set aside. Here one sees no generalizing arguments; unity is momentarily displaced to consider diversity.
D. Giving close attention to world view as expressed through customary daily procedure no matter how small or how seemingly irrelevant to larger societal issues (war, famine, etc.).
E. A turning from the theories of Marx and Weber; eschewing overdeterminism.
F. A turning to the French tradition represented by Durkheim, van Gennep, Mauss, and Bourdieu. Incorporation of ideas from symbolic anthropologists.

Burke's list has clear anthropological roots. Some anthropologists, however, would add additional elements such as the recognition that there is rarely a "first cause for any complex social phenomena [or] single organizing principle." New ethnographers also reject the usual distinction between histories of nonliterate peoples and societies with writing and collapse the boundaries between ethno-history, historical archaeology, and prehistory. Many would extend the reach of "historical" records to include oral tradition, art, and other less customary sources. They would explore the multiple realities, acknowledging that these are beyond the control of both scholars and the people of the past who left the material remains found at a particular site.[9]

No view, in other words, can be all-encompassing, and cultures, depending on one's point of view or position in society, possess different dimensions. No reality presented is, a priori, right; no reality is inviolate; cultures always change in one way or another through time and space. But to study change, "time must be stopped," Henry Glassie writes, "and states of affairs examined." Without this step, a scholar can never see her subject very clearly and is unable to understand why people shift, alter, and transcend old ways of doing things.[10]

Learning about culture change also involves isolating essential features. These vary from one culture to another, but as anthropologists inject a historical perspective into their work, they are also discovering that characteristic forms of behavior ("cultural schemas") sometimes have great time depth. In summarizing the characteristic forms of Balinese culture, Geertz concluded, "the scale of things varied, and their brilliance, but not, so far as I can see, between, say, 1343 and 1906, what they were all about." A six-hundred-year span of cultural continuity is *not* posited for the Chesapeake, for many characteristic forms underwent radical transformation. Yet some things stayed the same for several generations, some for longer, and always

Figure 15.1. A slave cabin from the nineteenth century shows its African and English heritage. For example, its wooden chimney echoes the chimney on the 1697 courthouse in Charles County, Maryland shown in fig. 1.1. (Photograph courtesy of the Virginia Historical Society.)

contrastive elements existed to set people apart by age, by skill, by social rank, and so on. Among these was the importance of clothing; what we recover at sites barely suggests its brilliance or critical role. But because it is described in such detail in probate inventories, it provides an excellent example of how people visually separated themselves within the society. It also presents a dimension of male activity that has slipped from view: men as peacocks, shining in finery, a competition in colorful silks and satins later replaced by Victorian black.[11]

For example, from detail in his inventory, it is easy to imagine the appearance of Edward Henry Calvert. This amiable, good-natured man was surely one of the town's brighter lights as he strode from the dusty streets leading up State House hill or crossed the Public Circle. Walking abroad, escorting Margaret Lee, meeting, conversing, and exchanging information with Annapolitan men, Edward Henry visually heightened the authority held by his brother and denoted the social distances, the different ranks that existed in the town by the way in which he dressed. Clothing in this era, Lawrence Stone observed, was "second only to hospitality as a status symbol." The validity of this can be seen vividly in the portraits of Edward Henry's niece and nephew.[12]

Edward Henry himself wore waistcoats of fine and gentlemanly fabric: cool, white calico; blue satin; yellow tabby; or scarlet camlet (a costly Eastern fabric). He owned no fewer than twenty-five shirts, at least ten pairs of variously colored britches, including one set made of buckskin which he wore with a red jacket; a dozen pairs of boots, pumps, and slippers; four dozen different pairs of silk or worsted socks and stockings; eight sets of gloves. Edward Henry had a scarlet cloak, coats of red, blue, brown, black, and yellow, and a wig for almost every day in the week. He could choose among a silver hilted sword, a new dagger, or two older swords and a brace of pistols if he wished to be armed. Some hint of the grand appearance he must have presented in the social landscape is gained from Devereux Jarratt's words on wigs: "A periwig in those days [ca. 1730] was a distinguishing badge of *gentle folk* – and when I saw a man riding the road, near our house, with a wig on, it would so alarm my features . . . that, I dare say, I would run off, as for my life." Kimber made the same association, combining it with an English perspective: "Tis an odd Sight," he commented, "that except some of the very elevated Sort, few Persons wear Perukes, so that you would imagine they were all sick, or going to bed . . . methinks, 'tis very ridiculous." One can only conclude that Edward Henry in his various hairpieces was a very fine man to see.[13]

That his appearance contrasted with many Annapolitans' can be seen in a list of clothing Charles Carroll left. Carroll, a merchant and lawyer, wore black silk trimmed with gold and suits of grey. Further hints can be gained by contrasting Edward Henry's dress with traditional patterns utilized by others of lesser rank in the Chesapeake. Attorney and poet Ebenezer Cooke in 1708 described Maryland's less distinguished farmers, maids, and servants garbed in scotch-blue. In a more controlled comparison, Susan Ostroff analyzed the cloth purchased in a Calvert County store between 1730 and 1734, and found that men usually avoided buying brightly colored cloth. Brown was the most popular shade, especially with plantation owners, although mariners preferred black, and government officials, physicians, or attorneys often selected blue.[14]

Extending her comparison to Philadelphia, Ostroff noted that the Deputy Governor, Robert Gordon, was "colorfully" clothed in a portrait where he wore a green coat lined with red and a waistcoat. Gordon's clothing contrasted with the brown fabrics favored by Philadelphia Quakers, making him distinctive. The relevant question, of course, is how much more colorful the two Calvert brothers appeared when he met with them in Annapolis in 1729 to negotiate the boundary dispute – an occasion duly noted in the *Maryland Gazette* (June 24, 1729) but without a description of dress.

Rhys Isaac wrote of the symbolic importance of making a proud entrance into the social landscape by riding a sleek, fast horse and, as noted earlier, Captain Charles Calvert owned one of the raciest gray stallions in town, a portent of the fame Maryland later attained for its thoroughbreds. There is insufficient detail in his inventory to know what the Captain wore or whether he favored the fashionable clothing that Edward Henry chose. And, since Benedict Leonard packed his wearing apparel and took it away on his journey home, there is no information on it either. But Benedict Leonard did leave behind a set of watered red bed curtains, pillowcases, and coverlet together with bolts of fabric in green, blue, brown, red, black, and yellow, which approximate the colors his brother wore. They foreshadow the range of colors that would become customary tones chosen by wealthy families in the Chesapeake for their clothing in the years to follow. In fact, there is much about the Calverts and their lifestyles that spoke of changing times, but one can see the give-and-take structure and cultural practice in the lives of ordinary Annapolitans too.

While societies can be bounded, political units, culture itself is not neatly closed. There are always transmissions of beliefs, goods, and peoples across the borders. One has only to acknowledge the presence in Annapolis of people with rich and varying ethnic backgrounds to realize that dominant Chesapeake culture in the early eighteenth century was in the process of assimilating new ideas and that acculturation was as much a part of daily life as enculturation. This was so whether or not it was consciously sought. At the same time, it had not abandoned the structure imposed by historical precedent.

William Creek was a Javanese servant/slave. His dilemma is a small example that suggests the accommodation between old and new. Historical precedent and the law in Maryland required (even though they were not routinely followed) that a man's personal possessions be appraised at his death and, if money was needed to settle his estate, sold at auction. What did not belong to a man could not be sold and was not appraised. The interplay between goods, values, property including items not shown, and "small things forgotten" had far-reaching significance. Because William Creek was not included on Samuel Chew's inventory of 1738, he obtained his freedom despite the fact that he was probably one of the two East India Indians appraised on Chew's father's inventory in 1718, but Creek had to sue for his freedom.

Rich Europeans kept servants and slaves wherever they sojourned (fig. 15.2), transporting such people immense distances at their pleasure. Depositions reveal Creek was carried from Java to England as a young boy and indentured to a London apothecary. Learning the craft, he greatly embarrassed his master's wife and daughter by selling a purgative drug as a love potion. He was then transported to save their face. His indenture was sold to Samuel Chew of Anne Arundel County. William Creek lived with Chew outside Annapolis for nineteen years. A week before his death, Chew ordered Creek to serve his grandson an additional four years. In court, Creek testified that he believed only slaves could be transferred from one generation to the next. As an East India Indian, William Creek argued, he was not African and therefore not subject to slavery. An Englishman, a friend well known to the family, testified on Creek's behalf that he had not been brought forth to be appraised at Samuel Chew's death.[15]

Creek's children did not become free because his wife was a slave; his children were listed on Samuel Chew's inventory: Peg, William, and Ned Creek. Maryland law decreed that any child born of a slave woman remained a slave for life as did any child born of a free woman wed to a slave. Their father escaped through a loophole and an awareness of the way the law should work. The judge's willingness to free him was in part based on the fact that he was a man and Asian, not African.[16]

Customary practice set the standards for inventory-taking. African-born and African-American slaves were listed, by age, sex, and health. Servants were listed by ethnic identity, age, sex, and years of service remaining. Inventories were used in court, but had folk-meaning outside court. Within the folk domain, members of the slave community recognized the significance of William Creek's absence from the Chew inventory; they somehow also *knew* of it. Someone gave Creek advice to appeal to the courts. This vignette, or "action-drama" in Rhys Isaac's words, reveals a great deal about the ways the society worked. It also speaks to the artifacts occasionally found at Chesapeake sites – small metal tokens with square holes – which archaeologists have identified as being made in the Orient, but enigmatic in the context of Chesapeake society. Inconclusive evidence by themselves, they are tantalizing hints that other people from the Far East also lived in Maryland and Virginia.

Adding women, merging cultures

In fact, if one looks for "others" in the Chesapeake, people from a wide variety of places begin to emerge. Initially, this startled me, for a nineteenth-century image of blandness originally colored my impressions of the region. And, like many women archaeologists, I had taken my male colleagues' presentations of data at face value, not fully realizing how little these showed of women. Recently, however, feminist archaeologists like Suzanne Spencer-Wood, Joan Gero, and Alison Wylie have suggested that we look at artifacts within the context of women's experience and begin to make women of all cultures more visible in archaeological interpretation.

In the pages of this book, the young Calvert women did not take center stage with their men. I am not sure why they never emerged in the research as equally vibrant. Their youth may have been one factor; the fact that they were primarily visible only

Figure 15.2. Javanese servant attends European merchant, ca. 1720. The servant shown in this East Asian drawing depicts a man from the island birthplace of William Creek, who lived in Anne Arundel County in the 1720s and 1730s. (Copyright British Museum.)

Table 15.1. *An observation on West African women by W. Bosman, 1705: 55*

Agonna begins with or about this Hill; and is at present, as it hath for some time past, been governed by a Woman with as much Courage and Conduct as other countries are ruled by men.

through texts written by Englishmen may be another. However, consideration of the Calvert women brought greater awareness of the impact of West African men and women on the data; techniques useful in eliciting information on women transferred readily to looking at slave culture. Artifacts that show the imprint of African beliefs bring to the surface dimensions of black life not highlighted in traditional histories. These are facets of slave life in essence their own and therefore extraordinarily meaningful (figs. 15.3 and 15.4). Black men and women in Annapolis did not share the culture of white Annapolitans; they shared an Afro-centric world view, a rich complex cosmology which contained guidelines for adaptation to the new circumstances each forced migrant faced. The artifacts from the site open windows to the accommodation on both sides – white and black – where the two cultures met. It was most informative about black women.

In trying to distill the essence of black womanhood in its first years in a strange land, I found that beads (chapter 9) and bones (chapters 10–12) broke the silence. They sparkled with cultural creativity. The tiny fragments revealed dimensions of women's lives that suggested a dynamic, willful personal resiliency which mirrors African myths wherein girls passed through cultural "tests" (i.e., quests), emerging as independent women. But to recognize the import of beads or bones, an archaeologist first has to accept that the cultural ideals African-born women strove to express in material form were different from the way rich, white men judged women. The European male-centered view of womanhood took as its ideal a loving mother, an obedient wife, a dutiful and subservient daughter with a chaste mind and quiet tongue. It valued gentle, charitable, modest, discreet, deferential, dependent women who put men's interests first. It defined women by their marital status and sexual availability (social rank as well as marital status affecting the latter), giving them few active roles and minimal status outside home or family. By way of contrast, when Panquash, "a great Doctor and chiefman among the Nanticoke Indians" on Maryland's Eastern Shore, realized what was happening to his people, he "fully instructed his daughter" with all the medical knowledge he knew. An Englishman would not have done that; cultures differ.[17]

So, like the English, African cultures elevated motherhood but also contained different notions of what comprised a family, of women's roles in the family, of cooperation among women, of women's roles in relation to exterior work space, especially the marketplace. It held in esteem women who exhibited an inner strength and vitality in daily life, and had no house space for the feminine passivity the dominant culture valued (Table 15.1). Beads and bones are commonplace items, but they show how the everyday world of black Annapolitans could be expressively African within an English frame. They represented transplanted African customs operative within the emerging black culture of the Chesapeake (figs. 15.5 and 15.6). But to see these, I had to consider events from the outside and the inside, and try to penetrate an African-derived world view.[18]

Reaching inside

One way to begin to penetrate a culture is to pay close attention to the folk beliefs and values that are revealed in texts. For example, Englishmen believed that air might be wholesome or, closed off by trees, unsafe. Dew could kill those who slept overnight on the ground. In fact, one is tempted to see in this belief a rationale for raising buildings on piers so that these simple homes, compared to "booths" at fairs,

Figure 15.3. Cowrie shells were used by West Africans as money, adornment, clothing. Their use was also seen in slave Chesapeake communities; recently more than 150 were recovered strewn across a town lot in Yorktown, Virginia, near Philip Lightfoot's eighteenth-century kitchen well, kitchen, slave quarters and garden; none were recovered from the grounds of his mansion across the street. (Nick Luccketti, personal communication, February 1992.) (Drawing by Julie Hunter-Abbazia.)

Figure 15.4. A lead counter with an "X" or Greek cross inscribed in its base may be of European derivation, but as Robert Farris Thompson stresses in *Flash of the Spirit*, the cross was also a highly charged symbol – the simplest manifestation of ritual space in the Kongo cosmology – and one used by Africans in the New World as well as the old. (Photograph by the author.)

Figure 15.5. A New Orleans black woman, possibly Marie Labeau, wore a carnelian necklace for her portrait drawn in 1844 by Adolph D. Rinck. Necklaces strung from carnelian beads were reputed to have been worn by African-American shamans and sorcerers, and they have been found in New World graves dating to the seventeenth and eighteenth centuries. The graves and the portrait bracket the period when the stone was recovered in Maryland. However, the stones could be incorporated as single elements in other forms of jewelry too. (Illustration courtesy of the University Art Museum, Lafayette, LA.)

Figure 15.6. Further evidence of the importance of bodily adornment within African culture can be seen in this drawing of a modern West African girl who wears necklaces, earrings, bracelets, rings, and a hat embellished by strings of glass beads and cowrie shells to signify her wealth and that she is now of marriageable age. There is cultural continuity centuries old in this tradition as there also is in her headgear which echoes that worn by Ayuba Ben Suleiman in 1733 as shown in Figure 1.10. (Illustration by Julie Hunter-Abbazia based on illustrations in Angela Foster's *Africa Adorned*.)

might be more habitable. Their form suggests some were barely that: "not lathed nor plaistered, neither ceiled nor lofted above . . . one window, but no glass in it, not even a brick chimney, and, as it stood on blocks about a foot above the ground, the hogs lay constantly under the floor." Cold in winter, hot in summer, they were not healthy places to live, but because the assessment of these "social facts" was made on different criteria, no connection was made in native minds. Money that could be better spent on buildings, to preserve health, was spent on tiny teacups whose role was more symbolic than practical.[19]

The importance of symbolic meaning is almost always skipped when archaeologists impose an economic framework on analysis. What is biggest, took the most labor to build, lasted longest, or was brought out first is not necessarily an artifact that held the most symbolic importance in a culture. Working from the outside, it is often easy to assess size, labor, durability, and purchasing patterns. Yet these do not necessarily draw us inside. "An appropriate understanding of a social fact requires that it be grasped totally, that is, from the outside, like a thing," but, Lévi-Strauss continues, "like a thing which comprises within itself the subjective understanding (conscious or unconscious) that we would have of it" if we were natives, not anthropologists. It is problematic because the insider's view, or grasp, or that of a researcher reliving the native's experience, also must be translated into a discourse that enables scholars to exchange their own ideas. The form of discourse varies, but it is always built from a grammar. If one also learns how the folk grammar works, it is possible to predict what "natives" may say and do in given situations.[20]

"Native" terms are visible in old texts, often appearing in unexpected places like inventory lists which contain words for pots, names of animals, and slaves. Some grab attention, making a reader instantaneously pause and think: "progging"; "soul-driver"; the "outbows" of trees. Others may slip past, such as anglicized African names, where, if one looks beneath the English homonyms, African names appear. These are names like Abby (*Abanna*), Hagar (for the Mandingo *Haga*), Jemmy (*Jeminah*), and Joe (*Cudgo*), or Cuffee (for Friday, *Kofi*). They are derived from naming patterns among different West Africa cultures.

Thus simple things like names on a list both hide and reveal cultural meaning, showing a nexus in daily life between two ethnic groups. Lorenzo Turner describes the African-American, African-rooted practice of naming children for conditions at their time of birth such as parental attitudes, appearance, weather, place, temperament, localities, or origins (cf., *Saltwater* for "from across the sea"). With this knowledge, one can take the Richmond, Virginia, man whose name is given in H. L. Mencken's list of unusual names – Chesapeake and Ohio Railroad Harry Stringfellow Johnson – and see the continuation of a practice with great time depth, tying him to people who lived in Maryland three hundred years ago such as Battle Creek Mary (1774), Saltwater John (1734), Limehouse (1729), London, Paris, or Bombay (1722). Conjoined to it would be a consideration of women's lives, accepting Russell Menard's position that birth rates are a sign of health, but adding the knowledge that because miscarriages and high rates of childhood mortality are not, these carry their own sorrow.[21]

Table 15.2. *Births and miscarriages among slave women*

Fanny has had six children; all dead but one.
Nanny has had three children; two of them are dead.
Leah, Caesar's wife, has had six children; three are dead.
Sophy . . . has had ten children; five of them are dead.
Sally, Scipio's wife, has had two miscarriages and three children born, one of whom is dead.
Charlotte, Renty's wife, had had two miscarriages and [is] with child again.
Sarah . . . had had four miscarriages, had brought seven children into the world, five of whom
    were dead and was again with child.
Sukey, Bush's wife . . . had had four miscarriages; had brought eleven children into the world,
    five of whom are dead.
Molly, Quambo's wife . . . Hers was the best account I have yet received; she had had nine
    children, and six of them were still alive.

This list is drawn from one made by Frances Kemble in 1838–9 at St. Simons, Georgia, but it is pertinent to Annapolis because it makes the point that much of what happened was unrecorded and gives some impression of the number of children born and those conceived who died in the womb to produce the eighteen living African or African-American children associated with the Calvert site ca. 1730. Archaeology becomes personal and humanistic as names and sometimes faces link in chains. Margaret Lee Calvert had at least three miscarriages, and one daughter who died. Rebecca Gerard Calvert had three or four children; one daughter lived to marriageable age. This is another side of history that begins to penetrate inside events to a degree, and bring forth lived experience. The "inside" differs from the exterior; it is not always possible for an archaeologist to see it. That does not mean the attempt should not be made, although whenever anyone does, the Chesapeake takes on the hues, sounds, odors, and sights of a vanished time, losing the hegemony of the modern world. Seeing it then becomes an encounter with the "others" anthropologists customarily study.[22]

Setting aside cultural complexity of African naming patterns or women's birth records as beyond their ken, an archaeologist might ask instead, is there an inside view to something simple like pots or animal bones? Since they were used in metaphor and embedded within cosmology, the answer is "yes." Native Americans believed bear meat enhanced male virility; the Virginian wives who became pregnant after their men returned from the forest, where Indian guides caught and served bear to the men, were seen as testimony of its power by William Byrd II. Among the English, animal meats were scaled in price, denoting their cultural evaluation: veal over lamb, sheep over cattle over pigs over goats over chickens. This evaluation guided their social use whereas little distinction was made in the ranking of body parts. To attribute dietary dependence on beef (measured as pounds of meat consumed) to a cultural preference misreads the inside or subjective role beef held in daily life.[23]

The inside view does not stop there. Maryland politicians could be scuttling crabs,

Table 15.3. *Extract from the* Maryland Gazette *of June 1727 from copy supplied by a London correspondent*

[Mr. Henley] proved very learnedly and metaphysically that everything was fish, and that the world is nothing but a great Fishpond, where Mankind laid baits to ensnare and catch one another. He observed very accurately that Politicians were Crab-fish, who go backwards and forwards, or a sort of Eel, that wriggle and twist, and skip through our fingers do what we will; or Pikes who tyrannize in the Water and devour almost every other fish that comes in their Way, especially Trouts and Gudgeons . . .

gullible gudgeons, or marauding pikes (Table 15.3). Maryland families ate crabs, ate pikes, but only used gudgeons for bait. Maryland men became lion-drunk, sheep-drunk, or swine-drunk on the town streets and in its taverns. One has to wonder if they ever thought of their eating habits in terms similar to Dr. John Rutty's: "ate as a swine"; "piggish at meals"; "a little swinish at dinner." Admitting to being "snappish on fasting," one is left to question if the physician was ever hoggish at breakfast or whether men in the Chesapeake, who were observed to "pig lovingly together" took these traits to the table too.[24]

The natural world penetrated the cultural and to write simply of adaptation hides the perceptions that guided behavior. In *Elementary Forms of Religion*, Durkheim wrote of the power a world view holds. Sahlins condensed and parsed it in *Historical Myths and Mythical Realities*. Since the universe does not exist except in so far as it is thought of, and since it is not always thought of in the way that it exists, people in the past could easily use a logic unfamiliar to modern men and women. Yet they still constructed cosmologies in which principles of contrast were operative and some of these contrasting elements can still be seen in the archaeological record. In the examples drawn from documents above, one also can discern other principles of contrast. These show how people separated one individual from another, revealing principles of social organization if interpreted in the context of the conventions of the day. They show that social people did not exist in isolation, but drew their positions in part from where they stood as members of groups.

The ways people did things, the ways they defined their groups, the traditions they drew on, the objects they adopted, left marks in the ground. Initially, they came from other places, on ships from Macao, Venice, Benin, Curaçao, Glasgow, and Liverpool. Joined together, they made the region their home, competed fiercely, rising and falling within different ranking systems. Overall they were Calvert's peoples, governed by their own rule and Lord Baltimore's. I began to understand these people and how they created their archaeological record by placing their culture in time and space. In doing so, I began to see how both the powerful and the powerless, relatively speaking, left independent traces in the ground.

Local context

This has relevance to the people who do contract archaeology in the Chesapeake. Moved from place to place and site to site with minimal time for involvement in either the historic or the archaeological record, the intimate involvement with a culture that ethnographers experience is impossible. Further, connectedness to local place or *communitas* (which still exists in modern society) is reduced and, as one consequence, the public sees what we do as simultaneously more specialized and mysterious, and of lesser import. They are readily aware that the form of today's world differs from that of the past, and so they see less reason why archaeological laws, which they gloss as "laws of the past" should have any bearing on what they plan to do *today* in their own local places. Replaced by the cultural resource manager's concern with "law-like" generalizations that emphasize the uniformity of man, the dialectic between cultural diversity and human unity is set aside.

This dialectic is what is implicit and critical in the Javanese proverb: "Other fields, other grasshoppers." Geertz uses the proverb to emphasize that "to be human [in Java] is thus not to be Everyman; it is to be a particular kind of man, and of course men differ." Among writers, H. L. Mencken put it this way: "A Baltimorean is not merely John Doe . . . exactly like every other John Doe. He is John of a certain place – of Baltimore, of a definite *house* in Baltimore. It is not by accident that all the peoples of Europe, very early in their history, distinguished their best men by adding *of* this or that place to their name." A black poet makes the same distinction: "Ye dark-skinned people, listen to me. Our fathers did not play about with names. To hear their names is to know their origin."[25]

Applying the concept in folklore, Henry Glassie studied Virginia's vernacular architecture by attending to the relationship expressed in objects between what he defined as "competence," that is, the ability to compose or create an object such as a building, and the social space (i.e., place) in which the building was set (cf., *Folk Housing of Middle Virginia*). He saw ability to create an object as mastery of a set of internalized, organizational rules that a person learned as he or she grew up within a social place. The rules related not only to the form of the object, but to the situations in which it was appropriate to use it, invoke it, creatively alter it, or destroy it. Explaining that context was not a difficult concept to grasp, Glassie also pointed out difficulties with its use:[26]

> a loose colloquial use can trick us into employing "context" to mean no more than situation. Then the power of the idea evaporates, and studying context we enlarge and complicate the object we described but come little closer to understanding than we did when we folklorists recorded texts in isolation. Context is not in the eye of the beholder, but in the mind of the creator. Some of context is drawn in from the immediate situation, but more is drawn from memory. It is present, but invisible, inaudible. Contexts are mental associations woven around texts during performance to shape and complete them, to give them meaning.

Mary Beaudry and her co-workers at Lowell expand this further: "context is where meaning is located and constituted and provides the key to its interpretation. Recovery of meaning is predicated on recovery of context . . . meanings cannot exist in the absence of context."[27]

Modern anthropologists provide similar observations of context, merging the concept of culture as pattern in the mind with that of culture as shared beliefs and patterns of activity. "Culturally patterned discourse, the common things that people say, derive not just from [internalized] rules of use; they also embody a sense of how and why to play, a style of action and understanding." Also, it is a discourse taking place in both public and private spheres. Martin Hall, for example, points out how the style of action incorporated in the design (1709–44) of William Byrd II's hierarchical eight-seater personal family privy built upon a Chesapeake world view and the need to imprint its structure on the physical fabric that surrounded his family's most private activities.[28]

"Discourse" was a word often used in the eighteenth century. The deposition of Eleanor Cushoca, 22 years of age, about an evening she spent in a kitchen quarter in the company of slaves from different plantations records that they were "discoursing of a negro man of John Miller's being returned from the [Indians at] Monocasy Mountains whose name was Harry." Here the meaning was simply to speak with someone and to listen to them. As used by archaeologists, such as Martin Hall, it carries much the same connotation, but is imparted a cultural framework:

> the material world can be seen as *texts without words*, and therefore particularly powerful in its meanings . . . A statement is a relation with a domain of objects, whether those objects be spoken words, written texts, or material artifacts. Discourse is formed from a sequence of such statements, and in turn gives regularities to statements. Because this notion of discourse emphasizes the importance of the sign, the semiotic insights that have flowed from structuralist projects in historical archaeology can be retained and enhanced.[29]

Thus archaeologists and anthropologists agree that cultural discourse utilizes metaphor to convey meaning. Symbolism and symbolizing, evident in metaphors, are pan-human activities; their cultural expressions are endlessly varied but historically situated. Firth wrote that one sees human thought and action when studying symbols and symbolism. In each instance, redundancy is built into the system. Thoroughly studied by linguists in verbal discourse, less is known about the symbolic dimensions of non-verbal phenomena and their role in cultural discourse. Hall suggests combining both – the material world and that seen in social action – and conceptualizing it as "discourse." In this light, the topic of this book has been a Chesapeake discourse: verbal evidence – the spoken or written words of a bygone people – and non-verbal statements – the shapes, forms, and spatial organization of things left in the ground and imprinted on the land. All are means to discover one Maryland family's power, status, and multicultural strands.

16

Archaeology, a topological discourse

> . . . in the documents surviving from the past, the social historian
> can everywhere find traces – occasionally vivid glimpses – of people
> doing things. The searching out of the meaning that such actions
> contained and conveyed for the participants lies at the heart of the
> enterprise.
>
> Rhys Isaac, 1982, *Transformation of Virginia*

Why archaeology?

The screen that archaeological records place on data is different and requires a
different translation than documents demand. Probate inventories, for example,
were one of the most informative written records. They told of Edward Henry's
colorful clothing. In the large quantities of common, ordinary cloth stocked, they
revealed what slaves wore. In its listing of slaves, Captain Calvert's inventory
gave names, sex, and age. Yet, as lists of material possessions inventories were
incomplete, compiled by men who paid less attention to the things women used in
their kitchens (which could not be resold) than to sheep in the field or the family
bed. Personal items belonging to mothers, wives, sisters, children, servants, and
slaves were not included in an inventory because they could not be sold. And there,
out the door and set aside, figuratively speaking, went many of the things archaeologists find at Maryland sites. So, it is archaeology and only archaeology that
enables scholars to see them with enough breadth to become aware of the pleasure
they once gave people and to know how they were as necessary, in some cases, as
basil in the garden or chicken in the pot (fig. 16.1).[1]

Within this context, historical archaeology is at once more complex than prehistory and yet simpler. Because it studies complex societies, historical archaeology
has to confront the variability created by different ethnic groups, by gender, by age,
by wealth distinctions, by a range of social ranking criteria, and by the interaction of
dominant elites and subordinate status groups. Today, it presents a series of challenges not seen in its 1930s infancy:

- How to discern material expressions of cultural diversity within complex
  societies.
- How to sort across communities for evidence of complementary social action.
- How to extract and transfer information from documents, drawing valid small-

scale generalizations to inform and expand information obtained from archaeology while simultaneously acknowledging the existence of variability.

- How to convince historians that the material dimension of life and that history from the bottom up yield as much insight, if not more, than the study of great ideas. Or, as James Deetz insists in *The Archaeology of Flowerdew Hundred*, that archaeology eventually may have more to say about a history of the inarticulate than all their sources strung end-on-end.
- How to cut time and transcend the difficulties of working within one's own culture so that it becomes possible to see and appreciate the "others" interacting with it on their own terms.
- How to bridge cultural domains – kinship, economics, politics, religion – while working from an object-oriented perspective.
- How to show that culture is the essence of humanity, an encompassing framework for daily life in ways that disparate scholars and lay people can appreciate.

These topics instill a strong anthropological thread into our field and require a holistic view of society. One focus could be social relationships, their organization, their expression, their cultural roots. These are structural relationships that exist in different cultures and can be symbolized in a variety of ways, although they "do" the same things in each. Leach defines the difference between culture and the social component of anthropology this way: "Culture provides the form, the 'dress' of the social situation." Marriage, for example, is a rite of passage that legitimates a change in status for women, giving children of a union both legitimacy and a set of rights and obligations with their mother's people and their father's people. Young girls and boys learned the form it would take as they grew up, enculturated into the ways of their people.[2]

Denied marriage ceremonies in the "dress" of their culture (i.e., in the known and familiar form in which it customarily existed), African-born women in the Chesapeake occupied an anomalous cultural position whether viewed from an Englishman's point of view or from within their own culture. African men replaced the "bride price" with small ceremonial substitutes: tiny trinkets and one-on-one talk, man and woman negotiating alone without the strength of kin. There was little else that could be done. The cattle, the pots, the "palaver," or conferences among two sets of families, no longer took place. The structure of the known and old social context was broken. Adaptive responses developed which, in part, redefined the meaning of marriage, symbolic and pragmatic, for African-Americans. Their social organization changed too. The drums that sounded in the Maryland night spoke of the difference, using traditional forms, carrying new messages. This is because black and white social structures were organized as much by kinship, gender, and age, especially in the early Chesapeake, as by the forces – modes of production and consumption – materialists privilege. To use a single focus to perceive how people and their possessions fit within a culture denies the density of cultural interaction and works against the grain, masking this group or that in the background.[3]

Table 16.1. *Conversations overheard in historical records*

They had first silver pipes. The ordinary sort made use of a walnut shell and a straw. I have heard my grandfather say, that one pipe was handed from man to man round the table . . . It was sold then for its weight in silver.[4]

For my commission and charges going to Hunger River to buy pork, one pound, four shilling, demanded Captain William Vernon, going to court to get his due.[5]

Six pence, wrote Humphrey Meredith, on John Dowley's account, "for one pint of rum, when you swore you'd have no more if you could get it."[6]

"For priming 18 yards of your shade; for priming 60 yards of your bedchamber, for priming 50 yards of paling; for painting inside of your porch blue."[7]

"Michael Macnamara and George Stuart to post a bond to keep the peace . . . especially with each other."[8]

"Take pity on my poor condition of having a husband, a poor crazy mad man not in his right senses for some eight years," pleaded Hester Robertson in requesting tax relief.[9]

Yet, whenever one does good historical archaeology, synthesizing written documents with the material remains, a range of people inescapably come into view. It would be difficult, indeed, not to give individuals who once lived in the Chesapeake thoughts and emotions, for these flow within the source material. No one reading the historical records of the Chesapeake can miss the people talking. It is a legacy of an oral culture where sight and sound often overrode the written word.

Elizabeth Wormsley, widow, "having scarce cloathes to cover my nakedness" pleaded for tax relief.[10] Thomas India, a mulatto, petitioned for his freedom because he was a "black" with non-African ancestry, his origins encoded in his name. Many archaeologists are unprepared for this and uneasy about incorporating this visual, vocal, emotive imagery into their research. With the exception of ethnoarchaeologists, they rarely hear people "speak" of the objects they study, but are dependent on other analytical devices to "read" material remains. The idea that "time sucks the meaning from things" is commonly held. Sometimes archaeologists avoid it by defining issues as pan-human problems unrelated to a specific people because this makes the issues timeless and hence relevant in modern life. When people are kept in the background, artifacts can appear to be larger than life.[11]

Archaeological facts do not speak for themselves, so they can be read with varying frames of reference. One commonly used analytical strategy is to take a model of culture and test the archaeological record against it to see if the archaeological data contain evidence that supports or disproves the model. An analyst knows beforehand what she wants to find, often in terms of precise data: plates of varying diameter; sets of matching teacups; ratios of hollow to flatwares; poor cuts of meat; geometry in the garden. In this generalizing mode of inquiry, the stress is on similarities – over time and over space – in social process or "behavior."

James Deetz, however, pioneered a view of artifacts in historical archaeology as components of a cultural discourse, defining culture as ideas, or folk models, that when put into action created different, diverging object forms, fabrics, and decorative details. In this, the ideal was the idea; the real was the form given it by a craftsman or -woman. The cultural dynamic flowed in the interplay (a) between idea and created object and (b) the way each was shared within society. In this framework, habitual ways of doing things reflect enduring patterns of social relations expressed in repetitive day-to-day activity, but are end products, constructed from cognitive structures – human creations – which may vary over time and space. In other words, Deetz made room for mental phenomena in archaeological interpretation and gave people active roles in shaping their culture.[12]

A humanistic orientation

The work of folklorist Henry Glassie also emphasizes subtle interactions between men, women, and material culture; it further illustrates the richness a historical framework brings to artifact analysis. Glassie and Deetz took the tenets of "history from the bottom up" and transferred them to the world of visible objects. Yet, the Calvert site was occupied by two governors of Maryland and thus associated with the wealthy, whereas an important goal in the counter tradition has been to "expand history beyond the control of a prosperous, literate minority." In other words, to take barns and fat pots, fence lines and quarters, sheep and pigs, and make them provide information about the lives of everyday people.

Glassie wrote: "Artifacts taught me that folklore and history are one." Following Glassie's lead, I gradually realized that the artifacts of the wealthy also spoke of the poor. Small things speak to big issues because the cultural framework of a society is encompassing. Nothing sits alone.[13]

Yet when historical archaeology serves as a handmaiden to history and occasionally to anthropology, its role is subordinate. Many of us would prefer to weld archaeology, anthropology and history to produce a synthesis – something greater than the sum of its parts – that could provide in an insightful, provocative, and imaginative manner a portrait of an earlier way of life; its big issues, its social conflicts, its men and its women. There are no hard and fast rules about how to do this. For most archaeologists, the guiding objective would be to illustrate and delineate the role of material culture within society, for artifacts are central to our field of inquiry and expertise.[14]

Still, historical archaeology remains a discipline few know intimately. It began in the Chesapeake with excavation of a Jamestown church by the Association for the Preservation of Virginia Antiquities (APVA) in 1901, but historical archaeology really took hold there in the 1930s with work by the National Park Service and through excavation in the service of restoration architecture at Colonial Williamsburg. By the 1970s, the Chesapeake was a hotbed of activity, a virtual cradle of the discipline. Relentlessly, anthropological interpretation was put in the back seat while practical forms of landscape and architectural information or public interpretation drove fieldwork. As a resource, archaeology's important contributions in the Chesapeake have been and are seen in this light. The strong museum base – Colonial Williamsburg, St. Mary's City, Flowerdew Hundred, the National Park Service at Jamestown – and the close ties to preservation agencies – APVA, Virginia

Historic Landmarks Commission, Historic Annapolis Foundation, the Center for Historic Preservation at Mary Washington – and historic houses or ancestral shrines – Mount Vernon, Monticello – dictated this. Yet the region has produced more than its share of outstanding archaeological studies by men like John Cotter, Ivor Noël Hume, James Deetz, J. C. Harrington, William Kelso, Mark P. Leone, Henry Miller, and Garry Wheeler Stone. Work in the region spans the scope of the discipline and has defined it in many instances.[15]

Many Chesapeake sites are rich in material remains: beads, buttons, shell and bone, toy marbles, broken brickbats, rose-head nails. Archaeologists commonly recover stems from clay tobacco pipes, bottle glass of Dutch, French, and English origin, coarse earthenware potsherds, and hand-painted oriental porcelain. They find etched glass, eye spectacles, human hair, gold sequins, wedding rings, tiny carved animals, and small bear jugs less often (fig. 16.2). Whatever the case, archaeologists are continually faced with the dilemma presented by data that in and of themselves are stark. The "bare bones" data for the Calvert site consist of tables that are not ethnographically informative. Archaeological material from a single deposit or stratum exists in association with material from different proveniences within the site and also in relation with material recovered from its contemporaneous sites. Like other Maryland families, the Calvert household existed in a cultural web formed by different sectors of a hierarchical society; the structure, culturally framed, of their interaction with these "others" created the changing

Figure 16.1. Shoes – the most ordinary of objects – of all sizes, some even with holes in their soles – were recovered from the Calvert well. (Photograph by Marion E. Warren.)

sequence of material remains found at the site. So too did the family's responses to new ways of thinking, broader knowledge, cosmopolitan world view, and privileged access to world markets.

What can one reasonably say about the Calvert family, servants and slaves, their beliefs, and their social relationships, after studying the things the household left behind? This book explored that question; its goals were twofold. First, I tried to illustrate how historical archaeologists use the independent lines of evidence in written texts and local lore. Second, I combined history and anthropology to build an ethnographic background, or local context, for the artifacts recovered from the site. This background could be extended, and has been to some degree, through the insertion of archaeological data from other sites in the region (cf. chapters 7 and 11).

The text shows how humanistically oriented archaeologists think about the relationships between two data sets: the hard data or tangible things recovered from below ground, and the complex ethnographic information contained in written texts and oral tradition, in history and in folklore. When looking at the data recovered through excavation, an archaeologist sees something that has already passed through two interpretive screens. The first, the one she sees during fieldwork is imposed by natural processes that cause the disintegration, fragmentation, and dispersal of artifacts, especially those of organic or fragile metal materials. As a result, various objects disappear from the archaeological record, especially plant remains (fig. 16.3).[16] As crucial, the data also have been mediated by the people whose culture we want to explore. Further, like living cultures, archaeologically visible cultures are multivocal. They yield no privileged position, no absolute perspective. Any image of the past as a knowable entity seen through archaeology is distinct from the past in itself which we will never know. Yet, as Glassie writes, "the past is not dead. It lives in mind, as mind . . . deeds emerge out of the past. Subtly or obviously, now is made of then." This recognition of the active role of the past in the present is reiterated by other folklorists speaking of the role of memory, the impact of homeland: "time and place have had their say."[17]

The archaeologist's bailiwick

Time and place, in mind and in matter, are the archaeologist's bailiwick. Archaeology, as shown here, is a potent means for recovering information about how earlier people lived their lives and the culture each possessed: the shared beliefs and the symbolic forms, material and immaterial, used to organize daily life. But all forms of archaeology are not alike. What defines historical archaeology as distinguished from its sister fields is that it stands at the interface of history and anthropology. At this interface scientific methods can be extremely useful, but alternative humanistic approaches to the past also enable scholars to comprehend different dimensions of past existence in ways that are coherent, reflective, and highly perceptive. This book has argued that interpretation within historical archaeology, like classic anthropological interpretation, is an art. Edmund Leach likens this to the ability to understand the nuances of a foreign language. What one gains through the translation is a measurably deeper understanding, an awareness of something lost or something found, a sense of the continuum that encompasses cultural time.[18]

To find something is to discover it; the core of a discovery can be intangible, expanding knowledge until modern men and women too appear in a different light. Anthropologists write of this as the awareness of one's own culture that emerges from an encounter with another way of life. It requires the contrast provided by

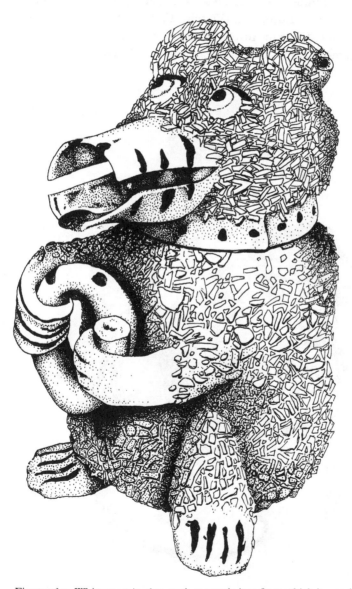

Figure 16.2. Whimsy set in clay, such as puzzle jugs from which it was difficult to drink or which were made in animal form, appealed to the earthy sense of humor in eighteenth-century men and women. Pieces of one such example – a fine white salt-glazed bear jug – had been scattered about the gate to the kitchen work yard. (Drawing by Julie Hunter-Abbazia.)

"others" whose cultures are foreign, exotic, or distant in time. To see one's culture as an anthropologist does, it is necessary to step outside it and look at how other people live. In this case I have looked at the past through a small town in Maryland whose society was extremely complex, although its inhabitants numbered fewer than a thousand. Annapolis was layered, a hierarchical community, home to people of varying social rank who came from many different cultures: Native American (Piscataway, Nanticoak, Shawnee, Iroquois), Asian, East Indian, West African (including but not limited to Senegalese, Gambian, Fulani, Dahomean, Asante, Yoruba, Bini, Congo), European (Dutch, French, German, Swiss, Italian or Swedish), and from different British subgroups – the Scots, Irish, Welsh and English. Some came via the Caribbean. Certainly the English culture was dominant,

Figure 16.3. A seed pod from the unicorn plant (identified by Dr. Donna Ware of the College of William and Mary) was recovered from a water-logged deposit in the well. Unicorn plants were grown for medicinal use in eighteenth-century gardens, but are now considered weeds. They can be seen along the sides of country roads throughout the south. (Illustration drawn by Julie Hunter-Abbazia.)

but society was in flux, and all of its members had their beliefs of what was appropriate behavior vis-à-vis the material world. By studying Annapolis ca. 1730, one gains a stronger respect for the way that ideas about behavior find expression in the archaeological record and for how objects, as a medium of symbolic exchange and communication, were negotiated and transferred from one group to another. Looking at Annapolis society imparts a poignant view of humanity, of cultures in contact, and a deepened awareness of the cultural pluralism that formed the building blocks for subsequent generations.[19]

The substance of archaeological discovery can also be seen as tangible, inspiring wonder at how objects survive time. This is what I felt when my field director, Gary Norman, recovered a gold-plated buckle dropped in a well ca. 1775, and held it out to me in the palm of his hand (fig. 16.4). The pleasure of discovery merges with intellectual satisfaction when an excavation unit comes down precisely on a buried feature such as a post hole, terrace slope, road or walk whose location was predicted by applying a way of thinking, an ancient or "dead" system of measurement no longer used, but one that determined placement of paths, garden beds, houses, barns and outbuildings in old landscapes.[20]

A critical element in the discovery process is that the more an archaeologist knows

Figure 16.4. A gold-plated buckle reflected light rays and glittered in the sun when it first came out of the mud in the well. It is similar to the smaller buckles worn by Charles Calvert in his portrait. (Photograph by Marion E. Warren.)

about the different aspects of past life, the more connections can be perceived between artifacts and the cultural milieu (or social context) in which they existed. The objects-in-life from which artifacts derive were elements in related sets of activities and in a sequentially-based cultural discourse; they were not isolates or specimens. Ivor Noël Hume, in his book, *All the Best Rubbish: . . . the Pleasures and Perils of Collecting Everyday Objects . . .* writes of the way some connoisseurs (pot-hunters too) value classical works of art and other "elderly" objects for their association with particular individuals, even countries, or events. Once known as "curiosities," these were among Benedict Leonard Calvert's passions (see Chapter 4, fig. 4.1), brought by him, his stepfather, and older brother out of Italy – boatloads of displaced art treasures to adorn English homes sold by impoverished Italians who could not, in Calvert's words, "roast a statue nor fricassee a Basso relievo [frieze]." Their *in situ* relationships or associations with other objects, artifacts, and features destroyed, the "curiosities" lost their analytic provenience; as a consequence, their informational content eroded. Although an object's age, beauty, and craftsmanship remained intact and appreciated, the relationships "curiosities" possessed as elements in cultural discourse or in a related grouping disappeared.[21]

Relationships among sets of artifacts and features are strategic in archaeology. These show how artifacts were tied to social action or were elements within cognitive models for social action that people applied in thinking through situations before acting upon them. The statues Benedict Leonard Calvert shipped home lost the original context (and were recontextualized) but the ones he described from the Great Duke's Gallery in Florence, Italy, retained some of their spatial organization in his letters: the statues of the emperors stand on one side, those of their wives and mothers line the other, intermingled among representations of ancient gods and goddesses. Walking the gallery, Benedict Leonard trod a path framed by gender, secular/religious, even political distinctions. By analyzing relationships between objects, people, and social space, it becomes easier to see how objects created one of the cultural frames that organized daily life and steered behavior. It becomes easier to see recursive relationships (i.e., the way a cultural framework brings about change in objects through the activities of men and women and social events; how these changes in turn impact the framework). This reciprocity is the unrelenting dialectic, or context, that surrounds material culture and gives objects their active roles in a culture. They lose much of it with passage into the earth.[22]

Weaving contexts

Archaeological interpretation starts with stratigraphy. Since fieldwork strategies and methodologies provide the foundation, archaeology is inherently topological, and field-related issues such as taphonomy are a critical factor in any explication. Archaeological analysis pushes beyond this constraint as examination of field data evolves into site interpretation, weaving knowledge of past social action within it. Simply put, the tangible remains of past life recovered through archaeology tell us little until the artifacts and features are cataloged, analyzed, and subjected to thorough interpretation. In most cases, the best sites are chosen for their research potential, for how they can answer this question or that, and not because a hotel is going to be built upon them. Like most historical archaeologists, the luxury of choosing my site was impossible. The archaeological study of the Calvert site in that sense is typical of much in our field; it represents an accommodation between the requirements of finely tuned research archaeology in an urban setting and the organizational constraints created by work in a construction environment.

This is a situation commonly seen. Sites are selected for historical archaeologists by the necessities of urban development, highway construction, museum research, public interpretation, preservation, even tourist incentives and local political needs; we accept them, based in part by our need to dig, but also because we must teach a fieldschool, train students, and put food on our tables. Although certain types of sites from select time periods are favored in different regions of the country (for example, the seventeenth century in Tidewater Virginia), the individual historical archaeologist also has less control over the era of the site he or she excavates than many people realize.[23]

Thus, despite a deep and abiding interest in the seventeenth century, I came to direct work at an eighteenth-century site even as a colleague trained as a prehistorian was faced with the interpretation of sites in New York city dating from 1650 to 1870, and another was given an industrial complex. The resolution of this unmatching of sites with ethnographic expertise means that an archaeologist, whether trained in one tradition or another, is faced with a set of artifacts and features left by people she does not understand, and asked to make sense of them. Research designs in such cases follow practicalities as often as they do genuine, long-term interests.

One way around the conundrum is to establish a tidy set of research goals, what Henry Glassie calls "a preconceived, trim and bounded entity, subdivided by firm categories in which illustrative anecdotes [i.e., data] can be crammed." This can constrain the discovery process and bring premature closure. Sometimes it makes archaeologists work against the grain, putting them on sites they have no business digging given their background and training. Glassie suggests that scholars "begin with texts [i.e., data], then weave contexts around them to make them meaningful," which is a humanistic process. One begins with a set of questions, revises them through inquiry, and, as Eliot wrote, the end becomes another beginning because the questions shift and change, responding to the data (table 16.2). Yet in no case will questions remain the same if one chooses an interpretive approach. In analyzing data from the Calvert site, I deliberately blurred genres to explore what historical archaeology would be like if it was fused with the constructs of anthropological history, to see if a deeper understanding of social process could be gained through an interpretive approach to archaeology. Now, the research questions with which I began the site are not the ones that intrigue me; these grew and evolved with knowledge of its local context. Yet they remain interpretively framed.[24]

Interpretive archaeology
Interpretive archaeology includes five main steps. First an archaeologist must gain access to the folk beliefs and ideas that comprised a culture (the emic perspective,

Table 16.2. *Extract from* Four Quartets

What we call the beginning is often the end and to make an end is to make a beginning . . . the end of all our exploring will be to arrive where we started and to know the place for the first time. T. S. Eliot (*Four Quartets*)

Table 16.3. *Dream of Quaker Robert Pyle in 1698*

I was myself and a Friend going on a road, and by the roadside I saw a black pot. I took it up, the Friend said give me part. I said not, I went a little further and I saw a great ladder standing exact upright, reaching to heaven, up which I must go to heaven with the pot in my hand intending to carry the black pot with me, but the ladder standing so upright, and seeing no man holding of it, it seemed it would fall upon me; at which I stepped down, laid the pot at the foot of the ladder, and said them that take it might, for I found work enough for both hands to take hold of this ladder . . . let black Negroes or pots alone.

Reprinted as "An early anti-slavery statement" edited by Henry J. Caldwell (*Journal of Negro History* 22: 492–3).

or natives' points of view). Then she must overcome the barrier of archaeological knowledge that is incomplete, not fully revealing of context. On the one hand, this requires recognizing limits: the fragmentary nature of data; the exclusivity of single-site assemblages. On the other, it demands awareness of possibilities, looking at the fragments for evidence of multiple realities, different points of view and unfamiliar contexts of use. One must remember that artifacts "do not come stamped with a guarantee of their sincerity." West African pots used to cook food, to trap bugs, catch fish, or shelter a soul may look alike; the guidepost that "things which *appear* similar *are* similar," that is so useful to archaeologists studying simple societies, cannot be transferred in toto to complex societies. The context of use determines what a pot is. In the example just here, Judy Sterner's interviews with local people enriched the field data from Cameroon. Her study reiterates that there are levels of knowledge no archaeologist can access.[25]

Yet in one transference, African-American folklore in the Chesapeake passes down tales of pots rising off the hearth to run away, which they surely could not do if they did not possess spirit (figs. 16.5, 16.6). Black pots, similar in shape and form to brown and red pots, served as metaphorical extensions of black people in the minds of Anglo-Americans (Table 16.3) who, however, did not extend the metaphor to designations of Native Americans, although large or great pots often graced euphemistic English-language statements about pregnant women of all races. Within the Chesapeake two eighteenth-century viewpoints – English and West African – almost fade into one another, but not quite. There is no cause and effect here; one cannot really speak of acculturation or assimilation vis-à-vis the two perspectives. In reality, both are present, interacting independently within eighteenth-century Maryland, as are the different passages through town and countryside described in Dell Upton's study of "black and white landscapes" and the different constructs of time in colonial Virginia that Mechal Sobel analyzed. Each world view drew on different heritages or sets of cultural precedents. The medium – European-made objects – was often the same, but the message varied, sometimes subtly and sometimes outrageously. Both co-existed simultaneously, different planes of existence observable in Annapolis ca. 1730.[26]

The lessons learned by Maryland's ethnohistorians are relevant: "The Piscataways were able to retain much of their precontact culture . . . a large measure of de facto independence. While absorbing elements of European culture that were useful to them, they rejected others that were not." Merrill also points out that these people were and are written out of many historical narratives, the "cultural conversations" in which they participated set aside. Still, historians are more willing to posit Native Americans as a strong and vital people whose culture contributed to the traditions of the Chesapeake than they are to see the convergence that took place between the

Figure 16.5. The element of fantasy that often resides in myth can be seen in this image of black pots running down a country road. While it is not an element visible in artifacts, the belief that pots could move about was expressed in folktales of the region. (Illustration by Julie Hunter-Abbazia.)

white and black cultures as time progressed. In this convergence, African culture influenced the ways people of English ancestry carried out traditional tasks. Over time, the source of influence was forgotten. Over time, what was once distinctively and unequivocally African was reworked. A distinctive African-Chesapeake culture emerged; the dominant culture helped write its parameters. The life of black Annapolitans differed in many ways after the Revolution from the experiences of their forbears who lived at the Calvert site ca. 1730. Neither culture, white or black, was the same ca. 1820 as it was a hundred years earlier. Yet they maintained a range of traditions in which each was distinct from the other. This is part of what cultures are: "equally significant, integrated systems of difference."[27]

Archaeologists approach ancient cultures first through soil levels, features and artifacts at individual sites. Yet no site is an isolate. The Calvert site was set inside Annapolis and the town provided the historical framework for it, the town that is, seen as consisting of both inhabitants and physical setting (buildings, gardens, walks, work areas, shops, streets, alleys, bogs, ravines, springs, and creeks). This larger domain is relevant to anything that occurred at the site and left a record in the ground because one cannot understand the parts of an entity without some sense of the whole they comprise, nor comprehend the whole until one has seen the parts from which it is made.[28]

Yet no city exists in isolation and thus the hermeneutic circle, logically followed, becomes progressively larger. Eighteenth-century Maryland contained a few size-able towns, many hamlets, far more plantations and farms. Its inhabitants shared a cultural affinity with people living in the settlements of Tidewater Virginia, another part of the encompassing circle within which the site and the town were set. To make sense of it, however, also implies some understanding of the wholes that comprised Anglo-American culture and its English counterpart, African-American culture and its West African counterparts. At the same time, one must recognize that Annapolis was distinct, a town unto itself, unlike any other in the Chesapeake.

In summary, the approach used here was interpretive, increasingly formed within a structuralist framework, and played out on different planes. Its roots lie in work by James Deetz and Rhys Isaac, who take as a method a careful search for the past in as many channels or discourses as possible – a tactic also used by Martin Hall and his students at the University of Cape Town – and in the reciprocal interchange between history and anthropology. Its emphasis on local context aligns it more closely with paradigms advocated by British archaeologist Ian Hodder than with many other approaches. Yet the approach used here differs significantly from Hodderian archaeology because it integrates the new history and new ethnography into consideration of local context, and participates in local history. Because of this, some archaeologists who read earlier drafts commented on extensive biographical chapters and the actors within them. "Do we really need to know these people?" one queried. It is the detail of their daily lives and the beliefs they espoused that were the springboards for material action in Annapolis; leave them out, or diminish what the historical record tells of them, and the ethnographic insight decreases. And as the ethnographic insight lessens, the artifact assemblage from the site becomes dry and flat, only a catalog. Nothing brought this home more clearly than the reading I did on West African cultures using travelers' accounts of the seventeenth and eighteenth centuries. It was the insight thus gained that enabled me to look again at objects I had thought of as securely British and see within them the residue that told of African behavior patterns (figs. 16.7 and 16.8).[29]

What is a rich site?

A site can be described as rich when it contains many artifacts and features, or when its artifact assemblages speak of wealth within the community. Using either criterion, the Calvert site fits within the framework. But in retrospect, the real reason why the word "rich" best characterizes the site is that it stretches the imagination. From the onset, it has provided a series of paradoxes. The first was simply that any

Figure 16.6. A small three-legged iron cooking pot from the site is functional evidence of food preparation (Photograph by Marion E. Warren.)

of it survived the activities of subsequent generations living right above it. The second was the contradiction between architectural style and material goods. A third was the presence of the most avant garde horticultural practice for its era recorded in Maryland to date (i.e., an orangery where exotic plants were grown). A fourth was the fact that the site apparently functioned as a family compound for a household whose social structure was extended by any definition of the term. Its members included siblings, cousins, nieces, in-laws, servants – English, Irish, and Italian – as well as one of the more unusual large groups (thirty-one) of slaves in the province. The Calvert slave-holdings in Annapolis were comprised primarily of young children, with a ratio of almost two adult women for each man. A fifth paradox is the degree to which the archaeological evidence suggests the continuation of African lifestyles.

These attributes were paradoxes because they turned upside-down conventional expectations based either on normative assessments drawn from quantitative social studies or on assemblages seen at other sites. In each case, the contradictions initially perceived were resolved as further evidence was gathered by following the Boasian dictum "to go out and find what is there." What the Calvert site represents is the home of a very wealthy, politically powerful family (broadly defined), intellectually curious and autocratic, that drew upon the services of a large support staff (upwards of forty people if one includes the slave children) to supply its needs. For its time (ca. 1730) within the province of Maryland, the household was probably unique, although its form and daily life were soon emulated. In many ways it was a catalyst in the eighteenth-century gentrification of tobacco planters.

I found the best way to grasp how the household fitted within the society is to fill in the hermeneutic circle starting with the region, adding the town, giving family members a cultural context (cf., Chapter 1). This context was expanded in the biographical chapters where the Calverts come forward (cf. Chapters 3 and 4). The Calverts were then placed on the lot in Annapolis through an analysis of the large features, ones that clearly showed the residual traces of a numinous life style (cf. Chapters 5 and 6). Smaller artifacts also readily showed how the Calverts used their material world to denote the power and prestige they felt themselves adorned with (cf. Chapter 7), and the accoutrements of gracious dining and social entertaining (cf. Chapter 8). These reveal the charismatic Calverts served images of power to Annapolitans at table and at play. All of this could have been readily forecast and was the stuff of which most socioeconomic archaeological studies consist.

The catalyst here for an interpretive study that moves beyond the bounds of the familiar was the addition of a year of independent research on the culture of slavery with a focus on black women. If one wants to think of this in structural terms, the Calvert men provided the known and familiar Euroamerican culture; the West African women, men, and children who lived at the site, introduced another ingredient, exotic, and distant. Their inclusion permitted me to see contrasting lifestyles and conflicting values. Each group left its impact on the archaeological record and each saw the other as foreign.

Thus the Calvert family incorporated exotic elements into their lifestyles through the display of African lifeways that their slaves created. Perhaps because they had travelled widely, Captain Charles Calvert and his cousin, Benedict Leonard Calvert, were better equipped to tolerate the difference introduced by the maintenance of non-English behavior patterns among their slaves than many Maryland families. Perhaps they were not more tolerant, but simply less able to enforce a standard behavior code. While this does not detract from the ugliness of slavery or the dehumanization wrought by oppression, my impression is that it was the former. In other words, the black slaves living at the site had both means and opportunity to recreate African lifeways, and to the extent that they could, they did. Although the evidence is diffuse and submerged within the whole, analysis of different elements within the artifact assemblages from the site suggest that through both food and dress, Africans kept elements of their cultural identities intact while living in the shadow of the State House and under the eye of the governor of the province. By extension, one also has to take this as evidence that they actively maintained other elements of their cultures as well.

But the artifacts do not tell only of those who lived on the site. By viewing them within the networks of individuals who brought objects to and fro in the community, other planes of social action can be seen to intersect with the daily activity at the Calvert site. This is one means to begin to see how the family fitted within the community at large. Another is to look at the ways they used objects to wield power, strengthen their authority, and denote leadership. Each brings a different facet of the data to light; each represents a strategy of interpretive research on culture and history.

Figure 16.7. For centuries, African women supported cooking pots over their fires using three stones as shown in this drawing based on a photograph by Merrick Posnansky. Once the fire went out, the stones were tossed apart; a technique that obscures evidence of the stones in the archaeological record since only the ashes or hearth remain intact. With the penetration of European markets into Africa, earthenware pots were gradually replaced with black iron pots that, initially, were identical to those used in the Chesapeake. (Illustration by Julie Hunter-Abbazia based on a photograph provided by Merrick Posnansky.)

The method followed was really quite simple: draw on all sources of information; do not artificially limit or constrain them. Take to heart what Dell Upton wrote recently. Consider Annapolis not as you would if you were a bird on high. Come down, look at the town with all your senses. Think of it as a sightscape, soundscape, smellscape, and insert into it animals – pets like dogs and cats; vermin like rats; edible creatures like Maryland's crabs, sheep, goats, and dung-hill fowls. Put the people in, too. Make the data tell about them. Add the weather, the conflicts, the inescapable characteristics of human society expressed in all small-scale communities. Take archaeology back to the people, black and white. Use it to add additional perspectives to traditional histories. Consider the things Annapolitans built with their hands and their souls, and the different social spaces they formed in their homes, on their lots, at the docks, in the market stalls, the churches, and the houses of government. Look at deep-time. Think of how artifacts express power, but also autonomy and aesthetic values. Look at areas of cultural continuity; look at those that change, consider what is traditional and what is variable.[30]

Moving on

Through all of the events – real, imagined, or surmised – that I have recounted here, there were certain nature universals. The sun did shine, the frosty wind appeared out of the northwest every fall, driving the large blue crabs down into "hidey holes" in the Bay, *cohoonks* (onomatopoeic Algonkian geese) loomed in the sky. It was so then, ca. 1730, and it is so now. Variations occur from year to year; the Bay may freeze, and fruit trees bloom in April. The crabs will not return until they are ready, and they are not ready until the water warms to a set temperature sometime in mid-May. As Collingwood observed, "The laws of nature have always been the same and what is against nature now was against nature two thousand years ago."[31]

Here where we are working, man has not dealt this land a tender hand, but has yanked from it whatever he could. Thus the environment shows the effect of human stewardship, and it has wrought change. Salinity in the Bay changed as Maryland families cut down trees, turning the land into farm fields. Increased run-off altered the ratios of salt- and freshwater, making some streams no longer hospitable zones for fish, but killing grounds instead. Some fisheries started to die ca. 1660; others showed the impact of intensive farming and its correlates: increased silt, muddier bottoms, turbid water, and reduced salinity by 1789 when the shad and herring fisheries on Pomonkey Neck were available to let. "The time is past, and not likely to return," wrote one farmer, when a profitable fishery could be carried out from this shore.[32]

If an archaeologist wants to understand what once was, can no longer be, and use it to read data, she has to plug in the environmental information, but there is more to reading the soil than meets the eye. The Maryland habitat offered a range of possibilities to its settlers while simultaneously imposing constraints on daily life. The interplay of culture and nature is one beginning to the study of time past.

However, it is the cultural information that takes historical archaeology to a different plane. Knowledge of the encompassing web of culture holding objects, plants, animals and peoples gives artifacts a new reality and casts fantasy aside. It presents a Chesapeake world that was task-organized, following work patterns set by the sun and the moon, begun at cock's crow and followed until the chickens, turkeys and guinea hens went back to their trees to roost; set by the changing tide, the predilections of an overseer, and the demands of king tobacco who wanted hard labor year in and year out, constant attention for months on end, only giving brief respite in the fall.

Hugh Jones wrote that Maryland was a place where "tobacco is . . . meat, drink, clothing, and money." By 1722, the legislators complained that better worm and rail fences were needed; there was not a horse in Maryland, they told their Governor, Captain Calvert, who did not nibble on its leaves. "Most or all horses have at this time taken to eating tobacco." 'Twas a sad sight to be sure, for tobacco was man's fodder and his future. The grammar of the culture decreed it was not fit for mares

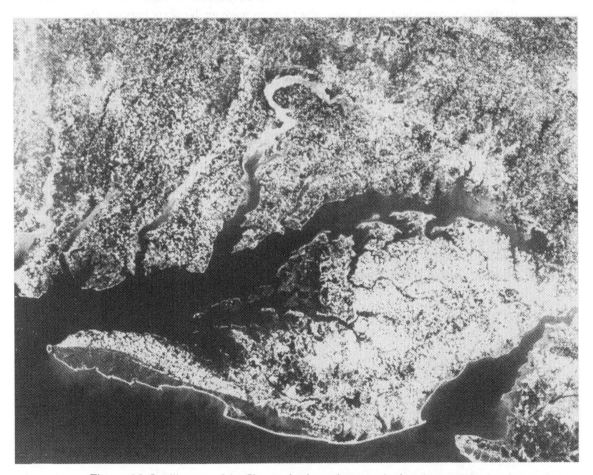

Figure 16.8. Satellite map of the Chesapeake shows the network of creeks, marsh land and rivers that line the Bay, one of the largest estuaries in the world. (Illustration courtesy of the Chesapeake Bay Foundation.)

and stallions. Even in the elevated circles that Benedict Leonard Calvert frequented, "conversation runs on planting Tobacco."[33]

Elsewhere, among ordinary folk, fantasy still rode the land on dark nights or at the moon's eclipse. Some believed the moon hid behind a cat's paw, and others that the sun had gone to war because the moon, bored, had struck out on a new path and had to be forced back. In this land without clocks, black slaves tended their own gardens under the stars, and a bright moonlit night could be taken for day as Benjamin Mifflin discovered to his chagrin upon awakening his household before dawn by thinking it was after.

These elements of past life disappear in the archaeological record unless one wants to reconstrue it to include documents. We cannot dig many of these facts up. They are the nuances and in their understanding anthropologists reach beyond data to men, to women, to humanity in its full and complex array. People appear as dim shades if we are content to use only artifacts for evidence when more is available. Their resonance is beyond the limits of archaeological knowledge until we learn how to use documents and break apart the barriers we have let texts impose. Perhaps we should say to students, "Explore a little, let the bones and pots talk by hearing how the natives have described them."

Follow a different anthropological lead. Make the imaginative effort to feel as a Chesapeake farmer felt, whether driving his cow into its pen at night, or weeding and hoeing his tobacco field. Picture the chickens, turkeys, and Guinea hens roosting in the trees. Listen to the laughing gull when it flies inland. Weed your tomato patch at night. Examine the magic the family used to plant and ensure a harvest. Consider the religious beliefs they drew upon in time of need, when great storms blew and sheets of rain poured down upon their fields. Think of how a man and his wife behaved in the areas of life that they controlled and take this fragile model to the places where they did not; see how the white society reacted first to the slaves and free blacks, and then how they responded to the reality of an increasingly biracial society where two speech communities interacted on a daily basis with a power structure built on fear. Then look at it from the other side. Bind science and art together. Listen to the many voices of Maryland.

Appendix A.1

Pottery and porcelain sold in Annapolis stores

Vessel form and ware	Charles Carroll	John Davisson	Amos Garrett	Thomas Bordley	Samuel Peele
Food preparation and storage					
Baking pans	—	—	—	X	—
Bowls, earthen	—	X	—	—	—
Bowls, black and white earthen	—	X	—	—	—
Bowls, wooden	—	X	—	—	—
Butter pots, brown (earthen)	X	—	—	X	—
Butter pots, non-specific	—	X	X	—	—
Butter pots, stone	—	—	—	X	X
Jars, large earthen	—	X	—	—	—
Jars, small	—	—	X	—	—
Milk coolers, wooden	—	X	—	—	—
Milk pans, earthen	—	—	—	—	X
Milk pans, large	—	—	X	X	—
Milk pans, small	—	—	X	—	—
Milk piggins, wooden	—	X	—	—	—
Pans, small earthen	—	—	—	X	—
Pans, assorted earthen	—	X	—	—	—
Patty pans, small	X	—	—	—	—
Patty pans, black and white earthen	—	X	—	—	—
Pipkins, brown (earthen)	X	X	X	X	—
Pots, earthen	—	X	—	—	—
Pots for potting beef	—	X	—	—	—
Pudding pans, brown (earthen)	X	—	X	—	—
Saucepans, 3 quart stoneware	—	—	—	X	—
Saucepans, large earthen	—	—	—	X	—
Saucepans, small earthen	—	—	—	X	—
Saucepans, assorted	—	—	X	—	—
Saucepans, children's	—	—	X	—	—
Sugar tubs, wooden	—	X	—	—	—
Jugs, smaller, blue and white	X	—	—	—	—
Jugs, smaller again, blue and white	X	—	—	—	—
Jugs, smallest, blue and white	X	—	—	—	—
Jugs, earthen	—	—	X	—	—
Jugs, large stone	—	—	X	—	—
Mugs, half pint, earthen	X	—	—	—	—
Mugs, pint, brown earthen	X	—	—	—	X
Mugs, quart (earthen?)	—	X	X	—	—

Vessel form and ware	Charles Carroll	John Davisson	Amos Garrett	Thomas Bordley	Samuel Peele
Mugs, small brown	X	—	—	—	—
Mugs, pint, stone	X	—	—	—	—
Mugs, quart, stone	X	X	X	X	—
Mugs, 8 wt, brown stone	—	—	—	—	X
Mugs, blue and white	—	—	—	—	X
Pannikens (drinking pots), earthen	—	X	—	—	—
Pannikens (drinking pots), stone	—	X	—	—	—
Syllabub pots	—	—	X	—	X
Punch bowls, large (delft?)	X	X	—	—	—
Punch bowls, small delft	—	X	—	—	—
Punch bowls, large and small	—	—	X	X	X
Punch bowls and ladles, lignum vitae	—	X	—	—	—
Coffee, chocolate, and tea related					
Teacups, non-specific	—	—	—	X	X
Tea saucers, non-specific	—	—	—	X	X
Teacups and saucers, stoneware?	—	—	—	X	—
Teapots	—	—	X	X	—
Milk pots, China	—	—	—	X	—
Sugar boxes, delft	—	X	—	—	—
Sugar dishes	X	—	—	X	—
Sugar pots, three sizes	X	—	—	—	—
Tea stands	—	—	—	X	—
Chocolate cups	—	—	X	—	—
Coffee cups	—	—	X	X	—
Other					
Basins, non-specific	X	—	X	X	—
Basins, earthen	—	X	—	—	—
Basins, delft	—	X	—	—	—
Basins, half-pint, delft	—	X	—	—	—
Basins, assorted white earthen	—	X	—	—	—
Chamber pots, non-specific	—	—	X	—	—
Chamber pots, coarse earthen	—	X	—	—	—
Chamber pots, white	—	—	—	—	X
Chamber pots, blue and green	X	—	—	—	—
Galley pots, blue and white	X	X	—	X	—

"X" denotes those stores which stocked the forms shown

Appendix A.2

Size of slave-holdings in Maryland

	0 slaves %	1–5 slaves %	6–10 slaves %	11–20 slaves %	21+ slaves %	50+ slaves %	
Annapolis and Londontown[a]							
1720–29 (N = 140)	not counted	14	0	26	61	0	100%
1730–39 (N = 175)	not counted	24	0	15	13	31	100%
Anne Arundel County[a]							
1720–29 (N = 445)	not counted	18	19	23	40	0	100%
1730–39 (N = 1104)	not counted	9	17	19	22	34	100%
Charles County							
1758 (N = 963)[b]	0	50.9	26.9	17.2	5.0	0	100%
by Household	382H	219H	36H	12H	2H	0	
Prince George's County							
1731–40 (N = 842)[c]	not counted	17	26	34	24	0	100%
St. Mary's County[c]							
1721–30 (N = 484)	not counted	26	21	25	28	0	100%
1731–40 (N = 524)	not counted	32	22	35	11	0	100%
Province-wide elite sample of decedents who left probated estates worth more than £650[d]							
1726–42	1	8	14	35	33	9	100%

[a] From Walsh 1984: Table 3 based on inventories
[b] From Lee 1986: 343 based on tax records
[c] From Kulikoff 1986: 331. No breakdown was given for slave-holdings above 20
[d] Burnard 1988: 58 based on inventories

Appendix A.3

Maryland population as reported in a 1755 "Account of the Number of Souls in Maryland"

	Southern Counties	Central Counties	Lower Eastern Shore	Upper Eastern Shore	Northern and Western Counties
Euroamerican					
Free men	4,099	3,049	6,289	3,199	6,908
Free women	4,222	3,219	6,803	3,290	5,986
Free children	8,695	7,329	12,517	6,851	15,295
"Poor" men	132	108	196	65	136
Servants, indentured					
Men	491	693	542	649	1,201
Women	331	148	360	340	645
Children	398	151	200	336	386
Servants, convict					
Men	234	257	34	369	613
Women	91	78	5	85	127
Children	31	17	2	14	24
Total white	18,194	15,049	26,948	15,198	31,321
African-American and Native American population					
Free black					
Men	19	11	24	18	47
Women	7	7	11	14	30
Children	37	15	29	17	13
"Past labor" or crippled	12	6	15	9	14
Black slaves					
Men	2,569	2,750	2,309	1,703	1,867
Women	2,230	2,111	2,039	1,095	1,363
Children	5,359	5,214	5,421	2,527	3,457
"Past labor" or crippled	120	180	155	67	73
Total black	10,353	10,294	10,003	5,450	6,864
Mulatto slave (black/white or black/red)					
Men	86	62	99	40	155
Women	64	54	107	41	126
Children	327	155	283	144	306
"Past labor" or crippled	34	22	20	15	8
Total	511	293	509	240	595
Free mulatto (black/white or black/red and all Native Americans)					
Men	100	33	87	26	61
Women	61	43	73	33	37
Children	232	133	246	90	184
"Past labor" or crippled	35	12	39	9	20
Total	428	221	445	158	302

Reprinted in the *Gentlemen's Magazine* 1766: 261

Appendix A.4

Domestic animals (excluding horses) owned by Captain Calvert at his death in January 1734

| | Anne Arundel County | | Prince George's County | | | | |
| | Farm | | House | Q#1 | Q#2 | Q#3 | |
	No.	%	No.	No.	No.	No.	%
Cattle							
Cows	3	33%	0	11	3	6	33%
Heifers (young cows)	2	22%	0	5	1	8	23%
Calves (less than a year old)	1	11%	0	3	3	2	13%
Yearlings (1–2 years old)	0		0	8	0	4	20%
Steers (2 to 5 years old)	2	22%	0	4	1	0	8%
Bulls	1	11%	0	0	0	1	2%
Subtotal	9	99%	0	31	8	21	99%
Sheep							
Sheep	23		0	0	0	0	
Lambs	16		0	0	0	0	
Subtotal	39						
Goats – none listed							
Swine							
Sows	10	42%	5	0	0	3	7%
Pigs	0		26	0	0	0	29%
Shoats (i.e., less than a year old)	13	54%	14	0		3	19%
Barrow (i.e., castrated boars)	0		2	0	0	0	2%
Boars	1	4%	0	0	0	0	
Hogs	0		0	0	29	9	42%
Subtotal	24	100%	47	0	29	15	99%
Poultry – none listed							

Appendix A.5

Domestic animals (excluding horses) owned by Col. Thomas Ennals, Esq. at his death in 1718

	No.	Percent
Cattle		
Cows	96	44%
Heifers(i.e., young cows)	7	3%
Calves (i.e., less than a year old)		
Two-year-old yearlings	25	12%
4 years old steers	22	
5 years old steers	16	
6 years old steers	13	
7 years old steers	28	
Steers (total)	(79)	37%
Bulls	9	4%
Subtotal	216	100%
Swine		
Sows	57	23%
Shoats (i.e., less than one year old)	108	44%
Barrows (i.e., castrated boars)	79	32%
Subtotal	244	99%

1. TRANSFORMING SPACE INTO PLACE

1 This viewpoint, eloquently expressed in Collingwood (1935, 1946), is a corner-stone of Henry Glassie's studies (e.g., Glassie 1975, 1982).

2 From Samuel Johnson's *The Rambler* as quoted by Noël Hume (1978: 39–40).

3 See Deetz (1977b) for a discussion of the wide-ranging parameters of material culture, or Deetz (1993) for a more recent overview of its Virginia dimensions. Deetz and scholars like Rhys Isaac also include speech utterances within this framework, but for the more timid, Isaac suggests instead we think of artifacts as "all enduring shaped products" (Isaac, letter, February 24, 1992).

4 For comprehensive overviews of Chesapeake history see the introductions in Tate and Ammerman (1979) or Carr, Morgan, and Russo (1988).

5 Quote is from Bloch (1985: 31).

6 Quotes are from Brait (1990: 1) and Dening (1988: 105). Also see Kimber (1746).

7 Quotes are from White (1989: 4); Cronin (1973: vii); Anonymous (1635: 81); Jones (1699: 216); Middleton (1953: 38, 41).

8 Quote is from White (1634: 40, 78).

9 Hammond (1656: 290). Hammond's description was an exaggeration of winter leisure; demands of tobacco cultivation took men into the fields in January and February at the height of winter cold; clearing fields was a year-long activity. For modern analyses of the labor involved in tobacco production see Morgan (1975); Rutman and Rutman (1984); Breen (1985); or, for Maryland, Carr, Menard, and Walsh (1991).

10 Original letter filed in the Dulaney Collection, Maryland Historical Society.

11 See White (1634: 40–4). Quote is from White (1634: 42). For an analysis of the greetings Native Americans gave the first European explorers and how they integrated these encounters into traditional belief systems, see Simmons (1992). Helen Rountree's study of the Powhatan (1989, 1990) provides a superb ethnographic account of Native Americans in Virginia and is an excellent introduction to the aboriginal culture of the Chesapeake. Feest (1978) records the movements of the Conoy Indians in the late seventeenth and early eighteenth centuries up river along the Potomac as proceeding from Harrison Island above the mouth of Goose Creek to Cony Island (now known as Heater's Island) where they were in 1712. By this time the population had been decimated by disease. By 1743, the

tribe had relocated to upstate New York, but not all went and some continued to live in Charles County and adjacent parts of Prince George's or St. Mary's near the rivers. The Anacostanks (in the vicinity of what is now Anacostia, a Washington, DC suburb) were a sub-tribe of this group. For Maryland's Piscataways see Merrill (1979); the archaeological record of the Yoacomaco village at St. Mary's City is described in Miller (1983: 18–40).

12 Notes outlining the petition are in the Bump Collection, Maryland Historical Society. The petition cites a population of 500 Native Americans, a number drawn from Hugh Jones' letter of 1698 which noted the presence of "Five hundred fighting Men" (Jones 1699: 441). However, Francis Jennings in *The Invasion of America* suggests adding four to five people for every adult warrior for more accurate estimates (Jennings 1975: 27). A third assessment is provided by Ubelaker and Curtin (1993: 11–12) who observe that an initial population of 45,000 in the Chesapeake "at the time of initial European contact were reduced to about 2,134 by about 1900." A list of trade furs is in Col. William Holland's inventory (Anne Arundel County Inventories, 1734, Liber 17: f. 454–62); for tomahawks see Samuel Young's inventory (Anne Arundel County Inventories, 1737, Liber 22: f. 432); for small Indian kettles see Henry Lowe's 1723 inventory (Kent County Box 5, Folder 63, Maryland State Archives). For Native American medicinal practice see the 1733 letter of Giles Falconer, of Kent County, MD, in the *Archives of the Royal Society* (LBC XV: 335–6). Also see the *Maryland Gazette* for advertisements of Seneca Indian rattlesnake potions.

13 James Merrill (1989) points out that the intersection of the two cultures is often inadequately covered by Chesapeake historians; there is also a false separation between historical archaeologists (who study Euroamerican or African-American sites) and those who work on Native American contact period sites.

14 Quotes are from Menard (1980: 110) and Greene (1988: 26–7).

15 For detail on seventeenth-century life in Maryland see Carr and Walsh (1977) or Carr, Menard, and Walsh (1991).

16 See Noël Hume (1982) for Martin's Hundred; H. Miller on the St. Mary's City chapel and its graves (1991); Bowen (1989) on the ages of livestock; Outlaw (1990) or Yentsch (1990b, 1991a) on pottery; Carr (1988a, 1988b), Carr and Walsh (1977, 1978), or Walsh (1979, 1983, 1988) for a range of different aspects of Chesapeake lifestyle and for economic consumption patterns.

17 Carr and Menard (1989: 408) on the economy; Carr (1988a, 1992); Carr and Walsh (1988a: esp. 144–7); Clemens (1980: 87–9); Hoffman (1988: 213); Land (1965, 1981); Russo (1989); Stiverson (1977). John Dowley's wife, for example, knitted stockings, mended shirts (for six pence) and/or made them (six pence apiece using oznabrig, an inexpensive, coarse linen). Anne Arundel County Judgments 1734, IBI: f. 43.

18 See Calvert entries in the *Biographical Dictionary of Maryland Legislators*, volume I (Papenfuse *et al.* 1979).

19 Those men without political office who wed the third Lord Baltimore's step-daughters were given positions on the Governor's Council almost as soon as the marriages took place.

20 Land (1981: 134).

21 Charles Carroll of Annapolis, for example, although he sold slaves, had only ten listed in his inventory; Thomas Bordley had nineteen. These were two of the wealthiest households in Annapolis (see table 3.4).

22 Margaret Lee was the daughter of Henry Lee and Charlotte Villiers, daughter of Barbara Villiers and King James II (*Smith's National Biographical Dictionary*). Inventory of Edward Henry Calvert, Anne Arundel County Inventories Liber 15: f. 570.

23 Ridgely (1841: 33–4); Reps (1972: 118).

24 McMahon (1831: 224); Baker (1984: 17; 1986). Carville Earle and Nancy Baker reconstructed the original town plan, using information in deeds and other documents under a 1977 research and development grant to Historic Annapolis, Inc. by the National Endowment for the Humanities, RS-0067-79-0738 (Baker 1984). Their work indicates use of a simple grid as does my later research (1983–6), and that of Anthony Lindhauer (Lindhauer, personal communication, March 1990). The grid was undoubtedly similar to that at Londontown where deeds (Nelker 1967) indicate many lots had dimensions that used the 9, 12 and 16 perch lengths that also shaped in Annapolis lots. See also Figures 77, 78 in Reps (1972) for the use of simple grid plans in other early towns.

25 Wealthy, prestigious Catholic men (usually related to the Calvert family by marriage) held many of the more important political positions in the government (Hoffman 1988: 212). Originally St. Mary's City, located halfway down the Bay at the southern edge of the province, was both more central to regional settlement and more accessible to the counties – St. Mary's and Charles – where the homes of Maryland's Catholic families were. They constituted 25% of the population (Carr and Jordan 1974: 33, note 64). Inhabitants of St. Mary's fought the relocation of the capital. They reiterated that their town was well watered, surrounded by a good harbor, defensible; they offered to provide additional material inducements. The Lower House spurned these efforts: "As to the great expenditure of money in improving the place and country around, it is against the fact, for more money has been spent here by the rest of the province, than its inhabitants and all the people for ten miles round are worth; and yet, after sixty years experience, and almost a fourth of the province devoured by them, they still, like Pharoah's kine, remain as lean as at first; and we are unwilling to add any more of our substance to such ill improvers" (*Archives of Maryland* XIX: 77). Henry Miller (1988b) reviews baroque elements incorporated in the plan of St. Mary's City. King (1994) describes the use of seventeenth-century ruins in the landscape.

26 Carr (1974: 125) explains the location of St. Mary's City. Quote is from Hawley (1635: 73). Quote by Cardross and Dunlop, 1685, as given in Wood (1974: 65). Oldmixon (1708, vol. I: 196). Land (1981) reviews the political context.

27 See Anne Arundel County Court Judgments, 1734, IB 1: f. 78 for a list of the county's public roads and ferries.

28 Benjamin Mifflin (1762: 431–2) described the town and its gatehouse: "There is but one way to it North, Leading under an old Frame Building to which is Fixt a Swing Gate to Keep the Cattle out of the Town . . . the streets are not paved." Town histories of Annapolis include Ridgely (1841); Riley (1887); Radoff (1954); Papenfuse (1975); Wright (1983); Walsh (1984a); Baker (1982, 1984, 1986); Middleton (1988).

29 Quote is from Jones (1699: 441). Deed from Sarah Perry now Evans, widow, to Charles Carroll (Anne Arundel County Deeds, 1700, WT#1: f. 55–6). A later deed (Cullen to Bruss and McNamara, Anne Arundel County Deeds, PK 1709–12: f. 139) specifies that "Perry the postman so called built a brick house." The stone house is described in a deed from Nathan Rigbie, son of James and Elizabeth, to Thomas Larkin (Anne Arundel County Deeds, PK 1718: f. 525) and is for a lot of land sold by "Robert Proctor to Mr. Jonathan Celly, merchant, and by him to his daughter, Katherine Celly, whose heir at law I am." The deed specifies that the land was included in the lot "numbered for the first lot in the town lying by the waterside and 20 feet from where a 44ft. stone house stood in the garden, and to the wharf east and south." Proctor was one of the first residents of the town (it was once called Proctor's Landing); his patents were filed in 1673 and 1680. Hugh Jones, a young minister sent by members of the Royal Society to gather floral and faunal specimens and collect information (1699: 441) was specific: "There are about forty Dwelling Houses, Seven or Eight whereof can afford good Lodging and Accommodations for Strangers. There is also a State House, and a Free-School built with Brick, which make a great shew among a parcel of wooden Houses, and the Foundation of a Church laid, the only Brick Church in Maryland." Also see Ebenezer Cook's 1708 description of Annapolis as "a City situate on a Plain, Where scarce a house will keep out Rain: The Buildings gram's with Cyprus Rare Resemble much our Southwark Fair."

30 Kimber in the *London Magazine*, July 1746. Kimber's account of booth-like dwellings at Snow Hill, on the lower Eastern Shore, is similar to Ebenezer Cook's 1708 description. Russell Wright (1983) describes the surviving buildings and discusses their aesthetic integration into the Nicholson town plan. Most families lived in homes without outbuildings, but some built a variety. For example, ca. 1730, John Chalmers had a bake-house; Thomas McNemara (by 1715) and Chalmers too had meat houses. As late as 1798 more than half the homes in Annapolis were wooden; the percentage of outbuildings and commercial structures made of wood was higher still (Yentsch and McKee 1987).

31 Quote is from Mifflin (1762: 433).

32 The improving quality of life is discussed by Land (1965; 1981: 119–22).

33 Quote is from Oldmixon (1708, vol. 1: 205).

34 Quote is from a letter of William Byrd to Johann Rudolp Ochs, July 15, 1736 (Byrd 1731–76: 490). See Records of the Annapolis Mayor's Court, 1722, f. 121 for Margaret Steele.

35 Suleiman's life was briefly reviewed by Middleton (1943) while a fuller transcript, with additional African data, is provided in Curtin (1967).

36 Quote is from William Green, *The Sufferings of William Green being a Sorrowful Account of his Seven Years' Transportation* . . . (London, 1774: 6).

37 See Anne Arundel County Court Judgments, 1734, IB 1: f. 54. Quote is from Hugh Jones (1699: 441).

38 Reference to the sandbank is in Anne Arundel County Deeds, AR 38: 334 (a deed for the Ship's Carpenter Lot, #12–18 Market Space), which was created by a stream emptying into the market space. The information on the shoreline comes in part from a deposition by Samuel Middleton in 1767 speaking of the harbor in 1742: "cove or salt water of the dock runs up above the place where said stump [lies] and did formerly run further up." Lease from Charles Carroll to Darby Callahan, Annapolis Mayor's Court Proceedings, 1729, Liber B: f. 180.

39 Inventory of John Davisson, Prerogative Court Inventories, 1721, Liber 7: f. 81.

40 Charles Carroll's inventory was never officially probated and is on file at the Maryland Historical Society (Ledger X, May 2, 1723, Carroll-McTavish Papers). For additional information on Carroll and his family see Rowland (1898) or the analysis of his political activities in Hoffmann (1988).

41 For William Peele's slaves – Bob, Sarah, and Saltwater John – see Anne Arundel County Judgments IB 1: f. 250. For Bess and Hannah see Anne Arundel County Judgments IB 1: f. 413. For the fine assessed Jane Govane, "being a person of ill fame," see Anne Arundel County Judgments IB 1: f. 379.

42 At times, prior to the new slave laws enacted in 1715, these men and women occasionally married, but the laws that prohibited this were harsh (Jordan 1962; Morgan 1975: 333–7). The case of Henry Tudor Williams can be found in Anne Arundel County Judgments, 1734 IB 1: f. 420.

43 Annapolis Mayor's Court Proceedings, 1722: f. 27–33.

44 Annapolis Mayor's Court Proceedings, 1722: f. 25 also records the abusive treatment of Agnes Callahan while f. 24 records what happened to Mary Holmes; 1722: f. 31 records drunken behavior; the breaking and entering is given on f. 2; the petticoat on f. 8. The woman involved, Eleanor Ferguson, received a relatively light sentence (fifteen lashes, paying its value fourfold) when one considers that three years later, a maidservant on the Eastern Shore was hung for stealing little more (Provincial Court Judgments, 1725, PL 7: f. 160).

45 See Annapolis Mayor's Court Proceedings, 1719: f. 5 for the theft of the plank.

46 Annapolis Mayor's Court Proceedings, 1745: f. 233 pertains to Tasker's agreement; 1745: f. 156 gives the land boundaries.

47 Davis (1803: 363). For the garden size, see lease between John Reynolds, barber and innkeeper, and Samuel Soumaine, goldsmith, dated 1742 recorded in the Mayor's Court Proceedings, 1742: f. 231. The rent was £14 and the lease was written for thirteen years; the tiny plot was "now enclosed in a garden belonging to the present dwelling house of John Reynolds." Reynolds was the father of William Reynolds who later built a large, two-story brick inn on Church Circle.

48 Ann Seaborn's age is given in Anne Arundel County Judgments 1734, IB 1: f. 375. Quote is from Davis (1803: 375, 237–8). In his introduction to *Brief Lives*, Aubry (1669–76) wrote "when I was a Boy every Gentleman almost kept a Harper in his home: and some of them could versified" (p. xxvii). Aubry was born in 1626 (Stephen and Lee 1917).

2. BEGINNING THE RESEARCH

1 Information is in Amos Garrett's will (Anne Arundel County Wills, Box 34, f. 2) and in Anne Arundel County Deeds WT 1: f. 275. The corner post stood on the Southeast Line that ran 16 perches west of Prince George Street (as originally laid out) and parallel to it (see also deed describing the slope of State House Hill bordering Nicholson's Cove – the town harbor – in Anne Arundel County Deeds, IB 2: f. 500). The most likely man is the son named Samuel Chew born in 1660 to merchant-planter Samuel Chew, Sr. Samuel Chew, Sr. was an original settler from Virginia who died in 1676/77. Chew's son and namesake, Samuel Chew, the second, was a wealthy Quaker merchant who became a County Court justice in 1685, and died in 1718, maintaining a primary residence at Herring Bay in Anne Arundel County. Biographical data are derived from Kelly (1963) and from *A Biographical Dictionary of the Maryland Legislature, 1635–1789* volumes I and II (Papenfuse *et al.* 1979/1985), hereinafter cited as BDML I or BDML II.

2 See Yentsch (1986: 12–13). The quantity of tobacco pipe fragments (330) seems low in comparison to St. Mary's sites, but many of these also served as inns or taverns when the General Assembly met. There is a difference in quantities of tobacco pipes found in association with taverns/inns (and in the inventories of their owners) and those from domestic lots. Rockman and Rothschild used samples from eighteenth-century taverns and inns containing 2,800 to 9,000 pipe sherds (Rockman and Rothschild 1984); Schrire *et al.* (1990) excavated a military outpost in South Africa and recovered 10,000.

3 Quote is reprinted in BDML II: 803. Taylard held the following clerkships: Prerogative Office, Secretary's Office, Lower House, clerk of St. Mary's County and, later, of Anne Arundel County (1699–1703). He was also elected to the Lower House from St. Mary's City from 1697/98 to 1700. Rev. Thomas Bray wrote that Taylard held a "commission by his Excellency's [Nicholson's] favor" (Steiner 1901: 230–3). The reasons why Taylard lost favor with Nicholson are unclear. It was during this era that Nicholson complained of "the great scarcity of good Clerks" and to improve the situation, established Maryland's first free school (Land 1981: 98). Only spartan details of the verbal sparring by Clarke are given in the legislative biographies (BDML I: 224, 233), but the legislative records themselves are filled with colorful details.

In later records, Taylard is described as a gentleman. His probate inventory contains few indications of wealth or the emerging modern lifestyle (Anne Arundel County Accounts and Inventories Liber 33A: f. 240), although it has some distinct oddities, such as a bird cage. His second wife, Audrey (widow of John Lewellyn who died in 1698), inherited his property in 1711 as well as his debts to neighbors Amos Garrett and Thomas Bordley. In 1718, his widow sold Lot 83 to Philemon Hemsley for £30 British sterling (Anne Arundel County Deeds IB 2: f. 542).

4 The Widow Taylard returned to St. Mary's City where she died in 1721, leaving an estate worth almost twice that of her second husband; most of her wealth was in livestock. Every indication is that she maintained a simpler life style after Taylard's death. Her cooking utensils were minimal; the birdcage was gone; only a single servant remained (St. Mary's County Inventories, November 1721, Liber 6: f. 220).

5 There are architectural details relative to the basement which provide one basis for believing that the original frame building may have been later encased in brick; a similar situation was observed at barrister Charles Carroll's house on Market Street (Russell Wright, personal communication) and has been reported at Holly Hill in Anne Arundel County (Carson *et al.* 1981).

Hemsley, a merchant planter in the London-Barbados trade, served as Justice of Talbot and Queen Anne's Counties. He lived on the Eastern Shore until his second marriage in 1709 to Mary Townley Contee, when he moved to his wife's plantation in Charles County. Through his second marriage, Hemsley gained control of the Contee estate, valued at £2,252 with over 3,500 acres of land. His widow inherited his Annapolis and his Western Shore estates whereas his son by a first marriage received the Eastern Shore estate. He appointed his wife executor. She refused this on December 23, 1719, rejecting the legacies bequeathed in the will, citing the deed of settlement executed before her marriage on October 23, 1711 (Queen Anne County, Box 26: f6). Further information on the Hemsley and Contee families can be found in BDML (vol. I: 230, 430).

6 Anne Arundel County Inventories Liber 4: f. 33, 38, 119.

7 Rogers was a young merchant-mariner in his mid-twenties from New England who later became Chief Clerk and Registrar of the Prerogative Court (1736–49). There is no record that Mary Townley-Contee-Hemsley-Rogers ever had a child, although she had a number of stepchildren whom she helped raise. While it is possible that the Hemsley children – William and Ann – may have spent time in Annapolis, it is doubtful that any of the wealthy Court family who were stepchildren of John Contee lived with her. Her nephew by marriage, Alexander Contee, became extremely well-connected politically through his marriage to Jane Brooke in 1721. Thereafter, he successfully contested the will of his uncle, confirmed in 1708 through an Act of Assembly while Seymour was still Governor, that gave the estate to Mary. Depositions taken in 1725 revealed that John Contee refused to sign the will, and a second Act of Assembly repealed the earlier confirmation on the basis of perjury, noting that it had passed through "means too shocking to be transmitted to posterity." Mary died May 24, 1725 (St. Anne's Parish Records in microfilm at the Maryland State Archives).

8 These included lots owned by Daniel Larke and Richard Bickerdike located on Maryland Avenue and/or on the sub-divided Stoddart Lot No. 82 (Anne Arundel County Deeds, RD 1: f. 84, f. 155, f. 158; see also Mayors Court Proceedings, Liber B: f. 176–7.

9 Correspondence from Charles Lowe, April 19, 1725, to Benedict Leonard Calvert reprinted in Steiner (1908: 287).

10 Quote is from Isaac (1982: 23–4). The value of a country estate is stressed by Stone (1967). For diary entries see Carter's Diary (vol. II: 1114); Maury (1853: 334); Boucher (1738–89). The estate account filed in 1737 contains listings of various debts paid for in tobacco and of tobacco traded with other individuals (Anne Arundel Accounts Liber 14: f. 359–65).

11 Carr (1988), Carr and Walsh (1988a, 1988b), Carr, Menard, and Walsh (1991) emphasize the conservative fiscal use of capital among Maryland families.

12 On housing, see Stone and Stone (1986). Also see discussions by Stone (1967); Mingay (1978); Beckett (1986).

13 The purchases began immediately after the fifth Lord Baltimore's visit to Annapolis in 1732–3. As a result, Captain Calvert's daughter inherited fifteen additional lots on the north side of Tabernacle Street (now College Avenue) which returned to Baltimore's side of the family with her marriage (1783 tax assessments for Anne Arundel County).

14 See Mingay (1978: 108–9). How the financial activities of individual members fit within the familial framework can be seen in various financial transactions. A trust established for Lord Baltimore's sister, Charlotte Brerewood, specified that her yearly allowance of £200 ceased when she died and could not be paid to her husband, poet Thomas Brerewood (Calvert Papers No. 90). The fifth Lord Baltimore's youngest brother, Cecilius Calvert, consistently loaned his nephews and nephews-in-law money as their unofficial banker. Servants and retainers frequently were related to the Calvert family in various ways, formal and informal, thus enabling the family to distribute wages among other kin. But these financial relationships did not incorporate provisions for in-laws except when there was continued and direct involvement with family members. The third Lord Baltimore gave a home to his widowed sister, Mary Calvert Blakiston, but filed suit to recover the expense from the Blakiston heir (see notes in the Bump Collection, Maryland Historical Society). A lawsuit brought by the Earl of Litchfield was filed to recover Lee family holdings at Woodstock Park when the first Benedict Leonard (who became the fourth Lord Baltimore) separated from his wife, Charlotte Lee (Treasury Papers 1702–7, pp. 318–19, published London 1874). Another example is visible in the set of lawsuits over "My Ladies Manor" filed by the Brerewoods and the sixth Lord Baltimore as different branches of the family sought to control this upper Maryland estate (now Monkton). The matter was finally resolved after the Revolution when the State, which seized the manor during the war, turned it over to the tenants who occupied it under Brerewood (Calvert Papers 658–61). Marriages were made as much for financial considerations as for love and affection.

15 Captain Calvert's inventories consist of three documents: one for his Anne Arundel County estate (Anne Arundel County inventories, L20: f. 153); one for the Prince George's County estate (Prince George's County inventories L20: f. 167); and an addition filed in 1737 (Anne Arundel County inventories, L22: f. 341). For Edward Henry Calvert's inventory see Anne Arundel County inventories L15: f. 570.

16 Prerogative Court Inventories, June 12, 1733, Liber 18: f. 18–19 (and filed while Lord Baltimore was in Annapolis). Benedict Leonard's wealth placed him in a category apart from almost all other Maryland men. As a younger son, however, his wealth was far less than that of his elder brother, Charles, the fifth Lord Baltimore, or other English peers. Beckett (1986: 288) indicates that "incomes in excess of £10,000 had become commonplace for peers above the rank of baron by 1710." For further information on the wealth of Maryland decedents see Carr and Walsh (1993) whose studies indicate that although by the 1730s more individuals owned small "luxuries" such as teawares than earlier, overall wealth levels for more than half the population still remained below £95.

17 For St. Mary's County see Carr and Walsh (1978), for Somerset County, see Car (1988). See also the work of Gloria Lund Main (1982) on Charles, Calvert, Anne Arundel, Baltimore, Kent, and Somerset counties; Alan Kulikoff (1986) for Prince George's County; Jean Russo (1989) for Talbot County; and for a study of the wealthiest decedents to file inventories in colonial Maryland, see Burnard (1988).

18 Carr and Walsh (1993).

19 Charles Carroll's inventory, May 2, 1723, is filed in Ledger x of the Carroll-Tavistock Papers at the Maryland Historical Society, Baltimore, Maryland.

20 For information on the modern index see Carr and Walsh (1993: 37).

21 Sir Henry Wooten, *Elements of Architecture*, as quoted in Mingay (1963: 149).

22 Stone and Stone (1986: 9).

23 Information on Blanche Arundel, grandmother of the third Lord Baltimore, is given in the English *Dictionary of National Biography* (Stephen and Lee 1917) as is the information on Thomas Hearne. John Aubry (1669–96) wrote about the trip made by Robert Talbot (husband or son of Grace Calvert Talbot). Lee was a cousin of Benedict Leonard and Edward Henry on their mother's side. Samuel Pepys in 1667 described the house that became the Calverts' Epsom home (Pepys 1660–9, vol. VIII: 338–9). The interconnections among the small group of English educated and elite gentlefolk were complex and far-reaching.

24 Land (1981) provides a detailed overview of Maryland history, while Hoffman (1973) concentrates on the period immediately preceding the Revolution; Carr and Jordan (1974) document the transition to a royal administration, and Papenfuse (1975) describes the economic background of the province and Annapolis at the height of its pre-Revolutionary prosperity.

3. *ON BEHALF OF HIS LORDSHIP*

1 See Hamilton (1874, vol. III: 442). Lord Baltimore's military service is noted in Beaton's Index and in Hayden's Book of Dignitaries (1890: 871). In September 1709, Charles Calvert Lazenby sold 1,000 acres of Portland Manor in Anne Arundel County to Col. Henry Darnall for £700 together with twelve African slaves and thirty head of black cattle for £300 (Anne Arundel Deeds, Liber PK: f. 191). The acreage was originally patented for the third Lord Baltimore who gave it to Lazenby in 1701 (Anne Arundel Deeds, Liber CD: f. 111). Witnesses to the 1709 deed were close associates or kinsmen of Lord Baltimore; the buyer, Henry Darnall, was a cousin.

2 See Hall (1904) or BDML I (under Calvert). Also see references cited in footnote 4.

3 Quote is from Hussey (1931: 230).

4 Material on the Calvert family is drawn primarily from the Archives of Maryland, from correspondence edited by Steiner (1898, 1908); from biographic data in Johnson (1905–8); Land (1968, 1981); William Nicklin (1980); Stephen and Lee (1917); Thomas Hearne's diaries, volumes 9–11 (Hearne 1678–1735); Calvert Memorabilia (Md. Historical Magazine X: 372–5; XI: 282; XVI: 38–388); and notes in the Bump Collection (Maryland Historical Society Manuscript Room).

5 Haslett (1983: 203). Among the Hydes were Lawrence, Earl of Rochester, who was High Treasurer to James II and Henry, Lord Cornbury, who was his brother; the family developed extensive mercantile connections from which Hyde descendants created a Maryland tobacco empire in the early eighteenth century; one of the Digges was an eminent mathematician; two were noted for their literary skill; Edward Digges who served as Governor to Virginia also provided Maryland with its branch of the family (Stephen and Lee 1917). For the third Lord Baltimore's network of political allies see Land (1968); Hruschka (1974); Hoffman (1988: 212).

6 Charles II gave this advice when word of Titus Oates' accusations against Catholic lords in 1678/79 became widespread. The third Lord Baltimore was a child during the Civil War of 1640–9, was in England at the time of the Titus Oates accusations, and during the Glorious Revolution (1685–9). In the late 1670s Charles Calvert was reported in Ireland where he was presumed to be plotting against the King (Bump Collection). He was also a nephew of Henry Arundel who was jailed for his presumed participation in plots against the king. Although there is no evidence that Calvert was ever involved in treason, English records indicate that he had to give affidavits concerning his loyalty in the 1670s and again in the 1690s. Hearne wrote that Benedict Leonard believed his grandfather returned to Maryland in 1679 "by the advice of King Charles" (Hearne, Diary, February 12, 1718/19, VI: reprinted in the *Maryland Historical Magazine* I: 277). There were two minor uprisings during his years in Maryland and, while he was in England in 1689 to defend the Province's northern boundaries against

William Penn's claims on behalf of Pennsylvania, the rebellion led by Coode took political control of the Province from his hands (see Carr and Jordan 1974 for a detailed study of the rebellion, or Land 1981 for an overview; Hoffman 1988 also summarizes his administration of Maryland). The third Lord Baltimore never returned to Maryland.

7 The Calvert family's English background has not been systematically studied by recent historians. Historians have also overlooked the importance of kinship connections on the matrilineal side of many families; Maryland histories of the Calverts, for example, do not discuss the heroism of Calvert's grandmother, Lady Blanche Arundel, when she held Wardour Castle for eight days, defending it against Cromwell's forces in 1643 with a very small force, and the help of many women and children. Yet knowledge of what his grandmother had done – it earned her fame as "the Defendor of Wardour" – must have shaped his life, as must the courage and heroism shown by his grandfather in England's civil war.

8 Steiner (1908).

9 The pertinent correspondence is a series of letters reprinted in the *Maryland Historical Magazine* (Steiner 1908: 209, 212, 321) to Governor Benedict Leonard Calvert.

Charles Lowe, September 12, 1723: Mother Calvert and Mrs. Ross are preparing for Maryland and go the latter part of this or beginning of next month, where I hope they will find the Governor and his lady well.

Charles Lowe, January 25, 1723/24: I have lately sent your letter to the Governor [Capt. Calvert] which came not to my hands till after his Mother and Mrs. Ross were gone.

Cecilius Calvert, May 16, 1724, also described the Countess Henrietta's behavior aboard ship while traveling to Maryland with Mrs. Ross in a letter to his brother. See footnote 35 below.

Charlotte Brerewood, June 30, 1728: I am sorry our Cousin the Captain had not . . . gratitude. I hear by Theda [Benedict Leonard's housekeeper in Annapolis was Theda Lawrence], the old countess his mother, is dead.

The wife of Henry Lazenby, the High Sheriff of Anne Arundel, was also Captain Calvert's kinswoman; the death of "Madame Margaret Lazenby, aunt to our present Governor, Charles Calvert" was recorded in the St. Anne's Parish Register on August 8, 1722. The death in May 1723 of Henry Lazenby, appointed High Sheriff of Anne Arundel County shortly after Captain Calvert arrived in the province, was noted in the St. Anne's Parish Register.

10 Stone and Stone (1986: 79–91).

11 Stone and Stone (1986: 152, 149).

12 Erickson (1959: 77). The regiment Captain Calvert belonged to was first raised by Charles II in 1656. In 1685 it was amalgamated with another regiment and renamed the Grenadier Guards (Bruce 1980). The regiment fought at Tournai in Belgium, at Malplaquet, Menin, and Douai and was under the command of Marlborough in 1714. In the 1720s Cecilius Calvert also purchased a commission in the same regiment. Blenheim Roll Records (Whitworth 1974: 19)

show the annual rates of pay its men received: Capt., Lt. Col. (£99); Capt., Lt. (£47); Ensign (£17); Adjutant (£12); Sgt. (£2-02-06d); Private (£01-02-06d). Lord Baltimore's rationale for appointing Captain Calvert as governor is given in the *Archives of Maryland* (XXXIV: 3–4).

13 Their letter, dated October 12, 1720, is in Proprietary Papers, Black Books, vol. I: 344.

14 Quote is from Land (1981: 129). Details of Captain Calvert's negotiations with Maryland Indians can be seen throughout the legislative records (*Archives of Maryland* XXXIV). It is former Maryland archivist, Phebe Jacobson's belief that the Calverts played a covert, protective role in relations with Native Americans by deliberately laying out manor lands and hunting reserves for the Proprietor close to traditional Indian villages. These, in essence, served as a mechanism to regulate development of tribal lands and to maintain their status as hunting preserves. In the 1690s, when land control is passed to the Crown, one begins to see a tacit acceptance of English encroachment onto these lands. A small flurry of protests by the sachems can be seen after the Calvert family regains control of the province in 1715, and these were one of the facets of Indian–English interaction that Captain Calvert negotiated.

15 *Archives of Maryland* (XXXIV: 4–5). Captain Calvert's statement, written on the back side of the Slye petition, is addressed to Thomas Bordley and reads: "Having read and considered the within petition of Mr. Slye, and upon his desire of your being counsel for him, if such a method is usual, I can't but think it very reasonable. March 16, 1720." Lewellyn had hired both Bordley and Daniel Dulaney to represent him. See Gratz Mss, Case 2, Box 29, Pennsylvania Historical Society, Philadelphia, PA.

16 Letter from Phillmon Lloyd to an unnamed relative included in the Calvert Papers (vol. II: 45–6).

17 It was advice given to the governor by Thomas Bordley, a member of the Lower House promoted to the Governor's Council in 1720–1, over dinner at his home that caused the furore (*Archives of Maryland* XXXIV: 277, 283). Shortly afterwards, Bordley's central role with the Country Party began. In 1722 he joined Daniel Dulaney on the Committee of Laws where "this pair took the lead in hatching a scheme that was to reverberate in local politics for years to come and more than once send echoes into the proprietary closet in England and beyond to Whitehall itself" (Land 1981: 131; see also BDML or Morton 1964). Yet the Captain and Bordley must have resolved their differences for there is evidence of continued financial transactions (e.g., Captain Calvert owed Bordley £300 at Bordley's death).

18 At the start of the 1721 session, Calvert announced to the legislature: "those little heats which lately disturb you are now happily at an end" (*Archives of Maryland* XXXIV: 124). See Land (1981: 134) or Charles Barker (1940) for a detailed analysis of the rights of the proprietary and how it meshed with the rights and interests of the colonists. Also see McMahon (1831: 283) and Everstine (1980: 243).

The English statutes provided security against some of the policies of the proprietary and also against the use of arbitrary power. Since none of the Calverts, unlike their grandfather, the third Lord Baltimore, were personally known in Maryland when they resumed administration of the Province in 1714, they were an unknown element in the provincial hierarchy. It was to be expected that Maryland's small planters might question their intentions. The issues raised concerning the statutes were not finally settled until 1776 when provisions in Article 3 of the Declaration of Rights in the new Constitution entitled the inhabitants of Maryland to the common laws of England and to its statutes (Everstine 1980: 244).

19 The dispute over who should pay this per diem first was raised in 1723; the Lower House (or House of Delegates) asserted that Lord Baltimore should do so when the Upper House met as the Council of State; the Upper House (or Council in its other role) disagreed. Baltimore refused to make any payments to them (Everstine 1980: 232–9). See *Archives of Maryland* (XXXIV: 592; XXXV: 393).

20 *Archives of Maryland* (XXXV: 256, 261, 265, 279).

21 *Archives of Maryland* (XXXIV: 378, 5; XXXV: 261).

22 See Land (1981: 129) and also his 1968 study of the Dulaney family. Owings (1953) contains a thorough listing of appointees to financially remunerative provincial offices.

23 Cecilius Calvert, October 1, 1728, correspondence with Benedict Leonard Calvert reprinted in Steiner (1908: 327). Charles Lowe, April 5, 1728, correspondence with Benedict Leonard Calvert reprinted in Steiner (1908: 311). Charles Calvert, fifth Lord Baltimore, April 5, 1728, correspondence with Captain Charles Calvert reprinted in Steiner (1908: 310).

24 There is some confusion about what the Captain should have received. A set of instructions dated March 14, 1726/27 from Baltimore to Benedict Leonard instructs him to take his salary of £1,000 out of the export tobacco duties, and also says that half of the three pence is to be given to Captain Calvert; if the bill then pending was dropped, they were to revert to the collection of quit rents (Slater Paper Prop. vol. 3, #2). Yet Benedict Leonard became angry once the Lower House passed the tobacco export duty which he was to share with Captain Calvert. The *Maryland Gazette*, February 17, 1728/39 (William Park, editor) reported Edward Henry's arrival in the Province.

25 Edward Henry Calvert, 1727, correspondence with Benedict Leonard Calvert reprinted in Steiner (1908: 298–9).

26 Cecilius Calvert, October 1, 1728, correspondence with Benedict Leonard Calvert reprinted in Steiner (1908: 327). Charlotte Brerewood, June 30, 1728, correspondence with Benedict Leonard Calvert reprinted in Steiner (1908: 322). The ball is described in the *Maryland Gazette*, March 4, 1728/30.

27 In 1718 Rev. Jacob Henderson of Annapolis gave Edward Henry a letter to take to Dr. Francis Asty which suggests Edward Henry made one trip abroad at the least (Steiner 1917: 130). Correspondence of Dr. Alexander Hamilton (Dulaney Collection, Maryland Historical Society Manuscript Collection). Benedict

Leonard Calvert correspondence with Charles Calvert, fifth Lord Baltimore (Calvert Papers No. 2: 79). Charlotte Brerewood, November 10, 1729, correspondence with Benedict Leonard Calvert reprinted in Steiner (1908: 331).

28 From the statement of the Upper House to the Governor made May 22, 1730 (*Maryland State Archives*, XXXVII: 8). The receipt book of Benedict Leonard Calvert, 1727–31, shows that on August 14, 1730 he "gave my Sister Margarett Calvert an Order on Capt. Hyde for Eighty pounds Sterling" (Document No. 910 in the Calvert Papers, Maryland Historical Society). Three graves have recently been found within the church at St. Mary's City containing the skeletons of a child, an adult man, and a young woman, each in a lead coffin (Miller 1991). Archaeologists from the St. Mary's City Commission believe they are the remains of Calverts who died in the Province in the 1680s; this finding prompts the question of whether or not Edward Henry would have been buried in the churchyard or laid to rest inside the first church on the Circle.

29 Quote by Commissary Johnson was made in reference to illness in South Carolina (quoted in Wood 1974: 71, from Klingberg 1946: 76). See epitaph of Rev. John Humphrey recorded in his own handwriting in the St. Anne's Parish Register.

30 Starting in the late 1600s, the British aristocracy were increasingly drawn to horse racing because of its popularity with monarchs such as Charles II (a great-grandfather of Benedict Leonard and Edward Henry discussed subsequently) (Reed 1984). Governor Francis Nicholson chose it as one means to bring Virginians of all social ranks together: "[Nicholson] studied Popularity, discoursing freely of Country Improvements. He made his Court to the People, by instituting Olympick Games, and giving Prizes to all those, that shoul'd excel in the Exercises of Riding, Running, Shooting, Wrestling, and Backsword" (Beverly 1705: 98). Keith Thomas (1983: 29) discusses how the symbolism associated with English horses gave an image of power to their riders. Horse racing, although popular with all the people, depended on the patronage of the gentry to make it a vital sport in part because of the cost of maintaining and breeding fast horses. Captain Calvert's future son-in-law Benedict Swingate Calvert became heavily involved in Maryland racing and, together with his brother-in-law, Governor Robert Eden, raced a winner of several Annapolis cups. But the earlier Calvert brothers were also intrigued by the sport. Steiner (1908: 291) contains a letter from Cecilius Calvert to Benedict Leonard that mentions Benedict Leonard's vivid description of "barbarous" Italian horse races. Stephen Patrick pointed out to me the timing between Captain Calvert's arrival and the town decision to award silver spoons to the winner of the race which is the first formalized notice of what became an annual event.

Quote from Jones (1724: 84); Elyot quote is reprinted in Thomas (1983). Although Virginia laws prohibited lesser folk from horse racing, and fined those individuals, such as tailors, who transgressed since it was "a sport only for gentlemen," no similar regulation is among Maryland's statutes (*Virginia*

Magazine of History and Biography II: 294). Also see Culver (1923) for a brief summary of horse racing in Maryland beginning in 1740.

31 Historians often cite the observation of Edward Kimber in 1736 (Kimber 1746: 158): "They are all great Horsemen, and have so much Value for the Saddle, that rather than walk to Church five Miles, they'll go eight to catch their horses." See Timothy Breen (1977). Quote from Isaac (1982: 99).

32 Quote from Land (1968: 49).

33 Footnote 37 from Jean Lee (ms. p. 249; forthcoming from W. W. Norton).

34 John Gerard was a merchant planter whose commercial activities included serving as local factor for Peter Paggen & Company of England. Among his Gerard ancestors was Thomas, Lord of St. Clement's Manor, a physician, one of the great seventeenth-century southern Maryland landowners (see Carr 1968; BDML I; or Walsh [1988] for an analysis of daily life on his estate). John Gerard's room-by-room inventory indicates that he was an educated man with literary and musical tastes. As a young man, he also became a justice of the county court, a position Carr (1968) observed wealthier men in a community often filled. She also points out that the young age at which he obtained the judgeship was another sign of his prominence and position in the Province. The Gerard patents included Swanston's Lot, Cool Spring Manor, the Garrison, and land on the Anacostia River reputed to have had "abundantly flowing springs, both wholesome and medicinal" (Hienton 1972: 37). Calvert repatented the Garrison in 1724 as the *Charles and Rebecca*, but informally it never lost its older designation (*Archives of Maryland*, XXXXII: 413; Prince George's County Court Records Liber H: f. 140). Stephen Patrick pointed out to me that it was called The Garrison when Calvert advertised for a runaway horse in the *Maryland Gazette* (May 20–7, 1729: 4). In 1742, a 60-acre portion of this patent was purchased from the Calvert estate and laid out as the town of Bladensburgh (Hienton 1972: 37).

35 See Land (1968: 50). Charles Lowe, September 12, 1723, correspondence with Benedict Leonard Calvert reprinted in Steiner (1908: 209). The infant died January 15, 1723/24 (St. Anne's Parish Church Records).

The voyage of the Countess Henrietta is colorfully described in correspondence between Cecilius Calvert and Benedict Leonard. "The countess Henrietta is arrived safe to Maryland but the Captain of the ship gave a sad account of her behavior during the voyage for when the ship went [to] one side, she raved att the Capt. and told him he was resolved to drowning her, and her goods, that he was a heathen and did not think that their was a God; and clapped her back to the side of the ship to support it from over setting. And if theire came any sudden squalls, she cried out for all ships crew to help her. As for Mrs. Ross she happen'd to laugh to see her in those agonies and she told her she was of the same principles as the Capt. was" (Steiner 1908: 220–1). St. Anne's Parish Register, 1708–85, pp. 69, 70, 159. The birth record of Elizabeth reads "baptised at her Father's house by the Rev. Mr. Vaughn (?) of Westminster Parish. Godfather, Benedict Leonard Calvert, godmothers Mrs. Elizabeth Garard and Mrs. Rebecca Dulaney" (p. 94).

36 This included 150 acres in Anne Arundel through forfeit of a mortgage and another 100 acres together with parcels such as Anglins' Discovery (60 acres) (Chan. Court Records #1–141, Maryland State Archives); Crouche's Calf Pasture (30 acres) (Chan. Court Records #1–104, Maryland State Archives), Martin's Nest (150 acres) (Chan. Court Records #1–112, Maryland State Archives)' and Cockson's Rest (355 acres) (Chan. Court Records #4–450, Maryland State Archives). In Prince George's County, he acquired Hoggyard (125 acres) (Chan. Court Records #4–414, Maryland State Archives).

Hienton notes that Captain Calvert was a Visitor of the Prince George's County Free School when the Visitors agreed to purchase 215 acres of land from Thomas Ricketts (Prince George's County Court Records Liber P: f. 288–91), but no longer on the Board when a lawsuit was filed in 1729 (Hienton 1977: 150). Residence in the county was supposed to be requisite for Visitors.

The 1737 estate account filed by George Plater and Onorio Razolini shows two farms/plantations, one rented by Thomas Nicholls (f. 361) and another by William Digges (f. 364). Rent on each was set at £12 (Anne Arundel Accounts, 1737, Liber 14: f. 359–65).

37 Anne Arundel County Court Judgments IB I: 248–50. All measurements are in feet. Moses and Charles Maccubbin were the sons of Thomas Maccubbin, and related to the Howards through the marriage of the widow Eleanor Maccubbin to John Howard. Their sister, Eleanor, later married Benjamin Howard. Benjamin Howard was possibly a son of Joseph who died ca. 1735/36. This family was closely connected to the Dorseys, the Hammonds, and also had ties to the Worthingtons (MBDL) while the Maccubbins became related to the Carrolls. Thus neither of the orphans was from a poor or even a middling-income family.

38 Other debts due included £152 from Robert Cruikshanks, £144 from John Digges; £117 from Samuel Chew (for tobacco); monies from other sales of tobacco; £10 from Samuel Ogle; £12 from John Ross; and £27 from George Plater. Digges was related to the Calvert family; Ogle was the governor who replaced Benedict Leonard Calvert in 1731; Ross was a Calvert placeman; and Plater served in a number of proprietary positions, including the Governor's Council. Total credits to the estate were £1,288-18-0d (sterling); £151-3-11 gold; £2,984-13-11d currency. These were partially offset by debts owed from the estate (Anne Arundel Accounts, 1737, Liber 14: f. 359).

39 Correspondence from Benedict Leonard Calvert, 1724, to the fifth Lord Baltimore (Dulaney Collection, Maryland Historical Society Manuscript Collections).

40 Anne Arundel County inventories L20: f. 153; Prince George's County inventories, L20: f. 167; and Anne Arundel County Inventories, L22: f. 341.

41 Normally early marriage led to high fertility with an average family size of nine to ten children. Survival rates for children were low in the last half of the seventeenth century (3.3) rising to 5.0 between 1700–50 (Kulikoff 1986: table 2, pp. 60–1). Close kin are defined here as grandparents, aunts, uncles, adult first

cousins where the blood tie is direct and not collateral. The fact that expenses incurred for Mistress Betsy were shown in the 1737 accounts, but not for Anne, suggests that Anne died too in the twenty-four months after her mother died (1734/35) and before the inventory was filed. The account also reports the deaths of six slaves in the same period. For general discussions of Chesapeake mortality see Rutman and Rutman (1976) and for Maryland orphans see Walsh (1979).

42 See Kulikoff (1986: 60–1).

4. *GOVERNOR BENEDICT LEONARD CALVERT*

1 Jourdain (1913). See also *Country Life* 1934, 75: 590–5.

2 George Mynne, brother (or nephew) of Lady Anne Mynne Calvert, had a daughter, Elizabeth, who married Richard Evelyn in the 1650s. Since Mynne had no surviving male heir, the property was transferred to Richard, who built Woodcote Park on the site of a monastic building. Richard was the brother of John Evelyn, the horticulturalist, whose diary (May 17, 1688) records his anger when his widowed sister-in-law first made plans to bequeath the property outside his family: "thro the fraude and unworthy dealing . . . [and] perswasion of my sister contrary to the intent of her husband my brother" (Bowles 1983: 357). Elizabeth did not leave the estate to her son-in-law (as initially planned), but left it instead to Charles Calvert specifying he was her "kinsman." The 1691 will of the older woman lists "my mansion house at Woodcote and my manor of Hanton late the inheritance of my Father, George Mynne, Esq., deceased" (Misc. Gen. & Heraldiea, edited by Joseph Jackson Howard, Publ. III, 2nd series, 769–70; London 1890). Notes on this are in the Bump Collection, Maryland Historical Society. See also Home (1901: 80). Quote is from Morris (1949: 342; also quoted in Harris 1961: 242). See also Morris (1949: 337–8, 350).

3 Stephen and Lee (1917). The abuse is reported by Hearne in his diary (reprinted in the *Maryland Historical Magazine*, 1915, 10: 373).

4 Notes on the lawsuit are in the Bump Collection. In 1718 Benedict Leonard wrote to Thomas Hearne just before he set sail for Calais, "From aboard ye Charlotte Yacht riding before Wolwich" (reprinted in Steiner 1908: 199).

5 *Archives of Maryland* XXV: 271.

6 McMahon explained why the third Lord Baltimore found no particular favor with the English kings. He was "too little of the libertine and sensualist for [Charles II] and yet too liberal and tolerant in his religious principles for [James II]. He rested for his protection solely upon the chartered sanctity of his rights, and the pleading of his wise and liberal administration of them" (1831: 218).

7 St. Omer's was also attended by a Maryland Catholic youth, Henry Carroll (born 1697 and only two to three years older than the Calvert boys [Rowland 1898, I: 9–10]), later by Daniel Dulaney's sons (Land 1968), and other young Catholic gentry from Maryland. Steiner (1917) writes that Rev. Jacob

Henderson, rector of St. Anne's in Annapolis, gave Edward Henry Calvert a letter to deliver to the Archbishop at Fulham Palace in 1718.

8 See discussion of education for British gentry in Mingay (1963), Cannon (1985), Stone and Stone (1984), and Beckett (1986). Correspondence, Benedict Leonard Calvert to Charles Calvert, 1724 (Dulaney Collection, Maryland Historical Society).

9 Correspondence Cecilius Calvert to Benedict Leonard Calvert, August 29, 1724 (Steiner 1908: 226–7); correspondence of Mary Granville Pendarvis, 1727 (Delany, 1861, vol. I: 148); Hearne Diary, January 11, 1725/26 (reprinted in Calvert Memorabilia, *Maryland Historical Magazine* 10: 373–4). Benedict Leonard became a member of the Royal Society in March 1731; his older brother joined in December after Benedict Leonard's death (*Records of the Royal Society of London*, 2nd edn., London, Harrison and Sons, 1901).

10 E.g., Harris (1961) reprints a bill from Brerewood to the sixth Lord Baltimore for work at Woodcote Park.

11 Much of the biographical information in this chapter comes from letters reprinted by Bernard Steiner in his article on Benedict Leonard Calvert in the *Maryland Historical Magazine* (1908). Steiner presents both family correspondence and early entries in Thomas Hearne's diaries relating to the Calvert family. Other diary entries are contained in Calvert Memorabilia (*Maryland Historical Magazine*, 10: 372–5; 16: 282–5, 386–8) while additional family data are in Nicklin's "Calvert Family" (*Maryland Historical Magazine*, 16: 389–91). Hearne (1678–1735), who kept a diary throughout much of his life, rose from a position as "assistant-keeper" at the Bodleian Library to its "second-keeper" in 1712, turning down an offer to become its primary "keeper" about the time he became acquainted with Benedict Leonard. Portions of the diary were first published in 1861 but the entire diary was published as a seven-volume set much later and hence was not fully accessible to Steiner. For quote see correspondence, Benedict Leonard Calvert to Charles Calvert, August 1724, where he also apologized for not writing sooner, "My time at Rome was so much taken up in seeing that it could not be employed in writing" (Dulaney Collection, Maryland Historical Society).

12 Correspondence, Benedict Leonard Calvert to Charles Calvert, August 1724 (Dulaney Collection, Maryland Historical Society).

13 Hearne, December 15, 1726/27 (*Maryland Historical Magazine*, 10: 375). For St. Paul's see correspondence, Benedict Leonard Calvert to Charles Calvert, August 1724 (Dulaney Collection, Maryland Historical Society); for Roman coins and Gloucester antiquities see Hearne diary (Steiner 1908: 197, 200). Quote from Plumb (1980: 129).

14 Johnson's Boswell (vol. III: 36); Addison (1718: unpaginated preface).

15 Addison described Leghorn at the end of the seventeenth century as a port town with an active market, a large Jewish population, and an enclave of English Catholic families (Addison 1718: 302–8).

16 Land (1966: 78); Carr *et al.* (1988: 10).

17 Correspondence, Charles Lowe to Benedict Leonard, July 5, 1725 (Steiner 1908: 293) and April 19, 1725 (Steiner 1908: 288).

18 Quote from correspondence of John Paston to Benedict Leonard Calvert (Dulaney Collection, Maryland Historical Society). Paston was married to Anne Calvert, youngest daughter of the third Lord Baltimore.

19 Vaughan (1611: 2, 8).

20 For a seventeenth-century list of things an ordinary family should bring see Hall (1925: 91–9).

21 Correspondence from Charles Lowe to Benedict Leonard Calvert, November 17, 1727/28 (Steiner 1908: 306). James Bowles' (d. 1727/28) first wife was Jane Lowe, a relative of Charles Lowe and the Calverts, whereas his second was Rebecca Addison, a daughter of Thomas Addison and Elizabeth Tasker Addison who was a niece of Benjamin Tasker, a wealthy planter and member of the Calvert circle. She held a life interest in the Sotterly plantation (MDBL II). One might assume that Benedict Leonard Calvert was at least partially successful in following the advice of Lowe, for in June 1729 Rebecca wed a second time, marrying George Plater, an influential member of the provincial government and a close ally of the Calvert family.

22 *Archives of Maryland* XXX: 461–2; XXV: 444–5; Radoff 1954: 51. Quotes from Radoff (1954: 49, 51).

23 *Archives of Maryland* XXV: 473, 474, 487, 504, 508, 514, 519

24 See Perry (1878: 55, 126); Allen (1857: 2–3); and the *Archives of Maryland*. Rhys Isaac (1992: 421) writes of the change between this form of government and one that primarily utilizes a written constitution (i.e., instructions, descriptions of what to do, open and accessible to anyone who could read or be read to) as a mechanism/machine for governance. The earlier form conceived of government and forms of the state as divine institutions incorporating within them "mysteries," and "arcana" (mysterious secrets) which would lose their powers were they readily accessible.

25 Correspondence of Samuel Ogle, January 10, 1731/32 to Charles Calvert, fifth Lord Baltimore reprinted in the *Maryland Historical Magazine* III: 127.

26 Correspondence from Benedict Leonard Calvert to Thomas Hearne, March 18, 1728/9 (*Maryland Historical Magazine* 10: 282).

27 See Norris (1937: 114). Throughout the eighteenth century, estate appraisers list the Lewis book – "The Mouse-Trap, or the Battle of the Cambrians and Mice: a Poem Translated from the Latin" – occasionally in probate inventories which give detail on the libraries of Maryland tobacco planters.

28 Correspondence from Benedict Leonard Calvert to Charles Calvert, fifth Lord Baltimore, October 26, 1729 (*Archives of Maryland* XXV: 601–10).

29 Thomas Hearne, June 24, 1724 (Steiner 1908: 222–5).

30 *Archives of Maryland* (XXXVI: 142, 309–10).

31 Calvert Papers No. 2, p. 79, Maryland Historical Society.

32 *Archives of Maryland* (XXXVI: 312–13).

33 For more background on the political situation see Barker (1940) or Land (1968,

1981). Correspondence of Benedict Leonard Calvert to Charles Calvert, fifth Lord Baltimore (*Archives of Maryland* XXV: 601–10).

34 Defoe 1724: 50 as quoted in Corfield 1987: 44.

35 *Archives of Maryland* (XXXVI: 109).

36 The clergy's petition was heard Saturday morning, November 2, and it was signed by all six rectors. The Upper House took pains to spell out that the proposed tobacco law was not an "offence to God or Destructive to Religion" (*Archives of Maryland* XXV: 102–3). Details of the planned uprising are in the Prince George's County Judgments 1728, Book 0: 413–15. For the discontent among the smaller country planters see vol. XXV of the *Archives of Maryland*.

37 Correspondence, Benedict Leonard Calvert to Charles Calvert, fifth Lord Baltimore as quoted in Land (1966: 78, 80 from *Archives of Maryland* XXV: 601–10).

38 See *Archives of Maryland* XXXVI: 357–8.

39 *Archives of Maryland* XXXVI: 357–8. Also see Barker's discussion of taxation in Maryland (1940).

40 Correspondence of Charles Lowe to Benedict Leonard Calvert, April 5, 1728 (Steiner 1908: 312).

41 Correspondence of Lord Baltimore to Benedict Leonard Calvert, March or April 1728 (Steiner 1908: 306).

42 Correspondence, Benedict Leonard Calvert to Governor R. Gordon of Pennsylvania. Ms. on file at the Historical Society of Pennsylvania.

43 Correspondence, Benedict Leonard Calvert to Governor R. Gordon of Pennsylvania. Ms. on file at the Historical Society of Pennsylvania.

44 Quotes are from correspondence of the third Lord Baltimore to William Penn dated July 19, 1683 and July 26, 1683 (reprinted in Fisk 1934: 38–9).

45 Baltimore's opinion was presented by Charles Lowe in a letter to Benedict Leonard Calvert dated November 17, 1727 (Steiner 1908: 306). See *Life and Correspondence of Mrs. Delaney* (Letter XV) wherein Lord Baltimore, low in spirits from a sports injury and other matters, "fitted up a little vessl" in 1727 and went abroad for three months (Delaney 1861, vol. I: 133). Baltimore also journeyed throughout Scandinavia and went as far east as St. Petersburg, Russia where he met with Frederick the Great of Prussia and opened up trade connections.

46 Correspondence of Samuel Ogle, January 10, 1731/32 to Charles Calvert, fifth Lord Baltimore reprinted in the *Maryland Historical Magazine* III: 127. Correspondence of Charlotte Brerewood to Benedict Leonard Calvert, June 7, 1727 (Steiner 1908: 298–9). More than three dozen delft galley pots as well as pill slabs and many small glass medicine vials were recovered from the site.

47 Correspondence of Benedict Leonard Calvert to Charles Calvert, fifth Lord Baltimore, October 26, 1729 (Calvert Papers No. 2: 79). Hamilton quote is from Bridenbaugh (1948: 198). Also see Kupperman (1984) for further information on climate and disease.

48 John Hart, 1720 (reprinted in *Maryland Historical Magazine* 29: 252). Bloodstones were usually jasper or other precious stones that had red streaks or

speckles within them. They were believed to stop bleeding and Lord Baltimore wore one that Mary Granville Pendarvis gave him while he recovered from his head injury (Delaney 1861, vol. I: 132). These stones, however, were not the same as the red carnelian ones used in West African jewelry described in Chapter 9 that were found at the site. Chinese stones which may also have been used for medicinal purposes were sold in eighteenth-century Annapolis stores.

49 For the barge, see Delaney (1861: 38–9).

50 Calvert Fund Publication No. 1 contains George Calvert's inventory. For Mary Darnall's see Prince George's County inventories.

51 Correspondence of Benedict Leonard Calvert to Thomas Hearne, March 18, 1728/29 (*Maryland Historical Magazine* 10: 282).

52 *Archives of Maryland* XXXVI: 34–5. Land (1968: 65–6, 121) notes Captain Calvert's popularity.

53 *Archives of Maryland* (XXXIV: 162).

54 He also subsidized the construction of a chapel in Centertown (Anne Arundel Accounts 1734/35, Liber 12: f. 233–7), although its location is now unknown. For Calvert's will see Original Wills, Box C, No. 1, Maryland State Archives. Also see Anne Arundel County Accounts, 1753, Liber 35: f. 57–8.

55 Quote is from Land (1966: 80).

5. "A HOUSE WELL BUILT AND WITH MUCH STRENGTH"

1 Quote from Kimber who visited Yorktown in 1736 (1746: 222).

2 Daniel Larke to Elizabeth Calvert (Anne Arundel County Deeds, 1747, RB 2: f. 566). Evidence for the gully can be seen in the deep levels of fill found on Lot 83 as documented in a 1982 engineer's report prepared for Paul Pearson (Test Bores B-4 and B-6), in the level of fill on State Circle northeast of the site, and in profiles from the north side yard. Governor Hart's approval of the siting is given in *Archives of Maryland* XXX: 465 (see also Radoff 1954: 49).

3 Possibly the central entrance to Bloomsbury Square as well as North and Francis Streets were among the smaller survivals from the older plan.

4 A Sassafras soil, geologists note that Collington sandy loam is an excellent one for gardening (Britton and Zappone 1917). The soil used as fill may have been obtained along the Severn River as similar soil was observed at the Bordley-Randall site and was used in a later eighteenth-century fill sequence on the Calvert site.

5 Anne Arundel County Inventories, Liber 4: f. 33, 38, 119; Anne Arundel County Court Judgments, November 1721 RC 2: 67.

6 Quote from Glassie (1982: 379).

7 Stone (1967: 251–3) provides information on the building craze. Haslett (1983) gives information on Kiplin. Jourdain (1913) describes Ditchley. See also Stuart (1979). Hearne visited Ditchley with Benedict Leonard on June 10, 1718, writing in his diary: "This old house is a very notable Thing, & I think I was never better pleas'd with any sight whatsoever than with this House, which hath been the

Seat of Persons of true Loyalty & Virtue." Hearne's Collections, *Proceedings of the Oxford Historical Society,* LXVII: 24–33 (reprinted for the Oxford Historical Society by Clarendon Press, pp. 188–9).

8 Quote from Reed (1984: 114). Correspondence from Cecilius Calvert to Benedict Leonard Calvert, dated April 30, 1725 reprinted in Steiner (1908: 291). Cannon (1985) believes this was true of the majority of the rebuilding in this era.

9 Correspondence from Cecilius Calvert to Benedict Leonard Calvert, dated April 30, 1725 reprinted in Steiner (1908: 291). Home (1901: 82) describes the view. Celia Fiennes' description of Woodcote Park is given in Morris (1949: 342). Correspondence from Cecilius Calvert to Benedict Leonard, July 6, 1725 (Steiner 1908: 293).

10 In writing about the French influence at Woodcote Park, architectural historian John Harris (1961) queries whether Isaac Ware might have influenced its architecture and introduced the French design details at a later time. However, Harris also points out the French table in the house shown in the portrait of Benedict Leonard Calvert painted 1726–7 (fig. 4.1). Lord Baltimore also married the daughter of a French immigrant, Mary Janssen (BDML I) and traveled extensively in France. Home (1901: 82) describes where the French influences can be seen inside the mansion and outside on its grounds. He also gives the oral tradition that links French craftsmen with some of the interior detail. I am indebted to John Harris for sharing with me information on the home's interior shown in a late eighteenth-century advertisement.

11 The mansion, "Place-house," was located in Horton, near Colebrook, Buckinghamshire (*Gentleman's Magazine* 41, August 1791: 713–16). I am indebted to Stephen Patrick for this reference. Harris' 1961 article also contains an invoice submitted by Brerewood for work about Woodcote Park in the 1750s.

12 See Carter Hudgins (1990) for information on Corotoman; Sanford (1990) for Germanna. Col. Holliday married the widow of Edward Lloyd, prominent in government and, briefly, acting Governor (BDML II). See Hollyday (1990) for further information on Readbourne.

13 Captain Calvert also enacted legislation which required Annapolis innkeepers to tear down wooden or cribbed chimneys and erect brick ones in their place.

14 Glassie (1982: 338) writes that "Hollow, every house is a tool" as well as an arena for social action. See also Goffman (1956).

15 Quote from Mr. Philemon Lloyd's 1690s description of Maryland used by Oldmixon (1708, volume I: 199). Stone (1967).

16 Hopkins (1986) in excavations at State House Inn located remains of these fenceposts as did excavation at the Calvert site. Descriptions of the activities on the circle are provided in Oldmixon (1708, vol. I: 333); Rebecca Key's remembrances (1919: 263); Ridgely (1841: 121–2).

17 Bayard, for example, commented on the odors of waterfront wharves at Baltimore and Philadelphia: "The wharves are constructed of trunks of trees. When the tides fall it exposes a slime which gives off foul odors" (1798: 160).

18 The use of central courtyards is seen throughout various parts of West Africa. Posnansky (1994) emphasizes their importance, the way they provide a space for different activities such as sleeping on hot nights, eating, dining, gossiping, socializing (for a discussion of their use among New World descendants of slaves from West Africa see Herskovits and Herskovits 1936). DeCorse (1994) cites descriptions from the early 1600s, quoting de Maree who saw houses linked to form a small square where "women have a place in the middle" for cooking. DeCorse also writes that the stone and packed clay floors uncovered at Elmina had been well swept with only tiny bits of residual primary refuse found packed into the clay and between the stones, which is much like what we found in courtyard space at the Calvert site.

19 Posnansky (1994: n.p.).

20 Oldmixon (1708, vol. II: 123).

21 Anne Arundel County Accounts, 1737, Liber 14: f. 359.

6. ORDERING NATURE: THE CALVERT ORANGERY, GARDEN, AND VISTA

1 Quote is from Glassie (1975: 175). But to understand fully why men attempt to control nature also requires a consideration of symbolic elements in western culture; Geertz (1973) provides one anthropological example of how anthropologists analyze power and symbolism; Kertzer (1988) brings it home to the U.S. in his study of *Ritual, Politics and Power*.

2 Geometry provided the architectural building blocks used in designing many English and European gardens in the Renaissance and post-Renaissance world (Wölfflin 1888); its use in the New World was first demonstrated by Paca-Steele and Wright (1987) who analyzed the William Paca Garden in 1980–2; their work is summarized in Leone (1984). The organizational principles they observed were archaeologically tested (i.e., excavation units were placed to recover belowground features) in mid-Atlantic gardens by Yentsch and her colleagues (Yentsch 1990a; Yentsch and Kratzer [1994]; Bescherer-Metheny *et al.* [1994]). The use of Euclidean geometry in creating garden perspectives has been applied at other gardens in Annapolis (Leone and Shackel 1990) and in Baltimore and southern Maryland (Weber *et al.* 1990).

3 Columella (1745; Miller (1724); Gibson (1796); Wright (1934); Jashemski (1979).

4 Bradley (1725). Quote is from La Quintinie (1693: 22).

5 Bradley (1724); Volckamer (1714).

6 Browne (1890: vi) described to the Maryland Historical Society how he found the Calvert Papers. The information on pineapples is drawn from a letter written by Elizabeth Key to her mother on February 9, 1735 in His. Mss. Comm. Rept. 15, Appl. 1896, vol. III of Earl of Dartmouth's mss at Patshall, p. 278 (as shown on notes by *Baltimore Sun* editor, Charles Bump; Bump Collection at the Maryland Historical Society).

7 Agricola (1719: 57); La Quintinie (1693). Quote from Loudon (1825: 310).

8 Bradley (1724); Miller (1724).

9 Quote is from Van Oosten (1703: 253–74).

10 Nichol (1812: 86).

11 Bradley (1724); Van Oosten (1703); Gibson (1796: 187).

12 For botanical analysis of the Calvert assemblage, see Naomi Miller (1988) and, for a published list of plant remains see Miller (1989: 53).

13 See de Serres (1607) and Van Oosten (1703: 241).

14 The need for skilled gardeners is noted in most discussions of the care and cultivation of orange trees (e.g., Evelyn 1693). See Black (1983) for Beddington. Quote is from Wright (1934: 54). Isaac (1992).

15 Van den Muijzenberg (1980) puts La Quintinie's accomplishment into perspective, but for a cross-cultural view of gardens see, for example, *Coral Gardens and Their Magic*. It provides a detailed account of the importance of gardens within small societies and of the ways in which customary procedure related to horticulture reached out into the community to permeate different domains of life (Malinowski 1935).

16 See Robert Beverley (1705: 298–9). Remains of peafowl (*Pavo real*) were identified among the faunal remains (see Table 11.1), but because they were normally present in pairs, we infer both a male (peacock) and a female (peahen) at the site.

17 Quotes are from correspondence of Benedict Leonard Calvert, 1724, to Charles Calvert (Dulaney Collection, Maryland Historical Society).

18 Letter from John Evelyn to Sir Thomas Brown, January 28, 1658 (Keynes 1964: 278); *The [1690–1710] Journeys of Celia Fiennes* (Morris 1949).

19 Very little is known about slave gardens; much of what is written emphasizes their role in providing food. However, Abrahams (1983: 137) points out that flowering hibiscus and colorful crotons were used as fences or boundary markers on the island of St. Vincent while Alice Walker writes of her mother's garden in South Carolina (1974: 241): "my mother adorned with flowers whatever shabby house we were forced to live in . . . Before she left home for the fields, she watered her flowers, chopped up the grass, and laid out new beds. When she returned from the fields she might divide the clumps of bulbs, dig a cold pit, uproot and replant roses, or prune branches from her taller bushes or trees – until night came and it was too dark to see. Whatever she planted grew as if by magic, and her fame as a grower of flowers spread over three counties." Richard Westmacott (1993) points out that distinctive patterns in the use of ornamental plants have evolved among the African-American communities of the deep South. These observations are hints that more than food was grown in the small gardens.

20 Three other important early eighteenth-century mansions stood on hills: Charles Carroll of Annapolis built a home that still stands on a hill by the harbor; Benjamin Tasker built one with a large garden along the shore on the north side of Market Street; Daniel Wolstenholme built one facing the bay which

eventually became the governor's mansion when it was purchased by Robert Eden. The hill Baltimore chose is where McDowell Hall now stands on St. John's campus. Ariana Jennings wrote it was "a very beautiful hill . . . with this spot his Lordship . . . [became] greatly enamored" (Gibson 1826).

21 Undeveloped when Lord Baltimore first saw it, a dismayed Bordley made it plain his lordship exerted pressure until Bordley agreed to sell his hill. Lord Baltimore then instructed his brother-in-law, Governor Thomas Bladen, to build a large mansion, using a legislative appropriation to cover its cost. Known for years as Bladen's Folly, the funding (£3,000) was insufficient to complete the ambitious plan and, refusing to raise additional funds, the Maryland legislature left it unfinished and roofless for many years. Adam Gordon wrote in the 1760s that its "timbers and roof though ready [were] never closed and shingled" (pp. 256–7). Also see the *Archives of Maryland* (XXXIX: 43); Land (1981: 177) or Radoff (1954: 77–9) for more detail. William Black, who saw it in 1744, described it thus: "the foundation of a very fine House Designed for the Governor was lying on a Beautiful Spot of Ground On the East side of the Town." He saw only three additional "very good Houses standing in the Middle of the Town," one of which belonged to Bordley (1744: 128). Today the tall Victorian mansions fronting Prince George Street hide the visibility of its hillside prominence.

22 "A Quaker Journal," Joseph Alibone, Historical Society of Pennsylvania, Philadelphia.

23 Repton (1816: 233).

24 Woolley (1930: 73); Taylor (1971).

7. TOUCHES OF CHINESE ELEGANCE: POTTERY AND PORCELAIN

1 Bed chambers were sociable spaces that often held goodly numbers of tables and chairs by modern standards. In wealthy families, wives had their own bed chambers where they kept personal items as well as teawares, the more expensive utensils, sometimes spices and other precious foodstuffs. The Widow Bowles, for example, had nine chairs in her room, three punch bowls, a teaset. Safe in her closet were rice, ginger, saucepans, the coffee mill and coffee pot, a tea kettle, three copper pepper boxes and one hundred candles. Mrs Thomas Addison kept the sugar, tea, raw coffee, knives and forks, fine white stoneware teapots, a 4-gallon stone jug, the silver plate, and gold buttons in her bed chamber. Later in the century, Governor Eden had his butler and the housekeeper sleep in their separate work areas: the dining-room pantry and kitchen storage chamber. And while the butler spent his nights on a flock mattress on the floor, and the housekeeper slept in a four-poster bed, he dreamed among china, silver, and crystal while she slept surrounded by queensware plates, butter boats, and the table linens (inventory of Mary Smith, 1723/24, Anne Arundel County Inventories, Liber 10: f. 23; inventory of James Bowles, 1727, Anne Arundel County Inventories, Liber 13: f. 79; inventory of Thomas Addison, 1727/28,

Prince George's County Inventories, Box 7, Folder 1; inventory of Robert Eden, 1776, AO 13/60: f. 205).

2 Information on this same topic, from a slightly different perspective, is provided in Steven Patrick's M.A. thesis (Patrick 1990).

3 See Breen (1985: 36) or Blaszczyk (1984). Philemon Lloyd described the retail trade for Oldmixon: "every considerable planter's ware-house is like a shop, where he supplies not only himself with what he wants, but the inferior planters, servants, and laborers" (Oldmixon 1708, vol. 1: 203). See Land (1965) for a good summary of the economic system and how these storehouses fit within it.

4 Quote is from Kimber, 1746: 126. See Stephen Patrick's master's thesis (1990) which discusses the contrast between store inventories and direct ordering in detail, especially with reference to the Annapolis Calverts. I am indebted to Stephen for his generous sharing of unpublished research throughout the Calvert project, and for several of the quotations presented in this section. See Blaszczyk (1984) for more information on rural stores in Maryland together with the Glassford Records; also MacMaster and Skaggs (1966/67) or, for Virginia, Soltow (1959) as well as the research of Jacob Price [e.g., Price 1980]. The distinction between store inventories in Virginia, individual probate inventories, and archaeological assemblages is presently the topic of dissertation research by Anne Smart Martin (1993).

5 Rhys Isaac (1982: 57).

6 Charles Carroll was an Irish Catholic, trained as an attorney, who gained admission to the Inner Temple in London in 1685 and migrated to Maryland perhaps at the urging of Lord Powis in 1688. He came with an appointment as Attorney General of Maryland, but the revolution of 1689 negated the appointment. Through an advantageous first marriage, he acquired the Ridgely-Underwood estate and with its support was able to become a merchant-planter. A second marriage, to the third Lord Calvert's niece, won him an appointment in the Land Office and helped place him at the center of land transactions. From this position, he began to acquire extensive land holdings of his own, but he also maintained his trade network. The small store that he operated from his Annapolis home was one result of his diversified economic strategy and by 1720, it had been open for approximately twenty-five years. Also see Rowland (1898), Land (1968, 1981) and Hoffman (1988).

7 Davisson specialized in wooden goods, and kept on hand more food-related utensils than any other Annapolis storekeeper in the 1720s and 1730s whose store inventory has survived. (Prerogative Court Inventories, 1721, Liber 7: f. 81).

8 Amos Garrett's experience as a supercargo on merchant vessels stood him in good stead, and his ability to acquire money was phenomenal. Beginning from relatively humble social origins, with few political connections to Baltimore's provincial government, Garrett amassed a fortune worth £27,000 at his death by dealing in land, lending money, securing mortgages, and working actively within

the town's political networks. A contemporary wrote that "he never [had] more than one ship or sea vessel, except small craft" (Papenfuse 1975: 13). Garrett's background and ambitions firmly grounded him in an entrepreneurial context that was as unlike the pedigree-conscious landed gentry as one could imagine. His probate inventory shows little indication that he sought a genteel lifestyle, and it is not surprising to see in the inventory that he had more "stylish" goods in his store than the planter gentry kept in theirs.

9 Bordley became an eminent member of the Maryland bar in the very early eighteenth century and established "a thriving and financially rewarding law practice" (Morton 1964: 10). Morton (1964: 1–12) argues that Thomas Bordley was an American member of the Inns of Court. Born in Yorkshire, where the Calvert family had its origins, his background and training gave his interests a breadth that extended beyond the confines of the province. In this, he was similar to the Calvert men. Bordley obtained positions of profit (Clerk of the Prerogative Court first, Commissary General later) and of political importance, serving as a delegate in the Lower House at various times in his life. For a brief time, as Commissary General and as Attorney General, he served in the Upper House and on the Governor's Council. The latter positions were given him by Baltimore as a means of enticing him from the political alliances and interests of the Country Party.

10 Patrick (1990) notes that contents of shipments were often chosen by British merchants and that local merchant-planters had little choice over the goods sent to be sold on consignment, whereas their direct orders for family supplies were filled with great care.

11 This was because it was recovered in such poor condition (i.e. without glaze) that few vessels could be separated on the basis of decorative motifs, although in well-preserved delft the hand-painted motifs would ordinarily provide an excellent basis for vessel identification. Vessel separation was done mainly using variations in base or rim profiles. It was different with the Chinese porcelain; its hand-painted motifs, even the simple decorations around cup or bowl rims, were so distinctive that they allowed easy minimum vessel designations.

12 See Yentsch (1990a, 1990b, 1991a) for further information on these points. It is intriguing that the ware composition and vessel counts for several features excavated in Philadelphia, a city with many small shops, matches closely that shown for the Annapolis merchants and the rural sites (Yentsch 1991a).

13 For earlier studies see Carson and Carson (1976), Carr and Walsh (1978), G. Miller (1974), and the several studies in Carson *et al.* (1993). Laborers and craftsmen consumed alcoholic beverages during the workday, deriving both modest nourishment and energy for work from the nutrients these contained. They drank coffee or tea less frequently because of its high cost. Quote is from Defoe (1724 as given in Corfield [1987]). The sample cited here was drawn by Karen Bescherer-Metheny and myself from inventories filed before 1740 in Annapolis, but was too small to be considered more than suggestive; work was not completed because of funding constraints.

14 See Hudgins (1982) for Corotoman.

15 Archaeologists such as Dennis Pogue (1991) are now investigating the differences between what appears in inventories and what is seen in the ground. Pogue suggests the inventory data may be biased against the more common earthenware and stonewares since these are found at virtually every historical-archaeological site no matter its age. They are, in fact, a major means (as artifact scatters in plowed fields) of locating sites.

16 Lois Carr (personal communication 1990) points out that Thomas Addison's home shows the impact of a radically different change in lifestyle from that practiced by his parents' generation.

17 *Life and correspondence of Mrs Delaney* (Delaney 1861, vol. 1: 210).

18 See *George Washington's China* (Detweiler 1982) for an understanding of the care status-conscious men took to obtain fine China.

19 See Norris (1937) for Richard Lewis' recollections of the conversations.

8. FINE FOODS AND DAILY BREAD

1 Mintz (1985: 3–4). For other relevant discussions of food see Richards (1932); Lévi-Strauss (1958, 1965); Douglas (1972); Firth (1975); Goody (1982); and Joyner (1971, 1984). Inventory of Charles Carroll, May 2, 1723, Md. His. Soc. in Ledger x, Carroll-McTavish Papers.

2 The information on Gov. Ogle's cook from the *Maryland Gazette* is reprinted in Windley (1983). Evidence that black women also cooked for wealthy families can be seen in a 1767 *Maryland Gazette* where Sarah Brice advertised a family slave, praising the woman as "an extraordinary good cook," who also washed, spun, ironed, sewed, but noting too her "impudent tongue" (Windley 1983). See will of Benedict Leonard Calvert (Anne Arundel County Wills, Liber 2: f. 496) for the legacies.

3 Root (1958: 41); Mennell (1986: 48); Carr and Walsh (1977, 1978, 1988b); Carr, Menard, and Walsh (1991) document its continuation in Maryland.

4 Mead (1931: 44).

5 Yentsch 1990b, 1991a, 1991b, 1991c. Data in Kelso (1984b) are also evidence of this, although Kelso does not present it as elite cookery. Inventory studies by Main (1982) and by Carr and Walsh (see note 3 above) are also pertinent. Anyone who wants to compare inventories directly could contrast the equipment in William Addison's 1727 inventory (Prince George's County Inventories, Liber 12: f. 295–313) with that of Henrietta Maria Lloyd dated 1697 (Talbot County Inventories, Liber 15: f. 198).

6 Miller (1986b, 1988a).

7 Thompson (1975); Thomas (1983).

8 Letter from Cecilius Calvert to Benedict Leonard, 1724, reprinted in Steiner (1908: 290).

9 Jarratt (1906: 14). Carr and Walsh (1977: 561–3). Lists of fruits and vegetables grown can be found in a number of different sources (e.g. Bolzius 1751: 239;

Jones 1724; Romans 1775: 115). Lawson (1709) is the source for the list here. Bolzius (1751: 239) observed that some traditional vegetables were no longer routinely grown in New World gardens. Thomas Lawrence's letter is given in Jordan (1978: 90). John Juitt's wife is mentioned in his plea for a tax abatement in Anne Arundel County Court Judgments (1734, IB I: 251).

10 Prerogative Court Inventories, 1721, Liber 7: f. 81. For an analysis of seasonal changes in food use see Bowen (1990).

11 Carson and Walsh 1981; Horn 1988a, 1988b; Miller 1984, 1988a. Carter (1772). For personal recipes see those of Gulielma Maria Springett Penn (Benson 1966), the *Receipt Book of Harriott Pinckney Horry, 1770* (published 1984) for South Carolina or *Nelly Custis Lewis's Housekeeping Book* for Virginia food ca. 1830 (Lewis 1830). Mrs. Lewis was the great-granddaughter of Captain Charles and Rebecca Calvert and the granddaughter of Martha Washington. Martha Washington's Cookbook (edited by Karen Hess) also includes seventeenth-century recipes from her grandmother. Mary Randolph's book (1824) was written for publication, but most manuscripts were privately kept, given from mother to daughter. Some of these, still in private hands, form the basis for an excellent Maryland cookbook, *Maryland's Way* (Andrews and Kelly 1963), which drew on family recipes from Miss Ann Chase's Book (1811); Mrs. Virgil Maxcy's Receipts (1820); Mrs. F. T. Loockerman's Book (1835); Josey's Way (1814). In handwritten texts such as these, women recorded instructions for dishes that were passed from generation to generation, while in families where women were illiterate, the information was conveyed through oral tradition. Kimber (1746: 145–6).

12 Paz (1972).

13 Henry Miller (1984: 126). Hudgins (1983: 30, Table IV-10). The use of wooden spits is recorded by an anonymous traveler (see "A voyage to Virginia" in Force, vol. III: 20) but note that this technique was adopted after their ship sailed off leaving the man and his companions on an uninhabited Eastern Shore island without supplies or equipment.

14 For Philemon Hemsley's inventory, see Anne Arundel County Inventories Liber 4: 33, 38, 119. For the Hominy Club see Chase (1868: 301).

15 The prices of the spices are found in Edward Henry Calvert's inventory while those of the beef are given in a lawsuit filed by Cornelius Brooksby (Anne Arundel County Court Judgments, 1721, RC: f. 86). This pricing scheme, in which sugar, spice, and fruit additions were costly, was used throughout the community and probably throughout the colonies. Beverage prices set by law indicate that tavern-keepers added to the cost of ordinary beverages whenever fruit or sugar was added. Among a tavern bill for 1722 appeared a bottle of English beer at £00-01-06d and another for English beer with sugar at £00-02-00d; the charge for a full week's diet was only £00-07-00d (Anne Arundel County Court Judgments 1721, RC 21: f. 63).

As one example of the new cookery, housewives were integrating tomatoes into the Italian cuisine, although they remained a novelty in England. Peter

Collinson, calling them "Apples of Love" wrote ca. 1740 that Italian women had begun to use them "to putt when ripe into their Brooths & Soops giving it a pretty Tart Taste. A Lady Just come from Leghorn says she thinks it gives an Agreeable tartness & Relish." (Coats 1973: 17; see also Tannahill 1989: 207).

16 See Mennell (1986: 33); Mead (1931); Earle (1989). Londontown merchant Samuel Peele stocked 122 lbs of pepper and 120 lbs of allspice in his 1730 store, but only a pound of nutmeg and 14 oz. of mace (Anne Arundel County Inventories, 1733, Liber 13: f. 166). Thomas Bordley had more mace (2.5 lbs), but had smaller quantities of cinnamon, nutmeg, and cloves (Anne Arundel County Inventories Liber 18: f. 12–18).

17 Black (1744: 126). Ice cream's popularity among Italians, Benedict Leonard's two-year stay in Italy, and the presence in the Calvert home of Onorio Razolini, a Venetian nobleman (undoubtedly familiar with Italian food delicacies) are tantalizing hints that it may have been served earlier in Annapolis than 1744. Favored flavors in the seventeenth and early eighteenth century were coffee, lemon, and chocolate (Simeti 1989; Wheaton 1983).

18 The linguist's definitions of pidgins and creoles are useful in understanding the evolution in food use because it is likely that food customs in the New World developed in a similar manner. According to Dell Hymes (1981: 3), "pidgins arise as makeshift adaptations, reduced in structure and use. They are no one's first language; creoles, however, are pidgins that become primary [or "first"] languages." See also Chapter 10, note 3.

Quote from Fox-Genovese (1988: 159) tells of Mandy Morrow whose mother and grandmother were "powerful good" cooks who passed their skills and knowledge to Mandy (1988: 159; see also Rawick 1972a: 139). In Anne Arundel County, Maryland, Caroline Hammond told a WPA interviewer that "Mrs. Davidson's dishes were considered the finest . . . Maryland's finest terrapin and chicken besides the best wine and champagne on the market" appeared on the Davidson table. Proudly, the black woman added, "All of the cooking was supervised by my mother." (Rawick 1972b: 19).

19 Alcey was a cook on a Mississippi plantation whose small rebellion against cooking was first described by Smedes (1889: 150–1) and then by Fox-Genovese (1988: 160). Landon Carter recorded thefts of milk in his diary (vol. 1: 353) as did Mrs. Carmichael (1833). Walsh 1984b (esp. 16–19) gives a good overview of the different tasks black women were assigned. Shammas (1985) and White (1990) are also pertinent. See Bush (1990) or Morrissey (1989) for the Caribbean.

20 Leach (1990: 229).

21 Glassie (1982: 80, 85–6).

9. THE FACE OF URBAN SLAVERY

1 At the same time, despite their numbers, slaves comprised a smaller segment (20%) of Calvert's total estate value than was characteristic of wealthy Maryland planters. His slaveholdings were only a third of those his descendants owned by

the end of the Revolution, an estimated 150 individuals who lived in "20 Negro houses" (Prince George's County 1798 tax assessments on file at the Maryland State Archives).

2 See Kulikoff (1986: 373) for children's work and Davis (1803: 379, 383). Snelgrave describes what children did in Africa: "When [the grain] is about a man's height, and begins to ear, they raise a wooden house in the centre of the field, covered with straw, in which they set their children to watch their corn, and fright away the birds" (quoted in Benezet 1788: 25 from Astley's Collection, vol. II: 651), a practice also recorded among Native American groups in New England. For tasks that young African children do today see Welbourn (1984). Klein (1967: 182) provides the vertical hierarchy among Chesapeake slaves.

3 Wax (1978); Menard (1975); Kulikoff (1986); Lee (1986).

4 For eighteenth-century laws concerning the different legal classifications for Africans and their American-born children, including mulattos, see Kilthy (1799–1800) and Jordan (1962: 184) or, for a woman's perspective, Clinton (1991). Quotes are from Davis (1803: 387) and Windley (1983).

5 Quote is from Davis (1803: 378). See Mullin's overview of Virginia slavery (1972) which can be applied to Maryland also. Mbiti (1969) describes pan-African cultural traits.

6 See Kulikoff (1986: 385) for the division of slave labor. Carr and Walsh (1977) note that English women also worked in the fields throughout the seventeenth century and continued to do so on the smaller tobacco farms where slave labor was unavailable, but neither black nor white women did any of the more "skilled" agriculturally-related tasks such as coopering, smithing, or being "drivers." Mann estimates that slave women spent up to thirteen hours a day in field labor, and observes that overseers made few distinctions between men and women, typically assigning jobs to women that included some of the hardest and dirtiest – clearing swamp lands, mucking out animal stalls (Mann 1989: 779, 781; also see White 1985, 1990, 1991). Hence the way work was apportioned among slaves did not use traditional English or European gender-based divisions of labor. Before the Civil War, Frederick Law Olmsted (1860: 14–15) described a group of African-American women returning from the Mississippi fields: "forty of the largest and strongest women I ever saw together; they were all in a simple uniform dress of a bluish check stuff; their legs and feet were bare; they carried themselves loftily, each having a hoe over the shoulder, and walking with a free, powerful swing like chasseurs on the march." Angela Davis points out that it was not necessary for these women to take pride in slave labor or its products for them to derive strength and self-confidence from their abilities to do the work (Davis 1981: 11). For the deplorable effect on slave women created by overwork, see Gunderson's discussion (1986) of birth rates in Virginia, or Morrissey (1989) and Bush (1990) on women in the Caribbean.

7 Bosman (1705: 178). Long (1774, vol. III: 427) noted African words for days of the week used as Jamaican names while Patterson observed in 1967 that some of these continued in use (Patterson 1967: 174). Lorenzo Turner (1949: 40–1) also

drew on modern linguistic evidence from the South Carolina sea islands to note cultural continuity in West African names used in this country: names that told of a child's physical appearance and condition; of temperament, capability, and character; of family lineage; animal names; names drawn from the Muslim faith or African myths; names of the day, week, year; place names; birth rank; weather at the time of birth or other aspects of the birth itself; objects in nature; occupations; objects used in daily life; and a variety of others (Turner 1949: 41). Mencken (1936) cited surviving examples elsewhere in America that also drew on African traditions of encoding birth conditions within a name: Highwater and Overflow, for two children born during a flood. But older evidence exists too.

Although the existence of African-centered names in the Chesapeake has been largely overlooked, there is also clear evidence in the Maryland court records that some Africans kept their own names. African names appearing on Captain Calvert's inventories include Mingo; Nom; Hann; Cubit; Girdle; Cusey; Tydoe. Many slave names on Chesapeake inventories are English, but Joyner (1984: 217–22), also Wood (1974: 182–3) and Dillard (1972: 129–30) believe that some English words/names were homonyms for African ones, used by slave-owners who "misheard" the English for the African. In line with this, easily recognizable African names or homonyms for those on the Calvert inventories would include: Liceta (for Lucy); Jeminah (for Jenny); Abanna (for Abigail or Abby); Pattoe (for Peter or Patty); Heke (for Hercules); Fany (for Frank); Sibby (for Liby); Esher (for Easter); Jaceo (for Jacob or Jack); Sawne, Sukie or Suti (for Sew); Nand (for Nan); Bungor (for Benja); Samba (for Sam or Sammy); Togi or Tobe (for Tony). One might note that the English names on the Calvert inventories which have no African homonyms were usually names of people in the Calvert family (i.e., Charles, Harry, George, Ned, Jane, Rachel, Rebecca).

The use of African names in the Chesapeake can be seen in other eighteenth-century documents; Captain William Rogers sold Onorio Razolini three negroes, including Cumorey (Anne Arundel County Deeds, 1740–4, RB 1: f. 409). Col. William Holland and Daniel Dulaney owned, in 1733 and 1764 respectively, significant numbers of individuals with African names. Some were clearly born on American soil (i.e., Cojo, a "very old" man had a son and daughter, Cojo, age 14 and Taby, age 12 in 1764; or the children of Rosa: Tetia, age 9, and Culey, age 6) (Inventory of William Holland, 1733, Liber 17: 454–60; Inventory of Daniel Dulaney, 1764, Liber 84: f. 32–5). A small sample of additional African names seen in other Maryland records dating to 1720–40 includes Toader, Fante, Sambo, Flowa, Dido, Poppaco, Doppaw, Pollopus, Polledoro, Sarakat, Abuer, Jam, Ockery, Hann, Southey, Cuffey, Festus, Sango, Colly, Gingoe, Pender, Jano, Cruali. Phebe Jacobsen kindly brought the Dulaney inventory to my attention.

8 *Maryland Gazette*, January 1728/29; for more general information on runaways in the 1720s see *Archives of Maryland* (XXXIV: 394–5); for Negro Stephen see *Maryland Gazette* advertisements, December 24 and 31, 1728 and January 21, 1728/29. For Governor Nicholson's encounter see *Archives of Maryland* (XXXIII:

498–9); also see Davis (1803: 383–4) and *Maryland Gazette* (1751) for Celia reprinted in Windley (1983).

9 Davis (1803: 385) defined the phrase "Negur day-time" as "a cant term among the Negroes for night; they being then at leisure." For an example of the co-existence of different cultural meanings see Sahlins (1981: 41–51) on the ways Hawaiians viewed nails and the bits of iron carried on British ships and its contrast with English symbolism.

10 Philadelphia legislated against these gatherings in 1693 (Dubois 1967: 12), but they continued in Washington Square through the eighteenth century. Latrobe (1819: 203–4) described the gatherings at Place Congo in 1819, but earlier accounts for New Orleans also exist (Donaldson 1984); Stewart (1823: 269–72) wrote of them in Jamaica.

Luisah Teisch (1985: 139–40) explains that "*gumbo ya ya* is a creole term that mans 'Everybody talks at once.'" Elsa Barkley Brown (1989: 925) points out that this non-linear poly-vocality or multiple rhythms is aesthetically expressed in music, *and* in material art forms such as quilts; it can be seen in textile designs on eighteenth-century rafia cloth. According to Brown, "to an outsider, *gumbo ya ya* can only sound like chaos. How can anyone be listening to everyone else at once while they are also themselves speaking? . . . this indeed is possible. In fact, the only time the conversation stops is when someone has asked a member of the group a question to which they do not respond . . . everyone is hearing themselves and everyone else at once."

11 Although Maryland acquiesced to Virginia, placing slave gatherings under legal jurisdiction, before the law became fully enforcible (if it ever actually was), it had to be rewritten twice – something Marylanders did not feel it necessary to do until the 1750s (Kilthy 1799–1800).

12 See Hawkins (1796: 141–3); Curtin (1967: 18); see the 1789 narrative of Ayuba Suleiman, known as Gustuvus Vasa by Europeans (Middleton 1943; Curtin 1967). Abu Bakr (born ca. 1790, a member of the *Shurfa* of the Western Sudan) wrote "on that very day they made me a captive. They tore off my clothes, bound me with ropes, gave me a heavy load to carry" (Wilks 1967: 162).

While enslavement was not new to the African continent, under the older institutions of slavery its rationale was politically and not economically motivated. Slaves were often war captives, slavery provided a means to watch carefully and to control them. Some slaves eventually became free members of their new communities; many were assimilated into families; others occupied high-status positions within households; and the Biblical injunction (Deuteronomy) to keep a slave no more than seven years was occasionally followed. Formal manumission was also praised in the Koran. African-based slavery was qualitatively and quantitatively different from the slave systems that arose in the New World (Bohannon 1964: 105; Oliver 1991: 119–21). In the latter, it became exceedingly difficult, often impossible, for African-Americans to maintain autonomous family units while wider kinship networks were continually fragmented. There were but few, circumscribed and limited, opportunities to obtain the practical benefits of freedom – mobility, skilled trade-craft, property; almost none for formal, juridical freedom. Jean Lee (1986) makes the point that children were economically separated from their mothers in southern Maryland, that men sometimes planned how they would dispose of the children while they were still in a woman's womb, and that they allocated the "future increase" of a slave woman much as they did that of the projected offspring from cows and heifers given as productive gifts and legacies to family members. Lee cites the examples of Elizabeth Atkins who bequeathed the first-born child of Cebberamous and another woman who bequeathed to a relative the first child that a slave woman, Sue, would bear if it lived a year and if not, then the next child (Lee, 1986: 359). This is one demonstration of the way slavery assumed an economic character similar to that which guided the European system of bond servitude.

13 Breen (1980: 146, quoting Michael 1901/2). Oldmixon (1708, vol. II: 117) gives a similar description for Barbados.

14 Although these descriptions are phrased in terms of color, which in some cases stood for country of origin, the distinctions people made in the early eighteenth century were not racial ones. The concept of race evolved in the nineteenth century as a justification for slavery and built upon the earlier designations based on skin complexion; it is, in Ashley Montagu's words, "of fairly recent origin" (Montagu 1942: 10). For descriptions of Africans given here see Jobson (1623: 33); Moore (1738: 30); Corry (1806: 94–6); Benezet (1788: 25); Crow (1830: 199–200); Horton (1868: 163). Most observers comment upon the physiognomy – attributing internal qualities to outward appearance was a common phenomenon of the time. See Horton (1868: 72, 148, 157, 163).

15 The visual imagery of scarification and the contrasts it created in Chesapeake society is discussed by Mullin (1972: 41–2) who also noted that it promoted social or corporate unity among members of a tribe or clan. These bonds, as African historians point out, extended from one generation to the next. Jobson (1623: 55) told of the pride women took in the distinctive marks: "And lastly, for her apparrell, it is loose clothes party-coloured, blew and white, whereof the women commonly weare but one tuckt about their middles, and from the waste upward, bare, in regard they are, for the most part, wrought, or rather printed upon the backs, . . . with work all over their backes, resembling right the printed lids and covers which we see laid and set upon our baked meats [i.e., decorated with a variety of dots and lines]: whereof it appears they take extraordinary pride, because they will turne themselves, wee should take notice of it, and be very well pleased, we should touch or handled it, as a matter to bee esteemed or set by." Quote is from Blier (1987: 208), but see also David, Sterner, and Gavua (1988) or, for visual depictions, Fisher (1984).

16 Hudson (1991: 238).

17 See Upton 1985 and 1990 for descriptions of how these varying geographic perspectives resulted in different views of and routes through the landscape. The hanging was ordered by Captain Calvert (Provincial Court Judgments, 1723,

Liber PL #7: f. 161). Kulikoff also described an African man who committed suicide; the overseer cut the man's head off and stuck it on a pole "to be a terror to others" (from an inventory of the estate of Edmund Jennings, 1712–13, quoted in Kulikoff 1978: 245). These punishments followed English justice which was harsh. A punishment that would strike terror in anyone who heard of it was probably what Benedict Leonard had in mind when he defined violent acts by slaves directed at slave-masters as petit treason and altered a customary English punishment for treason (hanging, drawing and quartering the body) and enacted it in 1729 into an even harsher law for slaves (Kilthy, 1799–1800, Chapters XXVI–XXVII). Its provisions were accurately known to African-Americans in Maryland as late as the 1930s when Dennis Simms recorded details of the "barbarous Maryland law" given him by a freed slave, Contee, from Prince George's County (Rawick 1972a: 61).

18 Records of using the moon to record the passage of time are given in Mullin (1972: 44–5). Francis Moore (1738) recorded West Africans' keen awareness of the phases of the moon, the placement of stars and planets in the sky. Hugh Jones (1724: 37–8) wrote of their enjoyment of the heat which Englishmen, who perceived heat as inducing ungovernable passions and fevers, found inexplicable.

Menard describes the "babel" of languages (1975: 35) then spoken in the Chesapeake as does Kulikoff (1978: 238; 1986) who may, however, overestimate the difficulties of communication among different African peoples. A letter of Stephen Bordley's mentions the "country language" used by slaves to plot rebellion; its contents imply slaves could effectively communicate (Stephen Bordley Letter Book, 1738–40: 55–8, Maryland Historical Society, reprinted in Land 1969: 228–30). African languages were complex, but in the linguistic system many African words were similar across different dialects (water is *minyi* in Eboe, *mingi* in Bonny, *Mindi* or *migi* in Nimbe, and *megi* in Oru) (Horton 1868: 156). Olaudah Equiano from Benin wrote that although he was "many days travelling [1755/56], during which I had often changed masters," still he was settled eventually in a country where the "people spoke exactly the same language with us" (Jones 1967: 86). Joyner (1984) discusses the difference between pidgins and creoles (see also Hymes 1981).

19 Klein (1967: 189–90). Mullin (1972: 94–6) provides the statistical information on runaways, concluding that one in four were house servants or slaves who "went by water." Kulikoff (1978: 239) described one runaway community among the Indians located beyond the Monocosy river in northwestern Maryland where the English population was small (Table A-3). See Brown (1991: 90–1) for the didactic uses of oral history that black mothers taught their daughters.

20 Walsh (1984c: 4). See Tate (1965); Chappell and Patrick (1991). Quote is from Berlin (1980: 48).

21 The small number of agricultural tools and the small amount of land owned in the nearby countryside implies that the household had minimal need for field

hands except on their Prince George's County estates. To gain an impression of the high fertility these figures imply see Morrissey (1989: 108–9).

22 Bohannon (1964: 105).

23 Davis (1803: 359).

24 See White (1985). Also see Callcott (1991) on the use of African-American midwives by the Calvert family.

25 The ways women worked together are described by White (1985, 1990, 1991).

26 Walsh (1984c). See Menard (1975) or Kulikoff (1986: 70–4) for discussions of birth rates. Jean Lee, however, contests their assumptions in a 1986 critique of the male-centered view of birth rates and other demographic factors among slave populations. The birth rate *was* demonstrably higher for native born black women. A similar situation is shown in the inventory of William Locke of Londontown, a physician, where children also were a disproportionate segment of the slave-holdings (fifty-two children, nineteen men, ten women).

27 Menard (1975); Oldmixon (1708, vol. II: 117); Kulikoff (1986: 334); Lee (1994).

28 This characteristic – the shared local knowledge – of seventeenth- and early eighteenth-century communities can be readily inferred from reading Court Records and from knowledge of contemporary small communities where information exchanges are rapid and detailed. As a case in point, the *Maryland Gazette* gave more column space to out-of-town events than to local news.

29 Crow (1830: 244); Jones (1967: 73, 78).

30 Walsh (1984c, table 4). Edward Kimber provided a 1730s description of a quarter (Kimber 1746) reprinted in the *Maryland Historical Magazine* in 1956 (51: 327) "a Negro Quarter, is a Number of Huts or Hovels, built some Distance from the Mansion-House; where the Negroes reside with their Wives and Families, and cultivate at vacant Times the little Spots allow'd them." Kulikoff found a plat of a quarter surrounded by fields in Moore v. Meek, Ejectment Papers, Box 30 at the Maryland State Archives. An excellent overview of Maryland slave housing can be found in George McDaniel's *Hearth and Home* (1982) with additional technical information given in his earlier dissertation (McDaniel 1979). To date, none in Maryland has been excavated archaeologically.

31 Key (1919: 264–5), but also see the version given in Ridgely (1841).

32 Armstrong (1990: 266).

33 Emerson (1988).

34 Quote from Jobson (1623: 122); Moore (1738: 76). Emerson (1988) draws on various types of evidence. His illustration of a pipe bowl with a lozenge motif (a distinctive line and stamped design surrounded by punched circlets) from a deposit at Jamestown bears remarkable affinities to decorative elements on Ashanti earthenware pots (Emerson 1988: 148, Figure 48). The example is not an isolated one. Similar connections can be drawn for pipes with "kwardaata" and double-bell motifs. The ideograms, symbolizing emotions, places, people,

and things, also appear in the New World among Caribbean peoples (Thompson 1984).

35 Armstrong (1990: 178–9, 272). See, for example, *Proceedings of the 1982 Glass Trade Bead Conference*, edited by Charles Hayes III (1983).

36 Handler, Lange, and Orser (1979) describe 900 beads from a Caribbean slave cemetery.

37 Opper and Opper (1989) discuss the Diakhité finds. DeCorse (1989) reviews the earlier evidence.

38 Jobson (1623: 36). Quotes from Matthews (1788: 108) and Bosman (1705: 102). See Moore (1738: 35, 75, 110), DeCorse's review of African beads (1989), but also see Dubin (1987) or Fisher (1984: 70–1 and her bibliography) for vivid examples of the visual imagery created by the use of beads in a variety of ways.

39 Quote is from Carmichael (1833: 146–7). For a summary of Caribbean glass beads see Armstrong (1990).

40 Handler and Lange 1978: 144–50, 274–81; Handler, Lange, and Orser 1979: 15–18. Quote from Handler, Lange, and Orser (1979: 16).

41 Adams (1987: 187, 197) discusses glass beads from Georgia slave sites; Smith concentrates on South Carolina (1983: Appendix F) where the eighteenth-century opaque red glass beads known as "cornaline d'Aleppo" – perhaps because these were made in imitation of carnelian – were found. Strangely, very few beads were recovered at the eighteenth-century free black site of Fort Mose located near St. Augustine, Florida (Deagan, personal commnication, March 1992), but a few have been found in post-1730 contexts at St. Augustine (Deagan 1987: 182) and in Haiti.

42 Quotes from Bosman (1705: 103); Davis (1803: 366).

43 Handler and Lange (1978: 149), Adams (1994) on blue beads; DeCorse's overview (1989) is particularly important; he critiques simplistic studies of beads found in the New World as well (DeCorse 1994). Quotes from Hammell (1983: 5, 28).

44 David, Sterner and Gavua (1988). Also see Fisher (1984).

45 Fisher (1984) gives examples of the various symbolic meanings attached to different stones, citing earlier studies while her photographs show the range of materials, innovative and traditional, adapted.

46 Dubin (1987) reviews the use of beaded jewelry among Europeans, although Jennifer Glassborough (Curator at the Maryland Historical Society) points out that Anglo-American children in colonial portraits sometimes wear coral beads. However, the global use of glass trade beads as a mechanism of exchange with native populations argues against their widespread use in the European population, especially among the wealthy.

47 The will of Rebecca Calvert is in Anne Arundel County Wills, 1734–5, Liber 21: f. 322; the account filed by Onorio Razolini gives the names of slaves who died (Anne Arundel County Accounts, 1737, Liber 14: f. 359).

48 Leach (1967: 151).

10. WEST AFRICAN WOMEN, FOOD, AND CULTURAL VALUES

1 It is clear from recent studies that elements of African culture were actively maintained in the slave culture of North America. Historians, drawing on Herskovits (1941), have put the issue to rest (Levine, 1977; Abrahams, 1983; Holloway, 1990; Philips, 1990), but it is not a fact that it was originally accepted. Lawrence Levine reprints a statement by Robert Park and observed it was typical of the historical view that guided much of twentieth-century scholarship: "The Negro when he landed in the United States, left behind him almost everything but his dark complexion and his tropical temperament . . . Coming from all parts of Africa and having no common language and common tradition, the memories of Africa which they brought with them were soon lost" (Levine 1977: 4, from Park 1919). This view was incorporated into some of the 1970s black feminist literature and still appears occasionally. One problem archaeologists stress (see the work of Merrick Posnansky and Christopher DeCorse) is the diversity of African culture – and the fact that one cannot draw simple one-to-one analogies as was sometimes attempted as evidence of carryovers from English tradition. However, archaeologists and historians working with Anglo-America have learned to assess the regional impact of English sub-cultures on New World settlements and it is possible to do this with African lifeways as well. The way both black and white traditions have meshed is well presented in a number of texts (cf. Philips 1990).

2 For the South, see studies by Reitz cited in Chapters 11 and 12; Singleton (1985; 1991); Ferguson (1992), and for the Caribbean, Armstrong (1990). Diane Crader (1984, 1989, 1990) reported upon the Monticello data.

3 See Axtell (1981: 9–11).

4 Creolization is a linguistic term used to indicate the merging of two different languages into a dialect that blends the two. Often these develop first as trade languages; Abrahams (1983: 26) cites the Mediterranean, Portuguese-based Sabir used in conversation between Europeans and West African traders in the fifteenth century. The dictionary defines the process as one whereby the language of the dominant group (or English in the Chesapeake) becomes the sole language (with modifications) of the dominated or oppressed group. This is a simplification, and the concept also extends to non-verbal elements of culture too. Take, for example, the process whereby African-born women living in the Chesapeake adapted elements of English cuisine with African cooking techniques and foodstuffs (whenever the latter were available). What Abrahams wrote about verbal performance in the Caribbean points the way to what happened with food: "many speech events called for the substitution of certain European forms because of the slaves' identification of the plantocrat's power with his European tongue. But this substitution was a selective process. The language of everyday discourse remained essentially creole. Only on certain ceremonial occasions was the European tongue called into play, and then only the most formal style of that speech system" (Abrahams 1983: 26).

African observers who described food customs include Olaudah Equiano, born in the 1740s in the Ibo region of Benin (now Nigeria), kidnapped and brought to Barbados in 1756 and then to Virginia. Bought by a Quaker merchant, he became a captain's assistant and purchased freedom (Jones 1967: 60–1). In 1789 Equiano (also known as Gustavus Vasa) wrote that Ibo vegetables were "mostly plantains, eadas, yams, beans, and Indian [New World] corn" (Jones 1967: 73). The list of vegetables provided by a Fulani, Salih Bilali, differs: red maize, millet, Guinea or African corn, beans, pumpkins, okra, tomatoes, cucumbers (Wilks 1967: 151). Bilali was born ca. 1770 on the Niger River near Mopti and transported to Georgia ca. 1800 (Hodgson 1844).

5 Quotes are from McCall (1964: 19) and Glassie (1975: 10); also see Bloch (1953: 60–9).

6 See *Geographica Nubiensis* (written in Arabic in the twelfth century) printed at the back of Francis Moore's account of Africa or Lewicki's (1974) summary of food descriptions in medieval Arabic texts. European accounts begin after 1450. Quotes are from Francis Moore (1738: 108) and Oldmixon (1708, volume II: 120–1). Also see Crow (1830: 253–4) or Jobson (1623: 131) for memorable discussions of distilling palm wine.

7 Quote from Moore (1738: 257).

8 Bosman (1705: 227). Quote from Achebe (1958: 117). African goats continue to have symbolic importance as an "animal most loved by the Earth and under-world goddess for the strong aroma of its meat . . . [and] as one of the first animals on earth." Blier (1987: 240).

9 Quote from Norris (1789: ix).

10 For dairying and other elements of diet see Jobson (1623: 36 and throughout; for rice also see Jobson). Quotes from Jobson (1623: 39) and Crow (1830: 250). The description of "creole ladies" is given in Grigson and Knox (1986: 70).

11 See Tannahill (1989), Hall (1991), or Sokolov (1991: 76–8). Costly imported iron kettles were bartered for slaves in Africa (Jones 1967: 68) even as they were used to purchase land from Native Americans. Quote from Birmingham (1967) as quoted in Hall (1991: 169). Labat (1693: 9) noted guards were necessary to preserve some edible plants.

12 Quote is from Jobson (1623: 155). The coarse yellow "Guinea" yam (*Dioscorea cayenensis*) arrived early in the slave trade and is described by Oviedo who saw it growing in 1514 (Parry 1955: 13); the white, floury great yam (*D. alata* or "*nymba*" in Mandingo) arrived later, but was seen by Sloane in 1687–9. Crow wrote of its use in Africa: "The country abounds with yams of all kinds, which when boiled with meat, peeled and dressed with salt and oil, are considered good and nourishing . . . the yam partakes of the colour of its skin; some being purple, others white; others of a mixed colour, according to the exterior dye or tinge. They are the common substitute for bread. When roasted they taste like an English potato" (1830: 256). In the New World, Romans evaluated yams by an "ascending scale of goodness": "Spanish, or the original root; Carolina, little superior to the first; Brimstone, from its internal colour, with a red skin; purple

potato, having that color throughout except a very little of the heart; Bermudas, or round white potato" (1775, I: 123). Ackee (breadfruit) appeared in the Caribbean by 1778 together with mango (*Mangifera indica*); Parry (1955: 16) notes that in parts of central Africa it lined the inland slave routes: volunteer plants dropped by people who marched as they ate.

Lawson (1714: 76) recorded Guinea corn in the Carolinas in 1709, used to "feed hogs and poultry" while Sloane saw both the Guinea corn and Guinea weed in Jamaica in 1687–9 (1707: xv, xvi, xix). Low country planters along the coasts of Georgia and South Carolina continued to cultivate the latter as a rice substitute. Henderson, for example, wrote: "there is a delicate white farinacious seed, called by some Guinea corn, which is raised, a few stalks in many of our gardens" (*Henderson's North Carolina Almanack of 1816*, quoted in Wood 1974: 120). Sesame seed grew in South Carolina by 1730 (Gray 1941, vol. I: 194) and probably by the 1690s; Sloane saw it before then in Jamaica (1707: xxi). Romans (1775: 130) wrote sesame was "the best thing yet known for extracting a fine esculent oil . . . Negroes use it as food either raw, toasted, or boiled in their soup and are very fond of it; they call it *Benni*." Romans also recorded that Africans brought ground-nuts, or peanuts, to the South (1775, I: 131; also see Morgan 1982: 573) while Sloane saw them in Jamaica a century earlier (1707: lxxiii).

13 Bosman (1705: 230); Sloane (1707: xvii). Consider here the style of cattle herding practiced in the Carolinas (Wood 1974) and the way domestic fowl were raised at slave quarters throughout the South.

14 See Jobson (1623: 133) for the bees. Bosman (1705) describes the trading at some length, but it is mentioned by most early travelers. For fish motifs see Elisofon (1958) or Fagg and Plass (1964). For trading at Jenne-jeno see McIntosh and McIntosh (1981: 7, 20–1).

15 Bosman (1705: 91, 106–7, 263). Christopher DeCorse, who has reviewed the faunal evidence as part of his research on Elmina, gave me information on shellfish utilization and its reduction in size (personal communication, March 1992).

16 See Sloane (1707: xviii); Carmichael (1833); Harris (1989).

17 Wax (1968; 477) on Annamaboo market. Also see Norris (1789: 145). Moore (1738: 108); Bosman (1705: 227). For Zaire see Caputo (1991: 26).

18 Adams (1987) for Georgia; Reitz (1991) for Fort Mose; Reitz, Gibbs, and Rathbun (1985) for the broader South. For Calvert data see Reitz 1988a, 1988b, 1989a.

19 Sylvia Leith-Ross (1939: 63) wrote that among the Ibo in Nigeria, fowls were seen "a little as one's own children"; a recognized time of day (when feasts ended, visitors left, and a house closed in for the night), was described as "on se couche avec les poules." Francis Moore compared Guinea hens favorably with the English pheasant (1738: 180). Tannahill (1989) provides information on Guinea hens and turkeys from the perspective of culinary history. Quote is from Mullin (1972: 61). For ways that gender distinctions are used to speak of distinctions among men see Bloch (1985).

20 For the perception that a master had to keep slaves occupied, see Bolzius (1751: 259). See Carmichael (1833: 136–7) for plants grown and Pulsipher (1990: 31) for the legislation and other contemporary evidence of slave plots. Frederick Douglass' account of his grandmother is given in Preston (1980: 20). Quote is from Hudson (1991: 217). See also Genovese (1974: 535–40) who notes men also helped cultivate small vegetable gardens in the New World. In Virginia, Landon Carter wrote in his diary of a conversation with a slave named Jack Lubber while Jack was tending his own melon and pea vines, the latter not yet hilled. Carter, who felt it was past time to do so, asked why not; Jack cited his experience in gardening and knowledge that they were still too young "to coat them closely with earth" (quoted in Sobel 1987: 42). For a woman's view of music and its feminine contributions, see Nikki Giovanni (1983: 78).

21 Quotes are from Jobson (1623: 124); Achebe (1958: 23); Crow (1830: 263–4). Corry (1805–6) also describes the women's traditional field labor.

22 Corry (1806: 64); Francis Moore (1738: 108).

23 The quote is from Moore (1738: 229). See Corry (1806: 39); Ferguson (1992: 90, 105, quoting Simms 1841: 122); Harris (1989: 5); Lewis (1988: 94–5). Olaudah Equiano (Jones 1967: 73) wrote of the women's pots he saw in childhood (ca. 1745–56). Today, African women still work with clay (Welbourn 1984; Sterner 1989), according to Posnansky (1994) "invariably so." For archaeological descriptions and the question of who made what pots in the New World see the extended discussion in Ferguson (1992), but note Posnansky's belief (forthcoming) that girls learned refinements of pottery making as women, i.e., later than the age when slavers took them from their homes.

24 Quotes are from Harris (1989: xxi); Kingsley (1897: 209). Barbot's description of North and South Guinea (1732: 378) includes the use of iron cooking pots in northeast Benin province where Olaudah Equiano also remembered their use in the 1740s (Jones 1967: 68).

25 Herskovits and Herskovits (1936: 14); Lewis (1988: 32–3); Hudson (1991: 123).

26 See Childs (1953: 78–9) and Hudson (1991: 123).

27 Achebe (1958: 78–9) and Kingsley (1897: 209).

28 Kingsley (1897: 208–10, 227). For the prevalence of male chefs at Caribbean plantations, see Carmichael (1833: 114).

29 Quote from Leith-Ross (1939: 65).

30 For Wye Island see Bescherer (1989). For Jamaica, Armstrong (1990: 98, 268).

31 Herskovits 1941; Mintz and Price (1976).

32 See Roger Abrahams (1983: xvii–xxii) on the transmission of oral and visual cultural elements to the New World. Also Mintz and Price (1976).

33 See Mintz and Price (1976). Quote is from Sobel (1979: xxi). See Miller (1989: 53) on the ethnobotanical interpretation. For the increasing range of African foodstuffs grown in the New World, there are a number of modern accounts (cf., Parry 1955; Sokolov 1991), but travelers' accounts should be read too: e.g., Romans (1775); Sloane (1707); Lawson (1709).

34 Oldmixon (1708: 119); Lawson (1709: 75); Jones (1724: 78); Bolzius (1751: 235).

35 Crader (1990: 703).

36 Quote is from Bolzius (1751: 236). Descriptive meat terms are from Wright (1990: 41).

37 Quotes are from Mrs. Carmichael (1833: 184–5).

38 See Yentsch (1992) on fishing and McKee (1987) on root cellars. On sanctioned food redistribution, Lady Nugent (1839) noted in her journal in 1802 that after a large party at the Governor's mansion in Jamaica, food was distributed to different individuals including slaves. But people who often were not fed adequately could not always wait for formal redistribution; they found unsanctioned and informal means. Orlando Patterson in *The Sociology of Slavery* quotes Stewart and Marly on the double standard vis-à-vis theft. These latter two writers provide the point of view of slaves: "When I take from my master, being for my use, who am his slave, or property, he loses nothing by its transfer" (Stewart 1823: 249). Or, in the words of a woman caught taking a calabash of sugar, "him no *tief* from Massa, him *take* from Massa" (my emphasis) (Marly 1828: 40–2). The distinction is subtle and pragmatic; it was also, in Patterson's belief, tacitly supported by all concerned. Slave owners who knew they were providing insufficient food also knew they could expect to have their own food supplies depleted. Oldmixon (1708, vol. II: 119) wrote that when any livestock – ox, bull, cow – died accidentally, the slaves feasted upon it and "white servants have often as not disdained to come in for a share."

39 The documentation on provision grounds is extensive over a wide geographic range of European slave-holding communities (see Morgan 1982; Berlin 1980). The practice also existed among slave households in West Africa in the early nineteenth century (Clapperton 1829: 214, quoted by Lovejoy 1979: 1284), in Brazil (Russell-Wood 1982), and in the West Indies. In the low-country south, Berlin observes that the purchase of or barter with black men and women on the part of owners and overseers "strengthened the slaves' customary right to their garden and barnyard fowl" (1980: 65). Further evidence of bartering and/or selling foodstuffs among Maryland's early African-American community is given in Chapter 12.

40 Carmichael (1833).

41 In Africa, Jobson wrote of the closeness with which African families and their birds lived; Leith-Ross (1939) demonstrated the continuity of the pattern (see note 18). In Jamaica, chickens were gathered and hung in baskets at night to protect them from rats; Guinea fowls roosted in trees near slave quarters (Barclay 1828: 515). Quote is from Gosse (1847: 326) who also observed that they flourished on Jamaica 150 years earlier. Lack (1976) noted that they became extinct in the late nineteenth century. Lewis (1976) records their presence in Virginia in the early twentieth century and writes that they now can be special-ordered from butchers' shops in the Carolinas (1988). As fellow archaeologists and students read drafts of this manuscript, they too commented on the presence of wild Guinea hens in the Chesapeake, in Georgia, and on Long Island, in some cases noting that the birds still roosted at night in trees next to farmhouses.

11. FAUNAL REMAINS: PUTTING MEAT ON THE BONES

1 This interpretation builds upon the thorough and excellent study of the Calvert faunal material by Dr. Elizabeth S. Reitz and Ms. Elizabeth Ruff at the University of Georgia and earlier work by Dr. Larry McKee (McKee 1985; Reitz 1988a, 1988b, 1989a, 1989b; Ruff 1989; Reitz and Ruff 1992). It also draws upon the comparative background provided by the research of Dr. Henry Miller, Dr. Joanne Bowen, and Dr. Diane Crader. Additional insight came from Crabtree (1989) which provides a broad overview of faunal analysis within historical archaeology; Zeder's work on procurement systems for town households in the Near East (1991); Reitz's work on southern and Caribbean faunal assemblages was essential (Reitz 1990; Reitz and Honnerkamp 1983; Reitz and Scarry 1985) while Reitz (n.d.) contained an essential overview and detailed bibliography of African-American food use based on faunal remains. Quote is from Mintz (1985: 3–4).

2 See Naomi F. Miller (1988 and 1989) for further information on the plant remains. To learn more about what dogs and squirrels can do to archaeological evidence, see "Ruby and how many squirrels? The destruction of bones by dogs" (Payne and Munson 1985).

3 In addition to the work by Reitz and Ruff, see McKee 1988: 96–108.

4 See McKee (1988) for the original chart on which this one is based.

5 See Miller (1984), summarized in Miller (1986b, 1988a). Also Joanne Bowen (1993), Gregory Brown (1989), David Landon (1992), Justin Lev-Tov (1990), Larry McKee (1987, 1988), and for a summary based on documentary sources, Carr (1992).

6 See Carr (1992) and Walsh (1984b: 5). At the same time, town records indicate a thriving tanning industry; at the start of the war in 1776, as the control of Lord Baltimore's civil government eroded, there were sufficient slaughterhouses in Annapolis to create an "intolerable stench," and the town instituted a three-month ban on the slaughter of "bullocks, muttons, or any kind of meat" (*Archives of Maryland* XII: 89; also see Ridgely 1841: 173; Papenfuse 1975: 10–12).

7 The rector at St. Anne's parish identified Cornelius Brooksby at his death as "a butcher," a fact not self-evident in his inventory; social historians have described Brooksby instead as a small, successful trader. The inventory evidence that he was a butcher is slim: one entry for five butcher's knives; another for twenty pounds of cheese; a third listing "a square table, two butcher's knives, and a butcher's steel" at 12 shillings. While hides and skins at the tanner's were also listed, Brooksby kept only two cows (Anne Arundel County Inventories 1723, Liber 9: f. 198–201). Many butchers, listed in the records as such, were relatively poor; they appear because they plead for tax relief or other forms of social aid when old or unable to work. The death of Charles Rive, goatkeeper, is recorded in St. Anne's Parish Register on March 8, 1721/22.

8 The Sullivan debts are found in Anne Arundel County Judgments, 1721, RC 21: f. 60–86; the Hammond ones in Anne Arundel County Judgments, 1735, IB 1: f. 329. For Reynolds see Reitz (1989b) and for St. Mary's City, see Miller (1984, 1986b, 1988a).

9 While we found modest midden-like deposits at Reynolds Tavern when I excavated there in 1982 and they were found at Gott's Court (Landon 1992), none was observed in the early layers near the main house at the Calvert Site until the 1790s when oyster shell began to accumulate behind an attached dependency. Although individuals could be fined (and the Calverts were) for disposing of trash in the streets, overall town regulations did not fully address garbage accumulation until the 1790s when they specified "no carrion, stinking fish flesh, dead creatures, broken glass bottles, loose oyster shell, or filth" was to lie on the streets or in passages next to houses for more than twelve hours. Also in 1792, Annapolitans were forbidden to dig "pits" for garbage, and were fined if they had a "bog-house, house of office shambles, or stalls" which was a nuisance. Unused wells were also ordered filled and shut (Proceedings, Mayor, Aldermen, and Councilor, 1720–1843, #84).

10 Miller first pointed out the importance of beef in the Chesapeake diet; Bowen's work on the myth of pork (1991) also indicates that beef was by far the more important source of meat protein.

11 Quote is from Bolzius (1751: 229).

12 Abstaining from meat during Lent was an English tradition which was customarily broken with the Easter feast. Hennisch writes that "any fish that finned its way obligingly within man's reach was welcome on fast days, . . . King herring mounted his throne on Ash Wednesday, and stayed there, however much his subjects grumbled, until Easter Sunday" (1976: 33). Bowen (1990), however, also points out that this fits with the natural seasonal cycle of birth and reproduction in animal herds and the constraints imposed by seasonal butchery schedules. For an example of how these "ethnographic" facts are used to pinpoint seasonal episodes of deposition see Langdon (1992).

13 See Crader (1990: 695–6) on sheep at Monticello where she concluded they were rarely part of the diet of ordinary slaves. Data from South Carolina was supplied by Dr. Reitz and can be found with more specificity in an on-going series of reports issued by the Charleston Museum, Charleston, South Carolina.

14 Hugh Jones wrote that Virginia pork was "famous, whole Virginia shoats being frequently barbecued in England" (1724: 79). Hilliard (1972) and Egerton (1987) provide regional information on barbecued pork. Slave narratives (Yetman 1970: 267) also mention that slaves butchered shoats to barbecue.

15 Edna Lewis provides information on the use of pig's head (1988: 76–7) and on hog butchery (1976: 181–5) for Virginia. Quote is from Carmichael (1833: 177); also see Wheaton (1983); Mennell (1985). Susannah Carter's 1772 cookbook recommends calves' head and pig's head in five different menus: one each for October, November, December, January, and February. Hennisch notes the ceremonial use of boars' heads at Christmas (1976: 229). Wilson repeats

Tusser's advice "at Michaelmas safely go sty up thy boar, Lest straying abroad ye do see him no more." (1974: 89).

16 Quote is from Ellis (1975: 14). Crabtree's (1989) review of faunal studies of assemblages from complex societies provides an overview of market-based analysis for European or Near Eastern assemblages; less attention has been paid to market constraints in historical archaeology, although Reitz's work on Charleston zeroes in on the problem (Reitz 1986). Two recent Ph.D. dissertations (Bowen 1990 and Landon 1991b) are also pertinent as are Nan Rothschild's (1990) and Haskel Greenfield's (1989) studies of eighteenth-century New York.

McKee (1985) began to analyze butchery marks on the Calvert bone to determine cuts of meat and food preparation techniques. It is unfortunate that limited funding precluded the completion of his analysis. Although at the time we felt fortunate to find funds to have the material identified; in retrospect and in light of the links between marks left on bone elements and different food preparation techniques which Landon (1991b) observed at the Spencer-Pierce Little homestead, it is clear that we would know more and might be able to distinguish more readily the utilization of haute cuisine, folk cookery, or West African influences had McKee been able to continue his study.

Reitz notes the greater variation in marine species living in southeastern waters as opposed to the narrow range of species present in Chesapeake Bay (personal communication 1991; compare, for example, the species lists in Adams [1987] or Reitz [1982] with fish found in Chesapeake deposits as given in Miller [1984]).

17 Kill-off patterns are derived from analysis of long bones where the epiphyses fuse to the shaft in prescribed sequence and from the study of dental eruption and tooth wear. A growing literature based on this type of analysis is reviewed by Crabtree (1989). Quote is from Jones (1724: 79). This was a prevalent opinion; Lord Adam Gordon wrote of Chesapeake beef and mutton as "excellent" whereas his ranking for the Carolinas placed poultry and pork as excellent, but beef and mutton as "middling" (Gordon 1764–5: 246, 255).

18 Various scholars attribute this to the climate and to the labor requirements on a tobacco plantation (Main 1982, Carson and Walsh 1981). It is also possible that the Calvert inventories show no cheese utensils because, familiar with the taste of English cheese, the Calvert men were not satisfied with its Maryland counterpart. The third Lord Baltimore's opinion on cheese is given in the Calvert Papers, I: 263.

19 One hint that the family did patronize local butchers is a small debt, 7 shillings, that Captain Calvert owed Cornelius Brooksby in 1722 (Anne Arundel County Court Judgments RC 21: 416).

20 Total meat poundage is in the range of 200 lbs, a figure significantly higher than the amount Hammond or Sullivan purchased in any single month. Ruff (1989) cites a weight of 600 lbs as an average weight for modern-day Holstein cows while archaeological data for Exeter cattle in England ca. 1500 indicate they

were much smaller; the Annapolis skeletal elements indicate animals that would fall in between these two size samples (Ruff 1989; see also Reitz and Ruff 1992).

21 In the first published cookbook by an American author, Carter (1772), for example, only lists mutton four times in her suggested menus whereas beef appears eight times and ham appears six times. Since veal, the more costly meat, was shown on seven menus, her criteria were not based on price.

22 Crader (1990: 696).

23 Only one lower vertebra was found. Reitz believes that this may be a bias introduced by preservational factors and/or by criteria used for identification. She is conservative in identifications of ribs and vertebrae, and requires morphological matches. While Reitz notes this excludes many fragments of ribs and vertebrae from being identified as other than Unidentified Large Mammal, she still found more ribs in deposits from the Reynolds Tavern site in Annapolis than from the early features at the Calvert site (i.e., from Feature 103 at Reynolds [table 7] there were one pig, eight cow, and one caprine rib; from Feature 106 [table 22] there were one pig and thirteen cow ribs, while in Feature 107 [table 16], there were none; Reitz 1989b); Hilliard (1972) notes the use of ribs as a freshly-cooked portion of the animal as does Crader (1990: 699). Hilliard also states preferred cuts were "the hams, shoulders, sausage and perhaps the tenderloin," but stresses that each part of the pig had its "own devotees" (1972: 44).

24 On the allocation of specific body parts to slaves see Joseph Ball's orders. Ball gave the "head and Pluck" from calves to the field hands, but dispensed a broader spectrum of hog-meat including neck, fat back, and other coarse parts (Mullin 1972: 50). Since the 1700s different parts of pigs have become associated with the food traditions of African-Amercians: the shoulders, the ham hocks, the feet ("trotters"), snout ("snoot") and the neck, backbone, stomach, and intestines (chittlins) (Wright 1990: 41).

25 The French pattern was based on butchered meats used during the fourteenth century in bourgeois households, not those used in aristocratic households that had better supplies of fowl and game and chose to feature these, as, apparently, did many in the later Chesapeake and in the far south. Among medieval English and French aristocrats, "butchered meats, especially beef, were used primarily in stocks, minced meat dishes, and slowly cooked stews" (Flandrin 1989: 272). For the provisioning of the indigent seeking medicinal cures at Cool Springs in the 1690s, see *Archives of Maryland* (XXII: 432).

26 Flandrin (1989). See, for example, Carter (1772), Randolph (1824) or Englishwoman, E. Smith (1742) whose cookbook was printed in Williamsburg, Virginia, as well as in England.

27 Bordley also ordered English hares (Gibson 1826: 103).

28 Browne (1884: 164) provides information on the suspected poisoning of the Governor and his Council at a 1678 meeting.

29 See Hilliard (1972); Otto (1984); Reitz *et al.* (1985).

30 Bolzius writes that a plantation should have seven men, three women, and one boy of 10 to 15 years to take care of the cattle and fowl (1751: 260). Olaudah

Equiano (1789: 86) writes that as a young slave in Africa, he was "sometimes employed in assisting an elderly woman slave to cook and take care of the poultry." Probably the critical factor is age, not gender, although young girls may have been more often assigned tasks inside the house. See Jobson (1623). For the New World see Wood (1974) for Guinea corn or Gray (1941) for a broader view. Also see Carmichael (1833: 263); quote is from an account of John Hatley Norton, 1782–4, quoted in Wood (1974: 49). See Sokolov (1990 or 1991) for the deep-fat frying and also Egerton (1987). Readers should note that southern fried foods do not use the standard English fat – butter – but depend on a lighter oil that could easily be an adaptation of palm-oil. Sesame, for example, was noted by Romans as a productive source of oil in the southeast in the 1760s. Deep-fat frying is also a technique used for small pieces of meat, usually fowl, shrimp, or crab (as in crab-cakes). Beef and lamb (two of the traditional English meats) are not cooked in this manner.

31 Medullary bone is a granular deposit found in many species of female birds formed in the narrow cavities of the bone a few weeks prior to the onset of egg-laying. It provides a supply of minerals necessary in the production of eggshell (Driver 1982: 251). At the Benjamin Banneker site, there were approximately 100 chicken bones recovered from a small excavation unit (6 ft × 8 ft) in a sealed cellar context (Robert Hurry, personal communication, June 1992).

32 There is an increase in the proportions over the eighteenth century that parallels the increase in the black population, and the increase is particularly visible at rural sites where plantation owners had large slave-holdings. Thus from a well at Kingsmill (ca. 1760) the MNI is four, but at the Bray well (ca. 1770–90) it is fourteen (Kelso 1984b: 220–1). Bowen also reports "many immature chickens" from a ca. 1770 slave quarter at Mt. Vernon (Bowen 1989: 4). The MacNamara henhouse is described in Chapter 3, table 3.4; for Rev. Humphrey's painting bill for "two hen coops and pidgeon house" see Anne Arundel County Judgments 1734 IB I: f. 387.

33 Birdcages appear in inventories for a number of wealthy decedents. Quote from a letter by John Montgomery, a Congressman from Pennsylvania, to Charles Thomas, Secretary of Congress, in 1784.

12. HUNTING, FISHING, AND MARKET TRADING

1 Greenfield (1989) provides information on transporting animals from farm to market. Fines assessed African-American Annapolitans may be seen in the records of the Annapolis Mayor's Court. See Oldmixon (1708) and Herskovits and Herskovits (1936) on the West Indies and Wood (1974) on Charleston.

2 Lawson (1709) wrote that colonists found goats "mischevious" because of their predilection for damaging orchards and consuming fruit. Information on the commercial activities of slaves can be found in Morgan (1982).

3 Blowing wind was clearly a subterfuge, but I have been unable to find a precise definition of it in dictionaries of slang or in the laws.

4 Sheep were not yet commonly raised and consequently were worth more than swine or goats. Grand Jury Presentments, July 1783, noted among Treasurer's Reports and Vouchers 1783–1829, Annapolis Mayor's Court II: 201–4. The case of Negro Frank is in Anne Arundel County Judgments, 1734, IB I: f. 187.

5 Oldmixon (1708, vol. II: 122); Wood (1974: 210). For Georgia see Berlin (1980: 63–5) and for the lowcountry south in general see Morgan (1982). For the Banneker family, see Hurry (1989: 362).

6 Carmichael (1833: 263–4); Sloane (1707, vol. II).

7 Davis (1803: 388); Equiano (1789: 72).

8 Horton (1868: 148).

9 See lawsuit of Eleanor Tracy vs. Robert Hugall, Anne Arundel County Judgments 1734 IB I: f. 467. See John Juitt's deposition, Anne Arundel County Judgments 1734 IB I: f. 251.

10 See Ridgely (1841) for a summary of the town regulations in 1717. For Charleston, see Wood (1974: 210–11). For Annapolis in 1787, see the Proceedings of the Mayor, Aldermen, and Councilmen, 1720–1843 (#84).

11 These ideas are drawn from Leach (1982). A statement by Leroi Jones (1963: 15) is also pertinent vis-à-vis the effects of culture contact: "A graph could be set up to show just exactly what aspects of African culture suffered most and were most rapidly suppressed [in the New World] . . . all forms of political and economic thought, which were two of the most profound sophistications of African culture, were suppressed immediately."

12 See A. J. Russell-Wood (1982: 36–7, 54–5) and Sokolov (1990). *Carurú* shows its African origins quite clearly; carura is the Brazilian word for okra; this dish is a variety of salad made with herbs, fish, shrimp, chicken, and seasoned with palm-oil and peppers. See also Freyre (1946: 464), an anthropologist trained by Boas, who also researched colonial records to include African-derived food use in Brazil for his *Masters and the Slaves*. *Aloa* is a drink made of rice flour or toasted corn with water and fermented with sugar in clay jars (Freyre 1946: 478).

13 Wood (1974: 211).

14 Dell Upton, letter June 1991; Wright (1921: 557–8).

15 Cleland is quoted in Thomas (1983: 145). Thomas Hearne's Collections, *Oxford Historical Society Proceedings* 65: 188–9.

16 *Archives of Maryland*, Council Proceedings, 1636–57: 45. Cedar Park in Anne Arundel County and Mt. Airy in Prince George's County are two examples, but neither appears old enough to be a place the third Lord Baltimore could have visited 1660–85.

17 The strategic use of wild food resources at important dinners given by English aristocracy is noted in Mead (1931) and Mennell (1985). Miller (1984) reviews the faunal evidence for hunting in the early Chesapeake. Fish and game are well represented at King's Mill (Barber 1976; McKee 1987) and Mt. Vernon (Bowen 1989) in post-1760 deposits.

18 The Virginia statutes record young Indian boys (of about ten years or less) "kept" by planters to fish, hunt, and carry messages (Emerson 1988: 164).

Lawson (1709: 86) also wrote that the Indians "hunt and fowl for us at reasonable rates." Quote is from Byrd (1733: 127, 134).

19 Byrd (1733: 135, 166, 181). See Lawson (1709: 120–1). Byrd saw them from a similar perspective: "ugly as a toad, and preserved to be looked upon, and good for nothing else."

20 In 1730 Maryland legislation was passed to preserve the deer because their numbers had lessened. Deer hunting was banned from January 1 to July 31 while female deer were with their young and "white men [were] not allowed to purchase deer or deer meat from Indians" at this season (Kilthy, 1799–1800).

21 Jones (1699: 441). Davis (1803). Brickell (1737). Landon Carter, quoted in Sobel (1987: 43). Information on the nocturnal habits of possums and raccoons can be found in Hilliard (1972: 80).

22 In South Carolina, the legislation forbidding guns to Negroes was impossible to enforce and it was subsequently changed to read "on the property" (Wood 1974: 127). This is the way it was first worded in the 1715 Maryland law (Kilthy, 1799–1800, Chapter XXXII).

23 Adanson (1759); Kimber (1746: 217). Lists of New World fish are given in almost every traveler's account. Many fish and shellfish in West African waters (e.g., mullet, flounder, shrimp, crab, lobster) were similar to those caught along the Atlantic coast. See Bosman (1705: 168–9) or Yentsch (1992). For women's participation see Preston (1980: 20).

24 Lévi-Strauss (1962: 5) and Wood (1974); Cronon (1983: 37). The planter's observation, drawn from a rice plantation in the Carolinas (Childs, 1953: 46), perhaps is not appropriate to the Chesapeake, although information in the *Maryland Slave Narratives* (Rawick 1972b) suggests it was.

25 For the archaeological evidence from African sites see DeCorse (1994) and Davies (1956) that show shellfish exploitation. DeCorse writes that although the indigenous fauna was over-hunted in the historic period, small game is still common today and some, especially grass cutters, continue to be regarded as delicacies.

For the dung see Brickell (1737: 186–7), who also described the migrations. In the 1670s Jasper Danickaerts wrote of numerous wild geese who "rose not in flocks of ten or twelve, or twenty or thirty, but continuously . . . and as they made room for us, there was such an incessant clattering made with their wings upon the water where they rose, and such a noise of those flying higher up, that it was as if we were all the time surrounded by a whirlwind or a storm . . . not only from geese, but from ducks and other water fowl." (Danckaerts 1679–80: 126). Similar observations of "black skies" can be seen in Byrd (1733: 152–3) and in the writings of later naturalists (cf. Matthiessen 1959).

26 Brickell (1737: 206). The official introduction of English pheasant is recorded much later, although correspondence by John Bordley asks for them to be sent to him from England in the 1700s.

27 Markham as quoted in Thomas 1983: 145.

28 See Martin Hall (1992: 392–5) for a South African example using archaeological data.

29 Brickell (1737: 181–2).

30 See Reitz 1988a. Original source material is from the Account Book of Charles Carroll where he entered in 1716: '12 turkeys bought by my wife at 2 shillings each: £1.04.00." (reprinted in the 1923 *Maryland Historical Magazine* 18: 220) and John Maccubbin Jr's inventory (Anne Arundel County Inventories, 1722, Liber 9: f. 169). Agricultural historian David Percy gave the planter's point of view: "lovers of roast turkey should not be put off from their feasting"; the gluts of worms which the turkeys ate came several months before the birds themselves were eaten (Percy 1984: 8).

31 Breen (1980: 156).

32 Geertz (1983: 125–9).

13. GENERATIONS OF CHANGE

1 Alexander Hamilton dedicated his *Itinerarium* to Razolini (Bridenbaugh 1948); the dancing lessons are mentioned in Homewood vs. Govane, Chancery Court Records, Liber IR: no. 5.

2 For information on the Stuart family see Stewart (1955). Margaret Callcott (1991) considered it unlikely that Admiral Vernon could have escorted Benedict because his naval duties took Vernon elsewhere in the late 1730s, but the critical years are before 1735 when there is some evidence that Vernon was in the colonies. More genealogical research is needed in English documents. In reading the court records about the 1735 assault (Anne Arundel County Court Proceedings, Judgments 1734–6, IB 2: f. 122), it is important to recognize that any minor (i.e., under the legal age of 18) was an "infant." The legal definition did not correspond with the folk use of the term *infant* for a very young child. Although no one knows who Benedict's mother was, rumors persist (Nicklin, 1980) that she was a sister of Prince Frederick, but this is unlikely for many reasons.

3 A coin dated 1752 was found in the clean sand placed at the base of the well after it was cleaned and repaired. Fines for tossing out broken bottles and other refuse "in the street before his door" were assessed against Benedict Calvert in 1754 and 1755 (Annapolis Records 1753–7: 32, 52). The fire is described in the *Maryland Gazette*, November 1, 1764 and was the second to strike the house.

4 See the addition to the inventory of Captain Charles Calvert filed in 1717 in Anne Arundel County Inventories, Liber 22: f. 341.

5 William Nevin first hired the stables and pastures (i.e., the land behind "Tabernacle" Street near St. John's) in 1764 (*Maryland Gazette* February 23, 1764); Richard Murrow leased them in 1766 (*Maryland Gazette* May 1, 1766). Wallace, Davidson, and Johnson advertised goods to be sold at the Calvert house in the *Maryland Gazette* (January 9, 1772; January 27, 1772).

6 For Governor Eden's garden see *Letters from America* (Eddis 1792). See Culver 1923. Culver describes Regulus as a black horse, son of Sharpe's Othello and sired by Godalphin; he draws on stud records kept by the Jockey Club of Maryland.

7 Owings (1953) gives the patronage jobs that Benedict Calvert held and also describes how the financial transactions in these offices produced incomes for Maryland men. Quote is from Abbé Robin (1783: 50–1). See *The Lords Baltimore and the Maryland Palatinate* (Hall 1904: 202) for a sanitized translation.

8 See Boucher (1738–89); Calvert (1885); and Stewart (1955).

9 Newman (1985: 164) reprinted information from the *Maryland Historical Magazine* that Alexander Stewart, a Jacobite, was sold to Benedict Calvert for £9, 6 shillings as soon as he arrived in 1747 and that "sympathetic friends purchased his freedom" immediately afterwards.

10 Quote from Abbé Robin (1783: 51). See Papenfuse (1975) for a detailed economic study of Annapolis' "Golden Era."

11 Owings (1953). Letter on file at the Historical Society of Pennsylvania (Grazt collection).

12 In 1770, during an impasse between the upper and lower house over fees, William Steuart, a clerk for Land Office judges, Benedict Calvert and George Steuart, accepted payments of fees larger than those designated by the Lower House (but of a size acceptable to the Upper House). When the Lower House jailed William Steuart (possibly George Steuart's youngest son) for doing so, Governor Robert Eden (Calvert's brother-in-law) prorogued the assembly, removed Steuart from its jurisdiction, and freed him (Hoffman 1973: 93). William accompanied his father to Scotland in 1775 and returned to Maryland after the War was over (Stewart 1955).

As collector of customs for the Patuxent, Calvert wrote to British authorities (Hoffman 1973: 133–8) describing the burning of the *Peggy Stewart*, whose owner, Anthony Stewart, had decided to pay the import fees on tea to the proprietary government; under threat from members of the popular party, Stewart burned the vessel and its cargo. By 1780, Maryland instituted a loyalty oath. Those who would not take it had to give parole for good conduct; their taxes were trebled, their arms were seized, and they were carefully watched (Hoffman 1973: 191). Maryland confiscated the land and other properties of 103 loyalists between 1781 and 1782 including those of Jonathan Boucher, Daniel Dulaney, and the Briscoes. More than 150 political dissenters saw their property seized by the end of the war, and approximately two third saw their lands and goods sold. Nonjurors (those who had not signed the Loyalty Oath) were among the first people approached when County commissioners had to obtain cattle, horses, or wagons for the military.

In 1780, Calvert added a codicil to his will that disinherited his son William. William does not appear in the family records afterwards.

George Calvert in his *Autobiographic Study* (1885) explained that Washington resigned his Commission at noon on December 23, 1783 and then left for home, but with night approaching and Mt. Vernon still 20 miles away, Washington decided to stay the night at Mt. Airy (Calvert 1885: 87).

13 George Calvert Sr. told his son how, at age 17–18, he "Used to start three hours before dawn, from his home, ride 20 miles to the Potomac, opposite Mt. Vernon, cross in the ferry boat, and fox-hunt with Washington alone . . . delighting in horses and outdoor life, the attraction was the hunt, not the renowned hunter." (1885: 85–6). Edward Henry married Elizabeth Briscoe, daughter of a loyalist.

14 Quote from Calvert (1885: 82). See Johnson (1905–8) or Callcott's (1991) *Mistress of Riverside* for further information on the nineteenth-century Calvert family.

15 Annapolis Mayors, Aldermen, and Councilman's Bylaws and Ordinances, 1779–1820 (MdHr 5157-1, #54); also see Annapolis Mayors, Aldermen, and Councilman's Proceedings, 1720–1843 (MdHr 5157-1: #84).

16 French troops, for example, damaged Logan's Wharf while leaving their transport ships; American forces did damage to the Carroll houses at their campgrounds on Charles Carroll the barrister's property, and elsewhere in Annapolis where officers were billeted, damages were paid. Sums ranged from £15 to £402 (see the initial accounts of the Treasurer of the Western Shore (MdHr 18: 9602) in 1781 and 1782 (folios 71, 82, 88, 109, 110, 113, 116) or the Auditor General's Ledger B2, 1 (1780–5: f. 342) for a summary (MdHr 18, 959), and include sums to Benedict Calvert for horses and for the house on State Circle. I am indebted to Andy Gallup for his initial work on this aspect of the study.

17 See Land (1981) and Hoffman (1973) for overviews of the political situation.

18 A similarly placed well was also filled and capped at State House Inn immediately after the War (Hopkins 1986).

19 The octagonal legislative privy was built in November 1786; its interior work was finished by cabinetmaker, John Shaw, for £100 (Radoff 1954: 45–6).

20 Sahlins (1985: xii).

21 See Sahlins (1985: xii).

14. CHARISMA AND THE SYMBOLICS OF POWER

1 Drawing on social theory, Geertz (1983: 123–46) applied the construct of charismatic power to anthropology; quote from Geertz (1983: 124).

2 Quotes from Geertz (1983: 124, 126–7).

3 Quote from Firth (1973: 40).

4 The social disorder that resulted in seventeenth-century Chesapeake society from high mortality, morbidity, an unbalanced sex ratio, an alien and hence unpredictable environment, and the ofttimes hostile indigenous natives provided ample opportunity to rework cultural practice into new forms.

5 See Land (1966) for a discussion of Maryland politics.

6 Bayard (1798: 35). Frances Trollope, who journeyed through Maryland in the 1820s found similar conditions (Trollope 1832: 241).

7 Quote from Isaac (1982).

8 Gilbert Falconer, a Quaker of Kent County, letter to Dr. Mortimer, Secretary of the Royal Society, May 14, 1733. *Archives of the Royal Society* LBC XV: 335–6.

9 See Anne Arundel Provincial Court Judgments, 1725, PL 7: f. 161. Unfortunately, it is one of the few places in the early documents where a particular set of activities can be seen and related to a specific black woman knowing that she exercised free choice. For this reason alone, the events surrounding Hannah's death are important. Yet, while the historical records of Hannah's trial do not give her motive, they do record how she did it. The murder was premeditated; she waited in the mansion house for Galloway until the early hours of the morning, and then she struck him with an ax, felling him with one strong blow to the head. While her motive is unknown, sexual abuse is one possibility. Estelle Freedman (1992: B2) notes that "during slavery, white owners assumed sexual access to black women." The idea that black women were sexual partners of slave-owners on a free and willing basis is one of the most trenchant elements of mytho-history. Angela Davis points out that sexual abuse was both used as a form of punishment by planters – "slavery relied as much on routine sexual abuse as it relied on the whip and the lash" – and that a fairly high incidence of testimony concerning it in slave narratives has been set aside in traditional historical literature (Davis 1981: 25, 175, but see Clinton 1991). In this case, as a Maryland slave, Hannah chose a particular form of action that many did not and would not; but it is important to acknowledge her choice, freely made, because it is evidence that women were capable of these choices. If women could exercise free choice in one realm, it also suggests that there were others – perhaps less visible in documentary records – where they may have behaved similarly. Toni Morrison wrote of such women as "salt tasters," willing to "take certain kinds of risks," to choose to behave in certain kinds of ways because they never lost their self-identity as a free person (Morrison 1983: 125).

10 See Bible, Book of Samuel (6: 14). Quote is from a letter by Elizabeth Spriggs to John Spriggs, Baltimore, 1756, reprinted in Cott (1972: 89–90) from: Isabel Calder (ed.) 1935, *Colonial Captivities, Marches and Journeys*, New York, Macmillan, pp. 151–2.

15. ARCHAEOLOGY AS ANTHROPOLOGICAL HISTORY

1 See Malinowski (1922: 25, 517) and Boon (1982: 8–20, also 156). Quote from Rabinow (1977: 150). Edmund Leach's *Social Anthropology* (1982) discusses these issues in a way that makes them easily understandable for non-anthropologists.

2 See Boon (1982: 6). Quote from Stanford (1986: 27) who draws on Holborn (1972: 79). Also see Sahlins (1985: 26–7).

3 See Carr (1961: 35) on the dialogue between past and present.

4 Young, quoted in Thomas (1963: 4); Gadamer (1979: 110).

5 Quote from Thomas (1989: 653). See also Leach (1982); Geertz (1973); Murphy (1971).

6 Quote from Geertz (1973: 52).

7 See Ortner (1990: 57). Quote from Sahlins (1985: vii).

8 Burke (1987: 31).

9 Quote is from Ohnuki-Tierney (1990: 24) whose introduction to *Culture Through Time* is pertinent.

10 Quote from Glassie (1975: 8).

11 Quote from Geertz (1980: 134), but the point is amplified in Ortner (1990: 60–3).

12 Quote from Stone (1967: 257).

13 Jarratt (1806: 14). For Edward Henry Calvert's inventory see Anne Arundel County Inventories, Liber 15: f. 570.

14 Cook (1708); Ostroff (1985: esp. p. 43).

15 Anne Arundel County Court Judgments Liber IB 2: f. 126.

16 See inventories for Samuel Chew (died ca. 1718) in Anne Arundel County Inventories, Liber 1; f. 469 and Samuel Chew (died ca. 1737) in Anne Arundel County Inventories Liber 23: f. 218–27 (esp. 223–4). For a discussion of Maryland's laws re children of mixed unions see Jordan (1962: 184) or Kilthy (1799–1800).

17 For quote see a letter to Dr. Mortimer, Secretary of the Royal Society, May 14, 1733, from Gilbert Falconer, a Quaker of Kent County, MD, *Archives of the Royal Society* LBC XV: 336. For the Eurocentric view of women see Power (1975), Lerner (1975), or Norton (1989).

18 For African folktales about women that contain values different from those in a European world view, see the work of Kosak (1986) or Kosak and Kosak (1988: 385). See Brown (1991: 76–8, 86–7); Collins (1991: 44–5); Greene (1990); Wade-Gayles (1991: 225).

19 J. F. D. Smyth (1784, vol I: 75).

20 Lévi-Strauss (1987: 30-1).

21 Turner (1949). Mencken gives the early twentieth-century name (1936: 525). Quote from Menard (1975: 39).

22 For list see Kemble (1863: 229–31).

23 See Byrd (1733: 184). Pottery is also a particularly rich source of symbolism in many cultures. For example, Barbara Babcock's description (1986: 326) of potter Helen Codiero makes it very clear that ceramics within Pueblo culture are not "mere things or lifeless artifacts." Among the Pueblo, every phase of pottery making includes interaction with "Clay Mother." Helen Codiero puts it this way: "I don't just get up in the morning and start making potteries. First, I go and talk to Grandma Clay." Babcock writes that "every piece of clay that is not used or that is sanded away or broken in the fire is carefully saved and taken back to the river," because the river is "the repository for all sacred substances no longer of use." Noting that this ritual destroys the ceramic debitage

archaeologists often study, Babcock draws attention to archaeologists' dependence on ceramic evidence while stressing that by considering only one facet of it, and by neglecting its social and mythic roles, pottery remains an under-utilized set of information about past lifeways. The point is important for historical archaeologists who work on Euroamerican sites because the type of relationship between substance and pot seen among the Pueblos did not extend to English potters, but may have characterized in different form that between African-born women and the pots they or their descendants made which appear on American sites associated with slavery. Africanists today note the symbolism of African pottery (cf., Blier [1987: 210] who found that "each of the principal female visual metaphors (the calabash, bowl, and the jar, among others) is circular. Accordingly, a frequent metaphor for the womb is a jar. "The jar has broken," one will say when a woman aborts.")

24 Quotes from the diary of Dr. John Rutty (1753–74), reprinted in Ponsonby (1923: 215–16). Table 15.3 is extracted from a 1729 essay by Rev. Henley reprinted on the front page of the *Maryland Historical Gazette* in July 1729, an issue that coincided with the opening of a legislative session under Governor Benedict Leonard Calvert.

25 See Geertz (1973: 53); Mencken (1927: 198–9); Tobosun Sowande, quoted by Stuckey (1987: 193).

26 Glassie (1982: 33).

27 Beaudry *et al.* (1991: 160).

28 Rosaldo (1980: 24). Quote in following paragraph is from the Prince George's County Court Judgments 1728, Book O: 413–15.

29 Hall (1992: 377) further contrasts discourse with structuralism: "A structuralist analysis of Westover would put the Byrds in the background to delight in the symmetry of facade and the house's offices, in the metaphor of height for status, and in the homologies of privy, house, and courtroom. This structured system would be seen as a material representation of the Enlightenment Mind, similarly represented by the Georgian mansions of England, Mozart's music, Jane Austen's novels, and formal gardens. A discursive analysis, in contrast, would thrust William Byrd and his son back into the foreground. It would see them as patriarchal members of a ruling class, using the semiotics of architecture over both family and their large holdings of slaves. It would introduce as evidence William Byrd II's diaries to show the conflict between his public emphasis on order and his continual debauchery, or the way his rampant sexuality complemented his material world in his struggle for control. Together, the material world of Westover and the actions of patriarch, family, and slaves would be statements in a discourse."

16. ARCHAEOLOGY, A TOPOLOGICAL DISCOURSE

1 It was fairly common to sell a deceased person's goods in Annapolis and the records contain accounts of these auctions. Governor Benedict Leonard

Calvert's property, for example, was sold and it is notable that the largest quantity was purchased by the new Governor, Samuel Ogle.

2 Leach (1976).

3 Leach (1982: 183) explains that the start of a marriage is frequently an "occasion for a transfer of valuables in the form of wedding presents, marriage settlements, token gifts." When these gifts are given by the groom's family to the bride's, anthropologists speak of them as a "bride-price." They confer legitimacy on the marriage and the higher their value, the more honor the bride possesses. These exchanges are seen cross-culturally. John Mbiti (1969: 140) explains their importance in African cultures: "The gift is in the form of cattle, money, food-stuffs and other articles. In some societies the families concerned may exchange brides. In others, the bridegroom (and his relatives) must in addition contribute labour; and in matrilocal societies the man lives with his parents-in-law working for them for some years in order to 'earn' his wife.

This marriage gift is an important institution in African societies. It is a token of gratitude on the part of the bridegroom's people to those of the bride, for their care over her and for allowing her to become his wife. At her home the gift "replaces" her, reminding the family that she will leave or has left and yet she is not dead. She is a valuable person not only to her family but to her husband's people. The gift elevates the value attached to her both as a person and as a wife. The gift legalizes her value and the marriage contract. The institution of this practice is the most concrete symbol of the marriage covenant and security . . . African words for the practice of giving the marriage gift are, in most cases, different from words used in buying and selling something in the market place . . . the girl's people also give gifts in return, even if these may be materially smaller than those of the man. The two families are involved in a relationship which, among other things, demands an exchange of material and other gifts."

4 Thomas Hearne quoted in Walker (1813: 512).

5 Anne Arundel County Court Judgments, 1734, Liber IB 1: f. 278.

6 Anne Arundel County Court Judgments, 1734, Liber IB 1: f. 43.

7 Anne Arundel County Court Judgments, 1734, Liber IB 1: f. 387.

8 Anne Arundel County Court Judgments, 1735, Liber IB 1: f. 428.

9 Anne Arundel County Court Judgments, 1734, Liber IB 1: f. 12.

10 Anne Arundel County Court Judgments, 1734, Liber IB 1: f. 13.

11 From Wallace Stegner's *Mormon Country*, 1942, Duell, Sloan & Pearce, Inc., quoted by Kluckhohn (1949: 47). The petition of "Indian Tom" can be found in Prince George's County Judgments, Book O: f. 413. "Thomas India" was given his freedom in October 1730 (Provincial Court Judgements, RB 2, 1: f. 571–2).

12 Deetz began this endeavor with his dissertation research of the 1950s, published as "*The Arikara*," (1964); it can be seen throughout his books (1967, 1977a, 1993).

13 See Glassie (1982: 11).

14 These ideas are laid forth in Harrington (1955) and Noël Hume (1978), both of whom adopt Childe's (1944) position that archaeology turns into history whenever it remembers that the objects it studies embody the thoughts and intentions of human beings and societies. Many, however, now emphasize the tie to anthropology. An early review of the two points of view was given by Schuyler in 1970 with the caveat that no matter how well trained in historiography an archaeologist might be, it would not make her a historian (cf., Schuyler 1978: 29). See Whittenberg (1982, 1987) for a different opinion.

15 For Jamestown, see Cotter 1958. For ways that Chesapeake archaeology initially defined the discipline, see Schuyler (1978), and the work of Ivor Noël Hume who insisted that historical archaeologists know their artifacts (Noël Hume 1969a) and how to tackle specific kinds of field problems (Noël Hume 1969b); for recent influences see Carson *et al.* (1981) or Upton (1982b, 1988) for architecture; Noël Hume (1982) for archaeological narrative and superb field techniques; Kelso (1984a) for thrusting landscape analysis forward, building upon A. Noël Hume (1974). Kelso and Most (1990) and Yamin and Metheny (1994) contain state-of-the-art garden archaeology for the region while Martin (1991) synthesizes it with garden history. For landscape's link with anthropology see Yentsch (1984a, 1990a); Yentsch *et al.* (1987), with Marxist analysis (Leone 1984; Leone *et al.* 1989; Kryder-Reid 1991, 1993), and with broad-based overview of the articulation of town plans or community foci see Yentsch (1984b, 1990d); Yentsch and McKee (1987); Miller (1988b). For an excellent study done in Anne Arundey County by a committed, but amateur archaeologist, see the study of Mareen Duvall's plantation by Doepkens (1991). And for one done by a past master see Deetz (1993).

Kelso (1984b) summarizes the work of the Virginia Historic Landmarks Commission at Kingsmill while Kelso (1986) reviews the beginnings of a growing interest in African Americans – a research area also given impetus by Deetz's students and colleagues (McKee 1987, 1988; Emerson 1988; Hall 1992); see also Yentsch and Beaudry (1992), Epperson (1990) or Singleton (n.d.) for reviews. King and Miller (1987) or Pogue (1988) are good explications of spatial and midden analysis; its genesis can be seen in the path-breaking work of Keeler (1978). Neiman's early work is also strategic (1978, 1980). A series of zoo-archaeological studies by Henry Miller (1984, 1986b, 1988a) provides the foundation for the Chesapeake while Bowen (1993) and Yentsch (1992) show the integration of textually-derived ethnographic observations into faunal analysis. Similar material and analysis appeared first in ceramic studies in the region (cf., Beaudry 1980, 1988; Beaudry *et al.* 1983; Stone 1977). Garry Wheeler Stone also published one of the first minimum vessel lists in historical archaeology (Stone *et al.* 1973); George Miller's stellar research on nineteenth-century ceramics derives from studies begun at St. Mary's City (Miller 1974). Closely allied with the archaeological studies of the Chesapeake are studies of vernacular architecture by Glassie (1975), Chappell and Patrick (1991) and

Upton (1982a, 1982c, 1987, 1988, 1990); this type of research is integrated with archaeology by Stone (1987, 1990). Feminist studies in the region started in the mid 1980s (cf. Gibb and King 1991; Yentsch 1987, 1990b, 1991b, 1991c). Leone brought critical theory into the fold (Leone 1984; Leone, Potter and Shackel 1987) while Little and Shackel (1989) and Kryder-Reid (forthcoming) show the growing influence of post-processual scholarship. The varied emphases of urban archaeology are captured in the work of Norman (1987) and Weber *et al.* (1990); Potter (1989) shows how urban archaeologists have merged their work with public interpretation. As well, there is a series of substantive reports produced by the major museums together with a healthy series of published studies on endangered sites (cf., Hazzard and McCartney 1987; Outlaw 1990; Pogue 1991) and a growing body of masters' theses and dissertations.

16 For a specific example of how taphonomic processes impacted the ethnobotanical remains at the Calvert site see N. Miller (1989); for an overview vis-à-vis faunal remains see Landon (1991a, 1991b).

17 The interpretive position is set forth by a number of scholars (cf., Rabinow and Sullivan 1979), including philosophers with knowledge of archaeology (Collingwood 1946), anthropologists like Clifford Geertz (1973), Paul Rabinow (1977); Greg Dening (1988); see also Marcus and Fisher (1986) or Clifford and Marcus (1986). The quotes are drawn from Glassie (1978:1) and Zora Mae Hurston (1942: 1).

18 Leach (1982) gives a synopsis of his perspective in a small, highly readable book, *Social Anthropology*, which comments briefly on the value of archaeological knowledge to anthropologists.

19 See Peacock (1986) or Rosaldo (1989). Also pertinent is Dening's warning: "be wary of the history that claims to be separate from the circumstances of its telling or to have only one meaning" (1988: 15).

20 See, for example, Yentsch (1990a), Yentsch and Kratzer (1994), Bescherer-Metheny *et al.* (1994).

21 Noël Hume (1974: 1–5). Letter from Benedict Leonard Calvert to Charles Calvert, August 1724.

22 Letter from Benedict Leonard Calvert to Charles Calvert, August 1724.

23 After a successful opening season in 1982 in which Archaeology in Annapolis drew thousands of visitors (tourists and townspeople) at sites in the Historic District, Governor Donald Schaeffer (then Mayor of Baltimore) quickly moved to institute a similar program in his city at sites in a downtown area where increased pedestrian traffic, drawn by the archaeology "exhibits," would have beneficial economic results for neighboring business establishments. Thus the Baltimore archaeological program was developed in the fall of 1982 with the opening of the Great Brewery Dig in the Jones Falls region of the city in 1983, but drawing fewer visitors than anticipated.

24 Quotes are from Glassie (1982: xvi).

25 Quote is from Patrik (1985: 52–4). A provocative discussion of pots as termite traps and shelters for the soul is contained in Jody Sterner's work (1989) which

turns around the methodological problems observed by Patrik (1985) and presents them in a slightly different way.

26 The connection between pots and people is one also made today in different African countries (cf., Welbourn 1984: 20; Blier 1987). Also see Upton (1988, 1990); Sobel (1979, 1988); Yentsch (1992) for the ways that African and European behavior patterns melded together, yet also co-existed, maintaining cultural integrity.

27 See Merrill (1989) and for quotes Merrill (1979: 567) and Boon (1982: ix).

28 See Taylor (1971).

29 Deetz (1977, 1993); Isaac (1982); Hall (1992); Hodder (1982, 1985 or 1987). Rhys Isaac helped me to clarify ideas on this topic and I thank him for doing so.

30 See Upton (1992).

31 Collingwood (1935: 11).

32 Quoted in Jean Lee, (1994), p. 313, footnote 83.

33 Quotes are from Oldmixon (1708, volume I: 206); Everstine (1980: 228) and a 1729 letter of Benedict Leonard Calvert to Thomas Hearne reprinted in the *Maryland Historical Magazine* (1916, 11: 282).

Abrahams, Roger D. 1983. *The Man-of-Words in the West Indies: Performance and the Emergence of Creole Culture*. Baltimore, Md., Johns Hopkins University Press.

Achebe, Chinua. 1958. *Things Fall Apart*. London, Heinemann.

Adams, William H., ed. 1987. Historical Archaeology of Plantations at Kings Bay, Camden County, Georgia. *Report of Investigations No. 5*. Report submitted to Naval Submarine Base, U.S. Department of the Navy, Kings Bay, Georgia, by Department of Anthropology, University of Florida, Gainesville.

Adanson, Michel. 1759. *A Voyage to Senegal, the Isle of Goree, and the River Gambia. Translated from the French with Notes by an English Gentleman who Resided Some Time in that Country.* London, J. Nourse.

Addison, Joseph. 1718. *Remarks on Several Parts of Italy, etc., in the Years 1701, 1702, 1703.* London, J. Johnson.

Agricola, G. A. 1719. *The Artificial Gardener: Being a Discovery of a New Invention for the Sudden Growth of all Sorts of Trees and Plants.* London (translated from the High Dutch).

Allen, Rev. Ethan. 1857. *Historical Notices of St. Anne's Parish.* Baltimore, Md., J. P. des Forges.

Andrews, Mrs. Lewis R. and Mrs. J. Reaney Kelly. 1963. *Maryland's Way: The Hammond-Harwood House Cook Book.* Annapolis, Md., The Hammond-Harwood House Association.

Anonymous. 1635. A Relation of Maryland. London. Reprinted in *Original Narratives of Early Maryland.* C. C. Hall, ed. Facsimile edition. Bowie, Md., Heritage Books, Inc., 1988.

   1755. An account of the number of souls in Maryland in the year 1755. *Gentleman's Magazine* 34 (June 1764): 261.

Armstrong, Douglas V. 1990. *The Old Village and the Great House: An Archaeological and Historical Examination of Drax Hall Plantation, St. Ann's Bay, Jamaica.* Urbana, University of Illinois Press.

Astley, Thomas, 1745–1747. *Collection of Voyages and Travels.* London. 4 volumes.

Aubry, John. 1669–1696. *"Brief Lives" Chiefly of Contemporaries, Set Down by John Aubry between the Years 1669 and 1696, Volume 1.* Andrew Clark, ed. Oxford, Clarendon Press, 1898.

Axtell, James. 1981. *The European and the Indian: Essays in the Ethnohistory of Colonial North America.* New York, Oxford University Press.

Babcock, Barbara A. 1986. Modeled selves: Helen Cordero's "little people". In *The Anthropology of Experience.* Victor W. Turner and Edward M. Bruner, eds., pp. 316–44. Urbana, University of Illinois Press.

Baker, Nancy T. 1982. The manufacture of ship chandlery in Annapolis, Maryland: 1735–1770. *The Chronicle of the Early American Industries Association* 34 (4): 61–71.

   1984. The early population of Annapolis: land development in Annapolis, 1670–1776. In *Final Report on NEH Grant RS-20199-81-1955: Annapolis and Anne Arundel County, Maryland: A Study of Urban Development in a Tobacco Economy, 1649–1776.* Lorena S.

Walsh, ed. Unpublished report on file at the Historic Annapolis Foundation, Annapolis, Maryland.

1986. Annapolis over the first two generations, 1695–1730. *Maryland Historical Magazine* 81 (3): 191–209.

Barber, Michael. 1976. The vertebrate fauna from a late eighteenth-century well: the Bray Plantation, Kingsmill, Virginia. *Historical Archaeology* 10: 68–72.

Barbot, John. 1732. A description of the coasts of North and South Guinea. In *A Collection of Voyages and Travels*. Awmsham Churchill, ed., London, volume 5.

Barclay, Alexander. 1828. *Slavery in the West Indies*. Reprint. Miami, Mnemosine Publishing Co., 1969.

Barker, Charles. 1940. *The Background of the Revolution in Maryland*. New Haven, Yale University Press.

Bartram, William. 1791. *The Travels of William Bartram*. Naturalist's Edition, Francis Harper, ed. New Haven, Yale University Press, 1967.

Bayard, Ferdinand M. 1798. *Travels of a Frenchman in Maryland and Virginia . . . in 1791 . . .*, Ben C. McCary, ed. and trans. Ann Arbor, Michigan, Edwards Bros., 1950.

Beaudry, Mary C. 1980. "Or What Else You Please to Call It": Folk Semantic Domains in Early Virginia Probate Inventories. Ph.D. dissertation. Department of Anthropology, Brown University. Ann Arbor, University Microfilms International.

1988. Words for things: linguistic analysis of probate inventories. In *Documentary Archaeology in The New World*, Mary C. Beaudry, ed., pp. 43–50. Cambridge University Press, Cambridge.

Beaudry, Mary C., Janet Long, Henry Miller, Fraser Neiman, and Garry Wheeler Stone. 1983. A vessel typology for early Chesapeake ceramics: the Potomac typological system. *Historical Archaeology* 17 (1): 18–42. Reprinted as Chapter 5 in *Documentary Archaeology in The New World*, Mary C. Beaudry, ed., pp. 51–67. Cambridge, Cambridge University Press, 1988.

Beaudry, Mary C., Lauren J. Cook, and Stephen A. Mrozowski. 1991. Artifacts and active voices: material culture as social discourse. In *The Archaeology of Inequality*. Randall H. McGuire and Robert Paynter, eds., pp. 150–91. Oxford, Basil Blackwell.

Beckett, J. V. 1986. *The Aristocracy in England, 1660–1914*. Oxford, Basil Blackwell.

Belden, Louise C. 1983. *The Festive Tradition: Table Decoration and Desserts in America, 1650–1900*. New York, W. W. Norton & Co.

Benezet, Anthony. 1772. *Some Historical Accounts of Guinea, its Situation, Produce, and the General Disposition of its Inhabitants with an Inquiry into the Rise and Progress of the Slave Trade, its Nature, and Lamentable Effects*. 1788 edition, London, J. Philips. Facsimile. London, Frank Cass & Co., Ltd., 1968.

Benson, Evelyn A. 1966. *Penn Family Recipes: Cooking Recipes of William Penn's Wife, Gulielma*. York, Pennsylvania, George Shumway Publisher.

Berlin, Ira. 1980. Time, space and the evolution of Afro-American society on British mainland North America. *Historical Review* 85: 44–78.

Bescherer, Karen. 1989. Report on field testing at the William Paca House on Wye Island. Report on file Historic Annapolis Foundation, Annapolis, Maryland.

Beverley, Robert. 1705. *The History and Present State of Virginia*. London, R. Parker. Edited with an introduction by Louis B. Wright, University of North Carolina Press for the Institute of Early American History and Culture, Williamsburg, Virginia, 1947.

Black, V. 1983. Beddington: "The first orangery in England." *Journal of Garden History* 3 (2): 113–20.

Black, William. 1744. Journal. R. A. Brock, ed. *Pennsylvania Magazine of History and Biography* 1 (2): 126–30 (1877).

Blaszczyk, Regina Lee. 1984. Ceramics and the sot-weed factor: the China market in a tobacco economy. *Winterthur Portfolio* 19 (1): 7–19.

Blier, Suzanne P. 1987. *The Anatomy of Architecture: Ontology and Metaphor in Batammaliba Architectural Expression*. Cambridge, Cambridge University Press.

Bloch, Marc. 1953. *The Historian's Craft*. Translated from the French by Peter Putnam. New York, Vintage Books.

Bloch, Maurice. 1985. From cognition to ideology. In *Power and Knowledge*, Richard Fardon, ed., pp. 21-48. Edinburgh, Scottish Academic Press.

Bohannan, Paul. 1964. *Africa and Africans*. Garden City, New York, Natural History Press.

Bolzius, Johann Martin. 1751. Reliable answers . . . [Johann Martin Bolzius answers a questionnaire on Carolina and Georgia]. Translated by Klaus G. Loewald, Beverly Starika, and Paul S. Taylor. *William and Mary Quarterly*, third series, 14: 218-61 [1957].

Boon, James A. 1982. *Other Tribes, Other Scribes: Symbolic Anthropology in the Comparative Study of Cultures, Histories, Religions, and Texts*. Cambridge, Cambridge University Press.

Bosman, William. 1705. *A New and Accurate Description of the Coast of Guinea . . .* 2nd edition. London, J. Knapton, 1721.

Boucher, Jonathan. 1738–1789. *Reminiscences of an American Loyalist, 1738–1789*. Edited by his grandson, Jonathan Boucher. Boston, Houghton Mifflin Company, 1925.

Bowen, Joanne V. 1989. Preliminary Notes on the House for Families Faunal Assemblage. Unpublished report on file at Mt. Vernon Ladies Association, Mt. Vernon, Va.

   1990. A Study of Seasonality and Subsistence: Eighteenth Century Suffield, Connecticut. Ph.D. dissertation, Department of Anthropology, Brown University. Ann Arbor, University Microfilms International.

   1991. The relative importance of beef and pork in the colonial diet. Paper presented to The 1991 Annual Meeting, Society for Historical Archaeology, Richmond, Virginia.

   1992. Faunal remains and urban household subsistence in New England. In *The Art and Mystery of Historical Archaeology: Essays in Honor of James Deetz*. Anne E. Yentsch and Mary C. Beaudry, eds., pp. 267-81. Boca Raton, Florida, CRC Press.

   1993. A comparative analysis of the New England and Chesapeake herding systems: the relative dietary importance of beef and dairy products. In *Chesapeake Archaeology*, Barbara Little and Paul Shackel, eds. Washington, D.C., Smithsonian Institution Press, forthcoming.

Bowles, John. 1983. *The Diary of John Evelyn*. Oxford, Oxford University Press.

Brackett, Jeffrey R. 1889. *The Negro in Maryland: A Study of the Institution of Slavery*. Reprint, New York, Negro University Press, 1969.

Bradley, Richard. 1724. *New Improvements of Plants and Gardening*. London, W. Mears.

   1725. *A Survey of Ancient Husbandry and Gardening . . . Collected from Cato, Varro, Columella, Virgil, and Others, the Most Eminent Writers among the Greeks, Romans: Wherein Many of the Most Difficult Passages in Those Authors are Explained*. London, B. Motte.

Brait, Susan. 1990. *Chesapeake Gold: Man and Oyster on the Bay*. Lexington, University Press of Kentucky.

Breen, Timothy. 1977. Horses and gentlemen: the significance of gambling among the gentry of Virginia. *William and Mary Quarterly*, third series, 34: 239-57.

   1980. *Puritans and Adventurers: Change and Persistence in Early America*. New York, Oxford University Press.

   1985. *Tobacco Culture: The Mentality of the Great Tidewater Planters on the Eve of the Revolution*. Princeton, Princeton University Press.

   1986. Creative adaptions: peoples and cultures. In *Colonial British America: Essays in the New History of the Early Modern Era*, Jack P. Greene and J. R. Pole, eds., pp. 195-232. Baltimore, Md., Johns Hopkins University Press.

   1988. Baubles of Britain: the American and consumer revolutions of the eighteenth century. *Past and Present* 119: 93-104.

Brickell, John. 1737. *The Natural History of North-Carolina*. London. New York, Johnson Reprint, 1969.

Bridenbaugh, Carl. 1948. *Gentleman's Progress: The Itinerarium of Dr. Alexander Hamilton, 1744*. University of North Carolina, Chapel Hill for the Institute of Early American History and Culture, Williamsburg, Virginia.

Britton, J. C. and C. R. Zappone, Jr. 1917. Soils of Anne Arundel County. In *Anne Arundel County*, pp. 133–61. Baltimore, Md., Maryland Geological Survey.

Brown, Elsa Barkley. 1989. African-American women's quilting: a framework for conceptualizing and teaching African-American women's history. *Signs* 14 (4): 921–9.

1991. Mothers of mind. In *Double Stitch: Black Women Write About Mothers and Daughters*. Patricia Bell-Scott, Beverly Guy-Sheftall *et al.*, eds., pp. 74–93. Boston, Beacon Press.

Brown, Gregory. 1989. The faunal remains from the John Draper well: an investigation in historic period zooarchaeology. Unpublished M.A. thesis, Department of Anthropology, San Francisco State University, San Francisco.

Browne, William Hand. 1884. *Maryland: The History of a Palatinate*. Boston, Houghton Mifflin & Co.

1890. *George and Cecilius Calvert*. New York, Dodd, Mead & Co.

Bruce, Anthony. 1980. *The Purchase System in the British Army, 1660–1871*. London, Royal Historical Society.

Burke, Peter. 1987. *The Historical Anthropology of Early Modern Italy: Essays on Perception and Communication*. Cambridge, Cambridge University Press.

Burnard, Trevor G. 1988. A Colonial Elite: Wealthy Marylanders, 1691–1776. Ph.D. dissertation, Department of History, Johns Hopkins University. Ann Arbor, University Microfilms International.

Bush, Barbara. 1990. *Slave Women in Caribbean Society 1650–1838*. Bloomington, Indiana University Press.

Byrd, William, II. 1733. History of the Dividing Line. Reprinted in *A Journey to the Land of Eden and Other Papers*. New York, Macy-Masius, 1928.

1731–1776. Correspondence. In *The Correspondence of the Three William Byrds of Westover, Virginia, 1684–1776, volume II*. Edited by Marion Trinley with a foreword by Louis B. Wright. Charlottesville, University Press of Virginia, 1977.

Callcott, Margaret. 1991. *Mistress of Riverside*. Baltimore, Md., Johns Hopkins University Press.

Calvert, George. 1885. *Autobiographic Study*. Privately printed [available at the Reference Library, Maryland Historical Society, Baltimore, Md.].

Campbell, Thomas E. 1954. *Colonial Caroline: A History of Caroline County, Virginia*. Richmond, Virginia, Dietz Press.

Cannon, John. 1985. *Aristocratic Century: The Peerage of Eighteenth-Century England*. Cambridge, Cambridge University Press.

Caputo, Robert. 1991. Zaire River: lifeline of a nation. *National Geographic* 180 (5): 5–35.

Carman, Harry J., ed. 1775. *American Husbandry*. London. Reprint. Port Washington, New York, Kennikat Press, 1964.

Carmichael, Mrs. A. C. 1833. *Domestic Manners and Social Conditions of the White, Coloured and Negro Populations of the West Indies*. 2 vols. London, Whittaker, Treache & Co.

Carr, Edward H. 1961. *What is History?* New York, Random House, Vintage Books.

Carr, Lois Green. 1968. County Government in Maryland, 1689–1709. Ph.D. dissertation, Department of History, Harvard University. Ann Arbor, University Microfilms International.

1973. Ceramics from the John Hicks Site, 1723–1743: The St. Mary's Town Landing Community. In *Ceramics in America*. Ian M. G. Quimby, ed., pp. 75–101. Charlottesville, University of Virginia Press.

1974. "The metropolis of Maryland": a comment on town development along the tobacco coast. *Maryland Historical Magazine* 69 (2): 124–45.

1987. Adaptation and Settlement in the Colonial Chesapeake. St. Mary's City Research Series No. 6. Historic St. Mary's City, St. Mary's City, Maryland.

1988. Diversification in the colonial Chesapeake: Somerset County, Maryland in comparative perspective. In *Colonial Chesapeake Society*. Lois Green Carr, Philip D. Morgan, and Jean B. Russo, eds., pp. 342–88. Chapel Hill, University of North Carolina Press for the Institute of Early American History and Culture, Williamsburg, Virginia.

1992. From servant to freeholder revisited: emigration to the seventeenth-century Chesapeake and the standard of living. Paper presented to the Washington Area Seminar in Early American History, February 6, 1992. Manuscript on file, Maryland State Archives, Annapolis, Maryland.

Carr, Lois Green and David W. Jordan. 1974. *Maryland's Revolution of Government, 1689–1692*. Ithaca, New York, Cornell University Press.

Carr, Lois Green and Russell R. Menard. 1989. Land, labor, and economies of scale in early Maryland: some limits to growth in the Chesapeake system of husbandry. *Journal of Economic History* 49 (2): 407–18.

Carr, Lois Green and Lorena S. Walsh. 1977. The planter's wife: the experience of white women in seventeenth-century Maryland. *William and Mary Quarterly*, third series, 34: 542–71.

1978. Changing life styles in colonial St. Mary's county. *Regional Economic History Research Center Working Papers* 50 (3): 72–118.

1980. Inventories and the analysis of wealth and consumption patterns in St. Mary's county, Maryland, 1658–1777. *Historical Methods* 13: 96–100.

1988a. Economic diversification and labor organization in the Chesapeake, 1650–1820. In *Work and Labor in Early America*. Stephen Innes, ed., pp. 144–88. Chapel Hill, University of North Carolina Press for the Institute of Early American History and Culture, Williamsburg, Virginia.

1988b. The transformation of production on the farm and in the household in the Chesapeake, 1658–1820. *Working Papers in Social History, Department of History, University of Minnesota* 1988 (3).

1993. Consumer behavior in the colonial Chesapeake. In *Of Consuming Interests: The Style of Life in the Eighteenth Century*. Cary Carson, Ronald Hoffman, and P. Albert, eds. Charlottesville, University Press of Virginia, forthcoming.

Carr, Lois Green, Russell R. Menard, and Lorena S. Walsh. 1991. *Robert Cole's World: Agriculture and Society in Early Maryland*. Chapel Hill, University of North Carolina Press for the Institute of Early American History and Culture, Williamsburg, Virginia.

Carr, Lois Green, Philip D. Morgan, and Jean B. Russo (eds.). 1988. *Colonial Chesapeake Society*. Chapel Hill, University of North Carolina Press for the Institute of Early American History and Culture, Williamsburg, Virginia.

Carson, Barbara, and Cary Carson. 1976. Styles and Standards of Living in Southern Maryland, 1670–1752. Paper presented at the Southern Historical Association, Atlanta, Ga., November 1976.

Carson, Cary. 1974. The "Virginia House" in Maryland. *Maryland Historical Magazine* 69: 185–96.

Carson, Cary, and Lorena S. Walsh. 1981. The Material Life of the Early American Housewife. Paper presented to the Conference on Women in Early America. Forthcoming, *Winterthur Portfolio*.

Carson, Cary, Norman F. Barka, William M. Kelso, Garry W. Stone, and Dell Upton. 1981. Impermanent architecture in the southern American colonies. *Winterthur Portfolio* 16: 135–96.

Carson, Cary, Ronald Hoffman, and Peter Albert. eds. *Of Consuming Interests: The Style of Life in the Eighteenth Century.* Charlottesville, University Press of Virginia, 1994

Carter, Landon. 1752–1778. *The Diary of Colonel Landon Carter of Sabine Hall, 1752–1778.* Jack P. Green, ed. 2 vols. Charlottesville, University Press of Virginia, 1965.

Carter, Susannah. 1772. *The Frugal Colonial Housewife or Complete Woman Cook.* American edition. Boston, Edes and Gill. Dolphin edition, Garden City, New York, Doubleday, 1976.

Chappell, Edward. 1989. Slave housing. *Fresh Advices*, A research supplement to *The Interpreter newsletter* (Colonial Williamsburg Foundation): i–iv.

    1989. Social responsibility and the American history museum. *Winterthur Portfolio* 24 (4): 247–65.

Chappell, Edward and Vanessa Patrick. 1991. Architecture, archaeology, and slavery in the early Chesapeake. Paper presented to the 1991 Annual Meeting, Society for Historical Archaeology, Richmond, Virginia.

Chase, T. L. 1868. Records of the Hominy Club. *American Historical Review for 1868*: 295–303, 348–55.

Childe, V. Gordon. 1944. *Progress and Archaeology.* London, Watts.

Childs, Arney R. ed. 1953. *Rice Planter and Sportsman: The Recollections of J. Motte Alston, 1820–1909.* Columbia, University of South Carolina Press.

Clapperton, H. 1829. *Journal of a Second Expedition into the Interior of Africa.* Philadelphia, Carey, Lea, and Carey.

Clemens, Paul G. E. 1980. *The Atlantic Economy and Colonial Maryland's Eastern Shore.* Ithaca, Cornell University Press.

Clifford, James and George E. Marcus. 1986. *Writing Culture: The Poetics and Politics of Ethnography.* Berkeley, University of California Press.

Clinton, Catherine. 1991. "Southern dishonor": flesh, blood, race, and bondage. In *In Joy and In Sorrow: Women, Family, and Marriage in the Victorian South.* Carol Bleser, ed., pp. 52–68. New York, Oxford University Press.

Coats, A. M. 1973. The fruit with a shady past. *Country Life*, May 1973: 17.

Collingwood, Robin G. 1935. *The Historical Imagination.* Oxford, Oxford University Press.

    1946. *The Idea of History.* Oxford, Oxford University Press.

Collins, Patricia Hill. 1989. The social construction of black feminist thought. *Signs* 14 (4): 745–73.

    1991. The meaning of motherhood in black culture and black mother–daughter relationships. In *Double Stitch: Black Women Write About Mothers and Daughters.* Patricia Bell-Scott, Beverly Guy-Sheftall, *et al.*, eds., pp. 42–62. Boston, Beacon Press.

Columella, L. J. M. 1745. *Of Husbandry in Twelve Books and His Book Concerning Trees (de Arboribus).* London, A. Miller.

Cook, Ebenezer. 1708. *The Sot-Weed Factor: or a Voyage to Maryland.* London. Reprint, Baltimore, Maryland, Maryland Historical Society Fund-Publication No. 36, 1900.

Corfield, P. J. 1987. Class by name and number in eighteenth-century Britain. *History, Journal of the Historical Association* 72: 38–61.

Corry, Joseph. 1806. *Observations upon the Windward Coast of Africa, 1805 and 1806.* Facsimile. London, Frank Cass & Co., 1968.

Cott, Nancy F., ed. 1972. *Roots of Bitterness: Documents of the Social History of American Women.* New York, Dutton.

Cotter, John L. 1958. *Archaeological Excavations at Jamestown, Virginia.* Archaeological Research Series No. 4, National Park Service, U.S. Department of the Interior, Washington, D.C.

Crabtree, Pamela J. 1989. Zooarchaeology and complex societies: some uses of faunal analysis for the study of trade, social status, and ethnicity. In *Archaeological Method and Theory*, vol. II, Michael B. Schiffer, ed., pp. 155–205. Tucson, University of Arizona Press.

Crader, Diane. 1984. The zooarchaeology of the storehouse and the dry well at Monticello. *American Antiquity* 49 (3): 542–58.

  1989. Faunal remains from slave quarter sites at Monticello, Charlottesville, Virginia. *Archaeozoologia* 3: 1–12.

  1990. Slave diet at Monticello. *American Antiquity* 55 (4): 690–717.

Cronin, L. Eugene. 1973. Foreword. In *The Chesapeake Bay in Maryland*, edited and illustrated by Alice Jane Lipson for the Natural Resources Institute of the University of Maryland. Baltimore, Md., Johns Hopkins University Press.

Cronon, William. 1983. *Changes in the Land: Indians, Colonists, and the Ecology of New England*. New York, Hill and Wang.

Crow, Hugh (edited by the Executors). 1830. *Memoirs of the Late Captain Hugh Crow of Liverpool comprising a Narrative of his Life together with Descriptive Sketches of the Western Coast of Africa, particularly of Bonny*. Liverpool, G. and J. Robinson. Facsimile. London, Frank Cass & Co., Ltd., 1970.

Culver, Francis B. 1923. *Blooded Horses of Colonial Days: Classic Horse Matches in America before the Revolution*. Baltimore, Md., Kohn & Pollock Press for the author.

Cumyn, Anna Key Bartow. 1984. *The Bartow Family: a Genealogy*, privately published in association with Longmeets, Montreal.

Curtin, Philip D. ed. 1967. Ayuba Suleiman Diallo of Bondo. In *Africa Remembered: Narratives by West Africans from the Era of the Slave Trade*. Philip D. Curtin, ed., pp. 17–59. Madison, University of Wisconsin Press [originally published 1734 as edited and written down by Thomas Bluett, London, Richard Ford, 1734].

Danckaerts, Jasper. 1679–80. *Journal of Jasper Danckaerts, 1679–80: Journey to the Southward*. B. B. James and J. F. Jameson, eds. New York, Scribners, 1913.

David, Nicholas, Judy Sterner, and Kodzo Gavua. 1988. Why pots are decorated. *Current Anthropology* 29 (3): 365–89.

Davies, O. 1956. Excavations at Sekondi, Ghana in 1954 and 1956. Unpublished report on file at the Department of Archaeology, Legon, Ghana.

Davis, Angela Y. 1981. *Women, Race, & Class*. New York, Random House.

Davis, John. 1803. *Travels of Four Years and a Half in the United States of America during 1798, 1799, 1800, 1801, and 1802*. Second edn. A. J. Morrison, ed. New York, Henry Holt and Co., 1909.

Deagan, Kathleen. 1987. *Artifacts of the Spanish Colonies of Florida and the Caribbean, 1500–1800. Volume I: Ceramics, Glassware, and Beads*. Washington, D.C., Smithsonian Institution Press.

DeCorse, Christopher R. 1989. Beads as chronological indicators in West African archaeology: a reexamination. *Beads* 1: 41–53.

  1992. Culture contact, change, and continuity on the Gold Coast, AD 1400–1900. *African Archaeological Review* 10: 163–196.

  1994. Oceans apart: African perspectives on New World archaeology. In *"I, too, am America": Studies in African American Archaeology*. Theresa Singleton, ed. Charlottesville, University Press of Virginia, forthcoming.

Deetz, James. 1965. *The Dynamics of Stylistic Change in Arikara Ceramics*. Illinois Studies in Anthropology 4. Urbana, University of Illinois Press.

  1967. *Invitation to Archaeology*. Garden City, N.Y., The Natural History Press.

  1977a. *In Small Things Forgotten*. Anchor Books, Doubleday, New York.

  1977b. Material culture and archaeology – what's the difference? In *Historical Archaeology and the Importance of Material Things*, Leland Ferguson, ed., pp. 9–12. Special Publication Series, No. 2. Tucson, Arizona, Society for Historical Archaeology.

1993. *Flowerdew Hundred*. Charlottesville, University Press of Virginia.

Defoe, Daniel. 1724. *The Great Law of Subordination Considered*. London, 1924.

Delany, Mrs. Mary Pendarves Granville. 1861. *The Autobiography and Correspondence of Mary Granville, Mrs. Delany* . . . The Right Honorable Lady Llanover, ed. London, R. Bentley. 1st edition.

Dening, Greg. 1988. *History's Anthropology: The Death of William Gooch*. Lanham, Maryland, University Press of America.

de Serres, O. 1607. *Le théatre d'agriculture et messages des champs*. Trans. by N. Goffe. London.

Detweiler, Susan G. 1982. *George Washington's Chinaware*. New York, Harry N. Abrams, Inc.

Dillard, J. L. 1972. *Black English*. New York, Random House.

Doepkens, William P. 1991. *Excavations at Mareen Duvall's Middle Plantation of South River Hundred*. Baltimore, Md., Gateway Press, Inc.

Donaldson, Gary A. 1984. A window on slave culture: dances at Congo Square in New Orleans, 1800–1862. *Journal of Negro History* 69 (2): 63–72.

Donnan, Elizabeth. 1933. *Documents Illustrative of the History of Slave Trade to America. Volume IV. The Border Colonies*. Reprint. New York, Octagon Books, 1969.

Douglas, Mary. 1972. Deciphering a meal. *Daedalus* (Winter 1972): 61–81.

1986. *How Institutions Think*. Princeton, Princeton University Press.

Driver, Jonathan C. 1982. Medullary bone as an indicator of sex in bird remains from archaeological sites. In *Ageing and Sexing Animal Bones from Archaeological Sites*. Bob Wilson, Caroline Grigson, and Sebastian Payne, eds., pp. 251–4. British Archaeological Reports, British Series 109.

Dubin, Lois Sherr (with original photography by Togashi). 1987. *The History of Beads from 30,000 B.C. to the Present*. New York, Harry N. Abrams, Inc.

DuBois, W. E. B. 1967. *The Philadelphia Negro: A Social Study*. New York, Benjamin Blom.

Durkheim, Emile. 1912. *Elementary Forms of Religious Life*. Translated by Joseph W. Swain. Glencoe, Ill., Free Press, 1954.

Earle, Carville V. 1975. *The Evolution of a Tidewater Settlement System: All Hallow's Parish, Maryland, 1650–1783*. University of Chicago Department of Geography Research Paper No. 170. 239 pp.

Earle, Peter. 1989. *The Making of the English Middle Class: Business, Society and Family Life in London 1660–1730*. Berkeley, University of California Press.

Eddis, William. 1792. *Letters from America, Historical and Descriptive: Comprising Occurrences from 1769 to 1777 inclusive*. London. Rev. ed., Aubrey Land, ed. Cambridge, Mass., Belknap Press, Harvard, 1969.

Egerton, John with Ann Egerton. 1987. *Southern Food: At Home, on the Road, in History*. New York, Alfred A. Knopf, Inc.

Elisofon, Eliot. 1958. *The Sculpture of Africa*. New York, F. A. Praeger.

Ellis, Donna M. and Karen A. Stuart. 1989. *The Calvert Papers Calendar and Guide to the Microfilm Edition*. Baltimore, Md., Maryland Historical Society.

Ellis, Merle. 1975. *Cutting-up in the Kitchen*. San Francisco, Chronicle Books.

Emerson, Matthew C. 1988. Decorated Clay Tobacco Pipes from the Chesapeake. Ph.D. dissertation, Department of Anthropology, University of California, Berkeley. Ann Arbor, University Microfilms International.

1994. African inspirations in a New World art and artifact: decorative clay tobacco pipes from the Chesapeake. In *'I, too, am America'': Studies in African American Archaeology*. Theresa Singleton, ed. Charlottesville, University Press of Virginia, forthcoming.

Epperson, Terrance W. 1990. Race and the disciplines of the plantation. *Historical Archaeology* 24 (4): 29–38.

1994. Constructed places/contested spaces: contexts of Tidewater plantation archaeology. In *"I, too, am America": Studies in African American Archaeology.* Theresa Singleton, ed. Charlottesville, University Press of Virginia, forthcoming.

Equiano, Olaudah [Gustavus Vassa]. 1789. *Equiano's Travels: The Interesting Narrative of the Life of O. Equiano or Gustavus Vassa, the African, Written by Himself.* London, for the author. Abridged with an introduction and note by Paul Edwards. London and Ibadan, Heinemann Educational Books, Ltd., 1977.

Erickson, Arvel B. 1959. Edward T. Cardwell: Pellite. *Transactions of the American Philosophical Society* 49 (2): 1–103.

Evelyn, John. 1693. A treatise on orange trees. In *The Complete Gard'ner; or Directions for Cultivating . . . Fruit Gardens and Kitchen Gardens by Jean de La Quintinie.* Made English by John Evelyn. London, Gillyflower and Partridge.

Everstine, Carl N. 1980. *The General Assembly of Maryland, vol. 1, 1634 to 1776.* Charlottesville, Virginia, Michie Co. Law Publishers.

Fagg, William and Margaret Plass. 1964. *African Sculpture: An Anthology.* New York, E. P. Dutton and Co., Inc.

Falconbridge, Alexander. 1788. *An Account of the Slave Trade on the Coast of Africa.* London, J. Philips.

Feest, Christian. 1978. Nanticokes and neighboring tribes. In *Handbook of North American Indians, Vol. 15, Northeast.* Bruce G. Trigger, ed. (William C. Sturtevant, series ed.). Washington, D.C., Smithsonian Institution.

Ferguson, Leland. 1992. *Uncommon Ground: Archaeology and Early African America, 1650–1800.* Washington, D.C., Smithsonian Institution Press.

Fernandez, James W. 1990. Enclosures: boundary maintenance and its representations over time in Asturian mountain villages (Spain). In *Culture through Time.* E. Ohnuki-Tierney, ed., pp. 94–127. Stanford, Stanford University Press.

Firth, Raymond. 1975. *Symbols, Public and Private.* Ithaca, New York, Cornell University Press.

Fisher, Angela. 1984. *Africa Adorned.* New York, Harry N. Abrahms, Inc.

Fisk, Mary. 1934. The Lords Baltimore. In *The Beginning of Maryland in England and America,* Mrs. A. A. Bibbins, ed. pp. 37–40. Baltimore, Md., N. Remington Co.

Flandrin, J. L. 1989. Distinction through taste. In *A History of Private Life, Vol. 3, Passions of the Renaissance.* Philippe Aries and Georges Duby, general eds.; Roger Chartier, volume ed., pp. 265–308. Cambridge, Mass., Belknap Press, Harvard (translated by Arthur Goldhammer).

Fleischer, Roland E. 1989. Gustavus Hesselius' letter of 1714 [translated by Carin K. Arnborg] and its contribution to current scholarship. *American Art Journal* 21 (3): 5–17.

Forman, Henry Chandler. 1934. *Early Manor and Plantation Houses of Maryland.* Haverford, Pennsylvania, privately printed.

1938. *Jamestown and St. Mary's: Buried Cities of Romance.* Baltimore, Md., Johns Hopkins University Press.

1956. *Tidewater Maryland Architecture and Gardens.* New York, Bonanza Books.

1967. *Old Buildings, Gardens, and Furniture in Tidewater Maryland.* Cambridge, Md., Tidewater Publishers.

Fox-Genovese, Elizabeth. 1988. *Within the Plantation Household: Black and White Women of the Old South.* Chapel Hill, University of North Carolina Press.

Freedman, Estelle B. 1992. The manipulation of history at the Clarence Thomas hearings. *The Chronicle of Higher Education,* January 8, 1992: B2–B3.

Freyre, Gilberto. 1946. *The Masters and the Slaves.* 2nd English language edition. New York, Alfred A. Knopf, 1971.

Gademer, Hans-Georg. 1979. The problem of historical consciousness. In *Interpretive Social Science, a Reader*, Paul Rabinow and William M. Sullivan, eds. pp. 103–60. Berkeley, University of California Press (originally published as *Le Problème de la conscience historique*, Louvain, Institut Superieur de Philosophie, Université Catholique de Louvain, 1963).

Geertz, Clifford. 1973. *The Interpretation of Cultures*. New York, Basic Books.

1980. *Negara: The Theatre State in Nineteenth-Century Bali*. Princeton, Princeton University Press.

1983. *Local Knowledge: Further Essays in Interpretive Anthropology*. New York, Basic Books.

Genovese, Eugene D. 1974. *Roll, Jordan, Roll: The World the Slaves Made*. New York, Random House.

Gibb, James G. and Julia A. King. 1991. Gender, activity areas, and homelots in the 17th-century Chesapeake region. *Historical Archaeology* 25 (4): 109–31.

Gibbs, M. J. 1987. Precious artifacts: women's jewelry in the Chesapeake, 1750–1799. *Journal of Early Southern Decorative Arts* 8 (1): 53–103.

Gibson, Elizabeth. 1826. *Biographical Sketches of the Bordley Family of Maryland for Their Descendents*. Edited by her niece, Elizabeth Mifflin. Philadelphia, Henry B. Ashmead, 1865.

Gibson, J. 1796. A short account of several gardens near London, with remarks on some particulars wherein they excel, or are deficient, upon a view of them in December 1691. *Archaeologia* 12: 181–92.

Giovanni, Nikki. 1983. Interview with Claudia Tate. In *Black Women Writers at Work*, Claudia Tate, ed., pp. 68–78. New York, Continuum.

Glassie, Henry. 1972. The nature of the New World artifact: the instance of the dugout canoe. In *Festschrift für Robert Wildhaber*. Walter Escher, ed., pp. 153–70. Basel, G. Krebs.

1975. *Folk Housing in Middle Virginia*. Knoxville, University of Tennessee Press.

1978. Meaningful things and appropriate myths: the artifact's place in American Studies. *Prospectus*, vol. 3: 1–49 (reprinted in *Material Life in America, 1600–1860*, Robert Blair St. George, ed., pp. 63–92. Boston, Northeastern University Press).

1982. *Passing the Time in Ballymenone*. Philadelphia, University of Pennsylvania Press.

1989. *The Spirit of Folk Art: The Girard Collection at the Museum of International Folk Art*. New York, Harry N. Abrams, Inc.

Goffman, Erving. 1956. *The Presentation of Self in Everyday Life*. Edinburgh, Edinburgh University Press. Rev. edition, Garden City, New York, Doubleday, 1969.

Goody, Jack R. 1982. *Cooking, Cuisine, and Class*. Cambridge, Cambridge University Press.

Gordon, Lord Adam. 1764–65. *Journal of an Officer in the West Indies who Traveled over a Part of the West Indies and of North America*. Portions reprinted in *Narratives of Colonial America, 1704–1765*. Howard H. Peckham, ed., pp. 233–94. Chicago, Lakeside Press, 1971.

Gosse, Philip H. 1847. *The Birds of Jamaica*. London, John van Voorst.

Gray, Lewis C. 1941. *History of Agriculture in the Southern United States to 1860*. 2 volumes. New York, Peter Smith.

Green, William. 1774. *The Sufferings of William Green, being a Sorrowful Account of his Seven Years' Transportation . . .* London.

Greene, Beverly. 1990. Sturdy bridges: the role of African-American mothers in the socialization of African-American children. *Women and Therapy* 10 (1/2): 205–25.

Greene, Jack P. 1988. *Pursuits of Happiness: The Social Development of Early Modern British Colonies and the Formation of American Culture*. Chapel Hill, University of North Carolina Press.

Greenfield, Haskel J. 1989. From pork to mutton: a zooarchaeological perspective on colonial New Amsterdam and early New York. *Northeast Historical Archaeology* 18: 85–110.

Grigson, Jane, and Charlotte Knox. 1986. *Cooking with Exotic Fruits and Vegetables*. New York, Henry Holt & Co.

Gundersen, Joan R. 1986. The double bonds of race and sex: black and white women in a colonial Virginia parish. *Journal of Southern History* 52 (August): 351–72.

Hall, Clayton Colman. 1904. *The Lords Baltimore and the Maryland Palatinate*. 2nd edition. Baltimore, Md., privately printed.

   1925. *Narratives of Early Maryland, 1633–1684*. New York, Charles Scribner's Sons. Facsimile edition. Bowie, Md., Heritage Books, Inc., 1988.

Hall, Martin. 1992. "Small Things" & "the Mobile, Conflictual Fusion of Power, Fear, & Desire." In *The Art and Mystery of Historical Archaeology: Essays in Honor of James Deetz*, Anne Yentsch and Mary C. Beaudry, eds., pp. 373–99. Boca Raton, Florida, CRC Press.

Hall, Robert L. 1989. Slave resistance in Baltimore city and county, 1747–1790. *Maryland Historical Magazine* 84 (4): 305–18.

   1991. Savouring Africa in the New World. In *Seeds of Change*, Herman J. Viola and Carolyn Margolis, eds., pp. 161–72. Washington, D.C., Smithsonian Institution.

Hamell, George R. 1983. Trading in metaphors: the magic of beads. *Proceedings of the 1982 Glass Trade Bead Conference sponsored by the Arthur C. Parker Fund for Iroquois Research, Research Records No. 16*. Charles F. Hayes III, ed., pp. 5–28. Rochester, New York, Rochester Museum & Science Center.

Hamilton, Sir Frederick William. 1874. *The Origin and History of the First or Grenadier Guards*. 3 volumes. London.

Hammond, John. 1656. *Leah and Rachel, or, The Two Fruitful Sisters, Virginia and Mary-land*. Reprinted in *Narratives of Early Maryland 1633–1684*. Clayton Colman Hall, ed. Facsimile edition. Bowie, Md., Heritage Books, Inc., 1988.

Handler, Jerome S. and Frederick W. Lange. 1978. *Plantation Slavery in Barbados: An Archaeological and Historical Investigation*. Cambridge, Ma., Harvard University Press.

Handler, Jerome S., Frederick W. Lange, and Charles E. Orser. 1979. Carnelian beads in necklaces from a slave cemetery in Barbados, West Indies. *Ornament* 4 (2): 15–18.

Harrington, Jean C. 1955. Archaeology as an auxiliary science to American history. *American Anthropologist* 57 (6): 112–30.

Harris, John. 1961. Clues to the Frenchness of Woodcote Park. *Connoisseur* 147: 241–50.

Harris, Jessica B. 1989. *Iron Pots and Wooden Spoons: Africa's Gifts to New World Cooking*. New York, Macmillan Publishing Company.

Harrison, Molly. 1972. *The Kitchen in History*. New York, Charles Scribner's Sons.

Haslett, Richard. 1983. Kiplin Hall, North Yorkshire, I and II. *Country Life*, July 28: 202–5; August 12: 270–81.

Hawkins, Joseph. 1796. *A History of a Voyage to the Coast of Africa and Travels into the Interior of that Country*. Plymouth, Clark, Doble & Brendon, Ltd. (Second edition, 1797). Facsimile. London, Frank Cass & Co., Ltd., 1970.

Hawley, Jerome. 1635. *A Relation of Maryland*. London, pp. 63–112. Reprinted in *Narratives of Early Maryland, 1633–1684*. Clayton C. Hall, ed. New York, Charles Scribner's Sons, New York, 1910. Facsimile edition. Bowie, Md., Heritage Books, Inc., 1988.

Haydn, Joseph T. 1786. *The Book of Dignities . . .* London, W. H. Allen.

Hazzard, David K. and Martha W. McCartney. 1987. Rescue efforts to save the vanishing traces of Gloucester town. *American Archaeology* 6 (1): 68–80.

Hearne, Thomas. 1678–1735. Remarks and Collections [Diaries]. *Oxford Historical Society* 65–7. (1718–1735 partially reprinted in the *Maryland Historical Magazine* as Calvert Memorabilia, vol. 10: 372–75; 16: 385–7.)

Henisch, Bridget Ann. 1976. *Fast and Feast*. University Park, Pennsylvania State University Press.

Herskovits, Melville J. 1941. *The Myth of the Negro Past*. New York, Harper Brothers. Reprint, Boston, Beacon Press, 1958.

Herskovits, Melville J. and Frances S. Herskovits. 1936. *Suriname Folk Lore*. New York, Columbia University Press. Reprint. New York, AMS Press, 1969.

Hienton, Louise Joyner. 1972. *Prince George's Heritage: Sidelights on the Early History of Prince George's County, Maryland, from 1696 to 1800*. Baltimore, Md., Maryland Historical Society.

Hilliard, Sam B. 1972. *Hog Meat and Hoecake: Food Supply in the Old South 1840–1860*. Carbondale, Southern Illinois University Press.

Hinks, Steven. 1988. Buttons from the Calvert Site. M.A. thesis, Department of Anthropology, College of William and Mary, Williamsburg, Virginia.

Hodder, Ian. 1982. The identification and interpretation of ranking in prehistory: a contextual perspective. In *Ranking, Resource, and Exchange: Aspects of the Archaeology of Early European Society*, Colin Renfrew and Stephen Shennan, eds., pp. 150–4. Cambridge, Cambridge University Press.

  1985. Postprocessual archaeology. *Advances in Archaeological Method and Theory* 8: 1–26.

  1987a. The meaning of discard: ash and domestic space in Baringo. In *Method and Theory for Activity Area Research*, Susan Kent, ed., pp. 424–48. New York, Columbia University Press.

  1987b. *The Archaeology of Contextual Meanings*. Cambridge, Cambridge University Press.

Hodgson, William B. 1844. *Notes on North Africa, the Sahara, and the Sudan*. New York, Wiley & Putnam.

Hoffman, Ronald. 1973. *A Spirit of Dissension: Economics, Politics, and the Revolution in Maryland*. Baltimore, Md., Johns Hopkins University Press.

  1988. "Marylando-hibernus": Charles Carroll the Settler, 1660–1720. *William and Mary Quarterly*, series 3, 45 (2): 207–36.

Holborn, Hajo. 1972. *History and the Humanities*. New York, Doubleday.

Holloway, Joseph E., ed. 1990. *Africanisms in American Culture*. Bloomington, University of Indiana Press.

Hollyday, Thomas. 1990. Readbourne Manor Revisited: Gleanings from an Eighteenth-Century Journal. *Maryland Historical Magazine* 85: 44–50.

Home, Gordon. 1901. *Epsom, Its History and Its Surroundings*. Epsom, Surrey, Homeland Association, Inc.

Hopkins, Joseph W. 1986. Preliminary Report on Excavations at the State House Inn, Annapolis, Maryland, 1985. Report on file, Historic Annapolis Foundation, Annapolis, Maryland.

Horn, James P. 1988a. Adapting to a New World: a comparative study of local society in England and Maryland, 1650–1700. In *Colonial Chesapeake Society*. Lois Green Carr, Philip D. Morgan, and Jean B. Russo, eds., pp. 133–75. Chapel Hill, University of North Carolina Press.

  1988b. "The Bare Necessities": Standards of Living in England and the Chesapeake, 1650–1700. *Historical Archaeology* 22 (2): 74–91.

Horry, Harriott P. 1770. *A Colonial Plantation Cookbook: The Receipt Book of Harriott Pinckney Horry, 1770*. Edited with an introduction by Richard J. Hooker. Columbia, University of South Carolina Press, 1984.

Horton, James Africanus Beale. 1868. *West African Countries and Peoples*. Reprinted with an introduction by George Shepperson. Edinburgh, Edinburgh University Press, 1969.

Hruschka, Peter. 1974. Acquisition and Maintenance of Position as an Economic Elite: A Study of Four Maryland Families, 1630–1960. Ph.D. dissertation, Department of Sociology, University of Wisconsin. Ann Arbor, University Microfilms International.

Hudging, Carter L. 1982. Archaeology in the "King's" Realm: Excavations at Robert Carter's Corotoman. Report on file, Virginia Department of Historic Resources, Richmond, Virginia.

    1983. Patrician Culture, Public Ritual and Political Authority in Virginia, 1680–1740. Ph.D. dissertation, Department of History, College of William and Mary. Ann Arbor, University Microfilms International.

    1990. Robert "King" Carter and the landscape of Tidewater Virginia in the eighteenth century. In *Earth Patterns: Essays in Landscape Archaeology*. William Kelso and Rachel Most, eds., pp. 59–70. Charlottesville, University Press of Virginia.

Hudson, Mark. 1991. *Our Grandmother's Drums*. New York, Henry Holt & Company.

Hunt, John Dixon and Peter Willis. 1988. *The Genius of the Place: The English Landscape Garden 1620–1820*. Cambridge. Ma., MIT Press.

Hurry, Robert. 1989. An archeological and historical perspective on Benjamin Banneker. *Maryland Historical Magazine* 84 (4): 361–9.

Hurston, Zora Mae. 1942. *Dust Tracks on the Road: An Autobiography*. Philadelphia, L. B. Lippencott, 1991 Harper Perennial Edition.

Hussey, Christopher. 1931. Kiplin Hall, Yorkshire. *Country Life* (August): 228–32.

Hymes, Dell ed. 1981. *Pidginization and Creolization of Languages*. Cambridge, Cambridge University Press.

Isaac, Rhys. 1982. *The Transformation of Virginia 1740–1790*. Chapel Hill, University of North Carolina Press, for the Institute of Early American History and Culture, Williamsburg, Virginia.

    1992. Imagination and material culture: the enlightenment on a mid-eighteenth-century Virginia plantation. In *Art and Mystery of Historical Archaeology: Essays in Honor of James Deetz*. Anne Yentsch and Mary C. Beaudry, eds., pp. 400–23. Boca Raton, Florida, CRC Press.

Jarratt, Devereux. 1806. *The Life of the Reverend Dr. Jarratt, Written by Himself*. Baltimore, Md., Warner and Hanna.

Jashemski, W. F. 1979. *The Gardens of Pompeii, Herculaneum, and the Villas Destroyed by Vesuvius*. Vol. 1. New Rochelle, New York, Caratzas Brothers Publishers.

Jennings, Francis. 1975. *The Invasion of America: Indians, Colonialism, and the Cant of Conquest*. Chapel Hill, University of North Carolina Press.

Jobson, Richard. 1623. *The Golden Trade*. London, Nicholas Oakes. Facsimile. Amsterdam, De Capo Press, 1968.

Johnson, R. Winder. 1905–1908. *The Ancestry of Rosalie Morris Johnson*. Philadelphia, privately printed.

Jones, G. I. 1967. Olaudah Equiano of the Niger Ibo. In *Africa Remembered: Narratives by West Africans from The Era of The Slave Trade*. Philip Curtin, ed., pp. 60–98. Madison, University of Wisconsin Press.

Jones, Rev. Hugh. 1699. Letter dated January 1698/99 to Benjamin Woodroffe at Oxford concerning Maryland. *Philosophical Transactions of the Royal Society for 1699*: 436–42.

Jones, Hugh. 1724. *The Present State of Virginia from whence is Inferred a Short View of Maryland and North Carolina*. London. Edited with an introduction by Richard L. Morton. Chapel Hill, University of North Carolina Press, 1956.

Jones, Leroi. 1963. *Blues People: Negro Music in White America*. New York, William Morrow and Company, Inc.

Jordan, David W. 1978. Maryland hoggs and Hyde Park duchesses: a brief account of Maryland in 1697. *Maryland Historical Magazine* 73 (1): 87–91.

Jordan, Winthrop. 1962. American chiaroscuro: the status and definition of mulattos in the British colonies. *William and Mary Quarterly*, 3rd series, 19: 182–200.

Jourdain, M. 1913. An early Georgian mansion: Ditchley. *Architectural Review* 33: 68–70.

Joyner, Charles. 1971. Soul food and the Sambo stereotype: foodlore from the slave narrative collection. *Keystone Folklore Quarterly* 16 (Winter): 171–8.

1984. *Down by the Riverside: A South Carolina Slave Community*. Urbana, University of Illinois Press.

Keeler, Robert W. 1978. The Homelot on the Seventeenth-century Chesapeake Tidewater Frontier. Ph.D. dissertation. Department of Anthropology, University of Oregon. Ann Arbor, University Microfilms International.

Kelly, J. Reaney. 1963. *Founding of Quaker Families in Anne Arundel County*. Baltimore, Md., Maryland Historical Society.

Kelso, William M. 1984a. Landscape archaeology: a key to Virginia's cultivated past. In *British and American Gardens in the Eighteenth Century*. R. P. Maccubbin and Peter M. Martin, eds., pp. 159–69. Williamsburg, Virginia, Colonial Williamsburg Foundation.

1984b. *Kingsmill Plantation, 1619–1800: Archaeology of Country Life in Colonial Virginia*. New York, Academic Press.

1986. Mulberry Row: slave life at Thomas Jefferson's Monticello. *Archaeology* 39 (5): 28–35.

Kelso, William M. and Rachel Most (eds.). 1990. *Earth Patterns: Essays in Landscape Archaeology*. Charlottesville, University Press of Virginia.

Kemble, Frances Anne. 1863. *Journal of a Residence on a Georgia Plantation in 1838–1839*, rev. edn., edited by John A. Scott. New York, A. A. Knopf, 1961.

Kent, Brent. 1988. Making dead oysters talk: techniques for analyzing oysters from archaeological sites. Report. 107 pp. Annapolis, Md., Maryland Historical Trust.

Kertzer, David. 1988. *Ritual, Politics, and Power*. New Haven, Yale University Press.

Kevill-Davies, Sally. 1991. *Yesterday's Children: The Antiques and History of Childcare*. Woodbridge, Suffolk, The Antique Collectors' Club Ltd.

Key, Rebecca. 1919. A notice of some of the first buildings with notes of some of the early residents. *Maryland Historical Magazine* 14: 258–71.

Keynes, Geoffrey. 1964. *The Works of Sir Thomas Brown*. Chicago, University of Chicago Press. 4 volumes.

Kilthy, William ed. 1799–1800. *The Laws of Maryland*. Annapolis, Md., Frederick Green, printer for the state.

Kimber, Edward. 1746–48. Observations in several voyages and travels in America in the year 1736. No. 5. Some account of a voyage from New York to Senepuxon in Maryland. *London Magazine* 1746: 125–8, 248, 322–30. (Reprinted in *William & Mary Quarterly* 1907, 15 (3): 1–17, 143–59, 215–24.)

King, Julia A. 1988. A comparative midden analysis of a household and inn in St. Mary's City, Maryland. *Historical Archaeology* 22 (2): 17–39.

1994. "The transient nature of all things sublunary": romanticism, history, and ruins in nineteenth-century southern Maryland. In *Landscape Archaeology: Studies in Reading and Interpreting the Historic Landscape*, Rebecca Yamin and Karen Bescherer-Metheny eds. CRC Press, Boca Raton, Florida, forthcoming.

King, Julia A. and Henry M. Miller. 1987. The view from the midden: an analysis of midden distribution and composition at the van Sweringen Site, St. Mary's City, Maryland. *Historical Archaeology* 21 (2): 37–59.

King, Noël Q. 1986. *African Cosmos: An Introduction to Religion in Africa*. Belmont, California, Wadsworth Publishing Company.

Kingsley, Mary. 1897. *Travels in West Africa: Congo Français, Corisco, and Cameroons*. 3rd ed. with an introduction by John E. Flint. London, Frank Cass & Co., Ltd., 1965.

Klein, Herbert S. 1967. *Slavery in the Americas: A Comparative Study of Cuba and Virginia*. Chicago, University of Chicago Press.

Kluckhohn, Clyde. 1949. *Mirror for Man*. New York, McGraw Hill.

Kosack, Godula. 1986. Njèkenè Mofa: Mafa Marchen, Geschichten, Fabelm. MS.

Kosack, Gerhard Müller and Godula Kosack. 1988. Comment on "Why Pots Are Decorated." *Current Anthropology* 29 (3): 384–5.

Kryder-Reid, Elizabeth. 1991. Landscape and Myth: A Critical Archaeology of an Annapolis Landscape. Ph.D. dissertation, Brown University. Ann Arbor, University Microfilms International.

1993. "As the gardener so is the garden": the archaeology of landscape and myth. In: *Chesapeake Archaeology*. Barbara Little and Paul Shackel, eds. Washington, D.C., Smithsonian Institution Press, forthcoming.

Kulikoff, Allan. 1977. The beginnings of the Afro-American family in Maryland. In *Law, Society, and Politics in Early Maryland*. Aubrey C. Land, Lois Green Carr, and Edward C. Papenfuse, eds., pp. 171–96. Baltimore, Md., Johns Hopkins University Press.

1978. The origins of Afro-American society in Tidewater Maryland and Virginia, 1700–1790. *William and Mary Quarterly*, series 3, 35: 226–59.

1986. *Tobacco and Slaves: The Development of Southern Cultures in the Chesapeake: 1680–1800.* Chapel Hill, University of North Carolina Press for the Institute of Early American History and Culture, Williamsburg, Va.

Kupperman, Karen Ordahl. 1984. Fear of hot climates in the Anglo-American colonial experience. *William and Mary Quarterly*, series 3, 41 (2): 213–40.

Labat, Jean Baptiste. 1722. *Nouveau Voyage aux Isles de l'Amérique (Antilles), 1693–1705*. Paris, P. F. Giffart. (Translated and abridged by John Eadenin, 1935, as *The Memoirs of Père Labat 1693–1705*.) London, Frank Cass & Co., Ltd., 1970.

Lack, David, FRS. 1976. *Island Biology, Illustrated by the Land Birds of Jamaica*. Studies in Ecology, vol. III. Berkeley, University of California Press.

Land, Aubrey C. 1965. Economic base and social structure: the northern Chesapeake in the eighteenth century. *Journal of Economic History* 25: 639–54.

1966. An unwritten history of Maryland. *Maryland Historical Magazine* 61: 77–80.

1968. *The Dulaneys of Maryland*. Baltimore, Md., Johns Hopkins University Press.

1969. (editor) *Bases of the Plantation Society*. New York, Harper and Row.

1981. *Colonial Maryland, a History*. Millwood, New York, KTO Press.

Land, Aubrey C., Lois Green Carr, and Edward C. Papenfuse eds. 1977. *Law, Society, and Politics in Early Maryland*. Baltimore, Md., Johns Hopkins University Press.

Landon, David B. 1991a. Pig's Feet and Pigeon Pies: Faunal Remains from the Spencer-Pierce-Little Farm Kitchen. Unpublished report on file, Department of Archaeology, Boston University, Boston, Mass.

1991b. Zooarchaeology and Urban Foodways: A Case Study from Eastern Massachusetts. Ph.D. dissertation, Department of Archaeology, Boston University. Ann Arbor, University Microfilms International.

1992. Diachronic Change in Urban Foodways in Annapolis, Maryland: Faunal Remains from the Gott's Court Site. Report on file at Goodwin and Associates, Towson, Md.

La Quintinie, J. de. 1693. *A Treatise on the Culture of the Orange Tree*. London, Matthew Gillyflower (translated by John Evelyn).

Latrobe, Benjamin Henry. 1818–1820. *The Journal of Latrobe: Being the Notes and Sketches of an Architect, Naturalist and Traveler in the United States from 1796 to 1820*. New York, B. Appleton, 1905.

Lawson, John. 1709. *A New Voyage to Carolina*. London. Printed for W. Taylor and F. Baker, 1714. Facsimile, Ann Arbor, University Microfilms International, 1966.

Leach, Edmund. 1967. The language of Kachin kinship: reflections on a Tikopia model. In *Social Organization: Essays Presented to Raymond Firth*. Maurice Freedman, ed., pp. 125–52. Chicago, Aldine Publishing Co.

1976. *Culture and Communication: An Introduction to the Use of Structuralist Analysis in Social Anthropology*. Cambridge, Cambridge University Press.

1982. *Social Anthropology*. Oxford, Oxford University Press.

1990. Aryan invasions over four millennia. In *Culture through Time: Anthropological Approaches*, E. Ohnuki-Tierney, ed. pp. 227–45. Stanford, California, Stanford University Press.

Lee, Jean Butenhoff. 1986. The problem of slave community in the eighteenth-century Chesapeake. *William and Mary Quarterly*, series 3, 43 (3): 333–61.

1994. *The Price of Nationhood: The American Revolution in Charles County*. New York, W. W. Norton, forthcoming.

Leith-Ross, Sylvia. 1939. *African Women: A Study of the Ibo of Nigeria*. 2nd edn. New York, Frederick A. Praeger, 1965.

Leo Africanus, Joannes. 1526. *A Geographical Historie of Africa, Written in Arabic and Italian*. Translated and collected by John Pory. London, George Bishop, 1600. Reprint. New York, De Capo Press, 1969.

Leone, Mark P. 1984. Interpreting ideology in historical archaeology: using the rules of perspective in the William Paca Garden, Annapolis, Maryland. In *Ideology, Power and Prehistory*, Daniel Miller and Christopher Tilley, eds., pp. 25–35. Cambridge, Cambridge University Press.

Leone, Mark P. and Paul Shackel. 1990. Plane and solid geometry in colonial gardens in Annapolis, Maryland. In *Earth Patterns: Essays in Landscape Archaeology*. William M. Kelso and Rachel Most, eds., pp. 153–68. Charlottesville, University Press of Virginia.

Leone, Mark P., Parker B. Potter, Jr., and Paul A. Shackel. 1987. Towards a critical archaeology. *Current Anthropology* 28 (3): 283–302.

Leone, Mark P., Elizabeth Kryder-Reid, Julie H. Ernstein, and Paul A. Shackel. 1989. Power gardens of Annapolis. *Archaeology* 42 (2): 35–9, 74–5.

Lerner, Gerda. 1975. Placing women in history: definitions and challenges. *Feminist Studies* 3 (1/2): 5–14.

Lévi-Strauss, Claude. 1950. *Introduction à l'oeuvre de Marcel Mauss*. Presses Universitaires de France (English translation, *Introduction to the Work of Marcel Mauss*, Thetford, Norfolk, Thetford Press Ltd., 1987).

1958. *Anthropologie Structurale*. Paris (English translation, *Structural Anthropology*, Garden City, New York, Basic Books, 1963).

1962. *La Pensée Sauvage*. Paris, Librairie Plon (England translation, *The Savage Mind*, Chicago, University of Chicago Press, 1966).

1965. The culinary triangle. *Partisan Review* 33: 586–95.

Levine, Lawrence W. 1977. *Black Culture and Black Consciousness: Afro-American Folk Thought From Slavery to Freedom*. New York, Oxford University Press.

Lev-Tov, Justin. 1990. Faunal Remains from the Jonas Green Site. Undergraduate Honors thesis, Department of Anthropology, University of Maryland, College Park, Md.

Lewicki, Tadeusz. 1974. *West African Food in the Middle Ages, According to Arabic Sources*. Cambridge, Cambridge University Press.

Lewis, Edna. 1976. *The Taste of Country Cooking*. New York, A. A. Knopf.

1988. *In Pursuit of Flavor*. New York, A. A. Knopf.

Lewis, Nelly Custis. ca. 1830. *Nelly Custis Lewis's Housekeeping Book*. Edited by Patricia Brady Schmit. New Orleans, Historic New Orleans Collection, 1982.

Little, Barbara J. and Paul A. Shackel. 1989. Scales of historical anthropology: an archaeology of colonial Anglo-America. *Antiquity* 63: 495–509.

Long, Edward. 1774. *History of Jamaica*. 3 volumes. London, T. Lowndes.

Loudon, J. C. 1825. *An Encyclopedia of Gardening*. London, Longham, Brown, Greene, and Longmans.

Lovejoy, Paul O. 1979. The characteristics of plantations in the nineteenth-century Sokoto caliphate (Islamic West Africa). *American Historical Review* 84 (5): 1267–92.

Lyman, R. L. 1987. On zooarchaeological measures of socioeconomic position and cost-efficient meat purchases. *Historical Archaeology* 21 (1): 58–66.

MacMaster, Richard K. and David C. Skaggs, eds. 1966–1967. The letterbooks of Alexander Hamilton, Piscataway Factor. *Maryland Historical Magazine* 61 (2): 146–66; 61 (4): 305–28; 62 (2): 135–69.

Main, Gloria L. 1982. *Tobacco Colony: Life in Early Maryland, 1650–1720*. Princeton, Princeton University Press.

Malinowski, Bronislaw. 1922. *Argonauts of the Western Pacific*. New York, Dutton, 1961 edition.
    1935. *Coral Gardens and Their Magic*. London, Allen & Unwin. 2 volumes.

Mann, Susan A. 1989. Slavery, sharecropping, and sexual inequality. *Signs* 14 (4): 774–98.

Marcus, George E. and Michael M. J. Fisher. 1986. *Anthropology as Cultural Critique*. Chicago, University of Chicago Press.

Marly. 1828. *Marly; or, The Life of a Planter in Jamaica, 1828*. Glasgow, R. Griffin. 2nd edn.

Martin, Ann Smart. 1989. The role of pewter as missing artifact: consumer attitudes towards tablewares in late eighteenth century Virginia. *Historical Archaeology* 23 (2): 1–27.
    1993. Consumerism and the Retail Trade in Eighteenth-Century Virginia. Ph.D. dissertation, College of William and Mary. Ann Arbor, University Microfilms International.

Martin, Peter. 1991. *The Pleasure Gardens of Virginia from Jamestown to Jefferson*. Princeton, Princeton University Press.

Matthews, John. 1788. *A Voyage to the River Sierra-Leone*. London, P. White & Son. Facsimile. London, F. Cass, Ltd., 1966.

Matthiessen, Peter. 1959. *Wildlife in America*. New York, Viking. Rev. ed., 1987.

Maury, Ann, ed. 1838. *A Tale of the Huguenots or Memoirs of a French Refugee family*. New York, J. S. Taylor.
    (ed.). 1853. *Memoirs of a Huguenot Family*. New York. Reprint. Baltimore Md., Geneaological Publ. Co., 1967.

Mbiti, John S. 1969. *African Religions and Philosophy*. New York, Praeger.

McCall, Daniel F. 1964. *Africa in Time-Perspective: A Discussion of Historical Reconstruction from Unwritten Sources*. Boston, Boston University Press.

McDaniel, George. 1979. Preserving the People's History: Traditional Black Material Culture in Nineteenth and Twentieth Century Southern Maryland. Ph.D. dissertation, Department of History, Duke University. Ann Arbor, University Microfilms International.
    1982. *Hearth and Home: Preserving a People's Culture*. Philadelphia, Temple University Press.

McIntosh, Roderick J. and Susan Keech McIntosh. 1981. The inland Niger Delta before the empire of Mali: evidence for Jenne-Jeno. *J. African History* 22: 1–22.

McIntosh, Susan Keech and Roderick J. McIntosh. 1979. Initial perspectives on prehistoric subsistence in the inland Niver delta (Mali). *World Archaeology* 11: 227–43.

McKee, Larry. 1985. Research notes on the faunal remains from Feature 121, the Calvert well. On file, Historic Annapolis Foundation, Annapolis, Md.
    1987. Delineating ethnicity from the garbage of early Virginians: faunal remains from the Kingsmill Plantation slave quarter. *American Archeology* 6 (1): 31–9.
    1988. Plantation Food Supply in Nineteenth-Century Tidewater Virginia. Ph.D. dissertation, University of California, Berkeley. Ann Arbor, University Microfilms International.
    1994. Plantation Food Supply in Nineteenth-Century Tidewater Virginia. In *"I, too, am America": Studies in African American Archaeology*. Theresa Singleton, ed., Charlottesville, University Press of Virginia, forthcoming.

McMahon, John V. L. 1831. *An Historical View of the Government of Maryland from Its Colonization to the Present Day*. Volume I. Baltimore, Md., Lucas, Cushing, & Sons, William and Joseph Neal.

Mead, William Edward. 1931. *The English Medieval Feast*. Boston, Houghton Mifflin Company.

Menard, Russell R. 1975. The Maryland slave population, 1658 to 1730: a demographic profile of blacks in four counties. *William and Mary Quarterly*, series 3, 32: 30–8.

1980. The tobacco industry in the Chesapeake colonies, 1617–1730: an interpretation. *Research in Economic History* 5: 109–77.

Mencken, H. L. 1927. *Selected Prejudices*. London, Jonathan Cape.

1936. *The American Language*. New York, Alfred A. Knopf.

Mennell, Stephen. 1985. *All Manner of Food*. Oxford, Basil Blackwell.

Merrill, James H. 1979. Cultural continuity among the Piscataway Indians of colonial Maryland. *William and Mary Quarterly*, series 3, 36: 548–70.

1989. Some thoughts on colonial historians and American Indians. *William and Mary Quarterly*, series 3, 46 (1): 94–119.

Metheny, Karen Bescherer, Judson Kratzer, Anne Yentsch, and Conrad M. Goodwin. 1994. Methodology in landscape archaeology: research strategies in a historic New Jersey garden. In *Landscape Archaeology: Studies in Reading and Interpreting the Historic Landscape*, Rebecca Yamin and Karen Bescherer Metheny, eds. Boca Raton, Florida, CRC Press, forthcoming.

Michel, Francis Louis. 1702. Report of the Journey of Francis Louis Michel from Berne, Switzerland, to Virginia, October 2, 1701–December 1, 1702. Translated and edited by William J. Hinke. *Virginia Magazine of History and Biography* 34 (1916): 1–43, 113–41, 275–88.

Middleton, Arthur Pierce. 1943. Job-Ben Solomon. *William and Mary Quarterly*, 2nd series, 5: 341–6.

1953. *Tobacco Coast: A Maritime History of Chesapeake Bay in the Colonial Era*. Newport News, Va., The Mariners' Museum. 2nd edn. Baltimore, Md., Johns Hopkins University Press, 1984.

1988. *Annapolis on the Chesapeake* [text]. Annapolis, Md., Historic Annapolis Inc. and Legacy Publications.

Mifflin, Benjamin. 1762. Journal of Benjamin Mifflin on a tour from Philadelphia to Delaware and Maryland, July 26–August 14, 1762. Edited by Victor H. Palsits. *Bulletin of the New York Public Library* 39 (1935): 431–4.

Miller, George L. 1974. A tenant farmer's tableware: nineteenth century ceramics from Tabb's Purchase. *Maryland Historical Magazine* 62 (2): 197–210.

Miller, Henry M. 1983. A Search for the "Citty of Saint Maries": Report on the 1981 Excavations in St. Mary's City, Maryland. St. Mary's City Archaeology Series 1, St. Mary's City Commission, St. Mary's City, Md.

1984. Colonization and Subsistence Change on the 17th Century Chesapeake Frontier. Ph.D. dissertation, Department of Anthropology, Michigan State University. Ann Arbor, University Microfilms International.

1986a. Discovering Maryland's First City: A Summary Report on the 1981–1984 Archaeological Excavations in St. Mary's City, Maryland. St. Mary's City Archaeology Series, No. 2. St. Mary's City Commission, St. Mary's City, Md.

1986b. Transforming a "splendid and delightsome land": colonists and ecological change in the Chesapeake 1607–1820. *Journal of the Washington Academy of Science* 76 (3): 173–87.

1988a. An Archaeological Perspective on Diet. In *Colonial Chesapeake Society*, Lois Green Carr, Philip D. Morgan, and Jean B. Russo, eds., pp. 176–99. Chapel Hill, University of North Carolina Press for the Institute of Early American History and Culture.

1988b. Baroque cities in the wilderness: archaeology and urban development in the colonial Chesapeake. *Historical Archaeology* 22 (2): 57–73.

1991. Archaeological investigations of the great brick chapel at St. Mary's City, Maryland. Paper presented at the Council on Northeast Historical Archaeology meetings, Newark, Delaware, October 1991. On file at Historic St. Mary's City, St. Mary's City, Md.

Miller, Henry M., Dennis J. Pogue, and Michael A. Smolek. 1983. Beads from the seventeenth century Chesapeake. In *Proceedings of the 1982 Glass Trade Bead Conference.* Charles F. Hayes III, ed., pp. 127–44. Rochester, New York, Research Division, Rochester Museum and Science Center.

Miller, Naomi F. 1988. Ethnobotanical Remains from the Calvert Site. Calvert Interim Report No. 7. Historic Annapolis Foundation, Annapolis, Md.

1989. What mean these seeds? A comparative approach to archaeological seed analysis. *Historical Archaeology* 23 (2): 50–9.

Miller, Philip. 1724. *The Gardener's and Florist's Dictionary, or a Complete System of Horticulture.* London, Folio.

Mingay, G. E. 1963. *English Landed Society in the Eighteenth Century.* London, Routledge and Paul.

1978. *The Gentry: The Rise and Fall of a Ruling Class.* Oxford, Oxford University Press.

Mintz, Sydney W. 1985. *Sweetness and Power: The Place of Sugar in Modern History.* Baltimore, Md., Johns Hopkins University Press.

Mintz, Sydney W. and Douglas Hall, 1960. The origins of the internal marketing system in Jamaica. *Papers in Caribbean Anthropology,* Yale University.

Mintz, Sydney W. and Richard Price. 1976. *An Anthropological Approach to the Afro-American Past: A Caribbean Perspective.* Philadelphia.

Montagu, M. F. Ashley. 1942. *Man's Most Dangerous Myth.* New York, Harper & Bros., 3rd edn., revised and enlarged, 1952 with a foreword by Aldous Huxley.

Moore, Francis. 1738. *Travels in the Inland Parts of Africa, . . .* London.

Morgan, Edmund S. 1975. *American Slavery, American Freedom: The Ordeal of Colonial Virginia.* New York, W. W. Norton & Company.

Morgan, Philip D. 1982. Work and culture: the task system and the world of lowcountry blacks, 1700–1880. *William and Mary Quarterly,* series 3, 39: 563–99.

Morris, Christopher ed. 1949. *The [1690–1710] Journeys of Celia Fiennes.* London, Cresset Press.

Morrison, Toni. 1983. Interview with Claudia Tate. In *Black Women Writers at Work.* Claudia Tate, ed., pp. 117–31. New York, Continuum.

Morrissey, Marietta. 1989. *Slave Women in the New World: Gender Stratification in the Caribbean.* Lawrence, University Press of Kansas.

Morton, Joseph C. 1964. Stephen Bordley of Colonial Annapolis. Ph.D. dissertation, University of Maryland. Ann Arbor, University Microfilms International.

Mullin, Gerald W. 1972. *Flight and Rebellion: Slave Resistance in Eighteenth-Century Virginia.* New York, Oxford University Press.

Murphy, Robert E. 1971. *The Dialectics of Social Life: Alarms and Excursions in Anthropological Theory.* New York, Basic Books, Inc.

Neiman, Fraser D. 1978. Domestic architecture at the Clifts Plantation: the social context of early Virginia building. *Northern Neck Historical Magazine* 28: 96–128. (Reprinted in Dell Upton and John Michael Vlach, eds., *Common Places: Readings in American Vernacular Architecture,* 1986, Athens, Georgia, pp. 292–314.)

1980. The Clifts Plantation. Unpublished report on file at the Virginia Historic Landmarks Commission, Richmond, Va.

Nelker, Mrs. Marshall N. 1967. This is London Town, Anne Arundel County, Maryland, U.S.A. Unpublished manuscript (#8121) on file at the Maryland Hall of Records, Annapolis, Md.

Newman, Harry Wright. 1985. *To Maryland from Overseas*. Baltimore, Md., Genealogical Publishing Company.

Nichol, W. 1812. *The Planter's Kalender*. Edited and completed by E. Sang. Edinburgh.

Nicklin, John Bailey Calvert. 1980. The Calvert family. In *Maryland Genealogies*, edited by Robert Barnes. Baltimore, Md., Genealogical Publishing Company.

Noël Hume, Audrey. 1974. *Archaeology and the Colonial Gardener*. Colonial Williamsburg Archaeology Series 7. Colonial Williamsburg Foundation, Williamsburg, Va.

   1978. *Food*. Colonial Williamsburg Archaeology Series 9. Colonial Williamsburg Foundation, Williamsburg, Va.

Noël Hume, Ivor. 1962. Excavations at Rosewell, Gloucester County, Virginia, 1957–1959. *United States National Museum Bulletin 225, Contributions from the Museum of History and Technology, paper 18*, Washington, D.C., pp. 154–228.

   1963. *Here Lies Virginia: An Archaeologist's View of Colonial Life and History*. New York, A. A. Knopf.

   1964. Archaeology: a handmaiden to history. *North Carolina Historical Review* 4 (2): 215–25.

   1969a. *Guide to the Artifacts of Colonial America*. New York, A. A. Knopf.

   1969b. *Historical Archaeology*. New York, A. A. Knopf.

   1969c. *Pottery and Porcelain*. Colonial Williamsburg Archaeology Series No. 2. Colonial Williamsburg Foundation, Williamsburg, Va.

   1974. *All the Best Rubbish: Being an Antiquary's Account of the Pleasures and Perils of Studying and Collecting Everyday Objects from the Past*. New York, Harper and Row.

   1978. Material culture with the dirt on it: a Virginia perspective. In *Material Culture and the Study of American Life*. Ian Quimby, ed., pp. 21–40. New York, W. W. Norton.

   1982. *Martins Hundred*. New York, A. A. Knopf.

Norman, Joseph Gary. 1987. Eighteenth-century wharf construction in Baltimore, Maryland. Master's thesis, Department of Anthropology, College of William and Mary, Williamsburg, Va.

Norris, Robert. 1789. *Memoirs of the Reign of Bossa Ahadea*. London, W. Lowndes. Facsimile. London, Frank Cass, Ltd., 1968.

Norris, Walter B. 1937. Some recently found poems on the Calverts. *Maryland Historical Magazine* 32: 112–15.

Norton, Mary Beth. ed. 1989. *Major Problems in American Women's History: Documents and Essays*. Lexington, Massachusetts, D. C. Heath & Company.

Nugent, Maria. 1839. *A Journal of a Voyage to, and Residence on the Island of Jamaica, from 1801 to 1805, . . .* London, T. and W. Boone.

Ohnuki-Tierney, Emiko (ed.). 1990. *Culture Through Time: Anthropological Approaches*. Stanford, Stanford University Press.

   1990. Introduction. In *Culture Through Time: Anthropological Approaches*. Emiko Ohnuki-Tierney, ed., pp. 1–25. Stanford, Stanford University Press.

Oldmixon, John. 1708. *The First British Empire in America*. 2 volumes. London.

Oliver, Raymond. 1991. *The African Experience*. New York, Harper Collins.

Olmstead, Fredrick Law. 1860. *A Journey in the Back Country*. New York. Reprint. Williamston, Ma., Corner House Publications, 1972.

Opper, Marie-José and Howard Opper. 1989. Diakhité: a study of the beads from an 18th–19th-century burial site in Senegal, West Africa. *Beads* 1: 5–20.

Ortner, Sherry B. 1990. Patterns of history: cultural schemas in the foundings of Sherpa religious institutions. In *Culture Through Time: Anthropological Approaches*. Emiko Ohnuki-Tierney, ed., pp. 57–93. Stanford, Stanford University Press.

Ostroff, Susan O. 1985. Gaudy Scarlet and Modest Browns: Searching for Meaning in Eighteenth-Century Clothing Color. M.A. thesis, American Studies Program, George Washington University, Washington, D.C.

Otto, John S. 1985. *Cannon's Point Plantation 1794–1860: Living Conditions and Status Patterns in the Old South*. New York, Academic Press.

Outlaw, Alain. 1990. *Archaeology at Governor's Land*. Charlottesville, University Press of Virginia for the Virginia Division of Historic Landmarks, Richmond, Va.

Owings, Donnell M. 1953. *His Lordship's Patronage: Offices of Profit in Colonial Maryland*. Baltimore, Md., Maryland Historical Society.

Ozanne, P. 1962. Notes on the early historic archaeology of Accra. *Transactions of the Historical Society of Ghana* 6: 51–70.

　　1964. Tobacco pipes from Accra and Shai. Manuscript on file at the Institute of African Studies, University of Ghana, Legon.

Paca-Steele, Barbara and St. Clair Wright. 1987. The mathematics of an eighteenth-century wilderness garden. *Journal of Garden History* 64 (4): 299–320.

Papenfuse, Edward C. 1975. *In Pursuit of Profit: The Annapolis Merchants in the Era of the American Revolution, 1763–1805*. Baltimore, Md., Johns Hopkins University Press.

Papenfuse, Edward C., Alan F. Day, David W. Jordan and Gregory A. Stiverson. 1979. *A Biographical Dictionary of the Maryland Legislature, 1635–1789, Volume I*. Baltimore, Md., Johns Hopkins University Press.

　　1985. *A Biographical Dictionary of the Maryland Legislature, 1635–1789, Volume II*. Baltimore, Md., Johns Hopkins University Press.

Park, Robert E. 1919. The conflict and fusion of cultures with special reference to the Negro. *Journal of Negro History* 4: 116–18.

Parry, John H. 1955. Plantation and provision ground: an historical sketch of the introduction of food crops into Jamaica. *Revista de historia de America* 39: 1–20. Instituto Pan-americano de Geografia e Historia, Mexico.

Patrick, Stephen. 1990. "Round the Social Bowl": Elite Ceramics at the Calvert Site and Other Patterns of Consumer Consumption in the Chesapeake. M.A. thesis, American Studies Program, College of William and Mary, Williamsburg, Va.

Patrik, Linda E. 1985. Is there an archaeological record? In *Advances in Archaeological Method and Theory, Volume VIII*, Michael B. Schiffer, ed., pp. 27–62. Orlando, Florida, Academic Press.

Patterson, Orlando. 1967. *The Sociology of Slavery*. Rutherford, New Jersey, Farleigh Dickenson University Press. 2nd edition, Cranbury, N.J., Associated Univ. Press, 1969.

Payne, Sebastian, and P. J. Munson. 1985. Ruby and how many squirrels? The destruction of bones by dogs. In *Paleobiological Investigations: Research Design, Methods and Data Analysis*, N. R. J. Fieller, D. D. Gilbertson, and N. G. A. Ralph, eds., pp. 31–9. Oxford, British Archaeological Reports, International Series 266.

Paz, Octavio. 1972. Eroticism and gastrosophy. *Daedalus* 101 (4): 67–86.

Peacock, James L. 1986. *The Anthropological Lens: Harsh Light, Soft Focus*. Cambridge, Cambridge University Press.

Pepys, Samuel. 1660–1669. *The Diary of Samuel Pepys*. Edited by R. C. Latham and W. Matthews. Berkeley, University of California Press, 1971. 11 volumes.

Percy, David O. 1984. Agricultural labor on an 18th-century Chesapeake plantation. Paper presented at the 45th conference on Early American History (The Colonial Experience: the Eighteenth Century Chesapeake). Baltimore, Md., September 13, 1984.

Perry, William Stevens, ed. 1878. Papers Relating to the History of the Church in Maryland. Vol. 4 of *Historical Collections Relating to the American Colonial Church*. 5 volumes. Hartford, Connecticut, Church Press Co., reprinted 1969.

Philips, John E. 1990. The African heritage of white America. In *Africanisms in American Culture*. Joseph E. Holloway, ed., pp. 225–39. Bloomington, University of Indiana Press.

Plumb, J. H. 1980. *Georgian Delights*. Boston, Little Brown & Company.

Pogue, Dennis J. 1988. Spatial analysis of the King's Reach Plantation homelot, ca. 1690–1715. *Historical Archaeology* 22 (1): 40–56.

    1990. *King's Reach and 17th-Century Plantation Life*. Jefferson Patterson Park and Museum Studies in Archaeology No. 1. Maryland Historical & Cultural Publications, Annapolis, Maryland.

    1991. Standard of living in the 17th century Chesapeake: patterns of variability between artifact assemblages. Paper presented at the Council of Virginia Archaeologists, Symposium V: The Historical Archaeology of 17th Century Virginia, Williamsburg, Va., May 11, 1991.

Posnansky, Merrick. 1994. West African Reflections on African American Archaeology. In *"I, too, am America": Studies in African American Archaeology*. Theresa Singleton, ed. Charlottesville, University Press of Virginia, forthcoming.

Posonby, Arthur. 1923. *The English Diary*. London, Methuen & Co.

Potter, Parker B. Jr. 1989. Archaeology in Public in Annapolis: An Experiment in the Application of Critical Theory to Historical Archaeology. Ph.D. dissertation, Department of Anthropology, Brown University. Ann Arbor, University Microfilms International.

Power, Eileen. 1975. *Medieval Women*. Edited by M. M. Postan. Cambridge, Cambridge University Press.

Preston, Dickson J. 1980. *Young Frederick Douglass: The Maryland Years*. Baltimore, Md., Johns Hopkins University Press.

Price, Jacob M. 1980. *Capital and Credit in British Overseas Trade: The View from the Chesapeake, 1700–1776*. Cambridge, Ma., Harvard University Press.

Pulsipher, Lydia M. 1990. They have Saturdays and Sundays to feed themselves: slave gardens in the Caribbean. *Expedition* 32 (2): 24–33.

    1991. Sundays at Galways Plantation [Montserrat] in the early nineteenth century. In *Seeds of Change*, Herman J. Viola and Carolyn Margolis, eds., pp. 153–55. Washington, D.C., Smithsonian Institution Press.

Rabinow, Paul. 1977. *Reflections on Fieldwork in Morocco*. Berkeley, University of California Press.

Rabinow, Paul and William M. Sullivan. 1987. The interpretive turn: a second look. In *Interpretive Social Science: A Second Look*, Paul Rabinow and William M. Sullivan, eds., pp. 1–30. Berkeley, University of California Press.

Radoff, Morris L. 1954. *Buildings of the State of Maryland at Annapolis*. Annapolis, Md., Maryland Hall of Records.

Randolph, Mary. 1824. *The Virginia House-Wife*. Baltimore, Md., Plaskitt & Cugle. Facsimile ed. with an introduction by Karen Hess. Columbia, University of South Carolina Press, 1984.

Rawick, George P. ed. 1972a. *Slave Narratives: Texas. Volume V*. Federal Writers' Project. Westport, Connecticut, Greenwood Press.

    1972b. *Slave Narratives. Kansas, Kentucky, Maryland, Ohio, Virginia, and Tennessee, Volume XVI*. Federal Writers' Project. Westport, Connecticut, Greenwood Press.

Reed, Michael. 1984. *The Georgian Triumph 1700–1830*. London, Paladin Books, Grenada Publishing Co.

Reitz, Elizabeth J. 1982. Availability and use of fish along coastal Georgia and Florida. *Southeastern Archaeology* 1 (1): 65–88.

    1986. Urban/rural contrasts in vertebrate fauna from the southern Atlantic coastal plain. *Historical Archaeology* 16 (2): 47–58.

    1988a. A Comparison of the Calvert Faunal Remains with Charleston and Caribbean Faunal Assemblages. Paper presented at the Annual Meetings, Society for Historical Archaeology, Reno, Nevada.

1988b. Preliminary Report on the Faunal Remains from the Calvert Site. Calvert Interim Report No. 6. Historic Annapolis Foundation, Annapolis, Md.

1989a. Final Report on the Faunal Remains from the Calvert Site. Calvert Interim Report No. 8. Historic Annapolis Foundation, Annapolis, Md.

1989b. Vertebrate fauna from Reynolds Tavern, Annapolis. Report on file, Department of Anthropology, University of Georgia, Athens, Ga.

1990. Vertebrate fauna. In *The Old Village and the Great House*. Douglas V. Armstrong, pp. 212–27. Urbana, University of Illinois Press.

n.d. Zooarchaeological Analyses of African American Foodways: Real Gracia de Santa Teresa de Mose. *Expedition* (in press).

Reitz, Elizabeth J. and Nicholas Honnerkamp. 1983. British colonial subsistence strategies on the southeastern coastal plain. *Historical Archaeology* 17: 4–26.

Reitz, Elizabeth J. and Barbara Ruff. 1992. Morphometric study of colonial New World cattle. Paper presented at the Annual Meetings, Society for Historical Archaeology, Kingston, Jamaica.

Reitz, Elizabeth J. and Margaret Scarry. 1985. *Reconstructing Historic Subsistence with an Example from Sixteenth-Century Spanish Florida*. Special Publication No. 3, Society for Historical Archaeology, Tucson, Arizona.

Reitz, Elizabeth J., Tyson Gibbs, and Ted A. Rathbun. 1985. Archaeological evidence for subsistence on coastal plantations. In *The Archaeology of Slavery and Plantation Life*. Theresa Singleton, ed., pp. 163–91. Orlando, Florida, Academic Press.

Reps, John W. 1972. *Tidewater Towns: City Planning in Colonial Virginia and Maryland*. Williamsburg, Va., Colonial Williamsburg Foundation.

Repton, Humphrey. 1816. *Fragments on the Theory and Practice of Landscape Gardening*. London, T. Bensley & Son for J. Taylor.

Richards, Audrey I. 1932. *Hunger and Work in a Savage Tribe*. Reprint. London, Routledge & Keagan Paul. Cleveland, World Publishing Company, 1964.

Ridgely, David, 1841. *Annals of Annapolis*. Baltimore, Md., Cushing & Brother.

Riley, Elihu S. 1887. *The Ancient City: A History of Annapolis*. Annapolis, Md., Record Printing Office.

Robin, L'Abbé. 1783. *Nouveau Voyage dans l'Amérique* . . . Philadelphia, Robert Bell. Facsimile. New York, Arno Press, 1969.

Robinson, W. Stitt. 1988. Conflicting views on landholding: Lord Baltimore and the experiences of colonial Maryland with Native Americans. *Maryland Historical Magazine* 83: 85–97.

Rockman, Diana deZerga, and Nan A. Rothschild. 1984. City tavern, country tavern: an analysis of four colonial sites. *Historical Archaeology* 18 (2): 112–21.

Romans, Bernard. 1775. *Natural History of Florida*. Facsimile. Gainesville, University of Florida Press, 1952.

Root, Waverly. 1958. *The Food of France*. New York, Random House.

Rosaldo, Michelle Z. 1980. *Knowledge and Passion: Ilongot Notions of Self and Social Life*. Cambridge, Cambridge University Press.

Rosaldo, Renato. 1989. *Culture and Truth: The Remaking of Social Analysis*. Boston, Beacon Press.

Rothschild, Nan A. 1990. *New York City Neighborhoods: The Eighteenth Century*. San Diego, California, Academic Press.

Rountree, Helen. 1989. *The Powhatan Indians of Virginia: Their Traditional Culture*. Norman, University of Oklahoma Press.

1990. *Pocahontas's People: The Powhatan Indians of Virginia Through Four Centuries*. Norman, University of Oklahoma Press.

Rowland, Kate Mason. 1898. *The Life of Charles Carroll of Carrollton 1737–1832 with His Correspondence and Public Papers*. 2 volumes. New York, G. P. Putnam's Sons.

Ruff, Barbara. 1989. Archaeological evidence for the size of American cattle in the eighteenth and nineteenth centuries. Paper presented at International Archaeozoological Congress, Washington, D.C., May 1989.

Russell-Wood, A. J. R. 1982. *The Black Man in Slavery and Freedom in Colonial Brazil*. New York, St. Martin's Press.

Russo, Jean B. 1984. The Structure of the Anne Arundel County Economy. In Final Report on NEH Grant RS-20199-81-1955: Annapolis and Anne Arundel County, Maryland: A Study of Urban Development in a Tobacco Economy, 1649–1776, Lorena S. Walsh, ed. Unpublished report on file at the Historic Annapolis Foundation, Inc., Annapolis, Md.

1988. Self-sufficiency and local exchange: free craftsmen in the rural Chesapeake economy. In *Colonial Chesapeake Society*. Lois Green Carr, Philip D. Morgan, and Jean B. Russo, eds., pp. 389–432. Chapel Hill, University of North Carolina Press.

1989. *Free Workers in a Plantation Economy: Talbot County, Maryland 1690–1759*. New York, Garland Publishers.

Rutman, Darrett B. 1983. Encounter with ethnography: a review of Isaac's *Transformation of Virginia*. *Historical Methods* 16: 82–6.

Rutman, Darrett B. and Anita H. Rutman. 1976. Of agues and fevers: malaria in the early Chesapeake. *William and Mary Quarterly*, series 3, 33: 31–60.

1984. *A Place in Time: Middlesex County, Virginia, 1650–1750*. New York, W. W. Norton & Co.

Sahlins, Marshall. 1981. *Historical Metaphors and Mythical Realities: Structure in the Early History of the Sandwich Island Kingdom*. Ann Arbor, Michigan, Association for Social Anthropology in Oceania and the University of Michigan Press.

1985. *Islands of History*. Chicago, University of Chicago Press.

Sanford, Douglas. 1990. The gardens at Germanna, Virginia. In *Earth Patterns: Essays in Landscape Archaeology*. William Kelso and Rachel Most, eds., pp. 43–58. Charlottesville, University Press of Virginia.

Scharf, J. Thomas. 1879. *History of Maryland from the Earliest Period to the Present Day in Three Volumes*. Vol. 1. Baltimore, Md., John B. Piet.

Schrire, Carmel, James Deetz, David Lubinsky, and Cedric Poggenpoel. 1990. The chronology of Oudepost I Cape, as inferred from an analysis of clay pipes. *J. Archaeological Science* 17: 269–300.

Schulz, Peter D., and Sherri M. Gust. 1983a. Faunal remains and social status in 19th century Sacramento. *Historical Archaeology* 17 (1): 44–53.

1983b. Relative beef cut prices in the late nineteenth century: a note for historic site faunal analysis. *Pacific Coast Archaeological Society Quarterly* 19 (1): 12–18.

Schuyler, Robert L. 1970. Historical and historic sites archaeology as anthropology: basic definitions. *Historical Archaeology* 4: 83–9.

1978. (ed.). *Historical Archaeology: A Guide to Substantive and Theoretical Contributions*. Farmingdale, New York, Baywood Publishing Co.

Shammas, Carole. 1985. Black women's work and the evolution of plantation society in Virginia. *Labor History* 26 (Winter): 5–28.

Shomette, Donald G. 1978. A reconnaissance of drowned cultural resources at Londontown, Maryland. Nautical Archaeological Associates, Inc., 125 pp. Report on file at the Maryland Historical Trust, Annapolis, Md.

Simeti, Mary Taylor. 1989. *Pomp and Sustenance: Twenty Five Years of Sicilian Food*. New York, A. A. Knopf.

Simmons, William. 1992. Of large things remembered: Southern New England Indian legends of colonial encounters. In *The Art and Mystery of Historical Archaeology: Essays in Honor of James Deetz*. Anne Yentsch and Mary C. Beaudry, eds., pp. 317–29. Boca Raton, Florida, CRC Press.

Simms, William Gilmore. 1841. Loves of the driver. *The Magnolia or Southern Monthly* 3: 222–3.

Singer, David A. 1985. The use of fish remains as a socio-economic measure: an example from 19th century New England. *Historical Archaeology* 19 (2): 110–13.

Singleton, Theresa ed. 1985. *The Archaeology of Slavery and Plantation Life*. Orlando, Florida, Academic Press.

1991. The Archaeology of Slave Life. In *Before Freedom Came: African-American Life in the Antebellum South*. Edward D. C. Campbell, Jr. and Kym S. Rice, eds., pp. 155–75. Richmond, Va., The Museum of the Confederacy and the University Press of Virginia (Charlottesville).

Sloane, Sir Hans. 1707. *A Voyage to the Islands of Madera, Barbados, Nieves, St. Christopher and Jamaica*. 2 vols. London, printed for the author.

Smedes, Susan Dabney. 1889. *A Southern Planter*. London, Murray.

Smith, E. 1742. *The Compleat Housewife or Accomplished Gentlewoman's Companion*. American edition. Williamsburg, Va., William Parks.

Smith, Marvin. 1983. Appendix F: bead analysis report. In *Yaughan and Curriboo Plantations: Studies in Afro-American Archaeology* by Thomas R. Wheaton, Amy Friedlander, and Patrick H. Garrow. Soil Systems, Inc., Marietta, Georgia.

Smollek, Michael A. and Wayne E. Clark. 1982. Spatial patterning of seventeenth-century plantations in the Chesapeake. Paper presented at the Annual Meetings, Society for Historical Archaeology, Philadelphia, Pa.

Smyth, John F. D. 1784. *A Tour in the United States of America*. 2 volumes. London.

Sobel, Mechal. 1979. *Trabelin' On: The Slave Journey to an Afro-Baptist Faith*. 2nd edition. Princeton, Princeton University Press, 1988.

1987. *The World They Made Together: Black and White Values in Eighteenth-Century Virginia*. Princeton, Princeton University Press.

Sokolov, Raymond. 1990. Soul food in the New World. *Natural History* 8/90: 74–9.

1991. *Why We Eat What We Eat: How the Encounter between the New World and the Old Changed the Way Everyone on the Planet Eats*. New York, Summit Books.

Soltow, J. H. 1959. Scottish traders in Virginia, 1750–1775. *Economic History Review*, series 2, 12: 83–98.

Stanford, Michael. 1986. *The Nature of Historical Knowledge*. Oxford, Basil Blackwell.

Stedman, John G. 1796. *Stedman's Surinam: Life in an Eighteenth Century Slave Society*. Abridged, modernized edition of *Narrative of a Five Years Expedition against the Revolted Negroes of Surinam*. Richard and Sally Price, eds. Baltimore, Md., Johns Hopkins University Press.

Steiner, Bernard ed. 1898. *Life and Administration of Sir Robert Eden*. Baltimore, Johns Hopkins University Press [as Johns Hopkins University Studies in History and Political Science XVI].

1901. *Reverend Thomas Bray*. Baltimore, Md., Maryland Historical Society Fund Publication No. 37.

1908. Benedict Leonard Calvert. *Maryland Historical Magazine* 3 (3/4): 191–227, 283–341.

1917. Some unpublished manuscripts from Fulham Palace relating to the Province of Maryland. *Maryland Historical Magazine* 12: 115–63.

Stephen, Leslie and Sidney Lee, eds. 1917. *The Dictionary of National Biography Founded in 1882 by George Smith*. Reprint. London, Geoffrey Cumberlege, 1950.

Sterner, Jody. 1989. Who is signalling whom? Ceramic style, ethnicity and taphonomy among the Sirak Bulahay [North Cameroon]. *Antiquity* 63: 451–9.

Stewart, James. 1823. *A View of the Past and Present State of the Island of Jamaica*. Edinburgh, Oliver and Boyd.

Stewart, Richard S. (compiled by A. B. Stewart). 1955. Dr. George Stewart of Annapolis and Doden, Anne Arundel County, and his descendants. Typescript, Maryland Historical Society, Baltimore, Md.

Stiverson, Gregory. 1977. *Poverty in a Land of Plenty: Tenancy in Eighteenth-Century Maryland.* Baltimore, Md., Johns Hopkins University Press.

Stone, Garry Wheeler. 1977. Artifacts are not enough. *The Conference on Historic Site Archaeology Papers 1976*, 11: 43–63.

    1987. Manorial Maryland. *Maryland Historical Magazine* 82 (1): 3–36.

    1990. St. Maries City; corporate artifact. In *New Perspectives of Maryland Historical Archaeology*, Richard J. Dent and Barbara Little, eds., pp. 4–18. Special Publication of the Maryland Archaeological Society 26 (1/2).

Stone, Garry Wheeler, J. G. Little, and S. Israel. 1973. Ceramics from the John Hicks Site, 1723–1744: the material culture. In *Ceramics in America*. Ian Quimby, ed., pp. 103–40. Charlottesville, University Press of Virginia.

Stone, Lawrence, 1967. *The Crisis of the Aristocracy, 1558–1641.* Oxford, Oxford University Press (abridged paperback edition).

Stone, Lawrence and Jeanne C. Fawtier Stone. 1984. *An Open Elite: England 1540–1880.* Oxford, Oxford University Press (abridged edition, 1986).

Stuart, David. 1979. *Georgian Gardens.* London, Robert Hale, Ltd.

Stuckey, Sterling. 1987. *Slave Culture: Nationalist Theory and the Foundation of Black America.* New York, Oxford University Press.

Tannahill, Reay. 1989. *Food in History.* Revised edition. New York, Crown Publishers.

Tate, Thad W. 1965. *The Negro in Eighteenth-Century Williamsburg.* Charlottesville, University Press of Virginia.

Tate, Thad W. and David L. Ammerman, eds. 1979. *The Chesapeake in the Seventeenth Century: Essays on Anglo-American Society & Politics.* Chapel Hill, University of North Carolina Press for the Institute of Early American History and Culture.

Taylor, Charles. 1971. Interpretation and the Sciences of Man. Originally published in *The Review of Metaphysics* 25 (1) and reprinted in Rabinow and Sullivan (1979, 1987).

Teisch, Luisah. 1985. *Jambalaya: The Natural Woman's Book of Personal Charms and Practical Rituals.* San Francisco, Harper & Row.

Thomas, David Hurst. 1989. *Archaeology*, 2nd edn. Fort Worth, Holt, Rinehart and Winston, Inc.

Thomas, Keith. 1963. The place of laughter in Tudor and Stuart England. *The Times Literary Supplement*, January 21, 1977: 77–81.

    1983. *Man and the Natural World: Changing Attitudes in England 1500–1800.* London, Allan Lane.

Thompson, E. P. 1975. *Whigs and Hunters: The Origin of the Black Act.* New York, Random House.

Thompson, Robert Farris. 1984. *Flash of the Spirit: African and Afro-American Art and Philosophy.* New York, Vintage Books.

Trollope, Frances. 1832. *Domestic Manners of the Americans.* Edited with an introduction by Donald Smalley. New York, A. A. Knopf, 1949.

Turner, Lorenzo D. 1949. *Africanisms in the Gullah Dialect.* Chicago, University of Chicago Press. New York, Arno Press Reprint, 1969.

Turner, Victor. 1986. Dewey, Dilthey, and drama: an essay in the anthropology of experience. In *The Anthropology of Experience*, Victor W. Turner and Edward M. Bruner, eds., pp. 33–44. Urbana, University of Illinois Press.

Ubelaker, Douglas H., and Philip D. Curtin. 1993. Human biology of populations in the Chesapeake watershed. To appear in an environmental history of the Chesapeake ecosystem, edited by Philip D. Curtin, Grace Brush, George Fisher, and Edward C. Papenfuse. Manuscript on file at the Maryland State Archives, Annapolis, Md.

Upton, Dell. 1982a. Slave housing in eighteenth-century Virginia. Report submitted to the Department of Social and Cultural History, National Museum of American History, Smithsonian Institution, Washington, D.C.

1982b. The origins of Chesapeake architecture. In *Three Centuries of Maryland Architecture*, pp. 44–57. Annapolis, Md., Maryland Historical Trust.

1982c. Vernacular domestic architecture in eighteenth-century Virginia. *Winterthur Portfolio* 17 (2–3): 94–119.

1985. White and black landscapes in eighteenth-century Virginia. *Places* 2 (2): 10–39. Reprinted in *Material Life in America, 1600–1860*. Robert Blair St. George, ed., pp. 357–69. Boston, Northeastern University Press.

1987. *Holy Things and Profane: Anglican Parish Churches in Colonial Virginia*. Cambridge, Ma., MIT Press.

1988. New views of the Virginia landscape. *Virginia Magazine of History and Biography* 96 (4): 3–67.

1990. Imagining the early Virginia landscape. In *Earth Patterns: Essays in Landscape Archaeology*. William M. Kelso and Rachel Most, eds., pp. 71–88. Charlottesville, University Press of Virginia.

1992. The city as material culture. In *The Art and Mystery of Historical Archaeology: Essays in Honor of James Deetz*. Anne Yentsch and Mary C. Beaudry, eds., pp. 51–74. Boca Raton, Florida, CRC Press.

Van den Muijzenberg, E. W. B. 1980. *A History of Greenhouses*. The Netherlands, Wageningen.

Van Oosten, H. 1703. *The Dutch Gardener, or the Compleat Florist* . . . Written in Dutch, trans. to English. London, D. Midwinter and T. Leigh.

Vaughan, Sir William. 1611. *Natural and Artificial Directions for Health*. 4th edn. London, F. Williams.

Volckamer, J. 1714. *Neurenbergische Hesperiden*. Neuremberg.

Wade-Gayles, Gloria. 1991. Connected to Mama's spirit. In *Double Stitch: Black Women Write About Mothers and Daughters*. Patricia Bell-Scott, Beverly Guy-Sheftall, *et al.*, eds., pp. 214–38. Boston, Beacon Press.

Walker, Alice. 1974. *In Search of Our Mothers' Gardens: Womanist Prose*. New York, Harcourt Brace Jovanovitch, 1983 paperback edition.

Walker, John ed. 1813. *Letters Written by Eminent Persons*. London, Longman.

Walsh, Lorena S. 1979. "Till death do us Part": marriage and family in seventeenth-century Maryland. In *The Chesapeake in the Seventeenth Century*. Thad W. Tate and David L. Ammerman, eds., pp. 126–52. Chapel Hill, University of North Carolina Press.

1983. Urban amenities and rural sufficiency: living standards and consumer behavior in the colonial Chesapeake. *Journal of Economic History* 43: 109–17.

1984a. (ed.). Annapolis and Anne Arundel County, Maryland: A study of the Urban Development in a Tobacco Economy, 1649–1770. Final Report for NEH RS-20199-81-1955 on file at the Historic Annapolis Foundation, Inc., Annapolis, Md.

1984b. Annapolis as a center of production and consumption. In Annapolis and Anne Arundel County, Maryland: A study of the Urban Development in a Tobacco Economy, 1649–1770. Lorena S. Walsh, ed. Final Report for NEH RS-20199-81-1955 on file at the Historic Annapolis Foundation, Inc., Annapolis, Md.

1984c. [Demographics] Annapolis and Anne Arundel populations. In Annapolis and Anne Arundel County, Maryland: A study of the Urban Development in a Tobacco Economy, 1649–1770. Lorena S. Walsh, ed. Final Report for NEH RS-20199-81-1955 on file at the Historic Annapolis Foundation, Inc., Annapolis, Md.

1988. Community Networks in the Early Chesapeake. In *Colonial Chesapeake Society*. Lois Green Carr, Philip D. Morgan and Jean B. Russo, eds., pp. 200–41. Chapel Hill, University of North Carolina Press for the Institute of Early American History and Culture.

Washington, Martha. [n.d]. *Martha Washington's Booke of Cookery*. Edited by Karen Hess. New York, Columbia University Press, 1981.

Watkins, Gloria. 1981. *Ain't I a Woman: Black Women and Feminism*. Boston, South End Press.

Wax, Darald C. 1968. A Philadelphia surgeon on a slaving voyage to Africa, 1749–1751. *Pennsylvania Magazine of History and Biography* 92: 465–93.

1978. Black immigrants: the slave trade in colonial Maryland. *Maryland Historical Magazine* 72: 30–45.

Weams, Renita. 1991. "Hush, mama's gotta go bye-bye." In *Double Stitch: Black Women Write About Mothers and Daughters*. Patricia Bell-Scott, Beverly Guy-Sheftall, *et al.*, eds., pp. 123–30. Boston, Beacon Press.

Weber, Carmen A., Elizabeth A. Comer, Louise E. Ackerson, and J. Gary Norman. 1990. Mount Clare: the Georgian landscape. In *Earth Patterns: Essays in Landscape Archaeology*. William M. Kelso and Rachel Most, eds., pp. 135–52. Charlottesville, University Press of Virginia.

Welbourn, Alice. 1984. Endo ceramics and power strategies. In *Ideology, Power, and Prehistory*, D. Miller and C. Tilley, eds. pp. 17–25. Cambridge, Cambridge University Press.

Westmacott, Richard. 1993. *The Gardens and Yards of African Americans in the Rural South*. Knoxville, University of Tennessee Press.

Wheaton, Barbara Ketcham. 1983. *Savoring the Past: The French Kitchen and Table from 1300 to 1789*. Philadelphia, University of Pennsylvania Press.

Wheaton, Thomas R., Amy Friedlander and Patrick H. Garrow. 1983. *Yaughan and Curriboo Plantations: Studies in Afro-American Archaeology*. Report on file at Soil Systems Inc., Atlanta, Ga.

White, Christopher P. 1989. *Chesapeake Bay: Nature of the Estuary, a Field Guide*. Centreville, Md., Tidewater Publishers.

White, Deborah Gray. 1985. *Ar'n't I a Woman: Female Slaves in the Plantation South*. New York, W. W. Norton & Co.

1990. Female slaves: sex roles and status in the antebellum plantation south. In *Unequal Sisters: A Multicultural Reader in U.S. Women's History*. Ellen Carol DuBois and Vicki L. Ruiz, eds., pp. 22–33. New York, Routledge.

1991. Female slaves in the plantation South. In *Before Freedom Came: African-American Life in the Antebellum South*. Edward D. C. Campbell, Jr. and Kym S. Rice, eds., pp. 101–22. Richmond, Virginia, The Museum of the Confederacy and the University Press of Virginia (Charlottesville).

White, Father Andrew. 1634. *A Briefe Relation of the Voyage unto Maryland*. London. Reprinted in *Narratives of Early Maryland 1633–1684*. Clayton Colman Hall, ed. Facsimile edition. Bowie, Md., Heritage Books, Inc., 1988.

Whittenberg, James P. 1982. But what does it mean? An historian's view of historical archaeology. In *Forgotten Places and Things: Archaeological Perspectives on American History*. Albert E. Ward, ed., pp. 49–54. Albuquerque, New Mexico, Center for Anthropological Studies.

1987. On why historians have failed to recognize the potential of material culture. *American Archeology* 6 (1): 4–9.

Whitworth, Major-General R. H. 1974. *The Grenadier Guards*. London, Leo Cooper Ltd.

Whorf, Benjamin. 1966. *Language, Thought, and Reality*. Cambridge, Ma., MIT Press.

Wilks, Ivor. 1967. Abu Bakr Al-Siddiq of Timbuktu. In *Africa Remembered: Narratives by West Africans from The Era of The Slave Trade*. Philip D. Curtin, ed., pp. 152–69. Madison, University of Wisconsin Press.

Wilson, Anne C. 1974. *Food and Drink in Britain from the Stone Age to Recent Times*. New York, Barnes & Noble.

Windley, Lathan A. ed. 1983. *Runaway Slave Advertisements: A Documentary History from the 1730s to 1790. Volume II, Maryland*. Westport, Connecticut, Greenwood Press.

Wölfflin, Heinrich. 1888. *Renaissance and Baroque*. Translated by Kathrin Simon with an introduction by Peter Murray. Cornell University Press, 1968.

Wood, Peter H. 1974. *Black Majority: Negroes in Colonial South Carolina from 1670 through the Stono Rebellion*. New York, W. W. Norton & Co.

Woolley, Sir Leonard. 1930. *Digging up the Past*. Harmondsworth, Penguin Books, 1956.

Wooten, Sir Henry. 1624. *Elements of Architecture*. London, John Bill.

Wright, James M. 1921. *The Free Negro in Maryland, 1634–1860*. Studies in Human Economics and Public Law 97 (3). New York, Longmans, Green & Co.

Wright, P. ed. 1966. *Lady [Maria] Nugent's Journal*. Kingston, Jamaica.

Wright, Richard. 1934. *The Story of Gardening from the Hanging Gardens of Babylon to the Hanging Gardens of New York*. London, George Routledge.

Wright, Russell. 1983. [Survey and Description of Sites and Structures in the Historic District of Annapolis for the Maryland Historical Trust]. Historic Annapolis Foundation, Annapolis, Md. Manuscript on file at the Maryland Historic Trust, Annapolis, Maryland. 62 pp.

Wright, Tanya Y. 1990. Soul food reconsidered. *New York Times Magazine*, Pt. 2, vol. 140, Issue 48381: 40, 41, 45, 48.

Yamin, Rebecca, and Karen Bescherer-Metheny eds. 1994. *Landscape Archaeology: Studies in Reading and Interpreting the Historic Landscape*, Boca Raton, Florida, CRC Press, forthcoming.

Yentsch, Anne. 1984a. Contrary to nature: the Calvert orangery as a symbol of power for a patrician household in Annapolis, Maryland. Paper presented at the 45th Conference on Early American History (The Colonial Experience: Eighteenth Century Maryland), Baltimore, Md.

1984b. Culture change and social process in the Georgian world of Annapolis, Maryland. Paper presented at the Eastern States Archaeological Federation Meetings, Annapolis, Maryland.

1986. The Earlier Posthole Buildings at the Calvert Site. *Calvert Interim Report No. 1*. Historic Annapolis, Inc., Annapolis, Md.

1987. Why George Washington's China is his and not Martha's. Paper presented at the Annual Meetings, Society for Historical Archaeology, Savannah, Georgia.

1990a. Historic Morven: the archaeological reappearance of an eighteenth-century Princeton garden. *Expedition* 32 (2): 14–23.

1990b. Minimum vessel lists as evidence of change in folk and courtly traditions of food use. *Historical Archaeology* 24 (3): 26–48.

1990c. The Calvert orangery in Annapolis, Maryland: a horticultural symbol of power and prestige in an early eighteenth-century community. In *Earth Patterns: Essays in Landscape Archaeology*. William M. Kelso and Rachel Most, eds., pp. 169–87. Charlottesville, University Press of Virginia.

1990d. An interpretive study of the use of land and space on Lot 83, Annapolis, Maryland. In *New Perspectives of Maryland Historical Archaeology*. Richard J. Dent and Barbara Little, eds., pp. 21–53. Special Publication of the Maryland Archaeological Society 26 (1/2).

1991a. Chesapeake artefacts and their cultural context: pottery and the food domain. *Post-Medieval Archaeology* 25: 25–72.

1991b. Engendering visible and invisible ceramic artifacts, especially dairy vessels. *Historical Archaeology* 25 (4): 132–55.

1991c. The symbolic division of pottery: sex-related attributes of English and Anglo-American household pots. In *The Archaeology of Inequality*. Randall McGuire and Robert Paynter, eds., pp. 192–230. Oxford, Basil Blackwell.

1992. Gudgeons, mullets, and proud pigs: historicity, black fishermen, and southern myth. In *The Art and Mystery of Historical Archaeology: Essays in Honor of James Deetz*. Anne Yentsch and Mary C. Beaudry, eds., pp. 283–314. Boca Raton, Florida, CRC Press.

Yentsch, Anne and Mary C. Beaudry eds. 1992. *The Art and Mystery of Historical Archaeology: Essays in Honor of James Deetz*. Boca Raton, Florida, CRC Press.

Yentsch, Anne and Judson Kratzer. 1994. Field Techniques for Recovering the Earlier Garden Landscapes of Morven. In: *The Archaeology of Garden and Field*. Naomi F. Miller and Kathryn Gleason, eds. Philadelphia, University of Pennsylvania Press, forthcoming.

Yentsch, Anne and Larry W. McKee. 1987. Footprints of eighteenth-century Annapolis, Maryland. *American Archeology* 6 (1): 40–50.

Yentsch, Anne, Naomi F. Miller, Barbara Paca, and Dolores Piperno. 1987. Archaeologically defining the earlier garden landscapes at Morven: preliminary results. *Northeast Historical Archaeology* 16: 1–29.

Yetman, Norman R. 1970. *Life Under the "Peculiar Institution": Selections from the Slave Narrative Collection*. New York, Holt, Rinehart.

Zeder, Melinda. 1991. *Feeding Cities: Specialized Animal Ecology in the Ancient Near East*. Washington, D.C., Smithsonian Institution Press.

INDEX

CPSIA information can be obtained
at www.ICGtesting.com
Printed in the USA
LVHW020118180123
737384LV00012B/951

9 780521 467308